G000059466

THE
DISPATCHES AND LETTERS
OF
VICE ADMIRAL
LORD VISCOUNT NELSON
WITH NOTES BY
SIR NICHOLAS HARRIS NICOLAS

VOLUME I

1777 TO 1794

Elibron Classics
www.elibron.com

Elibron Classics series.

© 2005 Adamant Media Corporation.

ISBN 1-4021-8709-2 (paperback)
ISBN 1-4021-2000-1 (hardcover)

This Elibron Classics Replica Edition is an unabridged facsimile
of the edition published in 1845 by Henry Colburn,
London.

Elibron and Elibron Classics are trademarks of
Adamant Media Corporation. All rights reserved.

This book is an accurate reproduction of the original. Any marks, names, colophons, imprints, logos or other symbols or identifiers that appear on or in this book, except for those of Adamant Media Corporation and BookSurge, LLC, are used only for historical reference and accuracy and are not meant to designate origin or imply any sponsorship by or license from any third party.

F.L.Abbott. pinx.ᵗ

S.Freeman. sculp.ᵗ

My Dearest Husband,

*I am now writing
opposite to Your Portrait — the likeness
is great — I am well satisfied with
Abbott................. Our Good Father was delighted with the likeness...................*

Your Affectionate Wife

*July 23ᵈ
[1798]*

Frances H Nelson

London. Henry Colburn, Publisher. 13 Great Marlborough St. 1844

THE

DISPATCHES AND LETTERS

OF

VICE ADMIRAL

LORD VISCOUNT NELSON,

WITH NOTES BY

SIR NICHOLAS HARRIS NICOLAS, G.C.M.G.

" The Nation expected, and was entitled to expect, that while Cities vied with each other in consecrating Statues in marble and brass to the memory of our NELSON, a Literary Monument would be erected, which should record his deeds for the immortal honour of his own Country, and the admiration of the rest of the World."—QUARTERLY REVIEW.

THE FIRST VOLUME.
1777 TO 1794.

LONDON:

HENRY COLBURN, PUBLISHER,

GREAT MARLBOROUGH STREET.

MDCCCXLV.

LONDON :

PRINTED BY G. J. PALMER, SAVOY ST. STRAND.

TO

HIS ROYAL HIGHNESS

FRANCIS ALBERT AUGUSTUS CHARLES EMMANUEL,

DUKE OF SAXONY, PRINCE OF SAXE COBURG AND GOTHA,

THIS WORK

IS, WITH HIS ROYAL HIGHNESS' GRACIOUS PERMISSION,

MOST RESPECTFULLY DEDICATED

BY HIS MOST FAITHFUL, OBEDIENT, AND HUMBLE SERVANT,

NICHOLAS HARRIS NICOLAS.

ADVERTISEMENT

SECOND EDITION.

———————

Since the publication of the First Volume of this Work, the Editor has been favoured with many communications, which have caused some additioal Letters to be inserted in the present Edition.

Through the influence of a friend, access has been obtained to the Papers of the late Dr. M'Arthur, which are now in the possession of his daughter, Mrs. Conway; but they contain few original documents relating to Lord Nelson, and scarcely any of the Manuscripts that were used in Clarke and M'Arthur's " Life of Nelson." If no other Papers of Dr. M'Arthur are in existence, the suggestion in the Preface that his family had retained Letters which were lent to him is without foundation; and the Editor, therefore, willingly recalls it. The fact, however remains, that many of the persons who lent original Letters to Dr. M'Arthur, never recovered them. It is therefore possible that they may have been lost.

Though the examination of Dr. M'Arthur's Papers was not attended with the expected result, some valuable original Letters, and Copies of a few others, have thereby been obtained. The original Letters were addressed to Lord Hood, during the Sieges of Bastia and Calvi, or to Dr. M'Arthur; and, (together with two Letters from other sources,) are inserted in their proper places in this Volume.

The most important document in Mrs. Conway's possession is, the *original* Manuscript of Lord Nelson's autobiographical "Sketch of his Life," which is now for the first time printed exactly as it was written.

The Editor is much indebted to Lady Bolton, a niece of Lord Nelson, for many Letters and Papers of great interest, which were obligingly communicated by James Young, Esq., of Wells in Norfolk. He has also to offer his best acknowledgments to the Dowager Lady de Saumarez, and to Lord de Saumarez, for Lord Nelson's Letters to that distinguished ornament of the Naval Service, the late Admiral Lord de Saumarez; to Mrs. Ellis, daughter of Admiral Sir Peter Parker, (Nelson's early patron and friend); to Admiral Sir Robert Otway, Bart., K.C.B.; to Colonel Hugh Percy Davison; to Captain Sir Andrew Pellet Green, K.C.H.; to the Reverend Henry Girdleston; to Captain Sir George Augustus Westphal, R.N.; to Captain Widdrington, R.N.; to Captain Robert Fitz-Gerald Gambier, R.N.; to Nathaniel Young, Esq.; and to the Reverend Edward Bushby, of St. John's College, Cambridge.

He also begs leave to thank Lord Stanley, for his permission to print Lord Nelson's Letters to the Secretary of State for War and Colonies, in the years 1803, 1804, and 1805, which, as stated in the Preface, are now in the Colonial Office.

Advantage has been taken of this Edition to supply some particulars of Lord Nelson's family, as well as of himself; to insert additional Notes; and to correct typographical and other errors.

January 13, 1845.

PREFACE

FIRST EDITION.

———————

THIRTY-NINE years have elapsed since the greatest of all the Heroes that adorn the Naval History of Britain closed a career of unprecedented triumphs, by a death which consummated his own glory, and rendered him, for ever, a paramount object of National pride, gratitude, and affection.

But though no language can adequately describe the effect of his transcendant services upon his Country, upon Europe, and indeed upon the whole civilized World, England is still more largely indebted to NELSON than even for his exploits. She owes to him a Name synonymous with Victory, which, with almost talismanic power, inspires her Sons in the day of battle with a confidence that ensures success; and She is indebted to him for an example to ages yet unborn, of the most ardent loyalty, the most genuine patriotism, the most conscientious sense of duty to his Sovereign and his Country, and of the highest professional skill, combined with the most generous disposition, the kindest heart, and the noblest aspirations, that ever graced a Public Man.

In the history of NELSON's career, Englishmen have always felt the liveliest interest; and their gratitude for his services has been shown by Parliamentary Grants to his family, and by Monuments to his memory. The Crown, though with a sparing hand, conferred various Honours upon NELSON, which were extended to his relations after his death; yet, with extraordinary inconsistency, his amiable Widow received no increase of Dignity; and no British Honours whatever have descended to the Hero's heir-at-law, and sole representative.

Before describing the present Work, it is desirable to take some notice of the various publications, professing to be LIVES of LORD NELSON, which have appeared:

I. "The Life of Lord Nelson," in the third volume of the "Naval Chronicle," apparently written by Dr. John M'Arthur, a Purser in the Navy, who had been Secretary to Admiral Viscount Hood, and who was personally known to Lord NELSON. For that work NELSON wrote, in October 1799, "The Sketch of my Life," which is now prefixed to his Letters. The Memoir was continued in the fourteenth, and concluded in the fifteenth, volume of the "Naval Chronicle," which valuable publication, as might be expected, abounds with Letters, Anecdotes, &c., of NELSON.

II. "Biographical Memoirs of Lord Viscount Nelson, with Observations, Critical and Explanatory. By John Charnock, Esq.," 8vo. 1802. This compilation was of no other value than that of containing such information of NELSON's early life as the Author's friend, Captain Locker, could contribute; together with many of the Letters from NELSON to Captain Locker, which form so interesting a part of the present Collection. It will be seen that the Editor has obtained access to the *Original* Letters; and he found that in no one instance had those Letters been accurately printed by Charnock. In many cases, important passages were omitted, because they contained NELSON's opinion of individuals; but most of the alterations were made with the intention of improving their style, in which absurd attempt much of the writer's spirit was lost, and his own natural and nervous words gave place to what was considered more *genteel* or more *elegant* expressions.

III. "The Life of Horatio Lord Viscount Nelson, by Mr. Harrison," two volumes 8vo., 1806.—This Memoir was written under the dictation of Lady Hamilton, with the view of supporting her claims upon the Government; and it is disgraced by disparaging, and unjust allusions to Lady Nelson. The work contains, however, some Letters, and a few statements not printed elsewhere; and though the Letters appear to be faithfully given, the statements, coming from so prejudiced a source, are extremely suspicious; and, if not without foundation, were, no doubt, very partially drawn. Alluding to the Author's assertion that he had been assisted by some of the Hero's " dear and intimate friends," the "Quarterly Review" observed, " It " seems as if these friends of Lord Nelson were in search " of a writer who would undertake to justify the only cul- " pable parts of his conduct, and found Mr. Harrison a " fit person for their purpose."

IV. " Memoirs of the Professional Life of Horatio Nelson, Viscount and Baron Nelson. By Joshua White,

Esq." 12mo. 1806.—A booksellers' work made up for the occasion, and of little value : it contains, however, one or two Letters, and perhaps as many facts, not printed elsewhere.

V. " Orme's Graphic History of the Life of Horatio Viscount Nelson:" folio, 1806.—A volume intended to illustrate a series of Engravings of NELSON's great battles. Neither the Memoir, which was written by Francis William Blagdon, nor the Plates, have any merit.

VI. " The Life of Lord Viscount Nelson. By T. O. Churchill." 4to., 1808.—A wretched compilation, intended as the vehicle of some equally wretched Engravings.

VII. " The Life of Admiral Lord Nelson, K. B., from his Lordship's Manuscripts. By the Rev. James Stanier Clarke, F.R.S., and John M'Arthur, Esq., LL.D., late Secretary to Admiral Lord Viscount Hood:" two volumes royal quarto, published in 1809, with numerous Plates, and since reprinted in octavo.—This is the standard Life of NELSON, and it has been largely used for all subsequent works. The Authors had access to the greater part of, but certainly not to all, the MSS. of LORD NELSON, then belonging to Earl Nelson; and a large body of Letters and Papers were sent to them by a great number of other persons, particularly by His late Majesty, and by a lady who possessed NELSON's interesting Letters to his Wife, before and after their marriage. The Memoir is principally made up of extracts from those Letters and Papers; but scarcely in any one of the numerous instances in which the Editor of this Work has had the opportunity of comparing the extracts printed by Clarke and M'Arthur with the original Letters or Papers, do those extracts entirely agree with the originals.

Dr. Clarke and Dr. M'Arthur seem to have been actuated by the same love of improving the Letters, which fell into their hands, as their predecessor Mr. Charnock; and though they, like him, thereby disregarded the first principle of Editorship, they are rarely open to the suspicion of having made the alterations from a worse motive than the desire to exhibit NELSON's productions in what, they considered, a fitting epistolary state; as if a Hero could never think, write, or speak naturally, but must always appear in full dress. Be the motive, however, what it might, the effect is, that no reliance can be placed on the literal fidelity of any one extract printed in their voluminous work.

VIII. " The Life of Nelson. By Robert Southey, Esq., LL.D., Poet Laureat." 12mo.— This, the most popular of all the Memoirs of NELSON, is an enlargement of its Author's article on Charnock's, Harrison's, Churchill's, and Clarke and M'Arthur's Lives of Nelson, in the " Quarterly Review " for February, 1810. It first appeared as a separate volume in 1813, and has passed through numerous editions.

IX. " The Life of Nelson. By the Old Sailor." 12mo., 1838,—which is the fullest collection of facts and anecdotes relating to NELSON yet given to the Public. Every printed authority has been consulted, and much new information inserted from the innumerable scattered Notices in Magazines, the " United Service Journal," Professional Newspapers, &c.

X. " The Letters of Lord Nelson to Lady Hamilton." In 2 vols. 8vo., 1814.—This work probably owed its existence to the distresses of the unfortunate woman to whom the Letters were addressed; and its appearance was justly and emphatically denounced in the " Edinburgh Review."[1] Such parts of those Letters as are unobjectionable will be found in this Collection.

With the exception of some Pamphlets, of which the most important were written by the late Vice-Admiral Sir Edward Foote, K. C. B., respecting the capitulation of the Castles of Uovo and Nuovo, at Naples, and the fate of Caraccioli, the preceding List seems to contain all the Works relating to NELSON that afford any information of his character or services.

But even if all those Works had been as well executed as their several plans admitted, the Biography of NELSON would still have been incomplete. The Life of a Man is best described by himself; either formally, in those pieces of autobiography which are perhaps the most attractive of all compositions, or, in the simple relation of his thoughts, conduct, and intentions, in Letters designed for the perusal of those only to whom they were addressed. A series of Letters is usually a Journal of the writer's actions, as well as of his feelings; and forms almost as complete a narrative of his career as a regular piece of autobiography. The very design of the Autobiographer, if he intend his work for publication, is scarcely consistent with an impartial exhibition of himself; and unless it be a Diary,

[1] For September, 1814, vol. xcvi. p. 398, et seq.

actually written at the time, and not afterwards altered, it cannot have the freshness and reality of a Letter to a near relation, or an intimate friend, conveying the impressions of the moment, and proceeding more from the heart than the head.

It is extremely well said, that " We feel especially that " *familiar* Letters, ' Epistolæ ad Quintum fratrem,' ' Epis- " tolæ ad Atticum,' the very effusions most likely to " escape us, are precisely what we chiefly long to seize " and to perpetuate. They are, indeed, windows through " which we look far into the heart—valves, at which " we observe the wayward ebullitions of temper es- " caping—meters, by which we calculate the mind's " elasticity, the intensity of passions, the oscillations " of the will. The easy private Letters of an individual " bear some analogy to the ballads of a Nation. They " embody and carry off, as the mood may be, softly or ner- " vously, jocularly or sadly, coarsely or elegantly, and " nine times out of ten, we believe, honestly, the whim " or resolve, enjoyment or anguish, rankling or effer- " vescence of the spirit, at the moment of their composi- " tion." . . . . . " What a flood of light has not " the twinkling star-ray of one Letter poured over the " previous gloom of a Nation's Annals ! With what a " cloud has not another obscured a hitherto sunny re- " nown ! And how much reality—fresh living truth, in " feature, costume, deportment, habits—is imparted by " these illustrative Portraits, as we may call them, to " the vague delineations of History, of which the high " and wide purpose seems to be fulfilled in present-

" ing to us the substance of the action, and only the
" shadow of the actor."[2]

Letters are therefore justly considered the most important, as well as the most interesting illustrations of character and talents; but the value of Letters for that purpose depends more upon the manner in which they are given to the world, than is generally supposed; and as the Editor's opinion on the subject has been acted upon in the present publication, it is proper to state it.

The principal questions, which an Editor of an extensive Correspondence has to decide, are—What Letters should be published? Whether the Letters should be printed entire, or whether certain passages should be omitted? Whether Names should be suppressed? Whether the Letters should be given literally, or be altered according to his own ideas of accuracy and elegance? Though in most cases it is, no doubt, necessary to omit many Letters that fall into an Editor's hands, on account of their want of importance, this does not always form a reason for withholding them; but it depends upon the interest attached to the writer, the distance of time at which he lived, and the number of such trifling Letters, to determine whether they should be printed.

Everything that proceeded from an illustrious Man, and especially in the early part of his life, has an interest which belongs not to the article itself, but is reflected upon it by his subsequent glory. No Letter of Chaucer or Shakespeare, for example, could be uninteresting, however trifling its contents ; and it is conceived that the familiar Letters of any Great Character, which describe his situation and feelings in the early stages of his career, — his hopes, his disappointments, and the efforts by which he surmounted every obstacle, and eventually chained fortune to his car,— yield only in interest, and in value, to Letters written after his powers had found adequate occasions for display, when he was in the full splendour of his renown, and when his Correspondence, from relating to great events and eminent individuals, not only commands attention, but becomes part of the History of his time.

Moreover, where Genius exists, and where one great and absorbing feeling occupies the mind, the most insignificant, as well as the most studied and important Letter, bears more or less of its impress: thus, there is scarcely a Note of NELSON's that does not contain some word, or line, or sentence, indicative of his predominant passions—Military Fame, and the Service of his Country.

It has been remarked by high literary authority, that " even the private habits of such a man as LORD NEL-" SON, when they are evidenced, as in this instance, by " the undoubted testimony of his own Letters, are matter " of History, and must pass as such into the records of " the age."

 ⁵ Edinburgh Review, for September 1814, vol. xlvi. p. 399. Article on Lord Nelson's Letters to Lady Hamilton.

It was, therefore, the anxious desire of the Editor to collect as many as possible of NELSON's early Letters; which though they can bear no comparison with the vivid interest of his later Correspondence, are very characteristic, showing the goodness of his heart, exhibiting the gradual development of his extraordinary powers, and bearing striking marks of that ardent zeal, which was afterwards so effectually manifested at St. Vincent, the Nile, Copenhagen, and Trafalgar.

At a very early stage of his labours, the Editor became convinced that the instances in which there would be a necessity to suppress any Letter of NELSON were extremely few ; that whenever they did occur, it would be more from public than from private causes ; and that the obligation would be imposed upon him by others rather than by his own conviction.   Though aware that he must occasionally print a trifling Letter, or Letters of which some part is of little value, he entertained the hope of being able to declare of NELSON what, he believes, has never been said by the Editor of the Correspondence of any other eminent Person,—that every Letter which fell into his hands, (except those addressed to the object of a passion as romantic as it was criminal,) extending over the whole period of the professional life of a man of ardent and irritable temperament, written under every variety of circumstances, and upon every conceivable subject, might see the light, with no other suppressions, than of a few lines relating to private expenses, and no other alterations, than the occasional correction of a loose orthography, which would have uselessly disfigured the page, and annoyed the reader.

Hitherto, the Editor has been able to carry out this design : he has every reason to hope he shall be able to pursue it; and if so, he confidently submits that it will redound to the honour of NELSON's heart, and shew the beautiful simplicity and integrity of his private character, in a far higher degree than all the eulogies ever composed on his merits, reflecting lustre upon even his matchless Victories. In what other instance, strictly parallel, has this ever been done? in how many would it be possible to do so without irreparable damage to the writer? and to accomplish it, who would not insert a few Letters which may seem trivial, and a few sentences which, being the momentary effect of irritation of mind or body, it might perhaps be wished had never been written?

This Collection of NELSON's LETTERS will consequently be the most genuine and truthful portrait of a Public Cha-racter that the world has ever seen. In most cases an Editor or Biographer selects only such Letters, or relates such facts, as place his hero advantageously before the world; and upon that plan, with the suppression of every unfavourable passage in the Letters that do appear, (and, perhaps too, without the least intimation that any thing is omitted,) every man can be made to represent himself as if there had not been one speck of human frailty in his nature. But though pure gold may be the apparent result of this literary alchemy, *truth* wholly evaporates in the process; and if the secrets of the laboratory be ever exposed, the artist, and his subject equally become objects of contempt.

With every allowance for the motives of such suppressions, nothing, however, can possibly justify the system of Charnock, Clarke and M'Arthur, and apparently of many other Editors, in having subjected what purports to be copies or extracts, to a refining process of their own, by which the text is so changed, that while the Reader imagines he is perusing what NELSON, or the party in question, actually wrote, he is in fact indulged with an *improved* and very different version of their Letters. The plan of the present publication is, it is believed, not only more satisfactory in itself, but it is consistent with the bold, uncompromising, natural character of NELSON. He now appears before his Countrymen in his writings, as he himself did in his lifetime, without concealment or disguise; and they will find in these Letters his own generous, and impetuous spirit, free from the alloy of Editorial adulteration, or Editorial squeamishness.

Every possible pains have been taken to print the Letters with the strictest fidelity. The text has, in almost all cases, been collated with the originals. The *brackets* show where words have been supplied; and the *italics* indicate the parts which were underlined by NELSON.

It was not, as might be supposed, the success that has attended the publication of the " Dispatches of the DUKE of WELLINGTON," or the powerful manner in which they have enhanced his Grace's fame, that induced the Editor to undertake the present work. Always an

ardent admirer of NELSON, and having in early life served
in the Profession of which he was the ornament, it has
long been his conviction that full justice had not been done
to NELSON, and that such justice could only be rendered
by NELSON himself.   The materials for the purpose
he knew were ample; but they have proved far more
extensive, and much more valuable than he expected.
The attempt of Clarke and M'Arthur to form the text
of NELSON's "Life" out of his Letters was a mistake,
which, on the appearance of their work, was pointed
out in the "Quarterly Review," where it was said, that
the Editors "having obtained an immense mass of documents, private and official, they had attempted to combine
two incompatible objects ; and that either a Life of Nelson should have been compiled from them, or the documents themselves should have been arranged and printed
as materials for History, under the title of the NELSON
PAPERS."   While referring to that admirable piece of
criticism, it is impossible to resist the satisfaction of ex-
tracting two or three other passages from it which show
the propriety of the present Work :

    " The time is not yet [in 1810] come when the Life of
" our great NELSON can be fully and faithfully related: his
" private history cannot be laid open without greater injury
" to individual feelings than the public has any right to
" inflict for the gratification of its curiosity; and of the po-
" litical transactions in which he bore so great a part, the
" views which he entertained, and the projects which he
" formed, there are some which could not be exposed
" without great and manifest imprudence."

As thirty-four years have passed away since the above confession of these imperfections was made, it is confidently hoped that the defects can now be supplied, with great advantage to History, and without injury to individuals, or to the Public; and that not only are NELSON's own Letters and Papers the proper materials for the purpose, but that they will form that " Literary Monument to the memory of our NELSON which the Nation expected, and which should record his deeds for the immortal glory of his own Country, and the admiration of the rest of the World."[4]

The sources from which the Letters have been obtained are very numerous; and though, in April last, the Editor commenced his labours without having one single Letter in his possession, enough have been already collected to form at least three volumes. This fact shows the care with which NELSON's Letters have been preserved, and the generous desire that prevails in the Public to enable the Hero to perpetuate his own fame. In most cases these Letters have been cherished as relics; and in some instances they were even glazed and framed, to adorn the apartments of their possessors.

In the first instance the Editor wrote to every person who, from connection with the friends of NELSON, was likely to have Letters, as well as to the Heads of the Public Departments with which he corresponded, especially the Offices of the Secretaries of State and the Admiralty. Some Letters were found in the State Paper Office, of which the Secretary of State for the Home De-

---

[4] Quarterly Review.

partment was so good as to allow him to have copies; and he has reason to hope that his application for transcripts of a valuable series in the Colonial Office will be successful.

To the Lords Commissioners of the Admiralty, and especially to Sir John Barrow, Bart., one of their Secretaries, the Editor cannot sufficiently express his obligations for the liberality and kindness with which he has been treated. Every facility to their records was afforded him; and this Collection is enriched by all the official Letters of any importance written by NELSON to the Board from the commencement to the close of his career. The few Letters preserved in the East India House were readily placed at his disposal: and for copies of them he begs leave to offer his acknowledgments to the Chairman and Court of Directors.

As a large collection of Letters were in the hands of Dr. Clarke and Dr. M'Arthur, it became the Editor's duty to endeavour to obtain access to the Papers used by those gentlemen in their " Life of Lord Nelson," with the hope of giving literally, and in full, those documents which they have printed partially and imperfectly. The attempt, however, utterly failed: the widow of Dr. Clarke said she knew nothing on the subject; while the widow of Dr. M'Arthur, after consulting some members of his family, admitted that they had papers relating to NELSON, but declined to allow them to be seen. The prudence of this resolution is greater than its courtesy; because the Editor learnt, in reply to his applications to many individuals, that all the Letters they possessed had been lent to Dr. Clarke and Dr. M'Arthur, and that they had not been restored.

It is, however, with reference only to two classes of
NELSON's Letters that the disappointment respecting the
M'Arthur Papers is of much importance: namely, the
Letters to Lady Nelson, and copies of the Letters to his
late Majesty King William the Fourth. Numerous inquiries
have been made after the former without success; and
though the original Letters to the late King are supposed
to have been in the possession of the Earl of Munster,
the Editor was informed by one of his Lordship's ex-
ecutors that there was no chance of finding them at this
moment. Those Letters, and some others, are therefore
necessarily reprinted from Clarke and M'Arthur's " Life
of Nelson," (which is expressly stated to be the authority
for each of them,) without collation with the originals;
and the Reader is reminded that though the substance,
and sometimes the words, may have been correctly given
in that work, yet, as a general rule, confidence cannot be
placed in the strict literal accuracy of any document
obtained from that source. A few Letters, of which the
originals could not be traced, are also reprinted, from the
" Naval Chronicle," Marshall's " Naval Biography," or
the other Works to which reference is made.

It is a pleasing task to acknowledge the assistance
which the Editor has derived, and for which he desires to offer his warmest thanks.

The *authority* for every Letter is given, and the persons in whose possession they are stated to be, are
assured that the Editor feels himself very much indebted
for them. But such important contributions have been
made, and such valuable aid afforded by many other individuals, that their kindness deserves a special acknowledgment.

The chief source has been " the NELSON PAPERS," which
consist of his Correspondence and other Documents, public
and private, part only of which was seen by Drs. Clarke
and M'Arthur. For these invaluable materials, the Public
and the Editor are indebted to Lord Bridport, who has them
in right of Lady Bridport, the only surviving child of
the late Earl Nelson, and the niece and heir-at-law of the
Admiral. To Lord and Lady Bridport therefore he cannot adequately express his obligations.

Another source was the " HOOD PAPERS," being
LORD NELSON's Correspondence with one of his early and
most constant friends, the celebrated Admiral Viscount
Hood, for which the Editor begs leave to offer his best
thanks to the present Viscount Hood. To Sir Alexander
Hood, Bart., he is also obliged for some Letters in his
possession.

" THE LOCKER PAPERS " are a collection of very interesting Letters from NELSON to Captain William Locker,
sometime Lieutenant-Governor of Greenwich Hospital,
extending from the year 1777, when he was a Lieutenant
in Captain Locker's Ship the Lowestoffe, until the death of
that able and highly respected Officer, in December, 1800.
He it was, NELSON says, " who taught me to board a
" Frenchman";—"who always told me to lay a French-
" man close and you will beat him;" and his affection for
his venerable preceptor, whom he attended to his grave, was
shown upon every occasion. The Collection belongs to his
son Edward Hawke Locker, Esq., F.R.S., who lately retired
from the office of Commissioner of Greenwich Hospital, in
consequence of ill health. Mr. Locker appears to have intended to write a " Life of Nelson;" and besides favouring

the Editor with these Letters, he had the goodness also
to lend him his MS. collections for that Memoir.

To the Earl of Minto, G.C.B., for a series of important
Letters to his distinguished father; to his friend Viscount
Strangford, G.C.B, as well for Letters addressed to his
Lordship as for invaluable assistance; to Viscount Mel-
ville, K.T; to Lord Bexley; to the Right Honourable
Sir George Rose, G.C.H.; to Rear Admiral Lord Rad-
stock, C.B.; to the Honourable Miss Addington, the
Honourable and Very Reverend Dr. Pellew, Dean of
Norwich, and Haviland John Addington, Esq., Trus-
tees of the Papers of the late Lord Viscount Sid-
mouth, for many Letters to his Lordship; to Vice-
Admiral Sir Graham Eden Hamond, Bart., K.C.B.;
to Sir William Keith Ball, Bart., for most valuable
Letters to his father, the late Rear Admiral Sir Alex-
ander Ball, Bart., the intimate friend of NELSON; to Cap-
tain Sir William Hoste, Bart.; to Rear-Admiral Sykes; to
Commodore Sir Francis Augustus Collier, C.B., K.C.H.;
to the Reverend Richard Keats, for Letters to his late
Uncle, the gallant Admiral Sir Richard Keats, G.C.B.;
to William Henry Whitehead, Esq.; to Dr. Lambton
Este; to Dawson Turner, Esq., F.R.S., of Yarmouth;
to Josiah French, Esq., of Windsor; to Captain James
Hope, R.N.; to Commander Thomas Pitt Robinson,
R.N.; to William Upcott, Esq.; to John Luxford,
Esq.; to William Masters Smith, Esq.; to William
Long, Esq., of Bath; to Henry William Johns, Esq., of
Blandford; to James Pulman, Esq., Richmond Herald;
to Albert William Woods, Esq., Lancaster Herald; to
Captain Ives Sutton, for several Letters to his late

father, Rear-Admiral Sutton; to Adam Bromilow, Esq., Barrister-at-Law, for Letters to the late Admiral Sir Ross Donnelly, K.C.B.; to John Barker, Esq., of Norwich; to John Bullock, Esq.; to Robert Baas, Esq.; to John Fitch, Esq., of Ipswich; to John Dillon, Esq.; to Thomas Duffus Hardy, Esq., Assistant Keeper of Records in the Tower; to John B. Heath, Esq., Consul General of His Sardinian Majesty; to Robert Cole, Esq.; to John Young, Esq.; to John Wild, Esq.; to Henry Phillips, Esq.; to Joseph Allen, Esq., of Greenwich Hospital; to Mr. Holloway; and to Mr. Empsom of Bath; and to many other persons the Editor's thanks are due for Letters of the highest interest.

A series of remarkable Letters from Lord Nelson to his maternal Uncle, William Suckling, Esq., was published in "the Athenæum" Literary Journal in 1834, which were followed by a few more to the late Dr. Baird, and to other individuals. For permission to reprint those Letters, the Editor begs leave to offer his acknowledgments to his friend Charles Wentworth Dilke, Esq.

To Page Nicol Scott, Esq., of Norwich, whose enthusiastic veneration for NELSON's memory was honourably shown by protecting the widow of the Hero's brave old follower, "Tom Allen," from the miseries of poverty in her old age, the Editor is under infinite obligations. He is on this, as upon every other occasion, largely indebted to his friend Sir Charles Young, Garter; and for much assistance in obtaining Letters or information, he is extremely obliged to Admiral Sir Philip Charles Calderwood Henderson Durham, G.C.B., to Dr. Sir George Magrath, K. H., who was for some time LORD NELSON's confidential Surgeon;

to Rear-Admiral Deans Dundas, C.B.; to Captain John Pasco, R.N., who was Signal Lieutenant of the Victory at Trafalgar; to Thomas Mee Lowndes, Esq.; to William Davison, Esq.; to Dr. B. Fonseca Outram; to Francis Bradley Dyne, Esq.; to John Barrow, Esq., Keeper of the Records, and Alexander Middleton, Esq., of the Admiralty; to Captain Montagu Montagu, R.N.; to George James Squibb, Esq.; to Bolton Corney, Esq., of Greenwich Hospital; and to Matthew L. Coleman, Esq., of the War Office.

It is gratifying to add that many of NELSON's Countrywomen have also shown great interest in the Work, by contributing valuable Letters; and the Editor takes the liberty of expressing his gratitude and respect to Her Grace the Duchess of Hamilton and Brandon, who has been so good as to favour him with copies of LORD NELSON's Letters to the late William Beckford, of Fonthill, Esq.; to the Lady Bridport; to the Honourable Miss Addington; to the Honourable Mrs. Newnham Collingwood, for the Correspondence with her celebrated father Vice-Admiral Lord Collingwood; to the Honourable Mrs. Wyndham, relict of the Honourable William Frederick Wyndham, sometime Minister at Florence; to the Lady Berry, widow of Rear-Admiral Sir Edward Berry, Bart., K.C.B., for many Letters to her late gallant husband, whose career is almost identified with that of NELSON; to the Lady Devonshire, widow of the late Rear Admiral Sir John Ferris Devonshire, K. C. H., an Officer who was said by the Earl of St. Vincent to have obtained every step of professional rank " by his good and gallant conduct;" to Mrs. Palmer, relict of Captain Edmund

Palmer, C.B.; to Mrs. Leake for LORD NELSON's private
Letters to the late William Marsden, Esq., Secretary to the
Admiralty ; to Mrs. Davies, for Letters to her late father,
Francis Drake, Esq., when Minister at Genoa; to Miss
Miller, the only daughter, and Mrs. Dalrymple, the sister,
of the late Captain Ralph Willett Miller, for Letters addressed to that brave and unfortunate Officer, who lost his
life by an explosion, when commanding the " Theseus," and
whom NELSON describes as " the only truly virtuous man he
ever knew;" and to Mrs. Locker, the wife of Edward Hawke
Locker, Esq., for much useful information. To Mrs. Horatia
Nelson Ward, (wife of the Reverend Philip Ward, Vicar
of Tenterden,) that " adopted daughter " whom NELSON,
only a few hours before he fell, so pathetically " left to the
beneficence of his Country," as one of "the only favours
" he asked of his King and Country when he was going
" to fight their Battle,"—he owes the most touching Letters
ever written by a father to his child, sending her, his
" parental blessing," in the last of them, written when the
Combined Fleets were coming out of Port.

This long list of Contributors shows how readily the
Editor's wishes and applications were acceded to; and
almost makes him forget that in some quarters, and those,
too, where the recollection of NELSON ought to have been
most cherished, (if not from affection, at least from gratitude,) his request was not complied with ; while in others,
it did not receive even the common courtesy of a reply.
In one solitary instance, copies of Letters were refused,
lest their publication might injure their pecuniary value
as autographs ! He now, however, ventures to appeal to
the feelings of all who may possess NELSON'S Letters, to

imitate the generous example of their Countrymen, by
enabling him to render this Collection as complete as
possible ; and the Prefaces to the subsequent Volumes will
enable him to record their names and their kindness.

Upon the general character of NELSON's Letters it is
hardly necessary to make any remark in this place,
since they will speak for themselves. But many of the
observations in the " Edinburgh Review" upon the very
worst and most objectionable specimens of them—his
Letters to Lady Hamilton—well describe the greater part
of his Correspondence : " They exhibit the picture of a
" warm, affectionate, and generous nature . . . .
" prone to pour forth without the least restraint the
" most hearty expressions of the sentiments that inspire
" it." After pointing out in strong terms, the defects of
the Letters to Lady Hamilton, the Reviewer adds, " But
" it is pleasing to observe so frequently the breaking
" forth of the only principle, amounting in him to a pas-
" sion, which could successfully combat his extravagant
" love,—we mean that mighty love of his Country, and
" that thirst for glory, which for the most part engrossed
" his soul—bearing his shattered frame through every
" suffering, mortification, and danger, and lifting him, at
" last, to the very height of renown, when it carried him
" to a death perhaps the most glorious that ever closed the
" existence of a warrior. There is something extremely
" affecting in the invariable constancy with which his
" military ardour rises superior to all his other pas-
" sions."

The Letters in this Volume extend from the year 1777
to the end of the year 1794. The first of them was

written to his brother, the Reverend William Nelson, a few days after he obtained his first Commission as a Lieutenant, wherein he says, "I am now left in the world "to shift for myself, which I hope I shall do so as to bring "credit upon myself and my friends." The private Letters were chiefly addressed to his family, to his maternal uncle, Mr. Suckling, to Mrs. Nelson, before as well as after his marriage, to his friends Captain Locker, Mr. Ross, and Captain, afterwards Lord, Collingwood, and to His Royal Highness the Duke of Clarence. They relate to everything in which he was personally concerned, as well as to most matters, especially Naval, of passing interest, forming a complete narrative of that period of his life, affording much information on professional matters, and displaying in warm colours the goodness of his disposition, and the strong and steady affection which he ever bore to his family and friends. Every impression of his mind is stated with pleasing frankness; and his language, though unstudied, is generally clear, and nervous.

The Official Letters within the same period were addressed to the Admiralty, and to the Admirals under whose command he was placed, on subjects connected with his Ship, and the Squadron under his orders on the Leeward Islands Station, its discipline and arrangements; and on various disputes with the Admiralty. It is very remarkable that one of NELSON's public Letters should describe an attack on the Enemy in the West Indies by a small Squadron under his command, which, though the earliest of his exploits, is unnoticed by all his biographers.

The other Official Letters were addressed to the Secre-

tary of State, pointing out the manner in which British
Commerce was injured by the admission of Foreigners to
trade in the Colonies, contrary to the Navigation Act, and
to the prosecutions to which his efforts on the subject had
exposed him, and which obliged him to present a Memorial to the King.   Frauds upon Government in the West
Indies to an enormous extent having been brought to his
notice, he communicated the discovery to the Prime Minister, the Master General of the Ordnance, the Comptroller
of the Navy, and to the Heads of other Departments, in
numerous Letters, all proving that he identified himself on
every occasion, and at all periods of his life, with the true
interests of his Country.

His Letters while on Half-pay, from 1788 to the commencement of 1793, show his earnest desire for employment;
and his Correspondence in 1793 and 1794, which chiefly
relates to his Action with a Squadron of French Frigates,
to the operations at Toulon, and to the Sieges of Bastia
and Calvi, in Corsica, form a complete vindication of
his claims to consideration, by placing his zeal, gallantry,
and talents, in the strongest light.

In all these Letters there appear the same devotion to
the service of his King and Country, the same energy of
character, and the same abilities, as were afterwards shown
on a larger field, and on more important occasions.

Every Letter, whether official or private, is placed according to its exact date, so that the thoughts and duties which
occupied his mind each day, and even at various times
of the same day, may be traced; and these transitions
are often extremely curious.   This arrangement has a
great advantage over any mere *classification,* not only

because the chains of thought and of events are alike unbroken, but the dry professional details of a Public Dispatch are often relieved by the more attractive contents of private and familiar communications.

In a few instances the Names of individuals have been suppressed, as their publication might be displeasing to their families, without any counterbalancing advantage; but it has not been thought right (except where conditions to that effect were imposed upon the Editor by those from whom he obtained the Letters) to omit any Name when it occurs in relation to Public affairs of importance; for NELSON'S opinions of the chief actors in the great events of his time, and of the events themselves, belong to History, and form the principal value of his Correspondence.

The Editor's NOTES do not contain a word more than is absolutely necessary to render the Letters understood, or to identify the persons mentioned. In some places the Text is illustrated by copies of, or extracts from, Letters addressed to NELSON; and particularly from his late Majesty King William the Fourth, Admiral Viscount Hood, and other eminent personages.

Where individuals are not identified, it is to be understood that accurate information respecting them could not be found; and the Editor will feel grateful for authenticated communications to supply the omissions, and for the correction of any error into which he may have fallen.

Complete Indexes will be given in the last Volume of the Work.

Torrington Square,
October 21st, 1844.

CONTENTS.

LETTERS

[The Letters thus marked * are inserted for the first time in this Edition; and this mark † indicates that the Letters were printed in the first Edition from Clarke and M'Arthur's "Life of Nelson," but that they have since been collated with the *originals*, and many additions made to them.]

1781 *continued.*

1782.

1783.

1784.

·

1786 *continued*.

1787.

1787 *continued.*

1793 *continued.*

1794 *continued.*

1794 *continued.*

1794 *continued.*

1794 *continued.*

ANALYSIS

OF THE

LIFE OF NELSON

FROM 1758 TO 1794.

YEAR.	MONTH.	FACTS.
1758.	September 29......*BORN.*	
1770.	About December ..Went to Sea as *MIDSHIPMAN* of the Raisonable.	
1771.	About June ......Joined a *Merchant Ship*, and went to the West Indies.	
1772.	July ....Became Midshipman of the *Triumph.*	
1773.	About August	Ditto	the *Carcass.*
1774.	About February ..	Ditto	the *Triumph.*
—	About March	Ditto	the *Seahorse.*
1776.	About August	Ditto	the *Dolphin.*
1776.	September 24......Appointed *Acting Lieutenant* of the *Worcester.*	
1777.	April 9th ....Passed his Examination for Lieutenant.	
—	April 10th ....Appointed *LIEUTENANT* of the *Lowestoffe*	
1778.	About July........Became Third Lieutenant of the *Bristol* at Jamaica.	
—	September 4th ....Appointed First Lieutenant of the *Bristol.*	

YEAR.	MONTH.	FACTS.
1778.	December 8th	Promoted to the rank of *COMMANDER*, and appointed to the *Badger* Brig, in the West Indies.
1779.	June 11th	Promoted to the rank of *POST CAPTAIN*, and Appointed to the *Hinchinbrook*.
1780.	January	Employed in the Expedition against St. Juan.
—	April	Appointed Captain of the *Janus*.
—	August 30th	Resigned the command of the *Janus* on account of ill health, and returned to England in the *Lion*.
—	Autumn	Arrived in England and proceeded to Bath.
1781.	January to August	On Half-Pay, and resided chiefly at Bath.
—	August	Appointed Captain of the *Albemarle* of 28 guns.
—	October to	Employed in the North Sea.
1782.	January	
—	January to April	At Portsmouth.
—	April 17th	Sailed for Quebec.
—	May 27th	Arrived at Newfoundland.
—	July 1st	Arrived at the Isle of Bic.
—	— 4th	Sailed on a Cruize.
—	August 14th	Fell in with a French Squadron.
—	September 17th	Returned to Quebec.
—	October 20th	Sailed with a Convoy to New York.
—	November 13th	Arrived at New York.
—	About December ..	Proceeded to the West Indies.
1783.	March 8th	Attacked Turks' Island.
—	June 25th	Arrived at Spithead.
—	July 3rd	Paid off the *Albemarle*, and was placed on Half-Pay.
—	November	Went to France, and arrived at St. Omer's.
1784.	January	Returned to England.
—	— 25th	Went to Bath.
—	March 18th	Appointed Captain of the *Boreas*, of 28 guns.

YEAR.	MONTH.	FACTS.

1784 *continued.* .... In command of the *Boreas.*

— May .... Sailed for the Leeward Islands, having on board Lady Hughes, wife of Rear-Admiral Sir Richard Hughes, Bart., the Commander-in-Chief on that Station.

June 1st .... Arrived at Madeira.

— — 26th .... Arrived at Barbadoes

to
1787. May } .... Employed in suppressing illegal traffic in the Leeward Islands.

— March 12th ...... Married.

— July 4th .... Arrived at Spithead, and was sent to the Nore.

— December
to } Paid off the *Boreas,* and was placed on Half Pay: resided principally at Burnham Thorpe, in Norfolk.

1793. January 26th...... Appointed Captain of the *Agamemnon* of 64 guns.

— May .... Cruizing in the Channel with the Squadron under Vice-Admiral Hotham.

— June .... Sailed for the Mediterranean under Lord Hood.

— July 16th to
August 25th } .. Off Toulon.

— September 11th .... At Naples.

— — 27th ...... At Leghorn.

— October 5th ...... At Toulon.

— — 22nd .... Engaged La Melpomene, one of a Squadron of French Frigates off the East End of Sardinia.

— — 24th ...... At Cagliari.

— November 1st to 30th In Tunis Bay.

— December
to
1794. February } .. Off Corsica, (occasionally touching at Leghorn,) and employed in harassing the Enemy in Corsica.

— — 6th .... Burnt four Vessels at Centuri.

— — 8th .... Attacked Maginaggio, and took or destroyed eight vessels.

— — 12th....... Personally engaged in a "very smart contest" at Capraja.

YEAR.	MONTH.	FACTS.
1794 *continued.*	...	In command of the *Agamemnon.*
—	— 19th	Took the Tower of Miomo near Bastia.
—	— 27th	Cannonaded Bastia.
—	April 4th to May 22nd } ..	At the Siege of Bastia.
—	— 23rd	Bastia Surrendered.
—	June (about the 4th.)	Sailed, with Lord Hood, in pursuit of the French Fleet, which took refuge in Gourjean Bay.
—	— 12th	Returned to Bastia.
—	— 13th	Sailed for Calvi.
— —	— 19th to August 10th }	At the Siege of Calvi; and on the 10th of July was severely wounded in the right eye.
—	— 18th	Arrived at Leghorn.
—	September 19th to 27th	At Genoa.
—	October	Off Gourjean Bay, with the Fleet under Vice-Admiral Hotham.
—	— 24th to 31st	At Leghorn.
—	November 3rd	Rejoined Vice-Admiral Hotham off Gourjean Bay, and was sent to reconnoitre Toulon.
—	— 10th	At St. Fiorenzo in Corsica.
—	— 28th	At Leghorn.

ILLUSTRATIONS TO VOL. I.

"SKETCH OF MY LIFE."

SKETCH OF MY LIFE:

[Autograph, in the possession of Mrs. Conway. This was written by Lord Nelson, and communicated, in October 1799, to John M'Arthur, Esq., Author (with Dr. Stanier Clarke) of the "Life of Nelson," (4to. 1809, and 8vo. 1840.) See Lord Nelson's Letter on the subject in its proper place.]

HORATIO NELSON,[1] son of the Reverend Edmund Nelson, Rector of Burnham Thorpe, in the County of Norfolk, and Catherine his wife, daughter of Doctor Suckling, Prebendary of Westminster, whose [grand]mother was sister to Sir Robert Walpole, Earl of Orford.

I was born September 29th, 1758, in the Parsonage-house,[2] was sent to the high-school at Norwich, and afterwards removed to North Walsham;[3] from whence, on the disturbance with Spain relative to Falkland's Islands, I

---

[1] All the biographers of Lord Nelson state that he was called after his *god-father*, Horatio *first* Lord Walpole of Wolterton; but that nobleman died on the 5th February 1757, seventeen months before Nelson was born. His Sponsors were Horatio, *second* Lord Walpole of Wolterton, Dr. Hamond, and Mrs. Joyce Pyle.

[2] Extract from the Register of the Parish of Burnham Thorpe, obligingly communicated by the Rev. W. H. Everard, Curate, on the 27th June 1844.

"1758. Horatio, son of Edmund and Catherine Nelson, born Septr. 29th, Baptized Octr. 9th, priv. Pub. Nov. 15th.

"ED. NELSON, Rector."

The following Note was attached to the Register by his brother, William, 1st Earl Nelson:

"Invested with the Ensigns of the Most Honourable Order of the Bath at St. James's, Sept. 27th, 1797. Made Rear-Admiral of the Blue, 1797. Created Lord Nelson of the Nile, and Burnham Thorpe, Oct. 6th, 1798.—Cætera enarret Fama!"

[3] He was also at School at Downham in Norfolk, and Captain Manby (so well known for his Invention to save Shipwrecked mariners) is perhaps the only one of his schoolfellows there, now living.

went to Sea [4] with my uncle, Captain Maurice Suckling, in the Raisonable of 64 guns. But the business with Spain being accommodated, I was sent in a West India Ship belonging to the house of Hibbert, Purrier, Horton, with Mr. John Rathbone, who had formerly been in the Navy, in the Dreadnought with Captain Suckling. From this voyage I returned to the Triumph at Chatham in July 1772;[5] and, if I did not improve in my education, I returned a practical Seaman, with a horror of the Royal Navy, and with a saying, then constant with the Seamen, '*Aft the most honour, forward the better man !*'—It was many weeks before I got in the least reconciled to a Man-of-War, so deep was the prejudice rooted ; and what pains were taken to instil this erroneous principle in a young mind ! However, as my ambition was to be a Seaman, it was always held out as a reward, that if I attended well to my navigation, I should go in the cutter and decked long-boat, which was attached to the Commanding officer's ship at Chatham. Thus by degrees I became a good pilot, for vessels of that description, from Chatham to the Tower of London, down the Swin, and to the North Foreland; and confident of myself amongst rocks and sands, which has many times since been of the very greatest comfort to me. In this way I was trained, till the expedition towards the North Pole was fitted out; when, although no boys were allowed to go in the Ships, (as of no use,) yet nothing could prevent my using every interest to go with Captain Lutwidge in the Carcass;[6] and, as I fancied I was to fill a man's place, I begged I might be his cockswain : which, finding my ardent desire for going with him, Captain L.[7] complied with, and has con-

[4] 1770, being twelve years old. He was rated " Midshipman," and served five months and one day in the Raisonable.

[5] Rated " Captain's servant " for one year, two months, and two days ; and " Midshipman " ten months, one week, and five days.

[6] He was rated " Midshipman," and remained in the Carcass five months and three days.

[7] Captain Skeffington Lutwidge, who is frequently mentioned in Nelson's Letters. He died an Admiral of the Red, in August 1814.

tinued the strictest friendship to this moment. Lord Mulgrave,[8] who I then first knew, continued his kindest friendship and regard to the last moment of his life. When the boats were fitting out to quit the two Ships blocked up in the ice, I exerted myself to have the command of a four-oared cutter raised upon, which was given me, with twelve men; and I prided myself in fancying I could navigate her better than any other boat in the Ship.

On our arrival in England, and paid off, October 15, I found that a Squadron was fitting out for the East Indies; and nothing less than such a distant voyage could in the least satisfy my desire of maritime knowledge : and I was placed in the Seahorse of 20 guns, with Captain Farmer,[9] and watched in the foretop; from whence in time I was placed on the quarter-deck : having, in the time I was in this Ship, visited almost every part of the East Indies, from Bengal to Bussorah. Ill health induced Sir Edward Hughes,[10] who had always shown me the greatest kindness, to send me to England in

---

[8] Constantine John Phipps, 2nd Lord Mulgrave in Ireland, Captain R.N., Author of " A Voyage towards the North Pole," 4to. 1773, describing his attempt to discover a N. E. passage into the South Seas. He died 10 Oct. 1793.

[9] He joined the Sea-Horse in October 1773, on which occasion Mr. Bentham, of the Navy Office, wrote the following Note (the original of which is now in the possession of Robert Cole, Esq., of Norton Street,) to Mr. Kee, a Navy Agent, to whom it appears to have been delivered by Nelson himself :—

" Mr. Bentham's Compliments to Mr. Kee; he understands he is Agent to Mr. Surridge, the Master of the Seahorse, should be obliged to him for a recommendation in favour of Horatio Nelson, a young lad, nephew to Captain Suckling, who is going in that Ship.

" The Master is a necessary man for a young lad to be introduced to, therefore Mr. Bentham will be obliged to Mr. Kee for a Letter. The Ships wait only for the Commodore's dispatches.

" Navy Office, 28th Oct. 1773."

Nelson was rated " Midshipman " in the Seahorse for five months, two weeks, and six days; then " Able" for one year, seven months, one week, and six days, and then again " Midshipman " for four months, three weeks, and two days. Captain George Farmer, of the Seahorse, gallantly fell in command of the Quebec, of thirty-two guns, which ship was burnt in action with Le Surveillante, French frigate of thirty-six guns, off Ushant, in 1779.

[10] Commodore Sir Edward Hughes, K. B., Commander-in-chief in the East Indies, who died an Admiral of the Blue in February 1794.

the Dolphin of 20 guns, with Captain James Pigot,[1] whose kindness at that time saved my life. This ship was paid off at Woolwich on the 24th September 1776. On the 26th I received an order from Sir James Douglas,[2] who commanded at Portsmouth, to act as Lieutenant of the Worcester, 64, Captain Mark Robinson,[3] who was ordered to Gibraltar with a convoy. In this Ship I was at sea with convoys till April 2nd, 1777, and in very bad weather; but although my age might have been a sufficient cause for not entrusting me with the charge of a Watch, yet Captain Robinson used to say, ' he felt as easy when I was upon deck, as any Officer in the Ship.'

[1] He served as Midshipman in the Dolphin, for six months, three weeks, and six days. Captain Pigot died a full Admiral.

[2] Vice-Admiral Sir James Douglas died an Admiral of the White in 1787.

[3] Captain Mark Robinson, who distinguished himself on many occasions, and lost a leg while commanding the Swiftsure, in Admiral Graves' action in September 1781, died a superannuated Rear-Admiral in 1799. He left a son, the late Admiral Mark Robinson, two Letters to whom, from Lord Nelson, in 1804 and 1805, will be found in this Work. For those Letters and for the following Extracts from Captain Robinson's Diary, relating to Nelson when Acting Lieutenant of the Worcester in 1776 and 1777, the Editor is indebted to that gallant Officer's grandson, Commander Thomas Pitt Robinson, R.N. :—

1776, October 8th.—Captain Robinson mentions that Mr. Nelson joined his Ship and brought letters from his uncle, Captain Suckling. The Worcester preparing for sea. October 9th.—Captain Robinson remarks his having, this day, introduced Mr. Nelson to Sir James Douglas, Commander-in-Chief at Portsmouth. "Wrote letter to Mr. Suckling. Worcester went out of harbour." October 10th.—" Mr. Nelson and Captain Varlo dined with me : very busy getting live-stock on board, and getting Ship ready for sea." October 11th.—" Dined on shore with my friend Mr. P. Varlo, Mayor of Portsmouth, in company with Mr. Nelson." October 17th.—" Dined and spent the evening with Mr. Nelson at Captain Varlo's."

1777, January 11th, at Gibraltar.—" Sent my letters on shore by Mr. Nelson to put into the Post for the British Consul, Mr. Hardy, at Cadiz." February 1st.— Captain Robinson mentions his having given Mr. Nelson four guineas. April 11th.—Captain Robinson confined to his room by illness at Portsmouth, received a letter from Mr. Nelson. April 12th.—Received a letter from Lord Sandwich in favour of his request: received a letter from Mr. Nelson, informing him that he had received his commission as Lieutenant of the Lowestoffe frigate. April 13th.—Captain Robinson remarks his writing to Mr. Nelson and sending Lord Sandwich's letter. April 15th.—Wrote to Lieutenant Nelson and enclosed his discharge, &c. September 29th.—" Received of Maurice Suckling, Esq., what I paid Mr. Dalrymple for Mr. Nelson—£1 14s. 6d."

On the 8th of April, 1777, I passed my examination[4] as a Lieutenant; and received my Commission the next day,[5] as second Lieutenant of the Lowestoffe frigate of 32 guns, Captain (now Lieutenant-Governor of Greenwich hospital) William Locker.[6] In this Ship I went to Jamaica: but even a Frigate was not sufficiently active for my mind, and I got into a Schooner,[7] tender to the Lowestoffe. In this vessel I made myself a complete pilot for all the passages through the (Keys) Islands situated on the north side Hispaniola. Whilst in this Frigate, an event happened which presaged my character; and, as it conveys no dishonour to the Officer alluded to, I shall relate it:

Blowing a gale of wind,[8] and very heavy sea, the Frigate captured an American Letter of Marque. The first Lieutenant was ordered to board her, which he did not do, owing to the very high sea. On his return on board, the Captain said, 'Have I no Officer in the Ship who can board the Prize?' On which the Master ran to the gangway, to get into the boat: when I stopped him, saying, 'It is my turn now; and if I come back, it is yours.' This little incident has often occurred to my mind; and I know it is my disposition, that difficulties and dangers do but increase my desire of attempting them.

Sir Peter Parker, soon after his arrival at Jamaica, (1778,) took me into his own Flag-Ship, the Bristol, as third Lieutenant; from which I rose by succession to be First.[9] Nothing particular happened whilst I was in this Ship, which

[4] Vide p. 21, postea.

[5] His Commission as Lieutenant was dated April 10th, 1777.

[6] Captain Locker is frequently mentioned in this work. Many of Nelson's Letters were written to him.

[7] "The Little Lucy;" so called after a daughter of Captain Locker.

[8] Between Cape Maize and Cape Nicola Mola, on the 20th October 1777. See another account of this occurrence in *Clarke and M'Arthur's Life of Nelson,* 4to, 1809, vol. i. p. 16.

[9] On the 4th September, 1778, Lieutenant Horatio Nelson, 3rd Lieutenant of the Bristol, was appointed 1st Lieutenant of that Ship, and Lieutenant James Macnamara (who attained the rank of Flag-officer, and died in 1802,) was appointed 3rd Lieutenant of the Bristol in Nelson's vacancy.—*Admiralty Records.* Vide p. 25, post.

was actively employed off Cape François, being the commencement of the French war.

On the 8th of December 1778, I was appointed Commander of the Badger Brig ;[1] and was first sent to protect the Mosquito shore, and the bay of Honduras, from the depredations of the American privateers. Whilst on this service, I gained so much the affections of the Settlers, that they unanimously voted me their thanks, and expressed their regret on my leaving them; entrusting to me to describe to Sir Peter Parker and Sir John Dalling[2] their situation, should a war with Spain break out. Whilst I commanded this Brig, H.M.S. Glasgow, Captain Thomas Lloyd, came into Montego Bay, Jamaica, where the Badger was laying: in two hours afterwards she took fire by a cask of rum; and Captain Lloyd will tell you, that it was owing to my exertions, joined to his, that her whole crew were rescued from the flames.

On the 11th of June 1779, I was made Post into the Hinchinbrook.[3] When, being at sea, and Count d'Estaing

---

[1] The following extract from a list of Officers appointed by Vice-Admiral Sir Peter Parker, Commander-in-Chief at Jamaica, from the 29th September 1778, to 21st February 1779, is highly interesting from its containing the names of *Nelson* and *Collingwood* in juxtaposition.

Time.	Persons' names.	Appointments.	From whence.	To what ship.	In whose room.	Occasion of the Vacancy.
8 Dec. 1778.	Lt. Horatio Nelson.	Commander.	1 Lt. of Bristol	Badger	Capt. Mich. John Everitt	Appointed Commander of the Port Royal
	Lt. James M'Namara.	1st Lt.	3 Lt. of Bristol	Bristol	Lt Horatio Nelson	Ditto of the Badger
	L. Cuthbert Collingwood.	2nd Lt.	2 Lt. of Lowestoffe	Ditto	Lt. John Pakenham	Appointed Lieutenant of the Hinchinbrook.

Lord Collingwood in his own account of his services says :—"In 1776 I went to Jamaica, Lieutenant of the Hornet sloop, and soon after the Lowestoffe came to the same station, of which Lord Nelson was Lieutenant. We had been long before in the habits of great friendship, and it happened here that Sir Peter Parker, the Commander-in-Chief, being the friend of both, whenever Lord Nelson got a step in rank, I succeeded him—first in the Lowestoffe, then in the Badger, into which Ship I was made a Commander in 1779, and afterwards the Hinchinbrook, a 28 gun frigate, which made us both Post-captains."—*Naval Chronicle*, vol. xxiii. p. 330.

[2] General George Dalling, Commander-in-Chief at Jamaica, was created a Baronet in March 1783, and died in 1798.

[3] He was succeeded in the command of the Badger, by Captain Cuthbert Collingwood.

arriving at Hispaniola with a very large Fleet and Army from Martinico, an attack on Jamaica was expected. In this critical state, I was by both Admiral and General intrusted with the command of the batteries at Port Royal:[4] and I need not say, as the defence of this place was the key to the Port of the whole Naval force, the Town of Kingston, and Spanish Town, it was the most important post in the whole Island.

In January 1780, an Expedition being resolved on against St. Juan's, I was chosen to command the Sea part of it. Major Polson, who commanded, will tell you of my exertions:[5] how

[4] Vide p. 31 post.

[5] In his official Dispatch, dated 30th April 1780, Colonel Polson said of Captain Nelson, "I want words to express the obligations I owe that gentleman. He was the first on every service whether by night or by day. There was scarcely a gun but what was pointed by him or Lieutenant Despard." General Dalling wrote a private letter to Lord George Germain, Secretary at War, pointing out his services, and "humbly entreating that his Majesty would be graciously pleased to manifest a satisfaction of Captain Nelson's conduct. Such minds, my Lord, are most devoutly to be wished, for Government's sake." In a note to Nelson, dated Kingston, May 30th, 1780, General Dalling said, "Thanks to you, my friend, for your kind congratulations: to you, without compliment do I attribute, in a great measure, the cause." [*Original* in the Nelson Papers.] His health suffered so severely from his exertions and from the climate, that he was compelled to quit his Ship, and return to Jamaica, attended by Mr. Tyson (afterwards his Secretary, and subsequently Clerk of the Survey in Chatham Dock Yard), in the Victor Sloop-of-War. Such was his debility from dysentery, that on his arrival he was obliged to be removed to the Lodging-house of Cuba in his cot.

Two Narratives of that Expedition have been published; one by Dr. Benjamin Moseley, in his "Treatise on Tropical Diseases," 8vo. London, 1803-4, and another by Dr. Thomas Dancer; entitled "A Brief History of the late Expedition against Fort St. Juan, so far as it relates to the Diseases of the Troops." 4to. Kingston, 1792. Early in 1803, Lord Nelson wrote the following remarks on this Expedition, for the second edition of Dr. Moseley's work:—

"Had the expedition arrived at San Juan's harbour in the month of January, the violent torrents would have subsided, and of course the whole Army would not have had occasion, which was the case in April, to get wet three or four times a day in dragging the boats. They would then have arrived at the Castle by the middle of February, and had between two or three months of fair season to have established themselves, with all the stores, in the healthy country of Granada and Leon: and then, I think, a road for carriages might have been made from Bluefields harbour, a healthier place than San Juan's to the Lake Nicaragua.

"The fever which destroyed the Army and Navy attached to that Expedition, was invariably from twenty to thirty days before it attacked the new-comers; and I cannot give a stronger instance, than that in the Hinchinbrook, with a complement of two hundred men, eighty-seven took to their beds in one night; and

I quitted my Ship, carried troops in boats one hundred miles up a river, which none but Spaniards since the time of the buccaneers had ever ascended that river. It will then be told how I boarded, (if I may be allowed the expression,) an out-post of the Enemy, situated on an Island in the river; that I made batteries, and afterwards fought them, and was a principal cause of our success. From this scene I was appointed to the Janus, 44, at Jamaica,[6] and went to Port Royal in the Victor sloop.

My state of health was now so bad, that I was obliged to go to England in the Lion, Honourable William Cornwallis, Captain; whose care and attention again saved my life. In August 1781, I was commissioned for the Albemarle; and, it would almost be supposed, to try my constitution, was kept the whole winter in the North Sea. In April 1782, I sailed with a convoy for Newfoundland and Quebec, under the orders of Captain Thomas Pringle. From Quebec, dur-ing a cruise off Boston, I was chased by three French Ships of the Line, and the Iris frigate: as they all beat me in sail-ing very much, I had no chance left, but running them amongst the shoals of St. George's bank. This alarmed the Line-of-Battle Ships, and they quitted the pursuit; but the Frigate continued, and at sun-set was little more than gun-shot distant: when, the Line-of-Battle Ships being out of sight, I ordered the main-top-sail to be laid to the mast; when the Frigate tacked, and stood to rejoin her consorts.

of the two hundred, one hundred and forty-five were buried in mine and Cap-tain Collingwood's time ; and I believe very few, not more than ten, survived of that Ship's crew ; a proof how necessary expedition is in those climates."

[6] Extract from a letter from Vice-Admiral Sir Peter Parker to the Secretary to the Admiralty, dated Jamaica, 7th April 1780. The vacancy was caused by the death of Captain Glover of the Janus :

" I have moved Captain Nelson of the Hinchinbrook into the Janus, and ap-pointed Captain Cuthbert Collingwood of the Badger Sloop, Captain of the Hinchinbrook, and Lieutenant Hood Walker, late first Lieutenant of the Niger, Commander of the Badger."—*Admiralty Records.*

The remaining part of Lord Nelson's Sketch of his Life, will be best illus-trated by the Notes to his LETTERS.

In October I sailed from Quebec with a convoy to New York, where I joined the Fleet under the command of Lord Hood; and in November I sailed with him to the West Indies, where I remained till the Peace; when I came to England, (being directed in my way to attend H. R. H. Duke of Clarence in his visit to the Havannah;) and was paid off at Portsmouth on July 3rd, 1783. In the autumn I went to France, and remained till the spring of the year 1784; when I was appointed to the Boreas frigate, of 28 guns, and ordered to the Leeward Island station.

This Station opened a new scene to the Officers of the British navy. The Americans, when colonists, possessed almost all the trade from America to our West India Islands: and on the return of Peace, they forgot, on this occasion, they became Foreigners, and of course had no right to trade in the British Colonies. Our Governors and Custom-house Officers pretended, that by the Navigation Act they had a right to trade; and all the West Indians wished what was so much for their interest.

Having given Governors, Custom-house Officers, and Americans, notice of what I would do, I seized many of their Vessels, which brought all parties upon me; and I was persecuted from one Island to another, that I could not leave my Ship. But conscious rectitude bore me through it; and I was supported, when the business came to be understood, from home: and I proved, (and an Act of Parliament has since established it,) that a Captain of a Man of War is in duty bound to support all the Maritime Laws, by his Admiralty commission alone, without becoming a Custom-house Officer.

In July 1786, I was left with the command till June 1787, when I sailed for England. During this winter H. R. H. the Duke of Clarence visited the Leeward Islands in the Pegasus frigate, of which he was Captain; and in March, this year, I married Frances Herbert Nisbet, widow of Dr. Nisbet, of the Island of Nevis; by whom I have no children.

The Boreas being paid off at Sheerness, on November the 30th, I lived at Burnham Thorpe, county of Norfolk, in the Parsonage-house. In 1790, when the Affair with Spain, relative to Nootka Sound, had near involved us in a war, I made use of every interest to get a Ship, *ay*, even a boat, to serve my Country, but in vain: there was a prejudice at the Admiralty evidently against me, which I can neither guess at, or in the least account for.

On the 30th of January 1793, I was commissioned in the very handsomest way for the Agamemnon, 64; and was put under the command of that great man and excellent officer, Lord Hood, appointed to the command in the Mediterranean. The unbounded confidence on all occasions placed in me by his Lordship, will show his opinion of my abilities; having served in the command of the seamen landed for the sieges of Bastia and Calvi. His Lordship, in October 1794, left the Mediterranean to Admiral Hotham, who also honoured me with the same confidence. I was in the Actions of the 13th and 14th of March 1795, and 13th of July in the same year. For the share I had in them, I refer to the Admiral's letters. I was then appointed by Admiral Hotham to co-operate with the Austrian General, De Vins, which I did all the time Admiral Hotham retained the command, till November; when he was superseded by Sir John Jervis, now Earl St. Vincent.

In April 1796, the Commander-in-chief so much approved my conduct, that he directed me to wear a Distinguishing Pendant. In June I was removed from the Agamemnon to the Captain; and on the 11th of August appointed a Captain under me. Between April and October, I was employed in the blockade of Leghorn, taking Port Ferrajo, the Island of Caprea, and finally in the evacuation of Bastia: when having seen the troops in safety to Port Ferrajo, I joined the Admiral in St. Fiorenzo, and proceeded with him to Gibraltar; from whence in December I was sent in La Minerve frigate, Captain George Cockburn, to Port Ferrajo, to bring down our Naval stores, &c. On the passage we captured a Spanish Frigate, La Sabina, of 40 guns, 28 eighteen pounders on her main deck, as will appear by my Letter.

From sailing from Port Ferrajo on the 29th of January 1797, to the finish of the Action, 14th of February, I refer to the account published by Colonel Drinkwater. The King for my conduct gave me a gold Medal, and the City of London a gold Box.

In April I hoisted my Flag as Rear-Admiral of the Blue, and was sent to bring down the garrison of Port Ferrajo: which service performed, I shifted my Flag from the Captain to the Theseus on May the 27th, and was employed in the command of the inner Squadron in the blockade of Cadiz. It was during this period that perhaps my personal courage was more conspicuous than at any other period of my life. In an attack of the Spanish gun-boats, I was boarded in my barge with its common crew of ten men, Cockswain, Captain Fremantle, and myself, by the Commander of the Gunboats. The Spanish barge rowed twenty-six oars, besides Officers, thirty in the whole; this was a service hand to hand with swords, in which my Cockswain, John Sykes, (now no more,) saved twice my life. Eighteen of the Spaniards being killed and several wounded, we succeeded in taking their Commander.

On the 15th of July, I sailed for Teneriffe: the event, I refer to my Letter of that Expedition. Having lost my right arm, for this loss and my former services his Majesty was pleased to settle £800 a-year; and by some unlucky mismanagement of it, I was obliged to go to England; and it was the 13th of December, before the surgeons pronounced me fit for service. On the 19th, the Vanguard was commissioned for my Flag-ship.

On the 1st of April 1798, I sailed with a convoy from Spithead: at the back of the Wight, the wind coming to the westward, I was forced to return to St. Helen's, and finally sailed on the 9th, carrying a convoy at Oporto and Lisbon. I joined Earl St. Vincent off Cadiz, on April 29th; being on the 30th ordered into the Mediterranean. I refer to a Book printed for my proceedings to the close of the Battle of the Nile.

On the 22nd September, I arrived at Naples, and was received as a Deliverer by the King, Queen, and the whole Kingdom. October 12th the blockade of Malta took place, which has continued without intermission to this day.[6] On the 21st December, his Sicilian Majesty and family embarked in the Vanguard, and were carried to Palermo in Sicily. In March, I arranged a plan for taking the Islands in the Bay of Naples, and for supporting the Royalists who were making head in the Kingdom. This plan succeeded in every part. In May I shifted my Flag, being promoted to be Rear-Admiral of the Red, to the Foudroyant; and was obliged to be on my guard against the French Fleet. In June and July I went to Naples, and, as his Sicilian Majesty is pleased to say, I reconquered his Kingdom, and placed him on his Throne. On the 9th August I brought his Sicilian Majesty back to Palermo, having been upwards of four weeks on board the Foudroyant.

On the 13th his Sicilian Majesty presented me with a Sword most magnificently enriched with diamonds, the Title of Duke of Bronté, and annexed to it the feud of Bronté, supposed to be worth £3,000 per annum. On the arrival

---

[6] i. e. The 15th of October 1799, when this SKETCH was written.

of the Russian Squadron at Naples, I directed Commodore Troubridge to go with the Squadron, and blockade closely Civita Vecchia, and to offer the French most favourable conditions, if they would evacuate Rome and Civita Vecchia; which terms the French General, Grenier, complied with, and they were signed on board the Culloden : thus a prophecy, made to me on my arrival at Naples, was fulfilled, viz. *that I should take Rome with my Ships.*

Thus may be exemplified by my Life, that perseverance in any profession will most probably meet its reward. Without having any inheritance, or having been fortunate in prize-money, I have received all the Honours of my Profession, been created a Peer of Great Britain, &c., &c. as set forth in the annexed Paper, and I may say to the Reader, ' Go thou, and do likewise.'

Presents received for my Services in the Mediterranean between October 1st, 1798, and October 1st, 1799 :—

From my own most gracious Sovereign, a Peerage of Great Britain, and a gold Medal.

From the Parliament of Great Britain, for my life and two next heirs, £2000 per annum.

From the Parliament of Ireland not known, but supposed the same as given to St. Vincent and Duncan, £1000 per annum.

From the Honourable East India Company, £10,000.

From the Turkey Company, a piece of Plate.

From Alexander Davison, Esq., a gold Medal.

City of London, a Sword.

The Captains who served under my orders in the Battle of the Nile, a Sword.

The Grand Signor, a Diamond Aigrette, or Plume of Triumph, valued at £2000. Ditto, a rich Pelisse, valued at £1000. The Grand Signor's Mother, a Box set with diamonds, valued at £1000.

Emperor of Russia, a Box set with diamonds, and a most elegant Letter—£2500.

King of the Sicilies, a Sword, richly ornamented with diamonds, and a most elegant and kind Letter, £5000 ; and the Dukedom of Bronté, with an Estate supposed worth £3000 per annum.

King of Sardinia, a Box set with diamonds, and a most elegant Letter, £1200.

The Island of Zante, a gold-headed Sword and Cane, as an acknowledgment that had it not been for the Battle of the Nile they could not have been liberated from French cruelty.

City of Palermo, a gold Box and Chain, brought on a silver waiter.

Port Mahon, October 15th, 1799.

It may be convenient to state here the following particulars of Lord Nelson's Family in illustration of this " Sketch of his Life," and of many of his Letters.

The family of NELSON were settled for several generations in Norfolk, and became connected with the noble house of Walpole in the following manner:— Robert Walpole of Houghton, in Norfolk, Esquire, had three sons and many daughters; viz.—1. Sir Robert Walpole, K. G., created Earl of Orford; 2. *Horatio*, created Lord Walpole of Wolterton, (ancestor of the present Earl of Orford,) from whose son, *Horatio*, 2nd Lord Walpole of Wolterton, *Horatio Nelson* derived his baptismal name ; 3. Galfridus, a Captain in the Navy, who distinguished himself and lost his arm in action, in command of the Lion. Of the daughters, Mary Walpole married Sir Charles Turner, of Warham, in Norfolk, Bart., and their daughter Ann became the wife of Dr. Maurice Suckling, Prebendary of Westminster, by whom she had two sons, viz. Captain Maurice Suckling, R.N., (who died in July 1778); and William Suckling, Esq. of the Custom-House, who died in November 1798 ; and a daugh_ ter Katherine, who married, 11th May 1749, the Rev. *Edmund Nelson*, Rector of Burnham Thorpe in Norfolk, son of the Rev. Edmund Nelson, who was Rector of Hilborough, in Norfolk, and died in 1747, æt. 54. The RE- VEREND EDMUND NELSON, (Lord Nelson's father,) wrote the following account of himself:—" I was born at East Bradenham, March 19, 1722,

[1722-3]. Educated at a school in the country, always a weak and sickly constitution. In 1742 admitted in Caius College, Cambridge, Doctor Gooch then Master ; my tutor Doctor Eglinton. Took a Bachelor's Degree at the usual time, was Ordained soon after, and at Michaelmas 1745, went as Curate to the Reverend Thomas Page, Rector of Beccles in Suffolk: there remained till October 1747. My father succeeded him in both his Livings—Hilborough, on my mother's presentation ; Spoole, the Provost and Fellows of Eton. The whole profit of Hilborough I gave up for the purpose of paying my father's debts, and the maintenance of my mother and her family. Spoole living is about £80 per annum. I resided with my mother at Hilborough; but in May 1749, married Catherine, daughter of Maurice Suckling, late Prebendary of Westminster, and Rector of Barsham and Wooten in Suffolk, and Ann his wife, daughter of Sir Charles Turner, Bart., of Warham. At Michaelmas 1749, went to housekeeping at Swaffham, and at Michaelmas 1753, removed into a hired house at Spoole. In November 1755, on the death of Thomas Smithson, Clerk, was preferred to the Rectories of Burnham Thorpe, on the presentation of the Honourable Horace Walpole, afterwards Lord Walpole, of Wolterton, and the Rectory of Burnham St. Albert with the Moieties of Ulp L. St. Margarets alias Norton."

He had issue—

1. Edmund, 2. Horace, who both died infants.

3. Maurice, born 24th May 1753, a Clerk in the Navy Office, who died without issue, 24th April 1801. He married Sarah Ford, who survived until 1810, and lived on an annuity allowed her by Admiral Viscount Nelson.

4. Rev. William Nelson, D.D., born 20th April 1757, afterwards *Earl Nelson*, who married on the 9th November 1786, Sarah, daughter of the Rev. Henry Yonge ; and had issue, Horatio Viscount Trafalgar, born 26th October 1788, and died 14 January 1808, unmarried ; and Charlotte Mary, wife of Samuel, the present Lord Bridport.

5. Vice-Admiral SIR HORATIO VISCOUNT NELSON AND DUKE OF BRONTE, K.B., born 29th September 1758, married 12th March 1787, Frances Herbert Woollward, only child of William Woollward, Esq., Senior Judge of the Island of Nevis, (widow of Josiah Nisbet, M.D.,) by whom, who died 4th May 1831, æt. 68, he had no issue.

6. The Rev. Suckling Nelson, died April 1799, unmarried.

7. Edmund, died unmarried, 12 December 1789.

8. George, died an infant.

9. Susannah, born 12th June 1755, married 5th August 1780, Thomas Bolton, Esq., and died 16th July 1813, leaving, besides other children, a son *Thomas*,

who became the *second EARL NELSON*, father of Horatio, the third and present EARL.

10. Ann, born 20th September 1760, died, unmarried, 15th November 1783.

11. Catherine, born 19th March 1767, and married 26th February 1787, George Matcham, Esq., by whom she has issue.

On the death of William Earl Nelson, without issue male, on the 28th of February 1835, the BARONY of NELSON, of Hilborough, the VISCOUNTCY of MERTON and TRAFALGAR, and the EARLDOM of NELSON, descended, pursuant to special limitations, to the son of his eldest sister, Mrs. Bolton, viz. *Thomas 2nd Earl Nelson,* who dying on the 1st November in the same year, was succeeded by his eldest son, HORATIO, the *third and present* EARL NELSON.

Mrs. Nelson, the Hero's mother, died on the 26th December 1767, when he was only nine years old. The inscriptions over her Remains and those of her husband at Burnham Thorpe, have been obligingly sent to the Editor by the Very Reverend and Honourable Dr. Pellew, Dean of Norwich :—

" Conservandæ Memoriæ causâ

C A T H E R I N Æ   N E L S O N,

Mauritii Suckling, D. D. filiæ,

Nepotis Caroli Turner, Baronetti,

Et primæ ejus uxoris,

Mariæ, filiæ Roberti Walpole

De Houghton Armigeri,

Uxoris Edmundi Nelson,

Hujus Ecclesiæ Rectoris,

xi liberos sibi peperit, viii supersunt.

Conjugali et maternâ affectione Christianâ charitate et verâ amicitiâ

Fuit prædita.

Obiit Decemb. 26,

Anno Salutis 1767.

Suæ Ætatis 42.

Let these alone—let no man touch these bones.''

On a marble slab against the North wall of the Chancel :—

" To the Memory of

THE REV. EDMUND NELSON, M.A.,

Rector of this Parish 46 years.

Father of Horatio first Viscount Nelson of the Nile, Duke of Bronte, &c. &c.,

Who died April 26th 1802, aged 79 years.

This Monument, the last mark of filial duty and affection,

Was erected by his surviving Children.''

Among the Nelson Papers are the following Memoranda, apparently in the writing of Lord Nelson's father :—

" Edmund Nelson, born at East Bradenham, March 19, 1722-3.

Catherine Suckling, born at Barsham, May 9th, 1725.

Edmund Nelson and Catherine Suckling were married at Beccles, 11 May 1749.

Their Issue.

* Edmund, born at Swaffham, 5 April, 1750.

* Horatio, ditto at   ditto,   28 July, 1751.

Maurice, ditto at   ditto,   24 May, 1753.

Susanna, ditto at Sporle, 12 June, 1755.

William, ditto at Burnham Thorpe, 20 April, 1757.

Horatio, ditto at   ditto,   29 September, 1758.

* Ann,   born at Burnham Thorpe, 20 September, 1760.

* Edmund, ditto at   ditto,   4 June, 1762.

* Suckling, ditto at   ditto,   5 January, 1764.

*George,   ditto at   ditto,   13 September, 1765.

Catherine, ditto at   ditto,   19 March, 1767.

Edmund, died 7 August 1752, buried at Hilborough.

Horatio, ditto 15 Nov. 1751,   ditto.

George, ditto 21 March 1766,   ditto Burnham Thorpe.

Catherine, their Mother, died 28 Dec. 1767, buried at Burnham Thorpe.

Ann Suckling, her Mother, died 3 Jan. 1768, buried at Barsham, Suffolk.

Poor *Ann Nelson, died 15 November 1783, buried at Bathford, Somersetshire."

[In another hand.]

" Edmund died 11th December 1790, buried at Burnham Thorpe, in the communion rails, south side." [1]

To these Genealogical Memoranda may be added the remarkable longevity of some of Lord Nelson's relations:

His grandmother, Mrs. Mary Nelson, (daughter of John Bland,) died at the age of 91 years and 3 months: his Father, the Reverend Edmund Nelson, died at the age of 79 years and 1 month : his Aunt, Mary Nelson, died at the age of 82 years and 2 months : his Aunt, Alice Nelson, (wife of the Reverend Robert

---

[1] In another Paper in the hand-writing of his father, he is said to have died on the 12th December 1789.

Rolfe, and grandmother of Sir Robert Monsey Rolfe, now one of the Barons of the Exchequer,) at the age of 93 years and 4 months: and his Aunt, Thomazine Nelson, wife of John Goulty, of Norwich, Gentleman, at the age of 89 years and 8 months, forming by five persons the extraordinary aggregate of 435 years and 6 months.

LETTERS,

Navy Office - April 14th 1777

Dear Brother

My Father arriv'd in Town on Friday
Evening in tolerable good health, my Sister & Brother are both
well & desire their love to you, I suppose you have not heard of
my Arrival in England yet, but we arriv'd on Thursday Week
but I been so full of business in prepareing to set out again that
I have not had time to write. I passed my Degree as Master of
Arts on the 9th Instand (that passd the Lieutenants Examination)
& Received my Commission on the following day for a fine
Frigate of 32 Guns. So I am now left in World to shift for
myself which I hope I shall do so as to bring Credit to
myself & Friends. Am sorry there is no possibility this
time of seeing each other but I hope that time will come
in a few years when we will Spend some merry hours
together —
        NB if it is not too troublesome turn over

Were we shall go at present I know not but were ever it

is I will always write to You, If You ever Chuse to

write Inclose either to may M.ʳ Suckling or my Brother.

as in all probability they will know were we are gone.

I leave London on Wednesday Evening & shall always

be glad to hear from You. Believing me to be

P.S pray give my best
respects to my Old School
fellow H. Hammond

Dear Brother

Your affectionate Brother

Horatio. Nelson

LETTERS.

TO MR. WILLIAM NELSON, CHRIST COLLEGE, CAMBRIDGE.

[Autograph, in the Nelson Papers. Mr. William Nelson, his second brother, soon after took Holy Orders. He succeeded as second Baron Nelson of the Nile, and of Hilborough, and was created Earl Nelson.]

Navy Office, April 14th, 1777.

Dear Brother,

My father arrived in town on Friday evening in tolerable good health; my sister and brother are both well, and desire their love to you. I suppose you have not heard of my arrival in England yet, but we arrived on Thursday week, but I have been so full of business in preparing to set out again, that I have not had time to write. I passed my Degree as Master of Arts on the 9th instant, (that is, passed the Lieutenant's examination,[1]) and received my Commission on the following day,

---

[1] The following copy of Nelson's "Passing Certificate," from the Record in the Tower, was communicated by Thomas Duffus Hardy, Esq., the Assistant Keeper. It appears that Nelson's examination took place on the *ninth*, and not as he states on the *eighth* of April, 1777.

"Lieutenants' Certificates. June 1762.—May 1777.

"In pursuance, &c., of the 5th April 1777, we have examined Mr. Horatio Nelson, who by certificate appears to be more than twenty years of age, and find he has gone to sea more than six years in the Ships and Qualities undermentioned: (viz.)

Raisonable	- -	Mid. - - -	0	5	0	1
Tryumph	- -	Captain's servant -	1	2	0	2
		Mid. - - -	0	10	1	5
Carcass	- -	Mid. - - -	0	5	3	0
Triumph	- -	Captain's servant -	0	0	1	5
Seahorse	- -	Mid. - - -	0	5	2	6
		Able - - -	1	7	1	6
		Mid. - - -	0	4	3	2
Dolphin	-	Mid. - - -	0	6	3	6
			6	3	1	6

for a fine Frigate of 32 guns.[2] So I am now left in [the] world to shift for myself, which I hope I shall do, so as to bring credit to myself and friends. Am sorry there is no possibility this time of seeing each other, but I hope that time will come in a few years, when we will spend some merry hours together.

N. B. If it is not too troublesome turn over.

Where we shall go at present, I know not, but wherever it is, I will always write to you. If you ever choose to write, inclose either to Mr. Suckling,[3] or my brother,[4] as in all probability they will know where we are gone. I leave London on Wednesday evening, so shall always be glad to hear from you. Believing me to be, dear Brother, your affectionate brother,

HORATIO NELSON.

P. S. Pray give my best respects to my old school-fellow, H. Hammond.[5]

" He produceth Journals kept by himself in the Carcass, Seahorse, Dolphin, and Worcester, and Certificates from Captains Suckling, Lutwidge, Farmer, Pigott, and Robinson, of his diligence, &c. : he can splice, knot, reef a sail, &c. and is qualified to do the duty of an Able seaman and Midshipman. Dated the 9th April 1777. M. S., Captain John Campbell, Captain Abraham North."

The letters " M. S." were the initials of Captain Maurice Suckling, Nelson's uncle, then Comptroller of the Navy, who is said by Clarke and M'Arthur to have been present at the examination by virtue of his office ; and of whom they relate the following anecdote : " Captain Suckling purposely concealed his relationship from the examining Captains. When his nephew had recovered from his confusion, his answers were prompt and satisfactory, and indicated the talents he so eminently possessed. The examination ended in a manner very honourable to him : upon which his uncle immediately threw off his reserve, and rising from his seat, introduced his nephew. The examining Captains expressed their surprise at his not having informed them of this before. ' No,' replied the independent Comptroller, ' I did not wish the younker to be favoured, I felt convinced that he would pass a good examination ; and you see, gentlemen, I have not been disappointed.' "—4to. vol. i. p. 14.

[2] The Lowestoffe, Captain William Locker.

[3] His maternal uncle, Captain Maurice Suckling, then Comptroller of the Navy, and M.P. for Portsmouth, by whom this Letter was franked.

[4] His eldest brother, Mr. Maurice Nelson, then Clerk for Foreign Accounts in the Navy Office. He died in April 1801.

[5] Apparently, his distant relation, Horace Hamond, son of his godfather, Horace Hamond, D.D., by Dorothy, daughter of Sir Charles Turner, Bart.—*Burke's Dictionary of the Landed Gentry.* Ed. 1844, p. 533.

TO CAPTAIN WILLIAM LOCKER.

[Autograph, in the Locker Papers.—Of Captain Locker, one of Nelson's dearest friends, from this period until his death in December 1800, very interesting Memoirs have been published by his son, Edward Hawke Locker, Esq. late a Commissioner of Greenwich Hospital, to whose kindness the Public are indebted for the interesting Letters addressed to his Father. Captain Locker then commanded the Lowestoffe, of which Ship Nelson was second Lieutenant. They sailed for the West Indies in May, and anchored at Barbadoes on the 4th of July 1777. On the 19th of that month the Lowestoffe arrived at Port Royal, in Jamaica. The address of this Letter is wanting, but it would appear to have been written during Captain Locker's temporary absence from his Ship in consequence of ill health.]

Lowestoffe, at Sea, August 12th, 1777.

My most worthy Friend,

I am exceedingly obliged to you for the good opinion you entertain of me, and will do my utmost that you may have no occasion to change it. I hope God Almighty will be pleased to spare your life, for your own sake, and that of your family: but should any thing happen to you, (which I sincerely pray God, may not,) you may be assured that nothing shall be wanting on my part for the taking care of your effects, and delivering safe to Mrs. Locker[6] such of them as may be thought proper not to be disposed of. You mentioned the word " consolation," in your letter—I shall have a very great one, when I think I have served faithfully the best of friends, and the most amiable of women.

All the services I can render to your family, you may be assured shall be done, and shall never end but with my life; and may God Almighty of his great goodness keep, bless, and preserve you, and your family, is the most fervent prayer

Of your faithful servant,

HORATIO NELSON.

P. S. Though this letter is not couched in the best manner be assured it comes from one entirely devoted to your service.

H. N.

---

[6] Lucy, only daughter and heiress of Admiral William Parry, whom he married on the 20th October 1770; and by her, who died in March 1780, he had five children; viz. 1, Lucy, who died unmarried; 2, William, a Major in the Army, who died in 1843 without issue; 3, John, late Deputy Register of the Admiralty Court at Malta, and died there in 1834, leaving several children; 4, Elizabeth, now living unmarried; 5, Edward Hawke Locker, Esq., F.R.S., above-mentioned.

TO CAPTAIN LOCKER.

[From Clarke and M'Arthur's Life of Nelson, 4to. vol. i. p. 17.   The original is not preserved in the Locker Papers.   This Letter was written while Nelson commanded the " Little Lucy," Tender to the Lowestoffe.]

9th February, 1778.   Off the West Corcos.

I am happy in having an opportunity of writing by Mr. Ellis, who comes down in the Abigail schooner from François, bound to Nantucket. We took her this morning at four o'clock, after a chase of eight hours. We are just come to an anchor; and the wind is got to the Northward, so that I must conclude, as we are now weighing. Pray give my compliments to my messmates.

TO CAPTAIN LOCKER, LOWESTOFFE.

[Autograph in the Locker Papers—without date of month or year.]

Bristol, Monday afternoon [apparently 31st August, 1778.]

Dear Sir,

Your goodness to me has been more than ever I expected, or had any right to think on in every respect. The man you mentioned I should be very happy to have with me, as the one is very assiduous, the other you know [is] one of my favourites. I will write to Mr. Hodgeson the first opportunity. One of these days we shall meet, but I know you would not have me ask where there is a probability of being refused. Dundas,[7]—I thought I had mentioned him before : he messes with us, and keeps the fourth watch : he agrees tolerable well, as he has been told the man he has to deal with, but I am sure he has wished himself often on board the Lowestoffe. Cuningham has sent me a jar of sweetmeats, which I am much obliged to him for. I heard of you by M'Namara yesterday. I hope it is not true the accounts we have here of the taking the Minerva.[8] May health and happiness attend [you] is the constant sincere wish of your humble Servant,

HORATIO NELSON.

[7] Thomas Dundas, who had been a Midshipman of the Lowestoffe : he was made a Lieutenant in 1798, commanded the Naiad Frigate in the Battle of Trafalgar, and died a Vice-Admiral and K.C.B. in March, 1841.

[8] On the 22nd of August 1778, the Minerva, 32, Captain John Stott, was taken by La Concorde, 40 ; and on the 2nd of September, in the same year, the Active, 28, Captain William Williams, was captured by the French Ships mentioned by Nelson.   Neither of the Captains survived their misfortune many weeks.

TO CAPTAIN LOCKER, LOWESTOFFE.

[Autograph, in the Locker Papers. Without date of month or year.]

Bristol, Saturday morning, [apparently 12th September 1778.]

Dear Sir,

Mr. M'Namara[8] came on board late last night, and I am very sorry to acquaint [you] of the Active's laying alongside the Minerva: she was taken by our friend the Disd a in, Cap tain M'Namara, and the Chamont. She had hove twelve of her guns overboard, in a gale of wind; and sprung her main-mast. Poor Captain Williams died about ten days ago of a broken heart:[9] the Tender that was sent after the Æolus is also taken, and our people were not permitted to see either the Officers or Seamen of the Ships. They say there is upwards of three hundred seamen in the jails. The Ships that went in the other day were the Concord and Disdain: they said once they thought of supping with us. They had been convoying twenty-four sail through the Caicos Passage, at half-past one A. M. they were within a mile of the Niger. Captain Caulfield and Mr. M'Namara are gone on board the Ruby.

May health and one [of] the French frigates attend you, is the sincere wish of yours faithfully,

H. NELSON.

TO CAPTAIN LOCKER, LOWESTOFFE.

[Autograph, in the Locker Papers.—Nelson was appointed Commander of the Badger Brig on the 8th December, 1778.]

Badger,[1] off the N. E. End, April 30th, 1779.

Dear Sir,

I hope with all my heart you are much better than when I left you, and that you will not be obliged to go home on ac-count of your health. I wish sincerely it was in my power in some measure to show some small return for the many favours I

---

[8] Vide page 7, note 9. He is frequently mentioned, and was Nelson's com-panion to France in 1783: he was made a Post Captain in 1781, and died a Rear-Admiral of the White in 1802, aged 65.

[9] Vide p. 24.

[1] The following Officers served with Captain Nelson in the Badger, from the 1st January 1779, to the 19th June following:—O. Edwards, Lieutenant; Fran-cis Foster, Surgeon; J. Wilson, Master; John Tyson, Purser.—*Clarke and M'Arthur*, vol. i. Appendix.

have received, but I am sure you do not think me ungrateful. If you come on the North Side, and I hear of it, I will come in. I know you will be pleased with this little earnest of success, but we have had a good deal of plague with her.[2] Two days before we could find the French papers, at last found them in an old shoe. There is a polacre coming this way ; I hope we shall fall in her way. I wish I could give a good character of Mr. Capper : he is a drunkard ; I need say no more. We shall part whenever he can get Mate of a Merchant ship. George Cruger behaves very well. If you have heard from Mrs. Locker, I sincerely hope she and all the family are in good health ; and that you and they may continue so, and enjoy every blessing of this life, is the real sincere wish of

> Your much obliged and faithful Servant,
> HORATIO NELSON.

News.—

The Punch killed one man, and wounded three, on board the Bourdeaux Snow. The Minerva sailed six days ago, with fifteen sail, for the Turks' Island Passage. The Tyger, Letter of Marque, belonging to Liverpool, of twenty-four guns, carried into the Cape. They mention an Action off Grenada, between the two Fleets.[3] The people say, Chambers searched them, and let them pass ; also a Kingston Schooner.

TO CAPTAIN LOCKER, LOWESTOFFE.

[Autograph, in the Locker Papers.]

Badger, Monday Evening, May 3rd, 1779.

Dear Sir,

I have just received your letter of the 29th, and this morning yours of the 24th, and hope you are much better than when I left you. Since I wrote last, we had very near taken a Schooner privateer, but it coming calm she rowed off. We

---

[2] On the 28th April 1779, the Badger captured La Prudente of eighty tons and nine men.—*London Gazette.*

[3] The Action fought on the 5th July 1779, off Grenada, between the English Fleet under Vice-Admiral Byron, and that of France, under the Comte d'Estaing.

have no accounts here of any Ships being cut out, but I shall sail in the morning and keep a sharp look out, and hope the next we see we shall be able to get alongside of. I am much obliged to you for taking care of Silvan: do as you please with him; I don't think he will ever stay with me now. May health, happiness, and every blessing attend you, is the real sincere wish of

Your much obliged and faithful Servant,
HORATIO NELSON.

———

TO CAPTAIN LOCKER, LOWESTOFFE.

[Autograph, in the Locker Papers.]

Badger, May 13th, 1779.

Dear Sir,

I am very sorry I made you so uneasy about the men that were pressed from the Amity Hall; but I will relate the story in particular, for Mr. Taylor's satisfaction, who I should be very sorry to disoblige, as he has been so exceedingly civil to me, and also upon your account.

When I first saw the Ships in Port Antonio, I took them for part of the Cork Fleet, and sent the boat for men, with orders not to press from homeward-bound Ships. They went on board two, and did not meddle with their people; but thirty-five men on board the Amity Hall tempted them to bring five; I was not pleased when they were brought on board, and came into Port on purpose to return them, for I had not a thought of keeping any of them; the Master came on board in a most impertinent manner, and with very abusive language told me he should take the Law, &c. I can't say but I was warm to be talked to in such a manner; however, I immediately returned two men and a Neutral, but told him I should keep the other two, for his impertinent behaviour. (This is all the matter.) If you tell the story, I beg you will mention, that the Master forgot to advertise that he had on board two deserters from the Badger. The Master is just coming on board, so I must stop a little.

The Master is just gone, and I never was more surprised than for him to deny the advertisement, that several circum-

4

stances were not what he had wrote about, in regard to the number, and to hinder his proceeding with the Convoy : he says he wrote to a gentleman in Kingston his account of the affair, and to beg he would get his men, or to take such methods that he might not [be] blamed if he did not fail. He tells me he never desired to be advertised, he has begged my pardon for his behaviour on that day, and we are parted very good friends (though I believe all he told me is false :) however, it will convince people what sort of a man he is. I am now completing our water, and shall sail in the morning. I intend going off the East End, to see if the report of the four-teen-gun Brig be true.

Since I wrote last I have lost a very fine Brig, who we chased twenty leagues to leeward of the Island, and lost, I am sure, for want of a night-glass. I intend to come in again on Tuesday to save post if possible, but for fear I should not, I leave this here. I see you are quite settled about going home,[5] which in all probability may happen before you can hear from me again; but I shall always write to you in England. I hope you will have a good passage, and find Mrs. Locker and all your family, in good health : I hope you will soon re-cover when you get home. The friendship you have shown me I shall never forget; and though I lose my best friend by your going, I would not have you stay a day longer in this country. I am very sorry indeed Captain Deane[6] is ill; I beg you will give my best wishes for his speedy recovery. May health and happiness attend you is the sincere wish of your

Much obliged and faithful Servant,

HORATIO NELSON.

I am afraid the Admiral has got the wrong end of the story about the men; if you think proper, mention it. I beg you [will] return Mr. Taylor my sincere thanks, for the kind part he has taken in this affair.

[5] On the 1st of May 1779, Captain Locker applied to the Admiral, Sir Peter Parker, requesting to be allowed to resign the command of his Ship on account of ill health.

[6] Captain Joseph Deane : he died Captain of the Ruby, on the 12th January 1780. *Vide* p. 33.

TO CAPTAIN LOCKER, LOWESTOFFF.

[Autograph, in the Locker Papers.]

Badger, off St. Ann's, June 7th, 1779.

Dear Sir,

I suppose before this you have heard of the fate of the poor Glasgow :[7] indeed it was a most shocking sight; and had it happened half an hour later, in all probability a great many people would have been lost. She anchored at half-past three, and at six she was in flames, owing to the steward attempting to steal rum out of the after-hold. Captain Lloyd is very melancholy indeed on the occasion, and I sincerely wish I was at Port Royal for his sake, and the Ship's company's, who are falling sick very fast, with the constant rains we have had since we left Montego Bay; and no place on board the Badger to shelter such a number of men. I suppose I have letters at Port Antonio from you, but I have not been there these three Posts; and am much afraid I shall be obliged to go round the West End, and attempt the South side, the current having set us nine leagues to leeward these last twenty-four hours, although we have had favourable winds: as I have heard of no Packets arriving, I hope to see you at Port Royal.

I beg you will remember me very kindly to Mr. Ross,[8] and Captain Deane, who I hope is got well. May health and happiness attend you, is the real sincere wish of

Your most humble Servant,

HORATIO NELSON.

The Lieutenant of Glasgow will take care of this: he is a very good young man I believe, and has not saved a rag but what was on his back.

[7] The Glasgow, 20, Captain Thomas Lloyd, while at anchor on the North side of Jamaica, was accidentally set on fire, and entirely destroyed; but the crew were saved, mainly by Captain Nelson's exertions.—See *Sketch of Life*.

[8] Hercules Ross, Esq., a merchant at Kingston in Jamaica, who is frequently mentioned in subsequent Letters.

TO CAPTAIN LOCKER.

[Autograph, in the Locker Papers.—Nelson was then Captain of the Hinchin-brook,[9] into which Ship he was promoted from the Badger, on the 11th June, 1779.]

Port Royal, July 28th, 1779.

My dear Sir,

We have nothing new here since I wrote you last by the Halifax Pacquet, except the safe arrival of the Lion, Captain Cornwallis,[1] in a very shattered condition. The news of the Action you have heard long before this comes to you. The Hinchinbrook is not arrived, although her cruise has been out these four weeks. Lady Parker is almost mad. The Admiral[2] tells me he will send me out in the Lowestoffe, to cruize for the Hinchinbrook, but I am afraid it will not be farther to windward than the Navassa. Captain Deane[3] wished much I should go with him off the Cape, but it will not do. No prizes to any of the Men-of-War except a few Americans. I sincerely hope you have had a good passage home, and that your health is recovered. I, you know, am never well in Port. Janus not arrived: a good deal alarmed for her. Ruby and Bristol sail on Sunday; the Captain of the latter[4] is in a bad scrape: you know Mrs. Browne's affair: he is arrested for 10,000*l.*, and went from the Marshal after being seized. They have petitioned the Governor not to permit him to leave the Island. He is now outlawed—I think the affair will end much to his loss. I beg I may be most kindly remembered to Mrs. Locker and all the family. I hope they and you will always enjoy health and happiness.

I am, dear Sir,

Your most faithful Servant,

HORATIO NELSON.

[9] The Officers who served with Captain Nelson in the Hinchinbrook, from the 1st of September 1779 to the 1st of May 1780, were—Lieutenants A. St. Leger, Geo. Harrison, C. Cunningham, Joseph Bullen, (now an Admiral of the Blue,) Peter Burns; Surgeon, Fran. Foster; Master, J. Walker; Purser, R. Huggens.—*Clarke and M'Arthur,* vol. i. in Appendix.

[1] Captain the Honourable, afterwards Admiral Sir William Cornwallis, G.C.B. particularly distinguished himself in the command of the Lion, 64, in the action between Vice-Admiral Byron's Squadron, and the French under Comte d'Estaing, off Grenada, on the 6th of July 1779.

[2] Vice-Admiral (afterwards Admiral of the Fleet) Sir Peter Parker, Knight, from whom, and from Lady Parker, Nelson received the greatest kindness during a severe illness at Jamaica.

[3] Captain Joseph Deane.   [4] Query Captain John Raynor.

I find this is not the time of year for shaddocks, but I will send some whenever they are in season; at present there is not one to be had. Captain Deane, &c. desire their compliments.

TO CAPTAIN LOCKER.

[Autograph in the Locker Papers.]

Port Royal, Thursday, 12th August 1779.

Dear Sir,

Jamaica is turned upside down since you left it. The Count d'Estaing is at the Cape with twenty Sail of the Line, and a Flag-ship, with eight or nine more, are at Port au Prince; the latter Fleet fell in with the Charon and Pomona, in the night, but they got off by good sailing. They say that there are 20,000 men at the Cape ready to embark, and 5,000 at Port au Prince. He arrived at the Cape last Saturday fortnight, with one hundred and twenty-five Sail, Men-of-War and Transports. He passed Captain Lambert's Squadron[5] on a very thick day, who arrived here yesterday; so that all our Ships are in Port, except Hinchinbrook, Hound, and Porcupine, who, we [have] reason to believe, are taken; as reports[6] are very strong from the Bahama Islands. As I have told you what we may expect, I will tell you the measures taken to defend the Island: 5,000 men are encamped between the Ferry and Kingston, 1,000 in Fort Augusta, 300 at the Apostles' Battery, and we expect to have 500 in Fort Charles, where I am to command. Lion, Salisbury, Charon, and Janus, in a line from the Point to the outer shoal; Ruby and Bristol in the narrows going to Kingston, to rake any Ships that may attack Fort Augusta; Pomona and Speke Indiaman above Rock Fort, and Lowestoffe at the end of the dock-wall. Expresses go to-morrow morning to all quarters. Resource and Penelope off the East End to cruise: four Fire-ships are down here, two of them commissioned. I have very fairly stated our situation, and I leave you

---

[5] Captain Robert Lambert of the Niger, who obtained that rank in February 1760. Charnock erroneously says, that he was not employed after 1770 until 1782, when he was appointed Commissioner of the Navy at Jamaica.

[6] The reports were unfounded.

in England to judge what stand we shall make; I think you
must not be surprised to hear of my learning to speak French.
I hope you have had a good passage, and are now in peace and
plenty with your family.   Ross has behaved in a very public-
spirited manner.   Has sent the Gayton and his vessels to the
Admiral, to send expresses, even his negroes into the batteries.   As the Packet sails to-morrow morning, and it was a
secret, I have not time to say any more; I know we shall
have your wishes for success.   May health, peace, and happiness always surround you and your good family, to whom I beg
to be kindly remembered, is the constant wish of

Your devoted humble Servant,

HORATIO NELSON.

TO CAPTAIN LOCKER.

[Autograph, in the Locker Papers.]

Port Royal, January 23rd, 1780.

My dear Sir,

I arrived here from a cruize in the middle of December,
and received your letter from London with great pleasure, as
I much feared you were in France; and on the 10th of this
month, I received your letter from Kent, dated October 3rd,
and am sorry you are not quite recovered. I sailed in the
Hinchinbrook from Port Royal in the middle of September,
to join the Niger and Penelope.   We took four Sail,
for which I shall share about 800l. sterling.   We left the
Penelope at sea, who soon afterwards took a Spanish privateer: the crew rose upon the Penelope, and have carried
her off: they certainly have killed poor Captain Jones and
his Officers.[7]

I know you will be sincerely sorry for the loss of poor
Hill, who died of a fever at Rattan.   He had entirely
recovered of his wounds.   I suppose you have heard he
lost his right hand in the action.   William Forrest, your
old Coxswain, is amongst the slain.   The Lowestoffe was the

---

[7] This report was not true; but the Penelope, Captain James Jones, foundered
with all her crew in that year.

first that stormed,[8] under the command of Dundas.[9] I am now going to tell what you and many others will be very sorry to hear—the death of that worthy, good man, Captain Joseph Deane. He died on the 12th of January, and was buried next day, at Green Bay, amidst the tears of his Officers and Ship's company, and his many friends. Captain Cowling [10] is appointed to the Ruby. Of that noble Ship's crew, three hundred took boats and are gone off. Every method has been used to bring them back, which I hope will prove successful. The Salisbury [1] has brought in a Spanish Store-ship, mounting fifty-six guns, four hundred men, from Cadiz to Port Omoa, after a smart action of two hours and a-half. The Salisbury lost nine men; the Don fifty men.

Our mess is broke up. Captain Cornwallis and myself live together. I hope I have made a friend of him, which I am sure from his character you will be glad to hear. Lambert has changed into the Leviathan, to go home. I have sent a cask or two of shaddocks by him, and Mr. Taylor sends to him this day, that if convenient to take two casks of old rum for you. I shall take your rum out of the Lowestoffe and keep it with me until you send for it. The Spanish Ship is to be made a Ship of 36 guns. The Admiral offered her to me, which I declined. He says he will give me the first Frigate. He has appointed me to go with an Expedition which is now on foot against the city of Grenada, upon the Lake of Niguragua.[2] How it will turn out, God knows. I do not expect to return before the beginning of June, but I shall always take every opportunity of writing to you. Collingwood [3] desires to be very particularly remembered to you and Mrs. Locker, to whom I beg you [to] give my best respects.

---

[8] On the 16th October, 1779, Captain the Hon. John Luttrell, in the Charon 44, with the Lowestoffe, Pomona, and Racehorse, attacked the Fortress of Saint Fernando de Omoa, which was gallantly stormed, and the Register Ships, which had taken refuge there, were captured.

[9] Apparently Mr. Thomas Dundas, vide p. 24.

[10] Captain John Cowling: he died in 1792.

[1] Commanded by Captain Charles Inglis, who died a Rear-Admiral, in October 1791.　The captured ship was the San Carlos, Don Juan Antonio Zavellata.

[2] Vide 'Sketch of my Life;' p. 9, ante.

[3] Captain Cuthbert Collingwood, afterwards Vice-Admiral Lord Collingwood.

The Admiral sails with the Fleet on Tuesday next, the 25th January, to meet if he can the Count de Grasse, who has been cruizing these some weeks past between Cape Nicola and Maize with five Sail of the Line.

You must not be surprised to see me in England after this trip; for if my health is not much better than it is at present, I shall certainly come home, as all the Doctors are against my staying so long in this country. You know my old complaint in my breast: it is turned out to be the gout got there. Kitty Crawford sends you two jars of tamarinds. Cuba, and all your old acquaintances in this part of the world, desire to be kindly remembered to you; and none more so than Captain Cornwallis, who has, I assure you, a very high esteem for your character. Caulfield is to stay behind this cruize to take his trial. Captain Pakenham [4] (Lord Longford's brother) goes in his Ship. Glover [5] is very ill; I hardly think he will get over this cruize. I have been twice given over since you left this country with that cursed disorder, the gout. I must make this a double letter, though against your desire. We have just heard the Penelope was carried into St. Jago, in Cuba.[6] She has been cruizing off the West end of Jamaica. I must now bid you Adieu, wishing you every thing you can wish in this life, and believe me to be with real sincerity,

Your much obliged and sincere friend,
HORATIO NELSON.

Captain Inglis [7] desires his compliments.

---

[4] Captain the Honourable, afterwards Admiral Sir Thomas Pakenham, G.C.B., who died on the 2nd February 1836.

[5] Captain Bonovier Glover, of the Janus, who died immediately before Captain the Honourable William Cornwallis' gallant action, "in the very hour he so wished to see," on the 20th March 1780. He was a son of the Author of "Leonidas."

[6] Vide p. 32, note.

[7] Captain Charles Inglis, of the Salisbury.

TO CAPTAIN POLSON.

[Autograph, in the possession of P. S. Benwell, Esq. This Letter was addressed to Captain John Polson of the 60th Regiment, who commanded the Expedition against Fort San Juan, near Grenada, assisted by the Hinchinbrook, Captain Nelson, and by some Ships under his orders. See the "Sketch of my Life," p. 9. Captain Polson obtained his Majority in the 92nd Regiment on the 20th October 1781.]

Port Royal, 2nd June, 1780.

Dear Polson,

I assure you nothing gave me more pleasure than to hear of your reducing the Fort, before the arrival of Kemble,[2] or any of the folks of the Second Division. When I arrived at Jamaica, I saw General Dalling[3] several times, and I told him of all your transactions from our first setting out; our troubles on the Mosquito Shore, &c., which I thought you would wish, as no letters had arrived. He expressed himself very much pleased with your conduct on every occasion, and expressed a very great regard for you, and was very sorry he was obliged to send down older Officers. But when the news arrived of the reduction of the Fort, I assure you he expressed the greatest pleasure it happened to you; and the news arriving of the plundering Black River by the Governor of Camayagoa, I told him of your sending back the Black River Company, and only taking 40 men from Tempest instead of 150; and advising to send 200 men to Black River; and that those 40 men had run away, so that not one Indian was taken to the Westward of the Cape. He was much pleased with those matters, as it takes off all reflection of taking the Inhabitants of the Shore to go upon the Expedition.

I am sorry you and so many of the Officers are not well;

[2] Lieutenant-Colonel Stephen Kemble, who commanded the 60th or Royal American Regiment, to which Captain Polson belonged.

[3] Governor of Jamaica. Vide p. 8, ante.

but I sincerely hope you are recovered before this. General Dalling will be with you by the middle of July, you may depend on it. Pray remember me kindly to the two Despards,[4] Bulkeley,[5] Harrison,[6] Mounsey,[7] and all my good friends about you ; and believe me with very great esteem,

Your ever well wisher,

And obedient Servant,

HORATIO NELSON.

TO HERCULES ROSS, ESQ., KINGSTON, JAMAICA.

[From a Copy in the Nelson Papers.]

Ad^{ls} Mountain, June 12th, 1780.

Dear Sir,

I got up here yesterday morning, and am but just got out of bed to answer your letter. I am exceedingly obliged to you for sending the letters. Oh, Mr. Ross, what would I give to be at Port-Royal. Lady P.[8] not here, and the servants letting me lay as if a log, and take no notice.

I am yours, most sincerely,

HORATIO NELSON.

[4] Captain Andrew Despard ; and Lieutenant, afterwards Colonel Edward Marcus Despard, of the 79th Regiment, who was executed for high treason in February 1803. Lord Nelson attended his trial, and gave satisfactory evidence of his bravery and character as an Officer. There was also a Thomas Despard, who was then an Ensign in the same Regiment.

[5] Captain Richard Bulkeley of the 79th Regiment.

[6] Apparently Captain William Causabon Harrison, of a " Corps serving in Jamaica."—Vide the *Army List* for 1780. A Lieutenant Robert Harrison was then serving in the same Corps.

[7] Captain-Lieutenant James Mounsey, or, Lieutenant Thomas Mounsey, of the 79th Regiment.

[8] Margaret Lady Parker, who was Miss Nugent, wife of Vice-Admiral Sir Peter Parker, Commander-in-Chief. This Letter appears to have been written in her house. They both lived to see Nelson a Peer; and in a beautiful Letter from Lady Parker after the Battle of the Nile, she told Nelson that they had always looked upon him as their son.

TO SIR PETER PARKER, KNIGHT, VICE-ADMIRAL OF THE BLUE,
AND COMMANDER-IN-CHIEF AT JAMAICA.

[Original, in the Admiralty.]

Port-Royal, Jamaica, the 30th of August, 1780.

Sir,

Having been in a very bad state of health for these several
months past, so bad as to be unable to attend my duty on
board the Janus,[9] and the faculty having informed me that I
cannot recover in this climate ; I am therefore to request that
you will be pleased to permit me to go to England for the re-
establishment of my health.

I am, Sir, &c.
HORATIO NELSON.[10]

TO WILLIAM LOCKER, ESQ., GRAY'S INN.

[Autograph, in the Locker Papers.—Captain Nelson, on his arrival in England,
in the autumn of 1780, proceeded to Bath for the recovery of his health,
and remained there several months.]

Bath, January 23rd, 1781.

Dear Sir,

I must crave your pardon for [not] having wrote to you before this, but I know you will readily believe the reason was

---

[9] He was removed from the Hinchinbrook to the command of the Janus
of 44 guns, early in April 1780.   The following Officers served with Captain
Nelson in the Janus, from the 2nd of May 1780 to the 19th of September fol-
lowing :—Lieutenants, Geo. H. Stevens, J. C. Haswell, C. C. Priswick, and
Henry Knight; Surgeon, T. Jameson; Master, J. Flenwick; Purser, W.
Hickman.—*Clarke and M'Arthur*, in Appendix.

[10] The Admiral in his reply, dated on the 1st September 1780, (in the
Nelson Papers,) said, " The Report of the Surgeons who have examined into
your complaints, confirms my opinion of the absolute necessity for your immediate return to Europe ; and you have therefore my leave to go to England
by the first opportunity, with my very sincere wishes for your speedy recovery ;
being with true esteem, Sir, your most obedient humble servant, P. PARKER."

inability; for I have been so ill since I have been here, that I
was obliged to be carried to and from bed, with the most ex-
cruciating tortures, but, thank God, I am now upon the mend-
ing hand.   I [am] physicked three times a day, drink the waters
three times, and bathe every other night, besides [*qu.* not]
drinking wine, which I think the worst of all.   I am sorry to hear
the account of your friend, Captain Sutton;[1] but I well know the
situation of a Ship just from the River, and I have no doubt
but the Court-Martial will consider it in that light.   Pray let
me know how it ends.   I suppose by this time you are alone
again ; when you write to Mr. G. Smith,[2] pray remember me
to him.   I wish much for a new Navy List: if it is convenient
to you, I should thank you much for one, for I do not know
how to get one.   I called upon Mr. Welch the day after I saw
you last.   I beg you will make my compliments to him, and
all other friends when you see them.   I hope your health is
better, at least that you have got rid of that cursed bile.
Adieu, and believe me to be, your

Devoted humble Servant,

HORATIO NELSON.

Mr. Spry's, Pierrepont Street, Bath.

If you write, direct for me only at Bath, then if I should
change lodgings, they will always come safe.

---

[1] Captain Evelyn Sutton, of the Isis, 50, on his passage from the Nore to Spit-
head, in December 1780, had a short and indecisive action with the Rotterdam,
Dutch ship of war of 50 guns, the Isis being sixty men short of complement.   A
Court of Inquiry into Captain Sutton's conduct was held at Spithead, which acquitted him of misconduct and cowardice; but he was afterwards tried by a Court-
Martial, and reprimanded.   The Rotterdam was captured in January 1781, by
the Warwick, 50, Captain the Hon. Keith Elphinstone, afterwards Viscount
Keith, K.B.   Captain Sutton, who died a Superannuated Rear-Admiral, is men-
tioned in a subsequent Letter.

[2] George Smith, of Camer in Kent, Esq.   His son, William Masters Smith of
Camer, Esq., states that his father once took a cruize in the Lowestoffe with Captain Locker, while Nelson was a Lieutenant of that Ship, when their acquaintance commenced.   Letters from Lord Nelson to Mr. Smith will be found in another volume.

TO WILLIAM LOCKER, ESQ., GRAY'S INN.

[Autograph, in the Locker Papers.]

Bath, January 28th, 1781.

Dear Sir,

I received your letter of the 22nd on the 25th, for which I am much obliged to you. Your scolding at my not writing I own I expected it, although I am convinced I did not deserve it; for even now, although I am much better, I am scarcely able to hold my pen. Your letter of the 25th, with the Navy List, I received last night, for which I am much obliged to you, as also for the Newspaper, though I would not have you be at the trouble of sending any more, as we receive all the Papers here in ten or eleven hours after they are published. I shall be very happy whenever I am appointed to a Ship, for as you will suppose, I do not set under the hands of a Doctor very easy, although I give myself credit this once for having done every-thing, and taken every medicine that was ordered, that Dr. Woodward, who is my Physician, said he never had a better patient.[3] I am sorry to see by yesterday's papers that Captain Pole[4] is come home, having lost his Ship, which I am sorry for: if he remembers me, make my compliments to him. Although I have not quite recovered the use of my limbs, yet my inside is a new man; and I have no doubt, but in two or three weeks, I shall be perfectly well, when nothing will give me more pleasure than seeing you in Gray's Inn, and finding you are appointed to a good Ship. Adieu, dear Sir, and believe me to be

Your most devoted Servant,

HORATIO NELSON.

---

[3] Of this generous member of the most liberal of all Professions, it is stated, that when Nelson expressed surprise at the smallness of his fees, and wished to increase his remuneration, Dr. Woodward observed, " Pray, Captain Nelson, allow me to follow what I consider to be my professional duty. Your illness, Sir, has been brought on by serving your King and Country, and believe me, I love both too well to be able to receive any more."—*Clarke and M'Arthur*, vol. i. p. 43, on the authority of Viscountess Nelson.

[4] His friend Captain Charles Morice Pole, whose Ship, the Hussar, was lost on the Pot Rock, in Hell Gates Passage, North River, America.

[Autograph, in the Locker Papers.]

Bath, February 15th, 1781.

Dear Sir,

It is really so long since I have wrote to you, that I am almost ashamed to write at all; but I know your goodness will forgive me, although I hardly deserve it. My health, thank God, is very near perfectly restored; and I have the perfect use of all my limbs, except my left arm, which I can hardly tell what is the matter with it. From the shoulder to my fingers' ends are as if half dead; but the Surgeon and Doctors give me hopes it will all go off. I most sincerely wish to be employed, and hope it will not be long. I have thought several times you were appointed to a Ship, else you would have wrote, if only to scold me for neglect: if I am not employed, I intend coming to town the beginning of March. I hope when I come to town to see a fine trio in your room. If Mr. Rigaud has done the picture,[6] send word in the next letter you write to me, and I will inclose you an order upon Mr. Paynter. Tell Mr. Rigaud I wish him joy of his picture being got to the Sardinian Ambassador's Chapel, and to hear it so well spoke of in the public Papers. Captain Kirke's [5] man has just been here to tell me his master, mistress, and family are come down. I am glad of it. I think the bathing will do infinite service to Mrs. Kirke. I must wish you a good night, and drink your health in a draught of my Physician's cordial and a bolus. Adieu, and believe me to be,

Your sincere friend and devoted humble Servant,

HORATIO NELSON.

Pray give my best compliments to Captain Pole, and tell him I hope we shall renew our acquaintance. When you get the pictures, I must be in the middle, for God knows, without good *Supporters*,[6] I shall fall to the ground.

[5] Captain James Kirke, a Commissioner of the Victualling Office: he was made a Post-Captain 23rd June 1748, and died in 1787.

[6] A Portrait of Nelson, by John Francis Rigaud, R.A., which was placed by Captain Locker, to whom it was presented, between the portraits of Captains, afterwards Admirals, Sir George Montagu and Sir Charles Morice Pole. It is now in the possession of Edward Hawke Locker, Esq., F.R.S.

TO WILLIAM LOCKER, ESQ., GRAY'S INN.

[Autograph, in the Locker Papers.]

Bath, February 21st, 1781.

Dear Sir,

I received your letter of Saturday last on Monday, and am sorry you cannot give a better account of your health. I wish you had come to Bath when your sons went to school, instead of being cooped up in Gray's Inn, without seeing any body. I am sure yours is a Bath case, and therefore you ought to come for a month or six weeks. Captain Kirke also is of my opinion, and desires me to say there is room for a lodger in the house where he is. As to my health, I thank God [it] is perfectly restored, although I shall remain here a few weeks longer, that it may be firmly fixed, as also to avoid the cold weather, which I believe is setting in, for you know this is like Jamaica to any other part of England.

As to my picture, it will not be the least like what I am now, that is certain; but you may tell Mr. Rigaud to add beauty to it, and it will be much mended. As to his inquiries about Lieutenant Haldimand, of the 60th regiment, I know no more than that he was given over when I left St. John's, which was the 2nd of May, and that I saw him in the Dead List a few days afterwards. I have recommended my Physician and Surgeon to Mrs. Kirke, and they are gone to her this day: perhaps I may hear their opinions of her case before night; if I do I will tell you.

I am, dear Sir,

Your very humble Servant,

Horatio Nelson.

TO WILLIAM LOCKER, ESQ., GRAY'S INN.

[Autograph, in the Locker Papers.]

Bath, March 5th, 1781.

Dear Sir,

I much fear that you are unwell, or out of Town, by your not answering my letter that I wrote last Thursday week; I hope the latter is the case. The Doctors and Surgeons here have pronounced Mrs. Kirke's case incurable, so they will return to London the latter end of next week. I am very sorry for her, poor woman; it must be a most lamentable situation to remain in her state, for the number of years she may live. I never was so well in health since you knew me, or that I can remember. It is a most precious jewel, which I will take great care of in future. I shall be in London on Thursday, the 15th of March, but as it will be too late to go to Mr. Suckling's[7] that night, I will, if you have a spare bed, and nobody to occupy it, sleep that night, if you will give me leave, at your house. I am sorry the wind hangs so much Western board, as it must hinder the sailing of the Grand Fleet. I hope to hear from you soon, and believe me to be,

Your most obliged obedient Servant,
HORATIO NELSON.

5th March.

I have now fixed to come to Town with Mr. Kirke and family, so that I cannot be certain of the day, but it will be on Wednesday or Thursday next, when, if [*illegible*], and you have a spare bed, I will beg leave to occupy it. I beg to hear from you, for something must be the matter, that I have not heard from you. Mr. Kirke desires his compliments.

TO CAPTAIN LOCKER, AT ROBERT KINGSMILL'S, ESQ.,
SIDMONTON PLACE, NEAR NEWBURY.

[Autograph, in the Locker Papers.]

Bath, March 9th, 1781.

Dear Sir,

Your letter from Sidmonton [8] I have just received: indeed I am glad you are got a little out of the air of Gray's Inn, for I do not think it the most wholesome of *any*. If you had come to Bath, I should have staid a few days longer. I set out for London on Monday morning with Mr. Kirke and his family, so shall be at Newbury between four and five in the

---

[7] His maternal uncle, William Suckling, Esq., Clerk of Foreign Entries, afterwards Deputy Collector Inwards, in the Custom House.

[8] Sidmonton Place, near Newbury, in Berkshire, the residence of Captain Kingsmill, afterwards Admiral Sir Robert Kingsmill, Baronet: he died in 1805.

afternoon, from whence I will do myself the pleasure of visiting Sidmonton Place, according to Captain Kingsmill's very civil invitation. I wrote you some days ago, that Mrs. Kirke's case was *incurable*. I have nothing more to add, only assuring you of the grateful sense I entertain of your kindness to me, and that I am your much obliged humble Servant,

HORATIO NELSON.

I beg my compliments to Captain Kingsmill.

TO CAPTAIN LOCKER.

[Autograph, in the Locker Papers.—No date of the month or year, but probably in May 1781.]

Wednesday, half-past ten.

My dear Sir,

I am very much obliged to you for your kind inquiries after me, and I most sincerely wish I was as well as your servant has reported me to be; but within these two or three days I have relapsed very much, attended with a slight fever. I shall visit Mr. Adair [9] at *one* this day; and if I have time will call upon you at Mr. Rigaud's.[1] I will wait upon you to-morrow, at eleven o'clock, and I am your much obliged Friend,

HORATIO NELSON.

I hope your Country trip has mended you.

TO WILLIAM LOCKER, ESQ., GRAY'S INN.

[Autograph, in the Locker Papers.—No date of month or year, but apparently written about May 1781.]

Thursday, two o'clock.

Dear Sir,

I thank you much for your kind inquiries after my health, which, I thank God, is very much altered for the better since

---

[9] Robert Adair, Esq., Surgeon-General to the Army : he married Lady Caroline Keppel, sister of George, 3rd Earl of Albemarle, and of Admiral Viscount Keppel. Mr. Adair died in March 1790.

[1] The Painter, vide p. 38.

I saw you. I did not intend to be in Town till Saturday, but as you have thoughts of going out of Town, I will do myself the pleasure of seeing you to-morrow morning, about ten o'clock.

I am, yours most sincerely,

HORATIO NELSON.

I saw Sir Richard Bickerton[2] on Tuesday: he is out of Town for a few days at Huntingdon. I am much obliged to C. Pole for his inquiries: if you write, I beg my compliments.

TO THE REV. MR. NELSON, BURNHAM, NORFOLK.

[Autograph, in the Nelson Papers.]

Kentish Town,[3] May 7th, 1781.

My dear Brother,

I have no doubt but you have scolded me pretty heartily for not having answered your letter before this time, and therefore I will begin to plead my excuse. In the first place, I was thirty miles on the other side London, and did not return here till the 30th of April, at night. On Thursday, I received your second, with the power of attorney, since which time I have been so much engaged that I really have not had a spare moment. I was with Lord Sandwich[4] yesterday, and he could fix no time when I should be employed, although he promised he would employ me the first opportunity, so all these matters are settled, and now you will say, Why does not he come into Norfolk? I will tell you: I have entirely lost the use of my left arm, and very near of my left leg and thigh, and am at present under the care of a Mr. Adair, an eminent Surgeon in London; but he gives me hopes a few weeks will remove my disorder, when I will certainly come into Norfolk, and spend my time there till I am employed. When you write to my father do not mention my complaints, for I know it will make him very uneasy, and can do no good; and if you tell it to my

---

[2] Captain afterwards Vice-Admiral Sir Richard Bickerton, Bart., who died Commander-in-Chief at Plymouth, in January 1792.

[3] The residence of his uncle, Mr. William Suckling, of the Navy Office.

[4] John, fourth Earl of Sandwich, then First Lord of the Admiralty.

sisters, desire them not to mention it. I saw Maurice[5] the other day: he is very well, and says he wishes much to pay a visit to Burnham. I beg you will remember me kindly to all those gentlemen who have been so good as to inquire after me, and believe me to be

Your affectionate Brother,

HORATIO NELSON.

Pray give my kind love to all my brothers and sisters.

TO THE REV. MR. NELSON, JUN^R., BURNHAM.

[Autograph, in the Nelson Papers. He was appointed to command the Albemarle, a small Frigate of 28 guns, early in August 1781.]

Kentish Town, August 24th, 1781.

Dear Brother,

According to my promise I sit down to write you an account of the Albemarle. Yesterday I went down to Woolwich with Maurice, and hoisted my Pendant; and I am perfectly satisfied with her, as a twenty-eight gun Frigate. She is in dock, alongside the Enterprize, and in some respects, I think, excels her. She has a bold entrance, and clean run. The Enterprize, a *lean bow*, which does not answer so well with copper, as they always allow for sheathing, which is upwards of an inch more in thickness, therefore, she wants that much. The Albemarle is not so wide, upon the gun-deck, by four inches, but the same beam; the gun-deck six feet high; between decks very low indeed, about five feet. She is now coppering, and will not be out of dock this fortnight, at least.

The Admiralty have been very civil, having given me the choice of all my Officers, which I am much pleased with. Now if you will ask Forster to enter for the Ship, he shall be rated Master's-mate, and receive five pounds bounty money; and if he can bring any Seamen with him, shall have two pounds for each man, and they will have the same bounty. They can come by any of the Wells' Ships, who shall be paid for bringing them. I have talked with Mr. Suckling about your going

---

[5] His brother, Maurice Nelson.

Chaplain in the Navy, and he thinks, as I do, that fifty pounds where you are, is much more than equal to what you can get at Sea; but in that I know you will please yourself, therefore shall not attempt to state any argument to *dissuade* you from it. Your own judgment must rule you. I beg my kind love to my father, and my brothers and sisters. Adieu, and assure yourself that I am in every respect your affectionate Brother,

HORATIO NELSON.

TO THE REV. MR. NELSON, JUN^R., BURNHAM

[Autograph, in the Nelson Papers.]

Woolwich, September 9, 1781.

Dear Brother,

I must beg your pardon for not having answered your letter before this time, but I assure you since last Sunday, when I wrote to my father, I have not had one moment's spare time: therefore in the first place let us mention your business. I have not seen one creature, since I have been in Town, that I could talk to upon the subject; but be assured I shall not forget you, but do what lays in my power towards the completion of your wishes. As to my real opinion, whether or no you will like it, I say, as I always did, that it[6] is five to one you will not. If you get with a good man, and with gentlemen, it will be tolerable; if not you will soon detest it. It is a chance, but I will let you know when I hear further upon the subject.

I am much obliged to you for having spoke to Forster, and I cannot promise that he can have the place I spoke of at first; but if he will come, I will do what I can for him, and if he does not like the Navy, he shall be discharged at any time. My Quarter-deck is filled, much to my satisfaction, with very genteel young men and seamen. My Lieutenants are appointed, but I have not seen either of them :[7] the second, a Mr. Osborne,

---

[6] Being a Navy Chaplain.

[7] The Officers who served in the Albemarle from the 15th August 1781 to the 3rd July 1783, were—Lieutenants, William Osborne, Martin Hinton, and Joseph Bromwich ; Surgeon, J. Armstrong ; Master, Don. Trail ; Pursers, H. Delamain and W. Easton.— *Clarke and M'Arthur*, vol. i. Appendix.

son of Sir Charles Hardy's[8] Secretary; an exceeding good Master, and good Warrant Officers, and pretty successful in getting men; not less than twenty volunteers have come to me already, most of them seamen. If any Ships are coming soon from Wells[9] to London, I beg the box of papers, &c. may be sent. If there is not within these three weeks, they must come by land. My wine from Portsmouth is sent for, though much I hear is lost. However, a moiety of it shall come to Burnham. The first week in October, I hope to be at the Nore. You must not forget me to your Wells' Club, nor any where else, where I am known. Adieu my dear brother, and believe me to be

Your affectionate Brother,
HORATIO NELSON.

Maurice is well. Give my duty to my father, and love to all.

P. S. If I do not give you the progress you will scold—She is rigged, and getting in her ground tier.

TO THE REVEREND MR. NELSON, JUN[R]., BURNHAM.

[Autograph, in the Nelson Papers.]

Albemarle, Woolwich, October 2nd, 1781.

Dear Brother,

I have received yours, as well as many more letters from Burnham, and which I have not had a moment's time to answer. In the first place my things came all safe by the Wells' ship. Your matter, as yet, I have made little progress in; but when I am amongst my Brother Officers, I shall then be able to judge better what can be done. My destination is fixed without anything particular happen, that is, the North Seas; and in that Fleet I know some of the Captains, and the Commodore, Keith Stewart;[1] but when I join them I will let you

---

[8] Admiral Sir Charles Hardy.

[9] The harbour of Wells is about five miles, and the Town three miles from Burnham Thorpe.

[1] Commodore the Honourable Keith Stewart, fourth son of Alexander, 4th Earl of Galloway: he died a Vice-Admiral in March 1795.

know what you may expect. Be assured it has been no neglect
of mine that you have not got it before this time, and I will
leave no method untried to accomplish it.

The day after to-morrow the Albemarle goes from here down
the River, and in the next week will be off the Nore. I received
a letter from Mun,[2] and am much obliged to him for the
trouble he has been at. All I shall say in answer to it is that
Mr. Wiseman is a *goose*. The Collector's letter I have received, and have sent for the young man: he will be here in
all probability before I close this letter. I have just seen
Val. Boyles,[3] who seems very sorry for what he has done,
but hopes that his father will be able to get Lord Townshend to give him a Lieutenant's commission, which will put
him in a very good line of life. Mr. Suckling is quite recovered.

I am, dear brother, yours affectionately,

HORATIO NELSON.

My kind love to my father, brothers, and sisters: and compliments to all. I have given Val. Boyles two guineas, as his
father requested.

TO THE REVEREND MR. NELSON, JUN[R]., BURNHAM.

[Autograph in the Nelson Papers.]

Sheerness, October 18th, 1781.

Dear Brother,

According to my promise, I sit down to write: I came
down to the Nore on Sunday last, and am now full manned, and
ready for any service. I have an exceeding good Ship's company. Not a man or Officer in her I would wish to change.
She appears to sail also very well. Where I am going, I
know not, but suppose I shall be gone from here in the next
week, when I will write again. I hope Mrs. Bolton's[4]
troubles are over. Give my kind love to her, and to my

---

[2] His brother Edmund, then a lad nineteen years of age. He died unmarried
in December 1789.

[3] Valentine Boyles, born in 1756, son of the Collector of the Customs in
Wells; vide. p. 49, post. George Viscount Townshend was then Master-General of the Ordnance.

[4] His eldest sister, Susannah, who was born 12th June 1755, and married

father, sister, and Mun ; tell him I would not take either Mr.
Wiseman or Walker. I hardly think I have so bad a man in
my Ship. I have got John Oliver, belonging to Wells, and
have made him a Quarter-master ; he is a very good man.

　　　　　　I am, dear Brother, yours affectionately,

　　　　　　　　　　　　　　　　HORATIO NELSON.

　Compliments to the Wells' Club, and all friends in
Norfolk.

TO WILLIAM LOCKER, ESQ., GRAY'S INN.

[Autograph, in the Locker Papers.—Two days after the date of this letter,
he received his Orders to the effect — that as the Russia Company had
represented, that besides the Fleet of Merchantmen under the Convoy of the
Africa, there would also be a very considerable number of Ships from the
different Ports of the Baltic at the Sound, laden with cargoes of the utmost
National importance, he was to take the Argo and Enterprise under his command, and proceed to Elsineur for the homeward bound trade, and having
seen them in safety to their respective places, he was to proceed to the Downs.
He was also informed, that he might, probably, be reinforced by some Ships from
Commodore Stewart's Squadron, which was off the Texel.—*Original* in the Nelson Papers.]

　　　　　　　　　　　　Albemarle, Nore, October 21st, 1781.
　My dear Sir,

　I arrived here this day week from Long Reach, and I
dare say you are almost scolding for my not writing before
this ; but, in the first place, I have been very busy in getting
my Ship's company in order for service. They are, in my
opinion, as good a set of men as I ever saw : indeed, I am
perfectly satisfied with both Officers and Ship's company. All
my Marines are likewise *old standers*. As another excuse,
which is much worse, I have been so ill, as hardly [to be] kept
out of bed. I have been but twice out of the Ship since her
arrival. I saw Mr. Belless[5] on one of those days ; he is pretty
well, and desires his compliments to you. Old Westcott, the
Master Attendant, is gone upon leave : he is very unwell. I am

---

5th August 1780, Thomas Bolton, Esq., of Cranwich, in Norfolk. She gave
birth to twin daughters on the 20th November 1781. Her son Thomas succeeded
as second Earl Nelson, and was father of the present Earl. Mrs. Bolton died in
July 1813.

　[5] Apparently, Robert Bellas, Surgeon of the Dock Yard at Sheerness.

sorry to hear poor Captain Sutton[6] is gone to the East Indies. That Johnstone must be a sad villain, he hopes to kill Sutton, to escape a trial. Pray let me know what you have heard of the matter.

What sad news from America: for my part, I cannot understand Mr. Graves'[7] letter; the French are here and there, I supposed in sight, to windward of him; at last a Frigate goes to look for them, and finds them very safe in the Chesapeake. I much fear for Lord Cornwallis: if something was not immediately done, America is quite lost. My orders are not yet come down, therefore hope you will give me a line, which will much oblige

Your much obliged Friend,
HORATIO NELSON.

Pray [give] my compliments to the Bradleys[8] and George Smith. I hope Mr. B. is better.

[6] On the 16th April 1781, the Squadron, under the command of Commodore George Johnstone, consisting, among other Ships, of the Isis, Captain Evelyn Sutton, (vide p. 36, ante,) was surprised and attacked in Porto Praya Bay, in the Island of Saint Jago, by a French Squadron under Monsieur de Suffrein. In his public letter, Commodore Johnstone accused Captain Sutton of neglect of duty, and stated that he had placed him under an arrest. He was accordingly tried by a Court-Martial, on the 1st October 1783, and honourably acquitted. Captain Sutton afterwards brought an action against Commodore Johnstone, which was the subject of two trials : by the first he obtained a verdict of 5000*l.*, and by the next 6000*l.* damages. The cause afterwards came before the House of Lords ; and in May 1787, Captain Sutton was defeated by a majority of thirteen votes. Commodore Johnstone died in the same month. In a satire published about this time called " the Norfolk Tripping Jury, by Dick Merryfellow," Commodore Johnson is thus alluded to :

> " Port Praya's tar who cannot *write*,
> Swears he'll make all his *Captains* fight ;
> For *Frenchmen* cares not a button—
> So he can lay the blame on Sutton."

[7] Rear-Admiral Thomas Graves, Commander-in-Chief in North America, afterwards Admiral Lord Graves. The Letter alluded to described his engagement with Count de Grasse, on the 5th September 1781, which caused much dissatisfaction in England.

[8] " The Bradleys" were three brothers ; viz. James, Henry, and Richard Bradley, and a sister, Frances. Being intimate friends of Admiral Parry, and consequently of the Lockers, (p. 23, ante,) Nelson, when a Lieutenant, became known to them, and always felt great regard for the family. Mr. James Bradley was appointed Secretary to the Board of Controul, on the institution of the Office, and died in 1800 without issue. His only sister, Frances, married, in

TO THE REVEREND MR. NELSON, BURNHAM.

[Autograph, in the Nelson Papers.]

Albemarle, Yarmouth Roads, December 18th, 1781.

My dear Brother,

I arrived here yesterday in my way to the Downs, but the wind has detained me here. I suppose our father is gone to Bath before this. I hope you have had a pleasant autumn, and plenty of game. Mr. Bracey I saw here yesterday; he tells me Charles Boyles[9] is in Norfolk; pray remember me kindly to him: I wish much to meet him. I hope you have lost all ideas of going to Sea, for the more I see of Chaplains of Men-of-War, the more I dread seeing my brother in such a disagreeable station of life.

Adieu, dear brother, and believe me to be

Your affectionate Brother,

HORATIO NELSON.

Love to Mun. I suppose all the Wells' house is flown.

TO WILLIAM LOCKER, ESQ., GRAY'S INN.

[Autograph, in the Locker Papers.]

Yarmouth Roads, December 22nd, 1781.

My dear Sir,

I would have wrote a line before this, but I expected every moment would have brought a wind that would have sent me to the Downs, where I am bound with a large Convoy of Store-Ships for Portsmouth and Plymouth. I assure you I have almost been froze on the other side the water: here we find it quite summer. We have not had any success; indeed, there is nothing you can meet, but what is in force: the Dutch have not a single Merchantman at Sea. One Pri-

1782, Andrew Hawes Dyne, Esq., of Gore Court, in Kent, and being heiress to her brother, her husband assumed the name of Bradley. Their eldest son, Francis Bradley, Esq., now of Gore Court, has lately resumed the name of Dyne.

[9] Charles Boyles, born in 1753, son of Charles Boyles, Esq., Collector of the Customs at Wells in Norfolk, was appointed to the Raisonable, Captain Suckling, at the same time that Nelson joined that Ship. He was a Lieutenant at the date of this letter; was made a Commander in April 1783; obtained Post rank in November 1790; and died a Vice-Admiral of the Blue, in November 1816.

vateer was in our Fleet, but it was not possible to lay hold of
him. I chased him an hour, and came fast up with him, but
was obliged to return to the Fleet. I find since, it was the
noted *Fall, the Pirate.*[1] Macbride[2] sailed from hence, yesterday, with his two Dutch prizes: they are fine Privateers,
Schooner-rigged, but very different to what you would suppose by his letter. Whoever gets them as fine Sloops of War,
will be very much disappointed when they see them. Dickson[3]
in the Sampson, was our Commodore. What fools the Dutch
must have been not to have taken us into the Texel. Two
hundred and sixty Sail the Convoy consisted of. They behaved, as all Convoys that ever I saw did, shamefully ill;
parting company every day. One hundred and ten Sail
are now in the roads.

I hope to hear that you have a Ship, at least that your
health will permit you to take one. I hope you are got into
Kent, but I shall direct it to the old place. If you are moved
they will send it. I hope Mr. James Bradley is got well. I
beg my compliments to all of them, [*a word illegible,*] my
dear Sir, and believe me to be

Your most obliged and very humble Servant,
                              HORATIO NELSON.

The Albemarle, although you abused her at Woolwich, has
some good sailing in her. The Argo, a new forty-four, we
can spare a good deal of sail; and I think we go full as well
as the Enterprise.[4] If you write a line to the Downs, I shall
get it there.

---

[1] This person, who commanded the Folkestone privateer Cutter, under French
colours, had menaced and fired upon several places on the coast of Scotland.

[2] Captain John Macbride obtained his Flag in February 1793, and died an
Admiral of the Blue, in 1800.

[3] Captain William Dickson. He died an Admiral of the Blue, in May 1803.

[4] The Argo 44, Captain John Butchart, (whose name immediately followed
Nelson's in the list of Post-Captains,) and Enterprize 29, Captain John Willett
Payne, who died a Rear-Admiral. Those Ships, with the Albemarle, sailed from
the Nore to the Baltic in October 1781.

TO CAPTAIN LOCKER.

[Autograph, in the Locker Papers.]

Albemarle, Yarmouth Roads, December 30th, 1781.

My dear Sir,

Mr. Mitchel, this morning, has shown me a letter from an uncle of his, which he received last night, telling him that he was to go out with Sir George Rodney, and that you had wrote to me in the Downs to discharge him. I therefore instantly discharged him, and have given [him] a boat to go on shore with his things, although it blows pretty hard. The wind, I am almost afraid, will not shift this change, for it has all the appearance of a Westerly and South-West wind. I have been once to Sea with the Convoy, and got pretty near Orfordness, but it coming to blow hard from the Southward, was very glad to get them safe into the Roads again. Mr. Mitchel, since he has been in the Albemarle, has acted as one of [the] Mates, and has always done his duty as an exceeding good Petty Officer, though I believe he thinks it high time that he was made a Lieutenant. I am puzzled where to direct to you, but shall continue it to the old place. If the wind continues to the Southward of West, I should be glad to know where you are, for we cannot stir with those winds. Adieu, my dear Sir, and believe me to be ever faithfully,

Your most obedient Servant

HORATIO NELSON.

Captain Dickson, of the Sampson, desired me, if I wrote to you, to make his compliments.

TO PHILIP STEPHENS, ESQ., SECRETARY TO THE ADMIRALTY.

[Original, in the Admiralty.]

Albemarle, in the Downs, 2nd January, 1782.

Sir,

I have to acquaint you, for the information of my Lords Commissioners of the Admiralty, that I arrived last night at dark, in the Downs, with the Argo and Preston,[5] and sixty-five Sail, mostly belonging to the Baltic Fleet, including ten Store-Ships for Portsmouth, and eighteen for Plymouth. Inclosed is the State and Condition of his Majesty's Ship under my command.

I am, Sir, &c.

HORATIO NELSON.

TO WILLIAM LOCKER, ESQ., GRAY'S INN.

[Autograph, in the Locker Papers.—Though dated in 1781, it is evidently a clerical error for 1782.]

Albemarle, Downs, January 2nd, 1781 [1782].

My dear Sir,

The instant I received your letter, the latter part struck me so very much, that perhaps I write to you sooner than otherwise I should have done. I need not say it to you, but what in the *name* of *God* could it be to me, whether a Midshipman in my Ship had not a farthing or fifty pounds a-year? therefore now I must tell you, as far as I know, his wish to leave the Ship. When he came on board, I sent him into Mr. Bromwich's[6] mess, where he was two or three days. In that time they spoke to me, that they hoped I would not take it amiss, but they could not think of keeping that young man (I forget his name) in their mess, as he could not pay his part of their small expenses. I am sure that you will not think I should attempt to force any person upon people who were behaving exceedingly well in the Ship, (which would have been *tyrannical* in the highest degree) against their inclination. Whether the lad sent to speak to me, or I sent for him, I do not recollect; but I told him of what the mess had said. He then seemed very uneasy at what I told him, and said he could not afford to live in a mess that cost anything; and then said he wished to leave the Ship. The next day he pressed me much to discharge him, as he could not live in any of the mid-messes. Much against my inclination I did *discharge* him. What he took the idea of 30*l.* a year from, I

---

⁶ Afterwards Lieutenant Joseph Bromwich, Warden of Portsmouth Dock-yard.

know not; for I declare I never opened my lips to him upon the subject. A youngster in the Ship, whose friends are Norfolk people, who had not made an allowance for their son, I took upon me to allow 20*l.* a year.

I assure you, I hold myself under very great obligations to you, that you asserted it was an *infamous lie:* had I in the least suspected the story he has told, he should staid on board, and might have lived as he pleased. It was my endeavouring to put him in a comfortable situation, that has made any person speak ill of me. If he had come into the Ship as many hundred youngsters of the kind do, and the Captain had [*a word illegible*] to him, or of him to anybody for . . . . . months, I should have had no trouble about him. I can't help being a little surprised that Captain Kirke should have such an opinion of me; and I am sure [I] shall always be happy to obey his commands in the fullest meaning of *the words.* I hope both he and Mrs. Kirke are well: if you should write or see them, I beg my best respects. I have never received your letter about discharging Mr. Mitchel; but you know he is, long before this. He is, as I wrote to you by him. I am sorry poor Bradley is taken, and that the other brother is so ill. Fortitude is not here, or I would send after *Jack Moore.*[7] Adieu, my dear Sir, and believe that I am

　　　　Your much obliged obedient Servant,

　　　　　　　　　　HORATIO NELSON.

I am much afraid we are fixed for the North Seas, as another has orders to take our Convoy.

TO THE REVEREND MR. NELSON, BURNHAM.

[Autograph, in the Nelson Papers.]

Deal, January 25th, 1782.

Dear Brother,

I have wrote at last. I am almost ashamed not to have wrote before, but I have been so unwell, and weather so bad, that I have not had patience to put pen to paper. On board I have wrote almost a sheet of *nonsense;* but in my great wis-

---

[7] It has not been ascertained who this person was. He is again mentioned in a subsequent Letter.

dom I was sent for on shore, and have left it on board : but I
was determined, as I had half an hour on dry land, to make
some use of it. Going well on for a month have I been laying here, and driving from one end of the Downs to the other.
Such weather I never saw in my life as has been for this
month past; nothing but wrecks all over the coast. I am ordered to Portsmouth with seven East India Ships ; whether I
shall stay to the Westward, or come back to the North Seas,
is quite uncertain. I must finish my letter, for I am disturbed
with a room full of company. Farewell my dear Brother,

And believe me, affectionately yours,
HORATIO NELSON.

Love to Mrs. Bolton, Kate,[7] and Mun, and compliments to
Miss Beck, and all your Wells' Club.[8]

TO THE REVEREND MR. NELSON, BURNHAM.

[Autograph, in the Nelson Papers.]

Albemarle, in the Downs, January 28th, [1782.]

My dear Brother,

I have no doubt but you have scolded me most heartily for
not having wrote before this, but I know *after a Storm comes
a Calm ;* so at this time I suppose you quite quiet and easy,
not expecting a letter : therefore I am determined you shall
have one. Now I'll begin excuses. In the first place, you did
not wish me to write till I knew where I was to [be] stationed ;
that I can't tell you, for I do not know myself. The Admiralty, I believe, are asleep, but if I can prognosticate, we are to
have the Downs Station for the present—(a horrid bad one).
I am glad you went on shore when you did, or you must have
come to the Downs with us, for we could not send a boat on

[7] His youngest sister Katherine, who was born 19th March 1767 : she married
on the 26th of February 1787, George Matcham of Ashford Lodge, and died 28th
March 1842, leaving a large family.

[8] The " Wells' Club" so often mentioned, was a Card Club which met on Mon-
days and Wednesdays at the Royal Standard and Three Tuns Inn alternately,
and consisted of the principal inhabitants of Wells and its vicinity. The Rev.
William Nelson, his brother-in-law, Mr. Bolton, and Mr. Boyles, the Collector
of the Customs, were among its Members. From the information of James
Young, Esq., of Wells.

shore all the next day. At eleven on Monday morning, we
sailed with sixty-five Sail, and next day, at noon, was at the
back of the Goodwin Sands. The Ships in the Downs took us
for a Dutch Fleet going down Channel; and many of
the Men-of-War were under sail to come after us, when a
Cutter went in, and told them who we were. We all got safe
in that night, and next, I delivered my charge up to the Admiral. Here I have been laying ever since without orders;
and in such a long *series* of bad weather as is seldom met
with. We have nothing but a coast full of wrecks,—twice we
have parted from our anchors; the North Seas are dreadful at
this season of the year. I'll wish you a good night, for I
must have some conversation with the Doctor, who, I believe,
has saved my life since I saw you.

All on the other side,[9] is what I told you in my last I
had left on board. At last I was ordered round to Portsmouth to take in eight months' provisions, and I have no
doubt was meant to go to the East Indies with Sir Richard
Bickerton, which I should have liked exceedingly, but
alas, how short-sighted are the best of us. On the 26th
January, at eight in the morning, it blew a hard gale of wind
at N.N.W., a large East India Store Ship drove from her
anchors, and came on board us. We have lost our foremast,
and bowsprit, mainyard, larboard cathead, and quarter gallery,
the Ship's head, and stove in two places on the larboard side,—
all done in five minutes. What a change! but yet we ought
to be thankful we did not founder. We have been employed
since in getting jury-masts, yards, and bowsprit, and stopping
the holes in our sides.[1] What is to become of us now, I know

---

[9] i. e. The preceding part of this letter.

[1] Clarke and M'Arthur thus relate the circumstance; but as they are wrong in
the date, they may have been misinformed respecting the particulars. It will be
observed that the accident happened at eight in the morning, and that Nelson does
not say a word of his being on shore at the time.—" The Albemarle arrived in the
Downs on the 3rd of January 1792, from Yarmouth Roads; when her Captain
went on shore to call on the senior Officer, the Hon. Keith Elphinstone. During
his absence from the Ship, there came on so heavy a gale, that almost all the
vessels on the station drove, and the Brilliant Store-ship, belonging to the Ordnance, came athwart-hawse of the Albemarle. Captain Nelson immediately ran
to the beach, and with his wonted contempt of danger, when any duty called for
his exertions, employed every method he could devise to return on board, fearing
lest the Albemarle might drive on the Goodwin Sands; but the dreadful surf

not. She must go into dock, and I fear must be paid off
she has received so much damage. But, however, we must
take the rough as well as the smooth: these are the blessings
of a Sea life. Remember me to Mrs. Bolton, Kate, and Mun,
and Mr. Bolton if at home; not forgetting Mr. Robinson
Boyles, and Charles Boyles² if he is there. Farewell, dear
brother,

And believe me to be your affectionate Brother,

HORATIO NELSON.

TO PHILIP STEPHENS, ESQ., SECRETARY TO THE ADMIRALTY.

[Original, in the Admiralty.]

Albemarle, at Spithead, 2nd February, 1782.

Sir,

I am to acquaint you, for the information of my Lords Commissioners of the Admiralty, that I arrived here this morning
in His Majesty's Ship Albemarle, under my command; and
inclosed I transmit you her State and Condition.

I am, Sir, &c.

HORATIO NELSON.

TO WILLIAM LOCKER, ESQ., GRAY'S INN.

[Autograph, in the Locker Papers.]

Portsmouth, February 5th, 1782.

My dear Sir,

Since I received yours, the Albemarle is much altered for
the worse. An East India Store-Ship came on board us in
a gale of wind, and carried away our foremast, bowsprit, head,
and quarter gallery, and done considerable damage to her
hull. We arrived here two days ago, and are now coming
into the harbour to be docked. I was ordered for Foreign ser-

and increasing gale, made even the skilful mariners of Deal regard the attempt
as utterly impracticable. At length some of the most intrepid offered to make
the trial for fifteen guineas; this produced a competition, and Nelson, to the
astonishment of all beholders, was long seen struggling with a raging and moun-
tainous surf, in which the boat was continually immerged. After much difficulty,
he got on board his ship, which lost her bowsprit and foremast."—Vol. i. p. 46.

² Mr. Robinson Boyles was probably the brother of Charles Boyles, so often
mentioned.

vice. Charles Pole[3] is here : he is going to Gibraltar with a
large Cutter, laden with Gun-boats; I wish he was safe back.
I think he runs great risk of going to Cadiz.[4]   Sir Richard
Bickerton[5] is here ;—*a great man*, he seems to carry it pretty
high with his Captains.   *Jack Moore* is with him, and I
heard him tell Captain Robinson, who was Admiral Parker's
Captain in the Fortitude, he would certainly provide for him.[6]
I shall certainly see you in Town before the Albemarle gets
out of the harbour.   Mr. White, the builder, has inquired
after you.   Farewell, my dear Sir, and believe me to be,

Faithfully yours,
HORATIO NELSON.

Compliments to the Bradleys, and all that ask after me.

TO THE REVEREND MR. NELSON, BURNHAM.

[Autograph, in the Nelson Papers.

Portsmouth, February 8th, 1782.

Dear Brother,

Your letter of January 30th I received two nights ago;
and am much obliged to you for it; I should have
wrote before I did from the Downs, only I expected my
orders every day, when I could have told you where I was to
have been stationed.   You have heard of the accidents that
have happened to the poor Albemarle, both by my letter and
the Papers long before this.   I was under orders for Foreign
service, and I fancy was going with dispatches to North
America.   I am now waiting at Spithead for a wind to bring
me into the harbour to be docked and repaired; what will
become of me afterwards I know not.   If I should touch at
any wine Countries, you may assure Lord Walpole I will purchase some of the best wines for him.   I beg you will make

---

[3] Captain Pole then commanded the Success frigate.

[4] i. e. Of being captured by the Spaniards.

[5] Wearing a Broad Pendant in the Gibraltar 80, and going with a Squadron to
India.

[6] Vice-Admiral Sir Hyde Parker.   Captain Mark Robinson is mentioned in p.
6, ante.

my best respects to him and Lady Walpole,[7] with many thanks
for their kind inquiries after me. I regret very much I had
not the pleasure of receiving Mr. Walpole on board the
Albemarle, or if he had been in Yarmouth, I should certainly have paid my respects to him. Apropos of wine:—in my
opinion, the expense of sending a cask of wine from this place
to Burnham is almost the original cost; but there it is, if you
please to have it; only send word. Charles Boyles sailed from
here the day before my arrival.

Whatever may be the opinion of the Wells people respecting
Captain Gardner's[8] behaviour in the matter of his Lieutenants
quitting his Ship, I will answer he was right. There is not a
better Officer, or more of a gentleman, this day in the Service.
I am much afraid poor Charles will wait a long while with
Mr. R—— before he gets promotion, for he is a great *liar*.
Sir Richard Bickerton, with the East India Fleet, sailed yesterday afternoon, with six Sail of the Line for India, and
three Sail of the Line and two Fifties, to go part of the
way with them. The West India Fleet is not yet ready:
they will sail Saturday or Sunday, if the wind is fair.

I wish I could congratulate you upon a Rectory instead of
a Vicarage: it is rather *awkward* wishing the poor man *dead*,
but we all rise by *deaths*. I got my rank by a shot killing a
Post-Captain,[9] and I most sincerely hope I shall, when I go,
go out of [the] world the same way; then we go all in the line
of our Profession—a *Parson* praying, a Captain fighting. I
suppose you are returned from Hilborough before this, and
taken *Miss Ellen* and the *Living*. As Miss Bec takes so
much notice of my respect to her, tell her I think myself
honoured by being in her favour. Love to Mrs. Bolton and
Mun, not forgetting little Kate. You have wrote so long a
letter, that I must get another half sheet to work.[1]

---

[7] Horatio, second Lord Walpole, of Wolterton, created Earl of Orford in
1806. He married in 1748, Rachel, daughter of William third Duke of Devonshire ; she died in May 1805. The Earl of Orford died in February 1809.

[8] Captain Alan Gardner, afterwards Admiral Lord Gardner.

[9] Captain Everitt who commanded the Hinchinbrook, joined the Ruby for a
cruize, in consequence of the illness of her proper Captain, Joseph Deane ; and
being killed by a random shot in capturing La Prudente, French Frigate, on the
2nd of June 1779, Nelson was promoted into the Hinchinbrook.

[1] The conclusion is not preserved.

[Autograph, in the Locker Papers.]

Portsmouth, March 10th, 1782.

My Dear Sir,

Your favour I received last night inclosing a letter from Ross,[2] of December the 31st. He has twice been on his passage for England, was once drove back by the French Fleet, and the other time shipwrecked; but he is going to make another trial, and I suppose will arrive in this Convoy. He desires his particular compliments to you: it is as friendly a letter as I ever received. I dare say you will see him very soon. In his postscript he mentions having received a letter from Mr. Higgins, saying that I was going to pay for a pipe of Madeira wine. He desires me, if I have paid it, to send for the money again, as there is no error existing but in Mr. Higgins' accounts; but, if you remember the circumstance, I did not pay for the wine.

All the Admiral's[3] family are well, enjoying the mountains, and daily increasing in wealth. General Dalling[4] landed here last night; he came home in the Ranger Armed Ship; one or two of the Convoy are also arrived. The Jupiter arrived yesterday morning, with a brig from St. Domingo, and a French privateer. I have just learnt that the Ranger's Convoy were most of [them] taken in the Gulf of Florida, by two Line of Battle Ships, and six armed Schooners, so I suppose Ross is carried into the *Havannah*. Adieu, my dear Sir, and assure yourself I am your

Most obedient Servant,

HORATIO NELSON.

[2] Hercules Ross, Esq., before mentioned.
[3] Sir Peter Parker.
[4] Vide p. 9, ante.

TO THE REVEREND MR. NELSON, AT JAMES COLDHAM'S, ESQ.,
BIRCHAM, NORFOLK.

[Autograph, in the Nelson Papers.]

Portsmouth, March 29th, 1782.

Dear Brother,

Yours of the 24th I received last night, as well as two letters
you wrote before to me. I have had so much business upon my
hands in fitting the old Albemarle once more for service, that
you must excuse my not having wrote. I shall sail, if the
weather is moderate, in the first week of April, from Spithead
to Cork, where I am to take a Convoy, and carry them to
Quebec. Whether I am [to] come home in the autumn or not is
uncertain. Perhaps, and I believe, your reasoning upon giving up the money to Mr. Bolton is very just, but yet I shall
sign the power of attorney, if it is sent me. If the children
have nothing else I am sure that is no object. Your argument that, if his trading schemes should fail, our family must
maintain her, and his children, I deny; I don't think myself
obliged to do any such thing. Perhaps our denying the
money to Mr. Bolton, may bring on a disagreement between
him and his wife: it is better for us to run the risk of the
sum, than that such a thing should happen. I beg we may
not interfere about the houses at Wells: if he don't do it
let it rest. I have burnt your letter. Oliver is still on
board the Albemarle, and well: he has wrote several times to
his wife, but has had no answer. I would, with great pleasure,
have sent you the wine, but a quarter cask cannot be entered
at the Custom House. I am very sorry you have not got New-
ton Living: I hope, now, Lord Walpole will look out for something for you. Make my compliments to all at Wells, &c., and
give my love to *Mun*. Adieu, dear Brother, and believe me
to be

Yours affectionately,
HORATIO NELSON.

Lord Howe is to command the Fleet.[1]

---

[1] Admiral Lord Howe hoisted his Flag in the Victory; and after cruizing in
the Channel for a short time, proceeded to the relief of Gibraltar in September
1782, with thirty-four Sail of the Line.

TO WILLIAM LOCKER, ESQ., GRAY'S INN.

[Autograph, in the Locker Papers.]

Portsmouth, April 2nd, 1782.

My dear Sir,

I ought to [be] scolded for not having wrote to you for this long time past: I can make but very lame excuses. The weather has been so bad for these ten days, and Southerly winds, that I have not been able to get old Albemarle out of the harbour. I am ordered to Cork to join the Dædalus, Captain Pringle,[5] and go with a Convoy to Quebec; where, worse than all to tell, I understand I am to winter. I want much to [get] off from this d——d voyage, and believe, if I had time to look a little about me, I could get another Ship. Mr. Adair, who attends on Mr. Keppel,[6] might tell him, that in such a Country I shall be laid up: for he has told me, that if I was sent to a cold damp climate, it would make me worse than ever. Many of my Navy friends have advised me to represent my situation to Admiral Keppel, and they have no doubt but he would give me other orders, or remove me; but as I received my orders from Lord Sandwich, I can't help thinking it wrong to ask Mr. Keppel to alter them.

Charles Pole tells me he wrote you yesterday. I am exceedingly happy at his success: in his seamanship he showed himself as superior to the Don, as in his gallantry; and no man in the world so modest in his account of it.[7] Admiral Pye[8] hoisted his flag to day. Admiral Barrington hoists his after the Court-Martial is assembled to-morrow, on board the Britannia.[9] Lord Longford[1] introduced me to him this

[5] Captain Thomas Pringle, who became one of Nelson's warmest friends. He commanded the Valiant in Lord Howe's Action on the 1st June 1794, and received the Medal; obtained his flag in 1794; and died a Vice-Admiral of the Red in December 1803.

[6] Admiral Keppel succeeded Lord Sandwich, as First Lord of the Admiralty, on the 30th March 1782. Mr. Adair, the Surgeon, was his brother-in-law.

[7] On the 16th March 1782, Captain Pole, in the Success, captured the Spanish Frigate Santa Catalina, after a gallant Action off Cape Spartel.

[8] Admiral Sir Thomas Pye, who died in 1785.

[9] Vice-Admiral the Honourable Samuel Barrington, then about to proceed to intercept a French Convoy bound to the East Indies: he died an Admiral of the White, in August 1800, æt. 71.

[1] Edward Michael, second Lord Longford, was made a Post-Captain in May 1776, and died in June 1792.

morning, and told him who I was : it is from that quarter,
could I stay long enough in Port, that I expect a better Ship.
Admiral Barrington takes twelve Sail of the Line, as soon as
ready; he is in very good spirits ; he gets amongst all the
youngsters here, and leaves out the *old boys*. We are all
alive here : I hope to hear, by next [post,] you have a Ship.
Farewell, my dear Sir, for I have been so idle, that I have
not had ten minutes to spare for this.

Yours most sincerely,

HORATIO NELSON.

Pringle would not have gone this voyage, but for a hundred
thousand pounds going out to Quebec, and he's got it all. See
what it is to be a Scotchman. I hope their times are over.
Sandys[2] desires his compliments. Ferguson[3] of the Berwick
was honourably acquitted, as also Thompson [4] of the Hyæna.

TO WILLIAM LOCKER, ESQ., GRAY'S INN.

[Autograph, in the Locker Papers.]

Portsmouth, April 16th, 1782.

My dear Sir,

I am very much obliged to you for the great trouble you
have given yourself, in trying to alter my destination. To-
morrow I sail, if the weather is moderate. If I can get home
in the *autumn* I hope I shall get a better Ship and a better

---

[2] Captain Charles Sandys, who is frequently mentioned. Vide p. 110.

[3] Captain James Ferguson, who particularly distinguished himself in Sir
George Rodney's action in April 1780. Charnock says he was not again employed until June 1782, when he was appointed to the Egmont, and takes no
notice of this Court-Martial. Captain Ferguson was tried for having sailed
from Spithead on the 11th of February to the Andromache's station, without
having joined that Ship or the West India Convoy. In 1784 he became Lieutenant-Governor of Greenwich Hospital, and died in February 1793.

Captain Edward Thompson, well-known for his literary talents, and who
was usually called "the Poet Thompson :" he obtained Post rank in April
1772, and was tried by a Court-Martial for having left his station in the West
Indies without orders, for the purpose of convoying a valuable fleet of Merchant
Ships to England. He died Commodore on the coast of Guinea, in January
1786. A Memoir of Captain Thompson is given in the sixth and seventh
volumes of the Naval Chronicle.

station. Pringle, in the Dædalus, is going to Newfoundland, after having seen the Convoy to Quebec. God bless you, and assure yourself

I am ever faithfully yours,
Horatio Nelson.

Remember me to the Bradleys. Charles Pole desires his compliments: his Ship is in the harbour. He is coming soon to London.

TO CAPTAIN LOCKER.

[Autograph, in the Locker Papers.]

Cork, April 20th, 1782.

My dear Sir,

After a very long passage of ten days, owing to very bad weather, we are at last got here; the Dædalus, our consort, arrived the same day. To-morrow we sail, if the wind continues fair. Captain Pringle goes upon the Newfoundland station, after having seen us to the entrance of the River St. Lawrence. Our Convoy is between thirty and forty Sail. I know your goodness will say, ' I wonder how Nelson does ?' I say, I am quite well, better than for a long time past. I hope by the time I get back, all your complaints will be removed. Remember me kindly to all the Bradleys, and don't forget me to Commissioner Kirke, nor to Charles Pole, when you see him : never a young man bore his own merits with so much modesty. Farewell, my dear Sir, and believe me to be

Ever faithfully yours,
Horatio Nelson.

The Preston, I understand, is to bring out the English Quebec Fleet. I should be happy to hear from you. Will you send to Mr. Paynter, and tell him I am at Cork?

TO WILLIAM LOCKER, ESQ., GRAY'S INN.

[Autograph, in the Locker Papers.]

St. John's Harbour, Newfoundland, June 1st, 1782.

My dear Sir,

We arrived at this disagreeable place last Monday, at day-light (the 27th) with four Sail of the Convoy; we parted from the Dædalus on the 7th of May, three hundred leagues to the Westward of Cape Clear, in a hard gale of wind. As the wind has blown strong from the Eastward, ever since our arrival here, I imagine that Captain Pringle could not fetch this Port, and is therefore gone on to the Westward; if he is, this wind will carry him to Quebec, while I am so unfortunate as to be kept here with a fair wind; for the entrance of this harbour is so narrow, that you cannot sail unless the wind blows right out: as soon as the wind changes I shall sail.

Leocadia arrived here three days before us with the Salt Ships from Lisbon. Captain Hope[5] desires his compliments; he took a Ship privateer, the day he made the land, of fourteen guns. We have heard the news from the West Indies, but not particulars: it is reported that the Duke blew up in the Action. I hope to God it is not true. I had rather the French were at the devil, than have lost Captain Gardner: he is a real loss to the service.[6] You know the particulars long before this. My second Lieutenant was appointed to the Preston, and left the Ship at Cork; the other Lieutenant not having joined the Ship, I gave Bromwich an order to act as a Lieutenant: it will in all probability get him some prize-money, and I hope get him confirmed a Lieutenant; he does his duty exceedingly well as an Officer: indeed I am very well off. They are all good.

As to myself, the voyage agrees better with me than I expected. I hope you are much better in your head than when

[5] Captain Charles Hope, grandson of Charles, first Earl of Hopetoun, and father of Captain Henry Hope, C. B. He was for some time Commissioner of the Navy at Chatham, and died in September 1808.

[6] Sir George Rodney's engagement with the French Fleet under Count de Grasse, on the 12th of April 1782. The report of the explosion of the Duke was unfounded. Captain Alan Gardner, who greatly distinguished himself in that battle, and on numerous other occasions, became an Admiral, was raised to the Peerage, both in England and Ireland, and died in December 1808.

I sailed, and that Mr. James Bradley is got from under the Doctor's hands. Remember me to them all, and all my old friends that you may see. I think the chance is much against your getting this letter, as it goes by the way of Lisbon.

Farewell, my dear Sir, and believe me to be

Your much obliged faithful Servant,

HORATIO NELSON.

Bromwich desires his best respects. You must not forget mine to Commissioner Kirke when you see him.

June 3. The remainder of the Quebec Fleet are arrived at a harbour a few leagues to leeward of this, and I am now getting under sail to join them with the other part of the Fleet from this place. The Irish Newfoundland Fleet arrived here on the 1st of June, and the Arethusa with the English Fleet at a place where the Quebec Fleet are, on the 2nd Instant, with their whole Fleets : not a Ship taken in any of the Fleets.

CERTIFICATE OF RELEASE OF AN AMERICAN PRIZE.

[From Clarke and M'Arthur's Life of Nelson, vol. i. p. 49, who state that on the 14th of July 1782, the Albemarle captured an American fishing Schooner, belonging to Cape Cod, and not having any Officer on board who was acquainted with Boston Bay and the adjacent shoals, Captain Nelson ordered Nathaniel Carver, the Master of the Schooner, to come on board the Albemarle, and act as her Pilot.

Having obeyed Captain Nelson's orders to his satisfaction, he said to him, "You have rendered us, Sir, a very essential service, and it is not the custom of English seamen to be ungrateful. In the name, therefore, and with the approbation of the Officers of this Ship, I return your Schooner, and with it this Certificate of your good conduct. Farewell! and may God bless you." The original MS. was framed and hung up in the house of Isaac Davis, Esq. of Boston. Judge Davis lately sent a copy of it to Page Nicol Scott, Esq., of Norwich.]

These are to Certify, that I took the Schooner Harmony, Nathaniel Carver, Master, belonging to Plymouth ; but, on account of his good Services, have given him up his Vessel again. Dated on board His Majesty's Ship Albemarle, 17th of August 1782.

HORATIO NELSON.

Boston Bay.

TO WILLIAM LOCKER, ESQ., GRAY'S INN,

[Autograph, in the Locker Papers.]

Albemarle, Isle of Bic, River St. Lawrence, Oct. 19th, 1782

My dear Sir,

My letter from Newfoundland, by the way of Lisbon, if you ever will receive, you have got long before this time; but this I most sincerely hope will not find you at Gray's Inn; but that Old England, at this time of need, will have the services of so good an Officer.

We arrived here with the Convoy on the 1st of July, and I sailed upon a cruise the 4th, and returned to Quebec on the 17th of September, knocked up with the scurvy; having [for] eight weeks, myself and all the Officers [lived] upon salt beef; nor had the Ship's company had a fresh meal since the 7th of April. In the end, our cruise has been an unsuccessful one; we have taken, seen, and destroyed more Enemies than is seldom done in the same space of time, but not one arrived in Port. But, however, I do not repine at our loss: we have in other things been very fortunate, for on the 14th of August, we fell in with, in Boston Bay, four Sail of the Line, and the Iris, French Man-of-War, part of M. Vaudreuil's Squadron, who gave us a pretty dance for between nine or ten hours; but we beat all except the Frigate, and though we brought to for her, after we were out of sight of the Line of Battle Ships, she tacked and stood from us.[7] Our escape I think wonderful: they were upon the clearing up of a fog within shot of us, and chased us the whole time about one point from the wind: the Frigate, I fancy, had not forgot the dressing Captain Salter had given the Amazon,[8] for daring to leave the Line of Battle Ships.

About a fortnight ago, when I was at Quebec, with no other expectation or desires than to return to England, arrives the Drake Sloop, and Cockatrice Cutter, with orders for the Transports to be fitted for the reception of Troops, and to

---

[7] Vide "Sketch of Life." p. 10.

[8] Captain Elliot Salter, in the Santa Margeretta, of 32 guns, and 220 men, captured on the 29th July 1782, after a gallant Action, the French frigate l'Amazone, of 36 guns and 301 men, off Cape Henry.

4

be sent to New York: in consequence thereof, old Worth, has given me orders to carry the Fleet to New York—a very *pretty job* at this late season of the year, for our sails are at this moment frozen to the yards. The wind has at this instant flew round from the Eastward to the N.W., and I have just made the Signal to unmoor: you shall hear from me again when I reach New York. Farewell, my dear Sir, and assure [yourself]

　　　　　　　I am your much obliged, and
　　　　　　　　　　Obedient humble Servant,
　　　　　　　　　　　　HORATIO NELSON.

Give my compliments to the Bradleys, Commissioner Kirke, or any others that ask after me.

TO THE REVEREND MR. NELSON, BATH.

[Autograph, in the Nelson Papers. The Reverend Edmund Nelson was then at Bath for the benefit of his health.]

　　　　　　　　　　　Albemarle, Isle of Bic,
　　　　　　　　River St. Lawrence, October 19th, 1782.

My dear Father,

I wrote to Mr. Suckling when I was at Newfoundland, but I have not had an opportunity of writing to you till this time. I expected to have sailed for England on the 1st of November, but our destination is now altered, for we sail with a Fleet for New York to-morrow; and from there I think it very likely we shall go to the *grand theatre* of Actions, the West Indies; but in our line of life we are sure of no one thing. When I reach New York you shall hear what becomes of me; but whilst I have health it is indifferent to me (were it not for the pleasure of seeing you and my brothers and sisters) where I go.

Health, that greatest of blessings, is what I never truly enjoyed till I saw *Fair* Canada. The change it has wrought, I am convinced is truly wonderful. I most sincerely wish, my dear Father, I could compliment you the same way; but

---

[9] Captain James Worth, of the Assistance of 50 guns: he was made a Post-Captain in November 1772, and died a superannuated Rear-Admiral.

I hope Bath has done you a great deal of good this summer. I have not had much success in the Prize way, but it is all in good time, and I do not know I ought to complain; for though I took several, but had not the good fortune to get one safe into Port, yet, on the other side, I escaped from five French Men-of-War in a wonderful manner. This is all the news I can tell you concerning myself. I can hardly say where you may write to me; but I should suppose you may soon learn where we are. If Nanny or Kate [9] are with you, give my kind love to them, and to all as you write to them. Farewell, my dearest Father, and assure yourself I always am, and ever shall be,

Your dutiful Son,
HORATIO NELSON.

If Dr. Woodward [1] is at Bath, give my compliments to him.

TO WILLIAM LOCKER, ESQ.

[Autograph, in the Locker Papers.]

Albemarle, New York, November 17th, 1782.

My dear Sir,

My letter, by the Assistance, you must [have] received long ago. It was directed to you at Gray's Inn, but I suppose they will send it to you. I arrived here with all my Fleet safe on the 13th, which is a very fortunate thing at this season of the year. Peacock [2] I saw and dined with the day I landed; I could not do less. He showed me a letter from you in August, where I was sorry to see you had not got perfectly well. Peacock has got the L'Aigle, a very fine Frigate, of twenty-eight, eighteen pounders, and three hundred and fifteen men. She had twenty-fours, but she is far preferable with eighteen pounders. I wish he may have health, or I am sorry to say, life to enjoy her. The day he went with me to show me his Ship, he was, to all appearance, perfectly well. He was seized with a fit of *apoplexy*, which, if there had not

---

[9] His sisters, Anne and Katherine.

[1] Vide p. 32, ante.

[2] Captain William Peacock was made a Post-Captain in January 1780, and died about 1783.

been a Doctor by, who bled him plentifully, might have carried him off: however, he is now pretty well, but not able to get out of doors. It is the second attack, but do not give him the least hint that you know it, as I fancy the Doctors have pretty well persuaded him it was only a *casual* fainting. He is very much beloved by everybody here; and I think, from my little personal acquaintance, he is a very genteel man.

I found Lord Hood [3] here upon my arrival, and I have requested him to take me with him to the West Indies: he has wrote to Admiral Digby [4] for me, and I was to have sailed with [the] Fleet as this day, but for some private reasons, when my Ship was under sail from New York to join Lord Hood, at Sandy Hook, I was sent for on shore, and told I was to be kept forty-eight hours after the sailing of the Fleet: it is much to my private advantage, but I had much rather have sailed with the Fleet: if there is wind enough they sail this day. I have told you all that concerns myself: if you write to me, direct it under cover to Mr. Hunt, Lord Hood's Secretary; he is a son of Hunt's, at the Navy Board. Charles Pilfold [5] is here, one of the first to be made a Lieutenant: he is a charming character, beloved by his Captain, and all his acquaintance. I have had him with me almost ever since my arrival: he is taller and stouter than me. Peacock has not got a third Lieutenant as yet; I wish he could get him. I shall speak to him this day about him. He has the same gentle disposition and modesty as when a youngster: you must remember the little fellow well. He desires to be particularly remembered to you. Pray wish Mrs. Dyne[6] joy for me, and my best compliments to the old lady and all the family.

I am a candidate with Lord Hood for a Line of Battle Ship: he has honoured me highly by a letter, for wishing to go off

[3] Rear-Admiral Samuel Lord Hood, who had been created a Peer of Ireland a few months before, was then proceeding with a large Squadron to the West Indies.

[4] Rear-Admiral the Honourable Robert Digby, Commander-in-Chief in North America: he attained the rank of Admiral of the Red, and died in February 1815.

[5] As the name of Charles Pilfold does not occur in the Navy Lists, he probably died, or retired from the Service, before he obtained his promotion.

[6] Miss Frances Bradley married on the 9th of July 1782, Andrew Hawes Dyne, Esq., and died on the 5th of August 1842. Vide p. 48, ante The "old lady" was probably her mother.

this Station, to a Station of Service, and has promised me his friendship. Princ William [7] is with him; I think it is a prelude to the Digby's going off this station; money is the great object here, nothing else is attended to. Peacock will write to-day, he tells me : he will, perhaps, tell you all the news of this place.

The French are still in Boston. The Packet sails to-morrow, and I have been so much employed in fitting my Ship, that I could not get time to write before to-day; and you must excuse me for not saying more, though I could fill another sheet very well. When I arrive in the West Indies you will hear from me.

Farewell, my dear Friend, and be assured
I am your obliged humble Servant,
HORATIO NELSON.

I have got but a corner, tell all my friends *"how do ye."*

---

[7] H.R.H. Prince William Henry, third son of King George the Third, afterwards Duke of Clarence, Admiral of the Fleet, and KING WILLIAM THE FOURTH. The Prince honoured Nelson with his warmest friendship, and many Letters in this Collection were addressed to His Royal Highness. The following description of Nelson by the Prince is extremely interesting :—

" I was then a Midshipman on board the Barfleur, lying in the Narrows off Staten Island, and had the watch on deck, when Captain Nelson, of the Albemarle, came in his barge alongside, who appeared to be the merest boy of a Captain I ever beheld : and his dress was worthy of attention. He had on a full-laced uniform : his lank unpowdered hair was tied in a stiff Hessian tail, of an extraordinary length ; the old-fashioned flaps of his waistcoat added to the general quaintness of his figure, and produced an appearance which particularly attracted my notice ; for I had never seen anything like it before, nor could I imagine who he was, nor what he came about. My doubts were, however, removed, when Lord Hood introduced me to him. There was something irresistibly pleasing in his address and conversation ; and an enthusiasm, when speaking on professional subjects, that showed he was no common being. Nelson after this went with us to the West Indies, and served under Lord Hood's flag during his indefatigable cruize off Cape François. Throughout the whole of the American war, the height of Nelson's ambition was to command a Line-of-Battle Ship ; as for prize-money, it never entered his thoughts : he had always in view the character of his maternal uncle. I found him warmly attached to my Father, and singularly humane : he had the honour of the King's service, and the independence of the British Navy, particularly at heart ; and his mind glowed with this idea as much when he was simply Captain of the Albemarle, and had obtained none of the honours of his Country, as when he was afterwards decorated with so much well-earned distinction."—*From Minutes of a Conversation with the Duke of Clarence at Bushey Park,* Clarke & M'Arthur, vol. i. p. 53.

TO WILLIAM LOCKER, ESQ.

[Autograph, in the Locker Papers.]

Albemarle, Off Cape Tiberoon, February 25th, 1783.

My dear Sir,

As I see the Packet is in sight astern, I ought not to miss this opportunity of writing, more especially as I did not write when in Port-Royal harbour, for I was so much hurried in getting my Ship in order for Sea, that I had not time to look round me.

The Fleet arrived the 4th instant, and I suppose will be ready for Sea the last day of this month, although stores are as scarce at Jamaica as ever: sixteen topmasts were wanted for the Line of Battle Ships, and there was not one in the Island of Jamaica; and the Fleet must have been sent to Sea short of masts, had not providentially a French-Mast ship, belonging to Monsieur Vaudreuil's Fleet come alongside the Albemarle, and was captured by her. She has nearly a hundred topmasts for large Ships, with a number of lower masts and yards. She will clear upwards of 20,000*l.* What a good prize if the Fleet had not been in sight. They do not deserve to share for her: we had chased to leeward, and she had passed every Ship in the Fleet without being noticed. The other Mastship that the French brought from America was run ashore, and entirely lost by the Fleet. They had parted from Vaudreuil in a gale of wind, and could not fetch St. John's, Porto Rico, which was their *rendezvous*, and therefore very fortunately came in our way. The French Fleet, finding we were off Monti Christi, went through the Mona Passage, and have been seen in sight of the Island of *Curaçoa*, but where they are God knows. I am sent out by Lord Hood to find them if I can.

We are all in the dark in this part of the world, whether it is *Peace* or War. If I should capture anything this cruize, I have made Hanbury and Shaw my Agents. Many inquiries were made after you at Jamaica, by people of all ranks and *colour*. Captain Reynolds, [8] I think, told me he had heard

---

[8] Apparently Captain Francis Reynolds, of the Monarch 74 guns, who was posted on the 12th of April 1762, and succeeded to the title of Lord Ducie. He is again mentioned.

from you lately, and that you were in good health, which, be
assured, gave me great pleasure. The Fleet fell in with Charles
Pole, but I was in chase, and could not see him. I had a
letter from him ten days ago by a Ship who parted from his
Squadron, for he is quite a Commodore here. He has been
pretty successful since he came upon this Station, and will be
very much so, if a *Neutral*, which he sent in, is given to him.
She is condemned in Jamaica, but they have appealed, and in
England we are afraid of the cursed Neutral flag.

My situation in Lord Hood's Fleet must be in the highest
degree flattering to any young man. He treats me as if I was his
son, and will, I am convinced, give me anything I can ask of him:
nor is my situation with Prince William less flattering. Lord
Hood was so kind as to tell him (indeed I cannot make use of
expressions strong enough to describe what I felt), that if he
wished to ask questions relative to Naval Tactics, I could give
him as much information as any Officer in the Fleet. He will
be, I am certain, an ornament to our Service. He is a *seaman*,
which you could hardly suppose. Every other qualification
you may expect from him. But he will be a *disciplinarian*,
and a strong one: he says he is determined every person shall
serve his time before they shall be provided for, as he is
obliged to serve his. A vast deal of notice has been taken of
him at Jamaica: he has been Addressed by the Council, and
the House of Assembly were to address him the day after I
sailed. He has his *Levées* at Spanish Town: they are all
highly delighted with him. With the best temper, and great
good sense, he cannot fail of being pleasing to every one.

But I must say God bless you, for the Endymion's boat is
just coming on board, who is Convoy to the Packet: they sailed
seven days before us from Port-Royal. You will remember
me kindly to all my acquaintance and friends that you meet
with. Farewell my good Sir, and assure yourself I am, and
always shall be,

Your most affectionate Friend and Servant,

HORATIO NELSON.

If I get safe back to Port-Royal (which is a matter of great
doubt to me), I shall get a cask of the best rum on board for
you. When you write, which I hope will have been long before

you receive this, you may direct them to the care of Mr. Joseph Hunt, Lord Hood's Secretary, which will be a sure way of my getting them. Bromwich is second Lieutenant of the Albemarle, and is a very good Officer. Not an Officer has been changed, except the Second Lieutenant, since the Albemarle was commissioned, therefore it is needless to say, I am happy in my Ship's company. Once more farewell.　　　H. N.

TO REAR ADMIRAL LORD HOOD, COMMANDER-IN-CHIEF IN THE WEST INDIES.

[Original, in the Admiralty. It is very remarkable that the attempt to re-capture Turk's Island, related in this letter, should not be mentioned by any of Nelson's biographers: nor does he allude to it in the " Sketch of his Life." The affair is noticed in Schomberg's " Naval Chronology," vol. i. p. 137, but he does not mention that the Albemarle or that Nelson was present, and leaves it to be inferred that the Ships were commanded by Captain King of the Resistance.]

Albemarle, March 9th, 1783.

My Lord,

On Thursday, the 6th Instant, a few leagues to windward of Monte Christi, I fell in with his Majesty's Ship Resistance, Captain King.[9] From him I received information that the French had taken the Turk's Island, on the 13th February, with one hundred and fifty Regulars, and three Vessels of War.

As it would be very little loss in my getting to the East-ward, making the Turk's Island, I determined to look what situation the French were in, and if possible to retake it. The Tartar,[1] who joined company a few hours afterwards, I ordered to put herself under my command, which, with the Resistance and La Coquette, a French Ship of War, prize to the Resist-ance, made a tolerable outward show. On Friday evening, the Albemarle, Resistance, and Drake,[2] anchored at the Island. The Tartar, Captain Fairfax, I imagine, could not

----

[9] The Resistance, of 44 guns, Captain James King, who had been one of the Lieutenants with Captain Cook, in his Voyages of Discovery : he died about 1786.

[1] The Tartar was commanded by Captain William George Fairfax, who was First Captain to Lord Duncan, in the Battle off Camperdown, in 1797. He received a Medal, and was Knighted for his services on that occasion, and died a Vice-Admiral in November 1813.

[2] The Drake, of 14 guns, Captain Charles Dixon : he was made a Post-Cap-tain in November 1790, and died in 1804.

keep his anchorage upon the bank. He went to Sea, nor have
I heard or seen anything of him since. I can have no doubt
but Captain Fairfax has good reasons why he did not join me
again. This reduced our small force one *third*, (the Coquette,
a larger Ship, kept off and on the whole time of our stay). I
sent Captain Dixon on shore with a flag of truce to demand a
surrender of the Islands. With much confidence of his superior situation, the Commander of the French troops sent an
answer that he should defend himself.

On Saturday morning, at daylight, one hundred and sixty-
seven Seamen and Marines were landed from the Ships under
the command of Captain Charles Dixon, who very much
obliged me by offering to command them. At eleven o'clock,
Captain Dixon thought a division of the Enemy's force might
be made by sending the Brigs off the Town, to give him an
opportunity of pushing on to the Enemy's works. I ordered
the Drake, under the command of Lieutenant Hinton, and
Admiral Barrington, Lieutenant Cunningham, who joined
at this instant, to go off the town, and batter it. Upon their
getting within shot, I was very much surprised to see a
battery of three guns open upon them, but notwithstanding
such an unexpected attack, they were both brought to an
anchor opposite the battery in a masterly manner; and the
steady constant fire they kept up for upwards of an hour, does
great honour to the Gentlemen who commanded them, and
to their Officers and Men. The Master of the Drake is
wounded, and the Boatswain and six men aboard the Admiral
Barrington. Captain Dixon at this time observed that the
guns were fought by Seamen, and that the Troops were
waiting to receive him with several field-pieces; and that
they had a post upon the side of the hill with two pieces of
cannon. With such a force, and their strong situation, I did
not think anything farther could be attempted.

I am, my Lord,

Your most obedient humble Servant,

HORATIO NELSON.

TO PHILIP STEPHENS, ESQ., SECRETARY TO THE ADMIRALTY.

[Original, in the Admiralty. Peace having been concluded with France in January 1783, Lord Hood's Squadron was ordered home ; and it arrived at Spithead the day after the Boreas.]

Albemarle, Spithead, June 25th, 1783.

Sir,

I beg you will acquaint my Lords Commissioners of the Admiralty of my arrival at Spithead, with his Majesty's Ship under my command. I parted with the Fleet under the command of Lord Hood, on the 14th of May 1783, in latitude 30° North, and longitude 80° West of London. Inclosed is the State and Condition of his Majesty's Ship under my command, and a copy of Lord Hood's Order for my proceedings.

I am, Sir, &c.

HORATIO NELSON.

TO WILLIAM LOCKER, ESQ., WEST MALLING, KENT.

[Autograph, in the Locker Papers.]

Portsmouth, June 26th, 1783.

My dear Friend,

After all my tossing about into various climates, here at last am I arrived, safe and sound. I found orders for the Albemarle to be paid off at this place. On Monday next I hope to be rid of her. My people I fancy will be pretty quiet, if they are not set on by some of the Ships here.[3]

I have on board for you, drawn off, twelve dozen of rum: I intend to put it for the present under Mr. White's care, as I dare say he will take care of it, (provided the Custom House do not seize it,) for I do not think rum is worth the expense of the duty. I hope this will find you in perfect health. Captain Gardner[4] tells me you still live at Malling. Farewell, my dear Sir, and assure yourself,

I am your affectionate Friend,

HORATIO NELSON.

[3] On the reduction of the Navy, in consequence of the Peace, the crews of several Ships were very insubordinate, insisting on being paid off at Portsmouth, instead of at Spithead ; and it was not until strong coercive measures had been adopted that the mutinous spirit was subdued.

[4] Captain, afterwards Alan Lord Gardner.

I suppose you have heard from Charles Pole; I left him exceedingly well, and very anxious to get Home. Make my compliments to all my acquaintance in your part of the world. Lord Hood's Fleet is just heaving in sight round St. Helen's.

TO PHILIP STEPHENS, ESQ., SECRETARY TO THE ADMIRALTY.

[Autograph, in the Admiralty. The Albemarle being paid off on the 3rd of July, Captain Nelson remained on half-pay until April 1784.]

No. 3, Salisbury-street, July 9th, 1783.

Sir,

I have to acquaint you that his Majesty's Ship Albemarle, late under my command, was paid off last Thursday.[5] I am, therefore, to request I may be put upon the half-pay list.

I am Sir, &c.

HORATIO NELSON.

TO CAPTAIN LOCKER.

[Autograph, in the Locker Papers.]

No. 3, Salisbury-street, Strand, July 12th, 1783.

My dear Friend,

When I look at the date of your letter I received at Portsmouth, I ought to be ashamed at not having wrote to you; but you always knew I was a careless fellow, although, be assured, my great esteem and respect for you can never be lessened. My time, ever since I arrived in Town, has been taken up in attempting to get the wages due to my *good fellows*, for various Ships they have served in the war. The disgust of the Seamen to the Navy is all owing to the infernal plan of turning them over from Ship to Ship, so that Men cannot be attached to their Officers, or the Officers care two-pence about them.

My Ship was paid off last week; and in such a manner that must flatter any Officer, in particular in these turbulent times. The whole Ship's company offered, if I could get a

[5] July 3rd.

Ship, to enter for her immediately; but I have no thought of going to Sea, for I cannot afford to live on board Ship, in such a manner as is going on at present.

Yesterday, Lord Hood carried me to Saint James's, where the King was exceedingly attentive: on Monday or Tuesday I am to be at Windsor, to take leave of Prince William, previous to his embarkation for the continent.

A Captain Merrick,[6] a young man of Lord Hood's bringing up, is to be with him. He is to go over in the Augusta yacht, Captain Vandeput.[7] *Maude*,[8] who you remember, is to be Lieutenant of the Yacht, (he came home third Lieutenant of the Barfleur,) and to be made a Captain upon his return. Bromwich came home second Lieutenant with me; he is an attentive good Officer, indeed nobody could be happier in their Officers than I was. Trail, who came down passenger in the Lowestoffe to Jamaica, has been Master ever since the Ship was commissioned. If I had interest with the Comptroller, I would wish to get him to be Superintendent of some of the Ships in Ordinary. He is the best Master I ever saw since I went to Sea.

Frank[1] tells me he has sent down by the Maidstone waggon, forty gallons of rum, directed for you: he has sent it not in the way I intended, but I must beg your excuse for it. London is exceedingly hot: I shall fly to the Country as soon as I can settle my little matters.

Farewell, my dear Sir, and assure yourself,

I am your sincere Friend,

HORATIO NELSON.

Make my compliments to Mrs. Bradley and all that family, if they are in your neighbourhood.

---

[6] Captain William Augustus Merrick, who was made Post in April 1782, but died about 1786.

[7] Captain George Vandeput, who died a Vice-Admiral, while Commander-in-Chief on the Halifax Station, in 1799.

[8] Apparently John Maude, who obtained Post rank in November 1790, and died in 1796.

[9] Frank Lepée, an old and faithful servant, who was with Nelson in the Expedition to San Juan: he is frequently mentioned.

TO THE REVEREND MR. W. NELSON, BURNHAM.

[Autograph, in the Nelson Papers.]

Salisbury-street, July 23rd, 1783.

My dear Brother,

Yours of the 19th I have received, for [which] I am much obliged to you. I should have wrote last night, but was agreeably surprised with the company of Mr. Bolton and Maurice, who was so good as to spend an hour with an invalid. A few days, however, I hope will allow me to get out of my room: and as soon as I get a little strength I propose spending a short time in Norfolk. If I can get strong enough, I would come down with Mr. B., who says he shall go in a few days; I had heard of Charles Boyles, which I am very glad of.[1] I wish it [*torn*] a good vacancy—though luckily for him . . . . . is in the Admiralty. I have not heard from . . . . . I hope she has wrote; the post has this [instant] knocked at the door, and delivered my [Sister's letter] which, tell her, I am much obliged for—in a day or two I shall certainly answer it. Nothing, I assure you can give me so much pleasure as hearing from my brothers and sisters. Mr. Suckling called the other day: he tells me Madam is laid fast with the gout. Farewell, my dear Brother, and assure yourself,

I am affectionately yours,

HORATIO NELSON.

Do not forget me to my Wells' acquaintance [*torn*] Dr. Poyntz, &c. My kind love to my Father, and Mrs. Bolton. I am sorry to hear my dear Kate is not well.

TO CAPTAIN LOCKER.

[Autograph, in the Locker Papers.]

Salisbury-street, July 31st, 1783.

My dear Friend,

Yours I only received yesterday morning, as I had been out at Mr. Suckling's[2] for a day or two, to breathe a little fresh

[1] Charles Boyles was made a Commander on the 11th April 1783.
[2] His uncle, at Kentish Town.

air, after having been cooped up for fourteen days in my room; luckily I have fell into the hands of an exceeding good Surgeon, who, I think, has made a perfect cure of me. I wish you had the segars with all my heart, especially as you have a West Indian with you. I have told Frank to send them down as soon as he can. Many thanks to you for having told George Smith where I lodged: he called on Monday last. Macnamara [3] is just arrived from Jamaica, where his Ship was sold. Gambier says he is to command there. Rowley [4] is to come Home in the spring. Lord Charles Montagu [5] is to be Governor, in the room of General Campbell, who has resigned. Have you heard from Simon Taylor lately? He was very ill when I left Jamaica: he seemed to me consumptive. He said he should come to England as soon as he had settled his affairs. I think if he don't make haste, he may stay a day too long. News here is very dead. I know nor hear any. Next week I hope to be able to get into Norfolk. Farewell, my dear Sir, and assure yourself,

> I am ever sincerely yours,
> HORATIO NELSON.

Make my compliments to Captain Williams, if he has not left you; and all my friends about you.

[3] Captain James Macnamara, vide pp. 7, 25, who had commanded the Nestor on the Jamaica station.

[4] Either Rear-Admiral Joshua Rowley, Commander-in-Chief in Jamaica, who was created a Baronet in 1786, and died in 1790: or, more probably, his second son, Captain Bartholomew Samuel Rowley, then Commander of the Diamond, who died an Admiral of the Blue, while Commanding in Chief at Jamaica, in October, 1811.

[5] Lord Charles Greville Montagu, second son of Robert Duke of Manchester: he did not become Governor of Jamaica, and died in January 1784. Major-General Archibald Campbell was succeeded by Brigadier General Alured Clarke, afterwards a Field-Marshal and Knight of the Bath.

TO HERCULES ROSS, ESQ.

[Copy, in the Nelson Papers.—Mr. Ross had been a Merchant at Kingston, in Jamaica.]

Salisbury-street, 9th August, 1783.

My dear Friend,

I am sure you are well convinced that nothing but my not knowing where to direct to you, could have hindered you from being troubled with my nonsense. Twice I called at your house, and they could only tell me you were in Scotland: the third time, a man told me he believed if I directed to Edinburgh, you would get the letter, therefore I determined to write, at all events. The innumerable favours I have received from you, be assured I shall never forget; and any opportunity that may offer of making some small return, you may always command: but I have done. You have always looked on me with a favourable eye, and I believe that I don't want gratitude.

I have closed the war without a fortune: but I trust, and, from the attention that has been paid to me, believe that there is not a speck in my character. True honour, I hope, predominates in my mind far above riches. I came home in the Albemarle, with Lord Hood, last from Jamaica, where I left Hanbury, as indefatigable in business as ever, (you know best), he is I hope, and think, in a fair way for making a fortune. Shaw was up at Porto Prince; he has, I fancy, done pretty well in the Neutral trade: all our other Jamaica friends are vanished. Wallcoff, who was Agent of Transports, I supped with him last night; he begged I would present his best compliments, and say everything that could be said of his sensibility of your civility to him; your health, I am told, is perfectly good: I hope it will always continue so.

Do you know Captain Pringle, of the Dædalus? He lives at Caroline Park, four miles from Edinburgh: he is my particular friend, and a man of great honour. I have had a very pressing invitation to come down to him: but, as I have not seen my relations, I cannot take this opportunity, which I sincerely regret, as it deprives me of the pleasure of seeing you so soon as I wished. In the winter, we shall meet in London, I have no doubt. I had a letter yesterday from

Locker; he is perfectly well. I have not seen any of the Parkers[7] since my arrival: they are in Essex, at an estate they have lately purchased, pulling the old house down and building a new one (thanks to Jamaica for the money.) An Irish Peerage is all that is wanted to complete them. Farewell, my dear friend, and assure yourself, I am, most sincerely,

Your devoted, humble Servant, .
HORATIO NELSON.

TO ADMIRAL VISCOUNT KEPPEL, FIRST LORD OF THE ADMIRALTY.

[Autograph, in the Admiralty.]

No. 3. Salisbury-street, August 20th, 1783.

My Lord,

What now obliges me to address you, is the unfortunate case of a gentleman who was second Lieutenant of the Albemarle,[8] by a commission from Lord Hood, approved by Admiral Pigot;[9] but, by an unfortunate event, his having been a Seaman and an Officer, is in a fair way to hinder his getting confirmed as a Lieutenant. I trust his story will make you his friend: from your generous disposition I expect everything.

When the Hector, Sir John Hamilton,[1] was ordered home from Jamaica, no Pilot could be got to carry the Ship through the windward passage. This gentleman being ordered a passage home in the Hector, and having been for several years upon the Jamaica station, Sir John requested, as appears by his certificate, he would take charge of the Ship. Sir John ordered him to be borne as Pilot, till the Ship got through the passage; but by a mistake of the Clerk's when he was discharged from being Pilot, he was not entered upon any of the

---

[7] Admiral Sir Peter and Lady Parker.

[8] Mr. Joseph Bromwich. The hardship mentioned in this letter could not be remedied, and he did not obtain his promotion until 1793.

[9] Admiral Hugh Pigot, who succeeded Lord Rodney as Commander-in-Chief in the West Indies. He died an Admiral of the White, in December, 1792.

[1] Sir John Hamilton, Baronet, to which dignity he was created for his services at the Siege of Quebec. He died in 1784; and was father of the present Admiral Sir Charles Hamilton, Bart., K.C.B., and of Vice-Admiral Sir Edward Hamilton, Bart., K.C.B.

Ship's Books for the remainder of the passage, by which loss of time, the Pilot's time not being allowed in his servitude, (and the mistake of not entering him upon any Books afterwards) instead of having served his time the 20th March 1783, five weeks previous to the date of his Commission, he had not served (by the Navy Board rule) his time till the 27th of June, a week before the Ship was paid off.

Depend upon it, my Lord, I should not have interested myself so much about this gentleman did I not know him to be a brave and good Officer, having been with me for several years ; therefore, I beg that, as my apology for troubling your Lordship with this letter. He has passed his examination at the Navy Office since the Ship was paid off.

I have the honour to remain,

Your Lordship's most obedient,

Humble servant,

HORATIO NELSON.

TO PHILIP STEPHENS, ESQ., ADMIRALTY.

[Autograph, in the Admiralty.—Having determined to remain unemployed during the Peace, (vide p. 77,) he resolved on going to France accompanied by his friend Captain James Macnamara, to acquire the French language. Not having received an answer to this Letter, he again applied to Mr. Stephens, for leave in similar terms, in a Letter dated on the 14th of October.]

No. 3, Salisbury-street, Strand, October 8th, 1783.

Sir,

I am to request that you will be pleased to move their Lordships to grant me six months' leave of absence, to go to Lisle, in France, on my private occasions.

I am, Sir, your most humble Servant,

HORATIO NELSON.

TO WILLIAM LOCKER, ESQ.

[Autograph, in the Locker Papers.]

St. Omer, November 2nd, 1783.

My dear Sir,

Our travels, since we left you, have been extended to a much greater length than I apprehended ; but I must do Captain

Mac the justice to say it was all my doings, and in a great measure against his advice ; but experience bought is the best; and all mine I have paid pretty dearly for.

We dined at Canterbury the day we parted from you, and called at Captain Sandys' house,[4] but he was just gone out to dinner, in the country, therefore we did not see him: we slept at Dover, and next morning at seven a clock, put to Sea with a fine North-west wind, and at half-past ten we were safe at breakfast in Monsieur Grandsire's house at Calais. His mother kept it when Hogarth wrote his ' Gate of Calais.' Sterne's Sentimental Journey is the best description I can give of our tour. Mac advised me to go first to St. Omer, as he had experienced the difficulty of attempting to fix in any place where there are no English; after dinner we set off, intended for Montreuil, sixty miles from Calais: they told us we travelled *en poste*, but I am sure we did not get on more than four miles an hour. I was highly diverted with looking what a curious figure the postillions in their jack boots, and their rats of horses made together. Their chaises have no springs, and the roads generally paved like London streets ; therefore you will naturally suppose we were pretty well shook together by the time we had travelled two posts and a-half, which is fifteen miles, to Marquise. Here we [were] shown into an inn—they called it—I should have called it a pigstye : we were shown into a room with two straw beds, and, with great difficulty, they mustered up clean sheets; and gave us two pigeons for supper, upon a dirty cloth, and wooden-handled knives—*O what a transition from happy England.*

But we laughed at the repast, and went to bed with the determination that nothing should ruffle our tempers. Having slept very well, we set off at daylight for Boulogne, where we breakfasted : this place was full of English, I suppose because wine is so very cheap. We went on after breakfast for Montreuil, and passed through the finest corn country that my eyes ever beheld, diversified with fine woods, sometimes for two miles together, through noble forests. The roads mostly were planted with trees, which made as fine an avenue as to any gentleman's country seat. Montreuil is thirty miles

---

[4] Vide p. 110.

from Boulogne, situated upon a small hill, in the middle of a
fine plain, which reached as far as the eye could carry
you, except towards the sea, which is about twelve miles from it.
We put up at the same house, and with the same jolly landlord that recommended Le Fleur to Sterne. Here we wished
much to have fixed, but neither good lodgings, or masters
could be had here ; for there are no middling class of people :
sixty noblemen's families lived in the town, who owned the
vast plain round it, and the rest very poor indeed. This is
the finest country for game that ever was ; partridges two-
pence halfpenny a couple, pheasants and woodcocks in proportion, and in short, every species of poultry. We dined,
supped, lay, and breakfasted next day, Saturday : then we
proceeded on our tour, leaving Montreuil you will suppose
with great regret.

We reached Abbeville at eight o'clock : but unluckily for
us, two Englishmen, one of whom called himself *Lord Kings-
land*, I can hardly suppose it to be him, and a Mr. Bullock,
decamped at three o'clock that afternoon in debt to every
shopkeeper in the place. These gentlemen kept elegant
houses, horses, &c. : we found the Town in an uproar; and
as no masters could be had at this place that could speak
a word of English, and that all masters that could speak
English grammatically, attend at the places that are frequented
by the English, which is, St. Omer, Lisle, Dunkirk, and
Boulogne, to the Northward of Paris, and as I had no intention of travelling to the South of France till the spring at any
rate, I determined, with Mac's advice, to steer for St. Omer,
where we arrived last Tuesday : and I own I was surprised
to find, that instead of a dirty, nasty Town, which I had always
heard it represented, to find a large City, well paved, good
streets, and well lighted.

We lodge in a pleasant French family, and have our dinners sent from a *traiteur's*. There are two very agreeable
young ladies, daughters, who *honour* us with their company
pretty often : one always makes our breakfast, and the other
our tea, and play a game at cards in an evening. Therefore I must learn French if 'tis only for the pleasure of talking to them, for they do not speak a word of English. Here
are a great number of English in this place, but we visit

only two families; for if I did I should never speak French. Two noble Captains are here—Ball and Shepard,[5] you do not know, I believe, either of them; they wear fine epaulettes, for which I think them great coxcombs:[6] they have not visited me, and I shall not, be assured, court their acquaintance. If Charles Pole is arrived, and you write to him, give my kind respects to him; I esteem him as a brother, even beyond what I ever felt for them: tell me where I can write to him. You must be heartily tired of this long epistle, if you can read it; but I have the worst pen in the world, and I can't mend it. God bless you, and be assured

I am your sincere Friend,

And affectionate humble Servant,

HORATIO NELSON.

Captain Macnamara desires his compliments to you: his and mine to Mrs. Bradley, Mrs. Dyne, &c.—Direct to me, ' A Monsieur Monsieur Nelson, chez Madame La Mourie, St. Omer, en Artois, France.'

TO THE REVEREND MR. NELSON.

[Autograph, in the Nelson Papers.]

St. Omer, November 10th, 1783.

Dear Brother,

As all Sea people are great travellers, I will give you a Journal of my proceedings since we parted. Before I left England I paid my visit of gratitude to Sir Peter and Lady Parker in Essex. I hope most sincerely that long before this you are perfectly recovered. Nothing, be assured, can give me greater pleasure than hearing of the welfare of all my bro-

---

[5] The two Captains were Alexander John Ball, afterwards a very distinguished Officer, a Rear-Admiral, and a Baronet, and Nelson's intimate friend, his Letters to whom are among the most interesting of this Collection; and Captain James Keith Shepard, who died a Vice-Admiral of the Red, in 1843.

[6] Epaulettes were first ordered to be worn, as part of the Naval Uniform, on the 1st of June 1795. The name shows that they are of French origin, and it appears from Nelson's Letter of the 26th November, p. 89, that they were worn by French Officers previously to the year 1783.

thers and sisters; and be assured, my only wish to be rich is to have an opportunity of serving our family. But enough of that subject : I believe my good intentions are not doubted.

On Tuesday morning, the 21st. ult., I set off from Salisbury-street, in company with Captain Macnamara of the Navy, an old messmate of mine. I dined with Captain Locker, my old Captain, at Malling in Kent, and spent the night at his house. The next day we slept at Dover, and on Thursday morning we left England with a fine wind. In three hours and twenty minutes we were at breakfast in Monsieur Grandsire's at Calais. The quick transition struck me much. The manners, houses, and eating, so very different to what we have in England. I had thoughts of fixing at Montreuil, about sixty miles from Calais, in the road to Paris. We set off *en poste*, they called it : we did not get on more than four miles an hour. Such *carriages,* such *horses,* such *drivers,* and such *boots,* you would have been ready to burst with laughing at the ridiculous figure they made together. The roads were paved with stones ; therefore by the time we had travelled fifteen miles, we were pretty well shook up, and heartily tired. We stopped at an inn, *they called it,*—a clean pigsty is far preferable. They showed us into a dirty room with two straw beds : they were clean, that was all they could brag on. However, after a good laugh we went to bed and slept very soundly till morning. How different to what we had found the day before at Dover.

At daylight we set off, breakfasted at Boulogne, and got to Montreuil in the evening. This day we passed through the finest country my eyes ever beheld : not a spot (as big as my hand) but was in the highest cultivation, finely diversified with stately woods. Sometimes for two miles together, you would suppose you were in a gentleman's park. The roads are mostly planted on each side with trees, so that you drive in almost a continued avenue, but amidst such plenty they are poor indeed. Montreuil is situated upon a small hill, in the middle of a large plain, which extends as far as the eye can reach, except towards the sea, which is about twelve miles from it. Game here was in the greatest abundance : partridges, pheasant, woodcocks, snipes, hare, &c. &c., as cheap as you can possibly imagine. Partridges, twopence halfpenny a brace; a noble turkey, fifteen pence; and everything else in proportion. You will suppose that it was with great regret we turned our backs upon such an agreeable place, but not a man that understood English, which was necessary to learn me French could be found in the place. Our landlord at the inn is the same man that recommended Le Fleur to Sterne.

From this place, we proceeded on to Abbeville, ninety miles from Calais. This was a large Town, well fortified, but even there I could not be accommodated to my wish: nor indeed, good masters, that is, that understood grammatically. At last, I determined to come here, which, indeed, is what we ought to have done at first: therefore by the time we arrived here, which was Tuesday week, we had travelled a hundred and fifty miles, but upon the whole I was not displeased with our excursion. This is by much the pleasantest and cleanest Town I have seen in France. It is very strongly fortified, and a large garrison. We have good rooms in a pleasant French family, where are two very agreeable young ladies, one of whom is so polite as to make our breakfast for us, and generally, when we are at home, drink tea and spend the evening with us. I exert myself, you will suppose, in the French language, that I may have the pleasure of talking to them; and French ladies make full as much use of their tongues as our English ones.

We have a most pleasant society of English at this place. We have seldom a day but we are invited somewhere, which I avoid as much as possible that I may acquire the French, and there are three families that I visit *en famille :* that visiting pleases me far beyond the other. My paper is done: in my next I shall proceed; I have much to say. To-day I dine with an English clergyman, a Mr. Andrews, who has two very beautiful young ladies, daughters. I must take care of my heart, I assure you. God bless you.

Your affectionate Brother,
Horatio Nelson.

Make my compliments to all in your neighbourhood. Love to Mrs. Bolton. Direct to me as follows: 'A Monsieur Nelson, chez Madame la Mourie, St. Omer, en Artois, France.'

TO WILLIAM LOCKER, ESQ., TOWN MALLING, KENT.

[Autograph, in the Locker Papers.]

St. Omer, November 26th, 1783.

My dear Friend,

Your kind letter I received last night. I concluded you were in London, as I had not the pleasure of hearing from you sooner. Since I wrote last I have been very near coming to England, occasioned by the melancholy account I have received of my dear Sister's death.[7] My Father, whose grief upon the occasion was intolerable, is, I hope, better; therefore I shall not come over. She died at Bath after a nine days' illness, in the 21st year of her age; it was occasioned by coming out of the ball-room immediately after dancing. Your time with Captain Reynolds must have been very agreeable: the good opinion he is pleased to entertain of me is highly flattering: it is more than my short acquaintance with him had a right to expect.

The French goes on but slowly; but patience, of which you know I have not much, and perseverance, will, I hope, make me master of it. Here are two Navy Captains, Ball and Shepard, at this place, but we do not visit; they are very fine gentlemen with epaulettes: you may suppose I hold them a little *cheap* for putting on any part of a Frenchman's uniform. Macnamara is very much obliged to you for the trouble you have taken about his picture: he will write a postscript at the end of the letter. Captain Young[8] visited me to-day, and to-morrow we meet at dinner; I shall certainly deliver your compliments:- he is come over to place his brother, who is a Lieutenant, in a French family. He returns immediately to England. Mac was last evening at a very elegant ball, but my mind is too much taken up with the recent account of my dear sister's death to partake of any amusements.

---

[7] His eldest sister, Anne Nelson, died at Bath, unmarried, on the 15th of November 1783. As she was baptized on the 20th of September, 1760, she was probably in her twenty-fourth, and not, as Nelson says, in her twenty-first year.

[8] Captain William Young, who obtained Post Rank in September 1778, afterwards Admiral Sir William Young, G.C B.: he died in October 1821.

I am much obliged to Charles Pole for his remembrance; I should have wrote to him if I had known where to have directed a letter. When you write to Captain Reynolds give my best compliments, and to Captain and Mrs. Gardner, when you write. If I am not in England before the winter is over, I shall go to *Paris* in the spring; where I have received a most polite invitation from the Officer who I detained off Porto Caballo.[9] I did not know his rank at that time, or after, till I came here : he went by the name of Count de Deux Ponts. He is a Prince of the Empire, a General of the French Army, Knight of the Grand Order of St. Louis, and was Second in Command at the capture of York Town. His brother is heir apparent of the Electorate of Bavaria, and of the Palatinate. The present Elector is eighty years of age, and this gentleman's brother is upon his death-bed ; so most probably I shall have had the honour of having taken prisoner a man, who will be a Sovereign Prince of Europe,[1] and brings into the field near a hundred thousand men : his letter is truly expressive of the attention that was paid him when on board my Ship. There are a vast number of English at this place ; I visit but few of them. In two of them I am very happy in their acquaintance ; one is the brother of Massingberd,[2] who was in the Lowestoffe ; who is very polite, and his lady a very complete gentlewoman ; here we are quite at home :—the other is an English clergy-man, who has a very large family, but two very agreeable daughters grown up, about twenty years of age, who play and sing to us whenever we go. I must take care of my heart

[9] In March, 1783, while cruising in the Albemarle off Porto Caballo in the Havannah, she captured a Spanish launch with several French Officers of distinction on board, who were making a scientific tour round Caracca de Leon, and whom he immediately released. Among them was Maximilian Joseph, second son of Frederic, Prince de Deux Ponts, a General in the French Army, who commanded the Regiment de Deux Ponts in the French Service in America. His eldest brother, Charles Duke de Deux Ponts, though supposed in 1783 to be on his death-bed, lived until 1795, when he died without surviving issue.

[1] Nelson's anticipations were greatly surpassed ; for the Prince de Deux Ponts not only succeeded to the Electorate of Bavaria 1799, but in 1806 became *King of Bavaria*. His Majesty died in 1825.

[2] Apparently Henry Massingberd, Esq. of Gunby, in Lincolnshire, who married Miss Elizabeth Hoare, and died about 1787. His brother, Thomas Massingberd, mentioned in this Letter, died a retired Commander.

I assure you.[3]   God bless you, my dear friend, and be assured,

I am yours most sincerely,

HORATIO NELSON.

[Added, in Captain Macnamara's hand.]

Captain Macnamara is exceedingly obliged to Captain Locker for the trouble he has taken respecting the picture; and begs that the picture may be done *justice to*, as a few guineas extraordinary will not be regarded.

TO THE REV. MR. W. NELSON, BURNHAM.

[Autograph, in the Nelson Papers.]

St. Omer, December 4th, 1783.

My dear Brother,

Yours I received a few days ago, and am exceedingly happy to hear of your preferment, as it will make you an independent man, and also give ease to our good Father. Fortune, you see, now favours us when we least expect it; but I hope this will not hinder the Walpoles giving you something if it should be in their power. I have not heard from our Father since our melancholy loss.[4] My fears from that account are great. Mr. Suckling wrote me the account of that shocking event the 20th of last month. My surprise and grief upon the occasion are, you will suppose, more to be felt than described. What is to become of poor Kate? Although I am very fond of Mrs. Bolton, yet I own I should not like to see Kate fixed in a Wells' society. For God's sake write what you have heard of our Father. I am in astonishment at not having heard from him, or of him by Mr. Suckling. If such an event was to take place, for with his delicate constitution, I do not think it unlikely, I shall immediately come to England, and most probably fix in some place that might be most for poor Kitty's advantage. My small income shall

---

[3] Those ladies were the daughters of an English clergyman of the name of Andrews, and the sisters of Captain George Andrews of the Navy, a follower of Nelson's, who will be again mentioned. It appears from a letter to his uncle Mr. Suckling, in p. 94, that he really intended to marry one of those ladies.

[4] The death of his sister Anne.

always be at her service, and she shall never want a protector and a sincere friend while I exist. But I will quit the subject.

The occasion of my fears will, I hope in God, soon be removed, by a letter from Mr. Suckling or my Father. St. Omer increases much upon me, and I am as happy as I can be, separated from my native Country. My heart is quite secured against the French beauties : I almost wish I could say as much for an English young lady, the daughter of a clergyman, with whom I am just going to dine, and spend the day. She has such accomplishments, that had I a million of money, I am sure I should at this moment make her an offer of them: my income at present is by far too small to think of marriage, and she has no fortune. Are our tickets drawn? I wrote you Mr. Paynter had them, and I told you the numbers, I believe, for I have quite forgot them. When you write tell me some Norfolk news. What is to become of Mr. Bolton? Where does he mean to fix? Is Little Brandon a pleasant village? Have you a good Parsonage house? not that I suppose you will go there while our father stays at Bath; and tell me, if he recovers, whether he means to return to Burnham in the summer. I hope most sincerely he does not, for the journey alone is enough to destroy him, and a Burnham winter must kill him. French goes on but slowly ; time can only make me master of it, and that a long one, some years probably. God bless you.

Your affectionate Brother,
HORATIO NELSON.

Make my kind love to Mrs. Bolton, Mr. Bolton, &c., and compliments to all my acquaintance at Wells, Burnham, and not forgetting Dr. Poyntz, who, I see by the papers, has at last got the Canonry of Windsor;[5] and if you reach Wolterton, make my best compliments. I have fixed a party for Paris in March or April if I *remain* in this Country ; and probably [shall] then proceed to the Southward. You have heard my account of taking the French Officers off Porto

---

[5] Dr. Charles Poyntz, afterwards Prebendary of Durham, brother of Georgina, Countess Spencer.

Caballo. I have had a letter from the chief of them, giving me an invitation to come to Paris. He is a much greater man than I suspected him to be: he is General in the French Army, Knight of the Grand Order of St. Louis, (similar to our Knights of the Garter,) was Second in Command of the French army in America, brother to the Prince De Deux Ponts, who is heir apparent to the Electorates of *Bavaria* and *Palatinate*, the present Elector upwards of eighty years of age, and the Prince, his brother, in a deep consumption; so that most probably I shall have had the honour of having taken prisoner a man who will be a Sovereign Prince of Europe, and an absolute *Monarch*, ruling a country as large again as England, and brings into the field near a hundred thousand infantry. My paper is full, therefore I must have done. A pretty good postscript!

TO THE REVEREND MR. NELSON, BURNHAM.

St. Omer, December 28th, 1783,
January 3rd, 1783, [1784].

Dear Brother,

Your Letter of the 15th, I received last post with infinite pleasure, as there was many pleasing accounts in it: if you get Sutton and Ulp secured for you, you are a lucky man indeed. And at a time when all your hopes were vanished—Who would be a Parson? was your tone a few months ago, now, I suppose, at least for the present—Who would not be a Parson? You will be surprised, but most probably my next letter may be from London, where I intend going on the first week in January. My health is not very stout this cold winter; and I must come over to get a little good advice from some of the London Physicians. At this place I am as happy in a friendly society as is possible. As you will suppose my time to have been pretty well taken up, as I have been so long in writing this epistle. The frost, thank God, is broke, which has made a vast alteration in me for the better; cold weather is death to me. I hope your plan of getting Ulp, &c., has been accomplished before this change in the Administration;[6]

---

[6] Mr. Pitt came into Office on the 27th December 1783.

if not, I suppose the Walpoles have lost the only opportunity that may present itself for a long time. The latter end of next week probably I may be in London, when you may depend I shall write to you; and, if you like it, I shall buy six or seven halves of tickets for the Irish Lottery. Something may turn up by having a number of chances. My stay in England will be but very short, without the First Lord in [the] Admiralty[7] thinks proper to employ me. I shall offer my services, and probably I shall stretch as far as Bath for a few days. Although I know I am very little further from London than you are at Burnham, yet what a distance I think is the journey. God bless you. I must conclude, as I am engaged to tea and spend the evening with the most accomplished woman my eyes ever beheld;[8] and when a Lady's in the case, all other things they must give place.

Make my compliments to all the Wells' party, and at Burnham, Dr. Poyntz; if Mr. Bolton has not left Wells give my kind compliments and love.

Yours affectionately,
HORATIO NELSON.

Do not forget me to Dr. Poyntz, if he is in Norfolk.

TO WILLIAM SUCKLING, ESQ.

[From the "Gentleman's Magazine," vol. xcv. part i. p. 196.]

January 14th, 1784.

My dear Uncle,

There arrives in general a time in a man's life (who has friends), that either they place him in life in a situation that makes his application for anything farther totally unnecessary, or give him help in a pecuniary way, if they can afford, and he deserves it.

The critical moment of my life is now arrived, that either I am to be happy or miserable :—it depends solely on you.

You may possibly think I am going to ask too much. I have led myself up with hopes you will not—till this trying

---

[7] Admiral Richard Viscount Howe, who succeeded Admiral Viscount Keppel, as First Lord of the Admiralty, on the 30th December 1783.

[8] Apparently Miss Andrews.

moment. There is a lady I have seen, of a good family and con-nexions, but with a small fortune,—100*l*. I understand.[2] The whole of my income does not exceed 130*l*. per annum. Now I must come to the point:—will you, if I should marry, allow me yearly 100*l*.[3] until my income is increased to that sum, either by employment, or any other way? A very few years I hope would turn something up, if my friends will but exert themselves. If you will not give me the above sum, will you exert yourself with either Lord North or Mr. Jenkinson, to get me a Guard-ship, or some employment in a Public Office where the attendance of the principal is not necessary, and of which they must have such numbers to dispose of. In the India Service I understand (if it remains under the Directors) their Marine force is to be under the command of a Captain in the Royal Navy: that is a station I should like.

You must excuse the freedom with which this letter is dictated ; not to have been plain and explicit in my distress had been cruel to myself. If nothing can be done for me, I know what I have to trust to. Life is not worth preserving without happiness ; and I care not where I may linger out a miserable existence. I am prepared to hear your refusal, and have fixed my resolution if that should happen ; but in every situation, I shall be a well-wisher to you and your family, and pray they or you may never know the pangs which at this instant tear my heart. God bless you, and assure yourself, I am,

> Your most affectionate and dutiful nephew,
>   HORATIO NELSON.

TO WILLIAM LOCKER ESQ., TOWN MALLING.

[Autograph, in the Locker Papers.]

3, Salisbury-street, January 19th, 1784.

My dear Friend,

I have been near a week without having wrote to my best friend; and you will be surprised, without doubt, to hear of

[2] Apparently Miss Andrews. Vide p. 91.

[3] The person who, under the signature "P," communicated this letter to the " Gentleman's Magazine," states that Mr. Suckling immediately complied with the request. If so, Nelson was probably refused by the fair object of his affec-tions.--See p. 99.

me at last from London. Some little matters in my Accounts obliged me to come over. The day before I came away, I received a letter of yours which had travelled nearly all over France; let that be my apology for not having wrote sooner. Yesterday I dined with Captain Kingsmill; he gives me some hopes of meeting you in Town, as soon as your boys[9] are gone to school. I should have had great pleasure in having crossed the country, and made Malling in my way to London, the weather was too cold. A few days, I hope, will bring you to Town; till then farewell, and be assured,

I am your most obliged, obedient Servant,

HORATIO NELSON.

Pray give my compliments to Mrs. Bradley, Mrs. Dyne, and my apology ought to be made to Mr. G. Smith ; I beg my kindest and best compliments to him.

TO PHILIP STEPHENS, ESQ., SECRETARY TO THE ADMIRALTY.

[Autograph, in the Admiralty.]

3, Salisbury-street, Strand, January 20th, 1784.

Sir,

Having received a letter a few days ago from Mr. Samuel Innis, Carpenter of his Majesty's Ship Albemarle, late under my command, requesting me to give him such a character as he deserved while under under my command, as he had wrote a petition to the Board requesting a larger Ship, I beg leave to acquaint you that he was nearly two years under my command, during which time he behaved as a good Officer, in which time the Ship was dismasted by a Ship's driving on board her in a gale of wind in the Downs ;[1] and that he fitted the Ship in twenty-four hours without any assistance whatsoever.

I am, Sir, &c.

HORATIO NELSON.

---

[9] Vide p. 23, ante. It is to the kindness and liberality of one of those *boys*, Edward Hawke Locker, Esq., Captain Locker's third son, late a Commissioner of Greenwich Hospital, that the Editor is indebted for these Letters to his Father.

[1] Vide p. 55, ante.

4

TO THE REVEREND MR. W. NELSON, BURNHAM.

[Autograph, in the Nelson Papers.]

3, Salisbury-street, Strand, January 20th, 1783, [1784].

Dear Brother,

I arrived in Town on Saturday week, but my time has been
so much taken up by running at the ring of pleasure, that I
have almost neglected all my friends;—for London has so
many charms that a man's time is wholly taken up. However, amongst other things which I have done, is that I have
received £16 16 for our lottery tickets. It ought to have
been £17 odd, but they reduce it fifty ways. I have lodged
the identical money with Mr. Paynter, tied up in a paper; I
have wrote upon it that we request him to purchase as many
halfs in the Irish lottery as it will produce—about six, I
fancy, or if there is no Irish one, to purchase in the English;
if you do not like that way, you can alter it if you please. I
received a letter from our Father last night, who says he is
perfectly well; I shall make him a visit before I leave England, which will be in about a fortnight or three weeks. I
can't write any more, for I am so unwell I know not how to
hold my head up. I caught a violent cold upon my first
arrival in England, which probably I should have got clear of,
had I not been fool enough to have danced attendance at St.
James's yesterday, where I increased my cold, till it has
brought on a fever, so much that I was obliged to send for
Dr. Warren[1] this morning. I hope a day or two will carry it
off. Let me hear from you soon. God bless you, and be
assured I am,

Your affectionate Brother,

HORATIO NELSON.

Give my compliments to all the good folks at Burnham,
Wells, &c. The present Ministry will stay in, there is no
doubt, in spite of Mr. Fox and all that party. If the Ministry
has not a majority to-day, it is confidently asserted the Parliament will be dissolved. I hope it will, that the people may
have an opportunity of sending men that will support their
interests, and get rid of a turbulent faction who are striving to
ruin their Country.

[1] Dr. Richard Warren, the celebrated Physician, father of the present Vice-
Admiral Frederic Warren.

[Autograph, in the Locker Papers.]

No. 3, Salisbury-street, January 23rd, 1784.

My dear Friend,

Your kind letter I received last night, but not soon enough to have sent you yesterday's Paper, as I dined out, and was not at home till late. You shall have one this night and to-morrow, which will most probably [be] well stuffed with the Debates.[2] To-night the Ministry will try their strength. Charles Phipps,[3] who was here just now, says, he believes Mr. Pitt will have a majority, but he speaks probably as he wishes, not as he thinks. I called at Captain Kingsmill's yesterday; he was out, therefore I do not know when he leaves Town. By his conversation, I did not think it would be this week or two. I will call to-morrow, and desire him to tell you. I shall have great pleasure in sending Newspapers, or anything else that is in my power. Unfortunately, on Tuesday I am going to Bath for a few days to see my Father, before I return to the Continent, or go to Sea. I have paid my visit to Lord Howe,[4] who asked me if I wished to be employed, which I told him I did, therefore it is likely he will give me a Ship. I shall not conclude my letter till late, as perhaps I may hear how matters are likely to go in the House of Commons. Lord Hood's friends are canvassing, although not openly, for his interest in case of a dissolution; and it is confidently asserted that Mr. Fox will never get Westminster again. I dined on Wednesday with his Lordship, who expressed the greatest friendship for me, that his house was always open to me, and that the oftener I came the happier it would make him. Ross[5] is in Town; I dined with him on Monday: he made many inquiries after you. Lutwidge[6] is in Town, but I have not seen him.

Ten o'clock. I have received a letter from St. Omer, Capt.

---

[2] On Mr. Pitt's East India Bill, when the Ministry were defeated by a majority of eight.

[3] The Honourable Charles Phipps, a Captain in the Navy, second son of the first Lord Mulgrave, who had strongly defended Mr. Pitt's measures in the House of Commons. He died in October 1786.

[4] First Lord of the Admiralty.

[5] Hercules Ross, Esq.

[6] Vide p. 4, ante.

Mac; he desires his compliments to you most particularly.
I can learn nothing from the Newspapers:—of to-morrow, will
tell you all, which, be assured, I shall send you. God bless
you, and be assured,

I am yours,
HORATIO NELSON.

Give my compliments to all your neighbours.

TO THE REVEREND WILLIAM NELSON, RECTOR OF BRANDON
PARVA, NORFOLK.

[Autograph, in the Nelson Papers.]

Bath, January 31st, 1784.

Dear Brother,

Yours I received the morning I left Town, for which I am
much obliged to you. You are an exact correspondent, therefore deserve to be wrote to. I wish sincerely your business
had been got through before the late Administration were
turned out. If you are not to get it before they come into
power again, I am afraid you will stay a long while. As to
your having enlisted under the banners of the Walpoles, you
might as well have enlisted under those of my grandmother.
They are altogether the merest set of *cyphers* that ever existed—in Public affairs I mean. Mr. Pitt, depend upon it, will
stand against all opposition: an honest man must always in
time get the better of a *villain*; but I have done with politics; let who will get in, I shall be left out.

I am happy I can say that our Father never was so well
since I can remember; he is grown quite lusty. His cheeks
are so much plumped out, that I thought they had been vio-
lently swelled when I first saw him, but it is all solid flesh. He
gets up to breakfast, eats supper, and never retires till after
ten. Keep his mind at rest, and I do not fear but he will live
these many years. We have fixed our plan for next winter: you
know I mean to come to you; we shall be quite a party. Poor
little Kate is learning to ride, that she may be no trouble to
us. She is a charming young woman, and possesses a great

share of sense. In about a week or fortnight I think of returning to the Continent, till autumn, when I shall bring a horse, and stay the winter at Burnham. I return to many charming women, *but no charming woman* will return with me. I want to be a proficient in the language, which is my only reason for returning. I hate their country and their manners. As to the lottery tickets, I can't trouble Mr. Paynter to do all that you wish. If an Irish lottery is fixed before I leave England, I will do it with pleasure. If you go to Wolterton, I beg my compliments, as also at Creek, Burnham, Wells, &c. Let me hear from you soon. Is the bank down at Wells? Tell me all your Norfolk news. God bless you, and rest assured,

I am your sincere and affectionate Brother,

HORATIO NELSON.

Kitty desires her love.

Rev. Wm. Nelson, *Rector*.[7]

TO THE REVEREND MR. NELSON, BURNHAM.

[Autograph, in the Nelson Papers. Captain Nelson was appointed to the Command of the Boreas Frigate, of twenty-eight guns, on the 19th March, 1784.]

London, March 19th, 1784.

Dear Brother,

It is so long since I wrote last, that I dare say you think I am lost, but behold, here I am, not against my own wish, but contrary to my expectation. Yesterday I was appointed to the command of the Boreas frigate. She is ready to sail from Woolwich, but to what part of the World I know not. My wish is to get the East India station. I have not taken possession yet, but I am told she is a very fine Frigate, well manned, and ready to sail, so that probably my next will be from the Nore or the Downs. I can't say any more at present,

---

[7] Nelson jocularly addressed his Letter to his Brother as " Rector," and under scored the word in this place, in consequence of Mr. Nelson having then obtained that rank in the Church, by becoming Rector of Little Brandon, in Norfolk.

being fully employed in spending my money to fit my Ship out.
God bless you, and be assured,

                    I am yours most affectionately,

                                HORATIO NELSON.

Direct under cover to Mr. Suckling.

TO WILLIAM LOCKER, ESQ., WEST MALLING.

[Autograph, in the Locker Papers.]

                    3, Lancaster Court, Strand, March 23rd, 1784.

My dear Friend,

Not having wrote for so long a time makes me almost
ashamed of telling you I am yet in Town.   On last Friday I
was commissoned for the Boreas, in Long Reach, at present
under command of Captain Wells,[8] (Lord Keppel's,) and I am
also sorry to say that the same day gave me an ague and
fever, which has returned every other day since, and pulled
me down most astonishingly.

I understand she is going to the Leeward Islands; and I
am asked to carry out Lady Hughes[9] and her family,—a very
modest request, I think : but I cannot refuse, as I am to be
under the command of this Gentleman, so I must put up with
the inconvenience and expense, two things not exactly to my
wish.   The Ship is full of young Midshipmen, and everybody is asking me to take some one or other.   I am told
she is well Officered[1] and manned ; I wish I may find her
so.   I have not seen her as yet, but shall go down to-morrow.
I met Mr. James Bradley to-day : he told me you were well.

----

[8] Captain Thomas Wells, who obtained Post rank in April 1782, and became
a Vice-Admiral in 1808.

[9] Wife of Rear-Admiral Sir Richard Hughes, Bart., the Commander-in-Chief
on that Station.   She was Jane, daughter of William Sloane, Esq., of South
Stoneham, in Hampshire.

[1] The Commissioned Officers who served with Captain Nelson in the Bo-
reas, from the 24th of March 1784, to the 30th of November 1787, were—
Lieutenants, James Wallis, Digby Dent, S. G. Church; Surgeon, T. Graham ;
Master, J. Jameson ; Purser, D. L. Peers.—*Clarke and M'Arthur.*

Your friend Captain Kingsmill was out of Town a few days ago, and I believe is not yet returned: he is looking out for a Seat in Parliament, but I suppose you know more of that matter than I do. I must conclude with saying, is there any young gentleman you wish me to take? I shall have great pleasure in paying every attention in my power to him. If I should touch at Madeira, shall I get you any wine? My head distracts me; therefore I must wish [you] a good night, and beg that you will rest assured,

I am yours most sincerely,
HORATIO NELSON.

Poor Bromwich[2] must go out as Master's Mate with me; he cannot get confirmed. I beg my compliments to all the Bradleys that are with you.

TO THE REVEREND MR. NELSON, BURNHAM.

[Autograph, in the Nelson Papers.]

Kentish Town, March 29th, 1784.

Dear Brother,

Yours of the 22nd I received yesterday, and have thought seriously on what you wished to have done upon the occasion.[3] As to the point of carrying you in my Ship, nothing could give me greater pleasure than to have it in my power to gratify any reasonable inclination of yours, but at the present moment I do not see how you can possibly remove from Burnham. My Father at Bath, and your own good sense, must point this out as an improper moment, but should I remain in England till June, when most probably our Father will be settled for the summer months, then, I think, there can be no possible objection to your taking a trip for a few months, and to return by the winter, to keep our Father and Sister company at that lonesome place.

My Ship probably will be at Portsmouth in the course

---

[2] Vide p. 81, ante.

[3] The Reverend William Nelson's wish to accompany his brother in the Boreas was gratified; but he returned to England a few months after her arrival in the West Indies.

of next week, when I shall be more able to tell you what
becomes of me. Common report says I am going to the
Leeward Islands, and am asked to carry out Lady Hughes
and her daughter, so that I shall be pretty well filled with
lumber. If I should go to the Leeward Islands, tell Mr.
Boyles I shall be happy to take any things he may wish to send
to his son Charles. You ask, by what interest did I get a
Ship? I answer, having served with credit was my recommendation to Lord Howe, First Lord of the Admiralty. Anything in reason that I can ask, I am sure of obtaining from
his justice. You had better direct your next to me at Portsmouth, or to Mr. Suckling, which you please. Remember
me to all at Burnham Wells, &c. I had a letter yesterday from
poor Kate: she is well, but mentions not having heard from
you for this some time past. For the present farewell, and
rest assured I am,

Your affectionate Brother,

HORATIO NELSON.

Mr. Suckling desires his compliments.

TO THE REVEREND MR. WILLIAM NELSON, CHRIST COLLEGE,
CAMBRIDGE.

[Autograph, in the Nelson Papers.]

April 2nd, 1784.

Dear Brother,

I shall not be from London on Sunday, but shall dine with
Mr. Suckling on Sunday. If you arrive on Sunday and come
immediately to Kentish town, you will be sure of finding me.
I hope sincerely you will vote for Mr. Pitt.[5]

Yours affectionately,

HORATIO NELSON.

We shall unkennel *Fox* in Westminster.

---

[5] Parliament was dissolved on the 25th of March 1784; Mr. Pitt was elected
for Cambridge. Mr. Fox was not *unkennelled*; as he was re-elected for Westminster with Lord Hood. Sir Cecil Wray, the defeated Candidate, demanded
a scrutiny; but Mr. Fox retained his seat.

Boreas, Downs, April 14th, 1784.

Sir,

I am to acquaint you, that this morning, I received information that sixteen of his Majesty's Subjects were detained by force, on board of a Dutch Indiaman, upon which I demanded and received them on board. The Master of the Ship has refused, notwithstanding all arguments that I could make use of, (by the Lieutenant,) to give up their chests, upon pretence they are in debt to [the] Ship, although most of them have been four or five months in the Dutch India Company's service. Having repeatedly refused to give up their clothes, I have ordered that no boats shall be permitted to go on board, or to leave the Ship; and have ordered the Nimble Cutter to put the above orders into execution. I must desire, as soon as possible, to have their Lordships' orders how to act upon this occasion.

I am, Sir, &c.

HORATIO NELSON.

I beg you will also assure their Lordships that every politeness and attention has been shown to the Dutchman upon this occasion. I have sent to acquaint him that he will not be suffered to leave the Downs till this matter is settled.

Boreas, Downs, April 14th, 7 P. M., 1784.

Sir,

I have the pleasure to acquaint you that all disputes with the Dutch East Indiaman are amicably settled, the Master having given up their clothes, bedding, &c.

I am, Sir, &c.

HORATIO NELSON.

TO PHILIP STEPHENS, ESQ., ADMIRALTY.

[Autograph, in the Admiralty.]

Boreas, Spithead, April 18th, 1784.

Sir,

I have the honour to acquaint you, that his Majesty's Ship under my command, arrived at this place yesterday, and enclosed is her State and Condition. Your answer to my last letter of the 14th, I received yesterday evening. I have therefore to suppose that my first of that day did not come to *hand.*

I am Sir, &c.

HORATIO NELSON.

TO WILLIAM LOCKER, ESQ.

[Autograph, in the Locker papers.]

Portsmouth, April 21st, 1784.

My dear Sir,

Since I parted from you, I have encountered many disagreeable adventures. The day after I left you, we sailed at daylight, just after high water. The d——d Pilot—it makes me swear to think of it—ran the Ship aground, where she lay with so little water that the people could walk round her till next high water. That night and part of the next day, we lay below the Nore with a hard gale of wind and snow; Tuesday I got into the Downs: on Wednesday I got into a quarrel with a Dutch Indiaman who had Englishmen on board, which we settled, after some difficulty. The Dutchman has made a complaint against me; but the Admirality fortunately have approved my conduct in the business, a thing they are not very guilty of where there is a likelihood of a *scrape.* And yesterday, to complete me, I was riding a *blackguard* horse that ran away with me at Common, carried me round all the Works into Portsmouth, by the London gates, through the Town out at the gate that leads to Common, where there was a waggon in the road,—which is so very narrow, that a horse could barely pass. To save my legs, and perhaps my life, I was obliged to throw myself from the horse, which I did with great agility : but unluckily upon hard stones, which has hurt my back and my leg, but done no other mischief. It was a thousand to one that I had not been killed. To crown all, a young girl was riding with me; her horse ran away with mine; but most fortunately a *gallant* young man seized her horse's bridle a moment before I dismounted, and saved her from the destruction which she could not have avoided.

Kingsmill came to Town on Sunday, and has taken possession of his Ship and Land Frigate again.[6] At Maidstone I see by the Papers, you have returned the old Members :[7] how consistently Mr. Marsham has behaved to support Mr. Fox, and then thank the King for turning him out. There can be no good at the bottom, I am afraid. Lady Hughes is here, but I have not received my orders. Give my compliments to Madam Bradley, &c. and rest assured

I am yours, most sincerely,

HORATIO NELSON.

Give my best compliments to George Smith : you can vouch for my intention to have visited him. Kingsmill desires his compliments. What inquiries you wish me to make about your land in Dominica, pray put upon paper.

TO THE REVEREND MR. NELSON, BURNHAM.

[Autograph, in the Nelson Papers.]

Boreas, Portsmouth, April 23rd, 1784.

Dear Brother,

Come when you please, I shall be ready to receive you. Bring your canonicals and sermons. Do not bring any

---

[6] Captain Kingsmill then commanded the Elizabeth 74, a guardship at Portsmouth. He was elected M.P. for Tregony. It does not appear what Nelson meant by "Land Frigate."

[7] Clement Taylor, Esq., and Gerard Noel Edwards, Esq. The Honourable Charles Marsham, (afterwards second Lord, and first Earl Romney,) who had taken an active part in the debates on the India Bill, was re-elected for the County of Kent.

Burnham servants.   I cannot say any more, being much hurried.

Yours affectionately,
HORATIO NELSON.

In less than a fortnight my Ship will not sail.   I have a fine talkative Lady[8] for you to converse with.

———————

TO PHILIP STEPHENS, ESQ., SECRETARY TO THE ADMIRALTY.

[Autograph, in the Admiralty.]

Boreas, Spithead, April 29th, 1784.

Sir,

Be pleased to state to their Lordships, that William Bell, Gunner of his Majesty's Ship Medea, who has formerly sailed with me, and for whom I have an esteem, and Thomas Harries, at present Gunner of the Boreas, who is in a very bad state of health, are desirous of exchanging Ships; and I shall deem it a particular favour, if their Lordships will approve of the exchange, and to appoint them accordingly.   Inclosed is their joint letter, and

I am, &c.

HORATIO NELSON.

———————

TO PHILIP STEPHENS, ESQ., ADMIRALTY.

[Original, in the Admiralty.]

Boreas, Spithead, May 10th, 1784.

Sir,

Their Lordships' orders of the 6th instant I have received ; and as soon as the Ship's company are paid their advance, shall put their Orders in execution with all possible dispatch.

I am, Sir, &c.

HORATIO NELSON.

———————

[8] Lady Hughes.

TO WILLIAM LOCKER, ESQ.

[Autograph, in the Locker Papers.—It seems to have been franked by Captain Kingsmill who wrote a few lines on it to Captain Locker: "Nelson's last, I imagine: he sailed to-day. He is a very good young man; and I wish him every enjoyment of life."]

Boreas, Spithead, May 14th, 1784.

My dear Friend,

The Commissioner is now paying my Ship, and I am making use of the time that I may be able to save Post, as none goes out to-morrow. I was agreeably surprised by your letter, as I did not expect to hear you was in London. I thank you much for your news, which if true, hostilities must commence soon again with the French : God send, I say. But if Cornwallis[9] is going out, I shall be a little vexed that I am not to be one of the Ships. Whenever I go to Dominica, you may be assured that every circumstance relative to your estate shall be inquired into. Jamaica is the place I wish to go to. I have not time scarcely to say, how much I am your devoted,

HORATIO NELSON.

I will write more by Sunday.

WALKING THE BOREAS' QUARTER-DECK ON THE 30TH MAY 1784, AT 7 IN THE EVENING.

[Autograph, in the Nelson Papers.—The great number of Passengers and Officers in the Boreas seems to have induced Captain Nelson to make the following List of them :]

Lady Hughes	Lieutenants Wallace [1]
Miss Hughes	Dent [2]
Captain Nelson	Jameson M.[3]
	R. Mr. Nelson [4]

[9] Captain the Honourable William Cornwallis.

[1] Lieutenant James Wallis, who was appointed by Nelson, Commander of the Rattler in May 1787, but was not confirmed until 1794. He was Posted in 1797, and died between 1806 and 1809.

[2] Lieutenant Digby Dent was made a Commander in 1797, and died 15th November, 1799.

[3] James Jameson, Master of the Boreas.

[4] Afterwards Earl Nelson.

Masters } Bromwich [5]	Mr. Boyle [14]
Mates } Powers [6]	Purefoy
Graham [7]	Batty [15]
Peers [8]	Parkinson, Senr.
Mrs. Peers [8]	Parkinson, Junr.
Mr. Lane, Marines [9]	Suckling [16]
Oliver [10]	Nowell
Hughes [11]	Stainsbury [17]
Jones	Brown
Bremer [12]	Tatham
Beale	Lock [18]
Bayntun	Morgan
Talbot [13]	Bishop.

[5] Joseph Bromwich; made a Lieutenant in 1793, and afterwards Warden of Portsmouth Dock Yard.

[6] He was discharged in the West Indies, and went to America. Vide p. 125.

[7] Surgeon of the Boreas.

[8] The Purser and his wife. Vide p. 132.

[9] Vide p. 132.

[10] Mr. Oliver was discharged from the Boreas, for being concerned in a duel. Vide p. 125.

[11] Richard Hughes, eldest son of Rear-Admiral Sir Richard Hughes: he was made a Lieutenant in November 1790, and died a Post-Captain in 1810.

[12] James Bremer, who afterwards commanded the Berbice Schooner, (so often mentioned in Captain Nelson's Letters,) Tender to the Flag Ship: he was made a Lieutenant in November 1790, and a Commander in August 1811, in which rank he died.

[13] Now Admiral the Hon. Sir John Talbot, G.C.B.

[14] The late Vice-Admiral the Hon. Sir Courtenay Boyle, K.C.H. Vide p. 247.

[15] Mr. William Batty.

[16] Maurice William Suckling, a distant relation of Captain Nelson, son of Mr. Suckling, of Wooton near Norwich. He was made a Lieutenant in March, 1794, succeeded to the estates of his family, and died without issue in 1820. Several notices of him occur in subsequent Letters.

[17] He was discharged because he had wounded Mr. George Andrews, a young Midshipman of the Boreas, in a duel. Vide p. 125.

[18] Charles Lock. He was made a Lieutenant on the 22nd of November 1790, a Commander in 1796, and appears to have died Captain of the Inspector in February 1800.

TO WILLIAM LOCKER, ESQ.

[Autograph, in the Locker Papers. The Boreas arrived at Madeira on the 1st of June 1784, and sailed on the 8th of that month for Barbadoes.]

Boreas, Madeira, June 7, 1784.

My dear Friend,

The opportunity that offers of a Vessel's sailing for London, makes me embrace the opportunity of writing to my friends; therefore you are sure of hearing, or I must be an ingrate indeed. I have received on board a quarter cask of wine for you from our friend Mr. Higgins, who has been vastly civil. Mr. Murray, the Consul,[1] I have not dined with, owing to a little etiquette about visiting. We arrived here on the 1st, after a pleasant passage, the Ladies[2] quite well, and satisfied with the Ship. To-morrow I sail,[3] for I am tired of this place, and Lady Hughes wishes to see her husband: and I shall not be sorry to part with them, although they are very pleasant good people: but they are an incredible expense. I beg the favour of Kingsmill to enclose this. By every opportunity be assured that I shall scrawl a line, for no man has a higher sense of the obligations he is under to you, than your faithful and devoted,

HORATIO NELSON.

I have had Scott from the Resource to dine with me, a very genteel young man he is: I wish he had been with me. Pray my compliments to Mrs. Bradley, &c. Your Dominica estate I shall be particular about. I take for granted Orde[4] will be civil about it, as I have taken on board for him four casks of wine.

[1] Charles Murray, Esq.: he declined returning Captain Nelson's visit because he had not been allowed a boat by the Government to go on board Ships of War.

[2] Lady Hughes and her family.

[3] The Boreas arrived at Barbadoes on the 26th of June 1784: and Nelson found himself Senior Captain, and Second in Command, on the Station.

[4] Captain John Orde was made Governor of Dominica in 1783: he was created a Baronet in 1790, and died an Admiral of the Red in 1824. He is frequently mentioned in Nelson's Letters after they had both attained their Flags: and is well known for his quarrel with the Earl of St. Vincent, in consequence of Nelson's having been chosen to command the Squadron which fought the Battle of the Nile.

TO WILLIAM LOCKER, ESQ., WEST MALLING.

[Autograph, in the Locker Papers.]

Boreas, English Harbour, September 24th, 1784.

My dear Friend,

I was in hopes that the first letter I should write you from this country would have given you some information of your Dominica estate, but that is not in my power. I was one day in Prince Rupert's Bay to wood and water; but there, you know, I could get no information. If Sandys[5] should go to Dominica, I shall give Bradley's letter to him, and write to Orde upon the subject. I have a right to trouble him in any business of that sort, as I took on board for him, at Madeira, four casks of wine, on purpose that I might have his hearty assistance in the business.

Collingwood[6] is at Grenada, which is a great loss to me; for there is nobody that I can make a confidant of. The little man, S——, is a good-natured laughing creature, but no more of an Officer as a Captain than he was as a Lieutenant. Was it not for Mrs. Moutray,[7] who is *very very* good to me, I should almost hang myself at this infernal hole. Our Admiral[8] is tolerable, but I do not like him, he bows and scrapes too much for me; his wife has an eternal clack, so that I go near them as little as possible: in short, I detest this Country, but as I am embarked upon this Station I shall remain in my Ship. Our ears here are full of Wars in the East; is there any likelihood of a War? I am in a fine [condition] for the beginning of one; well Officered and manned. I have not heard from a single creature in England since I arrived. I have [written] to everybody, and to you from Madeira, but not a line.

Give my best remembrance to Kingsmill, and my friends in his neighbourhood, not forgetting me to the Bradleys; and I

[5] Captain Charles Sandys, who is often mentioned, was made a Post Captain in January 1783, and then commanded the Latona. He became a superannuated Rear-Admiral in 1805, and died in April 1814, aged 62.

[6] Captain Cuthbert Collingwood, who then commanded the Mediator.

[7] Wife of Captain John Moutray, Commissioner of the Navy at Antigua.

[8] Sir Richard Hughes.

beg also that you will rest assured, I am, your devoted faithful Friend and Servant,

HORATIO NELSON.

TO THE REVEREND MR. NELSON, BURNHAM.

[Autograph, in the Nelson Papers.]

Windsor, [Antigua,] October 24th, 1784.

My dear Brother,

By this time I hope you are quite recovered, and drawing very near to old England.[9]　The weather here has been so very hot since you left us, that I firmly believe you would hardly have weathered the fever which has carried off several of the Boreas's Ship's company since you left us, and a Mr. Elliot, acting Lieutenant of the Unicorn, who you may remember. I have been living here for this week past, whilst my Ship has been painting. Yesterday, for the first time, I dined at Mr. Eliot's :[10] the Admiral and his family are there. They left Clarke's Hill the 15th, and come to Mr. Horsford's the 26th, where they are to remain till they sail, which is to be on the 1st of November.

We are all invited to a grand dinner on the 31st, on board the Adamant, and are to go strait to Barbadoes to get bread, for there is none at this Island. From Barbadoes I am to go to the Virgin Islands to examine them, by a particular order from the Admiralty. I suppose they wish to find some good lands for the poor American loyalists. I must make my letter short, for the Zebra sails to-morrow, and I have a number of letters to write. If you went to Portsmouth in the Fury, you would find Kingsmill, who would be vastly civil, I am sure. God bless you, and rest assured

I am your affectionate brother,

HORATIO NELSON.

---

[9] Mr. Nelson was obliged to leave the West Indies for England, in the Fury Sloop, on the 30th September 1784, on account of his health.

[10] Apparently Samuel Eliot, Esq., of Antigua, whose second daughter, Elizabeth, married in July 1791, Thomas Lord Le Despencer, grandfather of the present Baroness Le Despencer.

Mrs. Moutray desires her love to you, and I beg my best compliments to Wolterton, Wells, &c. I have seen Capt. B———, who is a friend of Mr. Walpole's. I do not like him at all: he is a self-conceited young man.

TO WILLIAM LOCKER, ESQ., WEST MALLING.

[Autograph, in the Locker Papers.]

English Harbour, November 23rd, 1784.

My dear Friend,

Your kind letter I received yesterday upon my arrival here, and though I cannot say much, as my time is very short, being obliged to sail this morning for the Virgin's. Your wine shall certainly be bottled, nor shall I forget the Dominica estate when I go there, which will be in about a month. I am heartily glad Bradley has got a place ;[1] I hope it will turn out a good one. Collingwood is here ; he desires to be kindly remembered. This Station is far from a pleasant one. The Admiral and all about him are great ninnies. Little S—— is in the L——. I am sorry to say he goes through a regular course of claret every day. Coll. desires me to say he will write you soon such a letter, that you will think it a history of the West Indies. What an amiable good man he is ! all the rest are geese. I have not had a letter from Kingsmill this Packet: when you write remember me to him.

I am in my way to examine a Harbour said to be situated in the Island of St. John's,[2] capable, it is supposed, to contain a Fleet of Men of War during the hurricane seasons. It is odd this fine Harbour, if such a one there is, should not have been made use of long ago ; but there is an order from the Admiralty to send a Frigate to examine it : it is said here to belong to the Danes ; if so, they will not let me survey it. I must have done, for the Signal gun is fired for Domingo to carry us out. God bless you, my dear friend, and believe

I am yours most affectionately,

HORATIO NELSON.

[1] Mr. James Bradley was appointed Secretary to the Board of Control on its formation in 1784.

[2] The Chart of this Harbour, signed "Horatio Nelson," is now among the Correspondence of 1785, in the Admiralty.

TO WILLIAM LOCKER, ESQ., WEST MALLING.

[Autograph, in the Locker Papers.]

Boreas, Basseterre Road, January 15th, 1785.

My dear Sir,

Your letter of the 16th November, I received a few days ago at Antigua, fortunately when I was in company with Collingwood, who is acquainted with Lieutenant-Governor Stewart. (I have not been at Dominica since the hurricane months, therefore have not been able to say anything to Governor Orde upon the subject of your estate.) He has wrote to him enclosing a letter I received in England from Mr. James Bradley, with all the particulars relative to the property; and as Collingwood is just going to Prince Rupert's Bay, he desires me to say, that if possible he will go to the spot, consequently will be able to say more upon the matter than I can at present. If the estate has not always had one family kept upon it, I fear there will be some difficulty in getting hold of it; for if it is good land, most likely some *genius* or other has got hold of it; and if it has never been inhabited since Admiral Parry[3] was here, the buildings must be gone to ruin before this time, but as it is you shall know very soon. Coll. will have information from Lieutenant-Governor Stewart, and I shall most probably be there in a month or two, when you may be assured I shall go to the spot and take a regular survey of it.

The longer I am upon this Station the worse I like it. Our Commander has not that opinion of his own sense that he ought to have. He is led by the advice of the Islanders to admit the Yankees to a Trade; at least to wink at it. He does not give himself that weight that I think an English Admiral ought to do. I, for one, am determined not to suffer the Yankees to come where my Ship is; for I am sure, if once the Americans are admitted to any kind of intercourse with these Islands, the views of the Loyalists in settling Nova Scotia are entirely done away. They will first become the Carriers, and next have

---

[3] Rear-Admiral William Parry was appointed Commander-in-Chief at Jamaica, and in the Windward Islands, in 1766, where he remained three years. He died an Admiral of the Blue on the 29th of April, 1799. His only child, Lucy, married Captain Locker, (vide p. 23, ante,) with whom he seems to have obtained the Dominica estate so often mentioned.

possession of our Islands, are we ever again embroiled in a French war. The residents of these Islands are Americans by connexion and by interest, and are inimical to Great Britain. They are as great rebels as ever were in America, had they the power to show it.

After what I have said, you will believe I am not very popular with the people. They have never visited me, and I have not had a foot in any house since I have been on the Station, and all for doing my duty by being *true to the interests of Great Britain*. A petition from the President and Council has gone to the Governor-General and Admiral, to request the admission of Americans. I have given my answer to the Admiral upon the subject ; how he will like it I know not : but I am determined to suppress the admission of Foreigners all in my power. I have told the Customs that I will complain if they admit any Foreigner to an Entry :—an American arrives ; sprung a leak, a mast, and what not, makes a protest, gets admittance, sells his cargo for ready money ; goes to Martinico, buys molasses, and so round and round. But I hate them all. The Loyalist cannot do it, consequently must sell a little dearer. I am happy in hearing Bradley has got so good a place. I beg my best compliments to him and all that family. God bless you, my dear Sir, and rest assured,

I am ever, your affectionate Friend,

HORATIO NELSON.

Remember me to the boys kindly.

TO REAR-ADMIRAL SIR RICHARD HUGHES, BART.

[Copy, in Captain Nelson's Narrative of his Proceedings in support of the Navigation Act. Vide p. 175, post.]

[January 11th or 12th, 1785.]

Sir,

I yesterday received your order of the 29th of December, wherein you direct me in the execution of your first order, dated the 12th of November, (which is in fact strictly requiring us to put the Act of Navigation, upon which the wealth and safety of Great Britain so much depends, in force,) to observe the following directions, viz. : To cause Foreigners to anchor by his Majesty's Ship under my command, except in cases of immediate and urgent distress, until her arrival and situation in all respects shall be reported to his Majesty's Governor or his Representative at any of the Islands where I may fall in with such Foreign Ships or Vessels; and that if the Governor or his Representative should give leave for admitting such Vessels, strictly charging me not to hinder them or interfere in their subsequent proceedings.

I ever have been, as in duty bound, always ready to co-operate with his Majesty's Governors or their Representatives in doing whatever has been for the benefit of Great Britain. No Governor will, I am sure, do such an illegal act as to coun-tenance the admission of Foreigners into the Ports of their Islands, nor *dare* any Officer of his Majesty's Customs enter such Foreigners without they are in such distress that neces-sity obliges them to unlade their cargoes, and then only to sell such a part of it as will pay the costs. In distress, no in-dividual shall exceed me in acts of generosity ; and in judging of their distress, no person can know better than Sea-Officers, of which I shall inform the Governors, &c., when they ac-quaint me for what reason they have countenanced the admis-sion of Foreigners.

I beg leave to hope that I may be properly understood, when I venture to say, that at a time when Great Britain is using every endeavour to suppress illicit Trade at Home, it is not wished that the Ships upon this Station should be singular, by being the only spectators of the illegal Trade, which I know is carried on at these Islands. The Governors may be im-posed upon by false declarations : we, who are on the spot, cannot. General Shirley told me and Captain Collingwood how much he approved of the methods that were carrying on for suppressing the illegal Trade with America; that it had ever been his wish, and that he had used every means in his power, by proclamation and otherwise, to hinder it : but they came to him with protests, and swore through everything, (even as the Sea phrase is, 'through a nine-inch plank,') there-fore got admittance, as he could not examine the Vessels himself; and further, by the Thynne Packet he had received a letter from Lord Sydney, One of His Majesty's Principal Secretaries of State, saying, that Administration were deter-

mined that American Ships and Vessels should not have any
intercourse with our West India Islands ; and that he had, upon
an Address from the Assembly, petitioning that he would relax
the King's proclamation for the exclusion of Americans, transmitted it to Lord Sydney to be laid before the King.   The
answer to General Shirley was that his Majesty firmly believed
and hoped that all his orders which were received by his
Governors would be strictly obeyed.

Whilst I have the honour to command an English Man·of-
War, I never shall allow myself to be subservient to the will
of any Governor, nor co-operate with him in doing *illegal acts.*
Presidents of Council I feel myself superior to.   They shall
make proper application to me, for whatever they may want
to come by water.

If I rightly understand your order of the 29th of December,
it is founded upon an Opinion of the King's Attorney-General,
viz. : ' That it is legal for Governors or their Representatives
to admit Foreigners into the Ports of their Government, if they
think fit.' How the King's Attorney-General conceives he has
a right to give an illegal Opinion, which I assert the above is,
he must answer for.   I know the Navigation Laws.

I am, Sir, &c.

HORATIO NELSON.

TO PHILIP STEPHENS, ESQ., ADMIRALTY.

[Autograph, in the Admiralty.—A Copy occurs in Captain Nelson's Narrative.
Vide p. 176, post.]

Boreas, Basseterre Road, St. Christopher's, January 18th, 1785.

Sir,

Inclosed I have the honour to transmit you, for their Lordships' information, (copy of which I have sent to the Commander-in-Chief upon this Station,) letters which have passed
between Captain W. Collingwood, Commander of His Majesty's
Sloop Rattler,[4] who is under my command, and Mr. Henry

---

[4] Captain Wilfred Collingwood was a younger brother of Captain Cuthbert (afterwards Admiral Lord) Collingwood.   He never obtained Post-rank, and
died in the West Indies on the 21st April 1787.   See Captain Nelson's Letter announcing his death to his brother (p. 230).   Captain Wilfred Collingwood's

Bennet, Collector of his Majesty's Customs at the Port of Sandy
Point, upon this Island, together with copies of the Registers
and Declarations of the Masters.

Being placed by the Commander-in-chief with the Rattler
Sloop upon this station, viz. Montserrat, Nevis, St. Christopher's, Anguilla, and the Virgin Islands, to protect the Commerce of Great Britain, and consequently, I take for granted,
to hinder illegal Trade or proceedings from being carried into
effect, which I have always supposed was our duty, and for
which purpose we are placed in this Country in times of Peace,
and sufficiently authorized by the Statutes which are sent us
by the Admiralty Board.

By the letters you will herewith receive, their Lordships
will be informed that Mr. Bennet, the Collector at Sandy
Point, doubts our having a right to ask reasons why Vessels
are admitted to receive Registers when we find they are Foreign
built, and some of them navigated entirely with Foreigners, so
contrary to the Act of Navigation, and all subsequent Acts of
Parliament for regulating the Plantation trade. By the copies
of the Vessels' Registers, their Lordships will also be informed
that the Vessels are all American built; and by the Declarations of the Masters and others, *were* and are now, in my
opinion, belonging to the Subjects of the States of America,
but wish to enjoy the privilege of British Subjects, by having
a free Trade with our West India Islands, to the prejudice of
British Ship-building, British Subjects, and the Colonies of
Nova Scotia and Canada. Their Lordships would not have
been troubled with this letter at *this time*, had not the said
Mr. Bennet declared in his letter to Captain Collingwood
that he thought himself legally authorized (having received no
Act of Parliament that hindered him from granting Registers
to any American Vessel, the Master and Owner taking oaths of
allegiance to his Majesty) to grant Registers to any Vessel on
those terms.

In consequence of this declaration, I have thought it my indispensable duty to make their Lordships acquainted with the
very illegal methods (I conceive) Americans get Registered at

extensive correspondence preserved at the Admiralty, respecting the illicit traffic,
shows that he was an able and zealous Officer.

these Islands, that they may take such measures as appear to them proper upon this occasion.

I am, Sir, with every respect,
Your most obedient and very humble Servant,
HORATIO NELSON.

I am very sorry it is in my power to say that at all the Islands on this Station, the illegal act of granting Registers to Americans, Subjects of the United States, is carrying on with great confidence.

TO JOHN MOUTRAY, ESQ, COMMISSIONER OF THE NAVY AT ANTIGUA.

[The points discussed in this, and in the following Letters, were ot mucn professional interest, viz. Whether a Captain holding the situation of Commissioner of the Navy was entitled to the same rank and authority as if he had been on full pay in command of one of the King's Ships? and, whether it was in the power of a Commander-in-Chief to give him such authority, and to hoist a Broad Pendant?

Captain John Moutray, the Commissioner at Antigua, was made a Post-Captain on the 28th of December 1758, and was by twenty-one years Nelson's senior Officer. It appears from Rear-Admiral Sir Richard Hughes' Letter to the Admiralty of the 14th February of 1785, complaining of Captain Nelson's conduct in refusing to receive orders from Commissioner Moutray, that he had authorised Captain Moutray to hoist a Broad Pendant in his absence from Antigua; that on the 29th of December 1784, he had given an order to all Captains "in his absence "or that of a senior Officer to Captain Moutray, to conform themselves to his "directions, and to apply to him for all necessary orders relating to the duty and "business of the Port, so far as the Ship under their several commands might be "concerned, and to show him all the usual marks of respect due to an Officer "wearing a Distinguishing Pendant;" and that on the 6th of February 1785, Commissioner Moutray issued a written order to Nelson, to put himself under his command. Nelson, it seems, was not the only Captain who doubted the Commissioner's authority.

Though inquiries have been made to ascertain in what manner the Admiralty disposed of the general question, their Lordships' decision has not been found; but they informed Nelson that he ought to have submitted his doubts to the Commander-in-Chief on the Station, instead of having taken upon himself "to control the exercise of the functions of his Appointment." It is, however, presumed that Captain Nelson's view of the subject was perfectly correct; and that unless (as is now the practice) a Commissioner of the Navy be placed on *full pay*, by being appointed to the command of a Ship, by the *Admiralty*, he is to all intents and purposes an Officer on *half-pay*; and that no Admiral commanding a Squadron or Fleet has the power to place him on *full-pay*, or to give him his Naval rank, and still less to authorize him to hoist a Broad Pendant. Captain Wallis, then First Lieutenant of the Boreas, wrote a

Narrative of Nelson's proceedings in the West Indies, apparently at the request of Dr. Clarke and Mr. M'Arthur, as it is largely quoted in their Life of Nelson. In the original MS., (which is now among the Nelson Papers,) Captain Wallis states that Nelson ordered the Broad Pendant to be struck, and returned to the Dock Yard; that to prove he was not actuated by personal motives, he dined on the same day with Commissioner Moutray, and gave him the first intelligence of what he had done; that the Admiralty approved of his conduct; and that the Pendant was never re-hoisted; but as Captain Wallis' Narrative is, in one part of this statement, inconsistent with Nelson's Official Report, it cannot be relied upon. Commissioner Moutray returned to England soon after.

Non-professional readers may require to be told that when a Captain who is senior on the List to him who wears a Broad Pendant, arrives, the Broad Pendant is immediately struck; and they will find some information on the subject of the National Ensigns, Admirals' Flags, Broad Pendants, &c., in a NOTE at the end of the present or of a subsequent Volume.]

Boreas; English Harbour, February 6th, 1785.

Sir,

Herewith I transmit you a copy of my letter to Sir Richard Hughes, Bart., Commander-in-Chief on this station, upon the subject of Distinguishing Pendants. My sentiments are still the same; that until you are in Commission, I cannot obey any order I may receive from you, but shall ever be studious to show every respect and attention which your situation as a Commissioner of the Navy demands; and at the same time let me beg you will be assured, with what personal esteem,[5]

I am your devoted, faithful, humble Servant,

HORATIO NELSON.

EXTRACT FROM CAPTAIN NELSON'S LETTER TO REAR-ADMIRAL SIR RICHARD HUGHES, DATED AND TRANSMITTED BY THE REAR-ADMIRAL TO THE ADMIRALTY.

[From a Copy in the Admiralty.]

Carlisle Bay, 12th February 1785.

" Some damages having happened to the Boreas, she was obliged to go into English Harbour, to get them repaired. The Latona was laying there, with a Broad Pendant flying at the main top-gallant mast-head. Upon inquiry, I found Commissioner Moutray had directed Captain Sandys to hoist it;

---

[5] His personal esteem for Commissioner Moutray, is shown by his Letter of the 16th of March 1785, in p. 128.

but as Captain Sandys had no orders from you to receive it, I did not think proper to pay the least attention to it, well knowing that Mr. Moutray was not second Officer in the Command in English Harbour during the hurricane season. Whatever he had been before I know not, but I looked upon him as effectually superseded by my sitting as President of Court-Martials when he was upon the spot, in his Naval uniform, and acting in an Official capacity as a Commissioner of the Navy.

I feel it a misfortune that so young a Captain should be the senior upon this station. Had it been otherwise, a man of more service must have been in the unpleasant situation in which I stand; but my best endeavours, however deficient they may be, shall always be exerted in supporting the dignity of my brother Captains, and I trust we shall also have the support of such a character of [as] Sir Richard Hughes.

I am, &c.,

(Signed)   HORATIO NELSON."

TO REAR-ADMIRAL SIR RICHARD HUGHES, BART.

[Copy, in the Admiralty.]

Boreas, Carlisle Bay, February 15th, 1785.

Sir,

Your letter of yesterday's date I have received. You have mistaken, Sir, the motives that influenced my conduct. I only disobeyed *any orders Commissioner Moutray* gave me. Whenever he is appointed a Commodore upon this Station, I must obey him, and I certainly shall not entertain a doubt upon the subject. I never looked upon Mr. Moutray in Commission, and my reasons for thinking so were, having sat as President of many Court-Martials, when he was upon the spot, acting only in the Civil Department of the Navy.

This, Sir, I hope you will transmit to my Lords Commissioners, that they, nor any other of my superior Officers, may have the smallest idea that I shall ever dispute the orders of my Superiors.

I am, Sir, with great respect,

Your most obedient Servant,

HORATIO NELSON.

TO PHILIP STEPHENS, ESQ., ADMIRALTY.

[Copy, in the Admiralty.]

Boreas, Carlisle Bay, Barbadoes, February 17th, 1785.

Sir,

Having lately held a correspondence with Sir Richard Hughes, and Mr. Moutray, a Commissioner of his Majesty's Navy, resident at the Island of Antigua, upon the subject of a Distinguishing Pendant which the said Commissioner thinks he has not only a right to hoist on board any one of his Majesty's Ships, but also to direct the operations of his Majesty's Squadron upon this Station in the absence of the Admiral, the whole of the papers upon this subject Sir Richard Hughes has done me the honour to say he shall enclose to you for their Lordships' information, therefore it is only necessary for me, Sir, to elucidate and explain the motives that have actuated my conduct through the whole of this business.

The matter is grounded upon my idea (for I never saw any Commission whatever) that Mr. Moutray is not Commissioned in such a manner as will authorize him to take upon him the liberty of hoisting a Broad Pendant, or the directing the Captains of His Majesty's Ships; but, Sir, let me first beg their Lordships will be assured that I never have received official information that Commissioner Moutray is appointed a Commodore upon this Station, or put in any Commission, but that of Commissioner of the Navy. I must beg their Lordships' indulgence to hear reasons for my conduct, that it may never go abroad into the World, I ever had an idea to dispute the orders of my Superior Officer; neither Admiral, Commodore, or Captain.

I arrived in English Harbour the 28th July 1784, to lay up for the hurricane season. Till the 1st of November 1784, numerous were the orders I received, and eventually with this direction, to "Horatio Nelson, Esq., Captain of his Majesty's Ship Boreas, and Second Officer in the Command of his Majesty's ships in English Harbour, Antigua." At this time, Sir, I need not to say that Mr. Moutray was not a Commodore: the whole of the Squadron did, I am sure, look upon

him as a half-pay Captain, Commissioner of the Navy. Thus,
Sir, the matter stood for three times that I went into English Harbour. At St. Christopher's I heard, as their Lordships will be informed, that Commissioner Moutray was authorized to hoist a Distinguishing or Broad Pendant. I did
not pretend to think upon the matter: it might probably be
so, and my answer to the Admiral was, that if Commissioner
Moutray was put into Commission, I should have great pleasure in serving under him. I have no doubt that Sir Richard
Hughes believed that Mr. Moutray was Commissioned as a
Commodore; but at the same time I trust that he thought
that the Officers under his command knew their duty too
well, to obey any half-pay Captain; and that he might safely
trust the honour of the Navy to those under him, (that
they would not act improperly upon this business,) and that
they would be well informed that the man who they received
orders from, was empowered to give them.

On the 5th of February, 1785, upon my arrival in English
Harbour, I found the Latona with a Broad Pendant flying.
As her Captain[7] was junior to me, I sent to know the reason
for her wearing it. Her Captain came on board, who I asked
the following questions:—

" Have you any order from Sir Richard Hughes to wear a
Broad Pendant?"

Answer—" No."

" For what reason do you then wear it in the presence of
a Senior Officer?"

Answer—" I hoisted it by order of Commissioner Moutray."

Question— "Have you seen by what authority Commissioner Moutray was empowered to give you orders?"

" No."

Question—" Sir, you have acted wrong, to obey any man
who you do not know is authorized to command you."

Answer—" I feel I have acted wrong; but being a young
Captain, did not think proper to interfere in this matter, as
there were you and other older Officers upon this Station."

---

[7] Captain Sandys, of the Latona, was by nearly four years Captain Nelson s
junior Officer.

I did not choose to order the Commissioner's Pendant to be struck, as Mr. Moutray is an old Officer of high military character; and it might hurt his feelings to be supposed wrong by so young an Officer.

When Commissioner Moutray sent me orders, I answered him, that I could not obey him till he was in Commission. As I never heard further upon the subject from him, I took for granted he saw I was perfectly right, or he would have produced his Commission, which would instantly have cleared up the business, if it was dated since I had, by orders from Sir Richard Hughes, executed the office of Second in Command in English Harbour.

This is the whole and every circumstance that has arisen upon this business, and have from time to time confirmed me in the opinion, that I am Second Officer in the Command of his Majesty's Ships upon this Station.

I am, Sir,

Your very humble Servant,

HORATIO NELSON.

Inclosed is a copy of my letter to Commissioner Moutray.[8]

TO THE REVEREND MR. NELSON.

[Autograph, in the Nelson Papers.]

Boreas, Carlisle Bay,
February 20th, 1785.

My dear Brother,

Your letter by the Camilla and by the Packet of December I received at the same time, upon my arrival here from St. Kitts, where I am stationed. Your friends on this side the Atlantic were very anxious to hear of your arrival. However, I give you credit for writing, although we did not hear for so long a time. I take for granted you are so much of a Sailor that you will like to hear of all our proceedings. We sailed for Barbadoes the 1st of November, as was intended when you left us: from thence the Ships were dispersed upon their se-

---

[8] Vide p. 119.

veral stations; the Admiral to visit all the Islands. My Lady and Miss left under the care of Lieutenant Gregory, who took possession of Constitution Hill. The Boreas was sent to explore a harbour in the Island of Saint John's, one of the Virgin's.

You may be certain I never passed English Harbour without a call, but alas! I am not to have much comfort. My dear, sweet friend[9] is going home. I am really an April day; happy on her account, but truly grieved were I only to consider myself. Her equal I never saw in any country or in any situation. She always talks of you, and hopes, if she comes within your reach, you will not fail visiting her. If my dear Kate goes to Bath next winter, she will be known to her; for my dear friend has promised to make herself known. What an acquisition to any female to be acquainted with: what an example to take pattern from. Moutray has been very ill: it would have been necessary he should have quitted this Country had he not been recalled. All my Children[1] are well

[9] Mrs. Moutray.

[1] Nelson's treatment of his Midshipmen, whom he affectionately calls his *Children*, is thus described by Lady Hughes, from her own observation while a passenger in the Boreas, in a Letter to Mr. Matcham, dated Clifton, June 24th, 1806:

"I was too much affected when we met at Bath to say every particular in which was always displayed the infinite cleverness and goodness of heart of our dearly beloved Hero. As a woman, I can only be a judge of those things that I could comprehend—such as his attention to the young gentlemen who had the happiness of being on his Quarter-Deck. It may reasonably be supposed that among the number of thirty, there must be timid as well as bold: the timid he never rebuked, but always wished to show them he desired nothing of them that he would not instantly do himself: and I have known him say—'Well, Sir, I am going a race to the mast-head, and beg I may meet you there.' No denial could be given to such a wish, and the poor fellow instantly began his march. His Lordship never took the least notice with what alacrity it was done, but when he met in the top, instantly began speaking in the most cheerful manner, and saying how much a person was to be pitied that could fancy there was any danger, or even anything disagreeable, in the attempt. After this excellent example, I have seen the timid youth lead another, and rehearse his Captain's words. How wise and kind was such a proceeding! In like manner, he every day went into the School Room, and saw them do their nautical business, and at twelve o'clock he was the first upon deck with his quadrant. No one there could be behind-hand in their business when their Captain set them so good an example. One other circumstance I must mention which will close the subject, which was the day we landed at Barbadoes. We were to dine at the Governor's. Our dear Captain said, 'You must permit me, Lady Hughes, to carry one of my Aid-de-camps with me:' and when he presented him to the Governor, he said, 'Your Excellency must excuse me for bringing one of my

except one, young Andrews.[2] He came out in the Unicorn:
do you remember him ? On the 11th of November last, he
was forced by Mr. Stainsbury to fight a duel, which terminated
fatally for the poor lad : the ball is lodged in his back, and
whether he will ever get the better of it God knows. He has
kept his bed ever since. His antagonist, and Mr. Oliver, his
second, are in irons since the duel. They will stand a good
chance of hanging if the youth should unfortunately die.
Wallace, Dent, Jameson, Doctor, often ask after you, and are
happy to hear of your safe arrival. Your singing friend,
Powers, was discharged at Antigua. Dick Hughes [3] is on
board, but I can neither make much of him or Suckling, but
the latter is the best of the two. Lady H. and Miss sailed
for Martinico two days ago. What a specimen of English
beauty : they are neither of them grown handsomer since
you left them. The Admiral doesn't go : Unicorn has the
Flag.

Come, I must carry you to our love scenes. Captain
Sandys has asked Miss Eliot—*refused.* Captain Sterling
was attentive to Miss Elizabeth E.;[4] but never having asked
the question, Captain Berkeley is, I hear, to be the happy man.
Captain Kelly is attached to a lady at Nevis, so he says: I
don't much think it. He is not steady enough for that passion to hold long.[5] All the Eliot family spent their Christmas

Midshipmen, as I make it a rule to introduce them to all the good company I
can, as they have few to look up to besides myself during the time they are at
Sea.' This kindness and attention made the young people adore him ; and even
his wishes, could they have been known, would have been instantly complied
with. It was your wish, Sir, to have the above particulars: an abler pen might
have described them better ; but I hope my simple narration may, in a faint
degree, describe his Lordship's excellent manner of making his young men fancy
the attaining nautical perfection was much more a play than a task. Who is
there but must allow these methods to be dictated by great skill, as well as great
goodness of heart that never caused a fear or disgust to any one ? How sincerely
is such a loss to be lamented ! But we have nothing to say, but—' The Lord
giveth and the Lord taketh away, blessed be the name of the Lord.'"—*Original,*
in the Nelson Papers.

[2] George Andrews ; he survived the wound, became a Post-Captain in 1796 ;
and is frequently mentioned : he died in July 1810.

[3] Sir Robert Hughes' eldest son, who died a Post-Captain in 1810.

[4] Afterwards married to Lord Le Despencer.

[5] Captain Nelson was, however, mistaken, for Captain Kelly did marry the
lady, who was a near relation of Mrs. Nesbit, afterwards Mrs. Nelson.

4

at Constitution Hill—came up in Latona. The Boreas, you
guessed right, at English Harbour. Rosy has had no offers: I
fancy she seems hurt at it. Poor girl! you should have offered. I have not gallantry enough. A niece of Governor
Parry's has come out. She goes to Nevis in the Boreas;
they trust any young lady with me, being an old-fashioned
fellow. My paper draws towards an end: to business. You
may be assured I will keep you upon the Books as long as I can,
but it depends entirely upon the Admiral, and we are not
upon the very best terms; but as I feel I am perfectly right,
you know upon those occasions I am not famous for giving up
a point. Should inclination or opportunity bring you here
again, towards the latter end of the Station, I shall be happy
to receive you. You will do as you please in that business.
God bless you. Adieu, and believe I am, your affectionate
brother,

HORATIO NELSON.

Remember me kindly to Charles Boyles. The Wells Club
must be strong this winter. *Noisy*, I'll answer, with you and
him.

[In continuation.]

Boreas, St. Kitts, March 16th, 1785.

My dear Brother.—Not having an opportunity of sending my
letter which was wrote at Barbadoes, I have added a new cover,
to acknowledge the receipt of yours of January 1st. Come
whenever you please, I shall be happy to receive you; but I
charge you, do not attempt to bring anything except a few books,
for I will not receive them. Do as you please about the tickets.
There is an Irish lottery. Whatever you do I shall approve. My sweet amiable friend sails the 20th for England.
I took my leave of her with a heavy heart, three days ago.
What a *treasure* of a woman. God bless her. She always asks
after you. She thinks you should have stayed with Dorothea.
When the twelve months are expired I will send your Certificate. I am not quite certain about the paying you; for the
Muster-Master has checked you absent with leave, since the

1st of October, nor can I help it.　All on board desire to be kindly remembered.　Farewell.

Yours affectionately,

HORATIO NELSON.

I shall not write to our Father this Packet, as I have done it to you and Kate.　Give my kind *love*.

TO WILLIAM LOCKER, ESQ., WEST MALLING.

[Autograph, in the Locker Papers.]

Boreas, St. Kitts, March 16th, 1785.

My dear Friend,

Since my last, I have been at Prince Rupert's Bay, and with great difficulty reached the house which Admiral Parry[7] built upon his land. The house is levelled with the ground, nor should I have known it was anything but a wood, had not my guide told me this was the estate.　I made every inquiry it was possible for me to do as to worth, or what could be done with it: from the whole I have heard it is not possible to sell or let it.　If you claim it, the taxes are far more than it is worth in its present state, and they have proclamations for giving the Loyalists land *gratis*, so much do they want settlers for the Island.　The soil is bad, so much so, that several mulattoes settled upon the cleared part after Admiral Parry left it, and lived in the house, but at last they abandoned it, not being able to get roots to grow in it.　Governor Stewart[8] has an estate at Prince Rupert's, but quite in another situation; am told he wishes for the money he has laid out upon it.

And now let me tell you a very extraordinary anecdote of Dominica.　When the English first took possession of it, they thought it a fine sugar Island; they built by far the best works of any Island in our possession, but time has proved that the soil is not proper for sugar, as it takes some hundred gallons of juice to make a hogshead more than at any other Island. Cotton and coffee are the only commodities it will produce in

---

[7] Vide p. 113.

[8] William Stewart, Esq., Lieutenant-Governor of Dominica.

perfection.   If ever I go to Rosseau, I will ask Governor
Stewart if anything can be done, and I will do what is right
in the business; but from what I have said, little can be expected.   News from this ill-fated corner you will not expect.
Moutray is gone home a few days ago, so that I lose my only
valuable friend in these Islands.   Every day convinces [me] how
superior the Jamaica Station is to this: everything is extrava-
gantly dear, and no comforts.   All the Navy are very unpopular, from the Governor downwards, for hindering the American
Ships from trading to the Islands.   I seldom go on shore, hardly
once a month.   Mr. and Mrs. Georges are the only people I
know upon this Island.   How have you been this winter?
quite stout, I hope, and all your children.   Collingwood recommends Lady Twisden,[9] he says you ought to marry her;
what a charming good man—he is a valuable member of
society.   Little C—— S—— is as usual—likes a cup of
grog as well as ever.   I think the chance is much against his
return to England. He has been paying his addresses to a young
lady at Antigua—but is refused.   She used to strike him
speechless every night.   What a pity he should have that
failing: there is not a better heart in the world.

Our Admiral with his family are just making the tour of the
Islands; they find, probably, more satisfaction in visiting
them than I do, for they are a sad set.   Yesterday
being St. Patrick's day, the Irish Colours with thirteen
stripes in them was hoisted all over the Town.   I was engaged
to dine with the President, but sent an excuse, as he suffered
those Colours to fly.   I mention it only to show the principle
of these *vagabonds.*   How does Mrs. B. and Mrs. Dyne?
Remember me kindly to all that good family.   Your wine is
well, and I will get some rum for you.   I suppose duty must
be paid for everything, as your friend Mr. Pitt has set his
face so much against smuggling.   God bless you—farewell;
and believe I am ever, your affectionate humble Servant,

HORATIO NELSON.

Collingwood desired me to make his compliments.   March
18th.

[9] Apparently Elizabeth, daughter of Mr. Waldash, and widow of Sir Roger
Twisden, who died in October, 1779, nine months after his marriage. Lady Twisden survived until February 1833.

TO LORD SYDNEY, SECRETARY OF STATE.

[Copy, in Captain Nelson's Narrative, vide p. 176 postea.]

Boreas, Basseterre Road, St. Christopher's,
20th March, 1785.

My Lord,

It is not to criminate any individual, but to vindicate my character as an Officer from the aspersions that are thrown on it by the inhabitants in general of this Island and Nevis,—I beg this may be my apology for troubling your Lordship. The character of an Officer is his greatest treasure: to lower that, is to wound him irreparably. But I trust as it is only by doing my duty that has caused these aspersions, the approbation of my Sovereign will make ample amends for the calumnies of the invidious.

In November last, I was appointed by the Commander-in-Chief to the Station at these Islands to protect the Commerce of Great Britain, which I have endeavoured to do by every means in my power. Americans at this time, I am very sorry to say, filled our Ports; but as I did not think it was a legal Commerce, I have constantly endeavoured to suppress it, the doing of which has so much hurt the feelings of the people in general, from the highest to the lowest, that they have not only neglected paying me that attention my rank might have made me expect, but reprobated my character, by saying that I am the injurer of this Colony, and that the Minister never intended to hinder Americans from coming into our Ports with any trifling excuse, only that the Trade was not be made free from all restraint. This did not appear to me to be the meaning of his Majesty's proclamation, or anything tending that way: consequently I have ever excluded all Vessels belonging to the United States from having a free intercourse with our Colonies, where the Ship under my command has been stationed. But although these Foreigners have been ordered away by me, yet, my Lord, astonishing to tell, these Vessels have almost always gone into some Port in this Island, and unladed their cargoes. What reasons they give to the Officers of the Revenue I know not; but almost uniformly are their reasons admitted to be good.

At times the King's Ship is obliged to sail to the neighbouring Islands to procure wood, water and provisions: constantly when I returned, have I been informed from good authority, that the Americans had free egress and regress to our Ports. The Custom-House do not admit them to an Entry, only the Master of the American makes a Protest (and what they say are ready to swear to) that their Vessel leaks, has sprung a mast, or some excuse of that sort. Then the Customs grant a Permit to land a part or the whole of their cargo to pay expenses, under which Permits they land innumerable cargoes: could the number of them be found out, which I fear cannot, your Lordship would be astonished. At this Island the Customs have refused to give answers to the King's Officers. I send for information, they have answered me, they do not know any right I have to ask; they are not amenable to a Captain of the Navy for their conduct.

Yesterday an American Brig came into this Port, said by the Master to be in distress. I told him he must not have any communication with the shore till I had ordered a survey upon his Vessel. People from the shore in boats had spoke to him, and he told them his distress. Now, my Lord, let my heart speak for me. It was dispersed all over the Island, (for my information came from Sandy Point, the extremity of it,) that in the night I intended to turn him out of Port, and that he would certainly sink before morning. There only wanted this report to represent me both cruel and unjust: the account was believed by great part of the Island. This, as the honour of my gracious King and my Country were at stake, has made me take the liberty of addressing your Lordship; for so far from treating him cruelly, I sent an Officer, a carpenter, and some men, to take care of his Vessel, which they did, by pumping her all night; and this morning I have moved him into a safe Harbour.

My name most probably is unknown to your Lordship; but my character as a man, I trust, will bear the strictest investigation: therefore I take the liberty of sending inclosed a letter, though written some few years ago, which I hope will impress your Lordship with a favourable opinion of me. I stand for myself; no great connexion to support me if inclined to fall: therefore my good Name as a Man, an Officer, and an Eng-

---

[1] This letter is not in the Narrative or Correspondence.

lishman, I must be very careful of. My greatest pride is to discharge my duty faithfully; my greatest ambition to receive approbation for my conduct.

I am, my Lord,

Your Lordship's most obedient Servant,

HORATIO NELSON.

TO THE REVEREND MR. NELSON, BURNHAM.

[Autograph, in the Nelson Papers.]

Boreas, St Christopher's, May 3rd, 1785.

Dear Brother,

Your letter of 26th February, I received three days after my Father's, of January, and let me assure you that your kind attention in writing by every Packet flatters me very much; and I congratulate you upon your friend Charles Fox being returned for Westminster. The Walpoles will be elated. Don't let them forget you in their prosperity. This Country appears now intolerable, my dear friend[2] being absent. It is barren indeed; not all the Rosys can give a spark of joy to me. English Harbour I hate the sight of, and Windsor I detest. I went once up the Hill to look at the spot where I spent more happy days than in any one spot in the world. E'en the trees drooped their heads, and the tamarind tree died :—all was melancholy: the road is covered with thistles; let them grow. I shall never pull one of them up. By this time I hope she is safe in Old England. Heaven's choicest blessing go with her.

We go on here but sadly. The Admiral I have not seen these three months. The family are visiting the Islands. They will be remembered, no fear, go where they will. The '*dear* Boreas' is quite forgot, very much disliked, and *entre nous*, I should not be surprised if the Admiral appoints another Chaplain to the Ship. I shall never ask a favour of him. Report says Captain Kelly pays great attention to Miss, and Sir Richard has said he will give her £5000. My

---

[2] Mrs. Moutray.

letter is broken in upon by a scoundrel of a *rebel*.   The whole
Island of St. Kitt's are on his side, and against me, but I am
in a fair way of casting them.   They make me so angry, that
I have no patience, and our Admiral does not support us.
He is an *excellent fiddler*.

Well, must I say any [thing] about your coming out? it shall
be short. Consider well before you set off upon such a wild-goose
chase; and at any rate don't think of coming by a Packet: a
Merchantman from the Thames is the proper mode of conveyance, and I charge you bring nothing but yourself.   Little
S—— is over head and ears in love; what will come of it
I know not, but he is in a sad way. Next hurricane months
will finish his life I should suppose. As to news, I can't tell
you any out of my Ship.   Old Jemmy Jameson[3] has got the
gout. Wallis, and Dent are well, and with Doctor Graham,
pay great attention to the Purser's wife. Mr. Lane is at sick-
quarters; let him stay, I never wish to see his face again.
Mr. Oliver and Stainsbury are discharged from the Ship
for being principals in a duel against young Andrews.   Mr.
Powers, I told you long ago, was discharged: he has gone
to America. Bromwich and all my dear good Children are
well, and all desire to be kindly remembered to you.   Lock
and Talbot are quite men; you will not know them. When
you go to Wolterton, remember me there, and at Norwich to the Boltons, and don't forget me to the Wells Club.
Where is Charles Boyles? Tell him Miss—— is waiting
for him : Fame says she is likely to have another child. She
often inquires after him. He might put a postscript in your
letter; tell him to do it. I wrote to my Father three days ago,
but this may arrive full as soon. God bless you. Adieu, and
believe I am, your affectionate Brother,

HORATIO NELSON.

May 12th.

The Packet has just arrived by which I send this letter.
Tell Kate I will write to her in a few days, for Ships sail every

---

[3] All Officers of the Boreas, and are mentioned in this Letter have been
already noticed. Vide p. 108.

day at this season. I am just come from Nevis, where I have
been visiting Miss Parry Herbert and a young Widow;[4] the
two latter known to Charles Boyles. Great inquiries after
him by the damsels in that Island. My trial comes on to-
morrow,[5] but I am sure of casting my gentleman.

TO THE REVEREND MR. W. NELSON, BURNHAM.

[Autograph, in the Nelson Papers.]

Boreas, St. Kitt's, June 28th, 1785.

My dear Brother,

Your letters up to the 1st of May I have regularly received, and many thanks I return for your kind remembrance
of me. This letter must be short, for my time for this six
weeks has been all Law. I will write more fully in about a
week; but I did not like to let a Packet sail without acknowledging the receipt of yours, my Father's, Mrs. Bolton's, and
Kate's letters. Tell them I will write the moment I have my
hands at liberty.

You ask when I may return to England? How can you
who have been at Sea ask such a question? How can I
possibly tell? and I never guess. If you sincerely ask my
opinion relative to your coming out to this infernal climate,
I can only tell you it is a thing I should never think

---

[4] Mrs. Nisbet, afterwards Viscountess Nelson. Vide p. 217, post. Mrs. Nisbet
had shortly before received the following account of her future husband in a letter
from a female friend :

"We have at last seen the Captain of the Boreas, of whom so much has been
said. He came up just before dinner, much heated, and was very silent; yet
seemed, according to the old adage, to think the more. He declined drinking any
wine; but after dinner, when the President, as usual, gave the following toasts,
'the King,' 'the Queen and Royal Family,' and 'Lord Hood,' this strange man
regularly filled his glass, and observed, that those were always bumper toasts with
him; which having drank, he uniformly passed the bottle, and relapsed into his
former taciturnity. It was impossible, during this visit, for any of us to make
out his real character; there was such a reserve and sternness in his behaviour,
with occasional sallies, though very transient, of a superior mind. Being
placed by him, I endeavoured to rouse his attention by showing him all the
civilities in my power; but I drew out little more than 'Yes' and 'No.' If
you, Fanny, had been there, we think you would have made something of him;
for you have been in the habit of attending to these odd sort of people.—*Clarke
and M'Arthur*, vol. i. p. 37.

[5] Vide p. 136.

of: nor would any that reflected one moment. All that I can say is, that if you come out, I shall be happy to receive you, and to make everything as pleasant as is in my power. The Admiral, Lady, and Miss, sailed from here yesterday. Joy go with them: I had rather have their room than their company. I can't write you any more; therefore pray excuse me. Give my kind love to our father, sisters, brothers, and respects to all who inquire after me; and do you be assured that I am, with sincere affection, your Brother,

HORATIO NELSON.

Entre nous.—Do not be surprised to hear I am a *Benedict*, for if at all, it will be before a month. Do not tell.

MEMORIAL TO THE KING.

[Copy, in Captain Nelson's Narrative, vide p. 178, post.]

29th June, 1785.

TO THE KING'S MOST EXCELLENT MAJESTY.

The humble Memorial and Representation of Horatio Nelson, Esq., Commander of His Majesty's Ship of War, the Boreas.

Sheweth,

That your Memorialist was, and is now, stationed in your Majesty's said Ship, the Boreas, together with a Sloop of War, at the Islands of St. Christopher's and Nevis, in the West Indies, for the protection of their Commerce, and the prevention of illegal Trade: in the execution of which trust, your Memorialist flatters himself he has ever conducted himself in such a manner as to meet his Admiral's approbation, and to merit your Majesty's consideration.

That in this situation your Memorialist soon found that your Majesty's proclamation prohibiting all Trade with America, to and from the West Indies, (except in British bottoms, owned and navigated by the people of your Majesty's Dominions and Territories,) was most shamefully evaded by colouring American Vessels with British Registers, by which means, through imposition on some, and connivance of others of the Officers of His Majesty's Customs in the West India Islands

nearly the whole Trade between America and your Majesty's
said Colonies was carried on in American bottoms.

That your Memorialist, in the performance of his duty kept
so strict an eye over this proceeding, that he shortly made
several Seizures, which were prosecuted by your Majesty's
Attorney-General and Counsel in the several Courts of Vice-
Admiralty of the said Islands of St. Christopher's and Nevis,
and there condemned upon the clearest evidence.

But these Seizures, and your Memorialist's unabating alertness to prevent this evasion of your Majesty's proclamation,
and put a stop to a mode of commercial intercourse so advantageous to America and prejudicial to Great Britain, failed
not to excite a rancorous disposition of some of the inhabitants
of the said Islands concerned in this illegal Commerce towards
your Memorialist, which, after having been shown in various
ways, has at length stirred up a persecution of your Memorialist, under colour of Law, upon the following occasion:

Your Memorialist being informed that four American Vessels under English colours had gone into the Road of Nevis,
and were trading there, went to the said Island and sent for
the Masters of the said Vessels on board your Majesty's Ship,
in order to inspect their Papers, and examine if they were properly qualified to trade in the British Colonies; three of which
said Masters accordingly, without force, or compulsion, or
even a refusal on their parts, readily came, and after answering
such questions as were thought necessary, (and put by your
Majesty's Counsel learned in the Law, who, at the instance of
your Memorialist, that he might be furnished with proper
legal advice on the occasion, had accompanied him from St.
Christopher's) were returned to their own Vessels again : that
the said Vessels being thought proper objects for Seizure, your
Memorialist, acting by the advice of your Majesty's Counsel,
seized them, and they were forthwith prosecuted and condemned as forfeited by the Court of Vice-Admiralty of Nevis.
This increased the ferment and irritation amongst the trading
part of the inhabitants against your Memorialist, and the several Masters of the said four Vessels have been instigated to
procure divers Writs for the arrest of your Memorialist, under
pretence of their having been assaulted and imprisoned by
him, to the amount of four thousand pounds damages, which

assault and imprisonment is no more than what your Memo-
rialist has before stated; and, moreover, one of the said
Masters never was on board the Boreas, or even seen by your
Memorialist.

That notwithstanding these glaring facts, which might be
proved in your Memorialist's favour upon a Trial, such is the
disposition of the generality of the people of the said Island of
Nevis, that your Petitioner is advised by your Majesty's Attorney-General, and your Majesty's Counsel, that it would be
unsafe, at present, to rely too much on the justice of his
cause, and put himself upon the Country for trial.

Thus circumstanced, your Memorialist is obliged to keep
himself confined to your Majesty's Ship, which, added to the
unhealthiness of a West India climate, has much impaired
your Memorialist's health. But he cheerfully submits to these
sufferings, incurred in your Majesty's Service, if they may be
allowed to claim your Majesty's attention and consideration,
which your Memorialist now, and on all future occasions, most
humbly presumes to solicit from your Royal goodness and
humanity. In confidence whereof, and in all duty, he thus ventures to lay before his Royal Master, not only the sufferings of
his faithful servant, but also the inquitous practices carried on
by the alienated Americans, and their adherents in the British
Colonies, in contempt to the Laws, and to the infinite prejudice of the Commerce of Great Britain.

                                        HORATIO NELSON,
June 29th, 1785.

A REPRESENTATION OF THE ILLEGAL TRADE WHICH IS
NOW CARRYING ON BETWEEN THE UNITED STATES OF
AMERICA AND THE ISLAND OF ST. CHRISTOPHERS; AND
ALSO THE PRACTICES OF THE OFFICERS OF HER MA-
JESTY'S CUSTOMS TO THAT ISLAND.

[This Representation was forwarded to the Admiralty, by Rear-Admiral Sir
Richard Hughes, on the 19th June 1785. A copy of it occurs in Captain Nelson's Narrative, vide p. 178 post.]

In November last the Rattler, Captain Wilfred Collingwood,
was put under my command by Sir Richard Hughes, Baronet,
Commander-in-Chief at the Leeward Islands, in order to pro-

tect the Islands of Montserrat, Nevis, St. Christopher's, and all the Virgin Islands. My orders to Captain Collingwood were, to protect the Commerce of Great Britain, and by every means in his power to hinder illicit Trade or proceedings from being carried into effect. In consequence of my orders the Rattler arrived in Basseterre Roads, on the 17th of November last. Upon examining those Vessels which had not shown their Colours to the King's Ship, the Ship Thomas, Thomas Kelly, Master, belonging to North Carolina, appeared to be one. When Captain Collingwood asked the Master why he did not hoist the Colours of the Nation to which he belonged, he answered that the Collector of the Customs had desired him not to do it. This Ship had received the sanction of the Customs to sell her cargo.

In December, upon the Rattler's arrival in Basseterre Roads from Antigua, Captain Collingwood found the Brig Chance, Stephen Pearce, Master, belonging to Rhode Island, and the Nanette Schooner belonging to Guadaloupe; all which Vessels had been importing goods and merchandise into this Colony, contrary to the Act of Navigation. But Captain Collingwood's humanity would not allow him to seize those Vessels as forfeited, as they had been led into the predicament in which they then lay by the Officers of the Customs.

On the 7th of January I arrived in Basseterre Roads, where was laying the Ship Fanny, Archibald Burnham, Master, belonging to Middleton, Connecticut. He had landed a part of his cargo under permission from the Officers of the Customs; but as the importation was illegal, I ordered her to sail, not choosing to seize her, as the Master had been led into the snare by the Officers of the Customs. These are only meant to fix the facts of the illegal Trade; for numerous indeed, I believe, are the American Vessels which have imported and exported merchandize into and from these Islands, for when ever the Men-of-War are absent for a few days, constantly, when I returned, have I received good information that three or four Americans had unloaded their cargoes and sailed.

And at Sandy Point I verily believe the case is still worse. There, I have every reason to think, that till very lately, the American Ships and Vessels have had free ingress and egress,

10

and I have good reason for believing that many Americans whom I would not permit to sell their cargoes at Basseterre, have often been permitted to do it at Sandy Point, and have also often procured Registers for their Vessels.

HORATIO NELSON.

June 1785.

TO WILLIAM LOCKER, ESQ., WEST MALLING.

[Autograph, in the Locker Papers.]

Boreas, English Harbour, September 4th, 1785.

My dear Friend,

Our friend Kingsmill will have told you of my captivity,[5] and of all the disasters which I have suffered by having acted with a proper spirit against the villanies of a certain set of men settled in these Islands from America and have brought their rebel principles with them. If Ministers do not support me, may they find the want of Officers to support them. You know, from this vile hole that we hardly hear of the arrival of the Packet at St. John's before her time of sailing arrives, therefore, from this place, you will not expect a long letter; indeed, my head has been so much taken up with Law, that I have very much neglected my best friends, who, I am sure, have great reason to complain of me; but I throw myself upon their generosity, and hope they will be sorry for the employment which has appertained to me this some time past.

On the 24th last, we had a most severe gale of wind; the mischief is great, but not so much as might have been expected. The Men-of-War rode out the gale, but very many small Vessels are lost about the Islands. At Martinico, we have a flying report almost everything is destroyed. From Barbadoes and Grenada we have not heard; I should hope they have escaped. I wish I could give you any good tidings relative to your Dominica estate, but you must not be sanguine about it: I was upon the property, but too certain. However; I have Mr. Bradley's letter with all the particulars by me, and, rest assured, what-

---

[5] Alluding to his being confined to his Ship to avoid an arrest at the suit of the owners of some American vessels which he had seized. Vide his Memorial, p. 136, and his Letter of March 5th, 1786, p. 156.

ever I can do, you may command me. When you see Commissioner Kirke, remember me kindly to him and his family. I feel much obliged by their kind inquiries. To the family of the Bradleys say every [thing] for me. How you surprised me about poor Mrs. Arbuthnot; that family has turned her brain. Farewell, my dear friend, and rest assured with what sincere regard and esteem, I am, your much obliged Friend and Servant,

HORATIO NELSON.

TO MRS. NISBET.

From Clarke and M‘Arthur's "Life of Lord Nelson, vol. i. p. 79.

[This Letter is the first of the series of Letters addressed by Nelson to the Lady who became his wife, (vide p. 217, post.) which are printed in Clarke and M‘Arthur's Life of Lord Nelson, who state that they received the Letters written before Mrs. Nelson's marriage from Mrs. Rose, her relation. They are now reprinted from that Work, every effort to obtain access to the Originals having failed.]

Boreas, English Harbour, 11th September, 1785.

Indeed, my dear Fanny, I had buoyed myself up with hopes that the Admiral's Schooner would have given me a line from you : but the tidings she brought of the release of poor Mrs. Herbert,[6] from this world, sufficiently apologize for your not thinking of an absentee. Yet ˙this believe from my heart, that I partake in all the sorrows you experience ; and I comfort myself, that however great your grief at this moment may be, at losing a person who was so deservedly dear to you, as your good Aunt ; yet, when reason takes place, you must rather have pleasure in knowing she is released from those torments she had undergone for months past. Time ever has, and in the present instance I trust may have, a tendency to soften grief into a pleasing remembrance ; and her unspotted character must afford you real comfort. Call Religion to your aid ; and it will convince you, that her conduct in this world was such as insures everlasting happiness in that which is to come.

I have received a letter from Mr. Herbert, in answer to

---

[6] Her Aunt, apparently the wife of the President of Nevis.

that which I left at Nevis for him. My greatest wish is to be united to you; and the foundation of all conjugal happiness real love and esteem, is, I trust, what you believe I possess in the strongest degree towards you. I think Mr. Herbert loves you too well, not to let you marry the man of your choice, although he may not be so rich as some others, provided his character and situation in life render such an union eligible. I declare solemnly, that did I not conceive I had the full possession of your heart, no consideration should make me accept your hand. We know that riches do not always insure happiness; and the world is convinced that I am superior to pecuniary considerations in my public and private life; as in both instances I might have been rich. But I will have done, leaving all my present feelings to operate in your breast:— only of this truth be convinced, that I am, your affectionate,

HORATIO NELSON.

P. S. Do I ask too much, when I venture to hope for a line? or otherwise I may suppose my letters may be looked on as troublesome.

TO WILLIAM SUCKLING, ESQ.

[This and the other Letters to Mr. Suckling were printed in " the Athenæum," in October and November 1834, Nos. 363-369, and are inserted with the obliging permission of Charles Wentworth Dilke, Esq.

Mr. Suckling, as has been already observed, was a brother of Nelson's mother and of Captain Maurice Suckling, with whom he first went to Sea.]

Boreas, English Harbour, September 25th, 1785.

My dear Sir,

Your kind letter of the 2nd of August I received upon the arrival of the Packet, and am much obliged for the intelligence it contains. I have not heard from Kingsmill that he is going to India: was he, I should have great pleasure in serving with him, for a more liberal man does not exist. Messrs. Marsh and Creed are my Agents, and I have said to them that you would give to them every information which lies in your power. What I wish them to know, and to be able to prove, is, that the Brig Hercules, who, by her Register, was a Schooner, taken as a prize in the War, was the Brig Neptune, and must have arrived in the Thames in the spring of 1783. Several Depositions go to this purpose by people who sailed in her, therefore we have only to prove the Register false, and the Appeal must fall to the ground, let her now belong to whom she will.

In your letter you say 'our Solicitor does not doubt our right of seizing the Ships, but wonders you would not take out a deputation from the Board of Customs, which would have left you independent of the Officers in this Country.' I must answer this question by asking another. Why should a Captain of the Navy, who is ordered by Acts of Parliament to take care that all Vessels which trade in the British Colonies are British built, or prizes taken from the Enemy, and that the owners are subjects of the King, and resident in his Dominions, &c. &c., do as a Deputy, what he is ordered to do personally, and has that right vested in him by Law? In some instances, I believe, a Captain of a Man-of-War cannot seize, only detain: for instance, a Ship arrives from England; upon examining her Papers I find everything regular and clear, but a man belonging to her says several tons of goods on board the Ship have not cleared from the Customs in England; this is a matter which perhaps none but Officers deputed by the Customs could actually take cognizance of. I could only detain the Vessel, and send information to the Customs. In the latter case, and making seizures on shore, which I think a Captain of a Man-of-War cannot do [illegible] if a Deputation is necessary I am ready to receive it. [illegible.] I shall then play the devil I am sure, particularly [illegible] where vast quantities of French sugars [illegible] put on board English Ships.

The Packet's stay here is so very short, that it is hardly possible to say much, but this I must tell you, that this Packet has brought a letter from Lord Sydney, signifying his Majesty's approbation of my conduct, and orders for the Crown Lawyers to defend me at his expense from all Civil prosecutions, and in case of unfavourable decree, advising me to Appeal. When Ministers support Officers, they will ever find alert and good ones. Bless you, my dear Sir, and believe I am,

With sincere affection,
Your dutiful Nephew,
HORATIO NELSON.

Suckling[7] is well, but home he must come in the Ship. Every Captain is so crowded with younkers that we cannot ask each other. A letter of yours, dated December 1784, I have this moment received, *via* New York. Best compliments to Mrs. Suckling, the Lieutenant, and the remainder of your good family, likewise to all my village acquaintance. You may make use of my name for a Deputation, as it may some time or other prevent some dispute with Officers of the Customs.

TO THE REVEREND MR. NELSON, BURNHAM.

[Autograph, in the Nelson Papers.]

Boreas, English Harbour, September 25th, 1785.

My dear Brother,

I am not certain that I answered your last letter, but you see my readiness to write by every opportunity, although I have not yet received your letters by the August Packet, which has not yet arrived at this Island, and when she comes, *you know* that the distance from English Harbour to St. John's, deprives us, without we are very alert, of the opportunity of answering the letters we receive by her. You are the most exact correspondent I ever knew. But come, we must yet to ourselves.

The Boreas has been hove down, and is now fitting for Sea, to sail the 10th of October. We are all well, and every person here desires their kind remembrances to you. Rosy —your Rose—is very unwell, and is obliged to apply to an Irish physician to cure her disorder, which is what the world calls Love. A bold Major Browne of the 67th regiment is the man,[8] and the Admiral sails on Tuesday in the Latona, to join them together. God help the poor man: has he taken leave of his senses? Oh what a taste. The mother will be in a few years the handsomest of the two. The old Admiral is quite elated upon the occasion. We are not upon the strictest intimacy, but his time will soon be out for this country as well as ours.

----

[7] Vide p. 108 ante.

[8] Rose-Mary, youngest daughter of Sir Richard Hughes, married Major John Browne, of the 67th Regiment: he appears to have quitted the Army in 1789 or 1790.

Summer, 1787, will, I venture to think, land me in England. Although nothing to look back to, yet an age to look forward to: therefore neither you nor myself can tell what we shall do at that period. You may be married, or, it is not impossible, I may, or ten thousand other things may happen. If we are *in statu quo*, I accept your kind offer with many thanks, and shall certainly not forget your commissions. I have received my Father's letter by this Packet, and hope by this time he is fixed at Bath. Everybody here desires to be kindly remembered. We are all the same as you left us. Bless you, and rest assured I am, your affectionate Brother,

HORATIO NELSON.

Remember me to all who inquire after me. In reading over the letter, I find that I have not mentioned that Lady and Miss Hughes are at Barbadoes. Tell our Father I will write him by a Ship in a week or two.

TO CAPTAIN COLLINGWOOD.

[Autograph in the possession of the Honourable Mrs. Newnham Collingwood, the only surviving daughter of Vice-Admiral Lord Collingwood.]

Boreas, English Harbour, September 28th, 1785.

My dear Coll.,

Although really I am half dead, yet I will not suffer Latona to sail without answering my good Friend's letter, were it only to show, that whatever Civil prosecutions may be carried on against Officers in the execution of their duty, Ministers will afford them the protection they stand in need of. It is a great consolation to Officers who mean to serve their Country faithfully. Wilfred[1] left me a letter to send by Sandys to Barbadoes, [which] he had better have kept, as I find he has gone there. I have had letters from Mr. Suckling, who belongs to the Custom House. He is a person who has been in that Office since a boy, and is consulted in all doubtful cases relative to that Board. His letter is as follows :—

' I am sorry the conduct of some people where you are stationed should compel you to exercise that authority, which the Legislative power has so wisely reposed with the Navy for

---

[1] Captain Wilfred Collingwood.

the protection of Navigation. I have spoken to our Solicitor in regard to your proceedings: he is clearly of opinion you are warranted in your seizure of the Ships; and he says you need not apprehend but that you will be effectually supported, and the business taken up very seriously, as soon as the Irish matters are settled.'

By these accounts, we know the mind they are of at home. Mrs. Moutray, I had a letter from; they are well, but you have heard, I doubt not. My first letter from her came to me with the wafer open, but I conclude it opened itself; but it is very odd both our letters should be in the same situation. They were welcome to read mine; it was all goodness, like the dear writer. I am to get to Nevis with all expedition to catch Yankees. My dear boy, I want some prize-money. I can't write more. Bless you. My head is so bad. I pray my compliments where you are, and to Kemble. Farewell. Send to me at Nevis and St. Kitts.

HORATIO NELSON.

TO WILLIAM SUCKLING, ESQ.

[From " the Athenæum."]

Boreas, Nevis, November 14th, 1785.

My dear Sir,

Not a scrap of a pen have I by the last Packet from any relation in England; but, however, you see I don't think I am forgot, more especially when I open a business which, perhaps, you will smile at, in the first instance, and say, ' This Horatio is for ever in love.'

My present attachment is of pretty long standing; but I was determined to be fixed before I broke this matter to any person. The lady is a Mrs. Nisbet, widow of a Dr. Nisbet, who died eighteen months after her marriage, and has left her with a son. From her infancy (for her father and mother died when she was only two years of age,) she has been brought up by her mother's brother, Mr. Herbert, President of Nevis, a gentleman whose fortune and character must be well known to all the West Indian Merchants, therefore I shall say nothing upon that head. Her age is twenty-two; and her personal accomplishments you will suppose *I think* equal to any person's I ever saw: but, without vanity, her mental accomplishments are superior to most people's of either sex; and we shall come together as two persons most sincerely attached to each other from friendship. Her son is under her guardianship, but totally independent of her.

But I must describe Herbert to you, that you may know exactly how I stand; for when we apply for advice, we must tell all circumstances. Herbert is very rich and very proud, —he has an only daughter, and this niece, who he looks upon in the same light, if not higher. I have lived at his house, when at Nevis, since June last, and am a great favourite of his. I have told him I am as poor as Job; but he tells me he likes me, and I am descended from a good family, which his pride likes; but he also says, ' Nelson, I am proud, and I must live like myself, therefore I can't do much in my lifetime: when I die she shall have twenty thousand pounds; and if my daughter dies before me, she shall possess the major part of my property. I intend going to England in 1787, and remaining there my life; therefore, if you two can live happily together till that event takes place, you have my consent.' This is exactly my situation with him; and I know the way to get him to give me most, is not to appear to want it: thus circumstanced, who can I apply to but you ? The regard you have ever expressed for me leads me to hope you will do something. My future happiness, I give you my honour, is now in your power: if you cannot afford to give me any thing for ever, you will, I am sure, trust to me, that if I ever can afford it, I will return it to some part of your family. I think Herbert will be brought to give her two or three hundred a year during his life; and if you will either *give me*, I will call it—I think you will do it—either one hundred a year, for a few years, or a thousand pounds, how happy you will make a couple who will pray for you for ever. Don't disappoint me, or my heart will break: trust to my honour to do a good turn for some other person if it is in my power. I can say no more, but trust implicitly to your goodness, and pray let me know of your generous action by the first Packet.

I shall send by this Packet some queries, which I must beg you will get your Solicitor to answer, for here are divided opinions in this Country as to the right of Admirals, Captains, &c., seizing Vessels to the King's use under the Navigation Laws; and the King's Order in Council, which is directed to the Admiralty, conjointly with the Treasury, and the Admiralty have sent it to the Admiral, with an order to give directions to the Commanders of the King's Ships to see that it is complied with. Does not 'complied with' certainly mean to imply, that if I find a Vessel breaking the proclamation, I am to bring her to punishment? or a circumstance may happen—for it has happened—a Vessel comes into the Roads or Bays, when the Ship may produce to the Officer an English Register: I tell him, 'Friend, you are an American bottom, and not qualified to trade in the British Colonies.' The Master naturally says, 'Sir, my owners have ordered me here to trade, and I can't carry the Vessel to a Foreign Island.' The Master will not go away—I can't let him stay; therefore must not the Vessel be tried in Admiralty, to know whether she is, or is not, a Vessel properly qualified to carry on trade with our Colonies? I do not seize as a Custom-House Officer, *qui tam*, &c. but transmit the circumstance of the Seizure to the King's Advocate General, who prosecutes for the King alone; and if she remains forfeited, she is wholly and solely his Majesty's: after which the King may, without prejudice to any individual, give the whole, or any part, to such persons as he thinks fit. Pray get me some Legal advice upon this subject, and send me out the King's proclamation for distributing Seizures. The mercantile lawyers say that the right of the King's Ships to make Seizures by the Navigation Act, is taken away by the 13th and 14th Charles the Second, chapter 11th, section 15th, where it says, 'None shall seize but Officers of the Customs, &c., or persons authorized by Warrant from the Treasury, or by Special Commission from his Majesty, under Great or Privy Seal, and all other Seizure shall be void,' &c.

I am clearly of opinion that we do hold our Commissions eventually under the Great Seal, for the Admiralty is only a Patent place during pleasure; and that the Act seems to think so,—read the next clause, 'an indemnification for all Officers of the Customs, or any Officer or Officers, person or persons authorized to put in execution the Act for increasing

Shipping and Navigation, their Deputies,' &c. What occasion could there be to indemnify the Officers enjoined to put the Navigation Act in force, if the power had been taken away by the preceding clause? It appears to me that the Parliament was afraid it might be wrong construed, therefore included them by name in a subsequent clause. Well done, Lawyer Nelson! The 3rd of George the Third, chapter 22nd, section 4th, recites, that it may be necessary to employ Men-of-War upon the coasts of Great Britain, &c. of the colonies, &c. Are not the King's Ships here employed to see the Navigation Act and the King's Order of Council carried into effect? Yes: the Admiralty has given the Admiral such orders, and the Admiral has given them to the King's Ships. Once more, get me some Legal advice upon all this matter. Best wishes for the happiness of every part of your family, and may they enjoy the happiness 'tis so much in your power to give me; but on every occasion believe that I am,

Your most affectionate
HORATIO NELSON.

I enclose some Queries, which pray have opinions upon from eminent Lawyers.—H. N.

TO LORD SYDNEY, SECRETARY OF STATE.

[Copy, in Captain Nelson's Narrative, vide p. 179 post.]

Boreas, Nevis, November 17th, 1785.

My Lord,

An Opinion which Doctor Scott[1] has given to some questions of the Officers of the Customs at Basseterre, St. Christopher's, doubting the right of the King's Ships to seize unless they are made as Custom House Officers, will once more stir up some people in this Country against me. What are they now saying? Has the Captain of a Man-of-War *no* right to seize our Ships, although they have transgressed the Navigation Laws? The Custom House officers tell *no; * Doctor Scott has given his Opinion against the right which the Act of Navigation had formerly given them. Thus circumstanced,

---

[1] Afterwards Lord Stowell, and Judge of the Admiralty Court.

your Lordship will not be surprised at receiving a letter from
me. I am apt to think that the Officers of the Customs
stated their queries as to seizures in general, and not upon
the Navigation Laws. Upon the former grounds, I should
answer *no*, we have no right. But I contend, that if I find
a Vessel trading in these Colonies, that is either not British
built, or solely owned by British Subjects, or not navigated
according to Law, that Vessel I am strictly required to seize,
and to carry her into the Admiralty Court to be proceeded
against.

The situation of Vessels where I conceive our right of
seizure does not extend, is as follows,—A Ship arrives in
port; upon being boarded by the Officers of the King's Ship for
to examine whether she is British built, owned, and navigated
as the Law directs, and finding that she is a Vessel duly
qualified to trade in the British Colonies, we can have no
more business with her, although we should be informed she
is loaded with contraband goods. What I should do would be
to inform the Revenue Officers, for Captains of Men-of-War
are not invested with power even to stop the Ship. That
part of the Navigation Act which relates to 'built,' &c., from
the situation of Great Britain for these last hundred years,
has had very little occasion to be attended to, as British Shipping was so much cheaper than any other; and there never
was a trial upon the first part of the Navigation Act in these
Colonies till I brought it forward: therefore here I stand, the
butt for every Lawyer that pleases to throw his venom at.

My former Letters and Memorial specified that his Majesty's
proclamation was most shamefully evaded, by connivance in
some, and imposition in others, of the Officers of the Customs;
so that nearly the whole Trade, between the British Colonies
and the United States of America, was carried on in American
bottoms. To see the American Ships and Vessels, with their
Colours flying, in defiance of the Laws, and by permission of
the Officers of the Customs, loading and unloading in our Ports,
was too much for a British Officer to submit to. I could not
even by a tacit acquiescence suffer a Commerce so prejudicial
to Britain to be carried on, legal or illegal: I was fully determined to suppress it.

We know that Commerce is the enricher of every Country; and where She flourishes most, that will be the greatest Country. I felt it my duty, and certainly it was my inclination, to preserve the Carrying Trade to our Country, as it encouraged British artificers, manufacturers, and seamen. At this moment, there are nearly fifty Sail employed in the trade, between the Islands of St. Kitts, Nevis, and America, which are truly British built, owned, and navigated. Had I been an idle spectator, (without, I hope, being accused of arrogance,) my firm belief is, that not a single Vessel would have belonged to these Islands in the Foreign trade. I could wish to have the Opinion of the Crown Lawyers in England touching these matters, and Doctor Scott's Opinion. A doubt is now started, (and I may probably be persecuted in this Country upon it,) that if the Custom-House give leave to a Foreigner to trade, I have no right to hinder him, but must look on as an idle spectator. I am furnished very lately, by the Admiral, with his Majesty's Proclamation: I should even have esteemed that, a sufficient authority for bringing to punishment all those who offend against it. But Doctor Scott has, by a General Opinion, put these Islands, (which had recognised my right, and were all quiet,) in a ferment against me.

I want not—I wish not—to be a Custom-House Officer; for however honourable the protecting the Revenue is, I must for ever derive my right of protecting it, from my commission as Captain in the Navy, and not by deputation from a Board, with which I can have no possible connexion in my professional line. My sincere wish and ambition are to prove myself a faithful servant to my Country, by preserving to her the Carrying Trade to and from her own Colonies. One thing more, although of a more private nature than the other parts of my letter, I trust to your Lordship's goodness in telling me, is, whether from untoward circumstances a prosecution at Law should commence against me, shall I (if I prove it happened through an earnest endeavour to do my duty properly) be supported by Administration? I have the honour to remain, with the highest respect,

Your Lordship's most obedient, humble Servant,

HORATIO NELSON.

TO THE REVEREND MR. NELSON, BURNHAM.

[Autograph, in the Nelson Papers.]

Boreas, English Harbour, December 15th, 1785.

My dear Brother,

You are so good a correspondent, that I fear I miss answering all your letters, but let me beg this may not hinder
your exactness; for I do not, be assured, miss intentionally.
You will have heard from my Father and Mr. Suckling—indeed, I think it was hinted to you, before the hurricane
months—that I am in a fair way of changing my situation.
The dear object you must like. Her sense, polite manners, and
to you I may say, beauty, you will much admire : and although
at present we may not be a rich couple, yet I have not the
least doubt but we shall be a happy pair :—the fault must be
mine if we are not. Your rum, &c. I shall certainly procure,
and everything you want from hence. I wish you were fixed
in your house, for really you begin to be too old to walk about
the world without a fixed residence of your own. Marry
Ellen, and then you are settled for life; but in all this you
will please yourself, I know.

I told you long ago, Miss Rosy was married to Major
Browne of the 67th. They live at St. John's, and were
they to stay there till doomsday I should not ride so
far to visit them. I have the Leeward Station still, but direct
as usual to Barbadoes. We are put in here by bad weather, having sprung our mainmast, and hurt the Ship a
good deal. We are all well on board, and everybody desires
their kind remembrance to the Bishop. You are still upon
the Books as Chaplain. You will accumulate a fortune if
you proceed this way. You shall give me a horse, however.
Remember me kindly to Mrs. Bolton and her family when
you see them; to the Walpoles, and all my old acquaintances.
Bless you, and believe I am, with great truth,

Your affectionate Brother,

HORATIO NELSON.

Herbert, President of Nevis, says you seem a good fellow;
he will make a cask of remarkable fine rum for you double-
proof.

TO THE REVEREND MR. NELSON, SWAFFHAM.

[Autograph, in the Nelson Papers.]

Nevis, January 1st, 1786.

My dear Brother,

Although I wrote to my Father and your Honour by the Packet which sailed from St. Kitt's only two days ago, yet as I have received a letter from you since my last, I shall send another across the Atlantic, to say I am well, and as merry as I wish. So I must be, you will conclude, sitting by the woman who will be my wife; and every day am I more than ever convinced of the propriety of my choice, and I shall be happy with her. You will esteem her for herself when you know her; for she possesses sense far superior to half the people of our acquaintance, and her manners are Mrs. Moutray's. The Admiral lives in a Boarding-house at Barbadoes, not much in the style of a British Admiral. Lady H., with her daughter, Mrs. Browne, in St John's, Antigua. They all pack off next May, certainly, and I hope most devoutly they will take the Admiral with them, but he wishes much to remain another Station. He is too much of a fiddler for me.

Am I to think you are in Norfolk, or at Bath? You may push for Miss Dorothea, and then you will soon be a Bishop, without any interest but money, which is indeed the strongest of any. To everybody that asks after me, say, ' how d'ye?' To Mrs. Bolton, Edmund, &c., &c., love and kind remembrances. Adieu, and believe me to be, your most affectionate Brother,

HORATIO NELSON.

Mr. Herbert says he will make some fine rum for you, and you must mind and have the Norfolk turkeys, fat, ready for eating. A merry Christmas, and a happy new year. To my father and Kate give my kind love.

TO LORD SYDNEY, SECRETARY OF STATE.

[Copy, in Captain Nelson's Narrative, vide p. 179 post.]

Boreas, Nevis, February 4th, 1786.

My Lord,

Herewith I transmit you a Register which was granted at
Antigua, to an American. His story is (I have no doubt)
fact. He arrived in May, 1784, at St. John's, with no Colours
or Papers, said he was obliged to leave the Continent, (this was
a long time after the evacuation of New York,) and the man
had never been in a British Port. He gets permission in the
first instance, by a Protest that his Vessel was not fit to keep
the Sea, to sell his cargo. He then asks if he can't obtain a Register; 'Yes,' was their answer; 'if you can swear to the best of
your knowledge, that the Vessel was taken and condemned,
and that you are an Englishman, we will give you a Register.'
They then, as your Lordship will see by the Register, permit
the man to swear that the Vessel was built in America, in 1782,
was taken, and legally condemned, although the man had told
them before he had no Bill of Sale, copy of Condemnation,
or any Paper whatever. The man perjured himself, there is
no doubt; but the Custom-House appears to me to have
very negligently filled the duties of their station.

But now I shall advance a little further, that your Lordship
may have every insight it is in my power to give. The Vessel
was very old: after her cargo was sold, if the Vessel had not
been permitted to a Register, she was not worth taking away,
and would have been sold for a hulk, but obtaining a Register
she is carried back to America, where a new Vessel of the
same description is put upon the stocks. The man then makes
another voyage to Antigua, that he may be looked upon without suspicion, and his Vessel be established in the Trade. He
then, in the winter, works himself, and in the Spring, 1785,
launches a new Vessel of exactly the same dimensions. He
has been trading to several of the Islands, but has at last
fallen under my inspection, and is condemned: the man not
claiming her, only saying, if the Custom-house at St John's,
Antigua, had not granted him a Register for his old Sloop, he
should still have had his property as an American, and that he

has a great mind to prosecute them for encouraging him in taking out a British Register.

I cannot help observing how ready the Custom-Houses of this Country are to grant Registers, Entries, &c. It certainly increases their fees: whether they get anything further, your Lordship must judge, as well as myself, for it is a matter that I cannot prove, whatever I may think. They have, hitherto, in all the Islands which I have been at, uniformly opposed the King's Ship under my command: first, upon a ground that I had no right to seize, (that was tried at St. Christopher's); secondly, that the Vessel was in Port, and that I can have no business with Vessels after Entry at the Custom-house; thirdly, it is making myself a judge of their actions, which I have no authority to do. But, my Lord, I shall still go on, and to the utmost of my power, protect to effect the Commerce, the Manufacturer, the Ship-builder, and the Seamen of Great Britain, and preserve them all for Her where I am stationed. If my conduct meets with approbation at Home, I mind not the epithets bestowed upon me by these Custom-Houses. My Lord, examine well all sides, and you will soon see, that in the first place, till exemplary punishments are inflicted upon those Officers who have encouraged the Foreigners to trade with our Colonies, the evil never will cease; and after that is done, it will be found necessary to call in all old Registers, and grant a new one, and of a new form. I should conceive something like the Mediterranean Passes, for very many old Registers are daily sold to Americans, and the Custom-Houses gloss over them, although they know how they are obtained.

I shall stand acquitted by your Lordship and my Country of any interested views in thus representing these malpractices, for I have no interest to obtain any place, nor do I ever expect any but what rises from a faithful discharge of my duty; and if I am taken notice of for that, I shall always endeavour to keep in view what preferment was given me for.

I have the honour, &c.

HORATIO NELSON.

TO MRS. NISBET.

[From Clarke and M'Arthur, vol. l. p 80.]

Boreas, English Harbour, 25th Feb. 1786.

My Dear Fanny,

We landed Mr. Adye[2] yesterday afternoon at St. John's; and after a disagreeable night, here we arrived this morning. Captain Collingwood is gone into the Country, therefore from this place I sail at daylight. You are too good and indulgent; I both know and feel it: but my whole life shall ever be devoted to make you completely happy, whatever whims may sometimes take me. We are none of us perfect, and myself probably much less so than you deserve. I am, &c.

HORATIO NELSON.

TO MRS. NISBET.

[From Clarke and M'Arthur, vol. i. p. 80.]

Off the Island of Deseada, 3rd March, 1786.

Separated from you, what pleasure can I feel? none, be assured: all my happiness is centred with thee; and where thou art not, there I am not happy. Every day, hour, and act, convince me of it. With my heart filled with the purest and most tender affection, do I write this: for were it not so, you know me well enough to be certain, that even at this moment I would tell you of it. I daily thank God, who ordained that I should be attached to you. He has, I firmly believe, intended it as a blessing to me; and I am well convinced you will not disappoint his beneficent intentions.

Fortune, that is, money, is the only thing I regret the want of, and that only for the sake of my affectionate Fanny. But the Almighty, who brings us together, will, I doubt not, take ample care of us, and prosper all our undertakings. No dangers shall deter me from pursuing every honourable means of providing handsomely for you and yours; and again let me repeat, that my dear Josiah shall ever be considered by me as one of my own. That Omnipotent Being, who sees and knows what passes in all hearts, knows what I have written to

---

[2] H. C. Adye, Esq., vide p. 177, post.

be my undisguised sentiments towards the little fellow. I am uneasy, but not unwell. Nothing but the Admiral's orders to be at Barbadoes at a given time, hindered me from coming down after my letters. Sir Richard Hughes, I am certain, would have overlooked my disobedience of orders, and have thought I had served the friend, who had neglected to bring my letters, very properly. But I cannot bear the idea of disobeying orders: I should not like to have mine disobeyed: therefore I came on. However, it was a toss-up, I assure you.

[Apparently in continuation.]

March 9th.

At last we are arrived; and as we came into the bay on one side, the Adamant [3] made her appearance on the other. Captain K— has brought me one letter from Antigua; for which one, although I know there are more, I retract all my mischievous wishes; and I have received several at this place from my sister and brother; the former from Bath, where my old friend Scriviner desires to be kindly remembered to me. I don't think my dear sister knows of my intentions of altering my situation, or she would have mentioned it. My friend M. [4] is still there: but I have not a line. It is wonderful, and I cannot account for it. I know myself to be so steady in my friendships, that I cannot bear the least coolness or inattention in others. My brother takes it for granted I am a married man, and in consequence desires his love. From my uncle Suckling I have a very kind letter, saying he will do everything in his power to add to my happiness; and if I should want it, that he will give me pecuniary assistance. [5] It is strongly reported that we are to sail from this Country in June next: if that is to be the case, my time is short. All this affects my spirits, and will not allow me to feel so pleasant as I wish; and makes me the more regret that I had not paid greater attention to getting money. But I will have done with this subject. You must write often, and long letters. I am, &c.

HORATIO NELSON.

[3] The Adamant, Captain David Knox, then a Commander: he was Posted on the 10th of February 1789.

[4] Apparently Captain Moutray, who died at Bath in 1785.

[5] "This was liberally done for some years by Mr. Suckling."—*Clarke and M‘Arthur*, vol. i. p. 81.

[Autograph, in the Locker Papers]

Boreas, off Martinico, March 5th, 1786.

My dear Friend,

Your kind letter of December 5th I only received a few days ago at Antigua, for the Post-Offices here are sadly careless of our letters, and if we do not happen to be at the Island where they arrive, they will not be at the trouble of forwarding them to us. You accuse me too justly of not writing; I know myself to be a sad careless fellow in that respect, and too often neglect my best friends; but really for this last year I have been plagued to death. This Station has not been over-pleasant : had it not been for Collingwood, it would have been the most disagreeable I ever·saw. Little ——, poor fellow, between Bacchus and Venus, is scarcely ever thoroughly in his senses. I am very sorry for him, for his heart is good; but he is not fit to command a Man-of-War. His Ship is the merest privateer you ever saw—such men hurt the Service more than it is in the power of ten good ones to bring back. The rest of the Captains I know nothing of; nor am I ambitious of the honour of their acquaintance. Sir Richard Hughes you know, probably better than myself, and that he is a fiddler; therefore, as his time is taken up tuning that instrument, you will consequently expect the Squadron is cursedly out of tune. I don't like to say much against my Commander-in-Chief; there has been too much of that the late War; but as I only tell it to you as a friend, you will not let it go further than you think right. Not that I can care who knows it; for I shall produce my orders whenever I come home, from some circumstances which has lately happened.

It was near the hurricane months when I arrived in this Country, consequently nothing could be done till they were over in November, when the Squadron arrived at Barbadoes, and the Ships were to be sent to the different Islands, with orders only to examine the anchorages, and whether there was wood and water. This did not appear to me to be the intent of placing Men-of-War in peaceable times, therefore I asked Collingwood to go with me (for his senti-

ments and mine were exactly similar) to the Admiral. I
then asked him if we were not to attend to the Commerce of
our Country, and to take care that the British trade was kept
in those channels that the Navigation Laws pointed out. He
answered, he had no orders, nor had the Admiralty sent him
any Acts of Parliament. I told him it was very odd, as every
Captain of a Man-of-War was furnished with the Statutes of the
Admiralty, in which was the Navigation Act, which Act was
directed to Admirals, Captains, &c., to see it carried into execution. He said he had never seen the Book ; but having produced and read the Laws to him, he seemed convinced that
Men-of-War were sent abroad for some other purpose than to
be made a show of. (The rebel Americans at this time filled
our Ports.) Sir Richard then gave Orders to all the Squadron
to see the Navigation Act carried into execution. When I
went to my Station at St. Kitts, I turned away all the rebels,
not choosing to seize them at that time, as it would have appeared a trap for them.

In December, to my astonishment, comes down an order
from him, telling us he had received good advice, and requiring us not to hinder the Americans from coming in,
and having free egress and regress, if the Governors
chose to allow them ; and a copy of the order he sent to
the Governors and the Presidents of the Islands. The General
Shirley[6] and others began by sending letters not far different from orders, that he should admit them in such and
such situations; telling me the Admiral had left it to them,
but they thought it right to let me know it. Mr. Shirley
I soon trimmed up and silenced.[7] Sir Richard Hughes' was a
more delicate business; I must either disobey my orders, or
disobey Acts of Parliament, which the Admiral was disobey-

---

[6] General Thomas Shirley was appointed Captain-General of the Leeward Islands, in 1781, and in June 1786, was created a Baronet: he died at Bath, in
February 1800. *Stemmata Shirleiana*, 4to. 1841, p. 245.

[7] Captain Wallis says in his Narrative, that Governor Shirley, feeling irritated
at Nelson's remonstrances, told him, " That old Generals were not in the habit
of taking advice from young gentlemen ;" to which Nelson replied, " I have the
honour, Sir, of being as old as the Prime Minister of England, and think
myself as capable of commanding one of his Majesty's Ships as that Minister is
of governing the State."—*Original*, in the Nelson Papers.

ing. I determined upon the former, trusting to the uprightness of my intention, and believed that my Country would not
allow me to be ruined, by protecting her Commerce. I first,
to Sir Richard, expatiated upon the Navigation Laws to the best
of my ability; told him I was certain some person had been
giving him advice, which he would be sorry for having taken
against the positive directions of an Act of Parliament; and
that I was certain Sir Richard had too much regard for the
Commerce of Great Britain to suffer our worst Enemies to
take it from us; and that too at a time when Great Britain
was straining every nerve to suppress illegal Trade at Home,
which only affected the Revenue; and that I hoped we should
not be singular in allowing a much more ruinous traffic to be
carried on under the King's Flag; and in short, that I should
decline obeying his orders, till I had an opportunity of
seeing and talking to him, at the same time making him an
apology.

At first, I hear, he was going to send a Captain to supersede
me; but having mentioned the matter to his Captain, he was
told that he believed all the Squadron thought he had sent illegal orders, therefore did not know how far they were obliged
to obey them. This being their sentiments, he could not try
me here, and now he finds I am all right, and thanks me for
having put him right. I told the Custom-Houses I should,
after such a day, seize all Foreigners in our Islands, and keep
them out to the utmost of my power till that time: the Custom-Houses fancied I could not seize without a Deputation,
therefore disregarded my threats. In May last I seized the
first: I had the Governor, the Customs, all the Planters upon
me; subscriptions were soon filled to prosecute me; and my
Admiral stood neuter, although his Flag was then in the Roads.
Before the first Vessel was tried, I had seized four others; and
having sent for the Masters on board to examine them, and
the Marines on board the vessels, not allowing some of them
to go on shore, I had Writs taken out against me, and damages
laid for the enormous sum of £4,000 sterling.

When the Trial came on, I was protected by the Judge
for the day; but the Marshal was desired to arrest
[me], and the Merchants promised to indemnify them for
the act; but the Judge having declared he would send him

to prison if he dared to do it, he desisted. I fortunately
attached myself to an honest Lawyer; and don't let me
forget, the President of Nevis [8] offered in Court to become
my bail for £10,000, if I chose to suffer the arrest. He
told them I had done only my duty; and although he suffered more in proportion than any of them, he could not
blame me. At last, after a Trial of two days, we carried our
cause, and the vessels were condemned. I was a close prisoner on board for eight weeks, for had I been taken, I most
assuredly should have been cast for the whole sum. I had
nothing left but to send a Memorial to the King, and he
was good enough to order me to be defended at his expense,
and sent orders to Mr. Shirley to afford me every assistance
in the execution of my duty, and referring him to my letters,
&c., as there was in them, what concerned him not to have
suffered.

The Treasury, by the last Packet, has transmitted thanks
to Sir Richard Hughes, and the Officers under him, for their
activity and zeal in protecting the Commerce of Great Britain. Had they known what I have told you, (and if my
friends think I may, without impropriety, tell the story myself, I shall do it when I get Home,) I don't think they would
have bestowed thanks in that quarter and have neglected me.
I feel much hurt that after the loss of health and risk of fortune, another should be thanked for what I did against his
orders. I either deserved to be sent out of the Service, or at
least have had some little notice taken of me. They have
thought it worthy of notice, and have neglected me; if this is
the reward for a faithful discharge of my duty, I shall be
careful and never stand forward again; but I have done my
duty, and have nothing to accuse myself of.

I wish I could tell you any [thing] pleasant about your Dominica estate I would not have you lay [*illegible*] of getting much
from it; however, when I go . . . . . . inquiries what it is
worth, and what taxes are due for it. The runaway slaves
have been very troublesome at that Island. Governor Stewart's estate is entirely ruined and all the white people
killed. He is at Grenada for his health, having had a para-

---

[8] Mr. Herbert, the uncle of Mrs. Nisbet.

lytic stroke which deprived one side of him of life : it is thought
he will not recover it.   Many thanks for the inquiries of those
who   remember me.   Pray present my best compliments,
and pray do as you intend, saying as many handsome things
as you please of me to the Kirkes, not upon Miss's account,
for most probably the next time you see me will be as a Benedict.   I think I have found a woman who will make me
happy ; I will tell you more of the matter shortly, for my
paper is full.   Remember me to Kingsmill ; he is much [more]
in use than myself as to writing.   To Lord Ducie9 say compliments ; why has he never sent the younker ?   I am sorry
he has left the Service.   Adieu, my dear Friend, and believe
that I am, with the most unfeigned regard and esteem,

Yours faithfully,

HORATIO NELSON.

Captain Sandys quitted the Latona on the 8th of March.

TO WILLIAM SUCKLING, ESQ.

[From " the Athenæum."]

Boreas, Carlisle Bay, March 9th, 1786.

My dear Uncle,

Your kind letter of January 3rd I received yesterday on my
arrival here from Nevis.   When I made application to you in
November, it was, I assure you, not so much considering you
in the light of a near relation as of a sincere friend, who
would do every [thing] which was proper for the happiness of
one who sincerely regarded and esteemed him, and whose
friendship was pure, without any interested views in it ; and
had it not been for one sentence in your letter, viz. 'Your application has in a great degree deprived me of my free agency,'
I should have been supremely happy ; but my feelings are too
quick, and I feel sharply what perhaps others would not, so

---

9 The Honourable Francis Reynolds, Lord Ducie, who was made a Post Captain in April 1762, and distinguished himself on many occasions, particularly in
Lord Rodney's action.   He succeeded as 4th Lord Ducie, in September 1785,
and soon after retired from the Service.   Lord Ducie died in August 1808.

they gained their ends. That sentence would make me suppose that you thought I conceived I had a right to ask pecuniary assistance: if you did think so, be assured you did me great injustice; for I was convinced, that whatever you might be kind enough to do for me, must spring from your own generous heart, and not from any shadow of right I could be fool enough to suppose I derived from our relationship.

Relations are not always the people we are to look up to for doing friendly offices. O my dear uncle! you can't tell what I feel—indeed, I can hardly write, or know what I am writing: you would pity me did you know what I suffer by that sentence —for although it does not make your act less generous, yet it embitters my happiness. You must know me, and consequently that I am guided by the strictest rules of honour and integrity; and that had I not been more ambitious of fame than money, I should not most probably [have] been under the necessity of making the present application to you. No dangers or difficulties shall ever deter me from doing my utmost to provide handsomely for my dearest Fanny, for with the purest and most tender affection do I love her. Her virtues and accomplishments are not more conspicuous than her goodness of heart and gentleness of disposition; and you will esteem her for herself when you know her.

Your readiness in giving, my dear Friend, will not make me more anxious to receive; for can I live without your putting yourself to the inconvenience of advancing me money, I certainly shall do it, for my disposition is not that of endeavouring to grasp all it can. The greatest felicity I can enjoy is to make her happy; for myself I can care but little when she is considered; and I could lay down my life with pleasure at this moment for her future happiness. After what I have written, you will believe my love is founded upon that strong basis which must have the appearance of enjoying happiness with her. I will endeavour, as much as my indisposed mind will let me, to answer all your questions about her son and herself.

When Mrs. Nisbet married, Mr. Herbert promised two thousand pounds with her; but as her husband settled in the Island, where he died a few months after, it never has been paid. Mr. H. told me he had given, and should pay to the child

one thousand pounds when he grew up; and that he should
bring him up at his expense, and put him in a way of providing for himself. Mr. Nisbet (the gentleman whose wife went
astray) was a brother. His estate, I understand from Mr.
Herbert, owes for money lent, and attending it as Doctor, about
300*l.* Currency; but Dr. Nisbet dying insane, without a Will,
or any Papers which were regular, has made this business
rather troublesome, as Mr. Nisbet wishes to pay as little as
he can help. Mr. Stanley, the Attorney General, whose property is next Mr. Herbert's and who is his particular friend,
has undertaken to settle it for her.

She will not get much; but it must, I conceive, make her
little fellow independent. Her Uncle, although he is a man
who must have his own way in everything, yet I believe has
a good and generous heart, and loves her and her son very
sincerely; and I have every reason to suppose is as much
attached to me as to any person who could pay their addresses
to his dear Fanny, as he always calls her. Although his income is immense, yet his expenses must be great, as his house
is open to all strangers, and he entertains them most hospitably.
I can't give you an idea of his wealth, for I don't believe he
knows it himself. Many estates in that Island are mortgaged
to him. The stock of Negroes upon his estate and cattle are
valued at 60,000*l.* sterling: and he sends to England (average
for seven years) 500 casks of sugar. His daughter's fortune
must be very large: and as he says, and told me at first, that
he looked upon his niece as his child, I can have no reason to
suppose that he will not provide handsomely for her. I had
rather wish, that whatever he may do at her marriage, may
flow spontaneously from himself.

I have not an idea of being married till nearly the time
of our sailing for England, which I did not think was to be till
1787; but report says, (which I don't believe, by-the-bye, but
you can ask Mr. Stephens,[1]) we are to go Home this summer;
but I thought it right to know every sentiment of my friends
upon a business of this moment. I have tried your patience
I am sure, therefore will have done. Pray send to Marsh
and Creed, my Agents, and ask if they have heard anything

---

[1] The Secretary to the Admiralty.

of the Appeal. I wrote to them what I would have done,
and I have not had a line from them to know, whether they
have ever received the letter. I can't write to my Father,
that perhaps you will have the goodness to say—I am well.

Pray remember me most kindly to all your family, and to
any gentlemen of the village[2] who do me the favour of asking
after me, and believe that I am with the greatest affection,

Your obliged Nephew,
Horatio Nelson.

Some time ago (two months), a Whaler called the Yorick,
arrived here from the Southern Fishery. He had no Register,
but had a Clearance from London, where he said he was
bound, and no other Papers whatsoever. Pray inquire if such
a Ship ever arrived, as I believe she is run away with, and
probably the Master got rid of by unfair means. If I had met
I certainly should have put a Lieutenant into her, and sent her
to London to have the business cleared up, as the man said
his owner lived there.

TO MRS. NISBET.

[From Clarke and M'Arthur, vol. i. p. 81.]

Boreas, Carlisle Bay, March 25th, 1786.

My dear Fanny,

Most probably, when the Packet arrives, the Admiral's
Schooner will be so soon hurried away, that I shall not have a
moment's time to write . . . . . The inhabitants here are
heartily tired of my company. I am ready to give them my
room; and they may assure themselves, I will not trouble them
one moment longer than I can help: for although my person
is with them, my heart, thoughts, and affections are far off.
Upwards of a month from Nevis. When I sailed, I hoped by
this time to have been there again: but how uncertain are
human expectations, and how vain the idea of fixing periods
for happiness. I am anxious, yet sometimes fear to receive
Mr. Herbert's answer to my letter: yet why I should fear, I

<hr style="width:30%">

[2] Kentish Town.

know not; for I conceive I wrote nothing but what was proper and right. What signify professions of friendship, if they are never to be put to the test? You, my dear Fanny, are all I care about: if you are satisfied, you will readily believe me, when I say, I shall. But I will give up the subject, and hope for the best.

The Admiral lives very retired. I have twice dined with him. We are good friends, nor do I think I should soon disagree with him. He seems ready to do everything I can wish him, and only wants to be well informed. The Governor[3] and Mrs. Parry are very civil: they have given me a general invitation, and always appear glad to see me. For the last week a French Man-of-War has been here:[4] and going about with them so much in the sun has given me violent headaches. I shall expect you will send me a long epistle.

March 29th.

I am involved in Law, and have Custom-House, &c. &c. upon me: but I fear not, being conscious of the rectitude of my intentions. The Admiral is highly pleased with my conduct here, as you will believe, by sending me such fine lines with a white hat. I well know I am not of abilities to deserve what he has said of me: but I take it as they are meant, to show his regard for me; and his politeness and attention to me are great: nor shall I forget it. I like the man, although not all his acts. If you should show the lines to any person, I desire it may not be to any Officers of the Squadron with you, as the compliment is paid to me at their expense. You will understand this as meant to extend to the very near relations of the parties: indeed, I do not wish to have them shown to any one. How is my dear Josiah? Bless you; and believe that I am, with the purest affection, yours most sincerely,

HORATIO NELSON.

---

[3] David Parry, Esq.

[4] It was probably this French frigate that was alluded to in Captain Wallis's Narrative, though from writing twenty years after the event, he places the transaction in 1785. " After the hurricane months were over, and the Boreas at anchor in Nevis Road, a French frigate passed to leeward close along shore. Captain Nelson had information that this Frigate was destined on a survey of our Islands, and had on board two General Officers and

TO THE KING'S ATTORNEY, AND ADVOCATE-GENERAL[5] AT BARBADOES.

[From a Copy in the Admiralty.]

Boreas, Barbadoes, April 6th, 1786.

Sir,

Having a Brig on the 15th of last month, as forfeited to the use of his Majesty, which I hear this day the Judge has refused to try unless I will seize her for myself as well as the King, therefore I think it right for me to acquaint you that the vessel was seized by me for the use of the King. You will, Sir, by your Office make such application to his Excellency the Governor, as you think fit, in order that the vessel may be tried, and his Majesty not lose his rights, through wilful neglect of any person.

I am, Sir, &c.

HORATIO NELSON.

some Engineers for that purpose, which information proved correct. Captain Nelson immediately determined to attend her, and prevent their intentions: therefore he immediately got under weigh and pursued her. On the next day we found her at anchor in the Road of St. Eustatia and the Boreas was anchored at about two cables' length on the French frigate's quarter. After a reciprocity of civilities, salutes, &c., had passed on all sides, Captain Nelson with his Officers were invited to meet the French Officers at dinner next day at the Dutch Governor's, which was accepted; and it was at this dinner that Captain Nelson made known his intentions to the Captain of the French Frigate. He said that understanding he intended visiting the English Islands, he thought it his duty to accompany him in the English Frigate, that attention may be paid to the Officers of his Most Christian Majesty, which he was sure every Englishman in the Islands would be proud of an opportunity of doing. This declaration did not appear palatable to the French Generals, and was politely refused by them as well as by the Captain of the French frigate, saying that their intention was only to take a cruize round the Islands, without stopping at any. However, Captain Nelson was determined not to be out-done in *civility*, and strictly adhered to his purpose. The Frenchman perceiving the English Commander's drift, in a few days abandoned his project, got under weigh, and beat up to Martinique. Captain Nelson availed himself of the same opportunity, and beat up to Barbadoes, by which he never lost sight of the French frigate until she got into Martinique, where she came from."

[5] Charles Brandford, Esq.

TO MRS. NISBET.

[From Clarke and M'Arthur, vol. i. p. 84.]

Boreas, Carlisle Bay, April 17, 1786.

My dearest Fanny,

I have been looking out anxiously for some time past, for the Adamant and Berbice, making sure of the pleasure of receiving a letter—but it is not to happen : therefore I must write what I know, and not answers to what you send. My letters from my sister and brother are very kind ; and, from the former, filled with every sentiment of affection for you. I am involved in Law : and although everything will go as I wish it, yet I fear it will keep me this fortnight. I shall wish the Vessels at the devil, and the whole Continent of America to boot.

Lord Hood has the command at Portsmouth. I had a letter from him by the Packet. I am all anxiety to hear and know what I have to hope for from Leeward.

April 23rd.

All the Squadron are now here holding Court-Martials, which will finish to-morrow, when they return to their respective Stations, except poor me, who am kept to take care of two Yankees ; I wish they were a hundred fathoms under water : and when I am likely to be released, I have not the smallest idea . . . . On Tuesday or Wednesday the Adamant sails for Antigua with Sir Richard—so much for the Flag-ship ; I should be sorry to have one : a Captain in her is never his own master. I am so much out of temper with this Island, that I would rather sacrifice anything than stay. I have been upon the best terms with the Admiral, and I declare I think I could ever remain so. He is always remarkably kind and civil to every one : I told him that no one could think otherwise but you, and I hoped you would be angry with him for keeping me away so very long. Whenever I can settle about my prizes here, I shall sail directly for Nevis.

How is my little Josiah ?—I sent yesterday, the moment the Admiral told me the Schooner was going to Nevis, for nobody but myself knew it, as polite a note as I was able to ———— . The servant brought word back, there was no answer; not even 'much obliged,' 'thank you,' or any other word but what I have told you: I may be uncivilly treated once, and then it is my misfortune: but if I put it in any person's power to be so a second time, it's my fault.—Farewell for a little time; and bless you, with all my heart and soul; and do believe, and never doubt, but that I am, with the most sincere affection, ever your

HORATIO NELSON.

TO MRS. NISBET.

[From Clarke and M'Arthur's Life of Nelson, vol. i. p. 84.]

Boreas, May 4th, 1786, Barbarous Island.

My dearest Fanny,

Never, never, do I believe, shall I get away from this detestable spot. Had I not seized any Americans, I should now have been with you: but I should have neglected my duty, which I think your regard for me is too great, for you to have wished me to have done. Duty is the great business of a Sea-officer. All private considerations must give way to it, however painful it is. But I trust that time will not have lessened me in the opinion of her, whom it shall be the business of my future life to make happy. Bless you, bless you. Ever, with the greatest affection, your

HORATIO NELSON.

TO THE DIRECTORS OF THE EAST INDIA COMPANY.

[Original, in the East India House.]

Boreas, Carlisle Bay, Barbadoes, May 5th, 1786.

Gentlemen,

A circumstance which has happened at these Islands, I think is of very material consequence to your China Trade, &c., therefore I take the earliest opportunity of acquainting you of it. Many persons have known of this event before it reached me, and I hope they have transmitted accounts of it to you; but, for fear they should not, I have taken the liberty of doing it.

A Mr. William Robinson of London bought, about two years ago, a twenty-gun Ship, (which was sold by [the] Navy Board,) called the Hydra. This Ship he fitted out in the Thames, loaded her with a cargo of goods, and cleared her at the Custom-house, London, for New York. A Mr. Green, late Secretary to Admiral Arbuthnot, is Supercargo of her. Instead of proceeding to New York, she has been trading upon the Coromandel Coast, at Bengal, and at China, under American Colours and Papers, and after a successful voyage arrived at St. Eustatia, the latter end of March, where she is dispersing her cargo of tea, saltpetre, &c., &c., over the British West Indies. A Mr. Hamilton of Nevis, I hear, has purchased upwards of one hundred tons of saltpetre out of her.

I understand she intends returning to London, and to play the same double game over again ; to prevent which I transmit you this account, and that you may take such measures as you think proper to prevent these iniquitous practices in future.

I can only lament that the King's Ship under my command was removed from the Station at St. Christopher's and Nevis, on the last of February to this Island, or let me assure you that I should have thought it my indispensable duty to have gone to St. Eustatia, and demanded the Ship and cargo, which I hope to have been able to prevail upon the Dutch to have given up, when I should have sent her to your House, to be dealt with according to Law.

I have the honour to remain, Gentlemen, &c.

HORATIO NELSON.

TO THE REVEREND MR. NELSON, HILBOROUGH.

[Autograph, in the Nelson Papers.]

Boreas, Barbadoes, May 5th, 1786.

My dear Brother,

Your letters of January and February are yet unanswered, nor is it through any fault of mine ; but I have been so much taken up here in a little business concerning Yankees. Everybody is against me, therefore I have a very unpleasant time, you will believe. But why should I carry my troubles

across the Atlantic? I will have done. I have been here
nearly three months, nor do I know when I shall be released.
Kelly [6] was married the 23rd of March, and he expects to sail
for England next month. Whether we go or not this year,
is quite uncertain. I am inclined to think we shall stay
another year, but Lord Howe [7] is so close, nothing is to be got
out of him. Sir Richard wishes to remain another Station,
perhaps more so, now Lady Hughes is gone home. She
was to sail from English Harbour in the Unicorn, which has
gone, I dare say, before this date. Mrs. Browne goes with her,
and carries a young Major. You will hear of them, I dare
say, before you are long in England.

We are as dead as to news, as you can possibly conceive, and telling only about ourselves is dull indeed.
Mr. Wallis [8] was left at Nevis, unwell, but he has been
so long there, that I am told he has got quite fat. Old
Jammy Jameson, [9] was down in the Berbice for the benefit of the Nevis hot-baths, as he had the rheumatism very
bad. All else are well. Sandys went home a passenger
in the Unicorn. I told you, I think, before, Captain
Berkeley [1] had the Latona, and Gregory [2] the Falcon. As
to myself, I am well, and notwithstanding all my struggles
in this country with bad people, I am perfectly at ease, so far,
as I am conscious of the rectitude and uprightness of my
conduct; and it is my not allowing them to continue inimical
to the Commerce of Great Britain that has drawn down the
displeasure of all the folks upon me. One sends me a
challenge; another Laws me: but I keep them all off, nor

---

[6] Captain William Hancock Kelly, third son of Arthur Kelly, Esq., of Kelly
in Devonshire. He was made a Post-Captain, 8th August 1783, married Sally,
daughter of Magnus Morton, Esq., a Judge in Nevis, and died a Vice-Admiral
of the Blue in May 1811.—Burke's *Dictionary of the Landed Gentry,* Ed.
1844, p. 667. Mrs. Kelly was a first cousin of Viscountess Nelson, their
mothers having been sisters of John Richardson Herbert, Esq., President of Nevis.

[7] First Lord of the Admiralty.

[8] First Lieutenant of the Boreas.

[9] Master of the Boreas.

[1] Captain the Honourable George Cranfield Berkeley, who was made a Post-
Captain in 1780, and died an Admiral and G.C.B., in 1818.

[2] George Gregory, who was posted on the 22nd November 1790: he commanded the Veteran in the Battle of Camperdown, and became a Flag Officer
in 1810.

have they been able to do the least thing to injure me.   I am
not married yet.   In England you think these matters are
done in a moment.   If you had considered I was a Sailor, and
what should I do carrying a wife in a Ship, and when I marry
I do not mean to part with my wife.   I can't say much, for
this comes by a Merchant-ship, and possibly it may never
reach you, but believe me always to be with real truth your
most affectionate brother,

HORATIO NELSON.

Remember me to all who inquire after me, to Mrs. Bolton,
Edward Suckling, &c., &c.   Everybody on board desires to
be remembered.

TO PHILIP STEPHENS, ESQ., ADMIRALTY.

[Original, in the Admiralty.]

Boreas, May 21st, 1786.

Sir,

Sir Richard Hughes having directed me to forward all such
other papers and letters, relative to the Vessels seized by me
in Carlisle Bay, Barbadoes, as had been written to, or received by me, since those transmitted by him, I do therefore
inclose all copies of papers and letters which I have in my
possession.[3]   I can't help observing there is in the Judge's
conduct what appears very extraordinary, and their Lordships will notice it, as well as myself.   In Captain Collingwood's cause, the Judge declared, that as Captain Collingwood had not a Deputation, he had no right to bring forward
an information for himself, as well as the King, for the Law

[3] The enclosures consisted of Informations (Captain Nelson's Letter to the
Attorney General, of the 6th of April, p. 166 ante); Letters from the Attorney
General to Captain Nelson, highly approving of his conduct, and censuring that
of the Judge; and other Papers on the subject, none of which are now of sufficient interest to justify their insertion.   In reply to a Letter from the Attorney-
General, Nelson said, on the 13th of April 1786, " I wrote to the Attorney-
General, telling him that as the Judge had ordered the Information to be
altered to a *qui tam* one, I supposed the Ship's company would not mind having
their names inserted; but that it was impossible I could give consent to have
mine mentioned, as I had seized the Vessels as forfeited to his Majesty."

says, I understand, that none shall file Informations, but Revenue Officers, or the King's Attorney-General. Now, in my cause, he declares, he will not receive an Information filed by the King's Attorney-General; what can I suppose, but that the Judge is determined not to try any Vessels seized by the Navy? I leave the propriety of such conduct to their Lordships, as he is an Officer immediately dependant on them.

I remain, Sir, &c.,

HORATIO NELSON.

CAPTAIN NELSON'S NARRATIVE OF HIS PROCEEDINGS IN SUPPORT OF THE NAVIGATION ACT FOR THE SUPPRESSION OF ILLICIT TRAFFIC IN THE WEST INDIES: APPARENTLY WRITTEN TOWARDS THE END OF JUNE 1786.

[From a Copy, signed by Captain Nelson, in the possession of William Henry Whitehead, Esq. This Copy was probably sent to Prince William Henry.]

The Boreas arrived in Barbadoes in June 1784. I very soon found that the Bay was full of Americans, who were lading and unlading without molestation. I inquired of Captain Sotherby, who had commanded a Post ship on this Station before the Peace, and of Captain Boston, who commanded the Latona, if the Americans traded with our Islands, and if they had no Orders from the Admiral to keep them from trading with the British Colonies. They both told me they had no Orders to hinder them from coming to our Ports, and they had never done it. Captain Boston showed me his Orders, which had not a syllable in them indicating a wish to see the Navigation Act was attended to.

Captain Collingwood[4] told me he was very much afraid that the Navigation Act was not in the least attended to by the Admiral, for the Colonies were full of Americans, which the Custom House encouraged (by their conduct) to trade to our Islands, instead of seizing them, which they ought to have done, agreeable to the Act of Navigation, their oath, and the instructions of the Board of Customs.

In July, the Squadron was laid up in English Harbour for

---

[4] Captain Cuthbert Collingwood of the Mediator, afterwards Vice-Admiral Lord Collingwood.

the hurricane season. I was once or twice at St. John's, at which place the American flags were by far the most numerous; and had it been possible I could have been set down from the air, I should most assuredly have been convinced I had been in an American, instead of a British Port.

I heard one of the Masters of these Americans say, he had given five joes for his permission to unload. I am convinced there had better not be any Officers than bad ones; for they encourage these people to transgress our Laws, which they dare not do so openly, if they had not permission. I told Sir Richard Hughes of what I had seen, but he seemed not to take any notice of it, more than saying, he believed it was the case in all the Islands; and to show Sir Richard Hughes's sentiments upon this matter more fully, the following is an extract of a letter from Captain Collingwood of the Mediator, at Grenada,[5] with the Admiral's answer:—

'I must inform you, Sir, that Ships and Vessels sometimes arrive here, and load, which I very much suspect to be the property of Americans. It is true they generally procure Papers and a Register, representing them the property of merchants in the Colonies, which may pass them on a cursory examination, yet they are not less Americans and navigated by Foreign seamen. It is from the idea that the greatness and the superiority of the British Navy very much depends on preserving inviolate the Act of Navigation, excluding Foreigners from access to the Colonies, that I am induced to make this representation to you, and to request that I may receive your particular instructions relative to them.'

Answer —'The circumstance you mention of a number of American vessels appearing to carry on a trade with these Islands, is, I find, common to the whole of them, and their admission into the several Ports, together with the disposal of their cargo, I conceive to rest entirely with the Civil Governors, and the Collector of the Customs, who have particular instructions on that behalf; and therefore I should not choose to interfere in any such matter, especially as I have no instructions so to do. But I agree with you, that the Americans have many methods of procuring Registers and other Papers to serve their particular purposes, and probably by very illegal and improper means.'

In the beginning of November 1784, the whole Squadron rendezvoused at Barbadoes to receive their Orders, when I received mine. I found no orders whatever relative to these Foreigners (Americans) trading to our Colonies. I found the orders of Captain Collingwood were similar to mine: there-

---

[5] Sir Richard Hughes.

fore, upon consideration with Captain Collingwood, we thought it proper and right to ask the Admiral what he would have us do, in regard to the Act of Navigation, which Act requires us to seize Foreigners trading to our Colonies, and was particularly directed to Admirals, Commanders, &c.

On the 10th of November, I went with Captain Collingwood to wait upon the Admiral, saying that as his orders had not mentioned anything relative to the trade of the Islands, I was come to ask him about it. With respect, I took the liberty of mentioning I thought that the Men-of-War were placed in this Country in times of Peace, not merely to guard against any sudden attack, but for the more especial purpose of taking care that our Trade was carried on through those channels which the Legislature had ordered, and that it was to be carried on in British built Vessels, Vessels entirely owned by British Subjects, and navigated with the Master and three-fourths of the mariners British, agreeable to the Act of Navigation, which I looked upon the wisdom of the Legislature had directed to us, knowing that Sea Officers must be the best of judges of Vessels, and the best investigators of everything concerning them; that I felt myself not only authorized, but required. The Admiral stopped me from proceeding, by asking me if I had got the Act of Navigation, that no Instructions had been sent from the Admiralty to him about those matters. I observed, that the Act of Navigation was furnished, I believe, to every Officer in the Navy, as were a number of Maritime Laws, in a book entitled 'The Statutes of the Admiralty.' He desired to see my book, for he had not one; and next morning desired to see Captain Collingwood and myself on the subject. We attended the Admiral, and showed him the Act of Navigation, which he said he had never seen or noticed before, but that he should now give orders to the Ships to see it carried into execution. Accordingly the following order was given to the Squadron :—

'By Sir Richard Hughes, Bart, &c. &c. &c.

'Whereas I think it my particular duty to take care that all the powers given and directed to be preserved and enforced by the Act of Navigation, passed in the 12th year of the Reign of King Charles the Second, entitled, An Act for encouraging and increasing of Shipping and Navigation, shall be regularly and constantly observed by the Squadron serving under my command, as far as the said Act relates to the exclusion of all Foreigners from trading with any of the West India Colonies belonging unto Great Britain.

'You are hereby required and directed (as far as shall unto you respectively appertain) to cause the said Act above-mentioned to be constantly complied with in all its force and forms, remembering that all the States of North America, which do not now remain under the Dominion of his Majesty, are to be considered as Foreigners, and excluded from all Commerce with the Islands in these Seas, in like manner as the prohibition extends to other Foreign Nations; and you are hereby authorised and required to proceed against all attempts of illicit Trade by the Americans, or any other standing in the above predicament, as the Act of Navigation commands and directs, For doing all which this shall be your order and sufficient warrant.

'Given, &c. Adamant, Barbadoes,
'12th November, 1784,
'By Command of the Admiral,   'RICHARD HUGHES.
'Leonard Horner.

'To Captain Nelson, Boreas.'

The Rattler Sloop, Captain Wilfred Collingwood, was put under my command, and we were stationed at the Leeward Islands, except Antigua.

I went to Tortola, &c., and came back to Barbadoes in December, where I began my career by turning away all the American Vessels who attempted to enter the Port. On the 4th of January [1785] I arrived at Montserrat, where I found an American Schooner, which had landed her cargo. I turned him away with a caution of never being found again amongst our Islands. I did not think proper to seize him, as the Custom-House was much more to blame than the man; for he was under his National Colours, and had no appearance of an attempt to impose on, or deceive, the Officers of the Revenue. On the 7th, I arrived at Nevis, where I found another American, who I turned away, not choosing to seize him for similar reasons. On the 9th, I went to Basseterre Road, St. Christopher's, where I found the Rattler. Captain Collingwood acquainted me of the numerous American Vessels who frequented that Island, and that he had turned away all he had found, but that if ever the Ship went out of Port for a few days, the Custom-House allowed them to fill again; that a Protest was all the Custom-House required, and the Americans were always very compliant in furnishing whatever the rules of Office required at the expense of any number and sort of oaths that were wished for.

Two days after my arrival, I received the following order :—

' By Sir Richard Hughes, Bart., &c.

' Whereas, since the delivery of my order to you of the 12th of November last, (relative to enforcing a due obedience to the Act of Navigation passed in the 12th year of the reign of King Charles II.,) I have more fully and maturely considered what is required and authorised to be done by his Majesty's Commanders and Naval Forces, conformable to the said Act, and having likewise received the Opinion of the King's Attorney-General upon that subject, I do now think proper to require you, in the execution of my first order here referred to, to observe the following directions, and in future to act agreeable thereunto.

' When any Foreign Ship or Vessel shall appear disposed to come into or anchor in any part of the British Leeward Islands, within the limits of your Station, or where you may occasionally be found with his Majesty's Ship under your command, you are to cause the said Ship or Vessel to be anchored near the King's Ship, and there order her to remain (except in case of immediate and urgent distress), until her arrival and situation in all respects shall be reported to his Majesty's Governor (or his Representative for the time being) at any of the British Islands where you may happen to fall in with the said Foreign Ship or Vessel ; and if after such report shall have been made and received, the Governor or his Representative shall think proper to admit the said Foreigner into the Port or Harbour of the Island where you may then be, you are on no account to hinder or prevent such Foreign Ship or Vessel from going in accordingly, or to interfere any further in her subsequent proceedings. For doing which, this shall be your order and sufficient warrant.

' Given, &c., Adamant, Barbadoes,
' By Command of the Admiral,   ' 29th December 1784,
' Leonard Horner.   ' RICHARD HUGHES.
' To Capt. Nelson,
' Boreas.'

Upon which I sent the following Letter.

[Vide Letter to Sir Richard Hughes, p. 114, ante.]

This order I was exceedingly sorry to see from the hands of Sir Richard Hughes. I was convinced that his easy temper had made him the dupe of some artful people, whose interest it so much was to see the Americans fill the Ports of our Islands. It attached the inhabitants to them; it also filled their pockets; and to fill them, it is my firm opinion they would not stop at any means, however injurious to Great Britain. These gentry well knew, that if the Men-of-War were once seriously determined to suppress this evil, that many emoluments would cease, and that they would in time be exposed by the tricks which had been played. It was their business, first of all, to insinuate we had no authority to seize; that the part of the Navigation Act upon which he had founded his Order of the 12th of November, was repealed; and that no person could seize Vessels of any description whatever, but by Deputation from the Board of Customs.

As by Law, I could not lay by and see these Foreign Vessels trade, which they would most certainly have obtained leave to do, had they any communication with the Shore, I constantly turned them away without allowing them to land. But whenever the Ship was absent, the Ports were filled, and upon the Man-of-War's coming in sight, they cut or slipped and got away. In January I sent the Rattler to Sandy Point to take copies of the American-built Vessels' Registers granted by the Custom-House of that place. All that were there, were American-built. In short, I found that all our Trade would be very soon carried on in American-built Vessels,—Vessels manned entirely by American seamen; and not only those disadvantages, they were, I believe I may say all, owned by the Subjects of the States of America, and only covered by British people, or Americans settled in our Islands. The Custom-Houses seemed to glory in the ruin they were heaping upon Great Britain, and seemed to think they were beyond the reach of power, for they minded nothing if the men would but swear official oaths. The following Letter I sent to Mr. Stephens, Secretary of the Admiralty:—

[Vide Letter to Mr. Stephen, dated 18th January 1785, p. 116, ante.]

Finding my character, both as a Man and an Officer, infamously traduced, I thought it proper to write the following Letter to Lord Sydney, Secretary of State.

[Vide Letter to Lord Sydney, dated 20th March 1785, p. 129, ante.]

Such being the conduct of the Officers of the Customs, I felt myself obliged, for the benefit of my Country, to declare that, after the 1st day of May 1785, I would seize all American Vessels trading to our Islands, let them be Registered by whom they might. The Custom-House laughed at my presumption (as I understood), and said I had no right, and dare not do it, for if I did it, that I should be sued, and cast in damages. To show my determination, on the 2nd of May 1785, I seized the Schooner Eclipse for being an American-built Vessel, owned at Philadelphia, and navigated entirely by Americans, although she was Registered at St. Christopher's. Upon laying the case before the Crown Lawyer, he doubted my right of seizing, as is seen by the following Letter:—

'Sir,

'I am just favoured with your letter, referring me to the Act of Navigation for the propriety of your making the seizure of the Schooner Eclipse or Amity, and your inference from that Act that the Custom-House have nothing to do with her. If you will attend to a subsequent Act made in the 5th year of his present Majesty, cap. 45, sect. 26, (as I make no doubt but you have the Acts of Trade on board), you will find that seizures made at Sea, nevertheless refer to an authority for making them, which is given by a proper Deputation from the Commissioners of the Customs for that purpose. I presume if you have not one yourself, some of your Officers on board have, as it is customary to have such in most of the King's Ships. (Captain Collingwood informed me he has one.) In this case you will have a right to prosecute without the intervention of the Custom-House Officers. I apprehend from a letter written by you to the Collector, which he has just brought to me, that you are of the same sentiments; and I shall therefore only add that I shall be happy on any occasion, in the prosecution of my duty, if the condemnation of this or any other seizure can be productive of an adequate compensation to you, for your zeal and activity in bringing offences of this nature to light.

'I am, Sir, your obedient humble Servant,
'A. C. ADYE.

'Basseterre, 3rd May, 1785.
'Captain Nelson.'

Notwithstanding Mr. Adye's doubts as to my right of seizing by virtue of my commission as Captain of the Navy, he proceeded in the suit. The Custom-House likewise came and seized her, as they asserted I had no right. On the 17th, the Trial came on against me. The Customs had retained several Lawyers. Mr. Adye said much as to seizing for the King, but in such a manner as appeared to me that although his inclination was the best in the world to serve the cause, yet he did not think my right of seizing could be established. I was therefore necessitated to plead for myself; and after much being said on all sides, the Judge thought fit to give it in my favour, by saying I had an undoubted right to seize Vessels transgressing the Navigation Laws. However, Mr. Adye might have been overseen in his Opinion as to the right of Seizure, in a few days, after studying the Maritime

Laws and his Majesty's Proclamation, he was perfectly convinced that I was right, and all the Lawyers, &c., wrong; and
by his manly, upright, honourable conduct since, in supporting the Rights of the Navy, he has made most ample
amends for any doubts he might at first have entertained.
In justice to him I must say, that by night as by day his
advice has always been ready, and that too without fee or reward.
On the 23rd I seized four Vessels at Nevis for carrying
British Registers, although they were American-built, navigated by all Americans, and some of them entirely owned by
Foreigners. Two of them were Registered at the Leeward
Islands; one at Dominica by Governor Orde; and the other
at St. Lucia during the time of the British, but had since
been trading at Barbadoes. On the 25th Sir Richard
Hughes arrived. He did not appear to me to be pleased
with my conduct; at least, he did not approve of it, but told
me I should get into a scrape. On the 27th, Writs were
taken out against me for four thousand pounds, and I understood subscriptions were set on foot in the Islands to carry on
the prosecution against me. Seven weeks I was kept a
close prisoner to my Ship; nor did I ever learn that the Admiral took any steps for my release. I had no alternative to
save myself from being ruined, but to lay my case in a Memorial before the King. My Commander-in-Chief did not
even acquaint the Admiralty Board how cruelly I had been
treated; nor of the attempts which had been made to take
me out of my Ship by force, and that indignity offered under
the fly of his Flag.

[See the MEMORIAL to the KING, in p. 134, ante. Then followed the Copy
of " A Representation of the Illegal Trade which is now carrying on between
' the United States of America and the Island of St. Christopher's," &c. inserted in p. 136, ante.]

After these Seizures I kept the coast clear of Yankees,
until the hurricane season, when I repaired to English Harbour. The Admiral seemed much pleased when I paid him
prize money; but to the end of the Station, his order of the
29th of December 1784, was never repealed, so that I always
acted with a rod over me.

In September I received a Letter from Lord Sydney, acquainting me that his Majesty had been graciously pleased to order me to be defended by his Lawyers.

On the 17th of October I sailed from English Harbour, and on the 21st I seized the Brig Active for being an American-built Vessel navigated contrary to Law. I found a violent ferment in men's minds relative to an Opinion which Doctor Scott had sent out to the Officers of the Customs of Basseterre; and great doubts had arisen as to the propriety of my seizing. I therefore wrote the following Letter to Lord Sydney:

[Vide Letter to Lord Sydney, dated 17th November 1785, p. 147, ante.]

In November, I received from the Admiralty the following extract of a Letter from Mr. Rose, Secretary of the Treasury, to Mr. Stephens, Secretary of the Admiralty:—

' I am commanded by their Lordships to desire you will acquaint the Lords Commissioners of the Admiralty that my Lords are of Opinion the Commander-in-Chief of the Leeward Islands and Officers under him have shown a very commendable zeal in endeavouring to put a stop to the illicit practices which were carrying on in the Islands, in open violation of the Law, and to the great detriment of the Navigation and Trade of his Majesty's Dominions.'

It is not from a wish that Sir Richard Hughes or any other person should not be thanked for the Services they have rendered, but I own I was surprised that the Commander-in-Chief should be thanked for an act which he did not order, but which, if I understand the meaning of words, by his order of the 29th December 1784, he ordered not to be. The Captains Collingwood were the only Officers, with myself, who ever attempted to hinder the illicit Trade with America; and I stood singly with respect to seizing, for the other Officers were fearful of being brought into scrapes. Thus much in justice to myself and the Captains Collingwood, I have thought myself obliged to say.

On the 2nd of February 1786, I seized at Nevis the Sloop Sally, for being an American Registered at St. John's, Antigua, by Governor Shirley, which Register I transmitted Home with the following Letter:

[Vide Letter to Lord Sydney, dated February 4th, 1786, p. 152, ante.]

[Then follow the Surveyor-General's charges against the Collector and Comptroller of Basseterre, St. Christopher's, on the representation of Captains Nelson and Collingwood, with the Answers of those Functionaries; and the Surveyor-General's letter to the Board of Customs in London : but it is not necessary to insert any of those documents.]

On the 9th of March 1786, I arrived in Carlisle Bay, Barbadoes. On the 10th I seized the Brig Lovely Lass for not being properly Registered, but the owner fortunately being on the spot, he was able to convince me there was no fraud in the Vessel, that she was *bona fide* an English Vessel, (a Prize,) and that he left New York when it was evacuated, as a Transport to carry the Loyalists to the Bahama Islands, since which time he had been allowed to trade with his New York Register, and he appeared by it as an inhabitant of that place. This conduct in the Customs was shameful, for by the Act of the 7 & 8 William III., chapter . . . , they are strictly required to new Register every Vessel that changes the place she formerly belonged to. How much more, then, was it necessary in this case, where the place became Foreign, and the Vessel stood as belonging to New York and owned there, consequently became to all appearance a Foreign Vessel. Mr. Keeling, the Collector of Customs, complained of my stopping this Vessel to the Governor; and the Admiral wrote to me upon the subject. But so well was the owner of the Vessel convinced that the Custom-House Officers had allowed him to continue in an error by permitting his Register to pass, that upon my giving up the Vessel, he not only publicly thanked me for undeceiving him, but lodged his former Register in the Custom-House, and proceeded to the Bahama Islands under a Pass from the Governor.

On the 15th I seized the Brig Jane and Elizabeth, registered in Dartmouth in England; but it appeared to me that she was an American Vessel, although covered by British Papers.

This Vessel had made several voyages to the West Indies, and was at Grenada when the Admiral was last there. In the issue it appeared to me by the Master's testimony, and by a letter from her owner, that she belonged to Portsmouth in New England, and was owned by James and William

Sheafe, merchants of that place. On the 17th I seized the Schooner Brilliant, Registered at Halifax by Sir Richard Hughes when he was Lieutenant Governor, and by her papers and log it appeared she came from Pasmaquada. Indeed all her Papers, even her Log-book, were so perfectly clear, that nothing but a presentiment that she was still an American could have induced me to seize her.

It appeared in the issue, by the Master's testimony, and her true Papers, that she belonged to Boston, owned by Paul Sarjent, and that she received her British Papers at Mount Desart, in the State of [*blank in the original*], and the Master declared to me that they were bought, he supposed, at the Custom-House, St. John's, Pasmaquada.

The following is my Deposition of the aforementioned Brig and Schooner, as I think I cannot show my transactions more clearly, nor represent the conduct of the Governor and the Judge of the Court of Admiralty at Barbadoes more fully, than by inserting it:

'THE KING AGAINST THE SCHOONER BRILLIANT, AND SUNDRY GOODS THEREIN LADEN.

' The Deposition of Horatio Nelson, Esq., Commander of his Majesty's Ship Boreas, taken before the Honourable John Ward, Esq., Judge of his Majesty's Court of Vice-Admiralty of the Island of Nevis.

' The said Deponent being duly sworn; maketh oath, that on the seventeenth day of March last past, upon his returning from the shore at the Island of Barbadoes, on board his Majesty's said Ship under his command, then lying in Carlisle Bay, he was informed by Lieutenant Dent of his Majesty's said Ship Boreas, that a Seizure had been made of the above-named Schooner by James Balentine, Gunner of his Majesty's said Ship, pursuant to his general Orders for the examination and seizure of Foreign Vessels trading with the British Colonies in America, and that Mr. William Batty, one of the Midshipmen of the Boreas, was then in possession of the said Schooner.

' That the said Deponent having examined the said Schooner's Papers, which had been delivered by the Master of the said Schooner to the said James Balentine, upon his making the

said Seizure, and having directed a Survey to be made of her
by the Master and said Gunner of his Majesty's said Ship, that
this Deponent, in consequence of their Report, approved of
the said Seizure, and directed that the said Schooner should
remain in the possession of the said Midshipman. That about
three hours after he saw the Custom-House boat of the Port
of Bridgetown at Barbadoes go on board the said Schooner,
but was not apprised, either from the information of any of the
Officers of the Customs there, or of this Deponent's own Officers, of any Seizure or pretended Seizure of the said Schooner
by the Custom-House. That having, on the evening of the
same day, discovered from the Master of the said Schooner
that there were other Papers on board which had been concealed, he, this Deponent, possessed himself of them, and as
soon as possible afterwards went with the said Papers to
Charles Brandford, Esq., his Majesty's Advocate General of
the Island of Barbadoes, whom he informed of his having made
the said Seizure, and desired he would take the necessary steps
for the prosecution of the said Schooner and her cargo. That
the said Advocate-General, having perused the said Papers,
directed the Deponent to leave them with the King's Proctor,
then, Mr. William Forbes, which this Deponent accordingly
did, and an Information in the King's Name was forthwith
made out by the said Advocate-General, which, upon its being
produced and read in the Court of Vice-Admiralty at Barbadoes, on the 6th day of April last, was rejected by the Judge
of the said Court as novel and improper, being only at the Suit
of the King, and was by him then, and at two other subsequent
times, directed to be amended, or otherwise qualified by making the Deponent and his Crew informants *qui tam*, &c., which
the Advocate-General peremptorily refused, as inconsistent
with, and a betraying of, the Right of the Crown.

'That this Deponent being apprehensive that the said Schooner
might receive damage by the delay occasioned by the Judge's
persisting in his refusal to receive and proceed on the information
aforesaid, he represented the same to his Majesty's said Advocate-General, who presented a Petition, as this Deponent hath
been informed, praying that the said Information might be
received, and the Schooner brought to a Trial, which the said
Judge still continued to refuse ; and peremptorily declared that

the said Information, in its then form, was inadmissible, and he could not answer to receive it as it then stood. That the said Advocate-General, as well as this Deponent, made frequent applications to David Parry, Esq., his Majesty's Governor of the said Island of Barbadoes for his interference, who declared his sentiments of the impropriety of the said Judge's conduct, and expressed his sorrow for the difficulties which had been thrown in the way of the said Deponent in the business of the said Seizure, but professed his inability to afford any relief on the occasion.

'That this Deponent having waited till the 20th day of May last, at which time he was under Orders to repair to his Station at the Island of Nevis, and finding from the Information of the said Advocate-General that the said Schooner was not likely to be brought to a Trial there, he informed the said Advocate-General, and also the said King's Proctor, of his intention to carry the said Schooner with the Boreas to the Island of Nevis; and received from the hands of the said Proctor the said Schooner's Papers, which he had delivered to him for the purpose of prosecuting her; and this Deponent saith, that not having been informed, or given to understand, either by the said Advocate-General or King's Proctor, that he, this Deponent, should be guilty of any illegality or irregularity in removing the said Schooner from the Island of Barbadoes, he sailed for the said Island of Nevis, and brought the said Schooner with him to be prosecuted in this Honourable Court.

'And this Deponent further saith, that upon the said Judge of the said Court of Vice-Admiralty of Barbadoes, his rejecting the Information filed against the said Schooner on behalf of the King as aforesaid, and the Advocate-General's declaring to the said Judge, that he would File no other, he, this Deponent, publicly in open Court declared to the said Judge his, this Deponent's, intention of carrying the said Schooner and the other Vessel which was under the same circumstances, in the said Court of Vice-Admiralty, into some other Court of Vice-Admiralty to be proceeded against, or the said Deponent expressed himself to that or the like effect; to which Declaration the said Judge made no manner of reply whatever to this Deponent; and this Deponent saith that the said

Schooner remained upwards of nine weeks after the Seizure of her as aforesaid, in the custody of this Deponent's Officer, Mr. William Batty, without any claim or application whatever made to this Deponent, either by the said Governor Parry, or Alexander Mallett, or any other Officer of the Customs of the said Island of Barbadoes; and this Deponent saith, that he more than once applied personally to the said Judge after he had rejected the said Information as aforesaid, expressing his, this Deponent's, apprehension of some damage or accident happening to the said Schooner and her cargo, if she continued to lay there, and desired to know of the said Judge, whether some Order could not be taken for landing and securing the cargo, or this Deponent expressed himself to that or the like effect; to which the said Judge replied to this Deponent, that as he had rejected the said Information and no other was Filed, he the said Judge did not consider the said Schooner and her cargo as before him, therefore he could not make any Order relative thereto: and this Deponent saith that the said Judge also told this Deponent that notwithstanding any Opinion he the said Judge might deliver upon the Bench, he the said Judge advised this Deponent never to consent that any *qui tam* Information should be Filed, or the said Judge expressed himself to this Deponent to that or the like effect.

'And this Deponent further saith, that finding that the people of Bridgetown in the Island of Barbadoes were very tumultuous, occasioned by his having Seized the Brig and Schooner, and thinking that an attempt would be made to take them forcibly from the Guard who had them in charge, and to prevent them ultimately from being successful, in the evening he ordered Lieutenant Dent to go on board the Brig and the Schooner, and to cut the Broad Arrow [6] deep into their masts, that he might, in case of an accident, be able to identify the vessels in a Foreign Port.

'HORATIO NELSON.

'Sworn the 26th day of June 1786, before me,

J. WARD.'

[6] The general mark of the King's Stores and other property.

On my arrival at Nevis, I stated the case of the two Vessels before the King's Counsel, and begged their opinions on the whole of the business, of which the following are copies:

[Here follow the Case and Opinion of his Majesty's Counsel; but as the facts of the transaction sufficiently appear from the Narrative, and from Captain Nelson's Letters, it is not necessary to insert them.]

On the 26th of June, 1786, the Vessels were tried and condemned, when Governor Parry appealed against the Decision, and claimed a third of the Brig, and two-thirds of the Schooner.

In July I seized an American Schooner under Spanish colours, as she was attempting to trade in the British Colonies, which was condemned.

A day or two after I arrived at Nevis, I received the following letters from Sir Richard Hughes:—

'Government House, 20th May 1786.

'Sir,

'Mr. Mallet, one of the Officers of his Majesty's Customs, having just acquainted me that a Schooner called the Louisa, against which he is informant as well for himself as the King and the Governor in the Court of Vice-Admiralty of this Island, is now to all appearances preparing for Sea, and is about to be taken from hence by Captain Nelson of H.M.S. Boreas.

'The duty I owe to the Crown, and the care of his Majesty's subjects claiming my protection, obliges me to require your Excellency to give Orders to Captain Nelson on no account to take away that Schooner.

'With respect to the Brig about to be carried off in like manner, events within my observation shall determine my particular conduct concerning her.

'I have the honour to be, Sir,

'Your Excellency's most obedient

'And most humble Servant,

'D. Parry.

'His Excellency Sir R. Hughes.'

'Government House, 20th May 1786.

'Sir,

'When your Excellency received my letter, the Schooner in question was in sight of Carlisle Bay. Captain Nelson could and ought to have informed your Excellency that Mr. Mallett had filed a Cross Bill against that Schooner; consequently the Captain's taking of her away in the manner he has done, is a direct violation of every existing Act and Statute in the Parliamentary and Constitutional Annals of Great Britain, for which he will, doubtless, on a future day, be made responsible; for the Laws of England are equally open to every man. What Declarations the Master of either Vessels may have made I know not; nor will it avail anything considering how they were obtained.

'The dispute between Captain Nelson and Mr. Mallett is not a matter of any concern to me, and the legality of Captain Nelson's mode of procedure is yet to be determined.

> 'I have the honour to be,
> 'Your Excellency's most obedient,
> 'And most humble Servant,
> 'D. PARRY.

'P.S.—I must also observe to your Excellency, that both the vessels were under *Appeal* in the Court of Admiralty, in Barbadoes; the legality of their removal I leave you to judge of.'

HORATIO NELSON.

TO WILLIAM SUCKLING, ESQ.

[From "the Athenæum."]

Nevis, July 5th, 1786.

My dear Sir,

This will be delivered to you by Mr. Suckling,[7] who has done me the favour of calling here on his way to England. He appears much improved since I last saw him, and seems to possess a modesty of behaviour, which must ever get friends and promotion for him.

My prizes were condemned on the 26th Instant, but an appeal is prayed by Governor Parry against the distribution, as he thinks that as Governor he is entitled to a third of all forfeitures, even though made by his Majesty's Ships; but he is grossly ignorant, and sets his face against the Navy, more particularly against me, as I will do my duty in despite of all machinations, even with Chiefs at the head of them.

I wish I could tell you I was well, but I am far from it. My activity of mind is too much for my puny constitution. I am worn to a skeleton, but I trust that the Doctors and asses' milk will set me up again. Perhaps you will think it odd if I do not mention Mrs. Nisbet ;—I can only assure you, that her heart is equal to her head, which every person knows is filled with good sense. My affection for her is fixed upon that solid basis of esteem and regard, that I trust can only increase by a longer knowledge of her. I have not a line from either

[7] Vide p. 108, ante.

my father or sister. My brother just mentioned it in a cursory manner as you did. I hope you and your family are well, and ever will continue so.

You have been my best friend, and I trust will continue as long so as I shall prove myself, by my actions, worthy of supplying that place in the Service of my Country, which my dear Uncle [8] left for me. I feel myself, to my Country, his heir; and it shall, I am bold to say, never lack the want of his counsel;—I feel he gave it to me as a legacy, and had I been near him when he was removed, he would have said, ' My boy, I leave you to my Country. Serve her well, and she'll never desert, but will ultimately reward, you.' You who know much of me, I believe and hope, think me not unworthy your regards. But I beg your pardon for this digression; but what I have said is the inward monitor of my heart upon every difficult occasion. Bless you, my best friend, and believe me most affectionately,

HORATIO NELSON.

TO MRS. NISBET.

[From Clarke and M'Arthur, vol. i. pp. 85, 86.]

Boreas, English Harbour, August 19th, 1786.

My dearest Fanny,

Having seen in this day's newspaper, that a Vessel cleared out from St. John's to Nevis a few days ago, I feel vexed not to have had a letter in the Office for you: however, if I can help it, I will not be behindhand again. To write letters to you is the next greatest pleasure I feel to receiving them from you. What I experience when I read such as I am sure are the pure sentiments of your heart, my poor pen cannot express, nor indeed would I give much for any pen or head that could describe feelings of that kind: they are worth but little when that can happen. My heart yearns to you—it is with you; my mind dwells upon nought else but you. Absent from you, I feel no pleasure: it is you, my dearest Fanny, who are everything to me. Without you, I care not for this

<hr/>

[8] Captain Maurice Suckling.

world; for I have found lately nothing in it but vexation and trouble.

These, you are well convinced, are my present sentiments; God Almighty grant they may never change. Nor do I think they will: indeed, there is, as far as human knowledge can judge, a moral certainty they cannot; for it must be real affection that brings us together, not interest or compulsion, which make so many unhappy.

I have not been able to get even a cottage upon a hill, not-withstanding my utmost endeavours; and therefore have been kept here, most woefully pinched by mosquitoes, for my sins, perhaps; so the generous inhabitants of Antigua think, I suppose: not one of whom has been here, or has asked me to leave English Harbour. But I give them credit for not paying attention to me to another cause—that I am a faithful servant to that Country which most of them detest, and to which all their actions are inimical: I wish not for a better proof from them of my having done my duty. These gentlemen I shall in my mind hold very cheap in future: but I will have done with such trash. I am not that jolly fellow, who, for a feast and a plenty of wine, would sacrifice the dearest interest of his Country; they are fond of those gentry.

Leave all Antigua by itself, 'tis not fit company for the other parts of the letter.

Monday, [21st August] seven in the Evening.

As you begin to know something about Sailors, have you not often heard, that salt water and absence always wash away love? Now, I am such a heretic as not to believe that Faith; for behold, every morning since my arrival, I have had six pails of salt water at daylight poured upon my head, and instead of finding what the Seamen say to be true, I perceive the contrary effect; and if it goes on so contrary to the pre-scription; you must see me before my fixed time. At first, I bore absence tolerably, but now it is almost insupportable; and by-and-by I expect it will be quite so. But patience is a virtue; and I must exercise it upon this occasion, whatever it costs my feelings. I am alone in the Commanding Officer's house, while my Ship is fitting, and from sunset until bed-time

I have not a human creature to speak to: you will feel a little for me, I think. I did not use to be over-fond of sitting alone. The moment old Boreas is habitable in my cabin, I shall fly to it, to avoid mosquitoes and melancholies. Hundreds of the former are now devouring me through all my clothes. You will, however, find I am better; though when you see me, I shall be like an Egyptian mummy, for the heat is intolerable. But I walk a mile out at night without fatigue, and all day I am housed. A quart of goats' milk is also taken every day, and I enjoy English sleep, always barring mosquitoes, which all Frank's[9] care with my net cannot keep out at present.

What nonsense I am sending you: but I flatter myself the most trivial article concerning me, you feel interested in. I judge from myself; and I would rather have what passes in your mind, than all the news you could tell me which did not concern you. Mr. Horsford, our neighbour, came to visit me, making many apologies for his neglect, and pressing me much to come to his house, which has Boreas in view. Also the Comptroller of the Customs, with fine speeches: he may go back whistling, if he pleases. I cannot add anything further, for I do not know if you would read more than a sheet full.

August 23rd.

At any rate, I will show some mercy. Berbice arrived yesterday. All at home are well. I am still apt to suppose this winter will carry me to England. Pringle[1] has been at Portsmouth, so says Lord Hood: he longs to see you. May every blessing attend my far better half, and may I soon be with you, is the sincere wish of

Your most affectionate
HORATIO NELSON.

---

[9] Frank Lepeé his servant.　　　[1] Captain Thomas Pringle, ante.

TO PHILIP STEPHENS, ESQ., ADMIRALTY.

[Duplicate, in the Admiralty.]

Boreas, English Harbour, Antigua, 27th August, 1786.

Sir,

The Board of Treasury having issued an Order in the year 1763, and signed by Mr. Grenville, for the admission of Spaniards bringing bullion to our Colonies, which order was sent to the different Custom-Houses in our Colonies, the money brought out of the Spanish territories not being allowed to be carried off by the Spanish Government, was, of course, clandestinely taken out of that Country, to the detriment of Spain, and the advantage of Great Britain. In return, the Spaniards received British manufactured checks and linens, which were carried into their own Country, in the same clandestine manner.

In a few years, our Custom-Houses admitted cattle, mules, and stock, to be brought by the Spaniards to our Islands, and they say it has the sanction of the Board of Customs, as an encouragement for the Spaniards to visit our Islands, and to take off our dry goods. At Jamaica, from my own knowledge, having been upon that station, the reasoning will hold good. To that Island very large quantities of dry goods used to be sent for the purpose of the Spanish trade; but the contrary is the fact in these Islands. No dry goods calculated to suit the Spaniards are sent here, nor is there a merchant which I have heard of, who deals in anything but American produce—rum, beef, pork, butter, &c., for the use of the small community living about them.

When I acquainted the Collector of Basseterre that I had seized a Spaniard bringing cattle and mules, he sent off the Treasury order of 1763, in which, besides bullion, was inserted in writing, 'live stock, &c.' In the Collector's letter he mentioned that he had sent off the Clerk of the Custom-house, as he had been twenty-one years in the Office, and could better answer any questions I might wish to ask than he could. When I observed the insertion of the writing, he declared it had been so ever since he had been in the Office, and that the Board of Customs approved of their admission.

7

This is the cloak which has hitherto been made use of for admitting every article in Spanish vessels. Money is always taken from these Islands instead of British goods, for we have none to sell, which money is carried to St. Eustatia, where they lay it out. Thus, instead of bringing bullion, they take it from us; and enrich the Dutch at our expense.

I must say a few words relative to the Island of Grenada. I understand that it is asserted the Spaniards take from that Island every year, large quantities of British manufactured dry goods. I think I may venture to say, that a great part of the dry goods given to the Spanish vessels, who visit Grenada, are of French manufacture.

Since the Peace, the Island of Trinidada has been declared a free Port. All imports are duty free; but on exports a duty of 15½ per cent. is paid.

As the American Vessels are now pretty tired of venturing too much amongst our Islands, their Vessels, after delivering their cargoes in the French Islands, or at the Dutch Settlements of Surinam, Demerara, &c., upon the Main, repair to the Island of Trinidada, where they obtain from the Governor a qualification to make their vessels Spanish for a given time. They, in general, take a Spanish Creole, or two, to give a colour to the fraud; and thus prepared, they, under Spanish Colours visit our Islands, and the Custom-Houses, under the cloak of the Order of [the] Treasury in 1763, and the sanction which they pretend to have from the Board of Customs, admit these Americans; and I have but little doubt, although their decks are loaded with cattle, that in their holds they bring American produce. Thus, after all the trouble which some of the Men-of-War upon this Station have had to hinder American Vessels from trading to our Islands, unless vigorous measures are made use of, they will again fill our Ports as much as heretofore.

I have seized one of these American Spaniards; but I might have had some difficulty in condemning her, had I not found the American Papers, and Orders of the owners for this transmogrification.

Their Lordships know my opinion of the Custom-House Officers in these Islands. They will allow all these kind of Vessels to be admitted, under the cloak of their being Spaniards, who may bring bullion, and are to be encouraged. I shall seize, and order Captain Collingwood to do so likewise, all these Trinidada Vessels who are American-built and navigated by Americans, and shall allow none to come to these Islands, but the small Spanish open Boats, which have hitherto been allowed; although I think, without any advantage to these Islands. If money is ever brought, those are the kind of Vessels which bring it; none other ever came to Jamaica.

I know the difficulties we shall meet with in having these Vessels prosecuted to condemnation. The Merchants and Landed people will be against us, for interest sake; the Custom-House Officers must be, as they admit them; and if they are condemned, it will show their bad conduct in too glaring colours.

I should not have sent Home this account, but have waited the arrival of the Officer who is to succeed Sir Richard Hughes in this Command, had I not thought it of such material consequence, that an account could not too soon be transmitted for their Lordships' consideration; and I beg leave to observe that already very numerous are the Americans who are covered by the Spanish qualifications, although the first of them which I have met with is only dated the 21st of May 1786. When I say one hundred, I am certain I am far within compass. Every American vessel who trades to the West Indies will call at Trinidada to receive Spanish qualifications.

This traffic, I must take the liberty of observing, brings to the King of Spain a considerable revenue; it will increase the Ship-building of America, and raise the numbers of her Seamen; while, on the contrary, it will decrease the British Shipping and Seamen in these Islands. These Americans will take off our rum, and carry it to America, so that our Vessels will shortly have no trade to those States. They will be again the Carriers between these Islands and America. For such is either the want of knowledge, or something worse, in most of our Officers here, that if a Vessel comes under Spanish colours, and produces anything Spanish, she must be a Spaniard; and as such, is granted certain privileges: for if under an English Ensign, must be a true Englishman.

Their Lordships will, I am sure, see the necessity of something being immediately done in this Spanish-American business; and I hope they will approve of what I intend doing.

> I am, &c.,
>
> HORATIO NELSON.

TO MRS. NISBET.

[From Clark and M'Arthur, vol. i. p. 79: but they do not give the date of his Letter. It was, however, written about August 1786.]

Boreas, English Harbour, [August 1786].

My dearest Fanny,

What can I say? Nothing, if I speak of the pleasure I felt at receiving your kind and affectionate letter; my thoughts are too big for utterance : you must suppose that everything which is tender, kind, and truly affectionate has possession of my whole frame. Words are not capable of conveying an idea of my feelings: nothing but reciprocity is equal to it; I flatter myself it is so. I have begun this letter, and left off, a dozen times, and found I did not know one word from another. Well, on the Saturday morning after the Berbice Schooner left me, Mr. Lightfoot came and paid me a visit, with an apology, of his having been confined to his house, or he would have done it before : that, not writing, he meant it as a mark of attention. He prevailed upon me to sleep at his house on Monday last, the day I dined with Sir Thomas Shirley.[2] This great attention made amends for his long neglect, and I forgot all anger; I can forgive sometimes, you will allow. I only came from thence this morning; it is nine miles, and with writing ever since my arrival, I feel a little tired; therefore expect nothing but sheer stupidity.

I have also seen the great Mr. ——; he says, he understood and believed I was gone to England—whistle for that! The Country air has certainly done me service. I am not getting very fat, my make will not allow it : but I can tell you, and I know your tender heart will rejoice, that I have no more

---

[2] Governor of the Leeward Islands. (Vide p. 157, ante.) He was created a Baronet in June 1786, which shows that this Letter must have been written some weeks after that date, though it is placed by Clarke and M'Arthur before Letters of February and March 1786.

complaint in my lungs than Captain Maynard, and not the least pain in my breast. Pray present my best respects to Dr. Jefferies; I am very much flattered indeed by his good opinion. Although I am just from salt water, yet, as I am in a hurry to get the Berbice away, that she may reach Nevis by the evening, I must finish this thing, for letter I cannot call it. I have a newspaper for Miss Herbert; it is all I have to offer that is worth her acceptance; and I know she is as fond of a bit of news as myself. Pray give my compliments to her, and love to Josiah. I am, &c.

HORATIO NELSON.

TO MRS. NISBET.

[From Clarke and M'Arthur, vol. i. 86.]

English Harbour, September 23rd, 1786.

On the 9th of October, barring something extraordinary, you will certainly see H. N. again; and, I need not say, if it be possible, with a stronger affection than when he left you. My letter is short, but my mind could say the paper full; therefore, don't let that be a reason for your writing either a short letter, or making the lines very wide from each other. . . . Believe that I am ever the same Horatio.

TO PHILIP STEPHENS, ESQ., ADMIRALTY.

[Original, in the Admiralty.]

Boreas, English Harbour, Antigua,
September 25th, 1786.

Sir,

I beg leave to acquaint you, that on the 23rd Instant, I received their Lordships' order of the 14th of July last relative to Harbours.

Inclosed, I transmit you the State and Condition of the Ships on this Station; and also a List of an Appointment made by me, with a Report of the Survey. And I am to request you will inform their Lordships, that in the beginning of September, I ordered the Rattler to the Island of Grenada to remain the rest of the hurricane season : I have also inclosed you as correct a List as I could procure of the French Squadron in these Seas, and have the honour to be, &c.,

HORATIO NELSON.

TO PHILIP STEPHENS, ESQ., ADMIRALTY.

[Original, in the Admiralty.]

Boreas, English Harbour, Antigua,
September 25th, 1786.

Sir,

Inclosed is a duplicate of my letter to you, of the 27th of August last,[3] by which you will see I made a mistake. It was a Treasury Order signed by Mr. Grenville in the year 1763, instead of an Order in Council. I remain, &c.,

HORATIO NELSON.

TO THE COMMISSIONERS OF THE NAVY.

[Original, in the Admiralty.]

Boreas, English Harbour. Antigua,
September 25th, 1786.

Gentlemen,

Inclosed, I beg leave to transmit you two letters which were sent by Mr. William Lewis, Surgeon of his Majesty's Sloop Rattler, to Captain Collingwood, and by him transmitted to me. The propriety of his writing such letters relative to the Commander of the Squadron, I leave to your consideration. The gentleman asserts that Captain Nelson will not believe his own representation, although he knows he never made to me in his life, either a verbal or written representation of his state of health. After the first Survey he writes his Captain, that he has received his letter, acquainting him of Captain Nelson's resolution of not signing a Ticket for him to go on shore to Sick

---

[3] The Letter printed in p. 190 was a Duplicate, in which he seems to have corrected the error in the Original.

Quarters, and much more improper writing, as in the former instance. I can only assure the Board that no Sick Ticket was ever presented for my approbation until he was invalided. I certainly did not choose to volunteer sending the Mate[4] of the Boreas on board the Rattler, for by it I left a hundred and eighty men under the care of a gentleman who has not the best state of health, and who told me his constitution was not equal to attending them if they were sickly. But when Mr. Lewis was by Survey judged an object to be sent to England, I appointed one in his room; and as there were not Ships enough to try Mr. William Lewis, I ordered him to be immediately discharged, and approved his Ticket to remain at the hospital, till an opportunity offered of his getting a passage to England. So far from treating him with inhumanity, I conceive I have shown him lenity after such expressions.

I have the honour to remain, &c.,

HORATIO NELSON.

TO THE REVEREND MR. NELSON, HILBOROUGH.

[Autograph, in the Nelson Papers.]

Boreas, English Harbour, September 25th, 1786.

My dear Brother,

Your kind letter of July 30th I received by Dent[5] from Barbadoes two days ago, and the last month those of May the 1st, June the 3rd, July the 2nd, I received here in due course. For not getting the two former I am obliged to Mr. Kelly, as well as not getting two from my father, and the same number from Kate. I am very angry with him; more so as there were many opportunities of sending them, and he told me there were none for me: not that I believe I could have wrote, for you cannot have an idea of the plague and trouble I have had with these Governors and people, and the number of letters I have been obliged to write upon those subjects. However, I have smoothed the way for those who may come after me. The Captains of Men-of-War are now invested with great additional powers, enough to carry on the business of doing good

---

[4] Surgeon's Mate, Officers now called " Assistant Surgeons."
[5] Second Lieutenant of the Boreas.

for the Nation, without interruption. When we are to come Home, that I believe, is only known at present to the Admiralty; but I take it for granted it will not be before the spring of the year. It would be cruel to give us, stewed mortals, a winter's passage. I can tell you nothing about myself, only that on the 9th of October I shall most willingly leave English Harbour —to Nevis naturally, you will suppose, first; and then (if I am Commanding Officer) to every Island in these Seas. This is my present plan, but may be altered in the turn of a straw.

News from this corner you will not expect. Rattler, Collingwood, is at Grenada; therefore, here have I been in this vile place without a creature near me. Your Warrant[6] I have in my bureau. When Sir Richard Bickerton arrives, probably you will be discharged. Indeed I think it a chance if they pay you now, as you have not actually been on board. However, that we'll try when Boreas gets home. Pray what do you know or hear of Maurice?[7] tell me. So Kate tells me she is to pass the winter with you: she will make Hilborough something pleasanter. Pray remember me kindly to your next door neighbours. I am sure you are very attentive to them. At Barbadoes, but the papers will tell you, they have had a little gale which drove some Ships on shore; but I have not heard of damage anywhere else. I have nothing to say, but that all on board desire to be kindly remembered, and Mr. Horsford often inquires after you. Adieu for a little, and believe me to be,

> Yours affectionately,
> HERATIO NELSON.

TO WILLIAM LOCKER, ESQ., WEST MALLING.

[Autograph, in the Locker Papers.]

Boreas, English Harbour, September 27th, 1786.

My dear Friend,

It is an age since I had the pleasure of hearing from you; but I know my deserts, and you have every reason not to be plagued with so bad a correspondent; yet be assured, my good

---

[6] As Chaplain of the Boreas.   [7] His eldest brother.

friend, that my gratitude for the many favours I have constantly received, does not fail. *No*, it is fresh in my remembrance; but if you got my letter from Barbadoes in May last (I ought to be ashamed of the date) you will have some idea of my troubles, nor will they ever end, I plainly perceive, while I am in this Country; for it will always be the case, where Officers neglect their duty, there rogues thrive; and God knows there is not a Custom-House Officer, Governor, &c., that I have met with, who have done their duty; therefore the latter party is kept up, and my hands full of business.

It is not more strange than true, that I was not only obliged to support myself against the most violent prosecutions that could be laid against an Officer; and instead of being supported by my Admiral, I was obliged to keep him up, for he was frightened at this business, which, although, I hope, completed now, he appeared ready, (I thought,) when he got Home, to receive any thanks which might be offered him for his alertness and attention to the navigation of Great Britain. God knows, I envy no man praises; but don't let him take what is due to others. Collingwood, I hope, has been down to see you; he will tell you a history. He seized a vessel at Barbadoes. When we are to expect Sir Richard Bickerton, [8] or when Boreas goes Home, I am all in the dark. As it is not in the autumn, I hope they will have mercy enough not to give us a winter's passage. I am sorry to tell you a good deal of your quarter cask of wine is leaked out: I had the remainder fined and bottled. Captain Erasmus Gower has likewise been a sufferer. Myself a great one, and also Lord Hood. Indeed all casks under pipes have not stood the heat, nor then without being new hooped. I am sorry for the losses of my friends' wine ten times more than my own; but I am sure you know that every care was taken. I have laid in a good supply of rum, and you shall have any quantity you please.

I think I have wrote lately to Kingsmill, but really I have been since June so very ill (till lately) that I have only a faint recollection of anything which I did. My complaint was in my breast, such a one as I had going

---

[8] The Successor of Sir Richard Hughes, in command of the Leeward Islands.

out to Jamaica: the Doctor thought I was in a consumption, and gave me quite up; but that Great Being who has
so often raised me from the sick bed, has once more restored me, and to that health which I very seldom enjoy. I
beg, whenever you see Commissioner Kirke, that you will
present my best respects to him : he has always been very kind
and polite. I hope Mr. Bradley is quite recovered: those
African voyages [9] do not seem to agree well with his constitution. He ought to get rich by them, but that, I fear, he
does not　To every other part of that family pray remember
me kindly, and to all other friends who may inquire after me,
and believe me to be, with the most unfeigned regard,

　　　　Your much obliged faithful humble Servant,

　　　　　　　　　　HORATIO NELSON.

TO PHILIP STEPHENS, ESQ., ADMIRALTY.

[Original, in the Admiralty.]

Boreas, English Harbour,
Antigua, 4th October, 1786.

Sir,

I beg leave to transmit you several letters, which Captain
Wilfred Collingwood, of his Majesty's sloop Rattler, has sent
me from the Island of Grenada.

Their Lordships will perceive the difficulties which Mr.
Byam [1] has thrown in the way to hinder Captain Collingwood
from performing his duty. Mr. Byam has thought proper to
be guided by an Opinion which Dr. Scott sent out to this
Country, although all good lawyers know it does not relate to
the Navigation Act. It has been the means of much trouble
to those Captains of the Navy who have endeavoured to suppress illegal Trade, for all those Lawyers make use of it, who
mean to throw every obstacle in our way to prevent us from

---

[9] Both Mr. Henry and Mr. Richard Bradley were enterprising men, and specu-
lated largely on the Coasts of America and Africa, where they obtained grants of
land.

[1] Ashton Warner Byam, Esq., Attorney-General at Grenada, who was
Knighted in October 1789.

securing the Navigation to Great Britain to and from these Colonies.

Mr. Byam, by demanding fees for advice, their Lordships well know, has thrown such an obstacle in our way, that very few Captains of Men-of-War can get over. Their Lordships will take some steps to obviate this difficulty. We cannot with propriety act without advice; nor have we ability to buy it. Had fees been demanded of me for the advice I have been necessitated to ask of the Crown Lawyers of the Leeward Islands, all my pay for the station would not have enabled me to ask it.

Mr. Byam their Lordships will recollect in the case of the brig Abigail, which Sir Richard Hughes sent home last April. How different is this gentleman's conduct from Mr. Stanley, Mr. Burke,[2] and Mr. Adye, the Crown Lawyers for the Leeward Islands. They are always ready to support and assist the Navy. This gentleman uniformly opposing them, and giving every countenance, I fear, to the admitting Foreign vessels to be registered in Grenada.

This prosecution is forced, you will perceive, upon the Attorney-General; and I should not be surprised, although the fraud is so very clear, if he should be acquitted. And although it is a prosecution at the suit of the Crown, yet the Solicitor-General has thought proper to oppose the Crown, by taking part on the other side.

It is presuming in me, and needless, I trust, to remark what zeal Captain Collingwood[3] has shown upon this occasion, in attempting to entirely hinder Foreigners from trading to our Islands; and with what perspicuity and clearness he has pointed out to the Crown Officer, the defects which the Vessels he seizes lay under. His conduct upon former occasions has not, I am certain, escaped their Lordships' observation; and I am sure such assiduity, alertness, and ability to serve his Country, will not pass unnoticed.

---

[2] In a Letter from Mr. Burke to Captain Nelson, dated November 29th, 1786, he said, " I am very much obliged to you for the two Acts of Parliament; and I am much mistaken if the Gentlemen of the Navy are not obliged to you, for the final settlement of the very important question, concerning the right of Seizure, without any authority from the Customs."—*Original*, in the Nelson Papers.

[3] Captain Wilfred Collingwood, of the Rattler.

Sir Richard Hughes has formerly, I doubt not, done Captain Collingwood that justice his conduct so well entitles him to. I feel great pleasure in their Lordships having left such an Officer under my command.

I have the honour to be, &c.

HORATIO NELSON.

TO PHILIP STEPHENS, ESQ., ADMIRALTY.

[Original, in the Admiralty.]

Boreas, Nevis, 3rd November 1786.

Sir,

Herewith I transmit you the remainder of Captain Collingwood's Correspondence at the Island of Grenada.

A total stop is put to our carrying on the Navigation Laws. The Custom-House Officers have the King's Chest to resort to; and if there is probable cause of Seizure, are allowed in their accounts the expense. As we have no such resort, their Lordships will consider this case, for it is out of our power to perform the duty imposed on us.

The President of the Island of Grenada has stopped the proceedings by virtue of a clause in the New Act.

Their Lordships will very soon find the ill effects of the Suspending Clause. Had the Governors, in the first instance, done their duty, in not granting Registers to Vessels who by Law were not entitled to them, the evil never could have arisen. I never expect to see any Vessels which are Registered in the Island condemned, if seized by the Navy. The interest of the Governors militates against it; and will Governors ever want a plausible tale to tell Ministers why they granted such and such Vessels Registers? No;—artful men will never want an artful story; and Oaths will not be wanting to confirm any tale. It would appear that the Suspending Clause has been got upon a fair American.

I have the honour to remain, &c.

HORATIO NELSON.

TO PHILIP STEPHENS, ESQ., ADMIRALTY.

[Original, in the Admiralty.]

Boreas, Antigua, 1st December 1786.

Sir,

Inclosed I transmit you, for their Lordships' consideration, an account of the difference of charges attending the Prosecution of two Vessels by the King's Advocate and Proctor, at the Island of Barbadoes, and those at the Leeward Islands. To the first, I stand pledged for payment; and the Cause is not yet finally decided. Therefore, the money must come from my pocket; and I am given to understand, that the Crown Lawyers of Barbadoes and Grenada will not proceed without being regularly paid, which is not in my power, or in that of very few Officers. Thus, an effectual method is fallen upon in those two Islands to hinder us from carrying the Acts of Parliament into execution. It can never be supposed that a Captain of the Navy, as a Custom-house Officer, seizes Vessels for their emolument, but as it is a duty imposed on them.

I shall continue to Seize, and must leave the Prosecution of them or not to the Crown Lawyers. I cannot pay them till the Vessels are sold, nor then if the fees are like those of Barbadoes and Grenada, for the value of most of the small Vessels does not amount to that sum.

Inclosed I also transmit you the State and Condition of his Majesty's Ships and Vessels in these Seas,

And have the honour to remain, &c.

HORATIO NELSON.

His Majesty's Ship Pegasus,[3] arrived the beginning of November: the Solebay arrived the latter end of November.

[3] Under the command of H. R. H. Prince William Henry.

TO MRS. NISBET.

[From Clarke and M'Arthur, vol. i. p. 88.]

Off Antigua, December 12th, 1786.

Our young Prince is a gallant man: he is indeed volatile, but always with great good nature. There were two balls during his stay, and some of the old ladies were mortified that H.R.H. would not dance with them; but he says, he is determined to enjoy the privilege of all other men, that of asking any lady he pleases.

Wednesday. We arrived here this morning at daylight. His Royal Highness dined with me, and of course the Governor. I can tell you a piece of news, which is, that the Prince is fully determined, and has made me promise him, that he shall be at our wedding; and he says he will give you to me. His Royal Highness has not yet been in a private house to visit, and is determined never to do it, except in this instance. You know I will ever strive to bear such a character, as may render it no discredit to any man to take notice of me. There is no action in my whole life, but what is honourable; and I am the more happy at this time on that account; for I would, if possible, or in my power, have no man near the Prince, who can have the smallest impeachment as to character: for as an individual I love him, as a Prince I honour and revere him. My telling you this history is as to myself: my thoughts on all subjects are open to you. We shall certainly go to Barbadoes from this Island, and when I shall see you, is not possible for me to guess: so much for marrying a Sailor. We are often separated, but I trust our affections are not by any means on that account diminished. Our Country has the first demand for our services; and private convenience, or happiness, must ever give way to the Public good. Give my love to Josiah. Heaven bless, and return you safe to

Your most affectionate,

HORATIO NELSON.

TO THE REVEREND MR. NELSON, HILBOROUGH.

[Autograph, in the Nelson Papers.]

English Harbour, December 29th, 1786.

My dear Brother,

Your letter of the 2nd and 31st of October I received a few days ago. So then you are at last become a husband;[4] may every blessing attend you. It is, I have no doubt, the happiest, or otherwise, state; and I believe it is most generally the man's fault if he is not happy. I most certainly have wrote repeatedly since August, which you say is the last time you heard from me. Your name is not now upon the Books:[5] you were discharged on the 4th of October. Your rum I have on board. I dare say you have many friends who, as you say, will gladly take what you can spare. You may tell them, the King's Ship, although she may bring a little for a brother, does not for any others. I begin to be very strict in my Ship, and as I get older, probably shall be more so. Whenever I may set off in another Ship, I shall be indifferent whether I ever speak to an Officer in her, but upon duty.

You know before this that his Royal Highness Prince William is under my command; and I wish that all the Navy Captains were as attentive to orders as he is. I had almost forgot to tell you that D—— is married, but to whom, or what, is out of my power. He has nothing left, in my opinion, but to put a pistol to his head: he is damned for ever. Pray where did you know Captain Holloway?[6] Do you know his wife, too? I don't take him to be a conjuror. I am truly happy to hear Mr. Suckling is married.[7] It will add to his felicity, for had he not done that, he must have kept a woman, which you will allow would have been very disagreeable. Pray give my best love and compliments where they will be well received; and believe me to be, your affectionate Brother,

HORATIO NELSON.

---

[4] The Reverend William Nelson married, on the 9th November 1786, Sarah, daughter of the Reverend Henry Yonge, Vicar of Great Torrington, in Devonshire, and cousin of Dr. Philip Yonge, Bishop of Norwich.

[5] Of the Boreas.

[6] Captain John Holloway of the Solebay, who died an Admiral.

[7] His uncle Mr. William Suckling of the Custom House, married on the 26th October 1786, Miss Rumsey of Hampstead.

TO WILLIAM LOCKER, ESQ., TOWN MALLING.

[Autograph, in the Locker Papers.]

English Harbour, December 29th, 1786.

My dear Friend,

I am sure it is a full twelvemonth since I have had a line: you will say I don't deserve it oftener than that, however, for since May, I know of three letters which I put myself into the Packet. If you think me unmindful of the favours and kindnesses I received at your hands, you do me injustice. I am at this moment more thankful for them than I was when they were granted: then I was not so capable of judging of their value. Let this be the opinion of your Horatio: and I trust it will be for the future.

You will know long before this reaches you, that Prince William is under my command: I shall endeavour to take care he is not a loser by that circumstance. He has his foibles as well as private men, but they are far over-balanced by his virtues. In his Professional line, he is superior to near two-thirds, I am sure, of the List; and in attention to orders, and respect to his Superior Officers, I know hardly his equal: this is what I have found him. Some others, I have heard, will tell another story. The Islanders have made vast entertainments for him. But all this you will see in the English papers.

I am in momentary expectation of Sir Richard Bickerton, from reports, for the Admiralty are wonderfully secret. I wish he was arrived, for this state of uncertainty is very unpleasant. The Prince is to remain in these Seas until May, when he returns to Nova Scotia, at which time I hope to set sail for Old England; for I am most heartily sick of these Islands. Heaven bless you, my dear friend; and believe that I am unalterably yours,

HORATIO NELSON.

TO MRS. NISBET.

[From Clarke and M'Arthur, vol. i. p. 89.]

1st January, 1787.

How vain are human expectations. I was in hopes to have remained quiet all this week : but to-day we dine with Sir Thomas ;[8] to-morrow the Prince has a party; on Wednesday he gives a dinner at Saint John's to the Regiment; in the evening is a Mulatto ball ; on Thursday a cock-fight, and we dine at Colonel Crosbie's brother's, and a ball : on Friday somewhere, but I forget ; on Saturday at Mr. Byam's,[9] the President. If we get well through all this, I shall be fit for anything ; but I hope most sincerely the Commodore[1] will arrive before the whole is carried into execution : in many instances it is better to serve than command ; and this is one of them. If the Commodore does not come down and relieve me, I think it likely we shall remain here all this month at least; for the Ship's company of the Pegasus are sick, and I cannot with propriety leave His Royal Highness by himself.

Should Sir Richard Bickerton come down, and I think he must be at Barbadoes, and send me to Nevis, I will bless him: yet I would sooner die than ask any favour. If he is polite, he will do it without ; if not, he would perhaps refuse me with asking, and I should not like the mortification. What is it to attend on Princes ? Let me attend on you, and I am satisfied. Some are born for attendants on great men : I rather think that it is not my particular province. His Royal Highness often tells me, he believes I am married ; for he never saw a lover so easy, or say so little of the object he has a regard for. When I tell him I certainly am not, he says, ' Then he is sure I must have a great esteem for you, and that it is not what is (vulgarly), I do not much like the use of that word, called love.' He is right: my love is founded on esteem, the only foundation that can make the passion last. I need not tell you, what you so well know, that I wish I had a fortune to settle on you : but I trust I

---

[8] Sir Thomas Shirley, the Governor.

[9] Edward Byam, President of the Council at Antigua, and Judge of the Admiralty Court : he died in February 1817.

[1] Alan, afterwards Admiral Lord Gardner.

have a good name, and that certain events will bring the other thing about: it is my misfortune, not my fault. You can marry me only from a sincere affection; therefore I ought to make you a good husband, and I hope it will turn out that I shall. You are never absent from my mind in any place or company. I never wished for riches, but to give them to you; and my small share shall be yours to the extreme. A happy New Year; and that many of them may attend you, is the most fervent wish of your affectionate

HORATIO NELSON.

TO PHILIP STEPHENS, ESQ., ADMIRALTY.

[Original, in the Admiralty.]

Boreas, English Harbour, Antigua, 7th January 1787.

Sir,

By my last from Dominica, of the 2nd of December, (in a Merchant-ship, having missed the Packet,) their Lordships will be informed of my taking the Solebay, Captain Holloway, and the Pegasus, commanded by His Royal Highness Prince William Henry, under my command, agreeable to their order by the respective Ships.

I was exceedingly sorry to find that the Pegasus was not only very leaky, but that there was every appearance her iron work was much corroded. After wooding and watering the Squadron in Prince Rupert's, I proceeded to this harbour, where I arrived on the 13th December. The Pegasus was immediately hauled to the wharf, and it was found that the leak was occasioned by her wooden ends forward being very open, nearly all her bolts about her bows were found very much corroded, and were so bad, that I have ordered her to be new bolted. The cheeks of her head have been taken off, and the seams were found so open, as plainly to show they had not been examined into at the Port she fitted out at: some of the chain plates have also been found unfit for service, and the generality of the bolts which hold them were so loose in the Ship, as to be drawn out by the hand. This has occasioned her to be so long in the harbour.

On the 11th, I shall sail for the Island of Barbadoes, to

which place I sent the Solebay in the last month, to look out
for Commodore Sir Richard Bickerton, who, I hear, from
private hands, is appointed to this Command.   I shall wait
there until the 20th, when, if I hear no confirmation of the
report, I shall proceed with the Pegasus and Rattler to the
Island of Grenada, leaving the Solebay to take care of the
Commerce at the Island of Barbadoes.   At Grenada I shall
leave the Rattler, and shall proceed with his Royal Highness
to visit the Islands of Montserrat, Nevis, St. Christopher's, and
the Virgin Islands, by which time I shall hope to be honoured
with their Lordships' commands; for since the 1st of August,
I have not received a line from the Board (except by the
Solebay and Pegasus) or an acknowledgement of a letter.   In
May, I wrote a very particular one,[2] by desire of Sir Richard
Hughes, inclosing an account of my proceedings at Barbadoes; but I do not know if it has been received, as it has
never been acknowledged.

Inclosed is the State and Condition of the Squadron on this
Station.

I have the honour to remain, &c.

HORATIO NELSON.

TO H. R. H. PRINCE WILLIAM HENRY,
CAPTAIN OF HIS MAJESTY'S SHIP PEGASUS.

[Transmitted to the Admiralty on the 10th July 1787, vide p. 242 post.]

Boreas, January 23rd, 1787.

Sir,

I have the honour of acquainting your Royal Highness that
in consequence of a letter which I have this day received
from Lieutenant Isaac Schomberg,[3] first Lieutenant of his

---

[2] Vide p. 170, ante.

[3] Lieutenant Schomberg's original Letter is in the possession of Dawson Turner,
Esq., F.R.S.; and it is only just to the memory of a zealous Officer of whose
general merits Nelson thought very highly (vide p. 250 post.) as well as to that
of the Prince, to state the particulars of the affair, more especially as it is the
subject of many other Letters.   Prince William's orders were as follow :

" Pegasus, English Harbour, Antigua, 23rd January 1787.
" From Mr. Schomberg's neglecting to inform me yesterday of his sending a
boat on shore, and Mr. Smollett doing the same, I think proper to recommend

Majesty's Ship Pegasus, under your command, I have thought proper to order him under an Arrest, and beg you will grant him such indulgencies, or lay such restrictions on him, during his Arrest, as his behaviour shall appear to you to deserve.

I have the honour to be, Sir,
Your Royal Highness's
Most obedient humble Servant,
HORATIO NELSON.

the reading over of these orders, with attention, to the Officers and Gentlemen ; as for the future, I shall make them accountable for their conduct in disobeying any commands or orders I may from time to time give out.

WILLIAM.

Mr. Schomberg, thinking he had not deserved this Reprimand, immediately applied to Captain Nelson for a Court-Martial:

Pegasus, in English Harbour, Antigua, 23rd January 1787.

Sir,

As His Royal Highness Prince William Henry, Commander of his Majesty's Ship Pegasus, has thought proper this morning to accuse me with neglect of duty, in the General Order Book, of which I do not conceive myself guilty, I must, therefore, in vindication of my conduct as an Officer, beg you will be pleased (whenever an opportunity may offer) to order a Court-Martial on me, to inquire into the charge alleged against me. Enclosed I have the honour to send you a copy of the accusation for your perusal.

I am, Sir, &c.
J. SCHOMBERG.

To Horatio Nelson, Esq., Captain of his Majesty's Ship
Boreas, and Senior Officer of the Leeward Islands.

No Court-Martial took place, the matter having been eventually settled by Commodore Alan Gardner. (See subsequent Letters.)

Lieutenant Schomberg attained the rank of Post-Captain in November 1790, and died one of the Commissioners of the Navy Board in January 1813. He was the Compiler of the "Naval Chronology," in 5 vols. octavo, 1802; from which laborious and useful Work much information for these Notes has been derived.

TO LIEUTENANT ISAAC SCHOMBERG, FIRST LIEUTENANT OF
H. M. S. PEGASUS.

[Original, in the possession of Dawson Turner, Esq., F.R.S. It is erroneously
dated in 1786.]

Boreas, English Harbour, January 23rd, 1786 [1787].

Sir,

I have received your letter of this day's date, desiring that
I would order a Court-Martial (when opportunity offered) to
be assembled, to inquire into the charge alleged against you
by his Royal Highness Prince William Henry, your Captain,
and inclosing me a copy of his Royal Highness's accusation
for my perusal.

In answer, I acquaint you that I shall order a Court-Martial to inquire into the charge alleged against you as soon
as possible. And, Sir, from the receipt of this letter you
are under Arrest, with such restrictions or indulgencies as his
Royal Highness, your Captain, may think proper.

I have the honour to remain, &c.,

HORATIO NELSON.

***

GENERAL ORDER.

[Transmitted to the Admiralty in a Letter dated 10th July, 1787, wherein
Captain Nelson explained his motives for issuing this Order. Vide p. 242
post.]

By Horatio Nelson, Esq.,
Captain of His Majesty's Ship Boreas.

For the better maintaining discipline and good government
in the King's Squadron under my command,

I think it necessary to inform the Officers, that if any one
of them shall presume to write to the Commander of the
Squadron (unless there shall be Ships enough present to bring
them to immediate Trial) for a Court-Martial to investigate
their conduct on a frivolous pretence, thereby depriving his
Majesty of their services, by obliging the Commander of the
Squadron to confine them, that I shall and do consider such
conduct as a direct breach of the 14th, and part of the 19th,
Articles of War; and shall order them to be Tried for the
same.

Given under my hand, on board His Majesty's Ship Boreas, at Antigua, the 28th of January, 1787.

HORATIO NELSON.

TO PHILIP STEPHENS, ESQ., ADMIRALTY.

[Original, in the Admiralty.]

Boreas, Antigua, February 4th, 1787.

Sir,

In September 1786, I transmitted to the Navy Board, for their consideration, several copies of letters,[9] which Mr. Lewis, late Surgeon of the Rattler Sloop, had sent to Captain Collingwood, and by him transmitted to me.

As I conceived them highly improper, and not having it in my power to try Mr. Lewis by a Court-Martial for his conduct, (for want of Ships,) I thought it proper to refer the propriety of his writing such letters relating to the Commander of the Squadron, to them, imagining at least they would not employ him until necessity might oblige them.

As detaining Mr. Lewis in this Country till the arrival of a sufficient number of Men-of-War, might have been the occasion of his death, I therefore could not, with humanity, prevent him from going to England; as by the Report of the Survey (which I had the honour of transmitting to you in October last) it was thought actually necessary for the re-establishment of his health.

In answer to which the Navy Board acquaint me they never interfere with Officers in Commission.

I have therefore thought proper to transmit to you, for their Lordships' information, copies of the whole correspondence, that they may take such steps as they may think proper on the occasion.[1]

I have the honour to remain, Sir, &c.

HORATIO NELSON.

[9] Vide p. 195, ante.

[1] Captain Nelson was informed, in reply, that the Admiralty had recommended the Navy Board not to employ Mr. Lewis until he shall have made a proper apology to him for the disrespectful expressions contained in his Letters. Vide p. 261, post.

[Original, in the Admiralty.]

Boreas, Antigua, February 8th, 1787.

Sir,

In September 1786, I appointed Mr. Thomas Morgan to act as Surgeon of the Rattler in the room of Mr. William Lewis, who was invalided to go to England for the establishment of his health.

Inclosed I send you the Navy Board's letter, and also one from Mr. Morgan. Mr. Morgan's situation is a hard one. The Appointment to the Rattler was an additional expense, which he would not have been subjected to had he remained in the Boreas. However, the Service obliged his going, and that was not to be considered; but Mr. Morgan had many and just reasons to refuse bringing a Medicine Chest and Instruments. The Rattler was expected to be ordered Home, and if she goes soon he will still be out of pocket by the Appointment; but Mr. Morgan would not allow the King's Service to be injured by his refusal to take the Medicine Chest and Instruments; hoping, and indeed I told him, that there would be no doubt of his being put on the Surgeons' List for his conduct, more especially as he had passed for Surgeon of a Third Rate, and had served all the War with an unexceptionable character. This, I hope, will weigh with their Lordships, and induce them to order Mr. Morgan to be put upon the Surgeons' List.

I have the honour to remain, &c.

HORATIO NELSON.

TO PHILIP STEPHENS, ESQ., ADMIRALTY.

[Original, in the Admiralty.]

Boreas, Antigua, February 9th, 1787.

Sir,

In January, the Rattler being at Barbadoes, seized a Schooner, being clearly by her papers an American Vessel.

I transmit you the several letters which have passed, and the Case laid before Mr. Charles Brandford, his Majesty's Attorney and Advocate-General of Barbadoes.

Their Lordships will see that he has refused his Opinion, unless accompanied by a proper fee. Captain Collingwood, not having money to pay for Opinions, could do nothing to the Vessel ; and she is now trading in these Seas.

I some time ago told you of Mr. Brandford's intentions; and a Captain of a Man-of-War that does not carry a long purse cannot prosecute Vessels under Mr. Brandford of Barbadoes, and Mr. Byam of Grenada. They, I am certain, do not deserve (and I hope their Lordships will think with me) to be his Majesty's Law Officers. But whilst I am complaining of Mr. Brandford of Barbadoes, let me do justice to Mr. William Forbes, the King's Proctor, who carried on this business without demanding any fees ; and how high does Messrs. Brandford and Byams' conduct place Mr. Stanley and Mr. Adye, who have ever carried on Prosecutions, and given opinions without fee or reward.

I am, &c.,
Horatio Nelson.

TO THE REVEREND MR. NELSON, HILBOROUGH.

[Autograph, in the Nelson Papers.]

Boreas, English Harbour, February 9th, 1787.

My dear Brother,

Your letter of December 4th, I received by the Packet, and do most sincerely partake of the happiness you enjoy by being united to an amiable woman. You will treat her kindly and tenderly, I have no doubt. A truly good husband is a good thing, and I hope to see it fully in you. I beg my best respects to the lady. The summer will probably bring me to England, but the time lays with the Admiralty. I fancy the King's Servants and the Officers of my little Squadron will not be sorry to part with me. They think I make them do their duty too strictly : and the West Indians will give a Balle Champetre upon my departure. They hate me; and they will every Officer who does his duty.

You know I have the honour of having Prince William under my command. In every respect, both as a Man and a Prince, I love him. He has honoured me as his confidential friend; in this he shall not be mistaken. I am sorry for poor Kate, but marriage is not a thing to be hastily entered into; and it's better to find a man to be good for nothing before, than after marriage. I am happy my Father has been able to make an addition to Maurice's allowance. I have never lost sight of his preferment in the line he is in, but my interest is but rising. I have already spoken to his Royal Highness about him, but it must take time to get on; and the Prince has it not in his power to do all he wishes at present. My time is short; therefore my letter must finish. Compliments to all I know, and believe me ever,

Your affectionate brother,

HORATIO NELSON.

TO WILLIAM LOCKER, ESQ., TOWN MALLING.

[Autograph, in the Locker Papers.]

Boreas, English Harbour, February 9th, 1787.

My dear Friend,

Your letter of November 29th I received by a Merchant-ship; it is the only one I have got, although I see you have wrote several desiring me to get things; but not a line has ever reached me till now. I was fearful I had unknowingly offended, but am happy to find it is not so. I am at a loss how to direct this letter, but shall send it to your Agent; for I have never heard of your removal to Kensington, nor am I certain you live there now, but it must take its chance. I am here without Ships enough to hold Court-Martials; and discipline, you know, cannot be kept up without that resort.

Mountserrat, February 13.

I am here with the Pegasus and Solebay; the Island has made fine Addresses and good dinners, &c. To-morrow we sail for Nevis and St. Christopher's, where the same fine things will be done again. His Royal Highness keeps up strict discipline in his Ship, and without paying him any compliment, she is one of the first ordered Frigates I have seen. He has had more plague with his Officers than enough : his First Lieutenant will, I have no doubt, be broke. I have put him under Arrest; he having wrote for a Court-Martial on himself to vindicate his conduct, because his Captain thought proper to reprimand him in the Order-book: in short, our Service has been so much relaxed during the War, that it will cost many a Court-Martial to bring it up again.

I am kept in utter darkness about who is coming to this Country. Since August, when Sir Richard Hughes left the Station, the Admiralty have not wrote me a single line, only to take the Pegasus and Solebay under my command. Many things have happened, and they have neither approved, nor otherwise, of my conduct. That Lord Howe[3] is a strange character—it may be all right, but I can't understand it. Pray remember me kindly to the Bradleys ; I am truly sorry for poor Dick. I had not heard of his death. To Lord Ducie,[4] and any others that may please to honour me with their remembrance. I am sorry for your wine, but I have five dozen of it saved and in bottles. Rum I have plenty of on board, and you shall have as much as you please; and whatever else I am in possession of, being, as I ought to be, with the truest esteem,

Your most faithful,

HORATIO NELSON.

TO MRS. NISBET.

[From Clarke and M'Arthur, vol. i. p. 90.]

Boreas, Montserat, 11th Feb. 1787.

My dear Fanny,
　　We are at last out of English Harbour again, and so far I am on my way to be with you. I anticipate with pleasure our

---

[3] First Lord of the Admiralty.　　　　[4] Vide ante.

meeting; for never do I feel truly happy when separated from you. Length of time often, too often, gives proof of the failings of human nature, and how difficult it is to be perfect. You have given me a proof that your goodness increases by time. These I trust will ever be my sentiments; if they are not, I do verily believe it will be my folly that occasions it.

Never think otherwise, than that I am, in the fullest sense of the word, most affectionately your

HORATIO NELSON.

TO PHILIP STEPHENS, ESQ., ADMIRALTY.

[Original, in the Admiralty.]

Boreas, Nevis, 15th February 1787.

Sir,

I beg leave to acquaint you for their Lordships' information that his Majesty's Ship Maidstone arrived here yesterday evening.

I have the honour to remain, &c.

HORATIO NELSON.

TO MRS. NISBET.

[From Clarke and M'Arthur, vol. i. p. 92.]

Boreas, 28th February 1787.

Indeed I am not well enough to write much, and I have a good deal of fag before me. Captain Holloway is gone from us. Captain Newcome[5] is laid up; therefore poor I must be worked: and I am the more mortified, as I purposed, when the Prince went over to the other side of the Island, to have escaped that trip, and have got a few hours to see you: but that is all over. It is possible His Royal Highness may stop at Nevis in his way up from Tortola. This, however, shall be his own act, and not mine. To-day we dine with the Merchants; I wish it over: to-morrow a large party at Nicholas Town; and on Friday in Town

---

[5] Captain Henry Newcome, of the Maidstone, of 28 guns, who was Posted on the 19th May 1782: he died about 1797.

here.　Saturday, sail for Old Road; Sunday, dine on
Brimstone Hill; Monday, Mr. Georges' at Sandy Point, and
in the evening the Freemasons give a ball.　Tuesday, please
God, we sail.　I did not like the cast of the day at Mr.——,
and I cannot carry two faces.　Farewell till to-morrow, and
be assured,

I am, ever your affectionate,
HORATIO NELSON.

TO MRS. NISBET.

[From Clarke and M'Arthur, vol. i. p. 92.]

March 3rd 1787.

My journey to Nicholas Town was too great a fag in the
height of the sun: I was very ill after it; and nothing but his
Royal Highness's attention and condescension, could or should
make me go through it.　However, I am quite well this morning; and as we shall be pretty quiet to-day, I hope to be able
to bear to-morrow and Monday, tolerably well.　We shall
most likely be at Nevis about the 18th; but keep this to yourself.

I am, &c.
HORATIO NELSON.

TO MRS. NISBET.

[From Clarke and M'Arthur, vol. i. p. 93. This was Nelson's last Letter to Mrs.
Nisbet before their marriage, which took place at Nevis, on the 12th of March
1787. The date of that event, (which is erroneously given, as well by Clarke and
M'Arthur, as in the Nelson Pedigree in the Genealogical Books of the Knights
of the Bath,) is shown to have been the *twelfth* of March, by the following passage in a Letter from Lady Nelson to her husband, written from Bath on the 11th
of March 1797, immediately after she had heard of the Battle of St. Vincent: ·

" To-morrow is our wedding day, when it gave me a dear husband, and my
child the best of fathers."

His Royal Highness fulfilled his promise, by giving away the bride.
Frances Herbert Woollward was the only child of William Woollward, Esq.,
Senior Judge of Nevis, by Molly, sister of John Richardson Herbert, Esq.,
President of the Council of that Island.　She was born about 1763, and married
first, Josiah Nisbet, M.D., who died eighteen months afterwards, leaving an only
child, Josiah.　At the time of her marriage with Captain Nelson, she was about
twenty-five years of age, and died on the 4th of May 1831, aged 68.　Her uncle,

Mr. Herbert, died on the 18th January 1793, leaving an only child, Martha
Williams, wife of Andrew Hamilton, of Nevis, Esq., who died without issue in
August 1819 ; and in the following year, Mr. Herbert's nephew, Magnus Morton
of Nevis, Esq., pursuant to directions in his Will, assumed the Name and Arms of
Herbert. He married Christian, daughter of George Forbes of Bush Hill, in that
Island, who is mentioned in one of Nelson's Letters.

Boreas, Sandy Point, 6th March 1787.

How uncertain are the movements of us Sailors. His
Royal Highness is rather unwell ; therefore I have given up the
idea of visiting Tortola for the present. To-day we dine with
Mr. Georges, at his Country-house. I am now feeling most
awkwardly : his Royal Highness has been with me all this
morning, and has told me, that as things here are changed, if
I am not married when we go to Nevis, it is hardly probable
he should see me there again ; that I had promised him not
to be married, unless he was present ; that he wished to be
there, to show his esteem for me, and should be much mortified if impediments were thrown in the way. He intends this
as a mark of honour to me ; as such I wish to receive it. Indeed his Royal Highness's behaviour throughout has been that
of a friend, instead of a person so elevated above me. He
told me this morning, that since he had been under my command he has been happy ; and that I should find him sincere
in his friendship. Heaven bless you ; and I need scarcely say,
how much I am

Your affectionate,
HORATIO NELSON.

TO PHILIP STEPHENS, ESQ., ADMIRALTY.

[Original, in the Admiralty.]

Boreas, Nevis, March 15th, 1787.

Sir,

February the 9th, I had last the honour of writing you
from English Harbour. On the 10th I sailed with the Solebay and Pegasus, leaving the Rattler at the wharf to be
repaired, she having been found exceedingly bad, and her timbers rotten. The builder, however, is of opinion that she may
be put in a state to undertake a summer's passage. I have
ordered her to be sheathed with wood, as the expense is so

much less, and the copper would be only taken out of this Country merely for a passage, when it must come off again. I hope their Lordships will approve of what I have done.

The Boreas, I must also observe, begins to get rather bad. In the beginning of May I shall carry her to English Harbour, to be made fit for a passage home, as I dare say their Lordship's intentions are not to keep her in these Seas longer than the hurricane season.

I have attended his Royal Highness since our sailing, to Montserrat, Nevis, and St. Christopher's, and shall sail for the Virgins on Monday the 19th instant, from whence, after calling at English Harbour for a few days, I shall attend his Royal Highness to Grenada, which will finish his tour. After wooding at Prince Rupert's and visiting Barbadoes, May will be advanced; and the Pegasus will be fitted for [her] voyage to the place mentioned in their Lordships' secret orders.

Herewith I have the honour to transmit you the State and Condition of his Majesty's Ships and Vessels on the Leeward Island Station.

I am, Sir, &c.

HORATIO NELSON.

TO CAPTAIN WILLIAM LOCKER, ROYAL NAVY, KENSINGTON.

[Autograph, in the Locker Papers.]

Boreas, on Her passage to Tortola, March 21st, 1787.

My dear Friend,

Your letter of December 26th I received a few days ago: as this is the second letter I have received, dated Kensington, I shall direct this thither. I wish I may be able to procure any of the things your friend wants, but I fear it is too late on the Station to expect much: indeed, my time since November, has been entirely taken up attending the Prince in his tour round these Islands. However, except Grenada, this is the last, when I shall repair to English Harbour, and fit the Boreas for a voyage to England. Happy shall I be when that time arrives: no man has had more illness or trouble on a Station than I have experienced; but let me lay a balance on the other side—I am married to an amiable woman, that far makes amends for everything: indeed till I married her I never knew happiness. And I am morally certain she will continue to make me a happy man for the rest of my days. I shall have great pleasure in introducing you to her. Prince William did me the honour to stand her Father upon the occasion, and has shown every act of kindness that the most professed friendship could bestow. His Royal Highness leaves this Country in June, by which time I hope my orders will arrive, or somebody be appointed to the Command of this Station. The wonder to me is, that any independent man will accept [it,] for there is nothing pleasant to be got by it. Farewell, my dear [*illegible*] and believe me to be

> Ever your affectionate
> HORATIO NELSON.

Remember me kindly to the [*illegible*] and Commissioner Kirke when you see him, and I am much obliged by their kind inquiries.

TO PHILIP STEPHENS, ESQ., ADMIRALTY.

[Original, in the Admiralty.]

Boreas, Antigua, April 14th, 1787.

Sir,

I have lately received a letter from my Agent acquainting me that the Navy Board had deducted £12. 18*s*. sterling, from my wages, for some Supernumeraries, which were borne for wages on the Books of his Majesty's Ship under my command. I must therefore submit the propriety of their conduct to my Lords' Commissioners of the Admiralty; as from the nature of the circumstances which obliged me to bear those men on the said List, I am confident their Lordships will allow I am not in the least culpable.

I must beg leave to acquaint you that on my joining the Boreas I found a vast number of men on board her who indeed appeared to me to have been very improperly entered into the Service, for several of them were fit objects to be invalided; and as the Boreas was ordered on a Foreign Station, I therefore sent them to the Hospital; at the same time discharging them to the Supernume-

rary List for wages (from whence they were D. S. Q.[6] before
the complement was full,) for if I had kept them on the Ship's
Books and carried them to a hot climate, the consequence must
have been dreaded. I therefore hope their Lordships' will
consider my conduct in this case as undeserving of pecuniary
punishment, for I could not have a wish to bear more Seamen
than my complement, as undoubtedly I knew it was contrary to
establishment, and that it would bring an additional expense
on Government.

I must also beg leave to acquaint you that the Navy Board
have likewise deducted £5. 18s. 9d. for some Supernumeraries
borne for victuals only, without order, part of which Supernumeraries were passengers going out to join Sir Richard
Hughes, one of them his own son, two Midshipmen, a servant
to Lady Hughes, and two boys, who were servants to the Gunner who deserted. If there is an error in respect to bearing
them without order, I am induced to think it is not their Lordships' desire that I should be amenable, by paying for their
victualling; for their being discharged to a King's Ship, with
their original entries, which is agreeable to the rules of the
Service in those cases, must entirely clear me; and I cannot be
supposed to be any longer responsible for them.

I must therefore request their Lordships will please to direct
that the Navy Board do grant a Certificate, that I may receive
my full wages.

I am, Sir, &c.
HORATIO NELSON.

In respect to Faster Doudle, one of the Supernumeraries, I
did not know of his being on board till the Ship was at Sea,
when I thought it rather hard that the man should be obliged
to serve his |King without receiving some gratuity or other.
I therefore entered him, as appears by the Books, but on the
Ship's arrival at Barbadoes, he deserted her, and consequently
his wages are forfeited.

---

[6] "D. S. Q," the indication of having been "Discharged to Sick Quarters."

TO PHILIP STEPHENS, ESQ., ADMIRALTY.

[Original, in the Admiralty.]

Boreas, English Harbour, Antigua, April 16th, 1787.

Sir,

Inclosed, I transmit you the Sentences of the Court-Martials held on some seamen of the Squadron. The two men belonging to the Solebay have received their punishment. William Clarke, the third, belonging to the Rattler, I have this day pardoned at the intercession of his Royal Highness.[7] John Woodhouse's sentence, with a Minute, is left for their Lordships' consideration.

I have the honour to be, &c.,

HORATIO NELSON.

TO PHILIP STEPHENS, ESQ., ADMIRALTY.

[Original, in the Admiralty.]

Boreas, Antigua, 16th April, 1787.

Sir,

Herewith I transmit you for their Lordships' information the State and Condition of his Majesty's Ships and Vessels in these seas.

I am, Sir, &c.

HORATIO NELSON.

N.B.—The Boreas is found to be rotten, and if she does not reach England before the hurricane season, she will be too bad for the voyage. The Rattler I shall order to sail from this Country on the 1st of June. She is quite rotten.

---

[7] It appears that Captain Nelson exceeded his authority in pardoning this culprit, who was condemned to death, though he might have suspended the execution of his sentence. The criminal was, however, pardoned by the Admiralty. Vide p. 253.

TO LIEUTENANT ISAAC SCHOMBERG.

[From a Copy in the Nelson Papers.]

English Harbour, April 18th, 1787.

Sir,

I am this moment honoured with your letter of this day's date, requesting that I would be kind enough to furnish you with the charge or charges which you suppose I mean to exhibit against you, that you may, whenever a Court-Martial offers, give as little trouble as possible; as you have reason to believe that your long and close confinement must arise from some other cause than that of your own wishes expressed to me in your letter dated January the 23rd.[8]

In answer, I beg leave to assure you that I never was more hurt, than that an Officer whom I very much respected, should do such an improper act as to deprive his Majesty of his services at a time they were wanted. My orders to the Squadron were to prevent other Officers from falling into the same error. I have not, nor can any other person, have any charge against you, until the Court-Martial which you desired to be held to investigate your conduct is over; and then I can tell you I have no charge whatsoever against you. Your confinement is your own. Had you not wrote to me for a Court-Martial, I dare say you never would have given me occasion to put you under Arrest.

Had I not ordered you into Arrest, you might then have accused me of having left you again to be unjustly accused, as set forth in your letter.

I am, Sir, &c.

HORATIO NELSON.

TO H. R. H. PRINCE WILLIAM HENRY.

[Original, in the possession of William Henry Whitehead, Esq., whose Father the late Alexander Whitehead, Esq., was Private Secretary to the Duke of Clarence, and Purser of His Majesty's Ships Pegasus, Andromeda, and Valiant, while those Ships were under His Royal Highness's command.]

Boreas, English Harbour, April 18th, 1787.

Sir,

Should any Dispatches from the Admiralty or other Public Boards be on board the Packet or other Vessels directed for

[8] Vide p. 209, ante.

me, I request that your Royal Highness will open them; and
as the contents may be, so you will regulate your proceedings.

> I have the honour to remain,
>> Your Royal Highness's
>>> Most obedient humble Servant,
>>>> HORATIO NELSON.

TO H. R. H. PRINCE WILLIAM HENRY.

[Original, in the possession of William Henry Whitehead, Esq.]

Boreas, Nevis, April 26th, 1787.

Sir,

By the death of my poor friend Collingwood,[8] a Vacancy has
arisen for a Commander and Lieutenant. In appointing Mr
Wallis [9] to the command of her, I hope I acted as you wish
me. The vacancy as Lieutenant, I leave to be filled up by
your Royal Highness. I inclose Mr. Gage's, and have desired Mr. Wallis to take a copy of my letter to him in answer
to his. I own I can't help saying his pretensions are not very
great, but this I leave to your consideration.

I hope your Royal Highness will allow me to beg for your
interest, should any difficulties arise about Mr. Wallis's being
confirmed, for he is a good Officer; and I am sure will do
credit to his Majesty's service. I left English Harbour yesterday, quite fitted up for my voyage Home. The business respecting the Fraud,[1] I have examined into as far as the parties
choose to disclose themselves. They are not disinterested.
They wish to be insured of so much per centage upon all sums
recovered; but they have given me a proof, by an account of
one quarter, viz. from March to June, 1782, of what Government was defrauded in that quarter; and I am most thoroughly
convinced they are enabled to prove Frauds to a very large
amount. I shall send the Accounts to Mr. Pitt, for Parliament

---

[8] Captain Wilfred Collingwood, of the Rattler, who died on the 21st April
1787, vide p. 230, post.

[9] James Wallis, then first Lieutenant of the Boreas, the writer of the Narrative
of Captain Nelson's Proceedings on the Leeward Islands Station, before referred
to.

[1] See many subsequent Letters.

must know of it, in order to enable Administration to send out persons vested with powers to make examinations in the West Indies.

No persons have died at the hospital, but none have recovered. I hope your Royal Highness has had a pleasant trip. We have yet heard nothing of the Packet. Sir Thomas Shirley is here, and Lord Ward[2] is appointed Chief Justice in the room of Mr. Dasent, deceased. I have the honour to remain, with the greatest respect,

Your Royal Highness's
Most obliged obedient Servant,
HORATIO NELSON.

The Gentleman you are pleased to appoint, which I take for granted, will be Mr. Church,[3] had better be appointed Second of the Boreas for the present; and I can make any arrangements your Royal Highness pleases, when I have the honour of seeing you.

———————

TO PHILIP STEPHENS, ESQ., ADMIRALTY.

[Original, in the Admiralty.]

Boreas, Nevis, 2nd May 1787.

Sir,

Herewith I have the honour to transmit you the State and Condition of his Majesty's Ships and Vessels on this Station; and also a list of Appointments made by me, and hope their Lordships' will approve of the Officers I have promoted.

I have the honour, &c.
HORATIO NELSON.

---

[2] John Ward, Esq., was appointed Chief Justice of Nevis, and it does not appear why Nelson should call him *Lord* Ward. The name of John Dasent occurs, however, as Chief Justice of Nevis, in the Royal Kalendar until 1799.

[3] Stephen George Church, afterwards a Post-Captain.

A List of the Appointments and Removals of Officers by Horatio Nelson, Esq., Captain of his Majesty's Ship Boreas, and Senior Officer, for the time being, of his Majesty's Ships and Vessels on the Leeward Island Station, between the 1st of April, and 2nd of May 1787.

Time when	Persons Names	Qualities	Appointments	From what Ship	To what Ship	In whose room	Occasion of the Vacancy
17 87. 21 April.	James Wallis	1st Lieut.	Commander	Boreas	Rattler	Wilfred Collingwood	Death
21 „	Digby Dent	2d Lieut.	1st Lieut.	Boreas	Boreas	James Wallis	Death
21 „	Stephen Geo. Church	Acting Lieut.	2nd Lieut.	Pegasus	Boreas	Digby Dent	Death

HORATIO NE SON.

TO SIR CHARLES MIDDLETON, BART.

[Original Draught, in the Nelson Papers.]

[Captain Sir Charles Middleton, afterwards an Admiral, and First Lord of the Admiralty, and who was created a Peer in 1805, by the title of Lord Barham, was then Comptroller of the Navy.]

Boreas, Nevis, 2nd May 1787.

Sir,

As a Fraud is likely to be discovered in the Naval Department under your direction, I think it proper to make you acquainted with it, that villany may be punished, and Frauds prevented in future.

Sir, before I proceed, I cannot help mentioning a circumstance which hurt me, when I was first left in the command here. The Deputy Naval Officer brought me Bills to sign for money which was owing for goods purchased. I insisted upon having the original Vouchers brought to me, that I might examine if they were really purchased at the market-price, and that Government was not cheated: this I could not obtain; and I wrote to your Board upon the subject of my approval of Bills, without being convinced that the former money I had approved of drawing for, was expended to my satisfaction, and that it was laid out in the most advantageous manner for Government. The answer seemed to imply, that you thought the old Forms were sufficient; which only was a certificate from the Naval Officer, and the Master Shipwright, that so much money was wanted. Since that period I have been less close in my examination, as I should have been very sorry to have incurred the displeasure of you, Sir, a gentleman who stands so high, both as a Professional man, and in the Department you fill with so much honour.

I enclose you the accounts of the Fraud[4] from March to June 1782. That the fictious name of 'Co. C.' stands for 'A. M.,' I am so little versed in mercantile matters, I will not take upon me to say, but all the credits due Cornelius Cole are carried in the Book to the account of Antony Munton. It will be necessary I should tell you who these gentlemen are, that have given this information: they were the partners of Mr. William Whitehead, under the firm of Whitehead and Co.: having separated, they have possessed themselves of all Whitehead's Books and Papers. Mr. Wilkinson was brought up under Muir and Atkinson, and is a very shrewd sensible man. Higgins is likewise a man of business. Wilkinson has been in various Departments of Government, in St. Lucia, Barbadoes, &c. and assures me, he can discover all the Frauds committed there, as easy as these, if Government think proper to reward them. Indeed they do not seem to be playing the fool; for if nothing is recovered, they desire nothing, and of what is actually recovered, only a certain per centage.

The business of Negro hire is yet not conducted in the manner you wish. If, Sir, when I arrive in England,[5] you choose to have any conversation upon this subject, I shall be happy to give you every information in my power. I have been merely a temporary Commanding Officer here, and have been expecting, since October, a Senior Officer; therefore I

---

[4] The *Original* communications from Messrs. Wilkinson and Higgins respecting these Frauds, which were the subject of so many Letters from Captain Nelson are still preserved among the Nelson Papers.

[5] On the 16th of August 1787, shortly after the Boreas' return to England, Sir Charles Middleton wrote to Captain Nelson in reply to this Letter, in which he said he had before written to request Captain Nelson would do everything in his power to collect evidence of those Frauds; that he had been in communication with Lord Howe on the subject; that the business should be taken up or his arrival in Town, when he wished to see him; and that he hoped he would, in the mean time, use every means to substantiate the charge which he had little doubt was well founded.—*Original*, in the Nelson Papers.

did not choose to enter into the minutiæ of the Yard, which, as Commander-in-Chief, I certainly should have done.

I have the honour to be, &c.

HORATIO NELSON.

TO VISCOUNT HOWE, FIRST LORD OF THE ADMIRALTY.

[Autograph draught, in the Nelson Papers. The date is not given, but it was probably written in May 1787.]

My Lord,

The subject of this Letter, I am sure, will require no apology for my addressing myself immediately to your Lordship, and not to the Board. Frauds upon Government there is no man who is not most thoroughly sensible of; but how to detect them has hitherto been a matter to be accomplished, but a door is opened here, which I hope will, if not the means of recovering back large sums of money, at least be the means of preventing Frauds in future.

On the 13th of April, a Mr. Higgins and Wilkinson came to English Harbour, and delivered me a Letter similar to the one enclosed to his Royal Highness, which was given me to present. His Royal Highness desired me to do what I thought proper and right on this occasion: in consequence, I have had several meetings with these gentlemen, and have examined the books and papers of Mr. Whitehead, (I must observe, these gentlemen were partners of Whitehead's, and have possessed themselves of all his books, papers, &c.,) by which I am most thoroughly convinced of the Frauds, and that to a very large amount. You will perceive these gentlemen expect to gain by this discovery. However, I suppose it matters but little the motive, if the business can be accomplished. I have got the Account of the Storekeeper for one quarter, which I inclose. Vouchers are looked upon in general as a sufficient check against Frauds. There is not a merchant in the Town of St. John's but will not tell you he never knows the Vouchers he signs; and what they tell me is the reason for their not looking at them is, that in this Country a thing is worth what it will bring, and every man is to sell for the most he can get. The fictious name of Cornelius Cole

6

standing for Mr. Munton, the Naval Storekeeper, I am so
little, as you will believe, versed in Merchants' Accounts, that
I do not absolutely say it is so, but there appears a circumstance which is very odd :—all the credits due to Cornelius Cole are carried to the account of Anthony Munton.

> I have the honour to remain, my Lord,
> > Your Lordship's, &c.
> > > HORATIO NELSON.

TO THE DUKE OF RICHMOND, MASTER-GENERAL OF THE
ORDNANCE.

[Autograph draught, in the Nelson Papers. The date is not given, but it was
probably written in May 1787.]

My Lord,

The subject of this letter will, I trust, render all apologies
unnecessary for my addressing myself to you. A few days
ago, Mr. Higgins and Wilkinson, merchants of St. John's, in
the Island of Antigua, came to English Harbour, to communicate to His Royal Highness and myself, that they were privy
to great Frauds which had been committed upon Government.
By agreements of a Mr. Whitehead, and various Officers of
his Majesty, employed in this Island, amongst others the
Storekeeper of the Ordnance. As this is in your Grace's Department, I shall not trouble you with any other, but be as
explicit as I am able.

As His Royal Highness could not attend to this business,
he desired me to make the necessary inquiries, and to take such
steps as I should think proper. These gentlemen were partners
of Mr. Whitehead under the firm of Whitehead and Co., they are
in possession of all Mr. Whitehead's books and papers, and
the agreement between your Storekeeper and Mr. Whitehead.
These gentlemen, as will appear by the inclosed letter, are
not publishers of this Fraud merely for the honour of serving
the Public; interest has its weight. I send you an Account of
one quarter's Fraud, and I examined several in the books:
but they declined my having more, till they were satisfied
Government would reward them in proportion to the Frauds
discovered. As a man who has more than once stood for-

ward to detect and bring to punishment those who are guilty of defrauding the Public, I may venture to express myself freely. Mr. Wilkinson was brought up in the house of Muir and Atkinson; has been employed under the different Officers in the Victualling, &c. He declares his knowledge of, and that he can bring to light, all the Frauds committed in those Islands, and even at Jamaica. He appears, as well as Higgins, a shrewd sensible man, and I believe can bring much iniquity to light. In Antigua, in the different Departments, at least, they say £300,000; at St. Lucia as much; at Barbadoes not far short; and at Jamaica, upwards of a million. What of this may be recovered, or if any, I know not: however, this good effect it surely will have, that of preventing the like in future.

More than probable, by the time your Grace receives this letter, the Boreas will have sailed for England, where I shall ever be ready to give your Grace any information you may wish to know of me. There is one observation, which I beg leave to make : it will be said, ' Vouchers are produced, and Merchants have attested that they are at the market-price.' In this Country the market-price is what an article will sell for ; and no Merchant in this Country, but will declare, that in signing Vouchers for each other, they never look at the articles, saying, a thing is always worth what it will bring: they are indeed, my Lord, no check, in this Country.

> I have the honour to remain,
> Your Grace's most obedient, &c.
> HORATIO NELSON.

TO CUTHBERT COLLINGWOOD, ESQ.

Autograph, in the possession of the Honourable Mrs. Newnham Collingwood.

Boreas, Nevis, May 3rd, 1787.

My dear Collingwood,

To be the messenger of bad news is my misfortune, but still it is a tribute which friends owe each other. I have lost my friend, you an affectionate brother.[6] Too great a zeal

---

[6] On the death of his brother Captain Wilfred Collingwood, of the Rattler.

in serving his Country hastened his end. The greatest consolation the survivor can receive, is a thorough knowledge of a life spent with honour to himself, and of service to his Country. If the tribute of tears are valuable, my friend had them.

The esteem he stood in with his Royal Highness was great. His letter to me on his death is the strongest testimony of it. I send you an extract of it:—'Collingwood, poor fellow, is no more. I have cried for him, and most sincerely do I condole with you on his loss. In him, his Majesty has lost a faithful Servant, and the Service a most excellent Officer.' A testimony of regard so honourable, is more to be coveted than anything this world could have afforded, and must be a balm to his surviving friends.

The Rattler has been refitting at English Harbour, and when I arrived there in the middle of April, Wilfred was a little complaining, but I did not think, at first, anything dangerous was to be apprehended. But in a few days I perceived he was in a rapid decline. Dr. Young told me to send him to Sea, as the only chance. He sailed on the Tuesday for Grenada, where I was in hopes, could he have reached Mr. Hume's, some fortunate circumstance might turn out; but it pleased God to order it otherwise. On Friday, the 21st of April, at ten at night, he left this life without a groan or struggle. The Ship put into St. Vincent's, where he was interred with all Military Honours; the Regiment President, and Council, attending him to the grave. I mention this circumstance to show the respect for his character. It is a credit to the people of St. Vincent's, which I did not think they would have deserved. I have directed Wallis[7] not to suffer a thing to be disposed of, but to have everything sealed up the moment he goes on board, and that I will take them on board the Boreas, and carry them home.

Adieu, my good friend, and be assured I am, with the truest regard, your affectionate friend,

HORATIO NELSON.

Mrs. Nelson desires to present her kind compliments and condolence.

---

[7] Lieutenant Wallis of the Boreas, whom Nelson had appointed to succeed Captain Wilfred Collingwood, in command of the Rattler.

[Autograph draught, in the Nelson Papers. The address of this Letter is not given.]

Boreas, Nevis, May 4th, 1787.

Sir,

As Frauds in the different Departments of Government are in a train to be discovered, and that to a very large amount, I have thought it proper to send all the papers and circumstances relative to it, at once to you. On the 13th of April, Messrs. Higgins and Wilkinson, merchants in the town of St. John's, in the Island of Antigua, gave his Royal Highness information that Frauds had been committed upon Government. As His Royal Highness could not attend to this matter, he desired me to do what was right in the business; since which time I have endeavoured to make myself master of this subject, and have examined a variety of books and papers, particularly those of a Mr. Whitehead, who appears a principal Agent. It is unnecessary to observe, that Higgins and Wilkinson were partners of Whitehead, under the firm of Whitehead and Co., but have now parted from ' him, and possessed themselves of all his books and papers, from which it appears, that Government has been defrauded in a most scandalous and infamous manner. The only emulation I can perceive is, who could cheat most. That the fictious name of Cornelius Cole stands for Antony Munton, his Majesty's Naval Storekeeper, I really am so little versed in Merchants' accounts, that I cannot assert (as these gentlemen declare) it does; but this circumstance makes a strong impression, that all the credits of Cornelius Cole are carried to the account of Antony Munton.

Vouchers have hitherto been deemed a sufficient check in the purchasing of Stores, that the market-price must be known: the Commissioners appointed to examine the Public Accounts of the Kingdom, in their sixth Report, were the first who doubted the credit of Vouchers. Although that Report was founded on Army Accounts, yet the same chain of reasoning will hold in the Naval Department abroad; for there is not a merchant in these Islands that does not always sign Vouchers whenever they are brought to them : they say, there is no fixed price for anything in this Country, that an article is worth what it will bring. These gentlemen have been in various employments in the different Islands, under those employed in the Victualling, &c. and they assure me, that they are certain they can discover frauds in Antigua to near £500,000; St. Lucia, £300,000; Barbadoes, £250,000; and at Jamaica, £1,000,000. The sum is immense. Whether they can make it out, time must determine. However, they only wish to be rewarded for what is actually recovered, and they are both shrewd sensible men ; and must know they are for ever ruined in this Country, if they do not make out what they have so boldly asserted. No. 1, is a letter to his Royal Highness; No. 2 is their letter of terms; Nos. 3, 4, 5, account of the Frauds; No. 6, a letter to me ; No. 7, an account of the method of cheating.

I hope, Sir, I am right in sending these Papers to you. If I have erred, be pleased to put a favourable construction on my intentions. I assure you, the ardent wish of my heart is to see defrauders of their Country punished. I shall most probably have sailed for England by the time you receive this letter, and shall always be ready to give every information you may wish to know of me.

I have, &c.,

HORATIO NELSON.

TO H. R. H. PRINCE WILLIAM HENRY.

[Original, in the possession of William Henry Whitehead, Esq.]

Nevis, May 7th, 1787.

Sir,

Nothing, I do assure your Royal Highness, could have given me greater concern than to find you are unwell, but rest, I most sincerely hope, will soon re-establish your health. Nothing else could have been of real service, for medicine in that disorder, without quietness, does more harm than good. I would instantly, upon the receipt of your letter, have sailed, but Herbert[7] is near going; and it is impossible to move a

---

[7] Apparently the President of Nevis.

female in a few hours—never yet having made the Boreas her
home. I therefore, with pain I assure you, accept your kindness in staying here. Church I have sent back in the Rattlea
with two Commissions. Mr. Rice, Wallis tells me, does
not now wish to go Home. I have sent the Maidstone among
the Bahamas, where I hear this Piratical fellow is gone; and
not having the smallest official intelligence that any Commanding Officer is coming out, will you turn in your mind
about going to Jamaica? If you should suppose there will
not be Ships enough on that Station, I will send Rattler with
you, and she may proceed from thence with your dispatches
for England. I should hope by the time Wallis reaches you
that you will be so much better, that I shall see the Pegasus
down here: but Sir, let me intreat that you will pursue such
plans as Fidge[8] has laid down for the re-establishment of your
health, which is the only consideration with me. Should you
not think it necessary to take the Rattler to Jamaica, I shall
send her to England in a few days after she joins me. I shall,
if possible, send you a copy of my letter to Mr. Pitt; but Sir,
allow me to say silence on this subject[9] is [the] best mode to
be pursued at present. Although every person is talking of
it, yet no person knows for a certainty where the blow will
fall.

I have sent to the Duke of Richmond and Lord Howe what
has fallen in their several Departments, and have not forgot
Sir Charles Middleton[9] about the Vouchers: to Mr. Pitt I
have sent everything; and an opinion, which perhaps I may be
wrong in doing, that if he is as thoroughly convinced of the
Frauds as I am, to pass an Act to prevent their making away
with their property from this time, till this business is inves-
tigated; or an Exchequer process will do as well. These
gentlemen wish to make terms, but only to receive upon
what is actually recovered, therefore, if they cannot make
good their assertions, they have no advantage, but are for
ever ruined: they possess a great deal of shrewd sense. It
is not within the bounds of a letter to tell everything, but I
will have all the papers ready for your Royal Highness, when
I have the honour of seeing you.

---

[8] Surgeon of the Pegasus.   [9] The Frauds.   [1] Vide p. 226, ante.

I have been very unwell since we parted: indeed, I attribute it to my frequent excursions to St. John's, to investigate this business. Poor Collingwood's death lowered my spirits. I considered our constitutions as nearly alike. Forbes desires me to present his most humble and dutiful respects. Mrs. Nelson returns her thanks with Miss Herbert[1] for your most polite remembrance of them; and be assured, that I am, with the highest respect,

Your Royal Highness's most faithful Servant,

HORATIO NELSON.

If your Royal Highness does not come down, I shall sail for English Harbour the moment Rattler returns.

TO H. R. H. PRINCE WILLIAM HENRY.

[Original in the possession of William Henry Whitehead, Esq.]

Boreas, Nevis, May 8th, 1787.

Sir,

I was yesterday afternoon honoured with your Royal Highness's letter acquainting me that from your state of health your Surgeon had judged it proper you should return to English Harbour. To express my concern, words are too weak; therefore I beg you will believe what I cannot express, but I trust that a few days' rest will perfectly restore your Royal Highness to that health I so ardently wish you.

Your Royal Highness having represented to me that Lieutenant Hope wished to exchange out of the Pegasus, I beg leave to acquaint you that I have appointed Lieutenant Stephen George Church, Second Lieutenant of his Majesty's Ship Boreas, to be Third Lieutenant of the Ship under your command. I hope this arrangement will meet with your Royal Highness's approbation. I am much obliged by your information of the irregularities in the Navigation at Grenada.

---

[2] Daughter of the President of Nevis, and Mrs. Nelson's first cousin. She married Andrew Hamilton, Esq., vide p. 218, ante.

As soon as I have a Ship to send, I shall order the Trade to that Island to be more strictly attended to.

I have sent the Maidstone amongst the Bahamas in search of this piratical Vessel under the British Flag. Although as yet he has only defrauded Foreigners, yet this doing it under our Flag, degrades it; and I conceive it is my duty, and that I am supporting the National honour, in searching out this miscreant, that he may not only be punished for the fraud, but for attempting to disgrace the British Colours.

Lieutenant Schomberg: There appears no opportunity of his being tried in these Seas: if your health would permit, I beg leave to submit to your consideration going to America by way of Jamaica, on which Station a Court-Martial can be held, which I believe cannot in America.

The Frauds discovered I will take care to have made out by the time I have the honour of seeing you, which I hope will be in a few days. If you think English Harbour a more healthy situation than this Road, I shall instantly join you upon the Rattler's return.

His Excellency Sir Thomas Shirley desires me to make his most dutiful respects; and [to say] that if you remain at English Harbour, he shall instantly return to Antigua.

I have the honour to remain, &c.

HORATIO NELSON.

TO COMMODORE ALAN GARDNER.

[Transmitted to the Admiralty in his Letter of the 10th July 1787. Vide p. 242, post.]

Boreas, Nevis, May 13th, 1787.

Sir,

Lieutenant Isaac Schomberg, First Lieutenant of his Majesty's Ship Pegasus, having, in his letter dated the 23rd of January last, requested that I would be pleased to order a Court-Martial to be held on him whenever the Service would admit of it, that he might have an opportunity of vindicating his conduct from the unjust accusation which he states his Captain made against him in the Public Order Book of the

Ship; I therefore, in order to prevent Lieutenant Schomberg from being again, as set forth in his letter, unjustly accused, ordered him into Arrest, in hopes there would soon have been a sufficient number of Ships on this Station to hold a Court-Martial.

But the time of the Pegasus's departure for America drawing near, and no probability of there being any more Ships (at present) on this Station, I have thought it right to order the Pegasus to Jamaica, in order that Lieutenant Schomberg may have the Court-Martial he requested, as I have reason to believe that there are not Ships enough on the American Station to hold a Court, and I conceive it would be highly improper in me to let an Officer go to that Country under Arrest, with my belief of the aforementioned circumstance. Herewith I transmit you Lieutenant Schomberg's letter to me, and a copy of the order he alludes to.

I have the honour to remain, &c.,

HORATIO NELSON.

TO COMMODORE ALAN GARDNER.

[Autograph draught, in the Nelson Papers.]

Private.   Boreas, Nevis, May 13th, 1787.

My dear Sir,

In a public letter, a Commander would be wrong to set forth all the reasons which influence his conduct: but as I hope to have your approbation, I take the liberty of mentioning a few circumstances.

His Royal Highness will give you an account of Lieutenant Schomberg's conduct, and of his having put him into Arrest for disobedience of orders, &c., and that on Mr. Schomberg's making proper apologies, he forgave him. Indeed, his Royal Highness's narrative is so explicit, that I cannot inform you so fully as that will.

His Royal Highness, I can have no doubt, gave the orders alluded to, although Mr. Schomberg might have misunderstood them. I am sure, Sir, you will consider his Royal Highness stands in a very different situation to any other Captain: his conduct will be canvassed by the world, when ours would never be heard of.

Mr. Schomberg was our friend Cornwallis's First Lieutenant in the Canada. I can only suppose that he thought the Prince was determined to take the first opportunity of bringing him to a Court-Martial, that he wrote for this for such a trivial matter. Indeed, what leads me to consider that as his motive was, when his Royal Highness told him how wrong he was to write for a Court-Martial on himself, he told him that every Officer who served under him must be broke, and the sooner he was from under his command the better; and that if a Court-Martial acquitted him he would write to quit the Ship. This matter has made the Prince very uneasy, for he says, no person can tell he gave Mr. Schomberg those orders but himself, and Schomberg denies them. The day the matter happened, his Royal Highness dined in the country, and I attended him. On the road he told me how unpleasant it was that Schomberg would act in that manner when he had only forgiven him a few days before; but he said, in future, if any person committed faults, he would insert it in the Public Order-Book of the Ship, which he did, on this occasion, the next day. On that evening when I returned from dining, I found Mr. Schomberg's letter. I immediately sent for his Royal Highness, and I told him that in his elevated situation in life the world looked more to him than any other person, that Mr. Schomberg had neither more nor less than accused him of putting his name to an untruth : therefore I thought it my duty, although the matter was so trivial, to take Lieutenant Schomberg from under his directions, by suspending him from duty, or it might be said I had left him in that disagreeable situation, merely because he served under the Prince; and that it very much concerned his Royal Highness to show the world he had put his name to nothing but the truth.

In order to show my disapprobation of Officers writing for Courts-Martial, to vindicate their conduct for trivial matters, I gave out the enclosed order,[3] that others might not fall into the same error. It might soon have risen to such a height, that if a topsail was not thought properly or briskly reefed,

---

[3] Vide p. 210, ante.

by a Captain, or some other trivial matter, and he reprimanded the Officer, the Officer would say, ' Sir, I think it
properly done, and I shall write for a Court-martial to vindicate my conduct from your unjust accusation.' If this was
to be allowed, farewell Discipline : the Service is ruined :
his Majesty may be deprived of the services of his Officers;
and the best-laid schemes may be frustrated by the malignity
of individuals, or pique against their Commanders.

As the Rattler is to sail for England on the 1st of June, I
have sent her down with his Royal Highness, not only as
there may not be Ships enough collected to hold a Court,
but to carry Home his Royal Highness's dispatches, which
he must be very anxious should reach the King before any
reports get to him. Extraordinary to tell, in the last month
Mr. Schomberg wrote me a letter,[4] requesting to know
what charges I intended to exhibit against him, as he supposed I was to be his prosecutor, having ordered him into
Arrest. My answer of course was, that I thought I had complied with his wishes in taking him from under the immediate
command of his Royal Highness, and that from the tenor of his
letter of January, I took for granted he meant to prove he
never had, in the instance alluded to, disobeyed his Captain's
commands, and it was therefore he supposed himself unjustly
accused. I am, &c.,

HORATIO NELSON.

TO HIS ROYAL HIGHNESS PRINCE WILLIAM HENRY,
CAPTAIN OF HIS MAJESTY'S SHIP PEGASUS.

[Transmitted to the Admiralty in Captain Nelson's Letter of the 10th July,
1787. Vide p. 242, post.]

By Horatio Nelson, Esq.,
Captain of his Majesty's Ship Boreas, &c.

You are hereby required and directed to take his Majesty's Ship Rattler under your command, her Captain
having my orders to follow your directions; and proceed

---

[4] Vide p. 223, ante.

with all possible dispatch to Port Royal in the Island of Jamaica.

When your Royal Highness has no further commands for the Rattler, you will order Captain Wallis to proceed to Spithead, making known his arrival to the Secretary of the Admiralty.

Given under my hand, on board his Majesty's Ship Boreas, in Nevis Road, 20th May, 1787.

HORATIO NELSON.

TO PHILIP STEPHENS, ESQ.

[Original, in the Admiralty.]

Boreas, Spithead, July 4th, 1787.

Sir,

I have the honour to acquaint you of the arrival of his Majesty's Ship under my command, in obedience to orders from Commodore Parker.

I am much distressed that their Lordships should think I had directed the Prince not to do what was right in respect to the Muster-Book for the Clerk of the Cheque at Antigua.[5] I assure the Board that I was guided, when his Royal Highness did me the honour of asking me relative to the Book, by the eleventh and fourteenth of the Captain's, and thirteenth Articles of the Purser's Instructions. If I have erred, I fear it has been by too strict a compliance with those Articles.

As I have been under the necessity of mentioning his

---

[5] In a Letter to Captain Nelson, dated on the 9th March 1787, the Admiralty said, that "they are much disappointed and dissatisfied at the little attention you have shown to the rules and practice of the Service, as well as the directions contained in the 10th and 11th Articles of the General Printed Instructions, in having authorized his Royal Highness to disregard the applications of the Deputy Muster Master to be furnished with a perfect Muster-book ;" and their Lordships added that " they are the less able to judge of your motives on that occasion as they conclude you have not been wanting yourself in furnishing such a Book on your first arrival on the Station, no complaint having been made to them by the Navy Board of the contrary."—*Original* in the Nelson's Papers.

Royal Highness's name, I feel I should be remiss in my duty, did I neglect to acquaint their Lordships that the Pegasus is one of the first disciplined Frigates I have seen; and his Royal Highness the most respectful and one of the most attentive obedient Officers I know of.[6]

I trust their Lordships have done me the honour of confirming the Appointments to the Rattler and Boreas,[7] which were made thirty days before Commodore Parker arrived at Barbadoes, as they were made agreeably to the Board's Instructions left with me by the late Commander-in-Chief at the Leeward Islands.

Having given Commodore Parker a Return of the Squadron, and the services they were employed upon, which doubtless he has transmitted, it is needless for me to trouble you with a repetition.

　　　　　　I have the honour to be, &c.,

　　　　　　　　　　HORATIO NELSON.

Herewith I transmit you the State and Condition of his Majesty's ship Boreas under my command.

────────

TO WILLIAM LOCKER, ESQ., KENSINGTON.

[Autograph, in the Locker Papers.]

　　　　　　　　　　Portsmouth, July 9, 1787.

My dear Sir,

Your truly kind letter I received last night: you are, as ever, too kind. What is to be my immediate destination I

---

[6] Another Officer of high reputation entertained a similar opinion of the Prince's merits. Captain the Honourable William Cornwallis, (afterwards an Admiral, and a Knight Grand Cross of the Bath, whose celebrated Retreat was more than equal to a Victory,) in a Letter to Nelson, dated Phœnix, Diamond Harbour, 13th August 1790, observed:—"Our Royal Duke is, I hear, almost tired of the shore, but how he will be able to employ himself in time of peace at sea, is not easy to determine. It would, however, be a pity that any of the zeal and fondness he has so evidently shown for the Service, should be suffered to abate, as there is every reason to believe that with his ability he will one day carry its glory to a greater height than it has yet attained."

[7] The Appointments were not confirmed, Captain Nelson not having had authority to make them.—Vide p. 245.

know not, but I rather think I shall go out with the Fleet now
at Spithead.   We are ultimately to be paid off at Woolwich.
I have rum and tamarinds for you, and in what quantity you
wish, for I have abundance.   My dear wife is much obliged
by your kind inquiries.   I have no doubt but you will like her
upon acquaintance, for although I must be partial, yet she
possesses great good sense and good temper.   We are at a
Court-Martial.

Ever yours truly,

HORATIO NELSON.

Charles Pole desires me to say everything kind for him.

TO PHILIP STEPHENS, ESQ., ADMIRALTY.

[Original, in the Admiralty.]

Boreas, Spithead, July 10th, 1787.

Sir,

As I understand that no official accounts are yet received
by their Lordships of the reasons why his Majesty's Ship
Pegasus, commanded by his Royal Highness Prince William
Henry, proceeded by the way of Jamaica to Halifax in Nova
Scotia, I think it my duty to acquaint the Board that on the
23rd of January last, Lieutenant Isaac Schomberg, First
Lieutenant of his Majesty's Ship Pegasus, wrote me a letter of
which No. I.[8] is a copy.   From his Royal Highness having
but a few days before released Lieutenant Schomberg from
Arrest, and from other antecedent circumstances, together
with the extraordinary attack of accusing his Royal Highness
of having put his name to what had not happened, I judged
it proper to suspend him from duty, and directed his Royal
Highness, as by No. II.[9]   Other reasons which influenced
my conduct were, by being convinced that it was impossible
Lieutenant Schomberg could ever serve properly after what
had happened; and I was not without hope that when a Commander-in-Chief arrived, some mode might be adopted by him

---

[8] Vide p. 209, ante,   [9] Vide p. 208, ante.

to prevent a Court-Martial, and to get Lieutenant Schomberg removed from the Pegasus. His Royal Highness also acquainted me that Lieutenant Schomberg had told him before the Officers of the Pegasus, that his Royal Highness was now grown so very particular that no Officer could serve under him, and that sooner or later he must be broke ; therefore he should stand a Court-Martial, and if they did not break him, he should apply to quit the Ship. This, I hope, their Lordships will consider a sufficient reason for my suspension of Lieutenant Schomberg. Indeed I was so much inclined to think that some other Officers would write for Court-Martials to vindicate their conduct, that I thought it proper to give out the Order No. III ;[1] and I was convinced from appearances that if I had not suspended Mr. Schomberg, I should soon have had an application from another quarter.

On the death of Captain Wilfred Collingwood, I sent a blank Commission to his Royal Highness, which he filled up. I thought it was the least compliment I could possibly pay him. By return of the Rattler his Royal Highness acquainted me that Lieutenant Hope wished to exchange out of the Pegasus into the Boreas. This request I thought proper to comply with.

I transmitted to Commodore Gardner by his Royal Highness their Lordships' secret orders. I also desired H. R. H. to give Commodore Gardner a copy of Commodore Sawyer's orders. If there were Ships enough assembled a Court-Martial might be held, the prisoner released, and H. R. H. made easy in his mind. If the Ships could not be assembled, H. R. H. had ample time to comply with Commodore Sawyer's orders. My reason for attending to the Commodore's order, although it was in some measure contrary to their Lordships' orders, was, that had the Pegasus fell in with the ice, and any unfortunate accident happened, it might have been said Captain Nelson should have paid more attention to what an old Officer and Commander-in-Chief directed. Their Lordships will not impute any other reason for my not sending the Pegasus away agreeable to their orders, as she sailed completely refitted for her voyage to North America, and every object of his Royal

[1] Vide p. 210 ante.

Highness's visit to this Station was accomplished.　Numbers IV. and V. are my letters to Commodore Gardner, and his Royal Highness's orders.

I have the honour to remain, Sir,

Your most obedient Servant,

HORATIO NELSON.

No. VI. are Extracts from his Royal Highness's Letters to me.[3]

---

[3] All the Letters referred to, except the following, have been already inserted : Vide pp. 223, 236, 237.

FROM H. R. H. PRINCE WILLIAM HENRY TO CAPTAIN NELSON.

Pegasus, May 3d, 1787.

Sir,

I this morning received your letter informing me of your having appointed Lieutenant Wallis to the command of the Rattler, and I have to own the receipt of the blank Commission, which you, in your usual polite and civil manner, have authorised me to fill up. I have appointed Mr. Stephen George Church to be second Lieutenant of his Majesty's Ship under your command, strongly recommending him to you as a deserving, diligent and attentive Officer, for the thorough knowledge I have of his character during eight years of service together. Lieut. William Hope, third Lieutenant of the Pegasus, having applied to me to request he may be allowed to exchange from the Pegasus into the Boreas, I beg leave, in compliance with Lieutenant Hope's application, to represent the matter for your decision. I have no objection to the exchange, as the request was made in a modest and proper manner.

W.

May 11th, 1787.

It is highly requisite for his Majesty's Service that Lieutenant Isaac Schomberg should be brought to trial, particularly after having been kept under suspension rather than confinement for one hundred and seven days. Justice calls loudly for a man so long in his situation to be as soon delivered from his captivity as possible. The only means to effect that must be a Court-Martial. You, Sir, are thoroughly acquainted with all the proceedings, and know the uneasiness of mind I have suffered, and the vast desire I must have to see the affair of this unhappy and deluded man settled ; and as you have mentioned to me in your letter that his Majesty's Ship Maidstone has gone in search of that piratical Vessel, and as no official accounts are yet come out concerning the approaching arrival of a Commander-in-Chief to his Majesty's Ships on this Station, and as the time is now almost come for his Majesty's Ship under my command to return to the Coast of North America, where it is likely that there will not be a sufficient number of his Majesty's Ships and Vessels to try the said Lieutenant Schomberg, I entirely coincide in opinion with you, Sir, that it is not only for the advantage of his Majesty's service, but that justice requires that his Majesty's Ship Pegasus should proceed, in her way to North America, to Jamaica. I am using the utmost

[Autograph, in the Admiralty.]

Boreas, Spithead, July 11th, 1787.

Sir,

I am just honoured with your letter of yesterday's date, wherein you inform me that as I was not duly authorised by their Lordships to fill up Appointments, they cannot by the rules of the Board be confirmed.

When Sir Richard Hughes, Baronet, resigned the Command of the Leeward Island Station in July 1786, which he informed me (by his order) was in obedience to the directions of the Admiralty Board, he left me the instructions of their Lordships to him, countersigned by himself, and, amongst others, the power of giving Commissions; also the power of holding Court-Martials, and directing them to be held; and also their Lordships' orders relative to improper Appointments. I therefore could not but suppose myself duly authorised, and with the sanction of their Lordships; or, otherwise, I should during the time of my command have been informed to the contrary.

If from this, what I supposed full, authority, my Appoint-

dispatch, and am confident I shall have the honour of paying my personal respects to you in a few days at furthest, my health being so much better that I am able to conduct the duty of the Ship.

W.

May 13th.

My going to Jamaica is really necessary, not only for my own ease and peace of mind, but for the King's service, to deliver this miserable object from his long confinement. The Sloop's going with me is a judicious arrangement of yours, to prevent delay. Gardner being an Officer of experience and judgment, will be able to give me good advice how to pursue the best mode through this difficult and disagreeable affair. I wish to God it had never happened, or that Schomberg had seen his error sooner.

W.

I thank you for allowing the Sloop's going to England. I am extremely anxious that the King should be as soon as possible acquainted with the issue of this trial.

W.

ments are not confirmed, I shall be looked upon in the Service
as an Officer who arrogated to himself powers with which he
was not invested, for the Service can never know what Sir
Richard Hughes left me.[4] Indeed the most serious consequences might have happened, and what might have embittered
my future days. Had there been Ships enough on the Station, I should not have sat at Court-Martials, and consequently
the Courts would have been illegal.

A man belonging to the Rattler was sentenced to death.
As Senior Captain of five Ships, or as an Officer detached from
the Fleet by a Commander-in-Chief, I had not leave to carry a
sentence of death into execution. Sir Richard Hughes's Flag
was struck, and I was only under the orders of their Lordships; therefore I felt myself empowered to carry any sentence of death into execution; which would have been the
case of the unhappy man belonging to the Rattler, had not his
Royal Highness interceded for his pardon.   Thus was I
near, if not cutting the thread of life, at least of shortening a
fellow-creature's days. The Law might not have supposed me
guilty of murder, but my feelings would nearly have been the
same.   I had always been bred up with the idea of obeying my
Commanding Officer most correctly; and what must I feel at
finding the Commander-in-Chief's directions a mere nullity?

I have heard that reports are circulated that I knew Commodore Parker was near the Station when I sent the Pegasus
and Rattler away, and that I knew he had been at the Island
of Madeira. I assure the Board the report is false.   Indeed,
on the day the Pegasus sailed, a report came from Antigua,
(said to be brought by a Ship that arrived there eleven days
before,) that the Jupiter sailed from Spithead the latter end of
March, but there appeared to me no foundation for it.   Indeed, since November last, I had almost always a Ship at Barbadoes, to look out for a Commodore, but I never had the
idea of the arrival of one about this time.

Their Lordships may be assured that one of the happiest

---

[4] The Appointments were not confirmed. Mr. Church was however made a
Lieutenant on the 15th of August 1787 ; but Lieutenant Wallis was not promoted to the rank of Commander until the 20th of January 1794.

acts of my life would have been to have resigned the Command before the Pegasus left the Station.

I have the honour to remain, &c.,

HORATIO NELSON.

TO THE EARL OF CORK.

[From the "Naval Chronicle," vol. xxx. p. 8. The Honourable Courtenay Boyle, third son of Edmund Earl of Cork and Orrery, was then a Midshipman of the Boreas. He died a Vice-Admiral of the Red, and a K. C. H. in May, 1844.]

Portsmouth, July 15th, 1787.

My Lord,

I am this moment honoured with your letter. I have great pleasure in doing what I know will give our dear Courtenay so much happiness. He is amiable in the truest sense of the word; and I feel real regret in parting from him. In his professional line he is inferior to none: his virtues are superior to most.

I am, &c.,

HORATIO NELSON.

TO PHILIP STEPHENS, ESQ., ADMIRALTY.

[Original, in the Admiralty.]

Boreas, Spithead, July 18th, 1787.

Sir,

I am this day honoured with your letter of yesterday's date.[5] I beg you will inform their Lordships that I duly observe the contents of it; and they may be assured that in future no consideration shall ever induce me to deviate in the smallest degree from my orders.

I have the honour to remain, &c.

HORATIO NELSON.

[5] In that Letter, Mr. Stephens informed him that—

"My Lords are not satisfied with the Reasons you have given for altering the destination of the Pegasus, and for sending the Rattler Sloop to Jamaica; and that for having taken upon you to send the latter away from the Station to which their Lordships had appointed her, you will be answerable for the consequence, if the Crown should be put to any needless expense upon that account."
—*Copy*, in the possession of William Henry Whitehead, Esq.

[Original, in the Admiralty.]

Boreas, Spithead, 20th July, 1787.

Sir,

Inclosed I have taken the liberty to transmit you a Passing Certificate, with two Warrants, for Mr. James Ballentine, Gunner of his Majesty's Ship under my command. I beg leave to recommend him as a sober, diligent, and careful man, and worthy of their Lordships' confirmation.

I have the honour to be, &c.

HORATIO NELSON.

TO THE REVEREND MR. NELSON, HILBOROUGH.

[Autograph, in the Nelson Papers.]

Portsmouth, July 21st, 1787.

My dear Brother,

Your kind letter of the 15th I have received; and indeed I have been so very unwell, with a violent cold, that I have scarcely been able to hold my head up till yesterday. What is to become of the Boreas, seems as yet uncertain. A Fleet seems necessary, and we are all ready to sail at a moment's warning. However, in my humble opinion, we shall not go to Sea this summer. The French have eight Sail in Brest Water, and we shall not be in a hurry to force them to Sea; but next summer I fear will involve this Nation in a War: it seems almost unavoidable. Although we are in a bad state for it, yet, thank God, the French are worse. So much for politics. Your Warrant[6] I have safe: what may arise from it, or if anything, I can't tell. I shall give it to my Agent when the Ship is paid off, and he will do what is proper. All on board are well, and desire their compliments. When I know what is to be our destination I will tell you. Adieu.

Ever yours,

HORATIO NELSON.

---

[6] As Chaplain of the Boreas.

TO THE EARL OF CORK.

[From the " Naval Chronicle," vol. xxx. p. 8 ; Vide p. 247, ante.]

Portsmouth, July 22nd, 1787.

In the first place, my Lord, it is necessary that he[7] should be made complete in his Navigation ; and if the Peace continues, French is absolutely necessary. Dancing is an accomplishment that probably a Sea Officer may require. You will see almost the necessity of it, when employed in Foreign Countries ; indeed, the honour of the Nation is so often entrusted to Sea Officers, that there is no accomplishment which will not shine with peculiar lustre in them. He must nearly have served his Time, therefore he cannot be so well employed as in gaining knowledge. If I can at any time be of service to him, he may always call upon me. His charming disposition will ever make him friends. He may as well join the Ship, when his brother goes to the Continent.

I have the honour to be, &c.

HORATIO NELSON.[8]

TO PHILIP STEPHENS, ESQ., ADMIRALTY.

[Original, in the Admiralty.]

Boreas, Spithead, July 26th, 1787.

Sir,

Inclosed I transmit you the Warrant of Charles Green, Boatswain of the Boreas, with the Certificates of his good character from others, his Captains ; and I beg leave to recommend him to their Lordships as worthy of having a confirmed Warrant.

I am, Sir, &c.

HORATIO NELSON.

---

[7] The Honourable Courtenay Boyle. Vide p. 247 ante.

[8] On the 26th July, Nelson wrote to Mr. Pitt, enclosing Papers on the subject of the Frauds in the West Indies, and was informed on the 31st of July, that his Letter and Papers were under the consideration of the Board of Treasury.

TO H. R. H. PRINCE WILLIAM HENRY.

[Autograph draught, in the Nelson Papers.]

Portsmouth, 27th July, 1787.

If to be truly great is to be truly good, (as we are taught to believe,) it never was stronger verified than in your Royal Highness, in the instance of Mr. Schomberg. You have supported your character, yet, at the same time, by an amiable condescension, have saved an Officer from appearing before a Court-Martial, which ever must hurt him. Resentment I know your Royal Highness never had, or I am sure ever will bear any one: it is a passion incompatible with the character of a Man of Honour. Schomberg was too hasty certainly in writing his letter; but, now you are parted, pardon me, my Prince, when I presume to recommend, that Schomberg may stand in your Royal Favour, as if he had never sailed with you; and that at some future day, you will serve him. There only wants this, to place your character in the highest point of view. None of us are without failings: Schomberg's was being rather too hasty; but that, put in competition with his being a good Officer, will not, I am bold to say, be taken in the scale against him.

I wish this matter could have been settled on my Station, and I am sure your Royal Highness will join me when I acquaint you, that I have been reprimanded by the Admiralty for allowing your Royal Highness to proceed to America by way of Jamaica. More able friends than myself your Royal Highness may easily find, and of more consequence in the State: but one more attached and affectionate, is, I am bold to say, not so easily met with. Princes seldom, very seldom, find a disinterested person to communicate their thoughts to. I do not pretend to be otherwise: but of this truth be assured by a man who, I trust, never did a dishonourable act, that I am interested only that your Royal Highness should be the greatest and best man this Country ever produced. In full confidence of your belief of my sincerity, I take the liberty of saying, that having seen a few more years than yourself, I may in some respects know more of mankind. Permit me then to urge, a thorough knowledge of those you tell your mind to. Mankind are not always what they seem. Far, very far, be it from me to mean any person whom your Royal Highness thinks proper to honour with your confidence: but again let me impress on your Royal mind what I have before mentioned.

As to news; from a much better quarter, most probably you will be furnished with that. However, Boreas is not paid off; but is kept in readiness to go to Sea with the Squadron at Spithead: but in my poor opinion, we shall go no farther at present. The French have eight Sail in Brest Water, ready for Sea: therefore I think we shall not court the French out of Port. The Dutch business is becoming every day more serious; and I hardly think we can keep from a War, without giving for ever the weight of the Dutch to the French, and allowing the Stadtholdership to be annihilated,—things which I should suppose hardly possible. I wrote to your Royal Highness, and sent a number of letters to Jamaica: Gardner,[9] I am sure, will forward them. When I go to Town, I shall take care to be presented to his Majesty and the Prince of Wales, that I may be in the way of answering any question they may think proper to ask me. Nothing is wanting to make you the darling of the English Nation, but truth. Sorry I am to say, much to the contrary has been dispersed. Lord Hood and the good Commissioner have made many inquiries about you. Permit me to subscribe myself,

> Your Royal Highness's attached and affectionate,
>> HORATIO NELSON.

TO WILLIAM LOCKER, ESQ., KENSINGTON.

[Autograph, in the Locker Papers.

Portsmouth, August 12th, 1787.

My dear Sir,

It is not kind in one's Native air to treat a poor wanderer, as it has done me since my arrival. The rain and cold at first gave me a sore throat and its accompaniments: the hot weather has given me a slow fever, not absolutely bad enough

---

[9] Commodore Alan Gardner.

to keep my bed, yet enough to hinder me from doing anything; and I could not have wrote a letter for the world;
now the wind has set in to the Westward, and the air is cool,
I am quite well again.

You have but too much cause to scold me for not writing,
but all my other friends have the same cause, if that is
any excuse. However, be assured that the things I have
for you are perfectly safe, and although I may be careless in not writing, yet your former kindness to me is never
out of my mind. Your sixty-gallon cask of rum is ready to
go to the Custom-house whenever Boreas goes up the River.
I have a hogshead of Madeira, which I intend you shall have
half of as soon as it can be drawn off. Tamarinds and noyeau I
must get smuggled, for duty on the former is so enormous,
that no person can afford the expense. The latter is not
enterable. I shall send up by Clarke's waggon a dozen bottles of *Veritable*, for when we get to Woolwich, the Custom-
House people will be so thick about us, and our time so short,
that most probably I shall lose it—and it's invaluable. I will
send you a line when it sets off, and it must take its chance.
Kingsmill [1] came, and staid a day or two here. I have not
heard of him since he went away. He was fortunate in his
wine; and I have given him a stock of rum, and a dozen
noyeau.

When Boreas is to be paid off, seems as uncertain as
ever. If we are to have a Bustle I do not want to come on
shore; I begin to think I am fonder of the Sea than ever.
Mrs. Nelson returns her best thanks for your kind inquiries;
I shall have great pleasure in making her known to so valuable a friend, but she knows you already most perfectly.
Charles Pole is gone to Southampton; he is perfectly well.
I beg my compliments to the Bradleys, and my kind remembrances to your sons, and believe me to be ever,

Your most affectionate,

HORATIO NELSON.

---

[1] Captain, afterwards Admiral Sir Robert Kingsmill, Bart, so often mentioned.

TO PHILIP STEPHENS, ESQ., ADMIRALTY.

[Original, in the Admiralty.]

Boreas, Portsmouth, August 17th, 1787.

Sir,

I am this moment honoured with your letter of yesterday, wherein you acquaint me of their Lordships' surprise at finding William Clarke[2] discharged from the Rattler by my order, and desiring to know my reasons for giving the order. In return, I beg leave to acquaint you, that it was at the request of the poor man, backed by the desire of the deceased Captain Collingwood. I certainly thought it was proper, as I exactly followed the steps of the late Commmander-in-Chief on the Leeward Island Station, in the case of William Ray, Seaman, deserter from the Unicorn.

I had also always understood, that when a man was condemned to suffer death, he was from that moment dead in Law; and if he was pardoned, he became as a new man;[3] and, there being no impress, he had the choice of entering or not his Majesty's Service. There was no want of a good man to supply his place.

If I have erred in discharging him, I am sorry; but I had at that time no doubts, as I conformed to the manner of the late Commander-in-Chief's treatment of a man in a similar situation; and I beg you will assure their Lordships, that I only wish to know the exact Rules of the Service in this respect, to have conformed most strictly to them.

I have the honour, &c.

HORATIO NELSON.

[2] The man who had been condemned. Vide p. 222, ante.

[3] It appears that even if the man had been properly pardoned, he had no claim to be discharged.

TO PHILIP STEPHENS, ESQ., ADMIRALTY.

[Original, in the Admiralty.]

Boreas, at the Nore, 20th August, 1787.

Sir,

I have the honour to acquaint you with the arrival of his Majesty's Ship under my command at this place. Inclosed is a State and Condition of his Majesty's Ship.

I am, &c.

HORATIO NELSON.

TO THE REVEREND MR. NELSON, HILBOROUGH.

[Autograph, in the Nelson Papers.]

10, Great Marlborough Street, August 25th, 1787.

My dear Brother,

Your letter of the 16th I received since my arrival at the Nore, where I arrived on the 20th. There is not at present the least probability of the Boreas being paid off: on the contrary, we are ordered to be in readiness to sail in a moment's warning. I have, therefore, been under the necessity of bringing my wife up to Town, till I can tell what is to become of me. I am much obliged about your inquiries at Bodney, but by your description the house seems too large for my purpose. It appears from the size, &c., very cheap, but I can't afford everything answerable to such a situation. I am much flattered by the honour you intend me if the young stranger should be a boy.

We beg our best compliments to Mrs. Nelson, and hope soon to hear of her safe delivery. Mr. Suckling will take care of Lord Walpole's wine when it is possible to get it to London. Maurice goes down with me to-morrow, and Mr. and Mrs. Suckling set off yesterday, just as I arrived in Town, so I shall have good company for a few days. Adieu. Yours, most affectionately,

HORATIO NELSON.

Love to your neighbours.

TO PHILIP STEPHENS, ESQ., ADMIRALTY.

[Original, in the Admiralty.]

Boreas, Nore, 29th August, 1787.

Sir,

I have received your letter desiring me to give my reasons why I appointed Joseph King, late Boatswain of the Boreas, Sail-Maker's Assistant of his Majesty's Yard at Antigua, not-withstanding the remonstrances of the Officers of the Yard, and notwithstanding it was in the Civil Department of the Navy, and not strictly within my authority.

I beg leave to observe that although the Civil Department of the Navy abroad is not strictly within the authority of Com-manding Officers, yet by vacancies which daily happen, it is a constant drain of our best artificers to supply the rooms of others.

I appointed Joseph King to the place of Sail-Maker's As-sistant, as, to my knowledge for some years, he was quite fit for the employment. I know not of remonstrances—I never allow inferiors to dictate. As to his being insane, and in con-sequence thereof, deprived of his employment as Boatswain, I beg to acquaint the Board that as he was squaring the yards he was struck with the sun, which, the Naval part of the Board knows, renders a man for some length of time wholly unfit for employment, that requires so much activity and exposure to the sun. He was always employed in the Sail-loft from the time of the Boreas's arriving in that Coun-try until he was at my recommendation made Boatswain of the Falcon; and when the Ship under my command required one, I applied to the late Commander-in-chief to appoint him to the Boreas, which he was rendered unfit for near a year afterwards by an unfortunate accident.

I did in him, as to all other Appointments, order the Officers of the Yard, more particularly the Deputy Naval Officer, to acquaint me if they behaved improperly, and I would [send] them so good a man, indeed so valuable a one being a Sail-maker as well as a seaman, that I shall be very glad to receive him as Boatswain, as a cold climate every one knows instantly relieves that complaint; and he never was affected in the under-cover employments. I am, Sir,

Your most obedient servant,

HORATIO NELSON.

P.S. I beg leave to acquaint the Board that the present Boatswain is a very valuable man.

TO PHILIP STEPHENS, ESQ., ADMIRALTY.

[Original, in the Admiralty.]

Boreas, Nore, 1st Sept. 1787.

Sir,

I beg leave to acquaint you that George Williams, a seaman belonging to his Majesty's Ship under my command, deserted yesterday morning from duty. I have therefore thought proper to send you his description, that their Lordships may, if they think fit, take such measures as may be necessary for apprehending him. I have no doubt of his having gone for London.

I have the honour, &c.,

HORATIO NELSON.

TO PHILIP STEPHENS, ESQ., ADMIRALTY.

[Original, in the Admiralty.]

Boreas, Nore, Sept. 9th, 1787.

Sir,

I beg to acquaint you that yesterday, a boat being on shore upon duty, William Pope, a seaman belonging to his Majesty's ship under my command, was arrested by Writ of the High Sheriff of Kent for a debt of £21 at the suit of John Rowe, a landlord of Gosport; and as I have reason to think that the reason of this arrest is only to give the people an opportunity of going to London and leaving the Ship, as William Pope has pay due from his Majesty's armed Store-Ship the Cyrus, which I understand the landlord means to make him receive, I have therefore to request their Lordships' interference, or

the Ship under my command may by this means be un-
manned; other publicans, as well as this man, having declared they have taken out Writs against several of the men,
and as the debts are far more than £20, they have a right
to take them out of the Ship. I beg their Lordships' orders
whether I am to give up these men, or in what manner I am
to act.

I have the honour, &c.,

HORATIO NELSON.

TO PHILIP STEPHENS, ESQ., ADMIRALTY.

[Original, in the Admiralty.]

Boreas, Nore, 21st September 1787.

Sir,

On the 4th of this month Joseph King was entered by the
Clerk of the Cheque of this Yard, as Boatswain of his Majesty's
Ship under my command, in obedience to a Warrant dated
at the Navy Office, the 27th August 1787, and discharged
Charles Green, acting Boatswain of the said Ship on the 3rd.

On the 20th, Charles Green, late acting Boatswain, was entered as Boatswain of his Majesty's Ship under my command,
agreeable to a Warrant dated at the Navy Office, the 13th
Instant. I am therefore requested by Joseph King to write to
their Lordships, to request they will be pleased to appoint
him to some other Ship, as he hopes he has done nothing
deserving of being superseded; and I beg leave to recommend
him as a most excellent gentleman.[1]

I am, Sir, &c.,

HORATIO NELSON.

[1] Professional readers will think this an extraordinary description of a
Boatswain; but Mr. King, who was a Portuguese, (and whose real name was
Joaquin,) was no common person. He was afterwards Boatswain of Gibraltar
dock-yard, where he distinguished himself by saving the life of a soldier, for
which the Earl St. Vincent presented him with a piece of plate, inscribed "for
preserving a soldier's life at the risk of his own." He died Boatswain of Pem-
broke Dock-yard, about ten years ago.—*From the information of Captain Hock-
ings of Norwich, and Tucker's Memoirs of Earl St. Vincent,* vol. i. page 383.

TO THE REVEREND WILLIAM NELSON, HILBOROUGH.

[Autograph, in the Nelson Papers.]

Boreas, Nore, September 23rd, 1787.

My dear Brother,

It is an age since I heard from you: not once since I came to this place. I hope nothing is amiss to deprive me of that pleasure, and that Mrs. Nelson is well. I don't know whether you have yet a son and heir. If you have, pray accept my congratulations on the occasion. We are here laying seven miles from the land on the Impress service, and am as much separated from my wife as if I were in the East Indies. A War seems at present inevitable. What the Marquis of Buckingham may be able to do, time must prove; but I dare say the French King has fixed his resolves and will not alter them. It looks like a general War.

I suppose Boreas will be paid off, and her men put into some other Ship, but what may become of me, depends on Lord Howe. I always was for actual service, and should not like to be an idle spectator. Jemmy Jamieson[4] is well, as we are all on board; and desire their compliments. I have this moment your letter of the 21st, and am happy to hear Mrs. Nelson is so well.[5] I beg my best respects to her. I am this moment getting under sail after some Ships.

Adieu, and believe me your affectionate Brother,

HORATIO NELSON.

TO PHILIP STEPHENS, ESQ., ADMIRALTY.

[Original, in the Admiralty.]

Boreas, Nore, September 30th, 1787.

Sir,

The bearer hereof, Joseph King, late Boatswain of his Majesty's Ship Boreas, under my command, who was superseded a few days past by their Lordships;—I beg leave to recommend him as one of the best Boatswains I have seen in his Majesty's Service.

I am, Sir, &c.,

HORATIO NELSON.

[4] Master of the Boreas.
[5] Mrs. Nelson gave birth to a daughter, Charlotte Mary, now Lady Bridport, on the 20th of September 1787.

TO CAPTAIN LOCKER, ROYAL NAVY, KENSINGTON.

[Autograph, in the Locker Papers.]

Boreas, Nore, October 3rd, 1787.

My dear Friend,

I have this moment your letter of the 1st. If the Regulating business[6] is a thing you like, most sincerely do I give you joy of it. Exeter, however, I should suppose, is as agreeable a place as you could wish to be at. I have no doubt but there are many very long faces at being left out. I have asked Lord Howe for a Ship of the Line, but Boreas is victualled for three months, and ready for Sea, ordered to hold myself in momentary readiness the moment my Orders come on board. Little S———, if he has left off grog, may do very well, but I never knew any of these grog-drinkers quit it. I wish he may, for no man has a better heart. My health, thank God, was never better, and I am fit for any quarter of the Globe. It rains hard, and I hope the wind will come to the Westward, and we have had very bad weather of late. My love to your boys, and believe me

Your most faithful
HORATIO NELSON.

I wish you had your rum and tamarinds, but I will take good care of them.

TO PHILIP STEPHENS, ESQ., ADMIRALTY.

[Original, in the Admiralty.]

Boreas, Nore, October 4th, 1787.

Sir,

I beg leave to acquaint you that Daniel Piercy, a seaman belonging to his Majesty's Ship under my command, absented

---

[6] Captain Locker was appointed one of the Captains for Regulating the Impressment of Seamen, and stationed at Exeter; but a War not taking place, he retained the situation a very short time.

himself from duty on shore last Monday, and his having received a Bill on the Pay Office in London, in part payment of his wages, will enable their Lordships to take such steps as are necessary for detecting him. Inclosed I transmit you his description, and have the honour to remain, &c.

HORATIO NELSON.

PHILIP STEPHENS, ESQ., ADMIRALTY.

[Original, in the Admiralty.]

Boreas, Nore, October 20th, 1787.

Sir,

Inclosed I transmit you two Notes for wages due to William Gaweas and William Caroline, for the Ship Wisk of Whitby, and have to request you will please to cause the said Notes to be immediately accepted, that the men may receive their wages.

I am, Sir, &c.

HORATIO NELSON.

TO THE REVEREND MR. NELSON, HILBOROUGH.

[Autograph, in the Nelson Papers.]

Cavendish Square, October 29th, 1787.

My dear Brother,

Many thanks for your kind inquiries about the School: it is quite the thing I wished for, and you will be pleased to tell the Master the child[7] shall come after the Christmas holidays. We are happy to hear Mrs. Nelson is about again, and desire to be most kindly remembered to her, with many thanks for her obliging offer, when the child may come to school: but we hope Boreas will soon be paid off, then we shall come into Norfolk directly. As to news, the Papers are all Peace; but, in my opinion, nothing can prevent a War. In the Naval

[7] His step-son, Josiah Nisbet.

line every exertion is made use of to man the Fleet.　Compliments to all about you, and believe me, ever

Your most affectionate Brother,

HORATIO NELSON.

Maurice is well.　He has been staying a few days on board with me.

TO PHILIP STEPHENS, ESQ., ADMIRALTY.

[Original, in the Admiralty.]

Boreas, Nore, November 4th, 1787.

Sir,

Mr. William Lewis,[8] late Surgeon of his Majesty's Sloop Rattler, having sent me a letter of October 23rd, (marked No. 1,) I returned for answer that as I could not wish to keep him from employment, although I conceived his conduct had been highly improper, yet whenever he acknowledged the impropriety of writing such a letter as his of August 27th, 1786, and that he was sorry for having written it, I should write to the Lords Commissioners of the Admiralty, I was satisfied. Having in answer thereto received a letter of October 26th, I transmit them both for their Lordships' consideration.　As far as relates to myself, I beg to acquaint their Lordships I am satisfied.

I am, Sir, &c.

HORATIO NELSON.

TO WILLIAM LOCKER, ESQ., KENSINGTON.

[Autograph, in the Locker Papers.]

Sheerness, November 27th, 1787.

My dear Sir,

I have sent your cask of rum to Chatham Custom-House, and it will come to London the first conveyance ; your tama-

---

[8] Vide p. 195, 211, ante.

rinds, sixty-five lbs., I have sent on board the Scipio.[9] Captain Lutwidge has promised he will get them up the first good opportunity.   Boreas is ready for paying off, but I understand we shall not be dismissed, at soonest, before Friday; perhaps, I am told, Monday next.[1] It would appear they don't like parting with our people. I hope your trip to Exeter has been pleasant. Mrs. Nelson has told me of your return; indeed I was in town for forty-eight hours last week. We are all gaping for the King's Speech. Our Admiral is rather surprised he has had no orders to strike his Flag, nor orders to pay off the Sandwich: she has near a thousand men on board. However, a few days must now determine matters. I shall then take the first opportunity of seeing you. I beg my compliments to Bradley, when you see him, and kind remembrances to your young folk; and believe me to be your most affectionate and attached,

HORATIO NELSON.

I had wrote the above before I received your letter. None of my things would be permitted to be sent to London Customhouse.   The duty, &c., I have given directions about paying,

---

[9] The Scipio of 64 guns, Guard-ship at Sheerness, commanded by Captain Lutwidge before mentioned.

[1] The Boreas was paid off early in December 1787.—The preceding Letters show that in the performance of arduous duties in the Leeward Islands, Nelson had received several rebukes or reprimands from the Admiralty; that his correspondence respecting frauds in the Public Departments had been then but coldly received; that he had incurred great anxiety, and exposed himself to heavy responsibility in supporting the commercial interests of his Country; and that on his return to England, the Boreas was made a Receiving Ship for impressed Seamen, at the Nore. This treatment is stated to have so irritated his mind, that he said to the Senior Officer in the River Medway, " I now rejoice at the Boreas being ordered to be paid off, which will release me for ever from an ungrateful Service, as it is my firm and unalterable determination never again to set my foot on board a King's Ship. Immediately after my arrival in Town, I shall wait on the First Lord of the Admiralty, and resign my Commission," a resolution which was happily prevented by his receiving a very civil letter from Lord Howe, desiring to see him in Town. The interview proved satisfactory to both parties, and Lord Howe offered to present him to the King on the next Levée day, when he was honoured with a gracious reception.—(See *Clarke & M'Arthur*, vol. i. p. 102.)   It is remarkable, if the anecdote be true, that there should be no allusion whatever to his feelings on the subject in his private correspondence; and in August of that year he had expressed his fondness for his profession. See p. 252, ante.

and it will come directed to Mr. Suckling at the Custom-House with my liquor. Mr. Bellas [2] has been for this month past in London. Nor is Mr. Prowse Master-Attendant here, but a Mr. Hemming from Halifax.

TO PHILIP STEPHENS, ESQ., ADMIRALTY.

[Autograph, in the Admiralty.]

No. 6, Princes Street, Cavendish Square, December 29th, 1787.

Sir,

Mr. James Jameson, late Master of the Boreas, having acquainted me of his applying to the Admiralty praying their Lordships to relieve him from the expenses and issue of a law-suit commenced against him by Thomas Watts, Purser's steward, for improperly correcting him; and having received their Lordships' answer, that it did not appear to them to be a proper case for their Solicitor to appear in, and Mr. Jameson having requested me to write to the Board concerning the matter, I take the liberty of requesting you to inform their Lordships that Mr. Jameson is by no means of a cruel or oppressive disposition, and I am afraid that if Mr. Jameson had confined the Steward till I came on board I should have punished him at the gangway.

He is of a bad character, insomuch that I have been obliged to punish him for suttling to the Ship's company, and making numbers of them drunk, and being impertinent. I therefore trust that their Lordships will not allow an Officer to be called before a Civil Tribunal, for acts committed under Martial Law, to which he was amenable, had the Steward ever complained to me, but which I never heard of till Mr. Jameson informed me of it; or if called, that they will have the goodness to allow their Solicitor to defend the suit.

I have the honour, &c.
HORATIO NELSON.

---

[2] Surgeon of the Dockyard at Sheerness.

TO CAPTAIN SIR CHARLES MIDDLETON, BART.,
COMPTROLLER OF THE NAVY.

[Original draught in the Nelson Papers. The exact date of this Letter does not
appear; but it was probably written in November or December 1787.]

Captain Nelson returns Sir Charles Middleton's Books,
with thanks for the perusal. Captain Nelson can most truly
say, that were those Instructions in any manner complied
with, it would have been impossible that the present charges
could have been brought forward. The mind that's callous
to the oath relative to the Negroes, would not scruple committing any act; and yet sorry am I to say, it is my firm belief,
that every Instruction relative to the hire of Negroes is broke
through. Captain Nelson has turned in his mind what Sir
Charles said about an examination abroad. In respect to
merchants vouching for the prices of goods, the fact, as far as it
goes, is most true. But any Vouchers may be got, signed in the
West Indies, and with propriety on the part of the merchant,
for there is no fixed market price, as in this Country. Everything is valued as the want of it occasions.

In respect to drawing Bills, I never saw an advertisement
in the Antigua papers for obtaining the best Exchange. It
came to my knowledge, in the first Bills to which my Name
was put on my having the Command, that two and a half per
cent could be got (it was offered to me by a Merchant) more
than the Exchange wrote on the Bills; and on my talking
to Mr. Dow, the Deputy Naval Officer, on this subject, he
gave as a reason that Mr. Charles Kerr, in whose favour
the Bills were drawn, had advanced this money and goods for
the use of the Yard before the Exchange had risen. These
were but bad reasons for his conduct, as I told him at the
time. I mentioned, that in future I should insist on money
being advertised for: but difficulties were started; nor was
ever any part of those Instructions communicated to me, but
such as either militated against the interest of the Naval
Officer, or (what I had ordered) might give some additional
trouble.

During the term of my Command, it may be found, that
from two and a half per cent, and in some instances seven per
cent., was obtained more for the Navy Bills, than was got for

private ones. I was satisfied with the conscious rectitude of
my actions; and only trouble you with this communication,
that, if possible, any improper mode of conducting this Department may be altered. The openings for fraud are so numerous, the facility of carrying it on so easy, and detection so
very difficult, (it being the interest of all parties to keep the
secret,) that I fear it is a difficult thing to find virtue
enough to withstand the temptation.

TO GEORGE ROSE, ESQ., SECRETARY TO THE TREASURY.

[From Clarke and M‘Arthur, vol. i. p. 104. The date of this Letter is not
given. It was probably written towards the end of 1787.]

Sir,

I yesterday received the enclosed letter from the Commissioners of the Customs. The exertions I made, whilst on the
Leeward Islands Station, in stopping the illegal Trade with
America, is not, I trust, forgotten by their Lordships. I have
therefore to request you will be pleased to move their Lordships, that they will order the necessary steps to be taken for
supporting the legality of the Sentences.

I am, &c.
HORATIO NELSON.

TO THE REVEREND WILLIAM NELSON, HILBOROUGH.

[Autograph, in the Nelson Papers.]

6, Princes-street, Cavendish-square, January 3rd, 1788.

My dear Brother,

Our little boy shall be at Hilborough on Tuesday or Wednesday next, escorted by Frank,[3] who I have desired to stay
two or three days till the child becomes reconciled. I am
assured of your and Mrs. Nelson's goodness to him—
that is, you will not allow him to do as he pleases: it's mistaken kindness where it happens. I wish him at school to have
the same weekly allowance as the other boys, and whatever
else may be proper for him.   We have been very unwell, and

[3] His servant, Frank Lepée.

shall go to Bath as soon as I can get out. Your rum will come down when I know the best conveyance: send me word. Your pay for the Boreas would not amount to the fees of Office.[4] In the Lottery, whatever part of a ticket, or in what proportion you wish to have one, shall be complied with. Maurice is well: he has just left us, and desires to be remembered. Our best compliments to Mrs. Nelson and the old ladies. The wine shall come as soon as I can get it from the Custom-house, and know the best conveyance. Adieu, and believe me ever, your most affectionate Brother,

HORATIO NELSON.

TO WILLIAM LOCKER, ESQ., KENSINGTON.

[Autograph, in the Locker Papers.]

Bath, January 27th, 1788.

My dear Sir,

Your kind letter I received yesterday, and am much obliged by your kind inquiries about a house. I fear we must at present give [up] all thoughts of living so near London, for Mrs. Nelson's lungs are so much affected by the smoke of London, that I cannot think of placing her in that situation, however desirable. For the next summer I shall be down in Norfolk, from thence I must look forward. I was rather hurried in getting down here, by Prince William having invited me to Plymouth. I was therefore glad to place Mrs. Nelson here at once, which not only saved me the expense, but the toil, of a journey three hundred miles. I returned from Plymouth three days ago, and found Prince William everything I could wish—respected by all. Those who knew him formerly say he is a most altered young man; and those who were prejudiced against him acknowledge their error. The Pegasus is allowed by every one to be one of the best disciplined Ships that ever came into Plymouth. But the great folks above now see he will not be a cypher, therefore many of the rising people must submit to act subordinate to him, which is not so

---

[4] As Chaplain.

palatable; and I think a Lord of the Admiralty[5] is hurt to
see him so able, after what he has said about him. He has
not certainly taken a leaf out of his book, for he is steady in
his Command and not violent. He has wrote Lord Hood
what I cannot but approve, yet am sorry about his taking
Lieutenant Schomberg.

When the Lists come out will you be good enough to send
me one? Kingsmill will frank it if it can come by the post.
I hope he is better; pray give my best wishes to him. Mrs.
Nelson desires the same, and unites with me in best wishes
to your family. I pray compliments to Bradley, Anderson, &c.
You are in debt to Mr. Suckling for the duty on the rum:
the wine I desire you will not pay. Charles Pole is not well,
I fear he is getting too fat. God bless you, my dear Sir,
and be assured

I am your most faithful and affectionate
HORATIO NELSON.

I beg my compliments to Lord Ducie when you see him.

TO PHILIP STEPHENS, ESQ., ADMIRALTY.

[Autograph, in the Admiralty.]

Bath, February 20th, 1788.

Sir,

I am this moment honoured with your letters of February
16th, acquainting me that if I had looked into the Instructions,
I should have seen that I ought to have sealed my Remarks and
Observations on board the Boreas up, and sent them under
cover directed to you. I beg you will inform their Lordships
it must have arisen from a mistake of my Clerk's, for that on
the day the Ship was paid off, I myself inclosed the Remarks and
Observations to you, and saw them directed. My Clerk was
sealing the official letters to the several Boards, for passing
my Accounts, which were to be put in a box with my books,

---

[5] The two Naval Lords of the Admiralty were Admiral Viscount Howe, and
Rear-Admiral the Honourable John Leveson Gower.

to be sent to my Agent's; and that I do assure their Lordships
I ordered him to put the packet into the Clerk of the
Cheque's Office after he had sealed it; and that I did not
know the Board had not received it till I received your letter.
And I beg you will assure the Board that no person wishes
to pay a more rigid obedience to his instructions than

Your most obedient Servant,

HORATIO NELSON.

TO WILLIAM LOCKER, ESQ , KENSINGTON.

[Autograph, in the Nelson Papers.]

Bath, April 3rd, 1788.

My dear Sir,

I have for this long time been very negligent about writing;
nor, thank God, have I the excuse of illness, for never was I
so well; but we have been for this last month at a relation's
near Bristol,[7] and am only just returned here, in order to drink
the waters another fortnight, after which we are going to Exmouth on a visit for a month; from whence we shall pass
through London on our way to Norfolk.   I am sorry the wine
has not turned out good. After my misfortune with your's, Captain Gower's, and my own wine, I bought this hogshead, and
was told it was the best quality : sure I am I paid the best
price. Captain Gower[8] is to have two dozen and four, but indeed
he ought to have what he pleases of it.   There is nothing to me
so distressing than losing anybody's wine, more especially one
who I am not very intimately acquainted with.   Pray remember me kindly to Captain Kingsmill.   I would direct this letter
under cover to him, but I am told he has let his house.   Our
Sea folks here are pretty numerous, but I am tired of this place,
and long to get into the country.   Our friend Charles Pole
has been fortunate in his trial; but the lottery is so very
much against an Officer, that never will I knowingly involve
myself in a doubtful cause.   Prize-money is doubtless very
acceptable; but my mind would have suffered so much, that
no pecuniary compensation, at so late a period, would have

[7] An Uncle of Mrs. Nelson's, at Redland.—*Clarke and M'Arthur*, vol. i.
p. 104.

[8] Captain, afterwards Admiral Sir Erasmus Gower.

made me amends. I am at this moment under a prosecution by some Americans, for seizing their Vessels in the West Indies: but I have wrote them word, that I will have nothing to do with them, and they may act as they think proper. Government, I suppose, will do what is right, and not leave me in the lurch. We have heard enough lately of the consequence of the Act of Navigation to this Country. They may take my person; but if sixpence would save me from a prosecution, I would not give it.

In some measure I agree with you about the Guard Ships and small Vessels; so far, certainly, that I would take half. of every Ship's company that are Cruisers in the Channel, and put them into the new-commissioned large Ships, and let the small ones raise more. What the Papers tell us is to be the conduct of this Country towards Russia is retaliation; at least, if our friendship is worth buying, we may have our own price. Spain appears fixed not to let their Fleet come into the Straits. The Empress's armed Neutrality falls most deservedly on herself. I think if her Fleet is able to get out of the Baltic, we shall have a Squadron of large Ships in Gibraltar Bay, either to keep the Peace, or assist one side or other. Something . . . . . [*torn*] . . . Mrs. Nelson desires her best . . . . . in which joins . . . [*torn*]

Compliments to Bradley.

TO MESSRS. WILKINSON AND HIGGINS, ANTIGUA.

[Original draught, in the Nelson Papers.]

Plymouth, 26th April, 1788.

Gentlemen,

This moment I have only been honoured with your letter of February 13th, and am surprised that you have not received a letter from me, dated at the Nore, in September last, more especially as I sent it to Sir Charles Middleton, (he having desired me to write you) stating, that a most honourable and liberal confidence might be reposed in him. Sir Charles has not only the abilities, but the power of doing more for you than I ever could have; and, I am assured has as much wish to bring these iniquitous Frauds to light. This is his public character, I have not the honour of knowing his private one. Repeatedly I have seen Sir Charles Middleton; and he told me that every step should be taken; nay, that one of the Officers was not likely to go out again to Antigua.

Lord Howe told me that he had consulted with the Navy Board, and they would receive any communication from you, or myself, and do what was right; and further said, that you was entitled, on making good these representations, to a most liberal reward.

From Mr. Pitt, I had an acknowledgment that the papers were received by him, and sent to the different Departments. The Victualling Board comes under the cognizance of the Admiralty. I don't recollect in that Department you gave me any proofs; but I will look when I go to Town; and if I have sent any of them (which I did if you gave them to me) I will see the Victualling Board on the subject. His Grace of Richmond has not honoured me with an acknowledgment of the receipt of them: in other people's Departments he is most rigid for justice; therefore I am the more surprised. I would have you write to him. The Sick and Hurt fall under the cognizance of the Admiralty; but a letter addressed to that Board cannot but be very proper. I shall go to Town very shortly, and shall see Sir Charles Middleton; and, if he thinks fit, I shall see your answer to the Navy Board. At all events, I shall desire it, and you may rest assured, that no steps shall be left undone by me to accomplish the discovery of these mal-practices; and to get you the reward, which I have not the least doubt you will so well merit: but I must apprise you that my interest in this Country is very small; therefore do not build that I can do much for you. Indeed, but little else than my integrity and public spirit can bring such an humble individual as myself into notice. But the goodness of the cause we are engaged in, will support itself at all times. More especially, I dare say, with such an upright character as Mr. Pitt.

His Royal Highness commands me to say, that was he placed in a situation where he could be of any service to this cause, most assuredly he would sift it to the bottom: but that

10

at present, (not having been from this Port since his arrival) he can only give his good wishes for the accomplishment of what you have begun. I am sorry any cause should be given for your suggesting to his Royal Highness your doubts of the propriety of conduct of so high a trust, and important an Officer,[9] as you mentioned, but I hope in this case you will be mistaken.

I am much obliged by your good wishes in respect to myself. All his Majesty's Navy Officers, I hope, will act the same upright part, which you are pleased to suppose I should. Any letters addressed under cover to Maurice Nelson, Esq., Navy Office, will find me out. And I beg you to be assured I am your sincere well-wisher, and most faithful, humble servant,

HORATIO NELSON.

TO . . . .

[Autograph draught in the Nelson Papers. The address is wanting.]

Exmouth, Devon, April 30th, 1788.

Sir,

My brother having written me that you wished to have the letter of Messrs. Wilkingson and Higgins to me, I have sent it. These gentlemen desire I will do them justice with your Board as to their ability to discover what they have pledged themselves to do. By the papers I saw, it conveyed to my idea most clearly the Frauds, (if they were not made for the purpose, which I cannot suppose,) and that it would be no very difficult matter to find it out. Nothing, I thought, could prevent these gentlemen bringing it to light, but what I mentioned to you when I had the honour of seeing you on this subject. These people must be fools indeed to effectually ruin themselves for a momentary reflection on the characters of these people. All their hopes of advantage certainly now arises from proving what they have alleged; and as they have only asked for rewards for what can be actually recovered, I

---

[9] Nelson originally wrote " that some of the Crown Officers, whose cognizance their situation might place," &c.

cannot suppose but they are most serious in the progress of this discovery. In the West Indies they are most effectually ruined as merchants. It has been alleged they are bad men, and were partakers in these Frauds. Admitting it to be so, much good often arises from bad motives; therefore to benefit the Public I should never ask or care from what motives the good arises. Their letters to his Royal Highness Prince William are only repetitions, I take for granted, of their Memorial and Petition to Mr. Pitt, and some compliments to my assiduity while in that Country. They are certainly men of strong natural parts, and appear wonderfully expert at the per centage.

I am, &c.
HORATIO NELSON.

TO THE COMMISSIONERS OF THE OFFICE FOR SICK AND HURT.

[Autograph draught, in the Nelson Papers. This letter was written in reply to one from the Commissioners, dated 22nd April 1788, (enclosing a Letter which they had received from Messrs. Higgins and Wilkinson of the 30th of January 1788, accusing their Officers of Fraud,) requesting Captain Nelson to favour them with his opinion whether the charges were likely to be true, as they had no other grounds for suspecting their Officers; and they were "not willing to institute an inquiry without a reasonable cause."]

[End of April, 1788.]

Gentlemen,

I was only this morning honoured with your letter of the 22nd instant, addressed to me at Bath. Messrs. Wilkinson and Higgins made their representations to His Royal Highness Prince William Henry and myself of various Frauds in several Departments of Government, in such a strong manner, as I humbly conceived fully authorised me to transmit them to the Minister and First Lord of the Admiralty, that they might direct such measures to be taken as appeared to them proper. It is a very delicate task to handle the character of any Officer, more especially one who most certainly pays very great attention to the sick and wounded Seamen placed under his direction, and is in every respect a most humane man to all who fall sick in the Fleet. In respect to myself, I feel under particular obligations to Dr. Y—— for his care and attention to me during my last Station. Mess. Wilkinson and Higgins have made in other Departments such proof of improper conduct, as I think certainly entitles them to a degree of credit in this case. Every honest man, after such a letter as is wrote you, I should conceive would wish a most strict inquiry into his conduct, rather than let the matter drop. Mess. Wilkinson and Higgins were merchants in St. John's, Antigua, and partners with Mr. Whitehead, Agent to the Hospital.

I am, &c.

HORATIO NELSON.

TO HERCULES ROSS, ESQ., ROYAL HOTEL, PALL MALL, LONDON.

[Original draught, in the Nelson Papers.]

Exmouth Moor, 6th May, 1788.

My dear Friend,

Your favour of the 1st found me in this remote corner, where I have been this last fortnight, enjoying the benefit of a first summer to a West Indian: no bad thing. However, as usual, my health is got up again, after the Doctors telling me they could do nothing for me ; Dame Nature never has failed curing me.

We shall rest all next Sunday at Bath, in our way to London, and I shall examine the Pump-Room, to see if you and Mrs. Ross are at Bath ; and should that be the case, I will have the satisfaction of taking my old friend by the hand. You have, as well as myself, undergone a great change, since we last met ; and I hope, and have been told, are united to an amiable woman, the greatest blessing Heaven can bestow. But in this next, my friend, you have got the start of me. You have given up all the toils and anxieties of business ; whilst I must still buffet the waves—in search of what? That thing called Honour, is now, alas ! thought of no more. My integrity cannot be mended, I hope ; but my fortune, God knows, has grown worse for the Service ; so much for serving my Country. But the Devil, ever willing to tempt the Virtuous, (pardon this flattery of myself,) has made me offer, if any Ships should be sent to destroy his Majesty of Morocco's Ports, to be there ; and I have some reason to think, that should any more come of it, my humble services will be accepted. I have invariably laid down, and followed close, a plan of what ought to be uppermost in the breast of an Officer: that it is much better to serve an ungrateful Country, than to give up his own fame. Posterity will do him justice: a uniform conduct of honour and integrity seldom fails of bringing a man to the goal of Fame at last.—But to what am I getting? Into a Sermon. Mrs. N. joins in best compliments to Mrs. Ross; and believe me ever, my dear friend,

Your affectionate,

HORATIO NELSON.

TO VISCOUNT HOWE, FIRST LORD OF THE ADMIRALTY.

[Original draught, in the Nelson Papers. No date, but probably written in May 1788.]

[May 1788.]

My Lord,

I have twice, since my arrival in Town, done myself the honour of calling at your Lordship's, in order to pay my personal respects; and to assure you, that as I have always been, so I continue, ever in readiness to undertake any service to which the Admiralty may think it proper to appoint me. My zeal for his Majesty's Service is as great as I once flattered myself your Lordship thought it.

I have had hopes that the Admiralty would have ordered me the same allowance at least, as was given to a junior Officer left in the command at Jamaica; and I hope your Lordship will give me countenance in an application for it. I trust it is incontrovertible, that I did my duty with the most rigid attention; and, that the business of the Naval Yard was never paid more attention to, than by myself. The Navy-Board, I am sure, at this moment, are inclined to believe, that the difficulties said by their Officers to be thrown in the way of their duty by me, arose only from my close investigation of their conduct; which prevented their impositions from taking effect. Every artificer and seaman employed in the Naval Yard receives additional pay; and shall the Officer who has the conducting of the whole business be the only one (in this instance) who is neglected? I trust, by your Lordship's answer, it will not be so. The trouble I was at in investigating these frauds, it is most true, was no more than my duty; but indeed, the expenses attending my going so often to St. John's, a distance of twelve miles, I little thought would have fallen upon me out of my pay as Captain of the Boreas.

I am, &c.

HORATIO NELSON.

TO H. R. H. PRINCE WILLIAM HENRY.

[Original, in the possession of William Henry Whitehead, Esq.]

No. 5, Cavendish Square, June 2nd, 1788.

My Prince,

It was not until a very few days ago, that I heard your Royal Highness was going the cruise with the Squadron now at Spithead. I am most sincerely glad to hear it, and am assured it is quite the thing you wish.

Your Royal Highness knows every thing relative to a single Ship; and it can only be by commanding a Fleet which will establish your fame, make you the darling of the Nation, and hand down your Name with honour and glory to posterity.

Indeed I have another very strong reason for being pleased at your serving near Home, which is, that the actions of all Officers, however brilliant, are wonderfully obscured by serving at a distance, for the capture of a Privateer makes more noise, taken in the Channel, than a Frigate, or even a Ship of the Line, afar off. Therefore, although the discipline and high order of your Ship is known to many others as well as myself, yet it will now be much more talked of; and the King will be more acquainted with the exact state of the Andromeda than [by] any representations made from abroad. I am most totally ignorant whether to expect you back with the Fleet, or if you proceed abroad; should the former be the case, if your Royal Highness comes within the reach of my purse, I shall most certainly pay my humble duty. Should the latter take place, I shall, as soon as I know to what part of the World you are destined, trouble your Royal Highness with letters, an honour which you have most condescendingly permitted me.

I am most truly sensible of your kindness to me on all occasions, and although Mr. Herbert was hard enough to withstand your solicitations, yet my obligation is the same: there may be a thing, perhaps, within reach of your Royal Highness; therefore, trusting to your goodness, I shall mention it. The Princess Royal must very soon have a Household appointed her. I believe a word from your Royal Highness would obtain a promise of a situation in her Royal Highness's Establishment not unbecoming the wife of a Captain in the Navy; but I have only ventured to say thus much, and leave the issue to your better judgment; being, with the highest regard and attachment,

Your Royal Highness's most faithful
HORATIO NELSON.

TO PHILIP STEPHENS, ESQ., ADMIRALTY.

[Autograph, in the Nelson Papers.]

Barton, near Norwich, Norfolk, August 8th, 1788.

Sir,

Having seen by the Gazette a new Board of Admiralty[9] is appointed, I feel it my duty to request you will be pleased to assure their Lordships of my readiness to serve whenever they may think proper to call for my services.

I am, Sir, &c.
HORATIO NELSON.

TO MRS. NELSON.

[From Clarke and M'Arthur, vol. i. p. 109.]

London, 26th August 1788.

I saw Lord Hood this morning; he made many inquiries after you, and was very civil. He assured me, that a Ship in

---

[9] The New Board was appointed on the 6th July 1788. The Earl of Chatham became First Lord; and the Naval Lords were Vice-Admiral Lord Hood and Rear-Admiral the Honourable John Leveson Gower.

peaceable times was not desirable: but that should any Hostilities take place, I need not fear having a good Ship.[1]

　　　　　　　　　　　I am, &c.

　　　　　　　　　　　　　HORATIO NELSON.

　　　　TO PHILIP STEPHENS, ESQ., ADMIRALTY.

　　　　　　[Autograph draught, in the Nelson Papers.]

　　　　　　　　　　　Burnham, December 26th, 1788.

Sir,

Having received a letter from Mr. Charles Lock,[2] late a Midshipman on board the Boreas, under my command, stating that on his going to be Examined touching his qualification as Lieutenant, the Comptroller of the Navy and the Passing Captains had refused to examine him, as he had been rated for a longer time Captain's Servant on board the Boreas, than they thought it proper, and requesting that I would state his situation to the Lords of the Admiralty, that they might be induced to give an Order to the Passing Board, that Mr. Lock might be examined.

I had occasion to write to the Board relative to Mr. John Talbot,[3] in a similar situation, and to that Letter I must beg leave to refer you; and have only to observe that I have always supposed that Servants were allowed for bringing up so many Seamen for the Navy, and that I thought I was performing a meritorious service, in taking for my Servants a set of young men to make Officers of, without a nursery for whom, I am well assured our Service must suffer. The want of good Petty Officers, and consequently good Lieutenants, is well known to have been most severely felt

---

[1] In October 1788, Nelson wrote to his friend Commodore Cornwallis, who was then going to the East Indies, expressing his desire to serve under him. In reply, dated on the 10th of that month, Commodore Cornwallis assured him that it would have given him the greatest pleasure to have him in one of the Ships, and though he remembered that Nelson was once partial to the part of the world to which he was going, yet his fireside was so changed since that time, that he durst not venture to name him; but that if more Ships were sent out, nothing could give him greater pleasure than to have the happiness of seeing him in one of them."—*Original*, in the Nelson Papers.

[2] Vide p. 108, ante.

[3] The present Admiral the Honourable Sir John Talbot, G.C.B.

during the late War, and if this young man is qualified, I humbly apprehend it can make no difference to the Service what pay he received. I have certified to the Passing Captains, and do now assure their Lordships that Mr. C. Lock was on board the Boreas during my whole command, three years and nine months, and did learn and perform the duties of Mate and Midshipman; and indeed, I cannot but help thinking that the Service would have suffered had I either rated these young men, or not taken more on board than the complement, viz. two Mates and four Midshipmen.

I am, &c.

HORATIO NELSON.

TO MESSRS. WILKINSON AND HIGGINS, ANTIGUA.

[Autograph draught, in the Nelson Papers.]

Burnham,[4] 24th January 1789.

Gentlemen,

Your letter of October, I received last night, and have sent the enclosed to Sir Charles Middleton this morning. I am most sincerely sorry for your situation,[5] and hope that

---

[4] On being placed on Half-pay, Captain Nelson intended to go to France with his wife, to acquire the French language; but they were persuaded by his father to reside with him at his Parsonage of Burnham Thorpe, where they remained until he was appointed to the Agamemnon, in January 1793. His Biographers say, "He employed himself with considerable zeal while at Burnham, in cultivating his father's garden, and in learning to farm the adjacent glebe; but the former was his principal station: he would there often spend the greater part of the day, and dig, as it were, for the purpose of being wearied. At others, he would renew the early pastime of their childhood, and with a simplicity that was peculiar to him, when his mind was not employed on the great objects of professional duty, would spend some part of the day amidst the woods, in taking the eggs of different birds, which, as he obtained, he gave to Mrs. Nelson, who always accompanied him. He sometimes also employed his time, when his eyes would admit of it, in reading the periodical works of the day, but oftener in studying charts, and in writing, or drawing plans. But the uniformity of a village life was occasionally diversified by professional calls to the Metropolis; by an annual visit, with Mrs. Nelson, to Lord Walpole, at Wolterton; and by occasional visits to Mr. Coke, at Holkham."—*Clarke and M'Arthur*, vol. i. pp. 109, 110.

[5] Mr. Wilkinson stated to Captain Nelson that he "wrote that letter from the gaol of the Island of Antigua, into which he had been placed by a quirk of the Solicitor General's," and he complained bitterly of the manner in which that Officer had treated him, which he attributed to his discovery of Mr. Whitehead's

Government will afford you every assistance, in bringing to maturity the good work begun under my auspices. But I would have you recollect, that although Government business may be slow, yet it is sure. I am assured the business will never be dropped ; and that all proper rewards and recompenses will be made you. His Grace of Richmond, after a long silence, has at last assured me,[6] that every proper measure shall be taken, and that you shall receive the reward you asked. All the other Boards will do you ample justice. I cannot but lament that your discovery should not have been made to a man of more consequence than myself; for in this Country I am not in Office, and am so much retired from the busy scenes of power, that although I have every inclination, I have not the ability of doing more than representing your situation, and which I have always done, expressing to all the Public Boards my belief of your ability and determination to lay all the Frauds open.

Rest assured, I am your Friend,

HORATIO NELSON.

TO . . . . .

[Autograph draught, in the Nelson Papers.]

Burnham, January 24th 1789.

Sir,

I received last night a letter from Mr. Wilkinson, Antigua, and as I suppose it was intended for your perusal by its being sent open, I hope you have done it, and have seen it contains only a melancholy *statement* of Mr. W.'s situation. I am sincerely sorry for his case, as I am sensible that the rigour which appears to be exercised against him in his private

Frauds. That the Solicitor General favoured that person, and that Whitehead had acted fraudulently, is shown by "A Resolution of the Honourable House of Assembly in the Island of Antigua, on the 4th day of June 1788—That it be resolved that William Whitehead, surviving partner of Francis Colley, has been guilty of gross imposition on the Committee of both Houses of the Legislature appointed to examine the accounts of Francis Colley and Co., and of a flagrant attempt to defraud the Public of this Island. 4th June 1788. Ayes 15. Noes 2." The two Noes being Mr. Solicitor General and Archibald Gloster, Esq.

[6] In a Letter (now in the Nelson Papers) dated 27th December 1788.

affairs is owing to his communication of Frauds, which I have
but little doubt set the greater part of the mercantile people,
who had to do with the Officers of Government against these
Gentlemen. And to myself, I cannot but help feeling that I
may have been in some measure accessory to these violent
measures, by my open attention, and I may say protection, and
promises of every encouragment which Government could
afford them. As Merchants they were from the moment of
discovery ruined. I am assured you will do what is right
and proper for these Gentlemen, and am with great respect,

Your most obedient Servant,

HORATIO NELSON.

TO MESSRS. WILKINSON AND HIGGINS, ANTIGUA.

[Autograph draught, in the Nelson Papers.]

Burnham, February 1st, 1789.

Gentlemen,

The following is an extract of a letter from Sir Charles
Middleton, January 27th: ' It is intended to try the business
at home, and which must be more satisfactory than doing it
abroad. In this case, Mr. Wilkinson, &c. will have notice by
summons: they are acquainted of this by the Navy-Board.'

I can only wish that all may end to your satisfaction.[7] You
see I have taken all opportunities in letting you know the
progress of your business, as soon as I was acquainted with it.
Being your sincere well-wisher,

HORATIO NELSON.

I have never seen the Letter you mention having wrote the
Navy Board, and which you say you wished me to read.

---

[7] On the 30th May 1789, Captain Sir Charles Middleton informed Nelson
that "the Navy Solicitor has received directions to send for Messrs. Wilkinson
and Higgins home, to make good their charge : and has wrote to them accordingly."—*Original Note*, in the Nelson Papers.

TO WILLIAM LOCKER, ESQ., KENSINGTON.

[Autograph, in the Locker Papers.]

Burnham, February 7th, 1789.

My dear Sir,

I received your favour of the 3rd, last night: the Madeira
I kept as a treat for some of my friends who are come here
to see us, when behold, on examination, instead of Madeira,
I found as good Port wine as ever was tasted. Your servant
I take for granted, has mistaken the binn. Your news in
respect to the Promotion, is great, but I can hardly believe
they can make Admirals so far as Lord Longford; we shall be
all Admirals![8] Pray thank Mr. Bradley for the Navy List he
was so kind as to send me. Pray remember me to Charles
Pole; I wish, if he likes it, he may get a Guardship at Plymouth.
Mrs. Nelson joins in best regards to yourself and family, with
your affectionate

HORATIO NELSON.

Pray don't forget me to Kingsmill and all our friends.

TO WILLIAM LOCKER, ESQ., KENSINGTON.

[Autograph, in the Locker Papers.]

Burnham, September 10th, 1789.

My dear Sir,

I was exceedingly happy to hear by your letter from Harro-
gate, that you was so much recovered, and by this time, I
take for granted, you are settled again at home, and I most
sincerely hope you will never be obliged again to travel
in quest of health. When we may meet, time must determine; at present, I have no appearance of being called up to
London. Not being a man of fortune is a crime which I cannot get over, and therefore none of the Great care about me.
I am now commencing Farmer, not a very large one, you will

---

[8] No promotion took place until September 1790, and only ten Captains
then obtained their Flags. In 1788 Lord Longford stood the 54th on the List
of Post-Captains; and he died a Captain in June 1792.

conceive, but enough for amusement. Shoot I cannot, therefore
I have not taken out a license; but notwithstanding the neglect I have met with, I am happy, and now I see the propriety
of not having built my hopes on such sandy foundations as the
friendships of the Great. The newspapers tell me of fine
frolics which both King and Prince of Wales have been
making.[9] Pray is Mr. Laforey[1] to be promoted, or is there to
be a promotion of Flags? Is there any idea of our being
drawn into a quarrel by these commotions on the Continent?
whenever that may be likely to happen, I will take care to
make my application in time. I wish our friend Kingsmill
would retract many of his generous expenses: it is his gifts
which has drawn him into difficulties, that I have little doubt
of, and not knowing the value of money. Pray, when you
write or see him, remember me kindly to him. Mrs. Nelson
desires me to present her best respects to you and family, and
believe me,

Your much obliged, and affectionate,
HORATIO NELSON.

[9] The Prince of Wales had just visited the North of England, and been entertained by Earl Fitzwilliam at Wentworth House; but it does not appear
what " fine frolics " of the King, were alluded to.

[1] Captain John Laforey. In 1779 this Officer, who commanded the Ocean in
Admiral Keppel's Action, was appointed Commissioner of the Navy at Antigua,
and in 1783, at Plymouth: he was passed over in the Promotion of Flag Officers
in 1787 on the ground that having accepted a civil Office, he was ineligible for
advancement in his profession. The question, which excited much interest in
the Navy, was warmly discussed between the Admiralty and Captain Laforey,
whose zealous conduct in support of Admiral Keppel at his trial rendered him,
it was supposed, unacceptable to the First Lord of the Admiralty, the Earl of
Chatham. His claims were, however, admitted, and he obtained his proper
rank, as Rear-Admiral of the Red, on the 10th November 1789, having a few
days before been made a Baronet. He attained the rank of Admiral of the Blue on
June 1795, and, dying on his passage from the West Indies, the 14th of June
1796, was buried at Portsmouth.—*Naval Chronicle*, vol. xxv. p. 182.

TO MESSRS. WILKINSON AND HIGGINS, ANTIGUA.

[Autograph draught, in the Nelson Papers.]

Burnham, November 28th, 1789.

Gentlemen,

I received your letter of the 11th of September, the beginning of this month, and sent it to Sir Charles Middleton, without any comments of mine; as, to me it seemed to require no explanation. When it was returned, it was wrote me that if I chose the letter should be made public, to send it to the Navy Board; reports having been circulated by high Officers, that they feared all this business would end in *smoke;* and that you had shifted your ground, and were very wavering in your opinions: for that at first you had said, that nothing was to be done in the West Indies; and now, that nothing could be done at four thousand miles' distance.

[As to] certain opinions which I had formed, although I am not a man who wishes to say much on anything without being asked, yet on this occasion, common justice would not allow me to be silent, when such (as appears to me) false reports, were in circulation. I therefore wrote to the Navy Board, of which the following is an extract: viz. ' Having heard a report that these Gentlemen had deviated from the first line of procedure they had adopted, it becomes, (I hope the Board will think) a line of justice in me to give my reasons why I do not think so. When the information was given, and in all their subsequent communications with me, they have uniformly and constantly protested against placing their confidence in his Majesty's Law-Officers in the West Indies. That a trial in England, although it might prove certain facts, yet was by no means the object they had in view when the information was given. Their object, I have constantly understood, was an inquiry and examination, on the large scale, of examining Merchants, their books, &c. and tracing the frauds *home* to every delinquent; who being made to refund, was the source from whence these Gentlemen expected their rewards to have arisen.'

On the 27th, yesterday, I received the following answer: ' We have sent the letters and enclosures to Mr. Dyson, our Solicitor, and desired him to lay them before the Attorney-

General for his Opinion as to what steps are proper to be taken thereon, and to use every means in his power to investigate and bring forward the whole of the business so soon as possible.' Retired as I am, upwards of one hundred and twenty miles from London, I can render you little if any assistance in getting forward in this business; and good wishes, without something more powerful, are of no avail in this Country. I can only sit down and *think*. Sir John Laforey is going out with the Command, and will probably be the man to investigate the frauds committed in the Naval Yard, &c. during the War. I am, &c.

HORATIO NELSON.[2]

TO THE COMMISSIONERS OF CUSTOMS.

[Autograph draught in the Nelson Papers.]

[Apparently in 1790].

I received your letter of the 20th yesterday, relative to the capture of the Hercules and Nancy Pleasant, American vessels, and desiring that I would acquaint you whether I have given

---

[2] This appears to be the last letter from Nelson respecting those Frauds; and his Biographers conclude the subject by observing: " Thus the very extensive public Frauds which had long been committed with impunity in the West Indies, were at length put in a proper train to be provided against in future. An immense saving was made to Government, and its attention directed to similar peculations in other parts of our extensive Colonies. No reward, however, nor any mark of commendation, seems in consequence to have been conferred on Captain Nelson;" and they add the remark of Mr. Rose, then Secretary to the Treasury, that Nelson's " representations were all attended to, and every step which he recommended was adopted. He thus put the investigation into a proper course, which ended in the detection and punishment of some of the parties whose conduct was complained of."—*Clarke and M'Arthur*, vol. i. pp. 106, 114. Southey says, as well in the "Quarterly Review" as in his "Life of Nelson," "that the peculators were too powerful; and they succeeded not merely in impeding inquiry, but even in raising prejudices against Nelson at the Board of Admiralty, which it was many years before he could subdue;" but he does not give any authority for the statement.

It is, however, proper to observe, that in 1788 and 1789, the Public Boards offered Nelson their warmest thanks for his zeal; and that the Duke of Richmond concluded his Letter of the 2nd of June 1789, in these words: " With respect to yourself, I can only renew the assurances of my perfect conviction of the zeal for His Majesty's Service which has induced you to stir in this business."—*Original*, in the Nelson Papers.

any orders, and what orders, for the support of the sentences of condemnation.

I beg leave to acquaint you that I did seize the above named Vessels, (with many others,) and that they were prosecuted in the name of, and by his Majesty's Attorney-General of the Leeward Islands, (John Stanley, Esq., of No. 10, Queen Ann Street, Westminster,) to whom I beg leave to refer you for farther particulars. Mr. Stanley has copies of the proceedings under the Great Seal of the Leeward Islands, and I did not imagine I could possibly have anything more to do in this business. The great exertions I made during the years of 1784, 85, 86, and 87, part of which I was on the Leeward Islands Station, in stopping the illegal trade with America, is not I hope forgot by the Board of Commissioners, and I have firm hope that they will order me to be defended, and that they will direct the legality of the sentence to be supported.

I am, &c.,

HORATIO NELSON.

TO GEORGE ROSE, ESQ , SECRETARY TO THE TREASURY.

[Autograph draught, in the Nelson Papers.]

[Apparently in 1790.]

Sir,

On yesterday I received the inclosed letter from the Commissioners of Customs. The exertions I made whilst on the Leeward Island Station, in stopping the illegal trade with America is not, I trust, forgot by their Lordships. I have, therefore, to request you will be pleased to move their Lordships, that they will order the necessary steps to be taken for supporting the legality of the Sentences.

I have the honour to, &c.

HORATIO NELSON.

TO PHILIP STEPHENS, ESQ., SECRETARY TO THE ADMIRALTY.

[Original, in the Admiralty. In reply to this Letter, he was informed that the Admiralty had referred his communication to the Treasury, with a recommendation that he should be defended at the Public expense.]

Burnham, Norfolk, March 21st, 1790.

Sir,

Last night I received a Letter (of which the inclosed is a copy,) the contents of which cannot but give me uneasiness.[3] Since May 1785, I have been continually harassed by my exertions in suppressing the illegal traffic which was carrying on between the States of America and the West India Islands, where I was stationed. These people seem determined to go lengths which must be very unpleasant to me, unless supported by Government. I feel happy that I never made a seizure whilst on that Station without the advice of the Attorney-General, or the Chief Law Officer of the Crown, where the case might happen; and in this particular I had the opinion of the Attorney-General and King's Proctor of Barbadoes. The Attorney-General and Senior King's Counsel of the Leeward Islands (where I was obliged from circumstances already known to their Lordships to carry her) to sanction my proceedings.

I trust their Lordships will think that, under such advice, I could not be supposed to err in stopping the Vessel; but that, on the contrary, I should have been guilty of neglect of duty, had I suffered her to trade unmolested, which she had repeatedly done since the Peace, (under false colours and papers.) I hope their Lordships will take my situation into their consideration.

I am, Sir, &c.
HORATIO NELSON.

---

[3] From Messrs. Venables, Buggin, and Bleasdale, Solicitors, (respecting proceedings against him for having seized the " Jane and Elizabeth,") on the 10th of March 1786.

TO PHILIP STEPHENS, ESQ., SECRETARY TO THE ADMIRALTY.

[Original, in the Admiralty.]

Burnham, Norfolk, April 26th, 1790.

Sir,

I wrote a short time since on the subject of the Vessel named in the inclosed papers.[4] This day I was served by a person from London with a notice, of which I send a copy. I trust to their Lordships' protection, hoping they will think I only performed my duty.

I have the honour to be, &c.

HORATIO NELSON.

TO PHILIP STEPHENS, ESQ., SECRETARY TO THE ADMIRALTY.

[Autograph, in the Admiralty. On hearing of the expected rupture with Spain, in consequence of the Affair of Nootka Sound, Captain Nelson immediately proceeded to the Admiralty, where this letter was written.]

Admiralty Office, May 8th, 1790.

Sir,

I have to request you will acquaint their Lordships, that immediately on my hearing of this bustle, I set off for Lon-

---

[4] Clarke and M'Arthur (vol. i. p. 110) state, that one day, while Nelson had gone to a fair to purchase a pony, two men served a " writ or notification" on Mrs. Nelson, on the part of some American Captains, who laid their damages at £20,000 : that on his return, while boasting of his pony, he was told of the transaction, and that he vehemently exclaimed, "This affront I did not deserve, but never mind, I'll be trifled with no longer : I will write immediately to the Treasury, and if Government will not support me, I am resolved to leave the Country :" that he informed the Treasury, if a satisfactory answer were not sent him by return of post, he would take refuge in France; and that he accordingly made arrangements for Mrs. Nelson's departure ; but that on the 4th of May he was told by Captain Pringle, that Mr. Rose, the Secretary to the Treasury, had said to him, " Captain Nelson is a very good Officer, that he need be under no apprehension, for that he will assuredly be supported by the Treasury." Clarke and M'Arthur have assigned this affair to the year 1788, instead of 1790 ; and they seem to have mistaken and exaggerated the facts, for it appears from the above Letters, that the " writ," or more probably a mere "notification of an action," was not served until the 26th of April ; and the Admiralty had informed Nelson, a month previously, that they had recommended that he should be defended by the Crown. Captain Pringle's Letter, which is among the Nelson Papers, has not the date of the year.

don, where I am just arrived; and that I am ready to undertake such employment as their Lordships shall judge most
proper.

I am, Sir, &c.

HORATIO NELSON.

TO H. R. H. THE DUKE OF CLARENCE.

[Autograph draught, in the Nelson Papers.]

Burnham, Norfolk, June 24th, 1790.

Sir,

I have seen by the papers of the Valiant's[5] arrival at Spithead; I hope she turns out everything your Royal Highness
expected of her. My not being appointed to a Ship is so
very mortifying, that I cannot find words to express what I
feel on the occasion; and when I reflect on your Royal
Highness's condescension in mentioning me to Lord Chatham,[6] I am the more hurt, and surprised. Sure I am, that
I have ever been a zealous and faithful Servant, and never
intentionally have committed any errors; especially as till
very lately I have been honoured by the notice of the Admiralty.

The attachment, which I trust has never been found to
vary, since I first was introduced to you by Lord Hood, had
invariably for its object one point—nothing else for myself did
I ever presume to solicit— that I might have the distinguished
honour of being one of your supporters in a Line of Battle:
then it would be shown, that no person had your Fame more
at heart than myself. I dare not venture a wish that your
Royal Highness should trouble yourself again in my behalf.
I trust most firmly on your kind recollection of me; and I beg
you to be assured, that

I am, as ever,

Your most attached and faithful,

HORATIO NELSON.

---

[5] Then commanded by the Duke of Clarence.
[6] First Lord of the Admiralty.

TO H. R. H. THE DUKE OF CLARENCE.

[Original draught, in the Nelson Papers. Another draught of this Letter, in which the expressions are slightly different, is also preserved.]

21st August, 1790.

Sir,

The retired situation which I am placed in, affords me seldom any other means of information but through newspapers; in which I read with sorrow, that your Royal Highness was prevented from being at Windsor on the Prince of Wales's birth-day by indisposition. It would give me real satisfaction to hear you are perfectly recovered. This, I recollect with pleasure, is your Royal Highness's birth-day : may many revolving years give me an opportunity of congratulating you on its return; and may each bring an increase of comfort, health, and honour to your Royal Highness, is the affectionate wish of

Your most faithful and attached,

HORATIO NELSON.

TO THE RIGHT HONOURABLE THE EARL OF CHATHAM, FIRST LORD OF THE ADMIRALTY.

[Autograph draught, in the Nelson Papers.]

Burnham, Norfolk, September 26th, 1790.

My Lord,

My wish to be employed is so great,[7] that I trespass on

---

[7] In November following Nelson requested his friend, Captain Lord Mulgrave, (p. 5 ante,) then one of the Commissioners for the Affairs of India, to use his influence in obtaining a ship for him. His Lordship replied on the 17th of that month:

"Dear Sir,—I have just received your very obliging Letter : had the Armament continued, I should have had the greatest pleasure in mentioning the just respect I entertain for your professional character, as well as my very sincere personal regard for you, with your very laudable claim for employment. I can only now repeat to you the assurances of the sentiments of esteem and friendship with which, I am dear Sir, most faithfully yours. MULGRAVE."—*Original*, in the Nelson Papers.

your Lordship's time with a Letter. I am sensible I have no great interest to recommend me, nor have I had conspicuous opportunities of distinguishing myself: but thus far, without arrogating, I can say, that no opportunity has been passed by; and that I have ever been a zealous Officer. I am sure Lord Hood [8] will bear testimony of what I have taken the liberty of saying. If the Raisonable[9] is not given away, I should esteem myself highly honoured by the command of her.

I have the honour to remain, &c.

HORATIO NELSON.

TO THE REVEREND MR. NELSON, HILBOROUGH.

[Autograph, in the Nelson Papers. Not a single Letter, written in 1791, has been found. During that year he resided chiefly at Burnham Thorpe.]

Burnham, February 5th, 1792.

My dear Brother,

I thank you for your letter. It was not my intention to have gone to the Coursing meeting, for to say the truth, I have seldom escaped a wet jacket and a violent cold; besides, to me, even the ride to the Smee is longer than any pleasure I find in the sport will compensate for. When I go to London I may possibly go by Hilborough; but, on the other side, I know you are so short of hay, that unless I could buy a little I don't like taking three weeks or a fortnight's keep at least, where it is impossible to replace it.

Mr. Suckling had not seen the present Earl of Orford[1] when he wrote to me. The following is an extract of his letter: 'I am sorry so much cause for warmth has been given to your family through the inattention and ignorance of Mr. Dashwood, in omitting the invitation to attend at the funeral of the late Earl of Orford,[2] which it was his duty to have

---

[8] Lord Hood was then one of the Lords of the Admiralty.

[9] The Raisonable, of 64 guns, in which Ship he first went to Sea.

[1] The celebrated Horace Walpole, who succeeded his nephew, George, the third Earl, as fourth Earl of Orford, on the 5th of December 1791.

[2] To whom the family of Nelson were related, vide p. 15, ante.

done, having taken upon himself to conduct the same, and you had an indisputable right to expect it. I have only seen the present Earl once since his accession to the Title, which was on the day of the interment. He then asked me if I knew who Mr. Dashwood was, and by what means he got hold of his Nephew, as he was perfectly unknown to him. He mentioned that he had received a letter from him respecting the funeral, to which he had returned an answer declining all interference therein.'

From this extract, I have no doubt but Dashwood thrust himself into the office, and was deputy for the Trustees, not for the present Earl, which, by his cards, he wished to be thought. However, the funeral is reprobated in this circle, a great deal of money thrown away, and no proper measure taken for a State funeral. Our news here is but little. Mr. Christian, of Brancaster, is presented to the Living of Workington, called £700 a year. The Martins[3] in the same state of uncertainty as when you were here. Dr. Poyntz told me a long story a little time past about walnut trees and red filberts; but really I can hardly tell you what he said. However I think he meant that he had not the trees you wanted, as he had planted them last year, but that he would send some which, if you planted five or six years in your garden, they would be fit to plant out. I told him I fancied you would never live to get many of the walnuts. I am sorry for Mr. Cauldwell, but hope he will not suffer much pain. Our father is very tolerable, except now and then colds, which we have also had.

I had letters from Commodore Cornwallis by the Swallow. He seems to have no doubt but that the War will soon be brought to an honourable conclusion. I wish it was over. It is thought he will stay there till it is finished, and then return Home, and no more Ships be sent out [at] present. I may now tell you, that if Kingsmill had gone to India, I was to have been his Captain, and the senior one sent out. However, that is over for the present. I had a letter from Maurice last night. The Navy is to be reduced to 15,000

---

[3] The family of Sir Mordaunt Martin, Bart., of Burnham Hall, in Norfolk.

men, but not the number of Guard-ships.   Suckling[4] returns
to Cambridge to-morrow.   Kind love to Mrs. Nelson, my
Aunt,[5] and Compliments to Mr. and Miss Randalls.

H. N.

I wish you much sport.   Tycho is very well, and has
afforded me a great deal of amusement.   Mrs. Nelson will be
obliged to Miss Randall to tell her where honey-water is sold
in Norwich.

TO H. R. H. THE DUKE OF CLARENCE.

[Autograph draught, in the Nelson Papers.]

[3rd November 1792.]

Sir,

Your Royal Highness[6] will not, I trust, deem it improper,
(although I have no doubt it will be thought unnecessary,) at
this time to renew my expressions of invariable attachment
not only to your Royal Highness, but to my King: for I
think very soon every individual will be called forth to show
himself, if I may judge from this County, where Societies are

---

[4] His youngest brother, who afterwards entered into Holy orders.

[5] Mary Nelson, his father's eldest sister, whom he frequently mentions
with great affection in his subsequent Letters.   She died unmarried in
March 1800, in her eighty-third year.

[6] Some animadversion having been made on the Duke of Clarence's Parliamentary conduct, Nelson appears to have written to his Royal Highness on the
subject, on the 12th of September 1792 ; and after acknowledging the receipt of
that Letter, the Prince said,

" I am so fully persuaded of your real regard for me, my good friend, that no
fresh mark can be wanting to convince me : still, however, at the present moment, when the public have two opinions, the one good, the other disadvantage-
ous of my Parliamentary conduct, I feel highly obliged to you, as a person qualified to judge, to deliver your sentiments.   I am by no means a friend to the
present Minister ; but my conduct can never militate against the good of my
Country, and I think it is the duty of every citizen to prevent, if possible, that
confusion which might throw our Kingdom into the wretched, deplorable state of
France.   Assure our common friends in the West Indies, that I will neither neglect nor desert them.   My best wishes and compliments attend Mrs. Nelson,
and ever believe me yours sincerely—WILLIAM." _Original_, in the Nelson
Papers.

formed, and forming, on principles certainly inimical to our present Constitution both in Church and State, of which our Dissenters are the head, and in this County they have great riches. Sorry am I to believe that others give a countenance to these Societies, who ought to conduct themselves otherwise.

In what way it might be in the power of such an humble individual as myself to best serve my King, has been matter of serious consideration, and no way appeared to me so proper as asking for a Ship; and on Saturday last Lord Chatham received my letter, asking for the command of one; but as I have hitherto been disappointed in all my applications to his Lordship, I can hardly expect any answer to my letter, which has always been the way I have been treated: but neither at sea, nor on shore, through the caprice of a Minister, can my attachment to my King be shaken; and which will never end but with my life.

I have been staying some time with my relation, Lord Walpole, near Norwich; at which place, and near it, the Clubs are supported by Members of the Corporation; and they avow that till some of the Nobles and others in Parliament are served as they were in France, they will not be able to get their rights.

I am, &c.
HORATIO NELSON.[7]

---

[7] In reply to a Letter which he had written to his friend Captain, afterwards Lord Collingwood, he received a long Letter, dated on the 14th of November, in which Collingwood said, "I am much obliged to you for your letter, which I received last month: it was particularly welcome to me, as it brought information of the good health of you and Mrs. Nelson. You must not be displeased that I was so long without writing to you. I was very anxiously engaged a great part of the time, and perhaps sometimes a little lazy: but my regard for you, my dear Nelson, my respect and veneration for your character, I hope and believe will never lessen. God knows when we may meet again; unless some chance should draw us again to the Sea-shore. I, however, hope to have long the happiness of hearing of your welfare."—*Original*, in the Nelson Papers.

TO H. R. H. THE DUKE OF CLARENCE.

[Autograph draught, in the Nelson Papers.]

Burnham, 10th December, 1792.

Sir,

I was honoured by your Royal Highness's letter last night ;[8] and it shall ever be my pride to deserve your Royal Highness's kindness. Respecting my present situation with Lord Hood, I can readily and truly answer. We have not for a long time had any communication with each other.[9] Our familiar correspondence ceased on a difference of opinion. In the Spanish armament, when almost the whole service were called forth, I asked Lord Hood to interest himself with Lord Chatham, that I might be appointed to a Ship.[1] His Lordship having declined doing it,[2] has prevented my troubling him again for his interest or influence. However, in consideration of our former intimacy, whenever I have gone to London, I have hitherto thought it right to leave my name at his Lordship's door. I certainly cannot look on Lord Hood as my friend ; but I have the satisfaction of knowing, that I never gave his Lordship just cause to be my enemy.

[8] His Royal Highness, in a Letter of the 6th of December, acknowledged the receipt of a Letter from Nelson, dated on the 3rd of that month ; and after expressing in strong terms his displeasure at Lord Chatham's treatment of Nelson, and his opinion of the state of Affairs, he generously added, " Should matters between the two Countries grow serious, you must be employed. Never be alarmed, I will always stand your friend : I wish you would write me word how you and Lord Hood stand at present."

[9] The cause of this coolness does not appear ; but it was of very short duration ; and Lord Hood's friendship for, and admiration of Nelson, was shown on every occasion during the remainder of his life. It was scarcely possible for two such Officers to have been long alienated from each other.

[1] After these words, Nelson originally wrote, " and made a speech never to be effaced from my memory, viz. that the King was impressed with an unfavourable opinion of me," but he struck out this remarkable passage, thinking, perhaps, that it was improper in a Letter to his Majesty's Son.

[2] Clarke and M'Arthur state, (vol. i. p. 121,) " That Nelson again applied to the Board for employment, on the 5th of December, and after earnestly requesting the command of a Ship, he added, ' Or, if your Lordships should be pleased to appoint me to a *cockle-boat*, I shall feel grateful ;' but that Letter has not been found either at the Admiralty, or among the Nelson Papers. There is, however, the following Letter from the Secretary to the Admiralty to Nelson, " Admiralty Office, 12th December 1792. Sir, I have received your Letter of the 5th instant, expressing your readiness to serve, and I have read the same to my Lords Commissioners of the Admiralty.' "

Our Lord Lieutenant has summoned a meeting of the Norfolk Justices on Tuesday next, the 11th; and I have no doubt but they will resolve to do collectively, what none of them chose to do individually—to take away the licenses from those public-houses who allow of improper Societies meeting at them, and to take up those incendiaries who go from ale-house to ale-house, advising the poor people to pay no taxes, &c. In this neighbourhood, a person of the name of Priestley, a clergyman, has held this language to a circle of ten miles round him; and, a few days past, I asked a Justice of the Peace, ' Why, as such a man's conduct was known, that he was not taken up?' His answer was, ' that no Justice would render himself unpopular at this time, by being singular; for that his life and property were gone, if the mob arose: but that when the Justices all agreed to act in an uniform manner, this man should certainly be taken hold of, if he went on with such conduct.'

That the poor labourer should have been seduced by promises and hopes of better times, your Royal Highness will not wonder at, when I assure you, that they are really in want of everything to make life comfortable.[3] Part of their wants, perhaps, were unavoidable, from the dearness of every article of life; but much has arose from the neglect of the Country Gentlemen, in not making their farmers raise their wages, in some small proportion, as the prices of necessaries increased. The enclosed paper will give your Royal Highness an idea of their situation. It is most favourable; but I have been careful that no Country Gentleman should have it in his power to say, I had pointed out the wants of the poor greater than they really are. Their wages have been raised within these three weeks, pretty generally, one shilling a week : had it been done some time past, they would not have been discontented, for a want of loyalty is not amongst their faults; and many of their superiors, in many instances, might have imitated their conduct with advantage. The wise precautions of Government have certainly given a vigour to the loyal of the Nation, who are most undoubtedly by far the majority;

---

[3] Nelson originally wrote, " Hunger is a sharp thorn, and they are not only in want of food sufficient, but of clothes and firing."

and the disaffected join them at present, for fear of being suspected ; therefore I have no doubt but our tranquillity will
be restored.

I am, &c.

HORATIO NELSON.

AN ACCOUNT OF THE EARNINGS AND EXPENSES OF A LA-
BOURER IN NORFOLK, WITH A WIFE AND THREE CHIL-
DREN, SUPPOSING THAT HE IS NOT TO BE ONE DAY KEPT
FROM LABOUR IN THE WHOLE YEAR.

[Enclosed in the preceding Letter to the Duke of Clarence.]

	£.	s.	d.
One pair of Man's shoes, 7s., one pair of Women's, 4s. 6d., one pair for each of the three Children, 10s. 6d., and £1 1s. for mending.			
Shoes and Mending	2	3	0
Shirts, two	0	10	0
Breeches or Jacket	0	3	0
Woman's and Children's clothes	1	6	0
Soap, 12 lbs.	0	8	10
Candles, 6 lbs.	0	4	0
Coals, one chaldron and a half	1	19	0
House Rent	2	0	0
	8	13	10

The advanced prices.

	£.	s.	d.
From Oct. 10th to March 31st, at 9s. per week	11	14	0
From March 31st to June 30th, at 8s. per week	5	4	0
From June 30th to Aug. 24th, turnip-hoeing and hay-harvest	3	0	0
Harvest	2	2	0
Woman's gleaning	1	1	0
Total earnings	23	1	0

				£.	s.	d.
Earnings	·	·	·	. 23	1	0
Clothes, &c.	·	·	·	. 8	13	10

For food, five people, 14　7　2

Not quite twopence a day for each person; and to drink nothing but water, for beer our poor labourers never taste, unless they are tempted, which is too often the case, to go to the Alehouse.

TO MRS. NELSON.

[From Clarke and M'Arthur, vol. i. p. 123.]

London, 7th January, 1793.

Post nubila Phœbus:—After clouds comes sunshine. The Admiralty so smile upon me, that really I am as much surprised as when they frowned. Lord Chatham yesterday made many apologies for not having given me a Ship before this time, and said, that if I chose to take a Sixty-four to begin with, I should be appointed to one as soon as she was ready; and whenever it was in his power, I should be removed into a Seventy-four. Everything indicates War.[5] One of our Ships, looking into Brest, has been fired into:[6] the shot is now at the Admiralty. You will send my Father this news, which I am sure will please him. Love to Josiah, and believe me

Your most affectionate,

HORATIO NELSON.

[5] War with France was declared on the 11th of February 1793.

[6] The Childers sloop, commanded by Captain, afterwards Admiral Sir Robert Barlow, G.C.B., was fired upon by the batteries at Brest, and one shot struck her.

TO COMMODORE LOCKER, SHEERNESS.

[Autograph, in the Locker Papers. Nelson was appointed to the command of the Agamemnon 64, on the 30th of January 1793. Captain Locker's Broad Pendant was then flying on board the Sandwich, as Commander-in-Chief at the Nore.]

Burnham, January 26th, 1793.

My dear Sir,

Lord Hood tells me that I am now fixed for the Agamemnon at Chatham, and that whatever men are raised for her, will be taken care of on board the Sandwich. I have sent out a Lieutenant and four Midshipmen to get men at every Sea-port in Norfolk, and to forward them to Lynn and Yarmouth: my friends in Yorkshire and the North tell me they will send what men they can lay hands on to the Regulating Captains at Whitby and Newcastle. The name of the Ship was fixed for the avowed purpose of my raising men for her, therefore I hope if any men from London are inclined to enter for her, you will not turn your back on them, as although my bills are dispersed over this County, &c. I have desired that no bills may be stuck up in London, till my Commission is signed. Lord Hood has been very civil indeed. I think we may be good friends again. From what Lord Howe writes me, I think the Ship will be commissioned within a fortnight, and I shall join her directly. Mrs. Nelson joins in kindest respect with

Your obliged and affectionate,

HORATIO NELSON.

TO COMMODORE LOCKER.

[From Charnock's " Biographical Memoirs of Nelson," Appendix, p. 43. The original Letter is not now in the Locker Papers.]

Navy Office, February 6th, 1793.

My dear Sir,

I shall join my Ship to-morrow, and if possible will get to Sheerness to pay my respects to you, but fear it must be Friday. The Lieutenant and Master join the Ship with me; and I have to request, as I hear an Admiral is coming down, that you will have the goodness to discharge Maurice Suck-

10

ling,[7] and such men as may be on board the Sandwich, into the Agamemnon. Pray have you got a Clerk which you can recommend? I want one very much: I urge nothing; I know your willingness to serve.

The Duke of Clarence desires me to say that he requests you will discharge Joseph King[8] into the Agamemnon, or that I am welcome to any other man, to assist me in fitting out: he is but poorly, but expresses the greatest satisfaction at the Appointment you are likely to succeed to,[9] and in which no one rejoices more than your affectionate,

HORATIO NELSON.

TO THE REV. MR. NELSON, HILBOROUGH, BRANDON.

[Autograph, in the Nelson Papers.]

Chatham, February 10th, 1793.

My dear Brother,

I have just received your letter. I shall be in town to-morrow, and speak about Mr. Mason; but I apprehend he must pass his examination at Surgeons' Hall, for which I will procure an order, and let you know. Surgeons' Mates are very scarce (keep that to yourself.) I have the pleasure of telling you that my Ship is, without exception, the finest 64 in the service, and has the character of sailing most remarkably well. I have only got a few men, and very hard indeed they are to be got, and without a press I have no idea our Fleet can be manned. The Lieutenants are Martin Hin-

---

[7] Son of his cousin W. Suckling, Esq., of Wooton, near Norwich: he is often mentioned. Vide p. 108.

[8] The Duke of Clarence, in reply to Nelson's Letter respecting this man, wrote, " My motive for discharging Joseph King, was in order to promote him; but if you think it will be in your power to be serviceable to him, keep him by all means; and ever believe me yours sincerely, WILLIAM."—*Original*, in the Nelson Papers. Joseph King has been already mentioned, vide p. 257.

[9] Lieutenant-Governor of Greenwich Hospital, which situation Captain Locker obtained on the 15th of February following, in the room of Captain James Ferguson, deceased, who is mentioned in Nelson's Letters, p. 7, ante.

ton,[1] first; Joseph Bullen,[2] second; third, vacant; W. Allison, fourth; Thomas Edmunds, fifth; John Wilson, Master; Custar, Surgeon; Fellowes, Purser; all good in their respective stations, and known to me, except the Surgeon.[3] I am obliged by Mr. Randall's good wishes. Pray remember me to them all. To all appearance, it will be the end of March before we leave the Medway. Love to Mrs. Nelson, and my Aunt, and believe me,

Your most affectionate Brother,
HORATIO NELSON.

Shall enquire about the Chaplain on Tuesday, but hear they are pretty full.

TO THE REV. MR. NELSON, HILBOROUGH.

[Autograph, in the Nelson Papers.]

February 14th, 1793.

My dear Brother,

We have nothing new here. I shall go down to my Ship to-morrow morning, but I hope to be able to get two days at Hilborough, whilst Mrs. Nelson is with you. Mr. Mason must pass an examination at Surgeons' Hall before he can be appointed, a thing by no means difficult. He must be in London before the 7th of March, as that is the examining day. I would advise him to be at the Navy Office the 5th, to get his order from the Board, without which they will not examine him. Tell Mr. Randall that his old shipmate,

[1] Promoted to the rank of Commander in 1795, for his services in the Agamemnon.

[2] This respected Officer is now an Admiral of the Blue.

[3] The Officers who served with Captain Nelson in the Agamemnon, according to *Clarke and M'Arthur*, from the 1st of January 1793 to the 10th of June 1796, were, Lieutenants, Martin Hinton, Wenman Allison, Thomas Edmunds, Joseph Bullen, George Andrews, William Lucas, Maurice W. Suckling, Edward Chetham, Peter Spicer, James Summers, James Noble, Henry Compton, James M'Arthur, and Edward Berry; Surgeons, John Roxburgh, Cornwall Reynolds, and Thomas Weatherstone; Master, John Wilson; Purser, Thomas Fellowes.

Captain Locker, is to be appointed Lieutenant-Governor of Greenwich Hospital. Love to all with you, and believe me,

Yours most affectionately,

HORATIO NELSON.

TO WILLIAM LOCKER, ESQ., KENSINGTON.

[Autograph, in the Locker Papers.]

Chatham, February 21st, 1793.

My dear Sir,

Most truly do I rejoice at your appointment, and hope you will derive every comfort from it. I am very much disposed to like Mr. Fellowes, [4] and have told him so, and that every protection of mine he shall certainly have, against a waste of his stores, &c.; but that he must be very careful that no just cause of complaint can be made against him, for I will not suffer any poor fellow to be lessened of his due. He seems perfectly to understand me, and I dare say we shall do very well together. Don't be in a hurry about the Charts. I shall see you before we sail. Remember me to your sons, and believe me,

Yours most affectionately,

HORATIO NELSON.

TO MRS. NELSON, AT HILBOROUGH.

[From Clarke and M'Arthur, vol. i. p. 124.]

Chatham, 15th March, 1793.

If the wind is to the Northward of West, we go down the River to-morrow, and are ordered to proceed to Spithead with all possible dispatch, as we are wanted, Lord Hood[5] writes me word, for immediate service; and hints, we are to go a cruise, and then to join his Fleet at Gibraltar: therefore I am anxious to get to Spithead. I never was in better health;

---

[4] Purser of the Agamemnon.

[5] Lord Hood, then Vice-Admiral of the Red, had shortly before been appointed Commander-in-Chief in the Mediterranean.

and I hope you intend a new lease of your life: the not tying up any of the money left you,[6] I consider as a confidence reposed in me, and I shall take care that it is not misplaced.

I am, &c.,

HORATIO NELSON.

———

TO MRS. NELSON, KENTISH TOWN.

[From Clarke and M'Arthur, vol. i. p. 124.]

Sheerness, April 14th, 1793.

Although I have not been out of the Ship since I wrote to you last, yet I know you wish to hear frequently from me. The wind is now got to the Westward, and we are unmooring to go out to the Nore, where I suppose our stay will be very short. I had a visit from the Admiral[7] yesterday, to examine my Ship; and I can say with truth, she is getting into high order, although we are upwards of a hundred short of complement; yet I think we shall be far from ill-manned, even if the rest are not so good as they ought to be. The Surgeon seems to be a very good sort of man : indeed I have reason to be satisfied at present with every Officer in the Ship.

I am, &c.,

HORATIO NELSON.

[6] By her Uncle, Mr. Herbert, President of Nevis, who died on the 18th January 1793.

[7] Apparently Vice-Admiral John Dalrymple, Commander-in-Chief, in the Sandwich, at the Nore.

TO GEORGE ROSE, ESQ., SECRETARY TO THE TREASURY.

[Autograph draught, in the Nelson Papers. The date of this Letter is not given, but the answer of the Lords of the Treasury, acquainting him that the Collector at Nevis could not legally be required by the Treasury to remit the proceeds in question, and recommending him to apply to the Collector himself, was dated on the 20th April, 1793. On the same paper, Nelson made a memorandum " to write to the Admiralty for an order to Captain Patrick Lynn, to receive my volunteers, and to pay their conduct money from the places they respectively enter with me."]

[April, 1793.]

Sir,

On an application made by me in the year 1789, (and on which Mr. Stanley, Attorney-General of the Leeward Islands, gave in a Report approving of the propriety of my application,) that the net proceeds of four American vessels seized by his Majesty's Ship Boreas, under my command, should be transmitted to the Receiver-General of his Majesty's Customs, and their Lordships having been pleased to give an order to that effect, I yesterday, (as two of the said Vessels, viz. the Hercules and Nancy Pleasant, were finally condemned by the Lords of Appeal, affirming the sentence of the Vice-Admiralty Court of Nevis,) made application for the moiety of the net proceeds of the said Vessels, when I was acquainted that the monies had not been transmitted to the Receiver-General of the Customs, but that since the affirming the sentence of condemnation, the Board of Customs had ordered the Collector and Comptroller of the Customs of Nevis to remit the King's share of those seizures, Hercules and Nancy Pleasant.

Now, I have to request that you will be pleased to move their Lordships that they will order the whole amount of the seizures, Hercules and Nancy Pleasant, to be remitted to England, that the Officers and Ship's company of his Majesty's Ship Boreas may be paid the prize-money due to them, and which they can hardly ever hope to obtain should my request not be complied with.

I have the honour to be, &c.,

HORATIO NELSON.

TO THE REVEREND MR. NELSON, HILBOROUGH.

[Autograph, in the Nelson Papers.]

Agamemnon, Nore, April 18th, 1793.

My dear Brother,

As I know you wish to hear how we go on, I write you, although as to news, can tell you none ; for we have not had a boat on shore this week past. Before this gets to you I dare say we shall be gone from hence, although my orders are not yet on board. I not only like the Ship, but think I am well appointed in Officers, and we are manned exceedingly well; therefore have no doubt but we shall acquit ourselves well, should the French give us a meeting. You will see by the Downs' List when we get there, and shall be glad to hear from you at Portsmouth, at which place we shall be by the time you see us in the Downs List. I understand from second-hand that we are to carry out the West India Convoy. To me it is perfectly indifferent to what quarter of the world we go: with a good Ship, and Ship's company we can come to no harm. We appear to sail very fast: we went, coming out, nearly as fast, without any sail, as the Robust did under her topsails. Josiah[8] is with me ; yesterday, it blowing a smart gale, he was a little sea-sick. Remember me kindly to Mrs. Nelson, and our Aunt, and believe me,

Your most affectionate Brother,

HORATIO NELSON.

TO MRS. NELSON.

[From Clarke and M'Arthur, vol. i. p. 124.]

Spithead, April 29th, 1793.

We arrived at Spithead last night, and this morning have got my orders to go to Sea until the 4th of May, when I shall be at Portsmouth. Lord Hood will then be there, and it is now certain that I am going with him. We are all well:

---

[8] Josiah Nisbet, his step-son, afterwards a Post Captain, who then entered the Navy.

indeed, nobody can be ill with my Ship's company, they are so fine a set. Don't mind what newspapers say about us. God bless you.

HORATIO NELSON.

Spithead, April 30th, 1793.

We should have gone to Sea yesterday,[9] but it blew so strong we could not get up our anchors; and to-day, unless the wind changes in the afternoon, we shall not get out to Sea, which is a great mortification to me; for something might be done, if we were at Sea, and I fear orders may come to stop us. I must be here on Sunday at the farthest, as Lord Hood sails, if the wind is fair, on Thursday, May 9th.

I am, &c.,

HORATIO NELSON.

TO MRS. NELSON.

[From Clarke and M'Arthur, vol. i. p. 124.]

Spithead, May 6th 1793.

I arrived here last night, and rather expected to have seen you here; but Mr. Matcham [1] told you right, there is no certainty in winds and waves. We had some blowing weather, but nothing for Agamemnon to mind. We fell in with two French[2] frigates, and two armed Vessels, who got into La Hogue harbour, where we could not follow for want of a pilot. I was again ordered to Sea this morning, but am now stopped, as my Ship wants many things before she sails for the Mediterranean. Lord Hood is expected to-night. Maurice[3]

---

[9] The late Captain Sir William Hoste, Bart., K.C.B., one of the most distinguished Officers in the British Navy, commenced his career in the Agamemnon at this time; and his Letters to his family while in that Ship, published in his "Memoirs," (8vo. 1833,) afford much interesting information respecting her proceedings.

[1] His brother-in-law, George Matcham, Esq.

[2] Mr. Hoste says the Agamemnon left Spithead on the 1st of May; and he calls those Ships "*Dutch.*"—*Memoirs*, vol. i. p. 9.

[3] His eldest brother Maurice Nelson.

came to me, and it blew so hard I could not land him: he consequently went to Sea with us.

> Believe me, most affectionately yours,
>
> HORATIO NELSON.

TO MRS. NELSON.

[From Clarke and M'Arthur, vol. i. p. 125.]

Agamemnon, twelve leagues N. W. of the Island of Guernsey,
18th May, 1793.

This is not the first Squadron sent out to do nothing, and worse than nothing. I suppose we are to stay here until Lord Hood arrives, which I think will not be this week to come. We have spoke many Neutral vessels from the French Ports, who tell us, that Nantes, Bourdeaux, and l'Orient, are filled with English prizes to the French privateers and Frigates. This information makes us feel more uneasy.

May 19th, off the Lizard.

We are going to-morrow to Falmouth, for further orders. I think we shall see Torbay before we leave England.

> I am, &c.,
>
> HORATIO NELSON.

TO THE REV. MR. NELSON, HILBOROUGH.

[Autograph, in the Nelson Papers.]

Agamemnon, S. B. E., ten leagues off the Lizard.
[About the 20th or 25th May, 1793.]

My dear Brother,

Although you will say, when you have read the letter, that I had nothing to communicate, yet I know you like to hear that nothing, though the postage will be so very great that I had thoughts of not writing. What we have been sent out for is best known to the Great Folks in London: to us, it appears, only to hum the Nation and make tools of us, for where we have been stationed, from ten to twenty leagues to the Westward of Guernsey, no Enemy was likely to be met with, or where we could protect our own trade. Thus five Ships have been sported with. I don't like it, nor does our Admiral.[4]

We are to be off Falmouth to-morrow, and expect fresh orders, or to be joined by Lord Hood. I think Torbay will finish this cruise. The French have eight Sail of the Line in different parts of the Bay, and six Frigates: three of each are always at Sea, and England not able or willing to send a Squadron to interrupt them. My Ship sails well; very few will outsail her, and she is very tolerably manned. Josiah is with me, and desires to be remembered. Give my best remembrances to Mrs. Nelson, and our Aunt. Believe me,

Your most affectionate Brother,

HORATIO NELSON.

————————

TO MRS. NELSON.

[From Clarke and M‘Arthur, vol. i. p. 125, where it is erroneously assigned to the 6th of July.]

5th June, S. W. sixteen leagues from Scilly.

I expected, when Lord Hood joined, that we should have gone to Gibraltar; but what his instructions or orders are, I cannot guess. I have not seen him since he joined us, a fortnight to morrow; nor had even a boat hoisted out. Our weather, although not bad, has been very unpleasant—foggy with drizzling rain. Agamemnon sails admirably; we think better than any Ship in the Fleet. Our force is eleven Sail of the Line, Frigates, &c. &c., and in very tolerable order. We have had some Naval evolutions when the weather would permit. I shall pay our Admiral a visit as soon as an opportunity offers, and leave this letter with Captain Knight.[5] God bless you.

I am, &c.,

HORATIO NELSON.

————————

[4] Vice-Admiral of the White, William Hotham, who was created a Peer of Ireland in March 1797, and died in 1813.

[5] Captain John Knight, Flag-Captain to Lord Hood, in the Victory. He commanded the Montague of 74 guns in the Battle of Camperdown, for which he received a Medal, and died Admiral Sir John Knight, K.C.B., in June 1831.

TO MRS. NELSON.

[From Clarke and M'Arthur, vol. i. p. 125.]

Off Cape St. Vincent, 14th June, 1793.

I sent you a few lines by a vessel in a Convoy we spoke this
day week off Scilly, and which turned out to be the Fleet we
were waiting to protect; and the East Indiamen passing us
the same evening, relieved us from a very unpleasant station.
We have had the finest passage and weather possible, but
have seen nothing except a poor miserable National brig,[6]
which one of the Ships took. I paid Lord Hood a visit a few
days back, and found him very civil : I dare say we shall be
good friends again. Six Sail of the Line have just parted
company, going to Cadiz to water, of which number is Agamemnon. We shall be in Cadiz to-morrow at twelve o'clock,
as well as Lord Hood at Gibraltar. We are all well; my Ship
remarkably healthy.

I am, &c.,

HORATIO NELSON.

TO THE REV. MR. NELSON, HILBOROUGH.

[Autograph, in the Nelson Papers.]

Agamemnon, ten leagues off Cadiz, June 15th, 1793.

My dear Brother,

After cruising off Scilly with Lord Hood for a fortnight,
in very unpleasant weather, the arrival of the Mediterranean
Convoy relieved us from a station where we could hardly expect to see an Enemy, and the last India Convoy passing us
in the evening, made Lord Hood quite satisfied. We are nine
days from Scilly; a very good passage for a Fleet : and
during our run have taken nothing but a miserable National
brig of eight guns. If we go on so, we shall soon make fortunes.

Last night six Sail of us parted from Lord Hood to
water at Cadiz, in order that no time may be lost in watering

---

[6] Le Vanneau of 6 guns, taken in the Bay of Biscay, by the Colossus 74,
Captain Charles Morice Pole.

so large a Fleet at Gibraltar.　This morning at day [light] we
fell in with a Spanish eighty-gun Ship, ninety mounted : there
being very little wind, and we the only Ship near her, and
fancying her to be French, we fully expected a trimming;
for we must have been in action near an hour before any
Ship could have come to our assistance.　However, as we sail
well, that is to come.　My Ship is remarkably healthy; myself and Josiah never better.　Letters directed for me at
Gibraltar will come safe : whether the Foreign postage must
be paid I don't know.　It will give me pleasure to hear from
you, and whenever I have an opportunity and anything to
communicate, you may be assured of hearing from me.　Give
my kind love to Mrs. Nelson and my Aunt, and believe me,

Your affectionate Brother,

HORATIO NELSON.

June 17.—The Cadiz Vessels just going to leave us.　The
Dons have twenty-three Sail of the Line ready to join us.
Time must discover what we are going after.

TO MRS. NELSON.

[From Clarke and M'Arthur, vol. i. p. 126.]

Agamemnon, at Sea, Sunday, 23rd June.

We came out[7] this morning, having completed our Ship
with everything except wine, which is to be done at Gibraltar.
The Spaniards have been very civil to us.　We dined on
board the Concepcion of one hundred and twelve guns, with
the Admiral ; and all restraints of going into their Arsenals and
Dock-yards were removed.　They have four First-rates in commission at Cadiz, and very fine Ships, but shockingly manned.
If those twenty-one Sail of the Line, which we are to join in
the Mediterranean, are not better manned, they cannot be of
much use.　I am certain if our six Barges' crews, who are
picked men, had got on board one of their First rates, they
would have taken her.　The Dons may make fine Ships,—they
cannot, however, make men.

[7] From Cadiz.

A bull-feast was exhibited, for which the Spaniards are famous; and from their dexterity in attacking and killing of these animals, the ladies choose their husbands. We English had certainly to regret the want of humanity in the Dons and Donnas. The amphitheatre will hold 16,000 people: about 12,000 were present. Ten bulls were selected, and one brought out at a time. Three cavaliers on horseback, and footmen with flags, were the combatants. We had what is called a fine feast, for five horses were killed, and two men very much hurt: had they been killed, it would have been quite complete. We felt for the bulls and horses; and I own it would not have displeased me to have had some of the Dons tossed by the enraged animal. How women can even sit out, much more applaud, such sights, is astonishing. It even turned us sick, and we could hardly go through it: the dead mangled horses with the entrails torn out, and the bulls covered with blood, were too much. However, we have seen one bull-feast, and agree that nothing shall tempt us to see another. The better sort of people never miss one, if within reach of them; and the lowest will sell his jacket, or go without his victuals, rather than be absent.

Gibraltar, June 24.

P.S.—We arrived here last night, and in a few days' sail shall be up the Mediterranean. God bless and preserve you.

HORATIO NELSON.

TO WILLIAM LOCKER, ESQ., KENSINGTON.

[From Charnock's "Biographical Memoirs of Nelson," Appendix, p. 45. The original is not now in the Locker Papers.]

Gibraltar, June 24th, 1793.

My dear Friend,

We arrived here last night from Cadiz, where six Sail of the Line have been to water. I have got for you a cask of, I hope, good sherry, which I shall take an early opportunity of sending home, and which I beg you to accept as a proof of my remembrance. We have done nothing, and the same prospect appears before us: the French cannot come out, and we have no means of getting at them in Toulon. We are to be joined off Barcelona by twenty-one Sail of the Line, Spanish: if they are no better manned than those at Cadiz, much service cannot be expected of them, although, as to Ships, I never saw finer Men-of-War. The Lord[8] is in a hurry to get from here: we think he is to hoist the Union. If anything interesting should happen, you may be assured I will let you know it, for believe me, with great truth,

Your most obliged and affectionate
HORATIO NELSON.

Remember me kindly to all your family, Kingsmill, &c.

TO H. R. H. THE DUKE OF CLARENCE.

[Autograph, in the Nelson Papers. It would seem from a Letter from Nelson to his Royal Highness, dated from the 14th of July to the 8th of August, (in Clarke and M'Arthur, p. 127,) that *this* Letter was not forwarded. The material variations between the two Letters are given in the Notes.]

Agamemnon, off Cape St. Sebastian,
14th July 1793, to 4th of August.

Sir,

The Fleet sailed from Gibraltar on the 27th June, (as I wrote your Royal Highness by Boyle,[9] was Lord Hood's intention,) and a Convoy of fifty Sail of Merchant Ships, with a brisk wind at West, and soon got off Cape de Gatte, since which time we have had either Levanters or calms. Off the Cape, L'Aigle was sent to Barcelona with letters for the Spanish Admiral, and the Iris to Tripoli, and the Convoy left with St. Albans, Castor, Bulldog, and some other Frigates. We have spoke very many Neutral vessels, but no information which, in my opinion, could be depended on; some saying, that Monsieur Egalité was beheaded, and the other Jacobins who were in confinement at Marseilles—that the French had taken three Spanish frigates, and had nearly thirty Sail of the Line ready for Sea at Toulon[10]—but as this last information

[8] Lord Hood never hoisted the Union Flag.

[9] The Honourable Captain Courtenay Boyle, (vide p. 247,) then a Lieutenant who was sent home from Gibraltar, with Despatches, in command of the Fox cutter.

[10] Vide p. 321.

we knew to be false, much credit has not, I suppose, been given to the other. Indeed, we now know that not a Spanish frigate has been taken.

We saw a Fleet off Alicant on the close of the 7th, and lay-to mid-channel between that place and Iviça. At daylight we formed our line, and soon perceived them to be the Spanish Fleet, twenty-four Sail of the Line. The Dons did not, after several hours' trial, form anything which could be called a Line of Battle ahead. However, after answering our private signals, the Spanish Admiral sent down two Frigates, with answers to Lord Hood's letters by l'Aigle, acquainting him, that as his Fleet was sickly 1900 men, he was going to Carthagena. The Captain of the Frigate said, "It was no wonder they were sickly, *for they had been sixty days at Sea.*" This speech to us appeared ridiculous; for from the circumstance of having been longer than that time at Sea, do we attribute our getting healthy. It has stamped with me the extent of their nautical abilities: long may they remain in their present state. It appeared odd to me that no salutes whatever took place. Leda[9] was sent on the 9th to Barcelona; and yesterday, the 13th, the Frigates joined the Fleet. Inglefield[1] brings nothing new respecting the Toulon Fleet, except that the French are preparing their Ships with forges for shot. This information I humbly think, (if true,) would have been as well kept secret; but as it is known, we must take care to get so close that their red shots can do no mischief. The Fleet received orders yesterday,[2] to consider Marseilles and Toulon as invested, and to take all Vessels of whatever Nation, bound into those Ports. This has pleased us; and may possibly induce these red-hot gentlemen to come out.[3]

Our Fleet is healthy: we sail in three Divisions, led by Victory, Colossus, and Agamemnon. We do not keep in so

---

[9] The Leda, 36 guns, commanded by Captain, afterwards Admiral Sir George Campbell, G.C.B.: he died in January 1821.

[1] Captain John Nicholson Inglefield, of l'Aigle, 36 guns, who was Acting First Captain of Lord Hood's Fleet, in 1794, was made Commissioner of the Navy at Corsica, and afterwards at Gibraltar.

[2] July 14.

[3] "If we make these red-hot gentlemen hungry, they may be induced to come out."—*Copy* in Clarke and M'Arthur, vol. i. p. 128.

compact an order as we ought, and the Lord does not spare signals.[4]

18th.—On the 16th, in the afternoon, we made Cape Sicie, two leagues from Toulon, and saw three Sail to leeward; the Leda and Illustrious were sent in chase. Between nine and ten at night, a firing of half-an-hour was heard from them; when, I believe, every person in the Fleet expected to have seen some of the Enemy's Ships brought in. It was the 17th at noon, before they joined us, with a Corvette[5] which Leda took that morning. The Ships they fired at the night before were three French frigates, who, after giving and receiving fire, got away from them. The account we have hitherto heard, has only been from a disappointed Flag-ship. I pretend not to give an opinion: the following circumstances are allowed to be facts; viz. that our Ships outsailed them, by getting alongside near enough to have men killed in each Ship (the Master of the Illustrious[6] one of them). It was a bright moon till twelve o'clock, and very little wind all night.[7]

We have not yet looked into Toulon, but are now, six P. M. 18th, only four leagues off. The Lord told us some days ago, that a Frigate was going to Genoa and Leghorn, by which conveyance I intended to have sent your Royal Highness this account of our proceedings. I conceive that every movement of this Fleet you will like to know. As I have before observed, those in the Fleet who are more able to write than myself, may possibly tell you these circumstances, and in a manner more concise for your Royal Highness' perusal. Mine is little else but a Journal, which I shall be glad if you approve of receiving.

On the 19th, the Fleet stood close into Toulon, and sent in a Flag of Truce,[9] which has given us information that the French have sixteen Sail of the Line in the outer road of Toulon, and five Sail fitting in the harbour. I think they will

---

[4] This passage is omitted.—*Ibid.*

[5] L'Eclair of 22 guns.

[6] The Illustrious 74, Captain Thomas Lennox Frederick, afterwards an Admiral.

[7] This Affair does not appear to be noticed by any of our Naval Historians.

[8] "It is an universal concern that they were not brought in, not that either party is absolutely blamed."—*Clarke & M'Arthur*, p. 128.

[9] "To propose an exchange of prisoners."—*Ibid.* The next paragraph, "which has given us information," &c., does not occur.—*Ibid.*

soon be so tired, and angry at being blocked up, that they will come out. We have experienced for three days[1] lately a very heavy gale of wind. We are much alarmed for the Berwick, who, by her signals, was in great distress, and bore away before the wind : a Frigate, (Tyler,[2]) was sent after her, but could not get to her.[3] Leda lost her mainmast and otherwise damaged, and got to Leghorn.

[[4] On the 25th of July the Flag of Truce joined from Toulon; the Enemy did not give us a clear answer whether they would exchange prisoners with us. They have seventeen Sail of the Line ready for sea and four fitting, the Commerce de Marseilles one of them : she carries 136 guns, having guns on her gangways : the prisoners believe her sides are so thick that our shot will not go through them; and that she can with ease take the Victory. We form various conjectures whether they will come out or not; in my opinion they will : when they have twenty-one Sail ready and we under twenty, the people will force them out.]

To this, 3rd of August, we have not heard of the Berwick. A Convoy was expected from Tunis of twenty-five Sail, with two Sail of the Line, three Frigates, and two Corvettes ; but I make no doubt they have information of our being on the Coast, and will unload their Merchant-ships, and secure the Men-of-War, as they have done at Genoa and Leghorn.

[August 5th.—From the 26th we have been lying off Toulon. Yesterday an express came from Captain Ingle-field, that he had been insulted by two French Frigates in Genoa Mole, who hauled alongside of him, entangled their yards, and in every way insulted him. The Alcide and two Frigates immediately sailed to liberate him.]

[August 8th.—We are steering to the Eastward, going to show ourselves off Nice, fifteen Sail of the Line : Fleet healthy.]

We[5] are in daily expectation of seeing his Royal Highness

---

[1] "Until the 23rd."—*Ibid.*

[2] The Meleager.

[3] " But unfortunately missed her in a heavy squall. Leda sprung her main and fore-masts, carried away her main-yard, and went for Leghorn, attended by the Romney."

[4] The paragraphs within brackets are inserted from Clarke and M'Arthur.

[5] This and the next paragraph are omitted in Clarke and M'Arthur.

Prince Augustus[6] in the Fleet, and shall then hope for an opportunity of sending this account.

August 4th.—Admiral Cosby[7] has just sent me word that his Royal Highness will not be many hours in the Fleet, and that he is to go to England in the Aquilon:[8] therefore I send this letter on board him, as I may be detached from the Fleet on the look out.　Believe me,

Your Royal Highness's

Most attached and faithful Servant,

HORATIO NELSON.

TO MRS. NELSON.

[From Clarke and M'Arthur, vol. i. p. 129.]

Gulf of Lyons, July 15th, 1793.

There seem to be no French Ships at sea, at least we have seen nothing like one.　We fell in with the Spanish Fleet a week ago, returning into Port, I believe glad we are arrived; and they mean to leave us the honour of keeping the French in order.　I really expect never to see them again.　Lord Hood is tolerably good friends with me.

18th.—We have just got a French Sloop-of-War of 18 guns, bound from Marseilles to Toulon.[9]　Remember me most kindly to our good father.

I am, &c.,

HORATIO NELSON.

[6] Created Duke of Sussex, in 1801.

[7] Vice-Admiral of the Blue, Phipps Cosby, in the Windsor Castle; and third in command of the Fleet: he died an Admiral of the Red in January 1808.

[8] Captain now Admiral, the Honourable Sir Robert Stopford, G.C.B., G.C.M.G., Rear-Admiral of England, and Governor of Greenwich Hospital.

[9] This capture is not noticed in the Printed List of Vessels taken during the War, nor in the London Gazette.

TO MRS. NELSON.

[From Clarke and M'Arthur, vol. i. p. 129.]

August 4th, off Toulon.

The Admiral has just sent us word, that the Aquilon will proceed to England with Prince Augustus, I therefore send this letter on board, in case Agamemnon should be on the look out; for as we sail fast we are always employed. Whether the French intend to come out seems uncertain: they have a force equal to us. Our Jacks would be very happy to see it; and, as our Fleet is in the fullest health, I dare say we should give a good account of them. I hardly think the War can last; for what are we at War about? How I long to have a letter from you: next to being with you, it is the greatest pleasure I can receive. The being united to such a good woman, I look back to as to the happiest period of my life; and as I cannot here show my affection to you, I do it doubly to Josiah, who deserves it, as well on his own account as on yours, for he is a real good boy, and most affectionately loves me. Captains Lutwidge[1] and Mann[2] have been very ill. Lord Hood has sent to offer me a Seventy-four, but I have declined it; as the Admiralty chose to put me into a Sixty-four, there I stay. I cannot give up my Officers. Lord Hood approved of my reasons; so far well. If I have not an opportunity of writing to my good Father, send my kindest remembrances to him. God bless you, and believe me,

Your most affectionate husband,

HORATIO NELSON.

[1] Afterwards Admiral Lutwidge, who is so often mentioned: he then commanded the Terrible, of 74 guns.

[2] Captain Robert Mann, of the Bedford, who will be again noticed. He died an Admiral of the Red, in September 1813.

TO H. R. H. THE DUKE OF CLARENCE.

[Autograph draught, in the Nelson Papers.]

Agamemnon, off Toulon, August 5th, 1793.

Sir,

I had wrote your Royal Highness two letters of our proceedings since the Fleet left Gibraltar, but having lost the opportunity of sending them when our different Ships went for Leghorn, I shall now only inclose you a kind of Journal of our proceedings which (if not received from others in the Fleet) you may wish to know. I am sure your Royal Highness will believe that if any communication from me can be satisfactory, that I have the greatest pleasure in ever anticipating your wishes. Lord Hood has given us notice that his Royal Highness Prince Augustus is expected in the Fleet and I hear Aquilon is to carry him to England, by which Ship I intend to send this letter.

I remain,

Your Royal Highness's most attached,

HORATIO NELSON.

TO CHARLES LONG,[3] ESQ., JOINT SECRETARY TO THE TREASURY.

[Autograph draught, in the Nelson Papers.]

Agamemnon, off Toulon, August 7th, 1793.

Sir,

Your letter,[4] dated April 20th, of which I enclose a copy, I did not receive till my arrival at Gibraltar: therefore it has been totally out of my power to take any steps to receive the prize-money due to the Ship's company under my command, nor is it possible that every poor seaman can go to Nevis, to receive his money from the Collector of the Customs. They look up to their Captain as their friend and protector, and it was my intention, if the money was paid me, to adver-

[3] Afterwards Lord Farnborough, G.C.B.
[4] Vide p. 303, ante.

tise the distribution of it in London, when every Officer
and Seaman, or their relatives, would be on the spot.

I must beg leave to observe that the amount was lodged in
the King's chest, sealed up in bags, as a place of security, till
the cause was determined. I humbly hope their Lordships
will be pleased to order the money to England, or such other
measures as in their wisdom they shall judge proper.

I am, &c.

HORATIO NELSON.

TO MRS. NELSON.

[From Clarke and M'Arthur, vol. i. p. 130.]

Agamemnon, off Nice, August 8th, 1793.

The French here are in a wretched state of confusion: an
Army is marched from Marseilles to Paris, and a Civil War
seems inevitable. The Aquilon is joining the Fleet.

August 20th, off Toulon.

The Convoy for England is just in sight, therefore I shall
not miss the opportunity of writing to you and my Father.
Marseilles, I am sure, would almost be put into our hands, if
we acted against it. They wish for nothing more than our
possessing it, when they would get something to eat: they in
general are now almost starving; only six days' provisions in
the place. Monsieur Egalité is still in the prison with his
daughter. They wish for Peace; and are, you know, at War
with the Parisians, with whom they have lately had an Action.
The Convention has denounced the Marseillois as traitors. If
Toulon joins them, they propose offering themselves to our
protection. I wish much to hear you are fixed at some place
to your satisfaction. Have you made a visit to Lady Walpole?

I am, &c.

HORATIO NELSON.

TO CAPTAIN LOCKER.

[From Charnock's " Biographical Memoirs of Nelson," Appendix, p. 45. The original is not now in the Locker Papers.]

August 20th, 1793.

My dear Friend,

I shall send by Trowbridge, if I can find his Ship,[4] a cask of sherry, which I hope will prove good. The Fleet has hitherto done nothing but look into Toulon. Lord Hood went with the Fleet ten days past to speak to the Genoese about supplying the French with corn, and bringing back French property under Neutral papers, for our being here is a farce if this trade is allowed. By all accounts we learn the district of Provence would gladly become a separate Republic under the protection of England. The people of Marseilles have said they would destroy Toulon to accomplish this measure. In short, France will be dismembered, but in all their misery they have no thought of Kingly government. Lutwidge and Mann have been very ill indeed, we had fears for them ; Lord Hood is very kind. Agamemnon sails well and is healthy, but we want to get into Port for refreshments. Remember me to Kingsmill ;[5] I hope his Flag is flying : also to all our friends, and kindly to your family. Believe me,

Yours most affectionately,

HORATIO NELSON.

TO THE REVEREND EDMUND NELSON.

[From Clarke and M'Arthur, vol. i. p. 130.]

August 20th, off Toulon.

My dear Father,[6]

No occurrence of a public nature has taken place since our arrival here, and our private ones are confined to a very nar-

---

[4] Captain, afterwards Rear-Admiral Sir Thomas Trowbridge, Bart., then commanded the Castor of 32 guns.

[5] Captain Kingsmill had obtained his flag as Rear-Admiral of the White, in the promotion of April 1793.

[6] Clarke and M'Arthur have printed some admirable Letters from the venerable Father of Nelson to his Son, which place the character of both in the most

row sphere, which yet I am sure will be considered by you a valuable one—*We are all well.* The affairs of France in this Country are worse than ever : the guillotine is every day employed. A Master of a Ship, whom we spoke from Marseilles, says, there are now only two descriptions of people in France—the one drunk and mad ; the other, with horror painted in their faces, are absolutely starving ; yet nothing brings them to their senses. A Peace with England is what they wish for ; and Provence would, it is said, willingly put itself, as a separate Republic, under the protection of England. In the winter we are to reduce Ville Franche and Nice for the King of Sardinia, and drive the French from Corsica. It seems of no use to send a great Fleet here, without troops to act with them.

I consider you now as at high harvest, and hope you have good weather and good crops. I hear Lady Spencer[7] and the party are at Lucca, a few miles from Pisa. I think we shall be in England in the winter or spring. If the Burnhamites inquire for me, make my compliments. Believe me,

Your most dutiful Son,

HORATIO NELSON.

pleasing light. The Letter in the text seems to have been in answer to the following, dated Burnham, 12th July 1793. (*Clarke and M‘Arthur*, vol. i. p. 127.)

" Every mark of my affection you may justly expect ; and it gives me satisfaction to reflect on the many proofs I have had of your disposition to observe those duties which each relation in life calls for. The approbation of your own mind is far more pleasing than any supposed partiality of mine ; though a reward infinitely short of what moral virtue, which is an attendant on true Religion, shall one day receive.—The principal domestic occurrence at this juncture is that of your brother's ordination, [Suckling Nelson]. Thus far, thank God, our design is accomplished : all proceeds favourably, and there is good hope he may prove a worthy member of society. Farming goes on well ; and at Christmas I look forward for the auditing my accounts to your own person ; Agamemnon and her crew being either honourably discharged, or laid up for the winter in safety. O England ! blessed art thou among the Isles, for thy internal prosperity. In peace and plenty may thy Counsellors preserve thee. . . . . . . As to myself, the material machine keeps pretty nearly the same periodical movement ; the repairs must be by a very nice delicate touch, and my mind is so fortified as to meet all common events with calmness : ever steady to my position, that the good of every man's life preponderates over the evil. God bless you."

[7] Georgiana, wife of John first Earl Spencer, daughter of Stephen Poyntz, Esq., and sister of Dr. Poyntz, so often mentioned.

LIST OF THE FRENCH LINE-OF-BATTLE SHIPS IN TOULON.

[Autograph, in the Nelson Papers, and referred to in pp. 311, 314 ante. Though this List may not have been compiled by Nelson, yet as it has been found in his own hand-writing, and as it illustrates some of his Letters, it is inserted. A List, with which this very closely agrees, except in the order of the names of the Ships, entitled " List of the French Line of Battle Ships, in the Great Road of Toulon, according to the order in which they anchored, from East to West, August 26th, 1793, together with remarks on the characters of their Captains, Officers, and Men," forms No. IV. of the " Toulon Papers," printed in the Naval Chronicle, vol. ii. p. 106. In this List, the orthography of Names, (which is very uncertain in Nelson's manuscript,) has been taken from the one printed in the Naval Chronicle.]

SHIPS' NAMES.	GUNS.	MEN.	MONTHS' PROVISIONS.	COMMANDERS.	REMARKS.
Le Commerce de Marseilles	100	700	4	Rear Admiral Trogoffe	Commander - in - Chief, formerly Captain, 2nd Captain of the Glorieux in the 12th April, and Captain Pasquier, both men of sound principles. Officers and men Clubbists.
Sans Culotte	100	7[00]			
Le Tonnant	80	400	4	Amiel	Formerly Captain of a Fire-Ship; doubtful.
Le Duguay Trouin	74	300	6	Not known	Her fore-mast out.
Le Lys, called Trois Color	74	600	4	Parquier	Clubbist; formerly a Pilot.
Le Centaure	74	550	4	Cassue	Formerly a Boatswain, very ignorant.
Le Pompée	74	600	6	Poulain	The Captain and Officers of good principles, particularly the Captain, who was formerly Director of the Port.
Le Destin	74	600	6	Heraut	Formerly a Pilot, good principles. Company doubtful, on shore.
Commerce de Bordeaux	74 [100]	600	4	Rear-Admiral Julion	Formerly Lieutenant de Vaisseau, Captain Barteret: the Officers and Company promoters of Opposition.
Le Patriote	74	500	4	Bouvet	Formerly Captain of a Fire-Ship.
L'Orion	74	500	4	Purin	Formerly Captain of a Fire-Ship: the crew stongly in opposition to Monarchy.

SHIP'S NAMES.	GUNS.	MEN.	MONTHS' PROVISIONS.	COMMANDERS.	REMARKS.
L'Héros	74	600	6	Simony	Formerly Lieutenant de Vaisseau; Sound principles: the Crew supposed to be the same.
L'Heureux	74	500	6	Gavoti	Formerly Captain of a Fire-Ship; believed of sound principles.
Le Scipion	74	500	6	Degoy	A good Officer, formerly Lieutenant de Vaisseau; sound principles. Crew doubtful.
L'Apollon	74	600	4	Imbert	Formerly Lieutenant de Vaisseau; Member of the Committee General of the Sections at Toulon; on board the Victory as a Commissioner from that Committee; good principles.
L'Entreprenant	74	500	4	Boubenck	Formerly a Pilot; very doubtful.
Le Généreux	74	600	6	Carotte	Formerly Officer of the Port; good principles.
Le Thémistocle	74	800	4	Duhamel du Desert	Formerly Lieutenant de Vaisseau; of sound principles—a Member of the Committee.

Ca Ira 74, Le Hardi (74), and two others of 74 guns; La Perle, a Frigate of 40 guns, having now the flag of Vice Admiral Trogoffe; and five other Frigates.

TO THE REVEREND MR. NELSON, HILBOROUGH.

[Autograph, in the Nelson Papers.]

August 20th, 1793, off Toulon.

My dear Brother,

Although no occurrence has happened since our sailing from Gibraltar worth mentioning, yet as I know you will like to receive a letter, I write literally only to say we are well. Lord Hood has gone to water the Fleet, and left three Sail of us here to watch the French Fleet. At Marseilles and Toulon they are almost starving, yet nothing brings them to their senses. Although the Convention has denounced them as traitors yet even these people will not declare for anything but Liberty and Equality. They would, we hear, gladly put themselves under our protection, but our Fleet is inactive. We have attempted nothing. Marseilles must fall if we attack it. Monsieur Égalité is still in prison at Marseilles with his daughter. We have taken nothing: my prize-money will not be twenty pounds. I recollect this is high harvest. I hope you have fine weather and good crops. Remember me kindly to Mrs. Nelson, and our Aunt, and to the children. Compliments at Swaffham. Believe me,

Your most affectionate Brother,

HORATIO NELSON.

TO MRS. NELSON.

[From Clarke and M'Arthur, vol. i. p. 132. On the 23rd of August 1793, Commissioners from Marseilles came on board the Victory, to treat for Peace, expecting to meet Commissioners from Toulon, on the basis of declaring a Monarchical form of Government in France—Lord Hood accordingly issued a Proclamation to the Inhabitants of the South of France; and General Carteaux's success at Marseilles so alarmed the Toulonese, that they placed the Citadel and Forts on the coasts provisionally at his disposal. On the 25th of August, Lord Hood directed Captain Nelson in the Agamemnon to proceed without a moment's loss of time to Oneglia, and to leave with the Vice-Consul there, his Lordship's despatches to Mr. Trevor, the Minister at Turin. From Oneglia he was to proceed to Naples, with despatches to Sir William Hamilton; after delivering which, and completing her water, the Agamemnon was to rejoin the Admiral in Hiéres Bay. He was further directed, on the 26th of August, to take the Sardinian Frigate under his protection to Oneglia, and thence to see her as far as Corsica, on her way to Sardinia.—*Copy*, in the Nelson Papers.]

Begun off the Island of Sardinia, 7th September; finished at anchor off Naples, 11th September, 1793.

My dear Fanny,

I sent you a line by Lord Conway,[8] who is gone Home with Lord Hood's dispatches.[8] As soon as the Treaty was con-

---

[8] Lord Hugh Seymour Conway, Captain of the Leviathan 74: he died a Vice-Admiral, in September 1801. Lord Hugh Seymour proceeded in the Tartar to Genoa, and meeting the Agamemnon at Sea on the 30th of August, he wrote to Nelson congratulating him on the surrender of Toulon; and added—"I have written to Sir William Hamilton, to press him to send as many Neapolitan troops to Toulon as possible, as Lord Hood means to make that request of the Court of Naples, being in the greatest want of them, to guard the very numerous and extensive Works which surround Toulon; and which the inhabitants think General Carteaux will endeavour to make some impression upon, after his success at Marseilles, where he has got the better of the party

cluded, Agamemnon, a fast sailer, was sent off with letters
to the Courts of Turin and Naples, for ten thousand troops, to
secure our possession. I should have liked to have stayed
one day longer with the Fleet, when they entered the harbour; but service could not be neglected for any private
gratification. I have only to hope I shall succeed with the
King of Naples. The last visit he had was from a French
grenadier [9] belonging to Monsieur Truguet's Fleet: how
differently he must feel at present !

What an event this has been for Lord Hood: [1] such an
one as History cannot produce its equal; that the strongest
place in Europe, and twenty-two Sail of the Line, &c. should
be given up without firing a shot. It is not to be credited.

On Sunday, August 25th, a party deposed Admiral Trogoff, and placed St. Julien at the head of the Fleet, manned
sixteen Sail of the Line, and were determined to come out and
fight us, who were only twelve Sail, Lord Hood having sent away
the other part of his Fleet, to give them the option: the Fleet
regret they did not: the issue we should doubtless have liked
better than laying them up dismantled. The perseverance
of our Fleet has been great, and to that only can be attributed
our unexampled success. Not even a boat could get into
Marseilles or Toulon, or on the Coast, with provisions; and
the old saying, ' That hunger will tame a Lion,' was never
more strongly exemplified. The Spanish Fleet arrived as ours
was sailing into the harbour, and joined in the general joy
which this event must give to all Europe. St. Julien, with
about four thousand men, left the Fleet as ours entered, and
·oined General Carteaux, who, I think it probable, by this
time, has attacked Toulon with the Parisian Army. They

---

with which we were in treaty. Pray press Sir W. Hamilton to hasten the Neapolitans, as I know it is Lord Hood's most anxious wish to receive them. I am
on my way to England with his dispatches, and will take your commands, if
you have any; but, in God's name, keep the boat as short a time as possible."
—*Original*, in the Nelson Papers.

It appears from the " London Gazette" of the 13th September 1793, that on
the 31st of August, Captain Nelson had sent an account of the surrender of
Toulon to Mr. Trevor, from Oneglia.

[9] Threatening him with War if he did not, within an hour, disavow his remonstrances against the reception of Monsieur Sémonville, at Constantinople.

[1] The surrender of Toulon.

have made sad work with the Marseillois in treaty with us:
hope to God our success may be so used, as to give peace to
that unhappy, distracted Country. Nice, Villafranca, Monaco,
&c. which were taken from the King of Sardinia, must revert
again to him, whenever our Fleet can be liberated from Toulon. I believe the world is convinced that no conquests of
importance can be made without us; and yet, as soon as we
have accomplished the service we are ordered on, we are
neglected. If Parliament does not grant something to this
Fleet, our Jacks will grumble; for here there is no prize-
money to soften their hardships: all we get is honour and salt
beef. My poor fellows have not had a morsel of fresh meat
or vegetables for near nineteen weeks; and in that time I
have only had my foot twice on shore at Cadiz. We are
absolutely getting sick from fatigue. No Fleet, I am certain,
ever served their Country with greater zeal than this has done,
from the Admiral to the lowest sailor.

Admiral Goodall [2] is Governor of Toulon: Elphinstone,[3]
Commander of the grand battery,[4] at the harbour's mouth.
I may have lost an appointment by being sent off; not that
I wish to be employed out of my Ship. I have sent in a
vessel from Smyrna bound to Marseilles, and I think it
probable she will be condemned, worth about 10,000*l.* I
hope she may, it will add something to our comforts. We
are now in sight of Mount Vesuvius, which shows a fine light
to us in Naples Bay, where we are lying-to for the night,
and hope to anchor early to-morrow.

I am, &c,

Horatio Nelson.

P. S.—We are in the Bay all night, becalmed, and nothing
could be finer than the view of Mount Vesuvius.

---

[2] Samuel Cranstoun Goodall, whose Flag, as Rear-Admiral of the Red, was
flying in the Princess Royal. He died Admiral of the White in 1801. Some
Letters to him from Nelson will be inserted in their proper place.

[3] The Honourable George Keith Elphinstone, Captain of the Robust 74, afterwards Admiral Viscount Keith, K.B.

[4] Fort la Malgue.

TO MRS. NELSON.

[From Clarke and M' Arthur, vol. i. p. 133.]

Naples, September 14th, 1793.

My other letter will arrive with this. Our news was received here with the greatest satisfaction. The King has twice sent for me, and I dine with him to-morrow, after he has made me a visit, which he is to do on board Agamemnon. We are called by him the Saviours of Italy, and of his Dominions in particular. I have acted for Lord Hood with a zeal which no one could exceed, and am to carry from the King the handsomest letter, in his own hand-writing, which could possibly be. This I got through Sir William Hamilton, and the Prime Minister,[5] who is an Englishman. Lady Hamilton[6] has been wonderfully kind and good to Josiah. She is a young woman of amiable manners, and who does honour to the station to which she is raised. I am to carry Lord Hood six thousand troops from hence. Remember me to my dear Father, also to Lord and Lady Walpole. Believe me, your most affectionate Husband,

HORATIO NELSON.

[5] Sir John Acton, Bart.

[6] It was on this occasion that Nelson first became known to Sir William and Lady Hamilton. Of this memorable circumstance, Mr. Harrison, who wrote his "Life of Nelson," under the immediate dictation of Lady Hamilton, has given the following account, which bears evident marks of that fascinating woman's usual exaggeration :— " Sir William, on returning home, after his first interview with Nelson, told Lady Hamilton that he was about to introduce to her a little man who could not boast of being very handsome, but who would become the greatest man that ever England produced. I know it from the very few words of conversation I have already had with him. I pronounce that he will one day astonish the world. I have never entertained any Officer at my house, but I am determined to bring him here ; let him be put in the room prepared for Prince Augustus." Nelson is stated to have been equally impressed with Sir William Hamilton's merits ; " You are," he said, " a man after my own heart ; you do business in my own way ; I am now only a Captain, but if I live, I will be at the top of the tree." *Harrison's Life of Nelson*, vol. i. p. 108.

TO WILLIAM SUCKLING, ESQ.

[Autograph, in the possession of Captain Montagu Montagu, R.N.]

Naples, September 14th, 1793.

My dear Sir,

I am here with news of our most glorious and great success, but, alas! the fatigue of getting it has been so great that the Fleet generally, and I am sorry to say, my Ship much so, are knocked up. Day after day, week after week, and month after month, we have not been two gun shots from Toulon. Famine has accomplished what force could not have done; not a boat has got into Toulon since our arrival, and we literally starved them into a surrender. The news here was received with the greatest satisfaction. The King was so anxious to hear of our success that he came afloat, and sent to me. He is to make me a visit on board to-morrow, and then I dine with him. I have already been to Portici with him. The Prime Minister, (who is an Englishman,) Sir John Acton, Bart., makes much of us. We are called the Preservers of Italy. I am to carry the handsomest letter that can be penned in the King's own hand to Lord Hood, and six thousand Neapolitan troops to assist in preserving our possession. Please to send the enclosed to Mrs. Nelson. Remember me kindly to Mrs. Suckling, Miss Suckling, and the Gentlemen; and believe me,

My dear Sir, your most affectionate,

HORATIO NELSON.

TO THE REVEREND MR. NELSON, HILBOROUGH.

[Autograph, in the Nelson Papers.]

Agamemnon, September 24th, 1793.
Off Leghorn, September 27th.

My dear Brother,

I have really been so actively employed, that I have not had time to think of writing letters except to my wife. At Naples, I hoped to have had a little time to rest my Ship's company, who are worn out with fatigue. Since the 23rd of

April to this day, we have only been twenty days at anchor,
and then, as may be supposed, fully employed. In the midst
of our employment an express came that a French Man-of-
war and three Sail under her Convoy, had anchored under
Sardinia. The Neapolitans have seven Sail ready for Sea,
the Spaniards a Frigate of 40 guns, but none of them were
sent. As the Prime Minister sent me the information, unfit
as my Ship was, I had nothing left for the honour of our
Country but to sail, which I did in two hours afterwards.
It was necessary to show them what an English Man-of-war
would do.

Fortune has not crowned my endeavours with success.
The French have either got into Leghorn, or are housed
in some port of Corsica. I am going into Leghorn, absolutely to save my poor fellows. Amongst those who have
fallen a sacrifice to our hard service, is poor Mr. Emerson. He died yesterday morning, and was buried off the
North end of Corsica.[6] You will readily believe my reception
at Naples was very different to the French Admiral's. The
King received me in the handsomest manner : I was three
times with him out of the four days, and once to dinner, when
I was placed at his right hand before our Ambassador and
all the Nobles present. He was to have visited my Ship the
day we sailed, when she was full of ladies and gentlemen.—
Sir William and Lady Hamilton, the Bishop of Winchester,[7]
Mrs. North and family, Lord and Lady Plymouth,[8] Earl
Grandison and daughter,[9] besides other Baronets, &c. I
gave them breakfast, manned Ship, &c., and was to have sent
them off at one o'clock, when the King was to come on board.
I had everything ready to have entertained him with a cannonading, and the Royal Standard of Naples ready to hoist,

[6] " Monday, 23rd September, 1793. Departed this life Mr. Joseph Emerson,
Surgeon's second Mate." " Committed his body to the deep."—*Agamemnon's Log.*

[7] The Honourable Brownlow North, second son of Francis, 1st Earl of Guilford:
his wife was Henrietta Maria, daughter and co-heir of John Bannister, Esq., by
whom he had Francis, present Earl of Guilford.

[8] Other, 5th Earl of Plymouth, who married Mary, eldest daughter and co-
heir of Andrew, 2nd Lord Archer: he died in June 1799.

[9] George Mason Villiers, 2nd Earl Grandison in Ireland : he died in July
1800, leaving by Gertrude, 4th daughter of Francis Earl of Hertford, an only
child, Gertrude Amelia, who married Lord Henry Stuart, and was mother of the
present Lord Stuart de Decies.

but this information sent me off in a very great hurry. It is hardly possible to conceive the state of my Ship: I have little less than one hundred sick. I purpose staying three days in Port, when I shall get to Toulon, for I cannot bear the thought of being absent from the scene of action. I shall finish this when I anchor.

I am still as busy as ever. A French 40-gun Frigate, and five hundred men, was ready to weigh when I hove in sight. I am obliged to keep close watch to take care he does not give me the slip, which he is inclined to do. I shall pursue him, and leave the two Courts to settle the propriety of the measure, which I think will not be strictly regular. Have been up all night, watching my neighbour; and I believe he would have gone to Sea, could he have cast without getting on board us, as the night was most favourable for the attempt—a gale of wind and thick weather. However we were ready to cut the moment he did.[1] Two days past, they turned their former Captain from his office, and he luckily got on shore, or they intended to have made him Sergeant of Marines. I sail for Toulon to-morrow. Remember me to Mrs. Nelson and my Aunt, and believe me, your affectionate Brother,

HORATIO NELSON.

TO MRS. NELSON.

[From Clarke and M'Arthur, vol. i. p. 134.]

Leghorn, September 27th, 1793.

My dear Fanny,

I am sorry to tell you the Vessel I sent in here is cleared ; so all my hopes, which I own were not very sanguine, are

---

[1] In a Letter from Mr. Hoste, without date, he mentions this capture, and a circumstance which is not noticed in Nelson's Letters, nor by his biographers: "On Sunday afternoon we saw two Ships close in shore, which we supposed were French Frigates. Accordingly we gave chase. They had, however, the good fortune to get under the protection of a Fort before we could cut them off. We stood in after them, but as it was late in the evening, and dark, we could not with safety go into the harbour, though we were almost within gun-shot. The Fort fired at us, but their balls fell short; we returned the compliment, and reached them. In the morning, Captain Nelson intended to send in our boats to burn them, but they thought proper to save us the trouble

gone. Prizes are not to be met with, except so covered by
Neutral papers that you may send in fifty, and not one turn
out good. I was hurried from Naples by information of a
French Ship of War, and three vessels under her Convoy being
off. I had nothing left but to get to Sea, which I did in two
hours: expedition, however, has not crowned my endeavours
with success; for I have seen nothing of them. I am here
plagued with a French 40-gun Frigate, who was to have
sailed the day I arrived, and will take the first dark moment
to get out. I am determined in my own mind to pursue
him. I hope to sail to-morrow if this gentleman does not;
and shall lie in his route to intercept him if he sails.

I have just heard, that last night the crew of my neighbour
deposed their Captain, made the Lieutenant of Marines
Captain of the Ship, the Sergeant of Marines Lieutenant of
Marines, and their former Captain Sergeant of Marines.
What a state! they are mad enough for any undertaking.
They say, as they have five hundred men on board, they
will go to Sea this night in spite of me : I shall be surprised
at nothing they may attempt.—I dined with the King of
Naples the day before I sailed, and was placed at his right
hand, and every attention paid me. He would have visited
my Ship the day I sailed; but I was hurried away unex-
pectedly.

September 28th. We have been looking out all night
for our neighbour to cut his cables, as it has blown a gale of
wind and rain: but he lay in such a position that he could
not cast his Ship without getting on board us, which he did
not choose to risk. I shall sail to-morrow for Toulon. God
bless you.

I am, &c.,

HORATIO NELSON.

---

by coming out of the harbour with five or six small vessels, in consequence of a
message Captain Nelson sent them by a neutral vessel, which had its effect.
They proved to be all Genoese, and therefore we could not make prizes of them.
They informed us the French had one man killed. The country people were
running up the mountain, crying out, "Mon Dieu!" very much frightened,
thinking we should land. Six hundred of the militia were sent down to oppose
our landing. The name of the harbour is Cagliari, about twelve leagues to the
East of Toulon. We have taken a prize valued at 15,000*l*. or 16,000*l*. I can
say no more, as the boat is going.''—*Memoirs of Sir William Hoste*, vol. i. p. 17.

TO MRS. NELSON.

[From Clarke and M'Arthur, vol. i. p. 134.]

Agamemnon, Toulon, 7th October, 1793.

As I never omit an opportunity of writing, I shall not let a Ship sail for Leghorn without a letter. I came here two days since, and shall sail on a cruise to-morrow. Lord Hood is much pleased with me. Our situation here is wonderful: the hills are occupied by the Enemy, who are erecting works for mortars and cannon. Whether we shall be able to maintain our most extraordinary acquisition, time only can determine: however, one hour will burn the French Fleet. You will not forget me to my Father.

I am, &c.,

HORATIO NELSON.

TO WILLIAM SUCKLING, ESQ.

[Autograph in the possession of Captain Montagu Montagu, R. N. On the 9th of October Captain Nelson received sealed orders from Lord Hood which he was not to open until he had arrived off the East end of the Island of Porquerol, one of the Hieres Islands, when he found he was to go to Cagliari, and place himself under the directions of Commodore Linzee in the Alcide.]

Agamemnon, off Corsica, October 11th, 1793.

My dear Sir,

I may possibly meet a vessel bound to Leghorn, when I may send this letter. Yesterday I spoke a Ship from Gibraltar, by whom I got your letter of 26th of July, the only one I have received since I left England; and I may not be in the way for some time to come of getting any. When you favour me with a letter, direct it to the care of Mr. Udney, Consul at Leghorn; and I believe some part of the postage must be paid in London.

I am on my way to Sardinia, and then have secret orders. If anything is to be got, I stand a fair chance. I was very few days in Toulon. The service for those landed is warm. On the 8th, at night, a very handsome action took place, commanded by a Lieutenant in the Navy,[2] and 450 men, in

---

[2] Lieutenant Walter Serocold, who was promoted, and fell at the Siege of Calvi in July 1794.

which 150 of the Enemy were killed, taken, or wounded,
3 mortars and 5 twenty-four pounders destroyed. The
Enemy possess the heights, from which shot and shells are
continually thrown into the harbour. When the English
troops from Gibraltar arrive to head the columns, something
very decisive will be undertaken. The Lord is very much
pleased with my conduct about the troops at Naples, which
I undertook without any authority whatever from him ; and
they arrived at Toulon before his requisition reached Naples.[3]
Only yesterday he told me he would make Suckling a Lieutenant as soon as possible. I think he will not be many weeks
in the Victory.

Our force now at Toulon, on shore, is 12,500 men, and
before November is out, will be 30,000, when the whole of
this Country will fall to us, for they hate the Convention. The
White Flag is flying in all the Ships and Forts, under which
we fight on shore. My health never was better than at present,
as is Josiah's ; but I cannot but feel uneasy at the accounts
you give me of Mrs. Nelson. I wish she was comfortably
fixed in a house or good lodgings, in a place she liked ; but
I hope, and indeed believe, she will recover herself at Kentish
Town,[4] where I am certain every kind attention will be shown
her. The Spaniards behave so infamously that I sincerely
wish not one Ship or soldier was in Toulon : they will do nothing but plunder and cut the throats of poor wretches who
have surrendered to the British. Remember me in the kindest
manner to Mrs. Suckling, Miss Suckling, and Horace. Best
compliments to Mr. Rumsey and family.

Believe me, dear Sir, your affectionate

HORATIO NELSON.

[3] On the 27th of September, 1793, the first division of Neapolitan Ships,
under Marshal Fortiguerra, the Commodore, had arrived at Toulon, with 2,000
troops, in two Ships of the Line, two Frigates, and two Sloops. On the 5th of
October, the second division of Neapolitan Ships, with 2,000 more troops,
arrived.—Lord Mulgrave's Dispatch of 27th September, and Lord Hood's of the
13th October 1793, in the London Gazette.

[4] Mr. Suckling's residence.

10

TO MRS. NELSON.

[From Clarke and M'Arthur, vol. i. p. 135.]

October 12th, 1793.

My dear Fanny,

I received a letter from Mr. Suckling yesterday, and was indeed truly sorry to hear you were not perfectly well. Why should you alarm yourself? I am well, your son is well, and we are as comfortable in every respect as the nature of our service will admit. Lord Hood is now quite as he used to be: he is so good an Officer, that every body must respect him. All the Foreigners at Toulon absolutely worship him; were any accident to happen to him, I am sure no person in our Fleet could supply his place. Every day at Toulon has hitherto afforded some brilliant Action on shore, in which the Sea-Officers have made a conspicuous figure: Elphinstone in particular, who is a good Officer and gallant man. I have only been a spectator; but had we remained, I should certainly have desired to be landed. Some of our Ships have been pegged pretty handsomely; yet such is the force of habit, that we seem to feel no danger. The other day we sat at a Court-Martial on board Admiral Hotham, when Princess Royal, a French 74, our friend, three Frigates, and four Mortar-boats, were firing at a battery for four hours, the shot and shells going over us; which, extraordinary as it may seem, made no difference. The Ardent, Captain Robert Manners Sutton,[6] brother to the Bishop, was much cut up, after behaving with the greatest gallantry and good conduct: near thirty of his men were either killed, or are since dead of the wounds. Indeed, wherever our Ships or Sea-Officers have had an opportunity, they have all behaved well. God bless you.

HORATIO NELSON.

[6] Third son of Lord George Manners, younger son of John, 3rd Duke of Rutland, brother of Charles, then Bishop of Norwich, afterwards Archbishop of Canterbury, and uncle of the present Viscount Canterbury. This gallant officer, who was born in 1754, perished with all his crew, in August, 1794, when the Ardent was lost off Corsica, it being supposed that she was accidentally blown up.

TO ADMIRAL LORD HOOD.

[Copy, in the Admiralty. On the 22nd of October, off Sardinia, the Agamemnon fell in with a French Squadron, consisting of three large Frigates, a
Corvette, and a Brig, under the command of Commodore Perrée, and after an
action of nearly four hours with one of the Frigates, the Enemy were so severely
handled as to decline a renewal of the engagement, and the Agamemnon was so
much cut up as to be unable to pursue them. The particulars of the affair are
related in the following Letters. Captain Nelson's official Letter was not published in the Gazette.]

Agamemnon, October 22nd, 1793.
At noon, Cagliari, W.S.W., 14 or 15 Leagues.[6]

My Lord,

Inclosed I send you an extract of our log, and hope you
will think the attempt to take one of those fine Frigates was
laudable ; and that circumstanced as I was, everything was
done which ought to have been done. Had not the wind
failed us, she must have surrendered or sunk, (which from the
appearance of her hull she was near doing,) for we were just
getting alongside when a light air headed us right off. The
Nemesis[7] most unluckily parted from me a few days ago.
Inclosed is an account of our deficiency of men. Every Officer and the Ship's company in general conducted themselves
entirely to my satisfaction. I shall be happy if my conduct
meets with your Lordship's approbation ; being, with the
highest respect,

Your most faithful, humble Servant,
HORATIO NELSON.

N.B. A very few hours at anchor will repair all our damages, when the Ship will in many respects be fitter for service than ever.

[Inclosure.]

At two A. M. saw five Sail standing across us to the N.
West by the wind. At half past two they tacked by signal
of rockets, then about three miles on our weather bow : at
four got within hail of a Frigate, but was careful not to
fire into her, thinking she might be a Neapolitan or Sardinian Frigate with a Convoy. On receiving no answer and
the Ship making sail, fired a shot ahead of her, when she set

---

[6] A glance at a Chart will show that this is an extraordinary *bearing*, inasmuch
as part of the Island lay between the Ship and Cagliari.

[7] Nemesis, of 28 guns, Captain, now Admiral, Lord Amelius Beauclerk, G.C.B.

all her sails, and steering two points from the wind, we after her with every sail set, keeping her two points on the bow, to prevent her from getting before the wind. The other Ships on our weather quarter steering after us. The Chase made many signals till daylight, when she hoisted National colours, and began firing stern-chasers, and by yawing, which her superiority in sailing enabled her to do, gave us many broadsides. We could only at times bring any guns to bear upon her, and then only a few of the foremost ones. At seven, took the Ships on our weather quarter to be one of the Line, two Frigates, and an armed Brig, but whilst the breeze continued fresh, the Chase and ourselves left them fast. At nine o'clock we run into almost a calm, the Ships on our quarter bearing N. W. by W., coming fast up with us; the Chase hauled up to join them, being in a shattered condition, and making signals to her consorts, who steered to join her when they brought to, hoisted out their boats, and sent to her. The Enemy were four Frigates, two of them carrying 28 eighteen pounders on their main-decks. The Enemy from this time till noon had the option of bringing us to action whenever they pleased; but we having our main top-mast shot to pieces, main-mast, mizen-mast, and fore-yard badly wounded, could not haul our wind till noon, repairing our rigging, masts, and yards, steering for Cagliari. Found we had one man killed, and six wounded. People employed knotting and splicing the rigging.

At noon, Cape Rosse, N. W., distance six or seven leagues.

Latitude observed 39° 34' N.

MEMORANDUM RELATING TO THE ACTION WITH THE FRENCH SQUADRON, ON THE 22ND OCTOBER 1793.

[Autograph, in the Nelson Papers.]

At seven o'clock sent for all the Officers to give me their opinion what the Ship on our Weather quarter was; they all agreed she was a Ship of the Line, of which opinion I was also.

At nine run into a calm, our head paid round to the Southward, the Frigates to the N. E. In about a quarter of an hour afterwards the breeze came again from the Northward:

sent for the Officers to give me their opinions what the Ship on the quarter was; they all agreed she was a Line of Battle Ship, of which opinion was myself.

Question.—" Do you think we can, by hauling our wind to the N. E., after the Frigate, close with her before she joins her consorts ?" *Answer.*—" No ; it is impossible."

Question.—" From what you see of the state of our Ship, is she fit to go into Action with such a superior force which is against us, without some small refit and refreshments for our people ?" *Answer.*—" She certainly is not."

My Orders.—Mr. Wilson,[8] wear the Ship, and lay her head to the Westward, (the Enemy bore N. W. by W. three miles,) let some of the best men be employed refitting the rigging, and the carpenters getting crows and capstern bars to prevent our wounded spars from coming down, and to get the wine for the people, and some bread, for it might be half-an-hour before we were again in Action.

H. N.

TO COMMODORE LINZEE.

[Autograph, in the possession of the Honourable Mrs. Gregory, sister of the present Viscount Hood. The Agamemnon joined Commodore Linzee at Cagliari, on the 24th of October. Vide p. 331.]

Agamemnon, October 24th, 1793.

My dear Sir,

I am sorry to have been so long in joining you, as I feel great satisfaction in being put under your orders. What has contributed to delay me a little, was four French Frigates and a Brig crossing me. A few shot was exchanged with one of them, who I left in a sinking state. We having lost the use of our main topmast, could not haul the wind to them, and they seemed to have got enough: therefore would not come down to me. Believe me yours most faithfully.

HORATIO NELSON.

Sailmakers would be of great service to us for a day, and some Carpenters with their tools: 24 hours will fit us for service.

Ten days past we boarded a Ship from Smyrna, but I think we ought not to be put into quarantine.

[8] Master of the Agamemnon.

TO MAURICE NELSON, ESQ.

[From Clarke and M'Arthur, vol. i. p. 136. The Agamemnon accompanied
Commodore Linzee in the Alcide to Tunis, on the mission described in Nelson's
letter to Captain Locker in p. 338, where she remained from the 1st to the 16th
of November, on which day she left Tunis Bay, and cruized off Cape Zibib until
the 26th. She then returned to Tunis; and on the 30th of that month, sailed for
Corsica.]

Tunis, 8th Nov. 1793.

On the 22nd of October, off the Island of Sardinia, having
only 345 men at quarters, the others being landed at Toulon
and in prizes, we fell in with, and chased the following
French Men-of-War from Tunis: Melpomene, 44 guns,
nine and eighteen pounders, 400 men; La Minerve, 44 guns,
nine and eighteen pounders, 400 men; La Fortunée, 44 guns,
twelve and thirty-six pounders, 500 men; Le Fouchet,[9] 24
guns, nine pounders, 220 men: Brig, 14 guns, nine pounders,
100 men. The Agamemnon, after a firing of near four hours,
so disabled the Melpomene she (as supposed) being apparently in a sinking state, that the other Ships declined bringing the Agamemnon again to Action, and, as it appeared, to
take care of their companion; since they had the option to
renew the engagement for three hours after the Melpomene
hauled from us. The Agamemnon was so cut to pieces, as
to be unable to haul the wind towards them. I am, &c.,

HORATIO NELSON.

TO WILLIAM LOCKER, ESQ., GREENWICH HOSPITAL.

[Autograph, in the Locker Papers.]

December 1st, 1793.

My dear Friend,

Your letter, of August 8th, I got two days past in Tunis[1]

[9] James, in his "Naval History," (vol. i. p. 106,) states that La Melpomene
carried 40, and the two other Frigates 38 guns each; that the Corvette was Le
Mignonne, of 28 guns, and not Le Fouchet; and that the Brig was Le Hasard.

[1] Mr. Hoste, writing to his father, on the 27th of November, says:

"We understood on our joining Commodore Linzee, that our destination
was for Tunis, to take out the Duquesne, a French 80 gun Ship, and four Frigates, then lying there waiting to Convoy a Fleet of Merchantmen to Marseilles, for which service the Commodore in the Alcide 74, was appointed by
Lord Hood, under whose command were the Berwick and Illustrious, 74 guns
each, ourselves, Lowestoffe, and Nemesis, Frigates.

Bay where Commodore Linzee has been negotiating for a
French convoy, under Le Duquesne, eighty guns, and a Corvette.   The English never yet succeeded in a negotiation
against the French, and we have not set the example at Tunis,
for the Monsieurs have completely upset us with the Bey ;
and had we latterly attempted to take them I am sure he would
have declared against us, and done our trade some damage.
Lord Hood has ordered me from Linzee's command, and to
take the command of a Squadron of Frigates off Corsica and
the adjoining shore of Italy, to look out for some French Frigates, who are in St. Fiorenzo in Corsica.   They are the
Ships I had a little brush with, joined with one or two others.
If they are active, they may do our trade some damage, but,
to say the truth, I believe they are more inclined to be passive
—at least they had much of that inclination when I saw them.
Lord Hood has written me a very handsome letter, and
given me this command.   At Toulon, I think they will have
plenty of fighting this winter.   Captain Torriano of the 30th,
I believe you know him, or some of his relations at Kensington,
is killed ; but shot and shells are very plentiful all over the
Harbour.   I wonder more damage has not been done.   General O'Hara, I hope, will be able to drive the French from the
heights near the Harbour, or we shall be unpleasantly situated ; not that I think Toulon is in the smallest danger.   At
all events, we can destroy the French Fleet and Arsenal in a
very short time : one Fire-ship will burn the Fleet and Arsenal.

"When we got to Tunis we found only the Duquesne and Merchantmen ;
the four Frigates were gone, which the Agamemnon had nearly been too sensible of, as those were the very Frigates we met in our voyage to Cagliari, which,
had they acted as they ought to have done, could have prevented our joining the
Commodore.   On our arrival at Tunis, we expected the Bey would have given
us leave to take out the Duquesne and Merchantmen, but we found he would
not allow the neutrality of the Port to be broken, however superior we were in
those seas ; nor would the Duquesne give herself up to the French King, notwithstanding all our negotiations to that purpose.   In consequence, the Commodore dispatched the Nemesis to Toulon for further orders.   On her arrival from
thence we found we were not to attempt anything.   She has brought orders for
Captain Nelson to take under his command the Lowestoffe on a cruize, but
where to, or on what service, remains a secret.   In the first part of my
Letter I told you that we left Toulon in company with the Nemesis.   Sailing
along the Island of Corsica we picked up a prize which we sent into Leghorn.
The day after we lost sight of the Nemesis."—*Memoirs of Sir William Hoste.*
vol. i. p. 18.

They are some of them the finest Ships I ever saw. The Commerce of Marseilles has seventeen ports on each deck. The Victory looks nothing to her. You know Pole[2] is gone to the West Indies. I have not seen him since his order, but I know it was a thing he dreaded.

Had I been at Toulon I should have been a candidate for that service, for I think our Sea-war is over in these Seas. Agamemnon has had her share of service; we have only had our anchor down thirty-four days since we sailed from the Nore, and then only to get water and provisions. I have now upwards of one hundred of my Ship's company absent;[2] we are not much better than a 50 gun Ship. Lord Hood has sent for Suckling, who was in the Sandwich, and I dare say has made him a Lieutenant[3] by this time. The Lord is very good friends with me: he is certainly the best Officer I ever saw. Everything from him is so clear it is impossible to misunderstand him. If I should go to Cadiz be assured I will get you a hogshead or two of sherry. Troubridge will tell you, I did not see him or his Ship, after my letter by St. Albans.

December 8th. — I am glad to see by the papers, that Kingsmill is to hoist his Flag. Pray, when you write to him, remember me kindly to him. Say, can I get him anything in these parts? if so, I will do it with real pleasure. I have been in sight of the French Squadron all day, and we hear they have been joined by a Frigate from Calvi; and really, I think that the Frigate who received most of our fire is not here; [that] they want one of their number, is certain. We have not, ever since the firing, wanted those who say they saw her sink.[4] I own it remains doubtful. Remember me kindly to all your sons and daughters, Mr. Bradley, and all friends, and believe me,

Your most affectionate
HORATIO NELSON.

---

[2] Captain Charles Morice Pole, then Captain of the Colossus, 74.

[3] "To another friend he jocosely observed on this occasion, that those he had were chiefly Norfolk men, and he always reckoned them as good as two others."—Harrison's *Life of Nelson*, vol. i. p. 112.

[4] Mr. William Suckling was made a Lieutenant in 1794.

[5] This was not the fact, as La Melpomene was one of the ships taken at Calvi. *Vide Postea.*

TO WILLIAM SUCKLING, ESQ.

[From "the Athenæum." On the 15th of November 1793, Lord Hood directed Commodore Linzee "to send Captain Nelson to cruise from Calvi to the Gulf of Especia, to look for the Frigates he had engaged on the 22nd of October, but not to let it be known where he was gone, and to take under his command such Ships as he might find on that Station, which were the Mermaid, Tartar, Topaze French frigate, and Scout Brig, and probably the Amphitrite: and in addition to looking out for the French Frigates, he was to direct him to prevent all Ships and Vessels from going to Genoa, as that Port was in a state of investment and blockade by a part of the Fleet under Lord Hood. In the execution of this service, he was to be as careful as possible not to give further offence to the subjects of such Powers, whose Vessels he might chance to fall in with, and whose Sovereigns were in amity with England, than making known to them the purport of those orders. But in case they should persist in going to the Port of Genoa, he was then to stop the said Vessels, and send them to Leghorn, or Porto Ferrajo, there to be detained."]

Agamemnon, December 5th, [1793,] off Corsica.

My dear Sir,

I am just returned from Tunis, where I have been under Commodore Linzee,[4] to negotiate for a French Convoy from the Levant. You will believe the English seldom get much by negotiation except the being laughed at, which we have been ; and I don't like it. Had we taken, which in my opinion we ought to have done, the Men-of-War and Convoy, worth at least £300,000, how much better we could have negotiated : —given the Bey £50,000, he would have been glad to have put up with the insult offered to his dignity. The French sent him very great presents ; and he bought, through fear of us, several rich cargoes, for one third of their value. The Ships of War so much believed we should have attacked them, that, at first, they hauled their Ships almost a-ground ; but

---

[4] Lord Hood's orders to Commodore Linzee, dated 15th of November, were "to expostulate with the Bey, in the strongest and most impressive manner, on the impolicy of his giving countenance and support to so heterogeneous a Government as the present one of France, composed of murderers and assassins, who have recently beheaded their Queen in a manner that would disgrace the most barbarous savages. The Bey of Tunis, who was possessed of superior abilities, is said at the Conference which Captain Nelson held with him, to have displayed such quickness as to have disconcerted even the Captain of the Agamemnon. On being told of the excesses which the French Government had committed, he dryly observed, ' That nothing could be more heinous than the murder of their Sovereign ; and yet, Sir, if your historians tell the truth, your own countrymen once did the same.' "—*Clarke and M'Arthur*, vol. i. p. 138.

latterly almost insulted us. Thank God, Lord Hood, whom Linzee sent to for orders how to act, after having negotiated, ordered me from under his command, and to command a Squadron of Frigates off Corsica and the Coast of Italy, to protect our trade, and that of our new Ally, the Grand Duke of Tuscany, and to prevent any Ship or Vessel, of whatever Nation, from going into the port of Genoa. I consider this command as a very high compliment,—there being five older Captains in the Fleet.

You will have heard of our little brush from Maurice,[1] whom I wrote to from Tunis, by way of Spain : that the Lord should be pleased with *our* conduct, you need not wonder at; I flatter myself he could not be otherwise. Had they been English, and we French, the case, I am sure, would have been different. I am now cruizing for them ; they are in St. Fiorenzo.

Corsica, December 8th :—I have been in sight of the French Squadron all day, at anchor ; they cannot be induced to come out, notwithstanding their great superiority. Remember me in the kindest manner to Mrs. Suckling, Miss Suckling, and all the family. Believe me,

Your most affectionate
HORATIO NELSON.

Pray don't forget me to Mr. Rumsey.

TO THE REV. MR. NELSON, HILBOROUGH.

[Autograph, in the Nelson Papers.]

Agamemnon, Leghorn, December 27th, 1793.

My dear Brother,

You may probably have heard of our evacuation of Toulon by last post, when I wrote Maurice a line, as the report then went. For England, the getting rid of such a place is a most happy event. Our money would have gone very fast. Even the Staff which was appointed from England was sufficient for Ireland, and other places, which was filling as fast as horses could draw them across the Continent, or they could find Ships to carry them to Toulon. The particulars

---

[1] Vide p. 337.

are as follows; that on the 13th a most numerous Army covered the neighbouring hills, that Lord Hood had given notice to the inhabitants of the probable evacuation of the place, that on the 17th at eight o'clock at night a general attack was made on all our outposts, which lasted all night; the Foreign troops quitted them sooner than they ought to have done, and the others were obliged to be abandoned the next morning, destroying the works, and spiking the guns, as well as a short time would allow.   Lord Hood attempted to rally the flying troops, but it was impossible: our Army retired into the Town and Fort la Malgue.   On the 18th the Neapolitan troops were ordered to embark, together with the Royalists in as many Ships as could be found.   Then began a scene of horror which may be conceived, not described. The mob rose; death called forth all its myrmidons, which destroyed the miserable inhabitants in the shape of swords, pistols, fire, and water.   Thousands are said to be lost.   In this dreadful scene, and to complete misery, already at the highest, Lord Hood was obliged to order the French Fleet, twenty Sail of the Line, twenty other Men-of-War, together with the Arsenal, (Dock-yard,) Powder-Magazines, &c., to be set on fire.   One half of the Town is said to have been consumed with them.   Only three of the French Fleet, one First-rate, one 80, one 74 and two Frigates, saved: all the Forts are blown up, and it is now strongly reported that Lord Hood has sailed for Hieres Bay.   Fathers are here without families, and families without fathers, the pictures of horror and despair.   Agamemnon is here getting provisions, but stationed with a Squadron off Corsica. Josiah is well, and desires to be remembered.   Don't omit my remembrance in the kindest manner to Mrs. Nelson and my Aunt.   I expect to see them soon, for this War cannot last much longer.   Hoste is a very good boy indeed, as is Bolton.[5]   Compliments at Swaffham, and believe me,

Your affectionate Brother,

HORATIO NELSON.

[5] Afterwards Captain Sir William Bolton, who was Nelson's Proxy at his Installation as a Knight of the Bath, on the 19th of May 1803.   He married, shortly before the Installation, his Patron's niece, Catherine, daughter of Mrs. Bolton, and died in December 1830.

I am glad to hear my mare is not sold. Lord Hood has not quitted La Malgue.—27th, 6 P.M.

Mrs. Nelson wrote about a fish dried called Tonges for Mr. Speed. I cannot find out any such fish. I think she must have mistaken the name. Be so good as to find out what it is, and let me know.

TO H. R. H. THE DUKE OF CLARENCE.

[From Clarke and M'Arthur, vol. i. p. 140.]

Agamemnon, Leghorn Roads, 27th December 1793.

Sir,

My last letter to your Royal Highness would convey to you my opinion of the impossibility of holding Toulon without a superior Army in the field : but the fall of it has been something quicker than I expected, owing to the Foreign troops having but very badly defended some of the outposts, as reported here by several vessels with some of the wretched inhabitants of Toulon. Lord Hood is said to have attempted rallying the flying troops, but in vain ; and that he exposed himself to great danger. The reports, although there is some difference in the telling, all seem to agree that the following are facts :—

That on the 13th a most numerous Army covered the hills ; that Lord Hood issued a Proclamation to prepare the inhabitants for what would probably happen, the evacuation of Toulon ; that on the 17th, at eight o'clock at night, the Enemy made a general attack on all our outposts, which lasted the whole night, many of which they carried with too much ease ; that the other outposts were obliged to be abandoned, and the troops to retire to Fort la Malgue ; that on the 18th, Lord Hood ordered all the Neapolitans to be embarked together, with as many Royalists as could find Ships to carry them ; and that our Fleet, with that of Spain, were anchored under La Malgue. On the 19th, in the morning, such a scene was displayed, as would make the hardest heart feel : the mob had risen, was plundering, and committing every excess ; many—numbers cannot be estimated—were

drowned in trying to get off; boats upset; and many put a
period to their existence.   One family, of a wife and five children, are just arrived—the husband shot himself.   Indeed,
Sir, the recital of their miseries is too afflicting to dwell upon.
In this scene of horror, Lord Hood was obliged to order the
French Fleet of twenty Sail of the Line, and as many other
Ships of War, together with the Arsenal and Powder Magazines, to be set on fire: report says one-half of that miserable
place is in ashes.

The Neapolitan Fleet, and near one hundred Sail with them,
are arrived in Port Especia, twelve leagues from hence.
What calamities do Civil Wars produce ; and how much does
it behove every person to give their aid in keeping peace at
Home.   It is the poor inhabitants at Toulon that I feel for.
The quitting Toulon by us, I am satisfied, is a National benefit; both in money, for our contracts will be found to have
been very extravagant, people seemed to act as if fortunes
were to be made instantly ; and in saving some of our gallant
English blood, which, when the muster comes to be taken,
will appear to have flowed plentifully.   The destruction of
the Fleet and Arsenal, and indeed of the harbour of Toulon,
for a number of years, is a great benefit to England.   I have
only to regret it could not have been done on the first day of
our entrance.   I expect Lord Hood here immediately, although they say he is in Hieres Bay, having blown up Fort
la Malgue.   I shall not close this letter till the moment of
the post going out.

Four Sail filled with wounded soldiers and sailors are just
arrived.   It is thought that the Governor here will not allow
the emigrés to land ; Leghorn being, as they say, in want of
provisions.   I have still a small Squadron blocking up the
Frigates in Corsica, who are in the greatest distress.   And I
remain, as ever, your Royal Highness's most dutiful and
faithful servant,

HORATIO NELSON.

TO MRS. NELSON.

[From Clarke and M'Arthur, vol. i. p. 141.]

Agamemnon, December 27th, 1793.

My dear Fanny,

Everything which domestic Wars produce usually, is multiplied at Toulon. Fathers are here without their families, families without their fathers. In short, all is horror. I have the Count de Grasse under my command, in a French Frigate:[6] his wife and family are at Toulon. Lord Hood put himself at the head of the flying troops, and was the admiration of every one; but the torrent was too strong. Many of our posts were carried without resistance; at others, which the English occupied, every one perished. I cannot write all: my mind is deeply impressed with grief. Each teller makes the scene more horrible. Lord Hood showed himself the same collected good Officer which he always was. I have only time to say, God bless you.

HORATIO NELSON.

TO MRS. NELSON.

[From Clarke and M'Arthur, vol. i. p. 144. Early in January 1794, Lord Hood concluded a convention with General Paoli, by which it was agreed that the British Forces should assist the Corsicans in expelling the French from possession of the Forts, &c.; and that Corsica should be ceded to Great Britain. Captain Nelson was' then cruising off Calvi with a small Squadron to prevent the French from receiving supplies; and he was in frequent communication with Paoli.]

Off Calvi, January 6th, 1794.

I left Leghorn on the 3rd, and very soon got off here, since which time we have had nothing but hard gales of wind, and the heaviest rains I almost ever met with. I am waiting anxiously for Troops from Lord Hood, to take St. Fiorenzo and the Frigates, which will fall into our hands a few hours after their arrival. I was most unfortunately driven a few miles to leeward two days ago, in the height of the gale; and a Frigate took that opportunity of sailing from

[6] La Topaze.

St. Fiorenzo to Calvi with provisions. One of my Frigates exchanged a few shot with her, but at too great a distance to prevent her getting in. I had so closely blockaded Calvi, that they must have surrendered to me at discretion; not a vessel had before got in for the six weeks I have been stationed here. This supply will keep them a week or two longer. We now know from a deserter, that it was the Melpomene who engaged us on October 22nd: she had twenty-four men killed, and fifty wounded, and was so much damaged as to be laid up dismantled in St. Fiorenzo. She would have struck long before we parted, but for the gunner, who opposed it; and when at length the colours were ordered to be struck by general consent, we ran into a calm, whilst the other Ships came up with a fresh breeze, and joined their consort. Admiral Trogoff[7] tells me she is allowed to be the finest Frigate out of France, and the fastest sailer: we were unlucky to select her—the others we could outsail. Had she struck, I don't think the others would have come down, and I should have had great credit in taking her from such superior force: now, of course, nothing can be known of that business, and I have to look out for another opportunity; which is very scarce here.

I have just received a most handsome letter from Lord Hood: he looks upon these Frigates as certain, trusting to my zeal and activity, and knows, if it is in the power of man to have them, I will secure them. Linzee [8] was to have been here for this service, and to settle plans with General Paoli, the Chief of the Corsicans, relative to landing the troops, &c. Andrews [9] is my ambassador. This business

[7] A French Rear-Admiral, who had zealously co-operated with Lord Hood at Toulon against the Republicans.

[8] Commodore Robert Linzee, in the Alcide 74: he died an Admiral of the Blue, in September 1804.

[9] On the 17th of January 1794, General Paoli wrote to Captain Nelson from Murato he had on the preceding day received his Letter by Lieutenant George Andrews, with whom he had agreed about the Signals. Paoli added, " A little before Mr. George [Andrews] came, were arrived here, Sir Gilbert Elliot, Colonel Moore, and Major Koehler: they are gone this morning to reconnoitre the environs of Saint Fiorenzo, and I hope they will bring a plan such as Lord Hood seems desirous to have."—*Original* in the Nelson Papers. Lieutenant, afterwards Captain, George Andrews, was the brother of the Miss Andrews mentioned in

going through my hands is a proof of Lord Hood's confidence in me, and that I shall pledge myself for nothing but what will be acceptable to him. I have promised my people, as soon as we have taken Corsica, that I would ask for a month's rest for them;—except to get provisions, I have not been one hour at anchor for pleasure, since April 23rd ; but I can assure you I never was better in health, as is Josiah. On Sunday I expect Lord Hood and the troops. Hoste is indeed a most exceeding good boy, and will shine in our Service.[1] We shall talk these matters over again in a winter's evening.

Yours, &c.,

HORATIO NELSON.

TO WILLIAM LOCKER, ESQ., LIEUTENANT-GOVERNOR OF THE ROYAL HOSPITAL AT GREENWICH.

[Autograph, in the Locker Papers.]

Agamemnon, St. Fiorenzo, January 17th, 1794.

My dear Friend,

I had some hopes of seeing my friends in England very soon ; but for the present they are at an end, and if I do not sail from this Country before the spring very far advances, I believe I shall give up all thoughts of going home till the Campaign is finished ; for I should be truly sorry to have the chance of laying by the walls for two or three months in the height of summer, and when probably we shall have active service in this Country. We are a week arrived here from a cruise of three weeks off Toulon, during which time we were fifteen days under storm-staysails,—indeed such a series of bad weather I never experienced ; the Ships most of them strained a good deal, but sustained no material damage, nor did a single Ship part company. We saw three French Frigates, but from the Admiral's anxiety to keep the Fleet together, he did not make the signal for the Frigates to chase

---

Nelson's letters from St. Omer, ante. An account of Captain Andrews's services is given by Clarke and M'Arthur, in a note to this Letter : he died in July 1810.

[1] No anticipation was ever more completely realized. Vide p. 355.

them till too late in the day, and they most unluckily escaped
One of them was a crippled Ship: Agamemnon was the next
to them by six or seven miles, but a Line-of-Battle Ship never
chases. I have no doubt but we should have taken one, if
not two, of them, for few Ships sail equal to us, none I believe
at present in this Fleet. The Admiral is anxious to get to
Sea again, to cover our Convoy and expected reinforcements
from England, and was only waiting till the Berwick, commanded by our shipmate Smith,[2] was got ready for Sea; but
waiting for her must now be at an end, for last night a very
heavy sea rolling into the Gulph, the Berwick not having, I
understand, her rigging set up, lost all her masts, and is now
a most complete wreck. I don't think our shipmate has
much improved in the art of seamanship since we parted.
The Admiral, as you will believe, is much out of humour with
him, thinking we have not a Seventy-four to spare, the French
Fleet in the outer road of Toulon being as follows: Sans
Culotte 120, Tonnant 80, Ca Ira 80, Languedoc 80, Géne-
reux 74, Censeur 74, Duquesne 74, Centaure 74, Commerce
de Bordeaux 74, Mercure 74, Conquerant 74, Guerrier 74,
Souverain 74, Heureux 74, Barras 74: in the inner, Hardi
64, Alcide 74; one eight of these very good, six bad, but will
to Sea, three very bad, with twelve Frigates in the harbour, and five Corvettes. Fifty sail of Marseilles Ships are
fitting for Transports: they have some expedition on foot,
most certainly,—I think Port Especia, many others, Corsica.
Remember me most kindly to all your family, and believe
me ever,

Your most obliged,

HORATIO NELSON.

[During great part of the year 1794, Captain Nelson kept, in three
forms, a Journal of his proceedings: *first*, Memoranda from the 21st of
January to the 13th of July, containing little more than dates and a brief notice
of occurrences; *secondly*, rather longer details of events from the 24th of
February to the 1st of April, 1794; *thirdly*, a regular Journal of the Siege of
Bastia, beginning on the 4th of April and ending on the 4th of July; and *fourthly*,
a Journal of the Siege of Calvi, ending on the 10th of August, 1794, a
copy of which he sent daily from the Camp to Lord Hood. The *first* and

---

[2] Captain William Smith, who with his First Lieutenant and Master, were dismissed the Ship by sentence of a Court Martial, for neglect of duty on the occasion.

second of those Papers, in his own autograph, are now in the Nelson Papers; but the *third*, which belonged to Lady Nelson, and was copiously cited by Clarke and M'Arthur, cannot now, unfortunately, be found; and the loss is the more to be regretted, because (besides the unjustifiable practice of altering words, and omitting passages) it is not always possible to decide, whether the statements printed by those writers actually occurred in the Journal, or were interpolated from other sources. Some difficulty arose as to the best mode of printing these Papers,—whether to give them entire, or to place each entry in the exact order of its date. The former plan was first adopted, but it was thought advisable to prefer the other arrangement, because the entries sometimes supply information not contained in the Letters, and often explain transactions mentioned in them. The JOURNALS will be distinguished by the letters *A*, B, and *C*; the letter "A" indicating the Memoranda from the 31st of January to the 13th July;—"B" indicating the Diary from the 24th of February to the 1st of April;—and "C" the passages in the larger Journal, quoted by Clarke and M'Arthur, from the 4th of April to the 10th of August, 1794. Some extracts from the Journal of the Siege of Calvi, not given by Clarke and M'Arthur, have been found in the Admiralty. Vide p. 407.]

JOURNAL A.

January 21st.—Landed about four miles from St. Fiorenzo. Burnt the only water-mill in that part of the country, much to the distress of the French.

TO MRS. NELSON.

[From Clarke and M'Arthur, vol. i. p. 146.]

Leghorn, January 30th, 1794.

I was blown off my Station on the 28th, in the hardest gale almost ever remembered here. The Agamemnon did well, but lost every sail in her. Lord Hood had joined me off Corsica the day before; and would have landed the Troops,[3] but the gale has dispersed them over the face of the waters. The Victory was very near lost; however, we are safe. A number of Transports are missing. I am fearful the Enemy will get their Troops from France before I can return to my Station, which will be a vexing thing after my two months' hard fag.

I hope to get my Ship to sea to-morrow. I direct this to Bath, where I desire you will not want for anything: my expenses are by no means great, therefore don't be afraid of money. A circumstance happened a few days past, which gave me great satisfaction. January 21st, the French having

---

[3] Lord Hood put to sea on the 24th of January, with sixty Sail, containing troops for the invasion of Corsica.

their storehouse of flour near a water-mill close to St. Fiorenzo, I seized a happy moment, and landed sixty soldiers and sixty seamen, in spite of opposition. At landing, the sailors threw all the flour into the sea, burned the mill—the only one they had, and returned on board without the loss of a man. The French sent one thousand men at least against them, and Gun-boats, &c.; but the shot went over them, and they were just within reach of my guns. It has pleased Lord Hood, but this dreadful gale may have blown it out of his memory.

Yours, &c.,

HORATIO NELSON.

TO THOMAS POLLARD, ESQ. LEGHORN.

[Autograph, in the possession of John Luxford, Esq., the nephew and legatee of Mrs. Pollard, whose husband was then a Merchant at Leghorn. This letter relates to the sale of some Prizes.]

3 P.M., Friday, January 31st, 1794.

Dear Sir,

We are now at sea, but call on Captain Wolseley, and tell him your offer; and if not sold at roupe before his arrival, have no objection to take your money, pledging myself for nothing but supposing the invoice to be right.

Your much obliged,

HORATIO NELSON.

1,400 chequins,   *Agree*,[4] W. WOLSELEY.
7,000*l.* sterling.

Pray send me a little paper by Lowestoffe.

JOURNAL A.

February 6th.—Landed at Centuri; burned four polaccas loaded with wine for the French Ships at Fiorenzo.

February 8th.—Landed at Maginaggio; burned eight Sail of Vessels, took four, and destroyed about 1,000 tons of wine.

4 Added by Captain William Wolseley, of the Lowestoffe, of 32 guns: he died a Full Admiral.

TO HIS EXCELLENCY GENERAL PAOLI.

[From a Copy, in the Nelson Papers.]

Agamemnon, between Bastia and Cape Corse,
February 8th, 1794.

Sir,

Yesterday at a place called Rocliniar,[6] or Porto Novo, they had the presumption to hoist National colours, as also the Vessels in the harbour. This morning I sent on shore a Flag of Truce, saying that I was come to deliver them from the Republicans, and wished to be received as friends, but that if any opposition was made to the landing of the troops I would burn the place. The answer to this message I have enclosed.[7] I landed and destroyed the Vessels, they having all National colours on board, with five hundred tons of wine, the National colours flying in the Town, and the Tree of Liberty planted, both of which I struck with my own hands. The people who left the town assembled on a hill, with the National colours flying.

When at anchor, a Vessel was seen at Sea. I sent a Cutter in chase of her, who took her. She was from Leghorn to this place, loaded with corn and salt fish, &c. She produced a Pass from your Excellency, dated in October last. I have sent the vessel to the Isle Rousse, that your Excellency may know to what an unworthy object your protection was bestowed; and I think you will agree with me, that she ought only to be considered as Enemy's property; for certainly only our Enemies could be benefited by her voyages to Leghorn.

I am, your Excellency's most obedient Servant,

HORATIO NELSON.

N.B. I am sorry the Ragusa Ship[8] has been for some time in Bastia: certain she is not in L'Avasina.

---

[6] *Sic* in the MS., but apparently a clerical error of the transcriber for " Rogliani."

[7] Vide p. 355.

[8] In a Letter from General Paoli to Captain Nelson, dated Murato, 24 January 1794, he said :—

" Les petits Corsaires de Bastia ont pris un batiment de Raguse chargé de coton, soie, sucre, caffé, et autres objets de valeur : cette prise est encore à cinq mille de distance du Port ou elle ne peut pas entre. Un marchand Anglois y est détenú prisonnier ;" and he added in a Postscript, " Le vaisseau de Raguse qui a été pris est dans la hause dite *L'Avasina* à cinq mille *Nord* de Bastia."—*Original*, in the Nelson Papers.

TO VICE-ADMIRAL LORD HOOD.

[Autograph, in the possession of Mrs. Conway.]

Agamemnon, at anchor, off Porto Novo, February 8th, 1794.

My Lord,

Yesterday at this place, they hoisted National colours as I passed, as also the Vessels in the harbour. I went to l'Avasina, but there is no Ship there. Captain Fremantle tells me, a Ship under Ragusa colours is in Bastia. This morning being very fine, I anchored here, and sent on shore a message to say I was come to deliver them from the Republicans, and wished to be received as friends, but that if a musket was fired, I would burn the Town. The answer[8] is literally as translated, viz.,

'We are Republicans; that is sufficient. It is not at Magina you ought to address yourself. Go to St. Fiorenzo, Bastia, or Calvi:—they will give you an answer such as you desire. The soldiers which I command are true soldiers of France. The Commander of the Military of Cape Corse.'

From this answer, I landed, and struck the National colours with my own hand, and ordered the Tree of Liberty to be cut down. The Commander retiring to a hill, with National colours, and his troops. We destroyed about five hundred tuns of wine ready to be shipped, and ten sail of Vessels.[9]

Just as we were coming . . [*The remainder is lost.*]

[7] The *original* Letter of the French Commandant is in the Nelson Papers:

"Nous sommes Republicains. Ce mot seul doit suffire. Ce n'est point au Maginaggio, lieu sans deffence, à qui il faut vous àdresser. Allez a St. Florent, Bastia, ou Calvi, et l'ou vous repondrá, selon vos desirs. Pour la trouppes que je commande elle est préte à vous montrer qu'elle est compose de Soldats Francais.

"Le Command^t. Militaire du
"Cape Corse."

[8] Maginaggio is about a mile from Rogliani.

[9] General Paoli writing to Nelson on the 13th of February 1794, said:—

"The punishment inflicted on the inhabitants of Rogliani with the burning of

JOURNAL A.

February 12th.—Attacked a French Courier-boat, whose crew got on shore at Capreia; after a very smart contest, in which I lost six men, carried her.

TO VICE-ADMIRAL LORD HOOD.

[Partly from Clarke and M'Arthur, vol. i. p. 148, and partly from an autograph draught.]

Agamemnon, off Cabrera, February 13th, 1794.

My Lord,

In addition to the paper I enclose for your Lordship's information, I have to acquaint you, that on Sunday the 9th, I anchored at Cabrera,[1] to see if any of the Enemy's privateers were lying in that port. I sent a message on shore to the Governor, to say, that the trade in these Seas had been very much annoyed by the Enemy's privateers which harboured in Cabrera, and that if any other Vessels were there belonging to the French, I should take them. The answer sent me was, that he had orders to admit of no search whatever in Cabrera; and that if I attempted it, he should repel me to the utmost of his power. My next message to him was, that I wished to be friendly, but unless he would give his word of honour that there were no Vessels in the Port under French Republican colours, I would search them. The Governor upon this gave his word of honour, and I did not think it right to proceed further.

This is a new Governor, the former one being turned out for allowing the Romulus and Meleager to take two Vessels out of the Port. Every person in the Island was under arms to oppose us. There are now lying in the

their Ships was well deserved by their cowardice in permitting that few desperate strangers should provocate your anger upon them. The inhabitants have certainly the best dispositions to come to us again, when they may expect to be supported, but the little resistance they made lately when the French established themselves again in Cape Corse has exposed them to all the misfortunes they now labour under. The answer to your offers from the Commanding Officer there was quite in a Guascon's way, and his flight afterwards well answered to the ostentation of his expression."—*Original* in the Nelson Papers.

[1] Generally called Capraja, a small Island, about three leagues E.N.E. from Cape Corse, of which the English, under Nelson, took possession in 1796.

port fifteen Sail of Vessels; their cargoes of flour were landed whilst we were there; several of them are under Corsican colours, which the French make all the Corsican boats carry, by which means they get free admission into Leghorn, and land corn: all the Genoese vessels are, I understand, also from Leghorn. I send you a Pass very improperly granted by the Sardinian Consul. Yesterday morning three sail of Boats under Corsican colours got into Cabrera: whenever we take them, they are Paoli's friends; when they get away, they are against him.

I had occasion yesterday to send my barge to the Gunboat at the farther end of the Island, passing a small Cove, where a boat was laying; she was fired on, and one of the men severely wounded. This was too much for me to suffer. I took the boats, troops, and Fox Cutter, and went to the Cove, where a number of people were posted behind rocks, (where we could not land,) who fired on us. It was a point of honour to take her; and after attempting in vain to dislodge the people, I boarded the Boat, and brought her out, I am sorry to say with the loss of six men wounded. She was a French Courier-boat from Bastia to Antibes; an Officer with a National cockade in his hat was killed, with several people. I don't think the Genoese troops came to assist them, at least none of their uniform was seen. I am, with great respect, &c.

HORATIO NELSON.

TO MRS. NELSON.

[From Clarke and M'Arthur, vol. i. p. 150.]

At Sea, February 13th, 1794.

I am just going into Leghorn to get water. Corsica I hope will fall in due time: Commodore Linzee has the command of the Sea-business, Lord Hood is in the offing. I have had the pleasure to fulfil the service I had been employed upon, since leaving Tunis, neither allowing provisions nor troops to get into Corsica, nor the Frigates to come out. I am next going to cruise off Bastia, to prevent succours from getting in there. Corsica is a wonderfully fine Island. We are anxious to hear how Parliament likes the War. I am still of opinion it cannot last much longer; not by the French having an absolute Monarchy again, but by our leaving them alone; perhaps the wisest method we can follow. You will remember me in the kindest manner to my Father. God bless you.

HORATIO NELSON.

TO THE REVEREND DIXON HOSTE, GODWICK HALL.

[Autograph, in the possession of Captain Sir William Hoste, Bart.]

Agamemnon, Leghorn, February 14th, 1794.

Dear Sir,

You cannot receive much more pleasure in reading this letter than I have in writing it, to say, that your Son[2] is every-

---

[2] The late Captain Sir William Hoste, Bart., K. C. B., who has been already mentioned, as having commenced his career with Nelson. He obtained Post Rank in January 1802, and after distinguishing himself on numerous occasions in the Amphion of 32 guns in the Adriatic, fought one of the most gallant Actions of the whole War, off Lissa, on the 13th of March 1811, when in command of a Squadron of four Frigates, he defeated a French and Italian Squadron of very superior force, destroyed one, captured two, and compelled another of the Enemy's frigates to surrender. On going into Action, Captain Hoste showed his affectionate remembrance of his immortal Patron by the Signal, " REMEMBER NELSON." He received the Naval Medal, was created a Baronet, and a Knight Commander of the Bath, and a Knight of the Imperial Order of Maria Theresa. Sir William Hoste died in December, 1828, leaving, besides other children, his Son, the present Captain Sir William Hoste, Bart., who has obligingly contributed the above, and other Letters. The following Letter to his late gallant Father, though not from Lord Nelson, is on many accounts too interesting to be omitted. Nelson, in his early Correspondence, frequently mentions *Charles Boyles*, the Son of the Collector of the Customs at Wells, in Norfolk. At the time of the Action off Lissa, *Charles Boyles* had his flag flying as a Rear-Admiral in the Canopus at Palermo; and he thus congratulated his friend and fellow Countryman on his brilliant achievement:

"Canopus, Palermo, April 2nd, [1811.]

"My dear Hoste,

"Nothing can be more grateful to my feelings than congratulating you on this most glorious occasion. Your gallant conduct and distinguished bravery will for ever immortalize your name, and make our County of dumplings and dripping, rejoice to think they have still preserved for its protection a brilliant spark from the shrine of our immortal Countryman, Lord Nelson. May you live long to continue your glorious career, and receive the most honourable rewards of a grateful Country.

"I have transmitted, by Eclair last night, to Cagliari, to intercept the Packet,

A A 2

thing which his dearest friends can wish him to be; and is a strong proof that the greatest gallantry may lie under the most gentle behaviour. Two days ago it was necessary to take a small Vessel from a number of people who had got on shore to prevent us. She was carried in high style, and your good Son was by my side:[3] we had six men badly wounded.

> I am, dear Sir, Your most obedient Servant,
>
> HORATIO NELSON.

I beg you will make my respects to Mr. Coke and to Mrs. Coke.[4]

JOURNAL A.

February 19th.—Landed at L'Avasina, took the Tower of Miomo, and drove the French within gunshot of the walls of Bastia.

TO VICE-ADMIRAL LORD HOOD.

[From Clarke and M'Arthur, vol i. p. 151.]

February 19th, 1794.

I had a good opportunity of looking at Bastia this morning; its means of defence are as follows: On the Town-wall next

copies of your Official Letters, Line of Battle, Lists of the killed and wounded, the Correspondence with the French Officer, and his answer, to the Secretary of the Admiralty, and the Originals of the whole to the Commander-in-Chief. I have likewise privately wrote to Mr. Coke, to give him an opportunity of telling your father and mother of your noble deeds.

"I hope this will find your wounds in a fair way of getting well, and that all those gallant Heroes, the companions of your Battle, are doing well. Pray present to Captains Whitby, Gordon, and Hornby, my warmest congratulations on their heroism so illustriously displayed on the 13th March 1811. May they receive every mark of Public approbation so justly their due, is my most anxious wish. Poor Clephane laments his misfortune in being so far from you, as not to participate in your glory. He is on board his new Ship, and desires to be kindly remembered to you.

"I hope this will find you all at Malta safe.

> "I am, my dear Hoste,
>
> " Your Sincere Friend, and (proud to say) Countryman,
>
> " CHARLES BOYLES."

[3] At Capreja, vide pp. 354 and 365.
[4] Of Holkham.

the sea, about twenty embrasures; to the Southward of the Town, two guns are mounted on a work newly thrown up, and an Officer's guard encamped there; they are also throwing up a small work commanding a large road to the Southward of the Town, which leads towards the mountains. I observed at the back of the Town four stone works, all with guns: two of them appeared strong, the others are stone guard-houses. In the Mole is La Flêche, 20 guns, which came out from Tunis with the other Frigates; she is dismantled, and her guns are put on the outworks.

Yesterday a Flag of Truce, with a Note from General Paoli, came off from a place called Erbalonga, to say they were friends of General Paoli's, and wanted muskets and ammunition. I asked them how long they had been our friends? one of them, who called himself General Paoli's commander of Volunteers on Cape Corse replied, ' Ever since the day you took Maginaggio.' They may be good friends, if it is their interest to be so; but I am rather inclined to believe they will always cry, ' Long live the Conqueror.' However, they are active fellows, and may be of great use, if we land near Bastia.

I had received information at Leghorn, that the cargo of the Ragusan vessel had been landed at l'Avasina. I therefore went on shore this morning,[5] but unluckily the cargo had been carried to Bastia thirteen days ago: had General Paoli's friends given him this information, we might have made a valuable capture. I carefully examined the landing-places near Bastia, and can take upon me to say, that troops and cannon may be landed with great ease to the Southward of the Town at any distance you please, on a level country. If I may be permitted to judge, it would require 1000 troops, besides seamen, Corsicans, &c. to make any successful attempt against Bastia. The Enemy, from all accounts I could learn, have about four hundred Regulars; and altogether 2000 men carrying muskets.

I am, &c.,
HORATIO NELSON.

[5] In his Journal (vide p. 356) Nelson states that on the 19th of February (the date of this Letter) he landed at L'Avisina, took the Tower of Miomo, and drove the French within gun-shot of Bastia. It is remarkable that he did not mention the circumstance in this Dispatch.

TO VICE-ADMIRAL LORD HOOD.

[Autograph, in the possession of Mrs. Conway.]

Agamemnon, February 22nd, 1794, between Cape Corse and Bastia.

My Lord,

I was honoured by your letter of the 19th, yesterday morning, by the Cutter, and beg leave most sincerely to congratulate your Lordship on the taking Fiorenzo.[5] We saw plainly, when evening set in on the 19th, the fire at Fiorenzo, and had no doubts but it was the Frigates on fire. We were close to Bastia. On receiving your letter, I bore away for the Cape, and at 4 P.M. joined Romulus. Captain Sutton had landed the arms, &c., before I got to him at the place he was ordered. I hope my letter sent by the Tartar, and, by Captain Fremantle put on board the Terpsichore, will convey to your Lordship the information you wanted about Bastia. I am now going to take another look at the place, when I shall send this letter. To the northward of the Town, at three miles distance, troops may be safely landed; and a good road for marching all the way to Bastia, but not for heavy artil-

---

[5] St. Fiorenzo was taken on the 17th of February; and the French having retreated to Bastia, Lord Hood proposed to Lieutenant-General Dundas (afterwards General Sir David Dundas, K.B.,) the Commander of the Forces, to reduce it. General Dundas, however, considering the plan impracticable, refused his co-operation without a reinforcement of 2,000 men from Gibraltar. Lord Hood determined to take Bastia with the Naval force only, and gave the command of the Seamen employed in the batteries to Nelson. Clarke and M'Arthur have printed the following remarkable Extract from Lord Hood's Letter to General Dundas respecting the operations against Bastia, dated Victory in Martello Bay, 6th March 1794: "I am honoured with your Letter of yesterday's date, in which you are pleased to say, 'after mature consideration, and a personal inspection for several days of all circumstances, local as well as others, I consider the Siege of Bastia, with our present means and force, to be a most visionary and rash attempt, such as no Officer could be justified in undertaking.' In answer to which, I must take the liberty to observe, that however visionary and rash an attempt to reduce Bastia may be in your opinion, to me it appears very much the reverse, and to be perfectly a right measure; and I beg here to repeat my answer to you, upon your saying, two days ago, that I should be of a different opinion to what I had expressed, were the responsibility upon my shoulders, 'that nothing would be more gratifying to my feelings, than to have the whole responsibility upon me;' and I am now ready and willing to undertake the reduction of Bastia at my own risk, with the force and means at present here, being strongly impressed with the necessity of it."

lery; but probably landing-places may be found to the northward of Bastia, much nearer than three miles. I see the little Camp with two guns, *en barbette,* is intended to prevent landing to the southward, as I dare say the shot will reach to the opening of the Lagoon : but then troops may land under cover of Gun-boats and other small Vessels, although Ships cannot get in. But every defence of Bastia is plainly to be seen from the sea, and in my opinion will soon fall. Yesterday morning, a very large Swedish ship from the Levant, loaded with corn, was within two miles of Bastia. I believe he intended for that Port; but if [he] had not, the boats would have carried her in, but we were between her and the Town. We could not get to his papers, except the common ones, as he is in quarantine. Nothing shall get in, you may be assured.

Saturday evening. I have just had a boat off from Erbalonga : they say that our landing at l'Avasina, and marching so near Bastia, has been of the greatest service to them, as the Enemy intended that night coming with Gun-boats and troops, and burning all the revolted villages. All the Corsicans, to the very walls of Bastia, have now declared for us, and they tell me not much less than 1000 are now under the outworks of Bastia; indeed we have seen the firing of musketry the whole evening.

Sunday noon. It is only just now I have been able to examine Bastia more closely. I find the Enemy every hour are strengthening their works. The two guns mounted *en barbette* are now making a half-moon battery. I passed close with Romulus and Tartar,[6] the Enemy opened their fire from the battery. We directly dislodged them, and they to a man quitted the works. The Town opened on us with shot and shells, but without doing us any damage of consequence : our guns were so exceedingly well pointed, that not one shot was fired in vain; a parcel of powder for one battery blew up, and did apparently considerable damage. Indeed, my Lord, I wish the troops were here : I am sure, in its present state it will soon fall. I don't think the Corsicans have the strong

[6] Romulus, 36, Captain John Sutton, afterwards Vice-Admiral Sir John Sutton, K. C. B. The Tartar, 28, was commanded by Captain, afterwards Vice-Admiral Sir Thomas Francis Fremantle, Bart., G.C.B., G.C.M.G.

post General Paoli mentions, or I think I must have known it. They tell me the garrison of Fiorenzo is got into Bastia.

I am, &c.,

HORATIO NELSON.

JOURNAL B.

February 24th.—The Enemy came out and carried off the guns from the work we fired on yesterday. A Ragusa Ship came out of the Mole, who informed us that our shot had done much damage, and killed several gunners.

February 25th.—Lord Hood, with five Sail in sight, to Leeward. Two Corsican boats came off to tell me our troops were on the hills (believe we see them), and to beg ammunition. Saw the French attack the Corsicans, and carry a village, which they burned to the ground. At half-past noon we being within shot of the Town, they fired on us with both shot and shells: did not return a single gun. Many went over us, and all round us, but not one struck the Ship. The bursting of one shell shook the Ship very much. The Enemy have begun a new work, just to the Southward of the Town. In the afternoon, at four o'clock, bore down to the Enemy's new work, and began to cannonade it, but it falling calm, could not perceive we did the Enemy much harm: hauled off. Being within shot of the Town, they fired on us with both shot and shells: returned the fire, and did good service.

JOURNAL A.

February 24th.[7]—Ran down the Town of Bastia, and cannonaded it for two hours.

February 26th.—Drove the French from a work they were making to the Southward of Bastia.

JOURNAL B.

February 26th.—Joined Lord Hood.

February 27th.—The Fleet blown off in a gale of wind: none but Agamemnon able to keep her Station.

February 28th.—Off Bastia: Lord Hood not in sight.

[7] Nelson seems to have run his pen through this date, and did not insert another.

TO MRS. NELSON.

[From Clark and M'Arthur, vol. i. p. 154.]

Off Bastia, February 28th, 1794.

My dear Fanny,

I write literally to say I am well, never better, and in active service, which I like. Lord Hood expresses himself on every occasion well pleased with my conduct. He is come on this side himself, but would not bring an older Captain than me; therefore the Naval service at Bastia is intrusted to my direction, under his Lordship. I have now six Frigates with me. Our little brush last Sunday, happened at the moment when part of our Army made their appearance on the hills over Bastia, they having marched over-land from St. Fiorenzo, which is only twelve miles distant. The General[8] sent an express to Lord Hood at Fiorenzo to tell him of it. What a noble sight it must have been! indeed, on board it was the grandest thing I ever saw. If I had carried with me five hundred troops, to a certainty I should have stormed the Town, and I believe it might have been carried. Armies go so slow, that Seamen think they never mean to get forward; but I dare say they act on a surer principle, although we seldom fail. You cannot think how pleased Lord Hood has been with my attack on Sunday last, or rather my repelling of an attack which the Enemy made on me. He is gone to Porto Ferrajo for some supplies, but will return in two days. I am to anchor, to have communication with the Army. Bastia is a large Town, and populous, having 10,000 inhabitants; there is a fine Mole for shipping. If we take Corsica, of which I have not the smallest doubt, I hope we shall keep it.

The Natives seem to hate the French, and are a brave people, and free. The attachment of the Corsicans to General Paoli is wonderful. When I took Miomo[9] near Bastia, the Corsicans all declared for the English; and a gentleman came down and said, ' I can now venture to say, how attached I am to Paoli;' upon which, taking a miniature of him from his bosom, he kissed it, and hundreds on their knees immediately

---

[8]　Lieutenant General Dundas.　　　　　　[9]　Vide p. 356.

begged to do the same. This is pure affection. Paoli has
nothing to give them, nor any honours to bestow. It is the
tribute of a generous people to a Chief who has sacrificed everything for their benefit. I hope he will live to see the
Corsicans truly free. It is a fine Island, and well culti-
vated, but the produce has been kept under by numerous
detachments of French soldiers. Their wines interfered with
those of France, and in consequence their exportation was
almost prohibited. Should it belong to us, it would soon be
a rich country; but would materially hurt the Italian
powers.

Yours, &c.

HORATIO NELSON.

TO WILLIAM SUCKLING, ESQ.

[Autograph in the possession of Captain Montagu Montagu, R.N.]

Agamemnon, off Bastia, March 1st, 1794.

My dear Sir,

We are still in the busy scene of war, a situation in which
I own I feel pleasure, more especially as all my actions have
given great satisfaction to my Commander-in-Chief. The
blocking up of Corsica he left to me: it has been accomplished in the most complete manner, not a boat got in, or a
single soldier landed, although eight thousand men were embarked at Nice.

On the 7th of February, Lord Hood took the command off St. Fiorenzo, and I went off Bastia. We have
had active service; four times I have been on shore with
the troops, always successful, and induced all the Corsicans
in this Port to declare for us. The French kept them in great
awe, by quartering troops in every village. On the 23rd
February we went against Bastia merely to reconnoitre: it
turned into a battle, which lasted one hour and three quarters. I had the Romulus and Tartar frigates with me. We
had a strong force against us; but the fire from Agamemnon
was so strong and close, that the Enemy ran from their guns,
and only fired when we were past. We totally destroyed a
battery of six guns just without the town. The Army is

within four miles of Bastia.   As soon as they are ready to
act, I have no doubt Bastia will very soon be taken, although
the Enemy have 62 guns mounted, besides mortars. Your
picture of Bastia is very like, only adding a Citadel.   We did
the Enemy great damage, as we learn from a Dane who
had been with a cargo of corn, but who was glad to get away.
Lord Hood is just arrived,[1] but has not brought an older Captain than myself with him.   I am to anchor and act with the
Army.   Maurice Suckling is not yet made a Lieutenant, but,
I hope, will in time.   Promotion is very slow now Toulon is
lost; and the additional Lieutenants being taken away from
the small Ships, will make it the longer before it comes to
his turn, as they are to be put into Ships as vacancies happen.
I should be glad he was made.   Your letters give me great
pleasure; and I hope, when you feel leisure, you will indulge
me by writing. The French have got three Sail of the Line in
the outer road of Toulon ready for Sea, a proof that all their
stores were not burnt.

I beg you will give my kindest remembrances to Mrs.
Suckling, Miss Suckling, and all your family.   Best respects
to Mr. Rumsey and family, who, I hope, are all well: shall
be very glad to take you all again by the hand.   Believe
me,

Your most affectionate,

HORATIO NELSON.

TO THE REVEREND MR. NELSON, HILBOROUGH.

[Autograph, in the Nelson Papers.]

Agamemnon, March 1st, 1794, off Bastia, in Corsica.

My dear Brother,

As Mrs. Nelson is removed from your neighbourhood, I
know you love to hear a little of what is going forward,
therefore shall send you some extracts of our Journal.   I
feel myself very much obliged by your offer about the farm,
but don't think I shall make prize-money enough to purchase
an estate; and if I do, must look out for a house and grounds

---

[1] See Nelson's Journal, vide p. 366, post.

in some measure ready made. It is too late for me to begin. I
assure you and Mrs. Nelson I feel myself very much obliged by
your attention to my Mrs. Nelson. Where is General White?
I suppose your letter came by him, but I have neither seen
or heard of him; but I must begin my Journal from January 21st. You must judge if we have been active.

January 21st.—Landed sixty troops and sixty seamen
within a very short distance of Fiorenzo with some opposition.
The soldiers stood guard, and the seamen destroyed a large
store of flour for the garrison, and set the mill on fire.
The Enemy sent 1000 men, but our activity had done the
job before their arrival, and they only got a few scattering
shot at us. I was not on shore, but may say it was amazingly well conducted. My merit, if that is any, was seizing
the happy moment. The Enemy lost many men; we had
not a man hurt.

February 5th.—Landed the troops, and anchored two Frigates off the port of Centuri. After a very trifling opposition, took possession of the Town and Harbour. It being
low water, was obliged to burn six Sail, four of them loaded
with wine for the garrison of St. Fiorenzo. Only one man,
belonging to a Frigate, was killed. Received the thanks of the
inhabitants for sparing the Town.

February 6th and 7th.—Lord Hood and the troops arrived,
landing near Mortella Tower. Left the Fleet, being ordered
to block up Bastia.

February 8th.—At eight o'clock anchored with the Tartar,
off the town of Maginaggio: sent a flag of truce on shore to
demand an immediate surrender. Having received a very
insolent answer, viz. ' We are Republicans, that is sufficient.
Go to St. Fiorenzo, to Bastia, or Calvi.—There you will get
such an answer as you desire: the troops which I command,
and which are ready to give you a meeting, are true French
soldiers.'[1] I immediately landed, when this famous Commander
and his troops ran away, and I had the satisfaction of striking
the National Flag with my own hand. We found the Town
full of provisions for Bastia, which we destroyed, and ten Sail
of Vessels. You will recollect our time could be but short.

---

[1] Vide p. 352, ante.

In a few hours, ten times our numbers could be got together to oppose *us ;* therefore we could carry nothing away.

February 9th.—Anchored in Capreia, a Genoese port. The Governor assured me there was no vessel under Republican colours there. Sailed next day.

February 12th.—Saw a small Dispatch-boat get into a Cove in Capreia. Sent the boats to attack her, but they were beat off. Went myself, boarded the vessel, and brought her off. We had six men badly wounded : we killed many of the French, and the Officer commanding her.

February 19th.—Went on shore with sixty troops five miles to the North of Bastia. Marched to within two miles and a half of Bastia, where we took the village and tower of Moimo, the French running away. These successes induced all the Corsicans in this part of Corsica to declare for us, and are now acting against the French. At night saw over the hills the Frigates on fire at Fiorenzo.

On the 21st received Lord Hood's letter, announcing the fall of Fiorenzo. 23rd, wishing to reconnoitre Bastia, and to the Southward of it close, I passed a battery of six guns, which began on us, the ships proceeding as named, Agamemnon, Romulus, Tartar. At the third shot we got the distance so exact, that we very soon drove the French out of the battery, and totally destroyed it, getting within shot of the Town. They began on us with shot and shells, and from the works over the Town. I backed our main top-sail, and passed slowly along the Town. The cannonading lasted one hour and three quarters. We did them great damage, as we see, and by a Dane who immediately came out, we hear they lost a number of men. We suppose they fired on us with twenty-seven guns and four mortars, besides those on the outworks; and although each Ship was struck in the hull, yet not a man was killed or wounded. Our troops were just in sight on the hills, having marched over-land from Fiorenzo, which is only twelve miles distant. General Dundas sent an express to Lord Hood to give him an account of it. It must have been a fine sight from the hills. On the 25th, getting too near in a calm, they fired on me with shot and shells, some of which burst very near us, so as to shake Agamemnon. Our troops are not yet got to work. I can't think what they are after. Give my kindest remembrances to Mrs. Nelson

and my Aunt, and your children, and compliments at Swaffham.   Believe me,

Your most affectionate Brother,

HORATIO NELSON.

Write to me, and direct to the care of John Udney, Esq.,
his Britannic Majesty's Consul at Leghorn: some postage
must be paid, but don't know how much.

JOURNAL B.

March 1st.—Off Bastia.

March 2nd.—Lord Hood in sight.

March 3rd.—Lord Hood made my Signal, and acquainted
me of the retreat of our Troops from the Heights, and of
their return to St. Fiorenzo.   Saw General Dundas's letter to
Lord Hood,[1] as also Paoli's.   What the General could have
seen to have made a retreat necessary, I cannot conceive.
The Enemy's force is 1,000 Regulars, and 1,000 or 1,500
Irregulars.   I wish not to be thought arrogant, or pre-
sumptuously sure of my own judgment, but it is my firm
opinion that the Agamemnon with only the Frigates now here,
lying against the Town for a few hours with 500 troops
ready to land, when we had battered down the Sea-wall, would
to a certainty carry the place.   I presumed to propose it to
Lord Hood, and his Lordship agreed with me; but that he
should go to Fiorenzo, and hear what the General had to
say, and that it would not be proper to risk having our
Ships crippled without a co-operation of the Army, which
consists of 1,600 Regulars, and 180 Artillery-men, all in good
health, and as good troops as ever marched.   We now know,
from three Ragusa Ships and one Dane, that our cannonade
on Sunday, the 23rd February, threw the Town into the
greatest consternation; that it almost produced an insurrec-
tion; that La Combe St. Michel, the Commissioner from
the Convention, was obliged to hide himself, for had he been
found and massacred, to a certainty the Town would have
been surrendered to me.   But St. Michel having declared
he would blow up the Citadel with himself was the only thing
which prevented a boat coming off to us with offers.   A magazine

[1] Vide p. 358.

blew up, and the people believe we fired nothing but hot
shot. The French shot were all hot; that by our cannonade
on Tuesday afternoon, the 25th February, the Camp was so
much annoyed that the French run, and in the Town they
so fully expected I should land, that St. Michel sent orders
for the La Fleche to be burnt, but it falling calm, I could
not lay near enough the Town to do good service. Many
people were killed and wounded, and the Master of the
Ragusa, who has been on board me, had a piece shot out
of his leg, and the man next him killed. I lament that
several women were killed, and a most beautiful girl of seventeen. Such are the horrors of war. My Ship's company
behaved most amazingly well. They begin to look upon
themselves as invincible, almost invulnerable : believe they
would fight a good battle with any Ship of two decks out of
France. Lord Hood offered me the Courageux 74, but I
declined it : shall stay by Agamemnon.

March 4th.—Close off Bastia. Romney joined.

TO MRS. NELSON.

[From Clarke and M'Arthur, vol. i. p. 155.]

Agamemnon, March 4th, 1794.

My dear Fanny,

You will be surprised to hear that the English General,
Dundas,[2] has retired from before Bastia without making an
attack. God knows what it all means. Lord Hood is gone
to St. Fiorenzo to the Army, to get them forward again. A
thousand men would to a certainty take Bastia: with five
hundred, and Agamemnon, I would attempt it. Lord Hood
said publicly, that if he thought it proper to give me
three Sail of the Line, and 500 men, he was sure I should
take the Town, although probably not the heights; but he
would not sacrifice his seamen and Ships in doing, what the
finest Army of its size that ever marched could, and wish to
do. General Paoli has told them, that if they don't keep my
force low, I shall take Bastia, before they pitch their tents
in St. Fiorenzo: however, these are only civil speeches.

---

[2] Vide p. 358, ante.

S

But we now know that I was very near getting possession on Sunday the 23rd. If I had force to go again and cannonade it, I believe I should yet get it. My seamen are now what British seamen ought to be, to you I may say it, almost invincible : they really mind shot no more than peas.

Yours, &c.

HORATIO NELSON.

TO VICE-ADMIRAL LORD HOOD.

[From a Copy in the Nelson Papers.]

Agamemnon, off Bastia, March 5th, 1794.

My Lord,

If your Lordship pleases to send me some Gun-boats I think they may be very useful this fine weather in harassing the Enemy.

By a Ragusa vessel come out since your Lordship's departure, I learn that the Enemy are in the greatest apprehension of our landing near the Town, which, in my opinion, would fall on the first vigorous attack. That the works on the hills would annoy the Town afterwards is certain, but the Enemy being cut off from all supplies (the provisions in the Town being of course in our possession) would think of nothing but making the best terms they could for themselves. The Enemy are now at work on the hill near Cardo, and are also beginning a work on a hill above it, and have made a road to the top of the mountains.

La Combe St. Michel[3] ordered the La Flêche to be got ready for burning on Tuesday the 25th. This Master was wounded, a piece being shot out of his leg.[4] He tells me that the inhabitants are in the greatest dread of being given up to the Corsicans. Some good use may possibly be made of this terror. I shall take care and keep rather to the Southward of Bastia, as your Lordship recommends. Your letter to Monsieur de Frediani[5] I landed yesterday. He wrote me he had something to communicate, and wished me to send a con-

---

[3] The French Commander, vide p. 366.

[4] Vide p. 367.

[5] J. de Frediani, Governor of the province of Balagne in Corsica.

fidential Officer, which I have done. He has not yet returned. Captain Clarke[5] of the 69th Regiment, having the charge of the Regimental accounts, has asked my leave to go to Fiorenzo, which I have permitted. He is the Officer I mentioned to your Lordship, and will be the bearer of this letter. The Enemy have just begun a battery in the Town, just to the Northward of the Mole, at the place I conceived our troops might have landed. The Romney has joined me. I hope very soon to see your Lordship and the troops, and that Bastia will be in our possession.

I am your Lordship's most faithful,
HORATIO NELSON.

TO VICE-ADMIRAL LORD HOOD.

[Autograph, in the Hood Papers.]

Agamemnon, off Bastia, March 6th, 1794.
4 P.M.

My Lord,

The Vanneau has just joined; and I have ordered Captain Paget[6] to proceed to St. Fiorenzo. I have just received a letter from Mons. J. de Frediani, to say, that their Camp will be lost, unless I can either destroy a battery which the Enemy made yesterday on the North of the Town, or land two eighteen-pounders, with men, ammunition, &c. I shall do either one or the other, or both, if possible. Bastia will be lost, if we are not active. I trust you will approve of my intentions: I see the necessity of something being done directly.

The Ragusa which I took on Tuesday morning has, I suspected, and have just received accounts, money and other valuable effects on board, besides a cargo of cotton, dyes, &c. I am anxious to see our troops over the Hill.

Believe me,
Your most faithful,
HORATIO NELSON.

---

[5] Captain-Lieutenant John Clarke of the 69th Regiment, who was severely wounded on the 12th of April. Vide p. 383.

[6] In the Romney.

JOURNAL B.

March 5th.—Close off Bastia.

March 6th.—Close off Bastia; the Enemy adding strong posts for the defence of the place. At this moment Bastia is stronger than when our troops retired from it; how that has hurt me. Received a letter from M. de Frediani, to request an interview, provisions, powder, shot, flints, and, if possible, two cannon. Sent an Officer overland to Lord Hood, with my opinion that it was yet possible to take Bastia with 500 Regulars and two or three Ships. Received a letter from Lord Hood, to say he would send me two Gun-boats, according to my desire. When I get them, the inhabitants of Bastia sleep no more. Sent the Romney to Lord Hood.

March 7th.—Close off Bastia.

March 8th.—Close off Bastia.

March 9th.—Went on shore to Erbalonga, and from thence to the Corsican camp; had a good view of all the Enemy's posts and the Town. I am yet of opinion that Bastia may be taken by our troops, although it is certainly stronger than when our troops retired, and every day adds strength to the place.

March 10th.—Got to my Ship.

March 11th.—Romney joined me from Lord Hood: brought me letters to say that General Dundas was going Home, and that he hoped and trusted the troops would once more move over the Hill. Sent the Rose Cutter to lay off Caprera for a day or two.

TO VICE-ADMIRAL LORD HOOD.

[From Clarke and M'Arthur, vol. i. p. 156.]

Agamemnon, March 11th, 1794.

My Lord,

You may be assured I shall undertake nothing, but what I have moral certainty of succeeding in: had this day been fine, it was my intention to have towed the Agamemnon in-shore, and to have destroyed the house which the Enemy has

fortified for musketry, and also the new battery which is
nearly finished: I think we should have been out of the
range of shot from the Town. When the Gun-boats arrive,
they may perhaps do it better; certainly with less risk than
ourselves. It must be destroyed, or the Corsicans will be
obliged to give up a post which the Enemy would immediately possess; and of course throw us on that side at a
greater distance from Bastia. I hope our troops will soon
join. If the Corsicans can, without them, keep the Enemy
from quitting their posts, and advancing into the Country,
what may we not expect when ours act with them? The
poor Corsicans know nothing, but how to fire a musket; yet
certainly a good use may be made of them. Bastia may be
easily bombarded from the North side, as also Fort St. Croix
which is the post commanding Bastia.

I am, &c.

HORATIO NELSON.

JOURNAL B.

March 12th.—Off Erbalonga, five miles from Bastia, getting off a little water. We are absolutely without water,
provisions, or stores of any kind, not a piece of canvas, rope,
twine, or a nail in the Ship; but we cheerfully submit to it
all, if it but turns out for the advantage and credit of our
Country.

March 13th.—Blowing strong the whole day: the Vigilant
Gun-boat joined me.

March 14th.—A strong gale all day with thick weather:
with difficulty cleared the shore towards Cape Corse.

March 15th.—More moderate: got up with Cape Corse.

March 16th.—Got off Bastia. Found that one small boat
with fifty-six sacks of corn had got in; that the inhabitants
are in the greatest distress for provisions, a small loaf selling
for three livres. The Petite Victoire having started a plank
was obliged to run on shore, and is hauled up; the Vigilant
and Fortunée Gun-boats not joined. The Romney, Tartar,
Vanneau, Fox, and Rose, with me. Sent off an express
to Lord Hood to tell him we have nothing to eat.

B B 2

TO VICE-ADMIRAL LORD HOOD.

[Autograph, in the Hood Papers.]

Agamemnon, off Bastia, 16th March, 1794.

My Lord,

The gale of the 14th came on at East, backing to the N.E.
which obliged me to carry a press of sail to clear the shore
towards Cape Corse; and so thick as to prevent our seeing
a Ship's length.

I send this over-land, and shall thank your Lordship to signify your wishes by the bearer of my letter. We are really
without firing, wine, beef, pork, flour, and almost without
water: not a rope, canvas, twine, or nail in the Ship.
The Ship is so light, she cannot hold her side to the
wind: yet if your Lordship thinks or wishes me to remain
off Bastia, I can, by going to Porto Ferrajo, get water and
stores, and twenty-four hours at Leghorn will give us provisions; and our refitting, which will take some time, can
be put off a little. My wish is to be present at the attack
of Bastia; and if your Lordship intends me to command the
Seamen who may be landed, I assure you I shall have
the greatest pleasure in doing it, or any other service where
you may think I can do most good: even if my Ship goes
into Port to refit, I am ready to remain. We are certainly
in a bad plight at present, not a man has slept dry for many
months. The two Gun-boats joined me in the gale. I hope
all my small Vessels are safe.

Believe me, your most faithful

HORATIO NELSON.

Romney ⎱
Tartar ⎰ With me.
Fox ⎰

Vanneau ⎱ In sight, off Cape Corse.
Rose ⎰

Petite Victoire—Hauled on Shore at Erbalonga.

Vigilant ⎱
Fortunée ⎰ Missing.

JOURNAL B.

March 17th.—Lieutenant Duncan,[7] of the Artillery, and a Mr. De Butts,[8] Engineer, came over to examine the ground I had thought eligible for erecting batteries to bombard the Citadel.

March 18th.—Went on shore with Mr. D. and Mr. D. to examine the ground. They both thought it an eligible situation for erecting a mortar battery: found a most convenient place for landing cannon and stores. At noon the Officers returned to St. Fiorenzo. At 4 P.M. received a letter from Lord Hood, desiring me to come to Fiorenzo; left the command with Captain Paget.

TO VICE-ADMIRAL LORD HOOD.

[Autograph, in the possession of Mrs. Conway.]

Agamemnon, off Bastia, 18th March, 1794.

My Lord,

Lieutenant Duncan and Mr. de Butts arrived on board me last night: this morning early I went on shore with them, and am sure their report will much please you. Bastia to the north is certainly not a place of strength: guns may be landed for less than one mile from where the battery will be erected, and I am sure with ease can be in the battery in twenty-four hours at farthest. I have never understood the force in Bastia to be more than 800 or 1,000 Regulars, and 1.200 or 1,500 Irregulars, Corsicans: ours are much better than those with the Enemy, who they do not trust, knowing their wish to desert. One Boat with 56 sacks of Corn got in the morning of the 16th. Bread is very scarce in Bastia— a small loaf selling for three livres. With fine weather, if it is necessary, I am certain we could starve Bastia. I am sure my hearty endeavours shall not be wanting to get it some way

---

[7] John Duncan, First Lieutenant of the Royal Artillery, who is frequently mentioned. He was promoted to a Company for his services during the Siege, and was spoken of in the most flattering terms in Lord Hood's Despatches announcing the surrender of Bastia and Calvi, as well as in those of General Stuart, on the latter occasion. He was made a Lieutenant-Colonel in October 1798: on the 30th December 1800, he was appointed Deputy Quarter-Master-General to the Forces under General Sir Ralph Abercrombie, and died in 1803.

[8] Now Lieutenant-General Sir Augustus De Butts, K.C.H.

or other ; for I consider, pardon the expression, it would be a National disgrace to give it up, without a trial. The Jean Bart and Swallow have this moment joined me: the St. Croix is in sight ; I shall return her this evening. The Petite Victoire was forced to take the shore in the late gale. : she is so much damaged that my Carpenter reports her unfit to be repaired. It was, I dare say, no fault of the officer command- ing her, for indeed it blew strong. I have taken the liberty of accepting your kind offer of sending letters. I now constantly keep a Ship off Caprera, joining me every twenty-four hours. I have just got your letter, by St. Croix, and am making the best of my way to Fiorenzo, where I hope twenty-four hours will fit me for sea again ; I am truly anxious to get off Bastia again. I have given Captain Paget all the necessary orders.

I am, &c.

HORATIO NELSON.

TO WILLIAM SUCKLING, ESQ.

[Autograph, in the possession of Captain Montagu Montagu, R.N.]

Agamemnon, off Bastia, March 18th, 1794.

My dear Sir,

I shall begin by saying what has given me pleasure, and I am sure will you, that Lord Hood has made Suckling a Lieutenant: I trust he will be confirmed.

We are still blocking up Bastia, the attack of which has been given up in a most extraordinary manner ; [I will make] what might, if it had not now met the sanction of men of science, have been deemed a most impertinent observation, viz. that Bastia, from a place I had found on a much closer examina- tion than our General Dundas, could be attacked to great advantage. I wrote Lord Hood requesting an Engineer and Artillery Officer might be sent to examine. To-day I have been with them, and their report is most favourable for an attack. Our weather is now but indifferent ; but hitherto I have so close blocked up the place, that one pound of coarse bread sells for three livres. If the Army will not take it, we must, by some way or other. General Dundas has quitted the command,[9] differing in opinion with Lord Hood.

---

[9] He was succeeded by Brigadier General Abraham D'Aubant, who was pro- moted to the rank of Lieutenant-General, and Colonel Commandant in the Royal Engineers, in 1802.

I have really nothing new to tell you: day after day we remain in the same state. Pray remember me to Mrs. Suckling, and kindly to Miss Suckling and all your family; and don't forget me to Mr. Rumsey and family. Believe me

Your most affectionate

HORATIO NELSON.

JOURNAL B.

March 19th.—At 8 A.M. got into Fiorenzo. Gave Lord Hood my free opinion that 800 troops, with 400 seamen, would take Bastia, and that not attacking it I could not but consider as a National disgrace. Found all the Army against an attack, and declaring the impossibility of taking Bastia, even if all the force was united. Getting water, provisions, and stores on board.

March 20th, 21st, 22nd, 23rd, 24th.—Ditto employed. The General absolutely refused to attack Bastia; but, wonderful to tell, he refused Lord Hood a single soldier, cannon, or stores, to assist in the Siege.

March 25th.—Sailed from St. Fiorenzo with Lieutenant Duncan, R.A.

TO THE REVEREND MR. NELSON, HILBOROUGH.

[Autograph, in the Nelson Papers.]

Agamemnon, off Bastia, March 26th, 1794.

My dear Brother,

Our General D'Aubant, with 2,000 as fine troops as ever marched, has thought it improper to attack Bastia, which has only 800 Frenchmen to defend it, and that as to taking it, that is impossible. As I had examined the ground, perhaps more than the General, Sir James Erskine St. Clair,[1] Major Koehler,[2] Colonel Moore,[3] or any other, I ventured to give my opinion very freely to Lord Hood, and that not to

[1] Then Adjutant-General to the Forces and a Lieutenant-Colonel; afterwards General Earl of Rosslyn, G.C.B.: he died in January 1837.

[2] Major George Frederick Koehler of the Artillery: he obtained the rank of Colonel in January 1800, and appears to have been the General Koehler who was sent to discipline the Turkish Army, and who died of the plague in Syria in 1801.

[3] Afterwards Lieutenant-General Sir John Moore, K.B., who fell at the Battle of Corunna in 1809.

attack our Enemy I should consider as a National disgrace. An Artillery Officer of great merit, Lieutenant Duncan, I requested his Lordship would ask the General to permit to come to me. He came with Mr. De Butts, a young Engineer. They agreed with me in opinion the place might be attacked, probably with success. Lord Hood sent for me to Fiorenzo to concert measures. The General has refused us a single soldier, and scarcely any stores. We have only about 700 men to land, troops who are embarked to serve as Marines, whilst the General has 1,300 Troops and Artillery, &c., to defend St. Fiorenzo.

I am to command the Seamen landed from the Fleet. I feel for the honour of my Country, and had rather be beat than not make the attack. If we do not try we never can be successful. I own I have no fears for the final issue: it will be conquest, certain we will deserve it. You will naturally be anxious about me. My reputation depends on the opinion I have given; but I feel an honest consciousness that I have done right. I am just sending a Ship to Naples, for mortars, shells, &c. We propose making on one point our attack with six mortars of thirteen-inch, and ten 24 pounders from my lower-deck to be landed. We must, we will have it, or some of our heads will be laid low. I glory in the attempt. I have not heard from you this age. Why don't you write? Pray remember me to my Brother at Burnham, and kindly to Mrs. Nelson, my Aunt, and the Children. Compliments at Swaffham. Believe me ever

Your most affectionate brother,

HORATIO NELSON.

TO THE HONOURABLE WILLIAM PAGET,[4] CAPTAIN OF H. M. SHIP ROMNEY.

[From a Copy, in the Nelson Papers.]

Agamemnon, off Bastia, March 27th, 1794.

Sir,

You will herewith receive two letters for His Excellency

---

[4] Younger brother of the present Marquis of Anglesea. On the 17th of June 1794, the Romney captured La Sybille of 46 guns, after a severe action. Captain Paget died soon after off Minorca: "he was a young officer of infinite merit in his profession, beloved and esteemed by all who knew him, and a public loss to his country."—*Naval Chronology*, vol. ii. p. 294.

Sir William Hamilton, his Majesty's Minister to the Court of
Naples, containing a request for mortars, shells, and Artillery-
stores, from the King of Naples. You will also receive on
board Lieutenant Duncan of the Royal Artillery, who is sent
to see that all the necessary stores are embarked; and as his
service is of the greatest importance, the Commander-in-Chief,
placing the highest confidence in your zeal and activity, has
directed me to send the Romney to Naples. On this [service]
I am sure it is unnecessary for me to acquaint you, that the
taking of Bastia may probably depend upon your expedition.
It is possible the mortars may be shipped on board a Neapolitan
Ship-of-War with shells, &c, : even should that be the case you
will take the proper measures to have them removed to the
Romney, unless you should meet her on her passage, when
you will desire her to join me off Bastia, proceeding yourself
to Naples, for the other stores. I hope that a very short time
will be sufficient to embark everything. If Craft are not lent
you to bring off the stores, &c., I desire that you will hire
what is necessary, and consider that expedition is to us invaluable. Having received the mortars, shells, stores, &c., you
will join me off Bastia. I am, Sir, &c.

HORATIO NELSON.

TO SIR WILLIAM HAMILTON, K.B., MINISTER AT NAPLES.

[Autograph draught, in the Nelson Papers.]

Agamemnon, off Bastia, March 27th, 1794.

My dear Sir,

Lord Hood having determined on attacking Bastia (contrary to the opinion of General D'Aubant,) from the reports of
Officers in whom his Lordship is pleased to place confidence,
he becomes in want of many things which I am rather
inclined to believe could have been supplied from the stores
at St. Fiorenzo.

As to the final issue of taking Bastia I have no doubt, although only with a small proportion of the Troops which were
at Fiorenzo, (those who are embarked to serve as Marines,) the
General thinking it right not to grant his Lordship a single
Soldier, and only a few Artillery-men. The General declares
the impropriety of even attacking Bastia, and that as to the
conquest it is impossible. But, my dear Sir, when was a

place ever yet taken without an attempt?[5] We must endeavour to deserve success; it is certainly not in our power to
command it.   Colonel Villettes[6] of the 69th regiment will
command the Troops.[7]   I shall certainly always be happy
to pay my respects to you, but if we are successful I shall
feel the greatest pleasure an Officer can, in taking you
by the hand at Naples, where my Ship has been ordered to
go to refit; but I own I cannot bear the thought of showing
myself in a Foreign port without its being known that the
British flag is respectable.[8]   I am just come from Lord
Hood at Fiorenzo.   His zeal, his activity for the honour and
benefit of his King and Country are not abated.   Upwards
of seventy, he possesses the mind of forty years of age.
He has not a thought separated from Honour and Glory.
May each opposer of such a Character have for their ac-
cusers their own minds.   I am sure that will be all sufficient.

My dear Sir, when was before the time that 2,000 British
troops, as good as ever marched, were not thought equal to
attack 800 French troops, allowing them to be in strong
works?   What would the immortal Wolfe have done? as he
did, beat the Enemy, if he perished in the attempt.   Our
Irregulars are surely as good as the Enemy's; and in numbers
we far exceed them.   I truly feel sorrow, but I have hope and
confidence that all will end well.   I beg leave to introduce Lieutenant Duncan to your notice.   He is by character an Officer

[5] Nelson originally wrote, " But, my dear Sir, we are to try; a place was
never yet taken," &c.

[6] He wrote here, but deleted, " I am to command the Seamen landed."

[7] Lieutenant-Colonel, afterwards Lieutenant-General, William Anne Villettes of the 69th Regiment, whom Lord Hood appointed Governor of Bastia on
its surrender.   He became an intimate friend of Nelson, and many Letters to
him will be found in this work.   The Troops which served at the Siege of
Bastia consisted of detachments of the 11th, 25th, 30th, and 69th Regiments,
which had done duty as Marines in the Ships under Lord Hood's command.
They had been landed with the Army, but when General Dundas obstinately determined not to co-operate with the Navy against Bastia, Lord Hood demanded
their return to the Ships.   Having received those Troops, together with two
Officers and thirty men of the Artillery, with some ordnance stores, and en-
trenching tools, the Siege of Bastia was undertaken and successfully completed
by the Officers and Seamen of the Fleet, while a large body of Troops were
allowed to remain wholly inactive at St. Fiorenzo, only six miles distant!
Nelson's indignation at the conduct of the General commanding the Forces is
expressed with his usual ardour in many of his Letters.

[8] The original word was " triumphant."

of great merit, and from the little acquaintance I have with him seems an amiable young man. His request for Artillery-stores is absolutely necessary; and I am sure your Excellency's zeal for the service of our dear Country will induce you to press for expedition.

I beg leave to present my most respectful compliments to Lady Hamilton, as does also my youngster. I assure you and her Ladyship that I remember with gratitude both your kindnesses to a stranger. Sir John Acton, being an Englishman, if he remember such an humble individual as myself, and it is not incompatible with your Excellency's situation, I beg to present my respects.

Believe me, my dear Sir,
Your most obliged,
HORATIO NELSON.

JOURNAL B.

March 27th.—At daylight got off Bastia. Sent the Romney to Naples for mortars, shells, field-pieces, and stores. Anchored the Tartar four miles to the Southward of Bastia, and the Scout off the tower of Miomo, three miles to the Northward of Bastia.

March 28th, 29th, 30th, 31st. — Close off Bastia; our boats rowing guard off the Mole and Town every night. Sent the Gun-boats to cannonade the town.

April 1st.—

TO COMMODORE LINZEE, ALCIDE.

[Autograph, in the possession of Page Nicol Scott, Esq., of Norwich.]

[Bastia, end of March or beginning of April, 1794.]

My dear Sir,

If you will order the Agamemnon to be supplied with two hundred fathoms of three and a half inch rope, and one hundred fathoms of two-inch rope, purchases will be rove to drag the guns. We have not a fathom of rope in the Ship. If you can spare us two three-fold blocks, and two two-fold blocks, I shall be much obliged. Believe me, dear Sir,

Yours most faithfully,
HORATIO NELSON.

TO CAPTAIN HANWELL.[8]

[From " Marshall's Naval Biography," vol. i. p. 542.]

Sir,   2nd April, 1794.

Lord Hood desires that you will move the Scout directly,
and anchor her as near the Tower which the Corsicans took
last night, as possible. I think you may anchor nearer Bastia
than the Tower we landed at yesterday: it is of the greatest
consequence maintaining the post taken by the Corsicans,
therefore I trust long before daylight you will be anchored
there. Believe me,

Yours truly,

HORATIO NELSON.

JOURNAL A.

April 3rd.—Landed for the siege of Bastia.

JOURNAL C.

On April 4th, 1794, at ten A. M. the Troops, consisting of
artillery and gunners 66; of the eleventh Regiment 257; of
the twenty-fifth 123; of the thirtieth 146; of the sixty-ninth
261; of the Marines 218; and of Chasseurs 112; total 1183,
and 250 Seamen, landed at the tower of Miomo, three miles
to the Northward of Bastia, under the command of Lieutenant-Colonel Villettes, and Captain Horatio Nelson, who
had under him Captains Hunt, Serocold, and Bullen. At
noon the Troops encamped about 2,500 yards from the citadel
of Bastia, near a high rock. The Seamen and Carpenters
were all night employed in cutting down trees to form an
abbatis, and also to clear the ground towards the tower of
Torga, whence the access to our Camp was by no means
difficult. A Captain's picket was always mounted at Torga,
with the sentry about a hundred yards in front of it.

---

[8] Captain Joseph Hanwell, who then commanded the Scout sloop, died an
Admiral.

TO MRS. NELSON.

[From Clarke and M'Arthur, vol. i. p. 161.]

April 6th and 16th, 1794.

We are in high health and spirits besieging Bastia; the final event, I feel assured, will be conquest. Lord Hood is at anchor near the Town, and our troops are active. Our batteries opened on the 11th, and apparently have done great execution. Time, I hope, indeed have no doubt, will crown our zealous endeavours with success. We are but few, but of the right sort: our General at St. Fiorenzo not giving us one of the five Regiments he has there lying idle.

Yours, &c.,

HORATIO NELSON.

TO WILLIAM SUCKLING, ESQ., CUSTOM-HOUSE, LONDON.

[Autograph, which was given to the Royal Navy Club, in Bond-street, by Captain Montagu Montagu, R.N. It was printed in "The Athenæum."]

Camp, near Bastia, April 6th, 1794.

My dear Sir,

Not knowing where Mrs. Nelson is, I shall trouble you to send my letter. You see by my date where we are, and hope in due time we shall be in Bastia. Our Army is still at Fiorenzo, nor can the General be induced to move. Colonel Villettes commands the Troops and Marines landed from the Fleet. What my situation is, is not to be described. I am everything, yet nothing ostensible; enjoying the confidence of Lord Hood and Colonel Villettes, and the Captains landed with the Seamen obeying my orders. We have been landed two days complete; are within 700 yards of the outworks, and 1,800 of the Citadel. Our battery will open in about two days, of eight twenty-four pounders and eight mortars. I have little doubt of our success; and if we do, what a disgrace to the Fiorenzo wise-heads:—if we do not, it can only be owing to their neglect in not attacking the place with us. Lord Hood has only just sent to tell me of the opportunity for England. Pray remember me to Mrs. Suckling, Miss

Suckling, and family, Mr. Rumsey, and all friends; and believe me,

Your most affectionate

HORATIO NELSON.

JOURNAL C.

From April 4th to the 10th, all the Seamen were employed in making batteries and roads, and in getting up guns, mortars, platforms, and ammunition; works of great labour for so small a number of men, but which was performed with an activity and zeal seldom exceeded. On the 9th, about eleven o'clock at night, the Enemy opened a very heavy fire upon our Camp, from their mortars and guns. The alarm was beat, and Captain Nelson fully expected an attack. This firing lasted until daylight; and yet, what was extraordinary, not a single man was hurt. The tents were much damaged; but from the troops being under arms, they escaped.

Lord Hood sent in a Flag of Truce on the 11th at seven o'clock in the morning, in one of the Victory's boats. The Officer on his landing was grossly abused, until the arrival of La Combe St. Michel, the Commissioner from the Convention, when the mob became quiet. Having offered his letters to St. Michel, our Officer was informed by the Commissioner, that he could not receive Lord Hood's summons: 'I have hot shot,' he exclaimed, 'for your Ships, and 'bayonets for your Troops. When two-thirds of our Troops 'are killed, I will then trust to the generosity of the Eng-'lish.' On the Officer's return with this message, Lord Hood hoisted a red flag at the main-top-gallant-mast head of the Victory; when our batteries opened on the Town, citadel, and redoubt of Camponella, English colours having been hoisted on the rock over my tent, and every man giving three cheers. In our batteries were two thirteen and two ten-inch mortars, one eight-inch howitzer, five twenty-four pounders, two eighteen-pounders, carronades, three twelve-pounders, one four-pounder field-piece, distant from the redoubt of Camponella 800 yards, from the Town battery 1800 yards, and from the centre of the Citadel 2300 yards. The Enemy returned a heavy fire during the whole day. The Proselyte frigate anchored off the tower of Torga, about 1200 yards from the Town battery. Captain Serocold informed me that she took fire from red-hot shot, and that as he found the impossibility of getting the Ship off the shore, he thought it right to set her on fire in several places, and she burnt to the water's edge.

April 12th. A heavy fire was kept up by us during the whole of last night and this day, apparently with good effect; the Enemy preserving a continued fire upon us. In the afternoon I went with Colonel Villettes, Lieutenant Duncan, R.A., and Captain Clarke, Brigade-Major, with a Corsican guide, to examine a ridge about one thousand yards nearer the Town than our present position, and on which the Corsicans kept a strong guard every night. The Enemy's continued fire of musketry and grape was poured on us during the whole evening. Unfortunately, the last shot they fired from Camponella killed the Corsican guide, who was standing behind Clarke, and shot off his right arm and a part of his right side: Clarke was looking over my shoulder at Camponella, whence we were distant about two hundred and fifty yards.

We began on the 13th of April a battery for three twenty-four pounders close to the Torga tower, which stands on the sea-side, 1230 yards from the Town battery, and 1600 from the Citadel; and, a little in the rear, a battery for two twenty-four pounders, a mortar battery for one fourteen-inch Neapolitan mortar, and for the two ten-inch mortars which are to be removed from the upper battery. We were employed in getting up the guns, mortars, shells, shot, powder, and platforms, and in making the batteries, until the 21st; as also a breast-work to cover a hundred men in case of an attack.

TO THOMAS POLLARD, ESQ., LEGHORN.

[Autograph, in the possession of John Luxford, Esq.]

Camp, April 17th, 1794.

Dear Sir,

I have to thank you for your remembrance of me: we want many good things; some porter, either a cask or bottled. I hope soon to have the pleasure of writing you from Bastia. You will be sorry for poor Clarke; but I have hopes he will live. Believe me,

Your obliged,
HORATIO NELSON.

Pray put my letter in the Post-office.

***

JOURNAL C.

The Torga battery opened on the 21st of April at daylight on the Town battery and Camponella, and apparently with good effect. The Enemy kept up a most heavy fire on us the whole day, with shells and shot, from the citadel, Town, Stafforella, Camponella, a square tower, and the two batteries newly raised under Stafforella. Brigadier-General D'Aubant came on the heights from St. Fiorenzo, with all the Staff and Field Officers of that Army, and a guard of fifty Corsicans.

The next day, the 22nd of April, the Enemy were hard at work on the heights, strengthening all their posts; the natural consequence of the parade of reconnoitering yesterday. A constant firing is kept up night and day. We are informed by several deserters, that our batteries have done great damage, and killed and wounded many of the Enemy. Our guns have twice totally demolished the Town-battery, and very much damaged Camponella, but from our not having a sufficient number of men to take advantage of this, the Enemy are enabled to repair them, and indeed make them stronger than ever. During this, and the succeeding night, our Corsicans made two false attacks on the upper posts, and those to the Southward, which must have harassed the Enemy considerably.

TO MRS. NELSON.

[From Clarke and M'Arthur, vol. i. p. 162.]

April 22nd, 1794.

I have great reason, my dearest Fanny, to be thankful to that Being, who has ever protected me in a most wonderful manner, and in none more than since my landing here.　If it is His good pleasure, I shall in nothing more rejoice, than in being once more with you; when we will talk over all these stories, and laugh at them.　We are here with a force not equal to our wishes or wants, and with only half of what is at present in this Island.　General D'Aubant will not attack our Enemy, with two thousand as fine troops as ever marched, whilst we are here beating them from post to post with one thousand. . . . .

The Island, however, is to belong to England; reinforcements are expected, and our Generals will, I am sure, be ordered to act.　My Ship lies on the North side of the town, with some Frigates, and Lord Hood is on the South side.　It is very hard service for my poor seamen, dragging guns up such heights as are scarcely credible.　The loss of the Enemy, we know, has been very great; report states it as much as five hundred killed and wounded, ours is not more than twenty.　The Agamemnon has to number five amongst them : they are not the men to keep out of the way.

Yours, &c.

HORATIO NELSON.

TO ADMIRAL LORD HOOD.[9]

[Autograph draught, in the Nelson Papers.　The preceding part of this Letter has not been found.]

*　　　*　　　*　　　*　　　*　　　*

may be of the greatest service to us, but I am sure the Colonel[1] will thank your Lordship for your information and

---

[9] Lord Hood was promoted from Vice-Admiral of the Red to be an Admiral of the Blue, on the 11th of April 1794; and changed his Flag accordingly on the 16th of May.

[1] Villettes.

be doubly on his guard against a surprise: besides, our *abatis* is already made. I have all my carpenters ready at dark to cut down more trees, and the piquet to-night is under the command of Major Smith, who is said to be a very good Officer. The Enemy are mistaken as to the impossibility of our troops getting down. In ten minutes at farthest, I am sure they would be at the bridge from the alarm-posts. I shall communicate your Lordship's letter to Colonel Villettes, and am sure he will take every precaution to prevent a surprise. I shall also communicate your ideas about Monserrat. Colonel Villettes intends writing your Lordship on his return from the heights.

H. N.

TO ADMIRAL LORD HOOD.

[Autograph draught, in the Nelson Papers.]

April 24th, 1794.

My Lord,

During the whole of yesterday no accident happened to any person here; and although I have no doubt but even remaining in our present situation, and by strict guard rowing close to the Town, and the Corsicans harassing them on the hills, and the Gun-boats by night, but that the Enemy must surrender before any great length of time, yet if force can be spared, a successful attack on the heights must much facilitate a speedy capture. I own it will give me the highest pleasure to assist in the attack.

Your Lordship knows exactly the situation I am in here. With Colonel Villettes I have no reason but to suppose I am respected in the highest degree; nor have I occasion to complain of want of attention to my wishes for the good of the service from any parties; but yet I am considered as not commanding the Seamen landed. My wishes may [be,] and are, complied with; my orders would possibly be disregarded: therefore, if we move from hence, I would wish your Lordship to settle that point. Your Lordship will not, I trust, take this request amiss: I have been struggling with it since the first day I landed.

The Gun-boats did not last night, or the night before, appear to us to be so near in shore as they might have been. I may be mistaken, but believe half the shot did not go on shore. Colonel Villettes desires me to say that three of the Chasseurs are gone off; but it is thought not to Bastia, but into the country. They are Corsicans.

I am, &c.
HORATIO NELSON.

TO ADMIRAL LORD HOOD.

[Autograph draught, in the Nelson Papers.]

April 25th, 1794.

My Lord,

I feel myself most exceedingly obliged by your kind letter of yesterday, and am happy that my ideas of the situation I am in here so perfectly agree with your Lordship's. Captain Hunt[1] is a most exceeding good young man, nor is any one more zealous for the service. I don't complain of any one, but an idea has entered into the heads of some under him, that Captain Hunt's command was absolutely distinct from me; and that I had no authority whatever over him, except as a request. It was even doubted whether I had a right to command the Officers and Seamen landed from the Agamemnon—that word, 'attached to the batteries,' was wrested to a meaning very different from your Lordship's thoughts.

Your kind intention to Captain Hunt I had the honour of telling your Lordship should be furthered by every means in my power; and my regard for him, I assure you, is undiminished. At present, no letter can be necessary, but when your Lordship may judge it proper, I will thank

---

[1] Captain Anthony Hunt, who brought home Lord Hood's Dispatch announcing the surrender of Bastia. He commanded the Amphitrite of 20 guns, when that Ship was lost in the Mediterranean, some months before. Lord Hood's strong commendation of Captain Hunt's services in his Dispatch occasioned Nelson some chagrin, as he conceived, and not without reason, that he was more conspicuously noticed than himself. (See *post.*) Captain Hunt conveyed the late Marquis of Wellesley to India in La Virginie, and died in May 1798, soon after landing the Governor-General at Bengal.

you for an order to command the Seamen without any distinction as to any particular services.

The conduct of Brigadier-General 'D'Aubant is so extraordinary, that anything he possesses[2] appears not sufficient to atone for such an expression as ' will not entangle himself in ' any co-operation.'[3] I am sorry to see and hear that Gardiola is so strengthened, the works now making in it, being, Lieutenant Duncan says, eighteen feet thick. In short, it is now much more difficult to take Gardiola than it would have been to have taken the Citadel immediately after the surrender of Fiorenzo. Colonel Villettes will write your Lordship on this subject; and in case of another refusal from Fiorenzo, what other steps may be proper to be taken. I rejoice to hear a Boat was taken last night: a close blockade will soon bring these people to terms. No accident whatever happened yesterday.

HORATIO NELSON.

JOURNAL C.

On the night of the 25th of February, La Combe St. Michel quitted the Town, and embarked in a Felucca for Cabrera, and got in, although chased by the Lugger : with him also went M. Rochon, the Commander-in-chief of the Troops, and some of our deserters.

TO ADMIRAL LORD HOOD.

[From a Copy,[4] in the Nelson Papers.]

Camp, April 26th, 1794.

My Lord,

The Enemy are still hard at work on the heights, and have put the battery at the Town in a tolerable state. Colonel

---

[2] Nelson wrote originally—"That anything he possesses, even his life, appears not," &c.

[3] Nelson here added, "To what is our Country fallen," but he struck out the words.

[4] The rough draught of part of this Letter, in Nelson's own hand, is in the Nelson Papers. It is here given, because it differs in some places from the above, which is taken from a *Copy* apparently made for Clarke and M'Arthur's

Villettes and myself must agree with your Lordship, that firing away many shot at it is almost useless till we have a force sufficient to get nearer. They reserve their ammunition; we will do ours, till more troops arrive, which I fear will not come from Fiorenzo. I am just going with Mr. Duncan to look for a road and to mark out a battery on the ridge above Camponella, where it is intended to mount the two eighteen-pound carronades. It will much annoy the communication between the Town and Camponella. I lost one of my best seamen repairing the lower battery in the night, by a shot from Camponella.

Believe me ever, your most faithful

HORATIO NELSON.

We are now removing an English twenty-four pounder from the upper to the lower battery, to knock down, if possible, Camponella.

TO THOMAS POLLARD, ESQ., LEGHORN.

[Autograph, in the possession of Josiah French, Esq. of Windsor.]

Camp, April 24th, 1794.

My dear Sir,

Will you have the goodness to put the inclosed in the Post-office, and to send me some good port wine and claret, if to be had, ten dozen together, a cask of good porter or beer : in short, whatever is good we want, some butter—fowls I have plenty at present.

work. The original Letter has not been found. In the draught the remarkable passage in brackets was struck out by Nelson himself :

My Lord,　　　　　　　　　　　　　　　　　[No date.]

We are in the same state as yesterday, except cne man killed belonging to Agamemnon. The Enemy are still hard at work on the heights. [It is sufficient to make any lover of his Country run distracted.] The battery at the North end of the Town the Enemy have put in a tolerable state of defence, and it appears almost useless to throw away many more shot on it. They reserve their ammunition ; we shall do ours till a sufficient force is given us to get nearer, which I fear will not come from Fiorenzo. I am just going with Mr. Duncan to mark out a battery on the ridge above Camponella, where the two eighteen-pound carronades may be mounted.

We are fagging, but not in much danger. Our loss has been most trifling since our landing ; the Enemy are said to have suffered much.

Believe me, your most obliged,
HORATIO NELSON.

Thank you for your present of peas and asparagus.

JOURNAL C.

On the 27th of April, we began the battery on the ridge for two eighteen-pound carronades, and one twelve-pounder on the spot where Captain Clarke was wounded ;[5] 250 yards from Camponella, 900 yards from the Citadel, 700 yards from the Town. The labour of getting up guns to this battery was a work of the greatest difficulty, and which never, in my opinion, would have been accomplished by any other than British seamen.

On the 1st of May the new battery opened : the 11th Regiment and Chasseurs were removed to the ridge for the protection of the battery, and the post was strengthened with an additional number of Corsicans. Forty-five Seamen under Lieutenant Andrews were also appointed to fight the battery.

TO MRS. NELSON.

[From Clarke and M'Arthur, vol. i. p. 164.]

May 1st to 4th, 1794.

My dear Fanny,

I need not, I am certain, say, that all my joy is placed in you, I have none separated from you ; you are present to my imagination be where I will. I am convinced you feel interested in every action of my life ; and my exultation in victory

---

[5] Colonel Villettes, in his Letter to Lord Hood, dated " Camp, near Pietra Negra, 13th April, 1794," said, " Exclusive of the concern which must arise from private esteem and regard, I lament most sincerely the loss of Captain Clarke's services on the present occasion. I had appointed him to act as Brigade Major since our coming here, and experienced the most real advantage from his assistance."

is two-fold, knowing that you partake of it. Only recollect that a brave man dies but once, a coward all his life long. We cannot escape death; and should it happen to me in this place, remember, it is the will of Him, in whose hands are the issues of life and death. As to my health, it was never better, seldom so well. I have no fears about the final issue of the Expedition—It will be victory, Bastia will be ours; and if so, it must prove an event, to which the history of England can hardly boast an equal. Time will show the Enemy's force; if it is small, the Fiorenzo Commanders ought to be blamed; if it is large, they are highly culpable, for allowing a handful of brave men to be on service unsupported. My only fears are, that these soldiers will advance when Bastia is about to surrender, and deprive us of part of our glory. The King, we trust, will draw the line of our deserts.

Bastia is a beautiful place, and the environs delightful, with the most romantic views I ever beheld. This Island is to belong to England, to be governed by its own laws as Ireland, and a Viceroy placed here, with free Ports. Italy and Spain are jealous of our obtaining possession: it will command the Mediterranean. I shall most probably be in England in August: if Lord Hood has a proper opportunity of sending me, I shall ask him, and am sure he will not deny me anything in reason. You may have heard rumours of the loss of the Ardent :[6] she was commanded by the Bishop of Norwich's brother, a gallant good Officer. Lord Hood has just sent me word that he fears there are no hopes of her being safe. I will tell you as a secret, Bastia will be ours between the 20th and 24th of this month, if succours do not get in. Our Ships are moored across the harbour's mouth, and three boats from each Ship row guard every night. Our loss has been very trifling; the Enemy's very great. Only think of a beautiful Town being bombarded and cannonaded for a month—what knocks it has had. We have many deserters, who paint the horrid situation the inhabitants are in, but they have behaved so ill to the Corsicans, that they are afraid to surrender. Josiah is very well; I have not seen him these ten days, but have written to invite him and Hoste to

⁶ Vide p. 384, ante.

dinner : that lad is a charming good boy.   You will write to
my father that I am well.

Yours, &c.,

HORATIO NELSON.

P.S.—If you write to Miss Walpole, I desire you will
remember me to all that good family.

TO THOMAS POLLARD, ESQ., LEGHORN.

[Autograph, in the possession of Josiah French, Esq., of Windsor.]

May 2nd, 1794.

My dear Sir,

The things you were so good as to send me by [my] servant
I have ; and shall receive in due time, the claret, butter, and
vegetables.   I have got the porter ; and port has not yet
appeared, but I dare say it is on board the Victory.   Please
to send me a cheese or two, Dutch ones.   Clarke is getting
well fast: Andrews[6] and Duncan[7] have been slightly wounded ;
and I have had my escapes.   The Agamemnon has been unlucky—eleven killed and wounded.   We shall be in Bastia
in about a week, where I shall be glad to see you, for

Believe me your much obliged,

HORATIO NELSON.

TO THE REVEREND DIXON HOSTE.

[Autograph in the possession of Captain Sir William Hoste, Bart.]

Camp, May 3rd, 1794.

My dear Sir,

Your letter of March 10th, I received only yesterday ; it
ought to have arrived near three weeks ago.   Your good
son had long ago received your letter relative to the melancholy event in your family, as I brought it from the Victory
for him ; and I am sure he has repeatedly wrote, because

---

[6] Lieutenant George Andrews.   [7] Lieutenant Duncan, R.A.

he has told me so, and I have not failed to remind him of the
pleasure his letters must give you. The little brushes we
have had since I wrote to you, only serve to convince me of
the great truth of what I wrote you. In his navigation,
you will find him equally forward : he highly deserves every
thing I can do to make him happy. Do not you spoil him by
giving him too much money ; he has all that he wishes—
sometimes more. I love him ; therefore shall say no more on
that subject.

You will have heard that we are before Bastia with
1000 Regulars and Marines, and 300 Seamen. We landed
on the 4th April. The Enemy have force, but what, we
cannot exactly say. General D'Aubant with 1100 as fine
Troops as ever marched will not join us, declaring that
our united force is unequal to the attempt. The Army here
is commanded by Lieutenant-Colonel Villettes, a most excellent Officer, and I have the pleasure of giving my assistance.
We shall in time accomplish the taking Bastia : I have no
doubt in the way we proposed to attempt it, by bombardment
and cannonading, joined to a close blockade of the harbour.
We now hear that General D'Aubant will take the field when
the reinforcements arrive from England. I am almost
afraid to say what I think such conduct merits. The King
cannot approve of it. Bastia is a large Town, walled in with
a battery to the North and South of it, a Citadel in the middle, defended by thirty pieces of cannon and eight mortars,
four stone redoubts on the nearest hills, and three other posts
above them. The Town contains about 12,000 inhabitants—
it is said 14,000. The Troops we differ about as to numbers.
Success, I trust—indeed have little doubt—will crown our
zealous and well-meant endeavours : if not, our Country will,
I believe, sooner forgive an Officer for attacking his Enemy
than for letting it alone. This Island, the finest almost in the
world, I hope will belong to England ; the inhabitants are
strongly attached to us, and it will give us the command of
the Mediterranean. The Italian States and the Spaniards, I
believe, are jealous of our taking it, well knowing its consequence.

The Agamemnon is moored off our Camp : your dear boy

wished much to come ashore with me, and if I had not
thought the danger was too great, I should have brought him.
However, he has been several times to see me.   The zeal of
our soldiers and seamen is, I believe, almost unexampled:
there is not one who does not consider himself as personally
interested in the event, and deserted by the General.   It has,
I am persuaded, made them equal to double their numbers.
The Enemy have made only two feint attempts at a sortie.

May 4th.—Your son has just left me.   He is writing you,
but may not be in time for this conveyance.   I beg to return
my thanks to Mrs. Hoste for her compliments.

I am, dear Sir,

Your very humble Servant,

HORATIO NELSON.

If you see any of my Burnham friends, I beg to be kindly
remembered to them.

JOURNAL C.

On the 3rd of May, we began a battery for one twenty-
four-pounder and a ten-inch howitzer, which was finished by
the 7th at night.   The Enemy from the 1st of this month
had shown several dispositions, as if they meant to attack
this post: but from some cause they never advanced.   Five
four-pound field-pieces, with good *abatis*, would in my
opinion, if the post had been well-defended, prevented their
making any impression on it.   The Seamen always slept on
the battery with their pikes and cutlasses.

Lord Hood on the 8th sent in another Flag of Truce
at eight o'clock, which was refused; the Mayor telling
the Officer, 'that they would return bomb for bomb, and
'shot for shot!'   Opened the twenty-four pounder and
howitzer with the greatest good effect; nor could all the
efforts of the Enemy knock down our works.   A continued
and increasing fire was kept up on the Town and outworks.

In the night of the 12th a large Boat came out of Bastia; she was closely pursued by our Guard-boats, and taken: in her were three deserters, the Captain of La Fortunée Frigate, twelve Seamen, eight Corsicans, and thirty wounded soldiers, going to Capraja. Her dispatches were thrown overboard; but in the morning of the 13th at daylight, Lieutenant Suckling of the St. Croix schooner saw the packet floating on the water, which he took up, and brought to me. Probably in the hurry of throwing them overboard, the weight that had been tied to them had slipped out of the string: they were all letters from Gentili, the Commander-in-Chief at Bastia, saying how much they had been annoyed by our fire, which had been opened on them near forty days, and that if succours did not arrive by the 29th of the month, they must look upon the Town as lost to the Republic. These letters were addressed to Salicetti, La Combe St. Michel, and Santelli. Lord Hood sent in the Boat with her crew and wounded men, with a week's provisions; and we this day got a nine-pounder on the ridge.

On the 14th of May, the Enemy displayed a picture on Camponella the whole day; they did not treat it with insult, and I think it was intended for Lord Hood.[8] Our batteries kept up an incessant fire. During the night of the 15th, our Guard-boats took a boat from Capraja with gunpowder on board, bound to Bastia, Galeazzini the Mayor's brother was in her: no despatches could be found. The Enemy were employed preparing Gardiola for a mortar.

On the 16th they got up a thirteen-inch mortar, which kept up a constant fire throughout the night. It blowing strong from the Northward, three Boats attempted to get into the Town with powder and provisions; two were taken, but one got in. From this day, until the 19th, the Enemy fired more than usual both night and day. We had also often five shells in the air all at once, going to Bastia.

On the 19th of May, some means had been taken to convey a message to Lord Hood, that if he would condescend to

[8] "By way of compliment for having returned the Boat with the wounded men." *Clarke and McArthur.*

send a boat with a Flag,[9] a negotiation would be entered into
for the surrender of the Town and its dependencies. In consequence, at four o'clock that evening, May 19th, a Flag of
Truce was hoisted on board the Victory, and a boat went from
her to the Town, and one from the Town to the Victory. The
Enemy from Camponella met us without arms, and our Officers
advancing, they shook hands, and were good friends: they
said it was all over, and that Bastia was ours. So many
interests, however, were to be consulted, that it was the 22nd,
in the evening, before our troops could take possession of the
out-posts. At five o'clock on the evening of the 19th, our
troops from St. Fiorenzo made their first appearance on the
hills; and on the 20th, General d'Aubant and the whole
Fiorenzo army, consisting of the 18th, 50th, and 51st Regiments, 12th Regiment of Dragoons, with 100 Artillery, came
on the hills to take Bastia.

---

[9] Mr. M'Arthur, who was Lord Hood's Secretary, has given the following
account of the circumstances that induced the Enemy to send the Flag of
Truce:

" The circumstance of a message having by some means been conveyed to
Lord Hood, on the 19th, was occasioned by one of those incidental events,
which have often so much influence on the transactions of men, and are too frequently concealed from the historian. . . . It has been just mentioned in Captain Nelson's Journal, that, on the night of the 15th of May, a Boat was taken from Capraja
laden with gunpowder, bound to Bastia, having on board Galeazzini, the Mayor's
brother. This prisoner was treated with great attention and kindness by the
officers of the Victory . . . . . Galeazzini, in a private conversation which he
held with Lord Hood's Secretary, on the afternoon of the 18th of May, had expressed his alarm at the deplorable situation in which his brother the Mayor, his
sisters, and family, would be placed, in the event of storming the Town, and
allowing Corsican troops to enter, and plunder the inhabitants. The Secretary
replied, that Lord Hood could not possibly prevent the consequences so justly
dreaded ; but that M. Galeazzini might be convinced of the justice of his appre-
hensions, and of what was seriously in contemplation by sun-set, when he would
behold the advanced body of the army from St. Fiorenzo take a position on the
heights ; and that probably by sun-rise the next morning he would see the whole
army in motion on the hills, from the Victory's quarter-deck : the Secretary
added, that nothing could avert the impending horrors, but a Flag of Truce with
proposals from the Town. Galeazzini with much agitation of mind, exclaimed,
' Entreat, Sir, the noble Admiral, for the sake of humanity, and in the name of
all that is dear to an unfortunate prisoner, to permit a Flag of Truce to be sent
on shore immediately, accompanied by an unsealed letter, in which I will state
my situation, and that no succours of gunpowder or provisions can be expected,
after the fate of the three boats which were captured on the nights of the 15th

TO MRS. NELSON.

[From Clarke and M'Arthur, vol. i. p. 168.]

Camp, May 20th, 1794.

I have the pleasure to tell you that yesterday afternoon, the 19th, the Enemy sent off a Flag of Truce to Lord Hood. The truce still continues, and I hope there will be a surrender of the Town in consequence. Our Fiorenzo army, hearing what was going on here, have marched to the tops of the heights, which will probably terrify the Enemy. I always was of opinion, have ever acted up to it, and never have had any reason to repent it, that one Englishman was equal to three Frenchmen; had this been an English Town, I am sure it would not have been taken by them. They have allowed us to batter it, without once making any effort to drive us away. I may say truly, that this has been a Naval Expedition : our Boats prevented any thing from getting in by Sea, and our Sailors hauling up great guns, and then fighting them on shore.

We expect to take 1000 Regulars, 1500 National Guards, and a large party of Corsican Troops, 4000 in the whole : these will lay down their Arms to 1000 Soldiers and Marines, and 200 Seamen. There is some difficulty about the terms, and hostilities may recommence for a day or two longer; but they must submit. Josiah has been with me at the head of the British grenadiers, taking possession of the Forts and Posts. When I reflect what we have achieved, I

and 16th.' The Secretary observed, that a proposal of this nature might be rejected by Lord Hood, after the indignities that had been offered to his former Flag of Truce, and the insults experienced by the Officer who had been the bearer of the summons. After further discussion, it was at length settled that the coxswain of Galeazzini's boat, who had a wife and family at Bastia, should be sent after sun-set with an ostensible passport, as if for some linen and other necessaries for himself, and his fellow prisoners who were on board the Victory, and be enjoined to return to the Ship by sun-rise the next morning : this proposal was then communicated to Lord Hood, who readily acceded to it. The coxswain was accordingly landed at sun-set about two miles to the southward of Bastia, he was admitted into the garrison that evening, and escorted under a guard to the General's quarters, whence he was conveyed to the Mayor's house; and early the next morning, May 19th, he returned, and was taken on board the Victory by one of her boats in waiting."—*Clarke and M'Arthur*, vol. i. pp. 166-168.

The proposal to surrender the Town was the result of this communication.

am all astonishment: Providence has ever been gracious to
me, and has been my protector from the many perils incident
to my situation.

Yours, &c.,

HORATIO NELSON.

JOURNAL C.

On the 22nd of May, our Troops at six in the evening
marched from their Posts, the band playing ' God save the
King.' At seven the French colours were struck upon
Camponella, Stafforella, Croix de Capuchin, Monseratto
Rock, Fort St. Mary's, and all the other out-posts, and the
British colours were hoisted under three cheers from every
Seaman and Soldier. The French Troops all retired to the
Town and Citadel.

May 23rd.—This morning the British Grenadiers took
possession of the Town gates; and the gate of the Citadel:
and on the 24th at daylight, the most glorious sight that
an Englishman can experience, and which, I believe, none
but an Englishman could bring about, was exhibited;—
4,500 men laying down their arms to less than 1,000
British Soldiers, who were serving as Marines. Our loss of
men in taking Bastia, containing upwards of 14,000 inhabitants, and which, if fully occupied, would contain 25,000,
was smaller than could be expected: Seamen killed, and
who died of their wounds, 12; wounded 14. Soldiers
killed, and who died of their wounds, 7; wounded 23.
Total killed 19, wounded 37. Officers wounded, Captain Rudsdale of the 11th Regiment, Captain Clarke of the
69th, and Lieutenant Andrews of the Agamemnon. By the
most accurate account we can get of the Enemy's killed and
wounded, they had, killed 203, wounded 540, most of whom
are dead. We consumed 1,058 barrels of powder, and fired
11,923 shot, and 7,373 shells.

TO ADMIRAL LORD HOOD.

[From Clarke and M'Arthur, vol. i. p. 169.]

[Apparently 23rd May 1794.]

My dear Lord,

With the most heartfelt satisfaction do I congratulate you on the great event of this day,[1] accomplished by that solid

[1] It is desirable to give Lord Hood's Dispatch, as printed in the London Gazette, on the surrender of Bastia, not only because it is a necessary illustration of an event in which Nelson performed so distinguished a part, but because the manner in which the services of the Officers was mentioned gave great umbrage to him, as he considered that his exertions had not been duly appreciated. (See some subsequent Letters.) That Lord Hood could not have intended to do him injustice is evident from his Lordship's high character, from his whole conduct towards him, and from his private Letters; but it is impossible to deny that Nelson, who was the mainspring of the Enterprize, and upon whom most of the responsibility and labour had fallen, deserved a distinct acknowledgment of his merits; and, at least, as strong an eulogium as a young Captain of Artillery, whom he had himself first brought to Lord Hood's notice.

" Victory, off Bastia, May 24th, 1794.

" Sir,

" I have the honour to acquaint you that the Town and Citadel of Bastia, with the several Posts upon the heights, surrendered to the arms of his Majesty on the 22nd. On the 19th I received a message that the garrison was desirous of capitulating upon honourable terms, in consequence of which I sent the enclosed note on shore. This brought on board the Victory three Officers, who informed me that Gentili, the Commandant, would assemble the Officers of the several corps and of the Municipality if a Truce took place, which I agreed to, a little before sunset. The next day I received a note from Gentili, which I also enclose, and sent Captain Young on shore on the morning of the 21st, who soon returned to the Victory with two Officers and two of the Administrative Bodies, which, with Vice-Admiral Goodall, Captain Young, Captain Inglefield, and my Secretary Mr. M'Arthur, settled the Articles of Capitulation, which were signed the following morning, when his Majesty's Troops took possession of all the Posts above the Town, the Troops in each retiring to the Citadel, from whence they marched to the Mole-head, where they grounded their arms and were embarked. You will receive herewith the Articles of Capitulation, which I hope his Majesty will approve.

" I am unable to give due praise to the unremitting zeal, exertion, and judicious conduct of Lieutenant-Colonel Villettes, who had the honour of commanding his Majesty's Troops : never was either more conspicuous. Major Brereton and every Officer and soldier under the Lieutenant-Colonel's orders are justly entitled to my warmest acknowledgments; their persevering ardour and desire to distinguish themselves cannot be too highly spoken of, and which it will be my pride to remember to the latest period of my life.

" Captain Nelson, of his Majesty's Ship Agamemnon, who had the command and directions of the Seamen in landing the guns, mortars, and stores, and Captain Hunt who commanded at the batteries very ably assisted by Captain Bullen and Captain Serocold, and the Lieutenants Gore, Hotham, Stiles, Andrews, and Brisbane, have an equal claim to my gratitude, as the Seamen under their management worked the guns with great judgment and alacrity. Never

judgment which no fears of others could warp from that duty, and love of our Country which has ever shone so conspicuous. My heart is too full to say all I think; but I must not for-

was an higher spirit or greater perseverance exhibited, and I am happy to say that no other contention was at any time known than who should be most forward and indefatigable for promoting his Majesty's Service; for although the difficulties they had to struggle with were many and various, the perfect harmony and good humour that universally prevailed throughout the siege overcame them all.

"I cannot but express in the strongest terms, the meritorious conduct of Captain Duncan and Lieut. Alexander Duncan of the Royal Artillery and Lieut. De Butts of the Royal Engineers, but my obligation is particularly great to Captain Duncan, as more zeal, ability, and judgment, was never shown by any Officer, than were displayed by him, and I take the liberty of mentioning him as an Officer highly entitled to his Majesty's notice.

"I feel myself very much indebted for the vigilance and attention of Captain Wolseley of the Imperieuse, and of Captain Hallowell, who became a volunteer wherever he could be useful, after being superseded in the command of the Courageux by Captain Waldegrave. The former kept a diligent watch upon the Island of Capraia, where the Enemy have magazines of provisions and stores, and the latter did the same by guarding the harbour's mouth of Bastia, with Gun-boats and launches well armed the whole of every night; whilst the smaller boats were very judiciously placed in the intervals between, and rather without the ships (which were moored in a crescent just out of reach of the Enemy's guns) by Captain Young of the Fortitude, the centre Ship, on board of which every boat assembled at sunset for orders, and the cheerfulness with which the Officers and Men performed this nightly duty is very much to be admired, and afforded me the most heart-felt satisfaction and pleasure.

"The very great and effectual assistance I received from Vice-Admiral Goodall, Captain Inglefield, and Captain Knight, as well as from every Captain and Officer of his Majesty's Ships under my command, have a just claim to my most particular thanks, not only in carrying into execution my orders afloat, but in attending to and supplying the wants of the little Army on shore. It is to the very cordial and decided support *alone* I had the honour to receive from the whole that the innumerable difficulties we had to control with were so happily surmounted.

"Major Smith and Ensign Vigoreux of the 25th Regiment, and Captain Radsdale and Lieutenant St. George of the 11th, not embarking with their respective regiments, having civil employments on shore; it is to their honour I mention that they relinquished those employments and joined their corps soon after the troops landed.

"It is very much my duty to inform you that I am extremely obliged to General Petrecono, Mr. Frediani, and all the Officers of the Corsicans serving with the Army, for their great zeal, ardour, and attention, in forwarding the reduction of Bastia by every means in their power, who were of infinite service by preserving good order in the troops.

"I transmit an account of the loss on the part of his Majesty in killed and wounded, which I am happy to say is inconsiderable, but the Enemy suffered much, their hospitals being full.

"At the commencement of the Siege the number of the Enemy bearing arms was three thousand.

get my friend Captain Duncan, who having attained that rank, I understand, for his services at Toulon, will, I trust, have another step through your Lordship's interest: the rank of Major is, as I am informed, not unfrequently given. I need say no more.

I am, &c.,

HORATIO NELSON.

TO THE RIGHT HON. SIR WILLIAM HAMILTON, K.B., MINISTER AT NAPLES.

[" Letters of Lord Nelson to Lady Hamilton." 8vo. 1814. vol. ii. p. 225.]

Bastia, May 24th, 1794.

My dear Sir,

Will you have the goodness to forward the inclosed to Mr. Brand, and to present my letter to Lady Hamilton?

Every lover of his Country will rejoice in our great and almost unexampled success, to the honour of my Lord Hood, and to the shame of those who opposed his endeavours to serve his Country. General Stuart,[2] I am happy to say, is just arrived.

We shall now join heart and hand against Calvi. When conquered, I shall hope to pay my respects to your Excellency at Naples, which will give real pleasure to your very faithful and obliged

HORATIO NELSON.

" By the first Ship that sails for England I shall have the honour of sending, to be laid at his Majesty's feet, the several stand of colours taken at Bastia.

" Captain Hunt, who was on shore in the command of the batteries, from the hour the troops landed to the surrender of the Town, will be the bearer of this Dispatch, and can give any further information you may wish to know respecting the Siege.

" I have the honour, &c.;

" HOOD.

" Right Hon. Henry Dundas."

[2] General the Honourable Charles Stuart, fourth son of John, third Earl of Bute, and father of the present Sir Charles Stuart, G.C.B., Lord Stuart de Rothesay,—" an Officer who, unfortunately for his Country, never had an adequate field for the display of those eminent talents which were, to all who knew him, so conspicuous."—*Southey's Life of Nelson.* General Stuart received the Order of the Bath in January 1799, and died in March 1801.

TO WILLIAM LOCKER, LIEUTENANT GOVERNOR, ROYAL HOSPITAL, GREENWICH.

[Autograph, in the Locker Papers.]

Agamemnon, Bastia, May 30th, 1794.

My dear Friend,

I am just got on board after eight weeks' service on shore, where I trust I have acquitted myself in a manner my friends will be pleased with. The more we see of this place, the more we are astonished at their giving it up, but the truth is, the different parties were afraid to trust each other; they can be justified on no other ground. I only yesterday got your letter of the 12th of December, which my brother sent in a box. I have now on board two Captains, twenty-four other Officers, and 300 Seamen of the Ships we fell in with last October.[1] The Officers abuse the crews, the people their Officers; all join against their Commodore for not coming down to us after we were crippled: not that I have any idea they could have taken us, but they certainly behaved shamefully ill. The Fortunée is burned, the Minerve and La Flêche taken;—the Melpomene is at Calvi, and I trust will fall into our hands. We are now taking on board shot, shells, powder, &c. for Calvi, which, although very strongly situated, will I believe soon fall, which when done, Agamemnon goes to Gibraltar to get something done to her, having now been without the slightest repair in hull or rigging, sixteen months. Bastia is most pleasantly situated, contains 14,000 inhabitants, and will hold 20,000. A few hours carries parties to Italy. If the Corsicans know their own interests they will be happy with us, but they cannot bear dependence. Remember me kindly to all your family, who I hope to see in August or September; and believe me,

Your most obliged and affectionate

HORATIO NELSON.

Direct me a letter to Gibraltar.

---

[1] Vide p. 334, ante.

TO THE REVEREND MR. NELSON, HILBOROUGH.

[Autograph, in the Nelson Papers.]

Agamemnon, Bastia, May 30th, 1794.

My dear Brother,

If you received my letter on our intention to land near Bastia, you will naturally have been anxious (more than common) for our success. If proofs were wanting to show that perseverance, unanimity, and gallantry, can accomplish almost incredible things, we are an additional instance. All has been done by Seamen, and Troops embarked to serve as Marines, except a few Artillery under the orders of Lord Hood, who has given in this instance a most astonishing proof of the vigour of his mind, and of his zeal and judgment. His thanks to the Seamen probably will find its way into the Newspapers:[3] they are as handsome as can be penned. 4,500 men have laid down their arms to under 1,200 Troops and Seamen: it is such an event as is hardly on record. Seventy-seven pieces of ordnance, with an incredible quantity of stores, are taken, with a Man-of-War of twenty-two guns. The Fortunée was destroyed at Fiorenzo, the Minerva taken, La Flêche here: therefore three out of four of my antagonists are gone. The Melpomene is at Calvi, and will, I hope, fall into our hands with Mignonne, a small Frigate. Thus I shall still have the satisfaction of seeing this Squadron taken, which could not have happened had they not fallen in with me. They were bound to Nice, but Melpomene being so much damaged, they were obliged to put into Corsica. I have now on board two Captains of the Frigates, twenty Officers, and 300 Seamen. All join in our praise,

[3] "Victory, off Bastia, 2nd May 1794.

"The Commander-in-Chief returns his best thanks to Captain Nelson, and desires he will present them to Captain Hunt, Captain Serocold, and Captain Bullen, as well as to every Officer and Seamen employed in the Reduction of Bastia, for the indefatigable zeal and exertion they have so cheerfully manifested in the discharge of the very laborious duties committed to them, notwithstanding the various difficulties and disadvantages they have had to struggle with, which could not have been surmounted, but by the uncommon spirit and cordial unanimity, that have been so conspicuously displayed, and which must give a stamp of reputation to their characters not to be effaced, and will be remembered with gratitude by the Commander-in-Chief to the end of his life."

"Captain Nelson."

but they accuse each other: the Officers saying the crew would not fight; the people abuse their Officers, and both parties join in abusing the Commodore, Captain of Fortuneé, for not coming down to us, when we were crippled. I don't think they are the men who would have taken Agamemnon, but they behaved shamefully in not trying. We are taking in stores for Calvi, which I trust will fall in a fortnight after we get our batteries erected. Agamemnon then goes to Gibraltar to get some refit, and I hope from thence to England: latter end of August, or beginning of September, I hope to be at Portsmouth. Remember me kindly to Mrs. Nelson, and to my Aunt, and children. Compliments at Swaffham. Believe me, your most affectionate Brother,

HORATIO NELSON.

TO MR. EVAN DAVIS, SWANSEA.

[From Clarke and M'Arthur, 8vo., vol. i. p. 252.]

May or June 1794.

From the nature of our profession we hold life by a more precarious tenure than many others, but when we fall, we trust it is to benefit our Country. So fell your Son[2] by a cannon-ball under my immediate command at the Siege of Bastia. I had taken him on shore with me, from his abilities and attention to his duty.

I am, &c.,

HORATIO NELSON.

TO MRS. NELSON.

[From Clark and M'Arthur, vol i. p. 171.]

Early in June, 1794.

We are just got to Sea after the French Fleet, which we hear is out of Toulon; our Squadron is after them, steering for Calvi, where I fear they will get, in spite of Admiral Hotham's endeavours. The Enemy are nine Sail of the Line, Admiral Hotham seven; two will join from St. Fiorenzo

---

[2] The Agamemnon's Log states that a Seaman called Thomas Davis, was killed during the Siege of Bastia.

and Lord Hood goes with six of us. If we have but the good fortune to catch them at Sea, we shall, I am sure, give a good account of them. Lord Hood only got the account last night at eleven o'clock, and by seven this morning we were all under sail. The Agamemnon had two hundred tons of ordnance to get out, and Lord Hood had given me orders to follow him as fast as possible: I was enabled to sail in half an hour after him, and we are now alongside the Victory. I pray God we may meet this Fleet.

If any accident should happen to me, I am sure my conduct will be such as will entitle you to the Royal favour : not that I have the least idea but I shall return to you, and full of honour ; if not, the Lord's will be done. My Name shall never be a disgrace to those who may belong to me. The little I have, you know I have given to you, except a small annuity. I wish it was more ; but I have never got a farthing dishonestly; it descends from clean hands. Whatever fate awaits me, I pray God to bless you, and preserve you for your Son's sake. I think always in the most affectionate manner of my Father; tell him so, and ever believe me your most affectionate husband,

HORATIO NELSON.

TO THE RIGHT HONOURABLE LORD HOOD.

[Autograph, in the possession of Mrs. Conway.]

Agamemnon, June 7th, 1794.

My Lord,

I have cleared our between decks of all our Ordnance stores, and sent them to the Dolphin. I have not touched those in our hold which, unless your Lordship chuses we should be entirely cleared of; all the stores, will I think be no great inconvenience for a short cruize. We are unmoored and short on our other anchor: will send for the Troops directly.

I am with great respect,
Your Lordship's most faithful Servant,

HORATIO NELSON.

I have wrote Captain Inglefield to request some of the Transports' boats may take some wads and platforms from us.

TO THE RIGHT HONOURABLE SIR GILBERT ELLIOT.

[Autograph, in the Minto Papers.—The Right Honourable Sir Gilbert Elliot, Bart., was sent to Corsica as Commissary Plenipotentiary. After the cession of the Island to Great Britain he became Viceroy, which office he held until the evacuation of Corsica in October 1796. On the 20th of October 1797 he was created a Peer, by the title of LORD MINTO, and obtained a Royal Grant of the Arms of Corsica, to be borne on a Chief, over his family Ensigns. His Lordship was Envoy Extraordinary to Vienna in 1799: in 1806 he was made President of the Board of Controul; and in 1807, Governor-General of India. In February 1813 his eminent public services were rewarded by the dignities of VISCOUNT of MELGUND, and EARL of MINTO. He died in June 1814, and was succeeded by his eldest Son, Sir Gilbert Elliot Murray Kynynmond, G.C.B., the present Earl of Minto, to whose kindness the Editor and the Public are indebted for this, and many other valuable Letters from Lord Nelson to his distinguished Father.]

Agamemnon, Bastia, June 12th, 1794.

Dear Sir,

As I am sure you must be anxious to hear of Lord Hood,[4] I shall, the moment I get on shore, desire a messenger to be dispatched to your Excellency with this letter. He did not (owing to little winds) join Admiral Hotham off Calvi till daylight on the 9th, and the Admiral had not been nearer the French Fleet than four leagues, and they had the wind of him, which induced him to steer for Calvi. At half-past nine o'clock, a Frigate was seen to the Westward, with the signal flying for the Enemy's Fleet to the Westward. Lord Hood instantly made the signal for a general chase. When the Frigate joined, Sir Charles Hamilton[5] acquainted his Lordship that he left the French Fleet at eight o'clock at night on the 8th, twelve leagues off the Island of Santa Margareta, laying to with their heads off shore. Lord Hood then made the signal for to chase N.W., which we did, till

---

[4] Intelligence having reached Lord Hood, at Bastia, that the French Fleet had put to Sea on the 5th of June, he immediately proceeded with the Squadron, consisting of thirteen Sail of the Line, including the Agamemnon, to meet them. On the 10th the Enemy were seen under the land of St. Tropez, but they succeeded in getting into Gourjean, where he resolved to attack them. It was, however, found impracticable to do so; and Lord Hood, leaving Vice-Admiral Hotham to watch them, returned to Bastia. The Agamemnon quitted the Fleet for Bastia on the 10th, as soon as the hopes of an Engagement were at an end, and she arrived there on the 12th of that month, to assist in the Siege of Calvi.

[5] The present Admiral Sir Charles Hamilton, Bart., K. C. B., then Captain of the Dido.

dark, when the Fleet was collected round the Victory, she carrying all her plain sails during the night, and having Frigates in every direction.

At noon, on the 10th, being nearly on the Station where the Enemy was seen, and in sight of the French coast, Lord Hood thought fit to order Agamemnon to Bastia, to convoy the troops to Mortella Bay, and to get everything in readiness to land them at Calvi at a moment's notice. Courageux is gone to Fiorenzo for stores, and comes round to Bastia. I lost sight of the Victory at half-past five o'clock on Tuesday afternoon, with thirteen Sail of the Line and several Frigates standing with an easy sail in shore. On the morning of the 9th, a heavy firing was heard by the Dido, and we fear the Sardinian Frigate is taken by them. By a Merchant-ship, spoke by the Fleet, we learn that the Convoy from England, with the troops, &c., and Thalia and Inflexible, are arrived in Gibraltar Bay. I hope they will not venture up till Lord Hood can get off Toulon, or wherever the French Fleet are got to. The Enemy are nine sail of the Line, and seven other Vessels. If Lord Hood can get hold of these gentry, he will give a most glorious account of them I am certain.

> Believe me, with the highest esteem,
>> Your Excellency's most obedient Servant,
>>> HORATIO NELSON.

JOURNAL C.

[From Clarke and M'Arthur, vol. i. pp. 172—189.]

[This Journal relates only to the Siege of Calvi. Captain Nelson sent a copy of it daily to Lord Hood, by whom it was transmitted to the Admiralty; but the only parts now in the Admiralty are those from the 28th of July to the 8th of August, for which period Clarke and M'Arthur have not given any extracts.]

June 13th.—Having ordered every Transport and Victualler, except the Ships in the Mole, to be ready to sail with me, and a Ship laden with empty casks, on the 13th of June, by eight o'clock every Soldier was embarked, amounting to 1450 men, exclusive of Officers. At noon made the signal to unmoor, and at four the signal to weigh. Sailed in company with his Majesty's Ships Dolphin, Gorgon, and twenty-two Sail of Vessels.

June the 15th, at seven o'clock in the morning, we arrived at Fiorenzo, and anchored in Mortella Bay. General Stuart came on board, and expressed himself anxious to go on to the attack of Calvi, if I thought it right to proceed with the Shipping, which I certainly did; placing the firmest reliance that we should be perfectly safe under Lord Hood's protection, who would take care that the French Fleet at Gourjean should not molest us. I therefore gave the necessary orders, and sailed the next day [the 16th] at half-past five in the evening from Mortella Bay, with the Dolphin, Lutine, and sixteen Sail of Transports, Victuallers, and Store-ships.

It was ten o'clock at night on the 17th, before any of the Ships could get to an anchor on the coast about four miles to the westward of Cape Revellata, the bottom rocky, and very deep water; the Agamemnon lying in fifty-three fathoms about one mile from the shore, opposite a little inlet called Porto Agro. This coast is so rocky, except in this inlet, that a boat cannot land stores on any other place; and it is with the greatest difficulty that a man can get up the cliffs.

June the 18th, in the morning, at half-past three o'clock, I went on shore with General Stuart to examine the Coast, with the hopes of finding a better landing-place; but we both agreed it could only be at the inlet called Porto Agro, though by no means a convenient place for landing guns or stores, as sunken rocks lie twenty feet from the shore, with deep water between them; and with a common sea-breeze such a swell sets in, as to prevent Boats from landing. This inlet is three miles and a half from the town of Calvi. Examined the Enemy's outposts, and found them as follows: Monachesco,[6] about 2200 yards from the Town, on the S. W. side of it. The Mozelle fort, West from the Town about 900 yards; and the Fountain battery in a shoulder of the hill, between Mozelle and San Francesco; which last stands on a rock on the north side of the peninsula, and is washed by the sea. The Town itself is apparently well fortified, but without any ditch.

---

[6] Called in General Stuart's Despatch " Mollinochesco."

June 19th.—The Troops were disembarked at seven o'clock on the morning of the 19th, under the direction of Captain E. Cooke,[7] with six field-pieces, which the seamen dragged up the hills. I landed in the afternoon with 250 Seamen, and encamped on the beach, getting on shore baggage for the Army. By the General's desire I sent the Fox Cutter, with directions for 180 of the Royal Louis, the 18th Regiment, and 100 of the 69th Regiment, to join as soon as possible. During the whole of the 20th and 21st it blew so strong, with a heavy sea and rain, and with such thunder and lightning, as precluded all intercourse with the Shipping, most of which put to sea. The Seamen were employed in making roads for their guns, and in getting up three twenty-six-pounders to the Madona, about two miles and a half from the landing-place, ready to act against Monachesco : the road for the first three quarters of mile led up a steep mountain, and the other part was not very easy. The weather became rather moderate in the night, but still with thunder, lightning, and rain.

TO ADMIRAL LORD HOOD.

[Autograph, in the possession of Mrs. Conway.]

Agamemnon, near Calvi, 19th June 1794.

My dear Lord,

Believing that what I should do would be of service to our Country, and of course meet with your Lordship's approbation, I have the honour to acquaint you that on my arrival in Mortella Bay, on the 15th instant, General Stuart was anxious to proceed on our expedition against Calvi, in which I own I most heartily concurred with him, believing ourselves safe under your Lordship's wing. I sailed on the 16th, in the evening, from Mortella Bay, and anchored here

---

[7] Captain Edward Cooke. This gallant Officer was severely wounded in command of the Sybille, in capturing La Forte, French Frigate, in the East Indies on the 28th February 1799. He died of his wounds on the 23rd of May following.

on the 17th, at night. Yesterday was taken up in looking at the Enemy, and this morning at daylight, the troops, 1,450 were landed, together with seventy volunteers from the Transports, thirty men which I took out of the Inflexible, and one hundred Seamen from the Agamemnon. I was obliged to use every effort to forward the service. The General, after looking at Calvi, wished to have some additional force; therefore I sent the Fox to Fiorenzo, with orders to Captain Wallis[8] to proceed to Bastia, for such troops as General Stuart wished to have. As the Gorgon had not men enough left her by your Lordship to take care of her, I was obliged to solicit volunteers from the Transports to bring her round with me, and therefore was under the necessity of desiring Inflexible to lend twenty men to assist in navigating the Ship. The Fox is to bring 150 of the Royal Louis. If the Victory does not join us before the Lutine is cleared I must send her for guns from the Commerce de Marseilles,[9] which are much wanted. Captain Cooke, who I found at Fiorenzo, with a zeal which will ever do him credit, wished to accompany me on the present Expedition. I not only have the greatest pleasure in having him with me, but his assistance to me has been very great; and as he is anxious to remain, I hope he will be allowed by your Lordship to stay with me till the Siege is over. I have much to say, but wish not to keep the Scout.

> Believe me, with highest respect,
> Your Lordship's most faithful,
> HORATIO NELSON.

General Stuart requests me to say that nothing particular has happened since our landing, and that he is really so busy that he cannot find time to write to your Lordship; but begs to refer you to me for particulars, which I have given in my letter.

[8] Captain James Wallis who served with Nelson as First Lieutenant of the Boreas. He then commanded the Gorgon, Store-ship.

[9] The Commerce de Marseilles of 120 guns, was one of the Ships brought from Toulon by Lord Hood in December 1793.

TO MAJOR-GENERAL STUART.

[From a Copy in the Nelson Papers.]

Camp, June 20th, 1794.

Sir,

The Shipping which sailed from hence this morning for Mortella Bay,[1] are the division under Lieutenant Harrison, who has landed as many Seamen as he could spare at present, and I was to send to Fiorenzo for more men as soon as the Fox Cutter returns to me. I was in the greater hurry to send these Vessels away, as their cables were much cut by the rocks, and it had the appearance of blowing weather. The others, which are under sail, are going to work up to a safer anchorage. If the weather put on a better appearance, abundance of Shipping will remain here to hold the troops in case any unforeseen event should render re-embarkation necessary. It is right to inform you, Sir, that if the present weather continue, it will, I think, be necessary for every Vessel here to put to sea. I can only assure you that every exertion of mine shall be made to comply with your wishes on every occasion, for I am, with the highest esteem,

Your most faithful Servant,

HORATIO NELSON.

I wished to have paid my respects to you this morning, but really have been so anxious to get a twenty-four pounder in the road, that I trust you will excuse me. The work of the day over, I shall do myself the honour of seeing you in the evening.

HORATIO NELSON.

[1] On the 20th of June General Stuart wrote to Captain Nelson, "that as he understood several Transports were sent from thence to Mortella Bay, he was under the necessity of asking how many Transports he meant to detain for the use of the Army in case of necessity, and what number he thought proper for its immediate protection, stating that in consequence of Lord Hood's absence, the Army was deprived of a powerful aid; that it was of the utmost consequence he should know how far he might depend upon Nelson's co-operation; that a tent was wanted for the Hospital; that 150 Seamen were unequal to the task of hauling up great guns in a short space of time; and wishing him to increase the number of men.—*Autograph*, in the Nelson Papers.

TO LIEUTENANT RICHARD SAINTHILL, AGENT FOR TRANSPORTS.

[From the " Memoir of Captain Richard Sainthill." That Officer was superannuated with the rank of Commander in 1814, and died in June 1829.]

You are hereby required and directed to land out of the Transports under your directions what studding-sail booms or other spars they can conveniently part with, to erect tents for stores, provisions, &c. for which this shall be your order.

Given under my hand, at the Camp before Calvi, this 20th of June 1794.

HORATIO NELSON.

TO ADMIRAL LORD HOOD.

[Autograph in the possession of Mrs. Conway.]

Camp, June 21st, 1794.

My Lord,

I did myself the honour of writing your Lordship by the Scout, who was in search of you here, to acquaint you of our situation. You will know from my letters to Captain Tyler[2] and Captain Wallis, of what I thought it right to order, in consequence of General Stuart's finding this place much stronger than he expected. As the General will write to tell you his wants and wishes, it is only necessary for me to say, that had not the weather been so bad as to preclude all intercourse with Ships for the last twenty-four hours, and still continues very bad, the Lutine would have been cleared of her stores and sent to Fiorenzo to request ten more guns from the Commerce de Marseilles, the General intending to have seventeen guns of the French against the Enemy, and three or four of my 24-pounders to fire shells from. Our landing-place is very bad ; the rocks break in this weather so far from the shore, and the mountain we have to drag the guns up so long and so steep, that the whole of yesterday we were only able to get one gun up, and then

---

[2] Captain Tyler of the Meleager of 32 guns. This gallant Officer, who was severely wounded in command of the Tonnant at the Battle of Trafalgar, died Admiral Sir Charles Tyler, G.C.B., in September 1835.

we have one mile and a half at least to drag them. I hope
before long we shall be able to land some to the eastward of
Cape Revellata; but it being within half gun-shot of the
Enemy, it cannot at present be done. General Stuart wishes
much for the Fortunée Gun-boat to lay in this Bay, to the
eastward of Revellata, to prevent the Enemy's Gun-boat
from coming in there to annoy our intended Battery, and purposes to place a heavy gun as a defence for her. She can lay
with another small Vessel under a high point of land between
her and the Enemy. I wrote to Lieutenant Fennell to try
and get some volunteers, and to bring the Gun-boat to me.
Your Lordship so well knows our want of seamen here,
that I am sure I need not mention it: we shall have more
than forty pieces of ordnance to drag over these mountains: my numbers are two hundred, barely sufficient
to move a twenty-four pounder. The two Vessels laden
with powder at Fiorenzo, the General will write you, I take
for granted, about. He says he shall want the powder they
have on board. Had not the weather been bad, I am sure
one battery against Monachesco would have opened to-morrow morning. Twenty-four hours, I think, will put us in
possession of it. We seem here determined to act with vigour,
and it is the only thing to get us on. The Enemy are hard at
work making batteries. I wrote your Lordship that Captain
Cooke is with me, who with great zeal and activity could not
think of laying idle at Fiorenzo, therefore offered his services
to me, which I cheerfully accepted. If it is not contrary to
your Lordship's plan for him, I believe he wishes much to
stay with me. He begs I will present his respects; and believe
me your Lordship's most faithful Servant,

HORATIO NELSON.

The Dolphin is in the greatest distress for men—not hav-

---

[3] On the 21st of June Lord Hood wrote officially to Captain Nelson from the
Victory in Mortella Bay :—

"Sir,—I am waiting with great impatience to hear from you, not knowing
what Stores you took with you, and what more may be wanted. The
additional troops General Stuart ordered from Bastia embarked this morning, and I expect to see the Ariadne and Transports to-morrow, when I
shall join and proceed with him. In addition to the men from this Ship
already on the expedition, I have sent fifty more under the command of

ing enough to weigh an anchor, so Captain May tells me. The Lutine shall sail the moment she is cleared of her stores.

Many of the Transports have been obliged to leave this anchorage, from the badness of the anchoring ground, none of which are now in sight.

TO ADMIRAL LORD HOOD.

[Autograph, in possession of Mrs. Conway.]

Camp, June 23rd, 1794.

My Lord,

The Agamemnon, who put to sea in the evening of the 21st, is, I hope, at Fiorenzo, and hope very soon to see her again with the Store-ships, who put to sea the day before. Not one Ship is returned to us. The General this morning sent Captain Stephens[4] of the Artillery to ask me, as more French twenty-pound shot could not be got, to give him my opinion what other guns could best be spared, and shot for them, to make up the original demand, all of which I am told will certainly be wanted. I endeavoured to fix on those sizes which I thought most likely to be obtained; and as the General wishes to write your Lordship, I send the Fox Cutter. The Lutine, if the weather moderates, will be cleared to-morrow, when I shall immediately send her to your Lordship at Fiorenzo, for these guns, &c. No more guns have been able to be landed, the swell has been so great: therefore the battery against Monachesco cannot be opened till another battery of four twenty-four pounders is erected to draw off the Enemy's fire. Twelve guns are judged necessary for the first parallel. If we cannot get on faster, we shall be a long while

Captain Hallowell, who is accompanied by Captain Serocold, both very able, willing, and zealous Officers, from whom you will have much assistance, and they are directed to follow your orders, which I am confident they will both do with great alacrity, and that all will go on with equal cordiality and good humour as at Bastia. I am, Sir, with great regard, &c., Hood. P.S. I tremble for what may have happened from last night's wind."—From a *Copy* certified by Nelson, in the Hood Papers.

4 Captain Edward Stephens of the Artillery, was the Senior Officer of that Corps at the Siege: he became a Lieutenant-Colonel in January 1794, and a Lieutenant-General in June 1813.

in getting possession, if the Enemy make an obstinate resistance. The Vessels with the powder having gone to sea, I have been obliged to order the Dolphin and Lutine to land powder, and Wolseley[5] having twenty-four barrels of prize powder, that is bought of him.

　　　I am, with highest respect,

　　　　　Your Lordship, your most faithful Servant,

　　　　　　　　　HORATIO NELSON.

Captain Cooke desires to present his respectful compliments.

TO THE HON. LIEUTENANT-GENERAL STUART.

[Autograph, in the possession of Mrs. Conway.]

June 23rd, 1794.

Two thirty-six pounders from Commerce de Marseilles, and 3000 shot.

Two twenty-four pounders from Agamemnon, and 2000 shot.

N.B.—The Agamemnon has not 900 shot of this calibre.

Four eighteen-pounders French, and 6000 shot, supposed from Pearl and Fiorenzo.

Three twelve-pounders French, and 4500 shot.

Two twenty-four pounders from Agamemnon for shells. These wanted, exclusive of the five guns and ten-inch howitzer on board the Victory.

I think these guns are more likely with the shot to be got than any others.

　　　　　　　　　HORATIO NELSON.

TO ADMIRAL LORD HOOD.

[Autograph, in the possession of Mrs. Conway.]

Camp, June 25th, 1794.

My Lord,

I am sorry your Lordship has not received my letters as I have wrote three since my landing. We go on well; and

---

[5] Captain of the Lowestoffe, vide p. 350, ante.

although we have, in appearance, a great deal of hard work to get through, yet I have no doubt but it will be accomplished in a proper manner.

The seamen are in want of tents, except the Agamemnon's ten, all the others (Victory's, who came yesterday, excepted) are lodged in sail tents, which are wanted for the Artillery Stores, Commissaries, and Hospitals. There being no houses near us, makes the application to the Navy very frequent and urgent. If those Ships who have tents can send us thirty, we want them. I have landed the Purser of the Agamemnon to issue provisions for the seamen. I have also to request that 300 pair of shoes may be ordered directly. I had not shoes more than sufficient for the Transport's people, and mine are barefooted.

I can assure your Lordship that I believe all will go on here with harmony and spirit. The General has an opinion of his own which is not to be drawn from its proper object by the talking of any people, and he keeps his opinion and intentions to himself; therefore prevents any opinions being given.

Captain Cooke goes in the Lutine to join your Lordship. His merits your Lordship is fully acquainted with, and I have only to say that they are certainly not lessened by his services under me. I send a Return of seamen. I am, with highest respect,

Your Lordship's most faithful Servant,
HORATIO NELSON.

Since writing, Lieutenant Fennell is just arrived in the Fortunée Gun-boat. No account of stores or troops being given me, it was impossible I could give your Lordship any account, or of what stores when wished, to be followed. I shall never omit writing your Lordship every occurrence.

The Tisiphone is just arrived. I have desired Captain Elphinstone to join Wolseley. Many thanks for the newspapers

TO THOMAS POLLARD, ESQ., LEGHORN.

[Autograph, in the possession of John Luxford, Esq.]

Camp, near Calvi, June 27th, 1794.

My dear Sir,

I have received your letter of June 10th, wherein you want a Prize-list for one vessel taken by Tartar and myself, which I believe Captain Fremantle[5] has settled about: if not, send the net proceeds to me, and I will give you a receipt; but the Tartar must be paid, as you could not have paid Andrews. You have only to class the proportions of Vessels as Captain Fremantle has told you them:—

1st Class $\frac{1}{8}$, Admiral, so much.

2nd ditto $\frac{2}{8}$, ditto.

3rd ditto $\frac{1}{8}$, therefore Captains must be alike.

4th ditto $\frac{1}{8}$, Lieutenants must be the same.

5th ditto $\frac{1}{8}$, Warrants do. Petty do.

6th ditto $\frac{2}{8}$, Seamen do.

Both Ships, the Cutter and Gun-boat, has, I am sure been settled by Fremantle, as Udney[6] has sent his very right, and I only wait yours to make a distribution. Respecting the Virgin del Porto, send the net proceeds to either Captain Wolseley here, or myself; and we will give you a receipt, and shall deliver the proper proportion to Lutine, Meleager, and Gun-boat which were in sight. I have received all the good things you have sent me, even to the last newspapers—a very great treat to us, Captain Hallowell,[7] and Captain Serocold. We are before Calvi, and shall have it in due time.

Believe me, your very much obliged,

Horatio Nelson.

[5] Captain Thomas Francis Fremantle of the Tartar of 28 guns, afterwards a Vice-Admiral, a G.C.B., Baronet, and G.C.M.G., who will be again often mentioned.

[6] John Udney, Esq., the British Consul and a Merchant at Leghorn, who, like Mr. Pollard, often acted as Agent for Prizes taken by the Squadron.

[7] Captain Benjamin Hallowell, afterwards Admiral Sir Benjamin Hallowell Carew, G.C.B. This distinguished Officer will be again frequently mentioned.

TO MRS. NELSON.

[From Clarke and M'Arthur, vol. i. p. 175]

Camp, near Calvi, June 27th, 1794.

My dear Fanny,

I sent you a few lines just as we landed, since which nothing particular has occurred. Dragging cannon up steep mountains, and carrying shot and shells, has been our constant employment. Josiah is very well, and I have no fears but he will be a good man. He is affectionate, though warm in his disposition, which nothing can cool so thoroughly as being at Sea, where nobody has entirely their own way. Corsica, in respect to prizes, produces nothing but honour, far above the consideration of wealth : not that I despise riches, quite the contrary, yet I would not sacrifice a good name to obtain them.

The French here do not know what to make of us. They hear we are landed, yet have not seen us, nor have they any idea about our batteries, which, when they open, will be heavy on them. That we shall take Calvi in due time, I have no manner of doubt. You know, probably, that George the Third is King of Corsica, chosen by the unanimous consent of the people themselves, the best of all Titles ; they are now our fellow-subjects. The first resolution of the Parliament of Corsica was to declare they were Englishmen : they might have been mistaken for Irishmen, by their bull. You will hear that Lord Hood fell in with the French Fleet, on the 10th ; but they were too near the shore for him to prevent their getting into Port. His Lordship wished to attack them ; a Council of Flag-officers prevented him.[8] You may be assured he will either take or destroy them, but I trust not before Calvi is ours, when I shall immediately join the Fleet. Be so good as to write a line to my Father, to say

[8] Nelson's dislike to " Councils of War " is emphatically shown by a Letter in a subsequent part of this work. Owing to recent promotions, there were in a Fleet of thirteen Sail of the Line, the extraordinary number of *eight* Flag

I am well, never better; also to Mrs. Bolton, and that I shall write soon. I expect this will find you at Mr. Matcham's, at Ringwood; remember me kindly. God bless you.

HORATIO NELSON.

June 28th.

Those people who so liberally abuse everybody but themselves, are probably the very persons who deserve abuse. I hope those who are to get so much money will make a proper use of it. Had I attended less than I have done to the service of my Country, I might have made some too: however, I trust my name will stand on record, when the money-makers will be forgot.

JOURNAL C.

On the 27th of June, we got up two ten-inch howitzers, and were employed all the day in carrying the heavy guns and carriages about three quarters of a mile forward, during a constant rain. Throughout the whole time, a gale of wind cut off all intercourse with the Ships. At one o'clock in the afternoon, the French came out, and made an attempt to turn both flanks of the Corsicans. A Gun-boat also came out to support their rear, and the Enemy advanced under cover of a heavy cannonade. Our Light Corps were under arms to support the Corsicans if necessary, and the Seamen got down two field-pieces and fired at the Gun-boat, which instantly rowed away. The Enemy rather forced our Corsicans to fall back, on which I went with General Stuart to them: they kept up a smart firing of musketry, and regained their post. Colonel Sabbatini,[9] their Commandant, was killed, with two or three others, and five or six were wounded. The Enemy retired to their works about four o'clock, and I believe have not the

Officers; namely, Admiral Lord Hood, Vice-Admirals Hotham, Goodall, and Corby, and Rear-Admirals Sir Hyde Parker, Linzee, Lutwidge, and Dickson.

[9] Called in General Stuart's Despatch in the London Gazette, " Lieutenant Colonel Senibaldi."

smallest idea of our intentions of bringing cannon over the mountains.

TO ADMIRAL LORD HOOD.

[Autograph, in the possession of Mrs. Conway.]

Camp, June 30th, 1794.

My Lord,

The General has thought, as we all did, of the necessity of landing two 12-pounders on the point near Revellata. A battery is made there, and I have put a Midshipman and twelve men to fight it: The General tells me he cannot afford men to encamp there for its defence. The 36-pounders, so soon as the Dolphin is cleared of shot and shells, I shall take out of the Gun-boat and put on board her. They are not to [be] landed at present, nor do I think they ever will. Two 26-pounders are to be landed from Lutine this morning, and the day after to-morrow our battery is to open against Monachesco; for it is found we cannot carry on our batteries against the Mozelle till that post is damaged. To our battery against Mozelle from the landing place is three miles. Wolseley, as soon as he has completed getting up the 12-pounders, tells me he shall go on board the Victory and acquaint your Lordship of his proceedings.

I am with highest respect,

Your Lordship's most obedient Servant,

HORATIO NELSON.

We want provision for the seamen on shore, particularly meat : our consumption of that article is very great. What Vessel would your Lordship wish me to find for it? if only to Fiorenzo, the Fox Cutter would very soon get it for us.

JOURNAL C.

July 3rd.—The Seamen were employed for six hours in bringing up stores from the landing-place, and at night carrying casks, sand-bags, and platforms, towards the intended battery. The French cannoneers and Royal Louis made the three-gun battery against Monachesco, which they are to have the fighting of.

TO ADMIRAL LORD HOOD.

[Autograph, in the Hood Papers.]

Camp, July 3rd, 1794.

My dear Lord,

I keep a regular Journal of each day's occurrence, which I will write out to-morrow and send your Lordship. In case you should send away before I can get my Journal to you, I beg leave to tell you that I arrived at Bastia on the 12th of June, in the morning; that all the Troops were embarked, 1450 men, on the 13th; that I sailed from Bastia the same evening; arrived at Fiorenzo on the 15th, in the evening; and having got all the stores embarked, I sailed with Dolphin and Lutine, with eighteen Sail of Transports and Store-ships, and anchored on the 17th, in the night, about four miles to the westward of Cape Revellata. The Troops were landed on the 19th, at four o'clock in the morning, in a Cove called Port Agro, about three miles and a half from the Town of Calvi, at which place all our Artillery and Stores are obliged to be landed. Particulars of our transactions I will, as I have before wrote, send to morrow, if possible. I beg leave most sincerely to congratulate your Lordship on the great news from England, though I am sure we shall all regret poor George Montague.[1]

Believe me with truest esteem,

Your most obliged,

HORATIO NELSON.

---

[1] The Battle of the 1st of June 1794; Captain *James* Montague fell, in command of the Montagu, of 74 guns.

By the ignorance and laziness of people in the different departments, the General is kept back much longer than he wished. Our advanced battery, I am sure, will not be made this night—much to his displeasure. All our guns are within three hundred yards of the intended battery against Mozelle: the battery against Monachesco was made last night in direct contradiction to the General's orders. The French¸ are of course firing at it, but it is thought right not to return the fire. We have nine twenty-six pounders, two twenty-four pounders, two eighteen pounders, three twelve-inch mortars, two ten-inch howitzers, one eight-inch howitzer, six field-pieces, all in their proper places.

I have sent for the Agents of Transports to send me an exact Return of what Ships are cleared; and what the other Ships have still on board, which I will send the first moment I get it.

TO ADMIRAL LORD HOOD.

[Autograph, in the Hood Papers.]

Camp, July 4th, 1794.

My dear Lord,

The Monachesco getting additional strength, the General ordered the three-gun battery which is manned by the Royal Louis, to open on them at daylight this morning. A great deal of the Enemy's battery is beat down, but I fancy it is not the General's intention to storm it to-night. I hope our advanced battery will be finished this night—at least for five guns, but we are very slow.

I have not yet quite wrote out my Journal, but will endeavour to do it this afternoon.

I am most truly your Lordship's faithful,

HORATIO NELSON.

A deserter came in this day: he says that two boats sailed for France within these three days past, that they do not come out by Cape Revellata, but go close round Cape d'Espano. The Brig would have gone last night, but the wind was unfavourable: she will go to-night if the weather is favourable.

JOURNAL C.

July 4th.—The Royal Louis Battery opened at day-light on Monachesco, and, before evening, did considerable damage to the Enemy's works. It being the General's intention to make our battery this night against the Mozelle, he judged it proper to endeavour to draw off the Enemy's attention from that place by a show of an attack on Monachesco.—In the evening the Royal Irish marched from the right, whilst the Light Corps moved to the left. The Corsicans also, as soon as it was dark, began to fire; which the Enemy thinking to be an attack on Monachesco, fired in all directions; not only from the latter place, but from the Mozelle, Fountain Battery, San Francesco, and the Town. In a short time, thinking, I suppose, that we were in possession of Monachesco, they directed their cannon against it; and their musketry was fired entirely across the isthmus, apprehending, doubtless, a general attack. It was General Stuart's orders, which were as plain as it was possible for orders to be, that the working parties should move forward with the sand-bags, casks, and platforms, after sun-set; and as soon as they were got a little forward, I was to have moved with the guns; but at half-past ten o'clock, when the General returned, not an Engineer had advanced : an attempt, however, was made to erect the battery, but by midnight it was found impossible to accomplish it, and mount the guns before daylight. The General, therefore, ordered all the materials to be taken back to the place whence they had been brought.

TO ADMIRAL LORD HOOD.

[Autograph, in the Hood Papers.]

Camp, July 5th, 1794.

My dear Lord,

I am sorry all the firing last night produced nothing. It was the General's intention, as he told me yesterday,[2] to make

---

[2] On the 4th of July General Stuart wrote to Captain Nelson:—

"Every time I write *delay*, my dear Sir, I suffer more than I can describe,

a feint of attacking Monachesco, which of course would draw off the attention of the Enemy from our people making the battery. From some cause it was eleven o'clock before the battery could be begun, and before twelve, from the impossibility of completing it, and getting the guns into it before daylight, every bag and cask was obliged to be carried back again. The failure of any plan must be distressing to him,— I am sure I feel it. Wherever it lays, it does not rest with us. We were at our posts one hour before any creature made their appearance. I think, from what the General told me last night, our battery will not be begun this night. A happy degree of irregularity I can't help thinking is sometimes better than all this *regularity*. I mentioned about the boats, as the way they securely go out, the same way they may attempt to get in, and the deserter said we guarded Cape Revellata, but not the other. Lieutenant Cox has his orders to join the Victory, and [is] getting some men to lay in the Cove with Mr. Fennel. I shall see the General before I close this letter, to know if he has anything to say to your Lordship. Believe me,

> Your most faithful
> HORATIO NELSON.

I am just come from the General, and I hope we shall get on better this night. He is very much displeased. The Return of Stores still on board the Transports the General wished to look over: therefore I have deferred sending them to your Lordship till to-morrow.

JOURNAL C.

July 5th.—Carrying junk for mortar platforms, and placing the mortars on their beds; getting also things forward for the advanced battery: one hundred seamen were

for it very little suits with my inclination or warmth of disposition. I must, however, crave it for one night more, and beg from you 100 men at eight o'clock this evening to forward shot still nearer the Enemy, while a hundred and fifty are employed by me in carrying other articles. Your very faithful servant, CHAS. STUART."—*Original*, in the Nelson Papers.

employed all night. Lieutenant Moutray made a battery for two eighteen-pounders inside Revellata, with twenty-five men.

TO ADMIRAL LORD HOOD.

[Autograph, in the Hood Papers.]

Camp, July 6th, 1794.

My dear Lord,

General Stuart is very anxious if your Lordship cannot get two eighteen pounders on the point inside Revellata, that one may be got, as it will take much fire from our battery, which I have now no doubt will be opened at daylight to-morrow morning. If opportunity offers during the feint of this night, Monachesco may probably be stormed. I send you my Journal, and an account of what is in the remaining Transports.

Believe me, your most faithful,

HORATIO NELSON.

JOURNAL C.

July 6th.—Procuring some planks, and preparing everything to be ready to work briskly in the evening. At half-past nine o'clock, a feint of an attack was carried on against Monachesco, which succeeded amazingly well. Not a shot was fired at us; for the Enemy turned their whole fire during the night towards the post which they imagined was attacked. By excessive labour, and the greatest silence in every department, the battery was completed for six guns, within 750 yards of the Mozelle, and without the smallest annoyance, before daylight.

On the 7th, and the guns brought close to it; but from unavoidable circumstances, the guns could not be mounted on the platforms until two hours afterwards. The Enemy did not fire at us until the fifth gun was getting into the battery, probably never thinking of looking so near themselves

for a battery, when they opened a heavy fire of grape
shot on us: but the Seamen did their duty. Considering our
very exposed situation, our loss was small in numbers;
yet amongst those who fell was Captain Walter Serocold,
of the Navy, who was killed by a grape-shot passing
through his head as he cheered the people who were
dragging the gun. In him, the service lost a gallant Officer,
and a most able Seaman. Three soldiers were also killed, one
of the Agamemnon's Seamen, and Mr. Thomas Corney,
Mate of the Grand Bay, Transport, who was one of the volunteers. A little before six o'clock, we got two English twenty-
four-pounders, and four twenty-six-pounders, mounted on
their platforms, in defiance of all opposition. At ten o'clock
opened our fire from this battery on the Mozelle and Fountain battery: not a gun from the Town can bear upon us,
being so much covered by the Mozelle. We also opened our
hill-battery of two twenty-six-pounders and a twelve-inch
mortar, fifteen hundred yards from the Mozelle, with the
Royal Louis battery of three thirty-six-pounders and two
twelve-inch mortars in the rear, and to the left of our advanced battery; all which kept up during the whole day a
constant fire on the Enemy. At three o'clock in the afternoon
the Enemy set fire to the fascines in Monachesco, and abandoned the post, which the Corsicans took possession of. We
had considerably damaged the works by night, during which
we fired occasionally on their batteries. The Enemy repaired
much of the fascine battery during the succeeding night.

TO ADMIRAL LORD HOOD.

[Autograph, in the Hood Papers.]

Battery, Noon, July 7th, 1794.

My dear Lord,

The feint on Monachesco succeeded most amazingly well.
Not a shot was fired at us, but from unavoidable circumstances our guns could not be mounted on the platforms till
two hours after daylight, and being within grape-shot of
the Enemy it is wonderful our loss has not been greater.

Your Lordship will be sorry to hear that Captain Serocold[3] is amongst the killed. The Agamemnon lost one Seaman, and a Mate of a Transport had his leg shot off. The Troops had a Sergeant and two Privates killed. Our battery seems to have had a good effect on the Cavalier of the Mozelle, the two guns facing us being silenced. I will send back your papers, with thanks, so soon as the General returns them: the others I gave to Captain Wolseley to return to your Lordship.

Believe me with truest esteem,

Your Lordship's most faithful Servant,

HORATIO NELSON.

Captain Hallowell and myself feel ourselves fully equal to the duty here. I send this Note, knowing your Lordship must be anxious to hear of us.

The Crescent is cleared of all her stores, if your Lordship wants her.[1]

―――――――

TO MRS. NELSON.

[From Clarke and M'Arthur, vol. i. p. 180.]

Camp, 8th July 1794.

My dear Fanny,

I long to hear from you, for a post has arrived without a letter. Our batteries opened yesterday, and it is possible you may have heard that a Captain of the Navy has fallen. To assure you it is not me, I write a few lines; for if such a

---

[3] Lord Hood thus replied to this Letter, on the 7th of July :—

" My dear Nelson,—You judge very right; I was anxious to hear from you, and all things considered from your statement, I wonder our loss has not been more considerable. But I feel struck for the fate of poor Serocold, as the King had not a more gallant and deserving Officer in the Navy, and I had a very sincere regard for him. If you, with the assistance of that brave fellow Hallowell, feel yourself equal to the service that may arise, I shall not send you another Officer, but I shall hold one ready to rejoin you whenever you wish it. There is a Transport not far off to which I have sent a boat, and I want its return to make a communication of her to the General, before I send away your messenger. Very faithfully yours, HOOD. Be so good as to order the Crescent to join me immediately, that she may be discharged. The Transport is the Jamaica from Bastia : the enclosed note specifies what she has on board."—From a *Copy*, certified by Nelson, in the Hood Papers.

[1] On the outside of this Letter, Nelson wrote in pencil, " To be sent off directly. H. N."

report should get about, I well know your anxiety of mind. We shall take Calvi in due time; and I hope without much loss of men. I am very busy, yet own I am in all my glory: except with you, I would not be any where but where I am, for the world. I am well aware my poor services will not be noticed: I have no interest; but, however services may be received, it is not right in an Officer to slacken his zeal for his Country.

Yours, &c.
HORATIO NELSON.

TO ADMIRAL LORD HOOD.

[Autograph, in the Hood Papers.]

My dear Lord,   Camp, July 8th, 1794.

I received your letter last night after dark, and having no light on the battery could not read it till daylight this morning. I shall send directly to the Crescent to join your Lordship. He desired from me, before we left Bastia, a written desire to sail with me: as he was under no Charter, it related I suppose to his insurance.

The Enemy abandoned Monachesco yesterday evening, setting all that would burn on fire. They have no shells but six and a-half inch, which is fired from a field carriage brought occasionally forward. Our exertions the night before must have surprised them, and had they believed their eyes at daylight they must have done us much damage, but it was a full hour before they fired a shot after the day broke. No person has been killed since our battery opened, and only two wounded, and they slightly. I sent off Mr. Cox to get ammunition, and if it is thought right, some men for the Gun-boats are wanted to come towards the Point near where we are, to prevent any of the Enemy's Gun-boats from flanking our battery. I believe the General intends erecting a battery to the left of our present one, and advanced about three hundred yards to knock down the Mozelle, which has already suffered greatly.

Believe me, with truest esteem,
Your Lordship's most faithful servant,
HORATIO NELSON.

Our Artillery Officers will use two wads for the guns—one we believe to be sufficient, but they don't seem to mind me. I have told Captain Stephens and Captain Wilkes,[4] who is on the battery, that they will, from using as many again as is necessary, be soon short of that article, which probably cannot be supplied them. A large packet I found in my Tent this morning from Sir Gilbert Elliot, which I send.

Since writing my letter I have received yours desiring one every morning. Ten o'clock is the hour I have appointed Sir H. Burrard[5] to have a person at my Tent. I was only just returned home, having been absent forty-eight hours, or should have wrote early in the morning.

I send this by L'Aimable as she is most likely to get to your Lordship before Mr. Cox.

JOURNAL C.

Throughout the whole of the 8th, both sides had kept up a constant and heavy fire. They totally destroyed two of our twenty-four-pounders, greatly damaged a twenty-six-pounder, and shook our works very much. One of their shells burst in the centre of our battery, amongst the General, myself, and at least one hundred persons, and blew up our battery magazine, but, wonderful to say, not a man was much hurt. We, on our part, did considerable damage to the Mozelle and Fountain battery ; but when any of their guns were disabled, they had others to supply their place. At night we repaired our works, and got two of the Agamemnon's eighteen-pounders to replace the twenty-four-pounder. During this day we had two Seamen killed, and three Soldiers wounded.

By ten o'clock on the 9th of July, we had evidently the superiority of fire, and before night had dismounted every gun in the Fountain battery and Mozelle, which bore upon

---

[4] Captains Edward Stephens and John Wilkes, both of the Artillery.

[5] Captain Sir Harry Burrard, Bart., of the L'Aimable of 32 guns. He afterward assumed the name of Neale, and died an Admiral of the Blue, a G.C.B., and G.C.M.G., in February 1840.

us: but the guns in Saint Francesco annoyed us considerably, being so much on our left flank, and at so great a distance, that we could not get our guns to bear on it with any effect. In the night, we mounted the howitzer of ten inches 150 yards in the rear, and a little to the left of our battery, both of which fired on the Enemy every three minutes during the night to prevent their working. Hallowell and myself each take twenty-four hours at the advanced battery. During this day one Soldier was killed, and one Soldier and two Seamen were wounded.

TO ADMIRAL LORD HOOD.

[Autograph, in the Hood Papers.]

July 9th, 1794.

My Lord,

I send you Captain Stephens' letter to me about wads. I spoke to the General, and he has directed that only one wad shall be used in future. If your Lordship will have the goodness to order two or three thousand to be made, we shall probably want them. The Victory has a Former for twenty-six pounders. The Agamemnon's two twenty-four pounders are both ruined: one split up to the rings; the other with the trunnion knocked so much off, that it is useless for shot. The Dolphin is in great want of wood. The Vigilant Gun-boat is laying here without men. Captain May[6] wishes, if you have no objection, to put some men into her, and send her for some wood to Port Galeria. I have just sent to the General to know when he wishes the powder to be sent. On shore they have probably sufficient: therefore it will be ordered to the Store-ships. We have no certain communication with Corte, although I should think a letter might be sent to Frediani, who I think would send a trusty Corsican with it.

Your most faithful
HORATIO NELSON.

Casualties—Three Seamen and two Soldiers wounded.

---

[6] Captain James May commanded the Dolphin Store-ship; he was Posted in 1794.

Battery, half-past ten o'clock.

I have this moment received your letter.   I should be sorry that any opinion of mine should cast a censure on an Officer; but at sunset the Seamen were ready to proceed with the guns: in about a quarter of an hour the General passed us with the Troops for the feint of an attack; in about a quarter of an hour afterwards, the Engineer, Captain Nepean,[7] came from towards the intended battery, and he did not go forward with the workmen till near half-past ten o'clock. The General's orders were clear, and were executed, as we know, the next night, and I know no reason but the Engineer's not going forward so soon as it was dark, that prevented the batteries being made one night as well as the other. The General is displeased, and it has given Captain Nepean a fit of the gout, so General Stuart tells me. I will, as your Lordship sends my Journal home, alter that part of it, if you will please to send it me, and put into it the exact time of the Agamemnon's parting from her anchor and return. Fox is returned.   I am getting the plank from her.   If sleepers can be got, the platforms are undoubtedly much the better for them. My Agamemnon's carpenter at Bastia made us much better platforms than these gentry.   The General's expression of anger, the night I mentioned — no Engineer to be found—was public : ' *not an Engineer to be found.*'   Hallowell and myself take, each one, twenty-four hours of duty at the advanced battery.

TO ADMIRAL LORD HOOD.

[Autograph, in the Hood Papers.]

Camp, July 10th, 1794.

My dear Lord,

I have just received your letter of last night,[8] and have to request that any part of my Journal which may relate to the

---

[7] Captain Thomas Nepean, elder brother of Sir Evan Nepean, Bart. He became a Major-General, and died in 1816.

[8] The Letter referred to is not among the Copies of Letters from Lord Hood to Nelson, now in the Hood Papers.

misconduct of any Officer, you will alter as you please. I write yours from my own, which contains nothing but the truth; and was intended by me as only a friendly not official communication to your Lordship. In my Journal it stands, —

'It was the General's orders, which were as plain as possible
' for orders to be, for the working party to move forward
' with the sandbags, casks, and platforms, and as soon as
' they were got forward, I was to move with the guns.
' At half-past ten not an Engineer had gone forward; and
' when the General returned, an attempt was made to erect
' the battery, but it was too late, and all the bags, casks, &c.
' were obliged to be brought back again.'

So stands my Journal. If your Lordship's is different, it was the writing of the moment; but the fact is the same, that by a quarter after nine, the Engineer ought to have done what he intended doing at half-past ten. The fact is as I have mentioned, but if your Lordship pleases to alter it, I shall be obliged, to,

' At half-past ten o'clock the working parties went for-
' ward, but it was too late, and all the bags, casks, &c., were
' obliged to be brought back again. In the afternoon of
' the 21st, the Agamemnon parted from her anchors, and
' went to sea. The others, two Men-of-War and four Trans-
' ports fortunately rode out the gale, for had they parted,
' being nearer in shore than the Agamemnon, every person
' must have perished.

' 24th.—The Agamemnon returned to her anchorage, as
' did every Transport.'

I enclose my Journal up to this morning. I will desire some of the plank which may come in the Brig, to be left on board her for the Victory.

I am to land, if possible, two thirty-six pounders this night in the bay close by our battery, and have to request from the Victory two coils of four-inch or four-and-a-half-inch rope: the Agamemnon now is exhausted of every thing. I beg they may be sent to the Gun-boat, and the Boats shall call for them as they row past her. So many and various are the stores which I have landed both at Bastia and here, and for which no regular receipts could be got, such as sails, ropes, blocks, wads, and a number of other stores, that I must request a General Order both for Bastia and this place; for every Ship near me has had Memorandums for many things being landed, and I shall get no pay unless you are pleased to give me some General Order. General Stuart is very well. He sleeps with us in the battery every night.

I find it so late, that I cannot send my Journal to-day, but will have it ready for to-morrow. Every thing mentioned, your Lordship may rely is most strictly correct; only we must recollect *the truth is not to be spoken at all times*, but with your Lordship I have no reserves.

Believe me with truest esteem,

Your most faithful,

HORATIO NELSON.

The Mozelle is much battered, as is the fascine battery. By ten o'clock yesterday morning we got the superiority of fire, and by dark the Enemy had [not] a gun in the Mozelle or Fountain battery to fire, all being either dismounted [or] disabled, and the embrasures blocked up. At San Francesco, they have one gun, which annoys us a good deal. They attempted to annoy us with large shells from the town, but very few came home to us, they mostly bursting as they leave the mortar. We kept firing grape and shells from the ten-inch howitzer, which we mounted last night to prevent their working; and their guns are in the same state as we left them last night. I think, if possible, the Mozelle may be breached by to-morrow night, but certain it will in one day after the thirty-six pounders get against it, as they are to be two hundred yards nearer.

One Soldier killed. 2 Seamen dead of their wounds. One ditto wounded.

———

JOURNAL C.

On the 10th at daylight, we opened our fire on the Mozelle, and occasionally a gun on the Fountain battery, and found that the Enemy had not done any work in that battery during the night, everything being exactly in the same state. At the Mozelle they had placed great numbers of sand-bags, to prevent our shot from striking under the arches of the bomb-proof of the cavaliere, which we did yesterday by beating down the merlins of the lower work. By seven o'clock in the morning the sand-bags were mostly beat down, and our fire went on without any opposition. By the evening, the Mozelle was much shaken, and I am sure a breach may be made practicable, whenever the General thinks it right to turn his attention to it. To the honour of General Stuart, he is not sparing of himself on any occasion : he every night sleeps with us in the advanced battery.

At ten o'clock on the same day, saw the Enemy carry off their field-pieces and howitzer, and totally abandon the Fountain battery ; which was no sooner done, than they opened a fire from the bastions of the Town over their old battery and the Mozelle, and although they could not see our battery, yet great numbers of their shot struck it. By the evening a very large breach was made in the lower work of the Mozelle ; and during the night, Lieutenant Moutray joined, with twenty-five seamen : at ten o'clock they got up two thirty-six pounders and one twenty-six-pounder. We had this day one Soldier killed.

TO ADMIRAL LORD HOOD.

[Autograph, in the Hood Papers.]

Camp, July 11th, 1794, 6 A.M.

My dear Lord,

The two thirty-six pounders were landed in the night. Our davit-cast unfortunately has broke its windlass, but if the carpenters can fix another before night, (I have sent for the windlass belonging to the Agamemnon's launch,) we shall, I dare say, get a battery made for them so near the Mozelle, as to insure a breach in the course of twenty-four hours' firing. The General seems as anxious as any of us to expedite the fall of the place ; and if I may be allowed to judge, he is an extraordinary good judge of ground. His object is to keep from the town-fire till Mozelle falls. I can only say, that every exertion of mine shall be used to facilitate its reduction. The Royal Louis are bringing the three guns entrusted to them down the hill to an advanced battery. We are now firing red-hot shot at the fascine battery, to endeavour to effectually destroy it, but I am rather inclined to think there is too much sand mixed with the fascines. I shall finish this in the battery.

The new battery cannot be made this night, but I hope all materials will be got forward. If the davit-cast is finished, I shall at all events get the guns forward. I have just sent for the two twenty-six pounders to be brought round to-night with shot and shells. With the highest respect, I am,

　　　　Your Lordship's most faithful Servant,

　　　　　　　　HORATIO NELSON.

JOURNAL C.

At daylight on the 12th, the Enemy opened a heavy fire from the town and San Francesco, which, in an extraordinary manner, seldom missed our battery ; and at seven o'clock, I was much bruised in the face and eyes by sand from the works struck by shot. The Mozelle was by this time much breached. At night replaced the guns destroyed, and fired a gun and mortar every three minutes. At half-past twelve the Town was on fire, and burnt for three hours. We had two Seamen and three Soldiers wounded.

TO ADMIRAL LORD HOOD.

[Autograph, in the Hood Papers.]

Camp, July 12th, 1794.

My dear Lord,

The Enemy yesterday afternoon abandoned the Fountain Battery, as I am sure they will Mozelle and San Francesco, when they come to be pressed. The bastions of the Town opened their fire upon us, but as they could not see our battery, could not do us much harm. In the night we got to the rear of our battery the two thirty-six-pounders : the twenty-six-pounders are landed, and one also got up. I send your Lordship Lieutenant Caines' letter. When I was on the beach, seeing how necessary it was to give encouragement to the Transport's people to exert themselves in getting Stores on shore, I gave them some wine and provisions rather than any delay should be made, but I did not feel myself justified in always continuing it. However, the people behaved well, and having worked all day probably, and ordered to work all night, if your Lordship will allow me, I will discretionarily order them a little wine as an encouragement. Reports, we know, get about, and as neither time, or many other circumstances, may be mentioned, it is best to say it myself—that I got a little hurt[9] this morning: not much, as you may judge by my writing.

Believe me with truest esteem,

Your most faithful,

HORATIO NELSON.

One Artilleryman killed.

JOURNAL C.

During the whole of the 13th of July, a constant fire was kept up from the Town, which struck our battery very often, and dismounted another twenty-six-pounder. This is the fifth gun which has been disabled since the 7th, when our battery opened, and having only six guns in it, is quite wonderful. At night we landed four eighteen-pounders, with a quantity of shot and shells, in Port Vaccaja, and were employed in getting them up to the rear of our work: and here I must acknowledge the indefatigable zeal, activity, and ability of Captain Hallowell, and the great readiness which he ever shows to give me assistance in the laborious duties that are entrusted to us. By computation, to this night, we may be supposed to have dragged one twenty-six-pounder, with its ammunition, and every requisite for making a battery, upwards of eighty miles, seventeen of which were up a very steep mountain.

[9] This "little hurt" caused him the loss of the sight of his right eye. Lord Hood thus expressed his concern at the accident on the 12th of July:—

"My dear Nelson,—I am truly sorry to hear you have received a hurt, and hope you tell truth in saying it is not much. I shall be glad you will order the Boats' crews of the Transports wine, upon any occasion you judge necessary. I shall send some one in the morning to know how you are, and whether you would not have assistance. Ever, my dear Nelson, most sincerely yours, HOOD."—*Copy* in the Hood Papers.

TO ADMIRAL LORD HOOD.

[Autograph, in the Hood Papers.]

Camp, July 13th, 1794.

My dear Lord,

Captain Knight will tell you that the Enemy dismounted one of our twenty-six-pounders yesterday, but another was got into the battery at dusk. We are now getting off the beach at Port Agro four eighteen-pounders, which are to be carried round in the evening. We are in want of eighteen-pounder shot for the two eighteen-pounders landed from Agamemnon. I have landed all but one thousand, but if your Lordship pleases, I will land such part of those as you may judge proper. They also want one barrel of pitch to pay the bottoms of tubs for the batteries. I have none; therefore request you will be pleased to order a barrel to be landed. If it is practicable, the General wishes to get Mozelle without erecting another battery, and then our efforts will all be against the Town-wall: eighteen-pounders to be left in our present battery, and the thirty-six and twenty-six-pounders carried forward. My eye is better, and I hope not entirely to lose the sight.

I shall be able to attend my duty this evening if a new battery is to be erected. Hallowell, who is a worthy good man, and myself, feel ourselves fully equal to whatever duty can be performed by our Seamen landed: should we want assistance I will acquaint your Lordship.

Believe me, with truest esteem,

Your most faithful

HORATIO NELSON.

Two Seamen slightly wounded. Three Soldiers ditto.

TO ADMIRAL LORD HOOD.

[Autograph, in the Hood Papers.]

Camp, July 14th, 1794.

My dear Lord,

We have been so unlucky with our guns in the advanced battery, five having been ruined out of the six mounted, that the General wishes, if the Victory has any of the Commerce de Marseilles' guns on board, that two or three may be landed.[1] I rather think the guns we have on shore are not those we had at Bastia; therefore I am in hopes they may be on board the Victory. The present battery will be continued complete, eighteen-pounders instead of the heavy ones. Not less than seven guns will be wanted against the Town, and we have got only six. I shall land one twenty-four-pounder from Agamemnon this night, as also some eighteen-pounder shot. I am sure we should get on much faster, but the General has not a person to forward his views—the Engineer sick, the Artillery Captain not fit for active service; therefore every minute thing must be done by himself, or it is not done at all. Last night we landed, and got to the rear of the battery four eighteen-pounders, and mounted a twenty-six-pounder in the room of the one dismounted yesterday. Our battery against Mozelle, if one is necessary, is, I understand, to be made this night. The General is not well. He fatigues himself too much, but I can't help seeing he is obliged to do it. I am sorry to hear your Lordship has not been so well as I most sincerely wish you to be; but I hope before this time the complaint is removed.

> Believe me, my dear Lord,
> With highest respect, your most faithful,
> HORATIO NELSON.

One Soldier killed.

I keep my rough Journal regularly on: a copy for your Lordship is rather behind, but to-morrow I hope to send it.

[1] To this request Lord Hood signified his assent, on the 14th of July:

"My dear Nelson,—You shall have three of the Commerce de Marseilles' guns on shore this evening. I grieve to hear the General is not well, but am not surprised at it, being sensible how much he is obliged to attend to himself, being so tamely supported; but if the Duncans keep well I don't care, as they are the men I depend upon. I cannot boast of my own health, but hope by care and attention to hold out to see Calvi reduced. From your rapid firing last night I flattered myself it was intended to walk into the Mozelle as this night. Captain Seccombe is here, whom I shall keep in case you should want his help. He is a very active fellow. Very faithfully yours, HOOD. You shall have two more of the Commerce de Marseilles guns to-morrow night, if the General wishes it."—*Copy*, in the Hood Papers.

TO THOMAS POLLARD, ESQ., LEGHORN.

[Autograph, (framed and glazed,) in the possession of Mr. Farrer, of Montagu
Street, Portman Square.]

July 14th, 1794.

My dear Sir,

I have to beg the favour of you to forward the inclosed for England. The money you mention as having sent by the Sincerity, Lieutenant Walker, is not received. You will be sorry to hear of the fate of Captain Serocold, but he fell as an Officer should, in the service of his Country. Hallowell and myself are both well, except my being half blinded by these fellows, who have given me a smart slap in the face, for which I am their *debtor*, but hope not to be so long.

Your obliged,

HORATIO NELSON.

TO MRS. NELSON.

[From Clarke and M'Arthur, vol i. 182.]

July 14th, 1794.

A fortnight will, I have no doubt, give us Calvi; but our efforts here are at such a distance, and so eclipsed by Lord Howe's great success at home, that I dare say we are not thought of: however, we must exert ourselves.

Yours, &c.,

HORATIO NELSON.

TO ADMIRAL LORD HOOD.

[Autograph, in the Hood Papers.]

Camp, July 15th, 1794.

My dear Lord,

We landed the guns, &c., as you will see by my Journal, which is up to this morning at daylight: the General is better; has spared himself a very little these two nights. He hopes to be able to take Mozelle without erecting another battery. I made, yesterday, thirteen scaling-ladders, on board Agamemnon, and landed them this morning, for I think the Troops will be troubled in getting up the wall, because the earth is too loose, and the weight of men will sink into it. The Enemy have heaped up a great quantity of sand-bags in the breach, and are aware of the General's intentions, I am sure by their conduct, although I have no doubt of our success. We changed the twenty-six-pounder in the battery last night for the eighteen-pounder. I shall rejoice to hear your Lordship is perfectly recovered,

Being, with the sincerest esteem,

Your most faithful

HORATIO NELSON.

TO ADMIRAL LORD HOOD.

[Autograph, in the Hood Papers.]

July 16th, 1794.

My dear Lord,

We can want no more guns on shore, having now seven twenty-six pounders, one twenty-four pounder, two thirty-six pounders, laying idle in the rear of our battery, besides three which the Royal Louis are in proper time, I suppose, to bring forward. The General did not think the breach practicable ; and I am rather inclined to think it will not be more so this evening, for we are battering against the solid rock, and the Enemy have filled up the space between the work and the Cavalier with sand-bags.

We must this evening either erect another battery for four guns, 250 yards nearer, which will knock down an angle, or mount the breach as it is. Two days I can't help thinking are already lost. Colonel Moore, as Colonel of the Flank Company, will have the command, and I think it is *he* who wishes the breach to be made wider. *We are slow,* which I am sorry for. Moutray, whose battery on the point seems now little thought of, wishes to come here. He says there is a careful Midshipman, therefore wishes to give his assistance here. Men we do not want : if your Lordship has no objection, I will occasionally take him over for a night's work now and then; but I would not do it without your approbation. We are all well. My eye is much better.

> Believe me, with truest esteem,
> > Your Lordship's most faithful,
> > > HORATIO NELSON.

No accident.[2]

TO WILLIAM SUCKLING, ESQ.

[Autograph, in the possession of Captain Montagu Montagu, R.N.]

Calvi, Camp, July 16th, 1794.

My dear Sir,

It is a little age since I have had the pleasure of hearing from you. A letter would give me real pleasure, and to say you are all well. I hear Captain Suckling[3] is gone abroad, where I am sure he will acquit himself with honour to himself and friends, amongst which I hope I am considered in the strongest degree. To an Officer, I feel, and [assure you] he does, that an opportunity to distinguish ourselves is our greatest happiness. What pleasure must those who are dear to us feel in reading of a gallant Officer's conduct.

I don't doubt but your son will return safe, and with every credit which an Officer can receive—that he may, I most sincerely wish.

You will probably have heard that I am landed here, although

---

[2] Lord Hood's answer to this Letter, dated July 16th, contains his opinion on an important question, to which Nelson alludes in his Letters of the same day:—

"My dear Nelson,—I am happy to hear you are better, and that no accidents have happened since yesterday. You are at liberty to make what use you please of Moutray, and I have told him so. Captain Seccombe is here, much disposed to be useful, and ready to obey your commands if you would have him. I am sorry the General and I differ with respect to Summoning the Garrison, having always understood that whenever an Army is before a place and does not Summon it, the besieged conclude no terms will be granted. I shall not, however, say another word upon the subject. I have given my reasons for the measure, and those increase daily, which makes the delay, even of a day, of importance to our Allies, consequently to his Majesty's service. But I say this to you alone. If things do not go altogether right no blame shall lay at my door. Ever faithfully yours, HOOD. L'Aigle is in sight from Leghorn."—*Copy* in the Hood Papers.

[3] A natural son of Mr. Suckling.

every person sees how much I am put in the back-ground at Bastia: yet my zeal for the honour of my Country ought not to abate. On the 7th ultimo, our battery opened. Captain Serocold of the Navy was killed on the 10th. You will be surprised when I say I was wounded in the head by stones from the merlon of our battery. My right eye is cut entirely down; but the Surgeons flatter me I shall not entirely lose my sight of that eye. At present I can distinguish light and dark, but no object: it confined me one day, when, thank God, I was enabled to attend to my duty. I feel the want of it; but, such is the chance of War, it was within a hair's breadth of taking off my head.

Lord Hood and myself were never better friends,—*nor, although his Letter does,* did he wish to put me where I never was—in the rear.[3] Captain Hunt, who lost his Ship,[4] he wanted to push forward for another—a young man who never was on a battery, or ever rendered any service during the Siege: if any person ever says he did, then I submit to the character of a story-teller. Poor Serocold, who fell here, was determined to publish an advertisement, as he commanded a battery under my orders. The whole operations of the Siege were carried on through Lord Hood's letters to me. I was the mover of it—I was the cause of its success. Sir Gilbert Elliot will be my evidence, if any is required. I am not a little vexed, but shall not quarrel. We shall be successful here; and a stranger and a landsman[5] will probably do me that credit which *a friend* and brother Officer has not given me. Best regards to every good friend.

Believe me your most affectionate
HORATIO NELSON.

[3] Vide p. 399, ante.   [4] Vide p. 387, ante.   [5] General Stuart.

TO ADMIRAL LORD HOOD.

[Autograph, in the Hood Papers.]

Camp, July 16th, 1794.

My dear Lord,

My letters, I am sure are considered as confidential :[6] therefore I write what I think, as your Lordship saw by my opinion this day. I have the pleasure to say the breaches, for there are *two*, are much enlarged this day, and the General has told me, in confidence, his plan for to-morrow night, when success will attend us, I have little doubt. The Enemy, by their mode of firing this day, are aware of our intentions, for they have tried the range of the different grounds we are to possess. I don't think it is always necessary to Summons a Place before an attack, nor that it precludes the besieged from honourable terms. I have served as Commanding Sea-Officer on shore, when we attacked, and the besieged, when they thought proper, sent out a Flag of Truce. At this place, if they had been aware of our getting so near them in the first position we could not have done it, the ground is so very unfavourable. The Town wall is well built, but after their guns are dismounted I think they will surrender. The

---

[6] From Lord Hood, " July 17th, 1794. My dear Nelson,—Not a soul knows anything of what you communicate except the casualties, and I am sorry for those of yesterday. I perfectly agree with you that a Town not being Summoned does not preclude the inhabitants from honourable terms, but according to the Rules of War generally practised, a Summons is sent, as it gives a fair opening to the besieged, if they are actuated by the same principles, that of sparing the effusion of blood, after security is offered to persons and property. At the same time in critical situations there may be objections to it, and I was convinced they existed in the first instance, but I am doubtful whether they do so now. However, I shall say not another word upon the subject, although the rapidity with which the French are getting on at Toulon, makes it indispensably necessary for me to put the whole of the Fleet under my command in the best possible state for service; and I must soon apply to the General for those parts of the Regiments now on shore, ordered by his Majesty to serve in lieu of Marines, to be held in readiness to embark at the shortest notice. I shall delay the application as long as possible, and I am now sending L'Aigle to look into Toulon. I write this in confidence. God send what is intended for this night may be successful. Ever faithfully yours, HOOD. P.S. I have no wish to send Seccombe, and only keep him in case he should be wanted. I have sent Sir Harry Burrard the last newspapers to be forwarded to you."—*Copy*, in the Hood Papers.

Frigates,[7] I am told, every evening are filled with people from the Town: therefore I don't think they intend to burn them.

I am sorry to conclude by saying that three Seamen and three Soldiers were blown up by some cartridges taking fire: two or three are in great danger. As I go out at nine o'clock, probably not to return till this business is over, I write this to be ready to close if nothing particular occurs in the night. Did we want assistance we could not object to Captain Seccombe:[8] quite the contrary, but too many Captains I have before felt are an inconvenience.

Believe me, with truest regard,

Your most obliged and faithful

HORATIO NELSON.

8 A. M. 17th.

Nothing new has occurred since my writing last night. Sandbags, &c., are carried forward to make a battery, which will open against the Town at daylight, or against the Mozelle, if we should by any accident miscarry.

One Seaman, blown up yesterday, *dead.*

TO THE RIGHT HONOURABLE SIR GILBERT ELLIOT, BART.

[Autograph, in the Minto Papers.]

Camp, Calvi, July 17th, 1794.

My dear Sir,

You may possibly hear both from Lord Hood and General Stuart of our operations; therefore I shall say little more of them, than that success, I have no doubt, will attend the General; and no Officer ever deserved it more. The place is strong, the access to it difficult; the great difficulties are, I hope, over. The Mozelle will be stormed this night, two breaches are made in it. The great fatigue General Stuart has undergone

---

[7] The French Frigates La Melpomene, of 44 guns, and La Mignonne of 32 guns, which were then in the harbour of Calvi.

[8] Captain Thomas Seccombe; he was Posted in 1796; and in January 1808 while commanding the Glatton, having gone to the assistance of the Delight, Sloop, which had grounded under the batteries of Reggio, he was mortally wounded and taken prisoner.

since our landing, has rather injured his health; but nothing
stops him from seeing every thing done himself. Our loss has
been trifling, not twenty killed and wounded : amongst the former is Captain Serocold, and amongst the latter, in a slight
manner, is myself, my head being a good deal wounded, and my
right eye cut down ; but the Surgeons flatter [me] I shall not
entirely lose the sight, which I believe, for I can already distinguish light from dark. It confined me, thank God, only one
day, and at a time when nothing particular happened to be
doing. I beg my respects to the Governor, if you see him. I
would write him a line, but have not time.

Believe me, dear Sir,

With the highest esteem,

Your most faithful Servant,

HORATIO NELSON.

TO ADMIRAL LORD HOOD.

[Autograph, in the Hood Papers.]

Camp, July 18th, 1794.

My dear Lord,

I am just come from the General, who seems better pleased
than he was last evening. He requests I will write to solicit from you 600 barrels of powder and 1000 English eighteen-pound shot. Now L'Aigle is gone, I am sure you cannot immediately supply that quantity. The Agamemnon has
500, 200 of which I have just ordered to be landed. We
shall find plenty about the Mozelle. I have also ordered 200
barrels of powder to be ready for landing from Agamemnon :
the powder to be landed where we now land all our stores in
Port Vaccaja. I shall thank you to tell me what shot the
Imperieuse can land, if any should be wanting. I send your
Lordship an account of what we have already expended : it
is I believe correct, or very near it. Many of our shot are
lost, probably on the roads, so that we cannot say the number remaining will all be forthcoming, by some hundreds.

Believe me, with truest esteem,

Your Lordship's most faithful,

HORATIO NELSON.

1 Artillery-man killed.

INCLOSURE.

An Account of Powder, Shot, and Shells, expended before Calvi between the 7th of July and the 17th, both days included.

		Barrels.	
Powder . . .		998	
Shells, 12-inch	.	1012	
Ditto, 10-ditto	.	424	
Ditto, 8-ditto	.	149	
Shot—			
26-Pds . .		5338	
18-Pds., French	.	2205	
18-Pds., English	.	1100	Remains :—

902 Barrels Powder.
1288 Large Shells.

Stores at landing :—			
Powder . . .		1900	Don't recollect { 8-Inch. 10-Inch.
Shells, 12 and 13-Inch		2300	
Shot, 26-Pds. . .		13,500	8162 26-Pdrs.
Ditto, 18-Pds., French		2600	315 18-Pdrs., French.
Ditto, 18-ditto, English		1300	200 18-Pdrs., English.

JOURNAL C.

July 18th.—The 50th Regiment were to assist in making a battery for three twenty-six pounders to the right of the Mozelle, at about the distance of 300 yards; the Seamen were ordered to carry forward the guns and mount them, and also one thirteen-inch mortar. Sixty seamen, under Lieutenants Edmonds and Harrison,[9] were to carry forward the field-pieces. The disposition of the Troops was as follows: Colonel Wemyss,[1] with the 18th Regiment, was to proceed by the left of our six-gun battery, with two field-pieces drawn by Seamen, and with fixed bayonets, was to take possession of the Fountain battery, which having carried, the Colonel was to direct his force against San Francesco, if it fired; when the

---

[9] Of the Navy : nothing has been found of their future career.

[1] Lieutenant-Colonel David Douglas Wemyss of the 18th, or Royal Irish Regiment. In 1795 he was made Governor of Calvi : he became a Major General in April 1802 ; Lieutenant-General in April 1808 ; and was subsequently Governor of Tynmouth Castle.—*Royal Military Calendar*, vol. i. p. 136.

troops under Colonel Moore, with two field-pieces drawn by
Seamen, were to move forward, under cover of the three-gun
battery, and carpenters under Lieutenant St. George,[2] were to
go before to cut down the palisadoes. A party under Major
Brereton[3] were to advance by the right of the Mozelle, and cut
off the Enemy's retreat from the Town. Colonel Moore's
party were to be supported by the 51st Regiment, the 50th
Regiment, having finished their work at the battery, was to
remain under arms; and the troops were to move forward
lying on their arms. We continued all night hard at work,
and landed one hundred and twelve Seamen from the Agamemnon, under Lieutenant Suckling.

TO ADMIRAL LORD HOOD.

[Autograph, in the Hood Papers.]

Camp, July 18th, 1794.

My dear Lord,

The General wishes that the battery of eighteen-pounders
on the Point may be able to open a fire to-morrow morning
at daylight. Moutray tells me he has only twenty cartridges of
powder and shot. It is necessary there should at least be one
hundred; therefore I shall be glad if your Lordship will order
a hundred shot and cartridges and some Match to be landed
in the night from L'Imperieuse, for these guns. I take for
granted we are to be active to-night.

I have received your Lordship's letter,[4] and shall take care,
if possible, to give no offence whatever.

Your most faithful,

HORATIO NELSON.

[2] Afterwards Major General Sir Thomas Bligh St. George, C. B., K. C. H.
He died in November, 1836.

[3] Major Robert Brereton. In 1793, he served in Lord Hood's Fleet, as
Captain of Marines; and in October of that year was appointed Major of the
30th Foot. He became, after much active service, a Lieutenant-General in June
1814. *Royal Military Calendar*, vol. i. p. 266.

[4] The following is the Letter alluded to :—

‘ TO CAPTAIN NELSON.

‘ Victory, 18th July 1794.

"My dear Nelson,—I thank you for your Letter, and desire to have a daily
account how things go on. I would not by any means have you come on board;
and do most earnestly entreat you will give no opinion, unless asked, what is

TO ADMIRAL LORD HOOD.

[Autograph, in the Hood Papers.]

Camp, July 18th, 1794.

My dear Lord,

When I wrote your Lordship last I had no idea I could have wrote again until the Mozelle was carried, *but such things are*. I hope to God the General, who seems a good Officer and an amiable man, is not led away; but Colonel Moore is his great friend.

Yesterday, at noon, I found all was given up as last night, that things might be got forward for the grand battery against the Town. In the evening the General took me aside to say I had got him nearly into a scrape, for that I had wrote your Lordship that the Mozelle was to be stormed as this night, for that a Corsican Colonel (I think) had landed from the Victory, and been to him to offer his services, and that he was told on board the Victory what was to happen. I told the General that I certainly had wrote so to you, but I was sure it went no further; and that as to the Storming, every body these three days past had fixed each night for the Storm. There seems a little jealousy of my communicating with you daily; and I rather think the question to me last evening was to know if I told you anything. We must go on, let Moore say what he pleases. We have lost several days already, and what was as extraordinary, last night not an article was carried forward: therefore we are in

right or not right to be done; but whatever that may be, keep it to yourself, and be totally silent to every one, except in forwarding all proposed operations. Have no jealousies, I beg of you, and avoid giving any most carefully. I have not seen a Corsican Officer to have any conversation with respecting Calvi. Colunna was here three days ago with some gentlemen and ladies, from Agiola, and this morning Tartarelli came on board, just to make his bow, and was not with me five minutes, and I said not a word to either about the Siege, and I do entreat you will not suggest the least hint to any person whatever about the Summons to the Garrison. The utmost caution is necessary in you to be silent: say so to Hallowell, or you will both get into a difficulty. You must, I am sure, see the force of what I say, as you cannot be insensible, from what you have said, that there is some of Saint Fiorenzo leaven existing. A word to the wise is sufficient. Ever faithfully yours,　　　　　　　　　　　　　　　　　'HOOD.

'P. S.—If you do not bring yourself into a scrape by *talking*, you may depend upon it I shall not do it, as I shall know nothing to the General of what you have ever written to me; but beware of the *Colonel* you mention. I can believe nothing dishonourable of Duncan: the situation in which he is placed makes *silence* highly prudent.'—From a *Copy*, certified by Nelson, in the Hood Papers.

the same state to-night. I was in the battery till one
o'clock. I should like to come off, if nothing was going
forward; but I am sure it would be a conversation that I
went to tell all I knew, which is very little indeed. However, I can always say what has happened.

Your Lordship will have an application for 600 barrels of
powder, and for 18-pounder shot, English. I have landed
500 since your letter, and have now about 500 18-pounder,
and 500 24-pounder shot in my Ship, and 300 barrels of
powder.

Your Lordship will be so good as not to notice any part
of this letter to the General; for you must feel that a more
free communication has not been kept up by the General; but
indeed I don't yet say he is to blame. I wish Moore was
100 leagues off: he will injure him with the Army I see
clearly. Captain Duncan is an Aide-de-Camp: therefore
says nothing. After Mozelle is taken, why might not the
Town then be summoned? at that time it might be proper,
although not in the first instance. I beg your Lordship to
burn this letter.

Believe me, with the highest respect,

Your most faithful,

HORATIO NELSON.

Duncan is, I think, a little altered; there is nothing like
kicking down the ladder a man rises by.

TO ADMIRAL LORD HOOD.

[Autograph, in the Hood Papers.]

Camp, July 19th, 1794.

My dear Lord,

I wrote you a scrap of paper this morning from the Mozelle, knowing how very anxious you must be to hear of our
situation. Every thing, I take for granted, answered the General's wish. The battery of San Francesco, I take for
granted, was abandoned soon after daylight. The Enemy
have fired smart since daylight, and several of the Royal
Irish have been killed and wounded by shells from the Town,
before they could get themselves under cover by an entrench-
ment. The Seamen were only sent with four field-pieces, and

the rest of us making the battery and getting the guns mounted, which was done by two o'clock. The Royal Irish were to attack the Fountain battery and Tower, and then to fire their two field-pieces at San Francesco. Colonel Wemyss certainly performed his part in an Officer-like manner : then the two field-pieces, with the Grenadiers under Colonel Moore, began to fire into the breach of the Mozelle, and the new battery opened at the same time. Carpenters went forward and cut down the pallisadoes, the Light Infantry went to the right of the Mozelle to cut off the retreat of the Enemy, but before our troops could get to the bottom of the breach all fled, except half a dozen, who threw over two thirteen inch shells. The Grenadiers only found two men in the place, who were killed ; and the Light Infantry got a few shots at the fugitives, and took two prisoners, who say they are told succours will certainly soon be sent them. Colonel Moore was hurt by a stone tumbled from the wall. He is come to Camp, but I have sent to the Surgeons, and they say he is not dangerously wounded. Captain M'Donald[4] is not much hurt. The Mozelle is absolutely a heap of ruins, and the breach easy of ascent. You may rest assured that no cause for jealousies shall arise from me, but I can't help thinking we are sometimes too active. I think General Stuart must be pleased with our services. I could have wished to have had a little part in the Storm, if it was only to have placed the ladders and pulled away the pallisadoes. However, we did the part allotted for us. Duncan, I dare say, will not act a dishonourable part ; but he has certainly grown a much greater man to me than he was formerly. His activity and bravery will I am sure remain with him, and I hope his gratitude.

Believe me truly,

Your Lordship's most faithful,

HORATIO NELSON.

Killed at Mozelle 4, 7 wounded.

Since 5, 7 or 8 wounded.

Capt. M'Donald at Mozelle. } Royals.
Capt. M'Kenzie,[5] since.

[4] Captain Colin Macdonald, of the Royals.

[5] Captain Patrick Mackenzie.

Duncan told me this morning, that he was sure we had not shot enough to breach the bastions, and that he supposed a mine would be run under one of them, that in the outer Town.

TO ADMIRAL LORD HOOD.

[Autograph, in the Hood Papers.]

Camp, July 20th, 1794.

My dear Lord,

When the Victory's were first landed our numbers victualled were 341, Captain and every body included: now from various causes, for which I can readily account, our numbers are only 223 working-men, as by the inclosed list. I will land all I can from Agamemnon. They shall, if possible, be here to-night. All our boats and the Transports have hitherto been employed every night it has been possible in carrying shot and shells and stores. I will take Moutray's men, as I think the General cannot now want the battery. I have no doubt but Calvi will be ours in spite of all endeavours to poison the mind of a good man. This application I thought was coming, but I do not see there can be any occasion for it; but *our* exertions must not slacken. Moutray some days ago said to Colonel Moore something that led Moore to say, ' Why don't Lord Hood land 500 ' men to work? our Soldiers are tired.' Here the *riddle* is fully explained.

I never write or open my mouth to any one but your Lordship. The permanent party for work is every person wanted; we don't portion our work: for instance, this morning we could have done much work, rested the afternoon, and work at night. Now, rumour says, for the General is asleep, that all is to go forward this night, which if we had 1,000 seamen is impossible; but no exertion of mine or Hallowell's is wanting. We are not firing: the Enemy are lining their merlons with sandbags, &c. The Dolphin's people I will send for, and an Officer. I shall see the General in the evening. Believe me,

Your most faithful,

HORATIO NELSON.

G G 2

INCLOSURE.

Seamen, exclusive of Officers, Servants, Cooks, attendant on the Provisions and Sick:—

				No.
Agamemnon	.	.	.	77
Victory .	.	.	.	39
Inflexible .	.	.	.	27
L'Eclair .	.	.	.	5
Transports .	.	.	.	75
Fit for duty .		.		223
On the Batteries		.	.	120
Remain .	.	.		103

Moutray—22 men for work.

H. N.

July 20th, 1794.

TO ADMIRAL LORD HOOD.

[From a Copy, in the Nelson Papers.]

Camp, July 20th, 1794.

My dear Lord,

Last evening I went to the General's as usual, and had not remained long before Sir James Esrkine arrived with two letters from Calvi, where it would appear he had been sent with a Flag of Truce. The General took me out to say that as he thought the taking the Mozelle was a proper moment to know the sentiments of the Garrison, he had sent in a letter just to ask if they had any terms to propose, and that the answer he had received was, that they were determined to hold out to the last extremity: therefore he wished me to write your Lordship and say what probably he has wrote. I could not help saying that in a business of such great moment, it would be improper in me to convey his sentiments, and submitted whether it would not be best for himself to write your Lordship. What seems wanting is more Seamen, a number sufficient to make the battery, and to drag the guns without any help, with all the supplies for those guns. The *Army* are *harassed* to death and the Enemy have, it seems, 2,000 men in arms at Calvi, therefore the General wants from your Lordship to make our number 500 working men. From various causes we are not more than 220 working men, and after 120 men are deducted for the present battery, we have not more than 100 working men.

The General is going to send to Bastia for 300 Troops to assist the Army in the land duty which they now have. Gunpowder is wanted, as also shot in such quantities as I fear it is out of your Lordship's power to supply, for we have no chance of success but by battering a breach, which without more ammunition could not be done; and it was come to the point either to go on or to give it up. I told the General that I was sure that if you had the means of supplying his wants I was certain he would have them; but I believed neither shot nor powder was to be got from the Ships. The General then said, as San Francesco was destroyed, why could not Ships be laid against the walls? I took the liberty of observing that the business of laying wood before walls was much altered of late; and that even if they had no hot shot, which I believe they had, that the quantity of powder and shot which would be fired away on such an Attack could be much better directed from a battery on shore. All our conversation was with the greatest politeness, and he thanked me for my assistance; but it was necessary to come to the point whether the Siege should be persevered in or given up. If the former, he must be supplied with the means, which were more troops, more seamen to work, and more ammunition. I observed that [even] if [neither] men nor ammunition could be supplied from the Fleet, or without sending to Gibraltar, [yet] that our present position might possibly be held.

I had wrote so far, when Sir James arrived to say he was going off to your Lordship. He, of course, is authorized to say everything.

Your most faithful,

HORATIO NELSON.

TO LIEUT. RICHARD SAINTHILL,

AGENT FOR TRANSPORTS.

[From " Memoirs of Captain Richard Sainthill."]

You are hereby required and directed to land out of the Transports under your direction all the empty Wine-pipes they have on board, for erecting batteries, for which this shall be your order.

Given under my hand, at the Camp before Calvi, this 20th July 1794.

HORATIO NELSON.

TO ADMIRAL LORD HOOD.

[Autograph, in the Hood Papers.]

Camp, July 22nd, 1794.

My dear Lord,

I am just come from the General, who intends getting things forward for this night, and to-morrow night purposes making a great effort to mount the seven heavy guns in their battery, and wishes to have near five hundred Seamen. We employ every man at the lower batteries all night, but there are eighteen at the upper battery which the General wishes to remain, in case of the Enemy opening a fire. If Fennel is here, he says he has thirty men, probably twenty-five effective. Except the Agamemnon's boats' crews and the Maltese, every man is landed from her. I should think I may take twenty-five of the boats' crews: the L'Aimable will probably, if you please, furnish the rest; and as it will take immediately sixty men in the batteries who must be relieved the next evening, we shall, I dare say, want more for the night after, and our having worked for four nights together, cannot have much strength remaining.

The six-gun battery is to be removed forward, and mounted, I hope. We alter our plans so often that it distresses us. We have been part of two nights carrying the large mortars and beds to the right, through very bad ground: it is now talked of, and I fear will be ordered to carry them all to the left. The ground is so bad, if we move them, that one night of every seaman fresh I don't think will more than effect it. However, I say nothing. The General asked me when I thought the powder and shot would be landed? I told him that I was sure your Lordship had sent for it, and I had no doubt it would soon arrive. I delivered Captain Knight's[6] message, as I understood it—that the General might depend upon every assistance in your Lordship's power to give him, and that I had directions for to furnish every wish of the General's as far as I had the power, and when I had it not, to acquaint your Lordship. He said he was sure of every assistance—that he never doubted. There is certainly no Treaty going forward. The General told me they thought they were gaining a great point by making more works, but it was useless for them—they only laid themselves more open to be knocked to pieces. If more men are wanted for the second battery to be erected, I will acquaint your Lordship as soon as possible. Believe me with truest esteem,

Your Lordship's most faithful,
HORATIO NELSON.

TO ADMIRAL LORD HOOD.

[From Clarke and M'Arthur, vol. i. p. 185.]

22nd July 1794.

We will fag ourselves to death, before any blame shall lie at our doors; and I trust, my dear Lord, it will not be forgotten, that twenty-five pieces of heavy ordnance have been dragged to the different batteries and mounted, and all, but three at the Royal Louis battery, have been fought by Seamen, except one Artillery-man to point the guns, and, at first, an additional Gunner to stop the rest ;[7] but, as I did not choose to trust a Seaman's arms to any but Seamen, he was withdrawn: all the mortars have also been worked by Seamen: every man landed is actually half barefooted. I am far from well; but not so ill as to be confined. My eye is troublesome, and I don't think I shall ever have

---

[6] Vide p. 307. ante.   [7] Sic, query, vent.

the perfect sight of it again. In one week at farthest after our batteries are open, I think Calvi will be ours.

I am, &c.

HORATIO NELSON.

TO LIEUTENANT SAINTHILL.

[From "Memoirs of Captain Richard Sainthill."]

Camp, July 22nd, 1794.

Sir,

As many of the largest and best empty casks as possible must be landed this evening. I think you have seventy on board the Ship which took them on board at Bastia; if not, apply to Captain May, who sent me word he had Wine-pipes. Less are useless.

Yours,

HORATIO NELSON.

TO ADMIRAL LORD HOOD.

[Autograph, in the Hood Papers.]

Camp, July 23rd, 1794.

My dear Lord,

We got four guns and a howitzer from the right of the Mozelle, where we had carried them two nights ago, to the left by the Tower, where a battery is making for seven 26 pounders; the two 36 pounders, and one 24, are to be to the right of the Mozelle. To-night we are to remove all mortars from the right to the left.[8] We shall want, if possible, fifty men from some Ship to-morrow night.

Yours most faithfully

HORATIO NELSON.

[8] On this day, 23rd of July, General Stuart wrote to Captain Nelson:

"My dear Sir,—As it will trouble yourself, and give labour to your men, to remove the mortars, &c., &c., from the situation where you have had the goodness to carry them, to the place where I judge it proper that they should remain, I

TO ADMIRAL LORD HOOD.

[Autograph, in the Hood Papers.]

Camp, July 24th, 1794.   4 A.M.

My dear Lord,

The General wishes for all the Wine-pipes which can be got to be landed directly at the place near the six-gun battery. We are just returned from work. The mortars carried into their batteries and the 18-pounders been taken from their six-gun battery to the three-gun battery, there mounted, and the 26 pounders carried into the Grand battery. Believe me, your most faithful

HORATIO NELSON.

I have sent to Dolphin and Agamemnon.

TO ADMIRAL LORD HOOD.

[Autograph, in the Hood Papers.]

Camp, July 25th, 1794.

My dear Lord,

I should not have troubled your Lordship for empty casks had any been within my reach, but the 400 brought round in the Transport from Bastia are all gone—where I cannot say, but such waste of everything I never was before witness to. I endeavour to keep pace with their wants but it is not always I am able to do it. Since our six-gun battery has been made, every Transport's boat, and Men-of-War's boat have been employed in bringing stores from the Ships and the other Cove; but if they come one trip from the Ships, then what they ought to have brought was things from the shore, and *vice versa*. The Agents have written desires from me to land everything as fast as possible. We ought to have 700, at least, barrels of powder. — I think 900 besides the 400 now landed. I have not yet landed the 200 which I told your Lordship I had on board Agamemnon, when 100 would

shall contrive for the soldiers to effect it to-morrow evening. Your very faithful CHARLES STUART.'

Added in Nelson's writing;—"Removed before this letter [was] delivered." —*Autograph*, in the Nelson Papers.

remain on board. I hope it will not be wanted. The General I am just going to, and will communicate his wishes about the powder so soon as I know them.

I am just come from the General, to whom I showed your letter of yesterday. He wishes for more powder, as he cannot tell how soon the Ships may be separated from him. I have at different times taken upon me to assure General Stuart of your inclination to forward his wishes in every respect. What is the matter I cannot tell, but he does not seem satisfied. All our spars, and those sent me, are in Tents, with every sail: therefore I have to request that with the powder may be landed a large sail to keep out rain, and proper spars to erect a Tent to hold it. He asked me if you were going to strip the Transports of the men, and supposed when the place fell, all the Transports would be taken from him. The General may have his causes to be displeased, but I am confident they cannot be caused by any part of the Naval Department. Our Seamen from noon yesterday till nine o'clock were employed carrying shot from the beach to the battery, mounting the guns on the seven-gun battery and mortars on theirs. This morning have been making a road to remove the Royal Louis battery, which is to be done with a party of seamen to-night. The others are now at work carrying shot. Be so good as to say the day my Journal ends, and I will send the remainder; but I did not mark it when it was sent, but think the 16th.

Believe me, with truest esteem,

Your most faithful,

HORATIO NELSON.

Pray what shot has L'Imperieuse landed, or some Ship? 32-pounders are landed, they tell me.

I don't think our batteries will open these two days.

TO ADMIRAL LORD HOOD.

[From a Copy, in the Nelson Papers.]

Camp, July 26th, 1794.

My dear Lord,

I am just honoured with your letter by Gibson, and do not conceive there can be a necessity for more powder: 900 on shore, 200 in Transports, and if distressed 200 in Aga-memnon. I am glad the Brig is taken; the other is ready for sea. Some *great men* of the Revolution may be on board her: might not some person from Calvi point them out? There is a Sergeant deserter on board the Mather Transport.

It is morally impossible the General can be out of hu-mour with your Lordship, or with any of us. He has never expressed a wish that has not instantly been complied with, in its fullest extent. I trust he will not forget our services; and when I recollect the morning of the six-gun battery, how he expressed his thanks for our Seamen drag-ging and mounting the guns under a heavy fire of grape-shot, I think he cannot. Sixty Seamen were with the field-pieces, and as exposed as any of the Troops the morning of the Storm, but no notice has been taken of them: but I shall not forget this fact, that every gun is dragged and fought by Seamen.

Believe me your most faithful,

HORATIO NELSON.

The Transports have not one empty cask: if the Victory has any we shall be glad of them.

TO ADMIRAL LORD HOOD.

[From a Copy, in the Nelson Papers.]

Camp, July 26th, 1794.

My dear Lord,

Except carrying shot, we had not last night much to do for the Victory's landed. In removing the Royal Louis bat-tery, the roads being so very bad, we were not able to get one gun to the battery, therefore I am necessitated to keep

5

the Victory's to assist us this night. I asked the General about the forty Royal Louis, in the Terrible. He does not want them, and if of no use on board, thinks they had better be landed at Fiorenzo with their Regiment. The General also requested me to say that the Cannoniers landed here belonged to the Commerce de Marseilles, that their wives and families and things were on board her, and that they were much distressed to know what was to become of them,— whether they were to join their Ship, or to have their families &c., landed? I am sorry to put all these questions, but the General asks me, therefore I am obliged to trouble you.

Our thirty-six-pounders are not to be mounted to-night. To-morrow night, the General says he hopes to be ready for them, but each day brings a further delay. The eighteen-pounders found in the Fountain battery, are to be turned against the Enemy, and one eighteen-pounder in the Mozelle. When all our batteries are completed, we shall have thirty-five pieces of ordnance playing on the Town, and I think a very few hours must bring them to terms. There are now on shore nine hundred barrels of powder, but from what I wrote yesterday they think they never can have enough of anything. To see the piles of shot at the back of the Mozelle, as I tell them, looks like Woolwich Warren. We must, thank God, be fast drawing to a close: it cannot be procrastinated many days longer.

Believe me, your Lordship's most faithful
HORATIO NELSON.

Captain Hallowell who is as active and good as ever, desires his best respects.

Stores expended.

Powder, barrels	1,090.
Shot, 26-prs.	6,175.
Do., 18 do	3,550.
Shells, 12 inch	1,150.
Ditto, 10 ditto	404.
Do., 8 do.	250.

To July 25th, 1794.[8]

---

[8] The proceedings on the 27th and 28th July are shown by the following Note from General Stuart to Captain Nelson, dated Sunday, July 27th :

TO ADMIRAL LORD HOOD.

[Autograph, in the Hood Papers.]

Camp, July 29th, 1794.

My dear Lord,

Since the Agamemnon has been here, two seamen, good men, have entered from the Changeable Transport into the Agamemnon. The Master came to me, and hoped I would give him two men in lieu. One, his Carpenter, was mutinous; and the other, his Second Mate; that he would be satisfied with an indifferent Carpenter, but he could not with propriety go to sea without one: that he would not ask for any one in lieu of the other, but he was very short-handed. I told him that if your Lordship had no objection I would discharge two men in lieu, but without that I did not feel justified, and desired him to take an opportunity of going on board, and asking Captain Inglefield[9] for an order.

Lieutenant H—— this morning came to me in a very uncivil way, that the Master of the Changeable had complained to him that [he] could not go to sea for want of two men in lieu; that if I would not give men in lieu to send them back,

---

"Dear Sir,—What I require from your people to-night, for the good of the Public service, in which I am sure of your kind assistance, is nearly as follows,—To place three eighteen-pounders upon their carriages, and in the batteries; to carry down, and place upon their respective platforms, two thirty-six-pounders and one twenty-six. Captain Stephens informs me that he has settled with respect to the number of Seamen we require on the batteries to-morrow, a little before day-break,—a number similar to that I had the honour of showing you some days ago, and which then appeared to me inferior to the service, but which upon a further explanation, I find to be sufficient from the number of additional guns added to them. May I entreat, for the safety of the whole, that no tobacco may be smoked by the sailors when upon this duty. I have the honour to be, your obedient servant, CHAS. STUART." *Autograph*, in the Nelson Papers.

[9] Captain John Nicholson Inglefield. Captain Sir Hyde Parker, First Captain to Lord Hood, having been promoted to Rear-Admiral, and wishing to hoist his Flag, (to which his Lordship consented,) Lord Hood issued an order dated "Victory, Hieres Bay, 19th June 1794," which, after stating those facts, and that from not having twenty Sail of the Line under his command, he did not feel himself entitled to appoint a First Captain in Sir Hyde Parker's room, "yet having a very urgent " and pressing occasion for assistance," he had " thought fit to authorize Captain " Inglefield to repair on board the Victory, and take upon him the duties of First " Captain, under the character of Adjutant-General of the Fleet." Captain Inglefield was afterwards a Commissioner of the Navy; and was placed on the Retired list of Post-Captains in February 1799.

and some other Man-of-War would. I told him, as I did the
Master, that as you was here, I should not do it without your
order. He said he had told the Master not to pay them their
wages, and that he would justify him by his instructions; in
short, he was very uncivil, but these Agents forget themselves
very much; and I have had more trouble with this Officer
about the Transports' people than a little. He is never satisfied: I only wish I had rejected his services; with the men I
should have had but little trouble. Cooke told me H——'s
character before he landed; but I thought the service would
have been forwarded by landing him, and I believe he took
more pains to get men from his own Division. If your Lordship pleases, I will discharge or lend two men in lieu.

Believe me, your most faithful,
HORATIO NELSON.

I send off my Journal to last night.

CONTINUATION OF CAPTAIN NELSON'S JOURNAL.

[From a Copy, in the Admiralty.]

29th July.—The Truce still continues: at 10 o'clock General Stuart went on board the Victory. At night four small
Vessels got into Calvi, and the Garrison gave three cheers.

30th.—At noon an Officer went into town with a Flag of
Truce. At half-past one he returned. Got everything ready
to recommence hostilities. At half-past five began firing.
The Garrison fired one general round, when they nearly all
left their guns, only now and then stealing a gun at us. By
dusk, three or four of their guns were totally disabled.
During the night the Enemy only fired three or four guns:
we fired a gun every three minutes.

Lieutenant Byron, of the 18th Regiment, and Ensign
Boggis, 51st Regiment, killed.

Lieutenant Livingstone, 30th Regiment, wounded; one
Seaman of the Agamemnon wounded.

TO ADMIRAL LORD HOOD.

[Autograph, in the Hood Papers.]

Camp, July 30th, 1794.

My dear Lord,

The General has desired me to send the Boreas Hospital Ship to Bastia, with sick soldiers ; as I cannot do it, your Lordship being present, I have, trusting it will meet with your approbation, ordered the Boreas to anchor off Revellata, and the sick to be embarked in the sandy Bay below our Camp ready to receive your Lordship's directions. At one o'clock this morning, I am sorry to say, the Enemy received some supplies. One whole Galley, two Half Galleys, as reported to me. They gave three cheers on the vessels' arrival.

I had established a signal with L'Amiable, a Dutch Jack inverted, when I wanted a boat. If the Ships near know the signal for a boat I can get one instantly, whenever I may want to send to your Lordship. The Corsican who brought the letter from Sir Gilbert Elliot yesterday afternoon, is waiting to know if any answer is to be sent.

Your most faithful

HORATIO NELSON.

TO ADMIRAL LORD HOOD.

[From a Copy, in the Nelson Papers.]

Camp, July 30th, 1794.

My dear Lord,

Many thanks for your letter. Every letter of yours which can require the least secrecy, I assure you is held sacred by me. The Enemy getting in these supplies, *four Vessels*, certainly will alter the face of the negotiation. Indeed, my Lord, I am sure that we have much more to fear from the climate than the Enemy. I own I should not have consented to have given them one day's Truce. I wish our batteries were open ; I think two days will sicken them. In our present state we cannot part with a man. 200 are on the batteries each day, thirty-three sick, and with Officers and servants 460. The Agamemnon cannot get under weigh : she has only her boats' crews and Maltese, besides idlers. The Seamen are very healthy in comparison with the Army, who in a week will be half sick. I attribute our healthiness to our hard work, and quantity of wine allowed.

Believe me your most faithful

HORATIO NELSON.

I have sent 10 sick men on board Agamemnon this morning.

TO THE RIGHT HONOURABLE SIR GILBERT ELLIOT, BART.

[Autograph, in the Minto Papers.]

Camp, July 30th, 1794.

My dear Sir,

You will probably have heard that Flags of Truce have been passing between us and the Garrison. What the basis is I am not exactly in a situation to be made acquainted with ; but if I am not mistaken, it is for a suspension of hostilities for a certain time, when, if no succours arrived, then to enter into a Capitulation. If this is the case, it is all over, for last night four Vessels arrived with supplies, and the Garrison gave three cheers. Indeed, my dear Sir, we have much more to dread from the climate than from the fire of the Enemy ; I would not give them one hour's Truce. They know their Climate, that it is an Enemy we can never conquer; for if the Siege is prolonged one week more, half this Army will be *sick.* Lord Hood is not well, or the General.

Believe me,

Your most faithful Servant,

HORATIO NELSON.

JOURNAL.

[From a Copy, in the Admiralty.]

31st July.—Our fire kept up very brisk during the whole day, the Enemy only firing from one gun on their left, and four or five howitzer shells. By sunset nearly all the Enemy's guns seemed disabled, and a great deal of the parapet wall beat down. The houses in the Citadel very much damaged, and on fire in three places, but the houses being all arched will not allow the fire to spread. At four o'clock a Flag of Truce came out to say two men had been killed in the Hospital, by a shot from our battery. At five the fire re-commenced. Mr. Bankes, Midshipman of the Victory, killed. One additional Gunner killed.

TO ADMIRAL LORD HOOD.

[Autograph, in the possession of Mrs. Conway.]

Battery, July 31st, 1794.

My dear Lord,

I own I rejoiced when our fire opened against the Enemy, being thoroughly convinced, all we have to guard against is unnecessary delay : the climate is the only Enemy we have to fear ; that we can never conquer. The garrison knew it, and wished to make use of their knowledge. Our fire has had all the effect which could be hoped for. Except one general discharge, and a gun now and then still at us, we have had no opposition. Every creature (very few excepted) of the Troops are in the lower Town, which we are to respect, it being full of black Flags.[1] Far be it from me to cast a reflection on the General's humanity ; I admire it, but there are times, and I think the present is one, when it would be more charitable to our Troops to make the Enemy suffer more, than for our brave fellows to die every hour, four or five of a day. Why might not the General send notice, that they must remove from the lower Town all their sick to the upper Town, for that it might be a necessary measure to destroy

[1] Indicating the hospitals.

it? In that case, they would be so crowded, the casements being filled with sick, that a few hours must make them submit to any terms. We cannot fire at the small craft which lay under the walls, for the lower Town, and these Vessels I dare say are filled with people or Troops.

The General is very unwell, not able to remain here last night; I have not heard of him this morning. This is my ague day, but I hope this active scene will keep off the fit. It has shook me a good deal; but I have been used to them, and don't mind them much. Lieutenant Byron,[1] heir to the title of Lord Byron, with an Ensign of the 51st, were killed yesterday afternoon, and one Officer wounded. I hope our Naples friend, Pierson,[2] will get a Commission : he is a very good young man. The Dolphin's men are on board ; and both her and the Agamemnon I ordered to be ready to weigh against they should receive your Lordship's directions. Hallowell is very well, and joins in best respects with your most faithful

HORATIO NELSON.

One Seaman slightly wounded.

JOURNAL.

[From a Copy, in the Admiralty.]

1st August.—Our fire kept up till eleven o'clock, when the Enemy hung out a Flag of Truce, and sent out a letter, requesting a suspension of Hostilities. Several Flags passed between this and the evening. Truce continued all night.

2nd. Truce still continues. During the day[2] many letters

---

[1] Lieutenant William Byron, of the Royal Irish Regiment, only son of the Honourable William Byron, (who died in 1776,) son of William 5th Lord Byron, was on his decease, heir apparent of his grandfather to the Peerage. The other Officer who fell was Ensign Boggis.

[2] He is frequently mentioned in subsequent letters.

On this day, General Stuart wrote to Nelson,

"August 2nd, 1794.—Dear Sir, I am happy to inform you that we *may venture* to-night to have only one half of the men on the batteries, but I earnestly intreat that no Officer or Sailor goes beyond the line of the batteries. Sir James St.

passed between the General and the Garrison. Sent in a bullock for the sick in the Hospitals. In the evening the Corsicans were ordered from their posts to the right and left, and sent to the hills, and the picquets reduced one half. An Officer went from the General to Lord Hood. Truce all night. A boat or two attempted to get out, but failed.

TO ADMIRAL LORD HOOD.

[Autograph, in the possession of Mrs. Conway.]

Camp, August 2nd, 1794.

My dear Lord,

I am just come from the General : asking him if he had any letter or message to send to your Lordship, as I was going to send the Cutter, his answer was, nothing. I therefore conclude you know of this Truce, and how it will end : probably till the time you granted them for receiving succours; if so, five days are elapsed. The Officers who came out were very inquisitive about the terms which were granted Bastia—whether they were not allowed to carry their Arms to the water-side. If there is no chance of firing, the keeping our seamen on the Batteries in the heat of the day is cruel. Sixteen fell ill yesterday, absolutely from the heat. I hope the Cutter has brought good news. Believe me your most faithful,

HORATIO NELSON.

The General is quite recovered.

I would not wish anything to be said to the General about our seamen. Hallowell and myself are always on the batteries with them, and our Jacks don't mind it.

Clair having a letter of importance to carry to the Victory, I request that he may have immediately a good conveyance. Yours very faithfully, CHARLES STUART."
Autograph, in the Nelson Papers.

TO MRS. NELSON.

[From Clarke and M'Arthur, vol. i. p. 186.]

4th August, 1794.

Except a very slight scratch towards my right eye, I have received no hurt whatever : so you see I am not the worse for Campaigning; but I cannot say I have any wish to go on with it. This day I have been four months landed, except a few days when we were after the French Fleet, and I feel almost qualified to pass my examination as a besieging General.

Yours, &c.,

HORATIO NELSON.

TO THE RIGHT HONOURABLE SIR GILBERT ELLIOT.

[Autograph, in the Minto Papers.]

Camp, August 4th, 1794.

My dear Sir,

The Victory, Britannia, and Agamemnon, are all gone from hence by the violence of the gale, which still continues. Since my last letter the Enemy getting four Vessels in, the truce was at an end. It suited their *convenience*. After thirty-six hours open batteries, another truce commenced, which has now lasted from August 1st, eleven o'clock fore-noon, I suppose on the same ground as the other, that if no succours arrived by a specified time, then the place to be surrendered. I dare say the General and Lord Hood have good reasons for their conduct, nor do I mean in the smallest degree to arraign them ; but I hope twenty-five years in the service will plead my excuse for giving an opinion, even to you, Sir, who will not let it go further.

What are the Enemys' inducements to get this kind of truce ? —their works are not going to ruin, you are getting, they know, every day more and more less able to act against them, and if the Convention can or mean to send them succours, it af-fords time for it : for if this lasts much longer, and a few Boats get in, you will not be in a condition to remain on this ground. I have no doubt but we could, after having ruined the defences of this place, have made a breach in the Bastion,—at all events have run a mine under it, and blown it into the air in less time than this Truce has lasted; and I own I had rather take a place by our own fire and efforts, than by the Enemy being starved and sickly. But I believe it is all over. The General sends them every day a bullock for their sick. This place taken, it will set Lord Hood at liberty to look at the French Fleet.[3] Reports say they are too securely moored to be got at in any way; but if they can, I am sure his Lordship will attempt something, in which I am sure he will have the support of every Officer in his Fleet. Laurels grow in the Bay of Biscay,[4]—I hope a bed of them may be found in the Mediterranean. The General, who is a worthy good man, and excellent Officer, has not been well, but he is better. I hope Lady Elliot[5] and your family will arrive in perfect health; for I assure you, Sir, that whatever will give you satisfaction, must always be pleasing to

Your most obliged, humble Servant,

HORATIO NELSON.

Perhaps my pen has been too free. Be so good as to burn my letter when read.

TO ADMIRAL LORD HOOD.

[Copy in the Admiralty, transmitted by Lord Hood.]

Camp, August 5th, 1794.

My Lord,

As the Officer of the Cutter has informed me he thinks it right to endeavour to find your Lordship, I take the opportunity of sending you a letter from Sir Gilbert Elliot, and to say we are in the same state you left us on the 3rd. I do not find the strong winds have lessened our sick. We now only

---

[3] In Gourjean Bay.

[4] Alluding to Lord Howe's Action.

[5] Maria, eldest daughter of Sir George Amyand, Bart. She died in February, 1829.

keep half our Seamen at the batteries, yet we have seventy sick on shore, and I sent thirty to the Agamemnon yesterday. The Troops are worse than ourselves by far.

As soon as the weather moderates, I shall get the Transports here ready to sail with this Garrison, as the General is desirous to get rid of it as soon as possible—even to think some may be sent away before the 10th. Should your Lordship not be here, I shall endeavour to act as I am sure your Lordship would have me, which is to comply with the General's wishes in everything; but I hope you will be here very shortly.

I have the honour to be, &c.,
HORATIO NELSON.

[On the same day Captain Nelson wrote a Private Letter to Lord Hood, which is now in the Hood Papers. It is in exactly the same words as the preceding, with these additions:]

I shall endeavour to act as I think you would wish me, which is to comply with the General's wishes in everything which is proper, but I hope to see you here before many days are past. Two Frigates keep their Station very well, and Fox and Lugger are here at anchor. Believe me with truest esteem,

Your Lordship's most faithful
HORATIO NELSON.

I have to request your Lordship to send my Letter to Mrs. Nelson by the Messenger, if he goes directly.

TO THE COMMANDING OFFICER OF HIS MAJESTY'S SHIPS AT FIORENZO.

[Autograph, in the Hood Papers.]

Camp, August 6th, 1794.

Sir,

Four Transports are wanted from Fiorenzo to carry to France the Garrison of this place, which the General wishes to get rid of the instant we get possession of the Town.   The Ships I have fixed upon as the most proper by the advice of Lieutenant Harrison, the Agent for Transports, are the Sovereign, Samuel and Jane, William, and Grand Bay, and I have sent such Seamen as are in health belonging to them, by the Fox.

If they should not be sufficient to navigate them, some men may be ordered from the other Transports, or should Lieutenant Elliot's Division of Ships be at Fiorenzo, it would save much time to send them here, as they must be ready, from having so lately carried the refugees.   It is necessary that these Ships should be well victualled and watered, for the Transports have no provisions on board, and to bring some provisions for these Ships—six in number, who are to carry 1250 men.   I have wrote to the Lieutenant of the Agamemnon to send by the Fox the men belonging to the Matther, Nancy, Camilla, Mary, Mary (4), and Scarborough, and should the Agamemnon not be in a state to be navigated here, without some assistance, I trust you will have the goodness to order her some, as we are really distressed by her absence.

                    I am, Sir,
                        Your most obedient Servant,
                            HORATIO NELSON.

TO LIEUTENANT SAINTHILL,
AGENT FOR TRANSPORTS.

[From the " United Service Journal " for 1830, part i. p. 36.]

                                                August 5th, 1794.

Sir,

You will let me know, in the course of the day, how many people each Ship of your Division will carry without inconvenience, for a very short voyage: also, if you have water and provisions for the number of people your Ships will carry : also let me know what men are on shore belonging to Ships of your Division, in case Agamemnon should not return before the Transports are wanted.   I wish to see you with the Return; and let me know if there are any Transports here, except of yours and Lieutenant Caines' Division.

I am, Sir, &c.

HORATIO NELSON.

TO LIEUTENANT SAINTHILL,
AGENT FOR TRANSPORTS.

[From the "United Service Journal," 1830, part i. p. 36.]

Camp, August 7th, 1794.

Sir,

All the Transports under your direction to be moved directly to this Bay, and anchored under our Camp. I have directed all the Transports' men here to be sent to your assistance; but you will get your Ships as ready to weigh as possible before their arrival.

I am, Sir, &c.

HORATIO NELSON.

JOURNAL.

[From a Copy, in the Admiralty.]

August 3rd.—A gale of wind all day. The Truce still continues.

4th, 5th, and 6th.—Gale continues: still a Truce.

7th.—Preparing Transports to carry the Garrison and Inhabitants to France. The Gale abated.

8th.—Fine weather. Victory and Ships in sight.

HORATIO NELSON.

TO ADMIRAL LORD HOOD.

[From Clarke and M'Arthur, vol. i. p. 187.]

8th August, 1794.

I rejoice to see the Victory in sight again,[6] and may now almost congratulate your Lordship on the final reduction of

---

[6] On this day Lord Hood communicated to Captain Nelson that, on the 30th

Corsica; an object which I know you had much at heart,
and which has been protracted beyond all bounds of calcu-
lation.　Captain Hallowell, I am sorry to say, is very unwell, and much reduced.　If Doctor Harness[7] is on board, I
wish he would come and look at Hallowell: I think, poor fellow, he would like it.[8]

I am, &c.,

HORATIO NELSON.

TO ADMIRAL LORD HOOD.

[From a Copy, in the Admiralty.]

Camp, August 8th, 1794.

My Lord,

Having transmitted my Journal of what the Seamen have
been employed upon during the whole Siege, I have now
only to acquaint your Lordship of the highly meritorious con-

---

of June, Parliament had voted its Thanks to the Officers, Seamen, Marines,
and Soldiers, who had been employed in the different operations against the
Enemy in Corsica.

[7] Doctor John Harness, the Physician to the Fleet, and afterwards Chairman
of the Board for Sick and Wounded Seamen.　To this zealous and intelligent
Officer the Navy is under the highest obligations.　His extensive and successful application of Citric Acid in the year 1793, induced the authorities at
Home, in 1795, to cause that article to form a necessary part of Medical Stores,
and to which the eradication of that fearful scourge, the scurvy, is to be attributed.
It was mainly through his exertions that the situation of the Naval Medical
Officers has been so much improved.　Dr. Harness died on the 3rd of January
1823. A Memoir of his Services will be found in the "Naval Chronicle," vol. xxxv.

[8] Lord Hood's reply was written on the same day, at 5 P.M.;—

"My dear Nelson,—I am grieved to hear Hallowell is not well, as I also am that
Colonel Wemyss is in the same state.　I wish both would come to the Victory this
evening or to-morrow morning.　Doctor Harness is not here, but I expect to see
him to-morrow.　In the morning early I shall send Captain Inglefield, or Captain
Knight to the General on the subject of Transports.　Much caution is necessary,
from the perfidious conduct of the Enemy : may the Transports go within reach of
the guns of Calvi? I am in perfect ignorance how matters stand.　The Boreas and
Jamaica, that carried the last sick to Bastia, may be expected here to-morrow. You
must undoubtedly take off all you put on shore unexpected ; so must the Victory,
and every other Ship, which you will prepare for.　I can only add, at present,
that I am ever and truly, your faithful humble servant, HOOD."—*Copy*, certified
by Nelson, in the Hood Papers.

duct of every Officer and Seaman landed under my command; to express my sincere acknowledgments for the very effectual support and assistance I have received from the ability, zeal, and activity of Captain Hallowell; and that Lieutenants Edmonds, Morgan, and Ferrier were constantly with the Seamen, fighting the batteries; to which were joined, on the last batteries, Lieutenants Hoy, Moutray, and Suckling. I must not also omit to acquaint your Lordship that Seamen being wanted for this service, the Agents for Transports raised 110 Volunteers from the Transports; and that Lieutenant Harrison, one of the Agents, and Mr. William Harrington, Master of the Willington, came on shore, and served with great credit during the whole Siege.

Herewith I transmit a list of killed and wounded Seamen.

I have the honour to remain, with great respect,

Your Lordship's most obedient

HORATIO NELSON.

TO ADMIRAL LORD HOOD.

[From a Copy, in the Nelson Papers.]

Camp, August 9th, 1794.

My dear Lord,

It was so dark when I got to Camp, and received your Lordship's letters from Mr. Hamilton, that I would not detain him for an answer, telling him that the Transports might anchor in perfect security in the Bay under our Camp. Sir James St. Clair, the Commissary, and Captain Stephens, with Mr. Bains, who is to be Town-Major, were all day in the Town, taking an account of Stores of every kind. The cannon, I find, are not very good—the iron particularly. They have only 217 barrels of powder, but plenty of shot and shells: one Coudrier mortar, which luckily for us was split by their putting thirty pounds of powder in it to fire at one of our Frigates. The place is a heap of ruins, the works much damaged; but it is the fashion to say it would have been difficult to make a breach. They went on board the Melpomene and Mignonne. All the latter's guns are landed,

5

and all but two of the former, but the greater part lay on the wharf. There is also a Gun-boat.

I have got the davit-casts ready to move the Agamemnon's guns, if we have strength enough, but I dread the getting liquor, after the Town is in our possession, which will completely kill our people. What we do must be as expeditious as possible. I have only two eighteen-pounders and one twenty-four-pounder to get on board Agamemnon, the other two twenty-four-pounders being disabled. One eighteen-pounder from the rear battery I got down to the landing-place this evening; the others we cannot move till Sunday morning. I had intended, when our troops took possession, to have sent Captain Hallowell, with an Officer and two or three careful men, to take possession of the Frigates and Gun-boat to prevent embezzlement, till your Lordship's arrival. You will now take possession in the way your Lordship judges most proper, but everybody at Bastia plundered La Fléche. Hallowell I hope is a little better, but I believe he will not be persuaded to go off till this business is closed. I send you, as a curiosity, an account of what Stores we have expended, and what has been landed, and what now remains.

> I am, with truest esteem,
>> Your Lordship's most faithful,
>>> HORATIO NELSON.

If I am not absolutely correct to a single shot and shell, I am within a dozen, except the $5\frac{1}{2}$, which is a guess, but I believe pretty near.

JOURNAL C.

August 10th, at nine o'clock, about three hundred Troops, a party of Seamen, some Royal Louis, and some Corsicans, were drawn up opposite the great gate to receive the Garrison of Calvi, who at ten o'clock marched out with two pieces of cannon, and the Honours of War; amounting in the whole to three hundred Troops, and two hundred and forty-seven armed Corsicans. I immediately sent Lieutenant Moutray and a party of Seamen, to take possession of the Frigates, Gun-boats, and Merchant vessels in the harbour, and I also ordered six Transports to come in ; and was employed all the day embarking the Garrison, the sick, and such inhabitants as chose to return to France. Out of their armed men the Enemy had three hundred and thirteen sick in their hospital. We have had six killed, six wounded, and two are missing. We expended 11,275 shot, and 2,751 shells.[9]

---

[9] In General Stuart's Dispatch, dated on the 10th of August, announcing the surrender of Calvi on that day, he detailed very fully the proceedings of the Siege. The following are the passages in which he mentions Captain Nelson : " Captain Nelson of his Majesty's Ship Agamemnon, consented, in Lord Hood's absence, to proceed to Port Agro, where a landing was effected on the 19th of June." " It is with sincere regret that I have to mention the loss of Captain Serocold of the Navy, who was killed by a cannon shot when actively employed on the batteries. The assistance and co-operation of Captain Nelson, the activity of Captain Hallowell, and the exertions of the Navy, have greatly contributed the success of these movements."—*London Gazette.*

Lord Hood's Dispatches were dated on the 5th and 9th of August. In the former, after describing his pursuit of the French Fleet, he stated :—

"Victory, Martello Bay, August 5th, 1794. My letter of the 15th of June would inform you that having forced the French Ships on the 11th, which sailed from Toulon on the 5th, to seek their safety within the shoals in the Bay of Gourjean, and under the protection of the batteries of the Islands of St. Honora and St. Margaretta, and on Cape Garoupe, that I had left Admiral Hotham to watch them, and that I was returning to Corsica to join Lieutenant-General Stuart for the reduction of Calvi, which I have the honour to. acquaint you is now, I believe, on the point of surrendering to the arms of his Majesty.

" Upon my junction with Vice Admiral Hotham off this Port on the 9th, I detached Captain Nelson in the Agamemnon to Bastia, with orders to embark the troops, and proceed with them to Martello Bay, where Lieutenant-General Stuart embarked on the 15th, and expressing a wish to proceed to the attack of Calvi immediately, Captain Nelson complied with it, and on the 19th all the troops were landed under the direction of Captain Cooke, in a small cove about three miles from Calvi.

" I anchored in Martello Bay on the 19th, and so soon as I had embarked the ordnance and other stores the General had desired, which the boisterous weather for some days prevented, and had forced the Agamemnon and several of the Transports from their anchors, but his Majesty's smaller Ships, and the rest of the Transports which were close under the land, and had not room to get under sail, very fortunately rode the gale out without an accident to either, the wind not blowing home to the shore with so much violence.

" On the 26th I sailed, having previously sent Captain Hallowell and Captain Serocold, (who were eager volunteers for the Service, as were also the Lieutenants Ferriers and Morgan,) with as many able Seamen as the Victory could then spare, to assist in dragging up the ordnance and serving the batteries.

" The Journal I herewith transmit from Captain Nelson, who had the com-

TO THE RIGHT HONOURABLE SIR GILBERT ELLIOT.

[Autograph, in the Minto Papers.]

Calvi, August 10th, 1794.

My dear Sir,

As the Corsican cannot enter the Town with me, I shall give him this letter the moment we get possession of the gates. The Garrison will lay down their arms at the water-side, and before night I hope to have them all embarked. The *business is certainly done*, and high time it is. We are all sick. Our Transports are in the harbour ; and I have an Officer and men ready to go on board the Frigates. The Enemy are said to have lost eighty killed and wounded,— the Town and Works much damaged.

Believe me, dear Sir,

Your very obedient Servant,

HORATIO NELSON.

Your letter of the 7th I sent on board Lord Hood the 8th, in the evening.

mand of the Seamen, will show the daily occurrences of the Siege, and whose unremitting zeal and exertion, I cannot sufficiently express, or of that of Captain Hallowell, who took it by turns to command in the advanced battery twenty-four hours at a time, and I flatter myself they, as well as the other Officers and Seamen, will have full justice done them by the General : it is therefore unnecessary for me to say more upon the subject. But I have to lament, and which I do most sincerely, the loss of a very able and valuable Officer, Captain Serocold, who was killed by a grape-shot whilst getting the last gun in its place soon after the Enemy had discovered our battery. The King has not a more meritorious young Captain in his Majesty's Navy. He commanded the floating-battery which was burnt by red-hot shot before Bastia, and afterwards served with infinite reputation at the batteries on shore. Independent of my regard and esteem for him, I feel his loss to be a public one.

" Much credit is due to Captains Wolseley, Hood, Sir Charles Hamilton, Sir Harry Burrard, Cunningham, Macnamara, and Robinson, for their vigilance in keeping succours out by a steady perseverance in preserving their respective stations under manifest difficulties, and I ought not to omit to mention my tribute of praise to Mr. Gibson, commanding the Fox hired Cutter, of whom all the Captains speak in the handsomest manner for his diligence and punctual obedience to orders. For near two months they did not receive at Calvi any intelligence from the Continent until the night of the 29th, when four boats got in, the Port not being then so well and closely guarded, having been obliged to send three Frigates to Naples, and other places for stores, which the General pressed for, and the night's being dark.

" On the 27th I arrived off Calvi, and have kept close off the Port ever

TO H. R. H. THE DUKE OF CLARENCE.

[From Clarke and M'Arthur, vol. i. p. 186.]

Camp before Calvi, August 6th and 10th, 1794.

Sir,

The Gazette will tell your Royal Highness the general out-lines of this Siege, which I believe is novel in its form. We landed about four miles to the Westward of Calvi on the 19th of June: on the 19th of July we were in full possession of every outpost of the Enemy, with very trifling loss. Our batteries were erected with impunity in situations which the Enemy ought to have prevented. Had they kept even a

since, in order to relieve the wants of the Army every morning, having stationed a Frigate at anchor off Cape Revellata, and another off Point D'Espana. I have landed from this Ship seven of her lower-deck guns, and from time to time all requisitions for various other stores, as well as for men, the General has made, have been complied with, under great inconvenience, that the operations of the Army should not stand still.

"On the 29th of last month, I had the honour of a visit from General Stuart, who brought letters that had passed between him and the Commandant of the French Troops, relative to a Truce for twenty-five days, which appearing to be inadmissible ; in the afternoon of the 30th of July, our batteries were opened, and on the morning of the 1st instant the White Flag was displayed on the Citadel under the National one, and the firing ceased."

In his Letter of the 9th of August, Lord Hood said :—

"Victory, off Calvi, August 9th, 1794. I herewith have the honour to trans-mit for the information of the Lords Commissioners of the Admiralty, duplicates of my Dispatches of the 5th from Martello Bay. I sailed on the 7th, and got off here the next morning, and herewith transmit a Copy of Captain Nelson's Journal from the 28th of last month to the 8th of the present one : also the copy of a Letter I have received from him highly creditable to Lieutenant Harrison, a Transport Agent, as well as to Mr. William Harrington, Master of the Willing-ton, and the Transports' men, who were all anxiously eager either to serve on shore or on board his Majesty's ships."—*London Gazette.*

By neither Commander was the severe wound which Nelson had received, and which deprived him of the sight of his right eye, even mentioned. With-out adopting the strong opinions of some of Nelson's Biographers at the manner in which his services at Calvi were treated in these Dispatches, it is certain that, as at Bastia, they were not duly appreciated, and that he deeply felt the neglect. He is stated by Harrison (vol. i., p. 127) to have said in a Letter to his eldest Sister, Mrs. Bolton, "They have not done me justice in the affair of Calvi ; but never mind, I'll have a Gazette of my own ;" and in a Letter to Captain Locker in May in the following year, he still more strongly expressed his dissatisfaction. Lord Hood, in a Letter to Nelson of the 1st of December 1794, censured General Stuart for not mentioning him in his Dispatch. (Vide p. 502.)

moderate look-out, our loss of men must have been great, every battery being within reach of grape-shot from its opponent. On the 19th of July, General Stuart sent in to ask, if they had any terms to propose to him; their answer was the Motto of the Town,—*Civitas Calvis semper fidelis.* We were then only 650 yards from the centre of the Citadel, and they allowed us to erect very strong batteries under a mask —they must, and ought to have known what we were after —without firing a single shot or shell.

On the 28th, in the morning, our batteries, 560 yards from the Citadel wall, were ready to open their force, consisting of twenty-one cannon, five mortars, and four howitzers. The General sent in to say that he should not fire on the black flags (hospitals). This Note produced a negociation, by which the Enemy wanted to obtain a Truce for twenty-five days; when, if no succours arrived, they agreed to surrender the Town, Frigates, &c. Lord Hood and the General agreed to give them six days; but, whilst this was going on, four small Vessels got in, which gave them hope, I suppose, of more effectual relief; for on the 30th of July they rejected our offer; and our fire opened with all the effect we could expect.

On the 1st of August, at eleven o'clock, when much of the parapet was beat down, and the houses in the Citadel were either in ruins or in flames, the Enemy hung out a White flag, and requested a suspension of hostilities for a few hours, to prepare terms. In twenty-four hours everything was settled,—That on the 10th of August we were to be put in full possession, and the Garrison, and such of the Inhabitants as chose, were to be transported to Toulon, without being Prisoners of War; provided no effectual succours were thrown in by the French. Thus is likely to end the attack of Corsica, the possession of which will, I hope, benefit our Country. Whilst there are such men as Sir Gilbert Elliot, to point out the advantages, it would be impertinent in me to attempt it. The loss to the French will be great: they got from it all the deals, that are excellent, for their decks, and timbers for their topsides, with pitch and tar, which, although of an inferior quality, they employed at Toulon for many uses. We also get the Melpomene, the most beautiful frigate I ever saw, fourteen ports, thirteen eighteen-pounders. The Mignonne with twelve-pounders, but not a very fine Ship, at least if compared with the other.

The climate here, from July to October, is most unfavourable for Military operations. It is now what we call the dog-days, here it is termed the Lion Sun; no person can endure it: we have upwards of one thousand sick out of two thousand, and the others not much better than so many phantoms. We have lost many men from the season, very few from the Enemy. I am here the reed amongst the oaks: all the prevailing disorders have attacked me, but I have not strength for them to fasten upon: I bow before the storm, whilst the sturdy oak is laid low. One plan I pursue, never to employ a Doctor; Nature does all for me, and Providence protects me. Always happy, if my humble but hearty endeavours can serve my King and Country.

The French Fleet are still at Gourjean Road, and so securely moored, that it is said we cannot get at them with our Ships. They are guarded as much as possible from Fire-ships by a line of Frigates outside the large Ships, and a line of Gun-boats outside them, and at night a line of Launches; the whole is protected by very formidable batteries. When they came out of Toulon, by some mistake, they were represented to Admiral Hotham as nine Sail of the Line, whereas time has shown they were only seven; which induced a most gallant Officer to bear up for Calvi, and there he intended to fight them, sooner than they should throw in succours: had he known they were only an equal force, I am sure he would have given a good account of them.

I have written thus much, that your Royal Highness may be assured of my compliance with your desire of knowing what we are about; and that I am ready to obey your orders; being, with the highest respect, your Royal Highness's most dutiful servant,

HORATIO NELSON.

TO ADMIRAL LORD HOOD.

[Autograph, in the Hood Papers.]

Camp, August 10th, 1794.

My dear Lord,

A bag of Letters are come from Mr. Hunter, of Bastia, which I send off with another letter left at my tent by a Corsican. Sir Gilbert Elliot's servant has just brought a letter for Lady Elliot, which he requests may be given to the Sea-Officer going to England. We took possession between ten and eleven o'clock, and I have endeavoured, as well as a momentary arrangement would allow, to dispose of the Garrison and Seamen, their baggage, &c., on the wharf, and the General, as well as the Governor, wished to get them on board as soon as possible. I therefore sent the Troops, 547 men, besides women and children, on board the Mather, and Alice and Jane, the Seamen, about three hundred, on board the Nancy. The Officers and Staff, with some of the principal Inhabitants, on board the Mary (4th,) 313 sick to be put as many as possible on board the Sovereign. If not able to hold them all, the Mary to take some. There are also 400 inhabitants to be embarked. The Transports here having no provisions, I ordered the Transports from Fiorenzo to bring provisions for 12,050 men, which can easily be removed out of them to these Transports. I have endeavoured to act as I think you would wish me.

I am the best in health, but every other Officer is scarcely able to crawl. I have got the Agamemnon's three guns to the water-side, but to-day it is as easy to keep a flock of wild geese together as our Seamen. We number ninety sick. Thirty of the Agamemnon's I shall send on board this afternoon if possible. Lieutenant Moutray took possession of the Melpomene and Mignonne, with the Gunboat, who has a fine brass-gun in her prow. Every sail is cut up for sand-bags, and delivered the Ships to Captain Wolseley. Mr. Harrington, Master of the Willington Transport, who has served his time in the Navy, and passed, has requested me to mention him to your Lordship. He is a deserving young man, and has been very active and attentive to his duty.[1] I could do nothing more than pro-

---

[1] Mr. Harrington was made a Lieutenant in 1796.

mise to mention him to your Lordship : he says he shall give up his Ship for a fair prospect of promotion. Your Lordship will excuse me for mentioning him. The moment the weather is fair I will go on board the Victory.

Believe me, your Lordship's most faithful,

HORATIO NELSON.

The Transports' people to-day had not one man for duty, many assisting to bring round the Transports.

Captain Hallowell's Division of Victory's 14.

Lieutenant Moutray's, 20.

Inflexible, 10.

Agamemnon, 120.

TO MRS. NELSON.

[From Clarke and M'Arthur, vol. i. p. 189.]

Agamemnon,[8] 11th of August, 1794.

As soon as I can get our guns on board, I shall go to Leghorn to refit ; my Ship's company are all worn out, as is this whole Army, except myself ; nothing hurts me. God bless you.

Yours, &c.,

HORATIO NELSON.

"CAPTAIN NELSON'S LETTER TO GENERAL STUART, AS NEAR AS HE CAN RECOLLECT."

[Autograph, in the Nelson Papers, and another Autograph, in the Hood Papers.]

Agamemnon, Calvi, August 13th, 1794.

My dear Sir.

Lord Hood has desired me to acquaint you,[9] that the King of Sardinia's Secretary of State, as well as our Minister at

---

[8] The Agamemnon's Log of the 12th of August, states that " Captain Nelson and Officers returned from the Batteries."

[9] In the following Letter, dated on the 12th of August :

" My dear Nelson,—I think it highly probable I shall be forced to bear up before daylight to-morrow, and have therefore sent you orders. I propose the Mignonne shall remain at Calvi, by way of Guard-ship for the present, and have appointed Captain May to her: the Dolphin is ordered to Bastia so soon as she has got your sick. I hope you procured as much powder from the shore, as you possibly could, as the King of Sardinia's Secretary of State, as well as our

Turin, have strongly requested of him to return the six hundred barrels of Powder which his Lordship had seized upon, as the Sardinian Army was much in want of it.

I have, therefore, to request you will have the goodness to direct such part of the powder as is not wanted for this place, to be delivered to me.

I am, dear Sir, &c., &c.,

H. N.

TO LIEUTENANT SAINTHILL, AGENT FOR TRANSPORTS.

[From a Fac Simile.]

Agamemnon, Calvi, August 14th, 1794.

Dear Sir,

Your readiness at all times to expedite the King's service, I shall always bear my testimony of, and therefore I have no doubt but you have got all the Barrel powder from the shore on board the Scarborough, which I hope is 500 barrels. If she should not be sailed for Fiorenzo, pray expedite her as soon possible, and don't keep her for a few barrels. I shall be off Revellata Point nearly all day to-morrow; let her join me, and I will see her safe into Port. Should the Agamemnon not be there, she will proceed by herself. I have written a line to Captain Mac Namara about her.

I am, dear Sir, very truly yours,

HORATIO NELSON.

Minister at Turin have strongly requested I would return the six hundred barrels I seized upon, the Sardinian Army being in want, which I desire you will make known to General Stuart; and you must manage to put all you can get into your bread-room. I propose to anchor in St. Fiorenzo for forty-eight hours, as Mr. Drake is arrived in Corsica from Milan for the purpose of communicating with me. If therefore you wish to see me, before you go to Leghorn, you know where you will probably find me. I shall be very glad to attend to your wishes in favour of your Surgeon's Mate immediately, and if you will send Mr. Fellows on board the Victory I will promote him as soon as I can. At present I have four or five Officer's sons upon my hands, whom I must attend to. Ever faithfully yours, HOOD.—Soon as Gibson has received your commands send him to me, and if the weather should not permit my being off Calvi in the morning, send Captain May in the Fox cutter to me, and I shall send back in her the Officers for the two French frigates."—*Copy*, in the Hood Papers.

TO LIEUTENANT SAINTHILL.

[From " Memoirs of Captain Richard Sainthill."]

Agamemnon, Aug. 14.

Dear Sir,

You are to come to Calvi harbour, and may be of use in carrying some of our poor fellows to Bastia, and where probably your Ship will be wanted with the forage. Many thanks for your getting off the powder. Capt. Wolseley will tell you what to do with the tent and spars.

Yours most sincerely,

HORATIO NELSON.

TO MRS. NELSON.

[From Clarke and M'Arthur, vol. i. p. 189.]

Off Leghorn, August 18th, 1794.

I left Calvi on the 15th, and hope never to be in it again. I was yesterday in St. Fiorenzo, and to-day shall be safe moored, I expect, in Leghorn : since the Ship has been commissioned, this will be the first resting-time we have had. As it is all past, I may now tell you, that on the 10th of July, a shot having hit our battery, the splinters and stones from it struck me with great violence in the face and breast. Although the blow was so severe as to occasion a great flow of blood from my head, yet I most fortunately escaped, having only my right eye nearly deprived of its sight : it was cut down, but is so far recovered, as for me to be able to distinguish light from darkness. As to all the purposes of use, it is gone ; however, the blemish is nothing, not to be perceived, unless told. The pupil is nearly the size of the blue part, I don't know the name.[1]

---

[1] Nelson received the following consolatory letter from his Father on the loss of his eye :

" My dear Horatio,—It is well known that the predestinarian doctrine is amongst the creeds of Military men. It may sometimes be useful : yet it must not exclude the confidence Christianity preaches of a particular Providence, which directs all events. It was an unerring power, wise and good, which diminished the force of the blow by which your eye was lost ; and we thank the hand that spared you, spared you for future good, for example, and instruction,

At Bastia, I got a sharp cut in the back. You must not
think that my hurts confined me : no, nothing but the loss of
a limb would have kept me from my duty, and I believe my
exertions conduced to preserve me in this general mortality.
I am fearful that Mrs. Moutray's[2] son, who was on shore
with us, will fall a sacrifice to the climate ; he is a Lieutenant of the Victory, a very fine young man, for whom I have
a great regard. Lord Hood is quite distressed about him.
Poor little Hoste is also extremely ill, and I have great fears
about him ; one hundred and fifty of my people are in their
beds ; of two thousand men I am the most healthy. Josiah
is very well, and a clever smart young man, for so I must call
him, his sense demands it.

Yours, &c.
HORATIO NELSON.

TO MRS. NELSON.

[From Clarke and M'Arthur, vol. i. p. 190.]

Leghorn, September 1st, 1794.

My dear Fanny,

You will be sorry to hear that young Moutray is dead :
he was Second Lieutenant of the Victory, and at this moment,
had he survived, would have been a Captain. What a shock

in many subsequent years. There is no fear that flattery can come from me ;
but I sometimes wipe away the tear of joy, at hearing your character in every
point of view so well spoken of. The Letters received from you, give me and
your good Wife the pleasing intelligence that your health has not suffered from
the long fatiguing service you are professionally obliged to go through ; and also,
that success has generally been the issue of your endeavours to make yourself
known to the world as a man of probity and judgment ; not only looking towards
the things that are your own, but to those of others also. Your lot is cast, but
the whole disposing thereof is of the Lord : the very hairs of your head are num-
bered—a most comfortable doctrine. Upon the whole, I am as strong as can
be looked for ; how many do I see, and hear of, that are either fallen, or much
more afflicted by age than myself. Bless God, my days are lengthened, I hope,
for some good purpose. Accept, my dear good Son, the usual but most hearty expressions of love and friendship from your affectionate Father, EDMUND NELSON."
—*Clarke and M'Arthur*, vol. i. p. 192.

[2] This gallant young Officer, who has been often mentioned, died the next day.

it will be to his poor Mother, who was all expectation to hear of his promotion; a very different account will now be told her. His amiable disposition will never be forgotten by those who knew him. Lord Hood was his godfather, and feels much for the loss of him.

The French Squadron is still in Gourjean Bay, blockaded by us and the Spaniards; but another month must liberate them, and they will get I dare say to Toulon. The opportunity was lost of fighting them when they first came out of port.

Yours, &c.,

HORATIO NELSON.

He was the only Son of Commissioner Moutray, and of the Lady whom Nelson so highly esteemed at Antigua, (vide *ante.*) The following Inscription to his Memory was placed by Nelson in the Church of St. Fiorenzo:—

[From a Copy, in Nelson's own hand, in the Nelson Papers.]

SACRED

TO THE MEMORY

OF

LIEUTENANT JAMES MOUTRAY, R.N.

WHO, SERVING ON SHORE AT THE SIEGE,

OF CALVI,

THERE CAUGHT A FEVER,

OF WHICH HE DIED,

SINCERELY LAMENTED,

ON AUGUST 19TH, 1794,

AGED 21 YEARS.

THIS STONE IS ERECTED BY AN AFFECTIONATE FRIEND, WHO WELL KNEW HIS WORTH AS AN OFFICER, AND HIS ACCOMPLISHED MANNERS AS A GENTLEMAN.

H. N.

TO MRS. NELSON.

[From Clarke and M'Arthur, vol. i. p. 190.]

September 12th, 1794.

I expect to see you in the fall of the year; and although I shall not bring with me either riches or honours, yet I flatter myself I shall bring an unblemished character. It always rejoices me to hear that you are comfortable, and that my friends are attentive to you. I hope we shall find some snug cottage, whenever we may be obliged to quit the Parsonage. My Ship's company are better, but still are in a very weak state. It is probable that we shall get to sea in about three days, and attend Lord Hood in the Victory to Genoa, Porto Especia, and Vado Bay; and then proceed off Gourjean Bay, Toulon, and I hope to Gibraltar and England.

When Lord Hood quits this station, I should be truly sorry to remain; he is the greatest Sea-officer I ever knew; and what can be said against him, I cannot conceive, it must only be envy, and it is better to be envied than pitied. But this comes from the Army, who have also poisoned some few of our minds. The taking of Bastia, contrary to all Military judgment, is such an attack on them that it is never to be forgiven.

Yours, &c.,

HORATIO NELSON.

TO ADMIRAL LORD HOOD.

[From a Copy in the Nelson Papers.]

Agamemnon, Genoa Mole, September 20th, 1794.

My dear Lord,

We arrived here[3] yesterday morning at ten o'clock in a very strong breeze, and thick weather. We were in the Mole before they saw us from the Signal-house. None of us having been here, I had the Signal up for a Pilot,[4] which, by the

---

[3] On the 18th of September Captain Nelson was ordered by Lord Hood to proceed to the Mole of Genoa with Dispatches for Mr. Drake, Minister at that place, and to wait for further instructions.—*Original*, in the Nelson Papers.

[4] The Signal for a Pilot was then, and is still, the *Union Jack* at the fore-top-gallant-mast-head. The mistake mentioned in this Letter, is only one of many

Consul's account, they took for the Flag of a Vice-Admiral ; and although it was struck a full quarter of an hour before they saluted, which they did with fifteen guns, and I returned an equal number. If the salute was not intended from the Private Ship, I shall probably hear more of it. Mr. Drake has not arrived, but expected this evening. By a letter from him to the Consul, I find he has got the King's leave to return to England, and that he sets off from this place on the 1st of October, but returns on the 1st of March. There are two small Privateers of the Enemy here, who occasionally go to sea, and have taken two Vessels, one a Ragusa with Spanish property, the other some other Nation, both I understand from Spain, and bound to this Port. Only three English Vessels are here, and had we more, they could not stir for these Vessels. I shall mention it to Mr. Drake.

The Government have called upon me to pledge my honour, which I did, that I would not break the Neutrality of the Port. I shall do every thing which is proper, you may rest assured, to bring this Government into good humour with us. I don't think they can ever be mad enough to allow the *Sans Culottes* to enter Genoa. Here would be glorious plunder for them : it exceeds in magnificence any place I ever saw. I shall not close this letter till evening, in case any thing new should occur.

6 P. M.—No news yet of Mr. Drake. I am to pay my respects to the Doge at seven o'clock to-morrow evening.

> Believe me,
> Your Lordship's most faithful,
> HORATIO NELSON.

The Agamemnon lays at her own anchors, and so may the Victory and Britannia.

instances of the inconvenience of using the *National Flag* for *Signals,* and of the inconsistency of distinguishing British Admirals by any other Flag than that of their Country.—See a NOTE on this subject at the end of one of the subsequent Volumes.

TO WILLIAM SUCKLING, ESQ.

[From "The Athenæum."]

Agamemnon, Genoa Mole, September 20th, 1794.

My dear Sir,

Agamemnon is still on the wing, and will not rest, most probably, till she gets into Portsmouth, which I hope will be no great length of time, as Lord Hood is inclined to take me Home with him, and turn us into a good Seventy-four; for although I have been offered every Seventy-four which has fallen vacant in this Country, yet I could not bring myself to part with a Ship's company, with whom I have gone through such a series of hard service, as has never before, I believe, fallen to the lot of any one Ship.

We are sent here to keep peace and harmony with Genoa; and I believe none has been injured by the blockade but ourselves: for I am assured here it never was felt; for all Ships which did not escape the vigilance of our Cruisers, went into the neighbouring Ports, and small Vessels carried their cargoes along shore, the underwriters paying the expenses. The breaking the Neutrality of the Port in small States must ever be impolitic in the English, as we have more to lose by such a conduct than any other Nation. The taking the Frigate[5] was useless to us, and gave the French party here great cause to complain of us. Our forcing the Tuscans into a war, was, in my opinion, equally impolitic. The Italian States must be claimed when the French turn their thoughts towards Italy; and, if you will allow them, will all unite against their common plunderers. Genoa is too rich and magnificent to allow (if anger does not get the better of their interest) the Sans Culottes to enter their City. This is an Aristocratical Government, and therefore must be subverted instantly. I am the first Ship here since our hostilities, and believe they are inclined to be civil.

I beg my best compliments to Mrs. Suckling, Miss Suckling, and family; and I hope Captain Suckling was well when you heard last from him—don't forget me at Hampstead. Believe me,

Your most affectionate,

HORATIO NELSON.

[5] L'Imperieuse of 40 guns: taken by a Squadron under Vice-Admiral Gell, out of Spezzia, in the Genoese Territory, on the 11th of October, 1793.

TO MRS. NELSON.

[From Clarke and M'Arthur, vol. i. p. 191.]

Genoa, 20th September, 1794.

This City is, without exception, the most magnificent I ever beheld, superior in many respects to Naples, although it does not appear quite so fine from the sea, yet on shore it is far beyond it. All the houses are palaces on the grandest scale. However, I trust we shall soon quit these magnificent scenes, and retire to England, where all that I admire is placed.

Yours, &c.

HORATIO NELSON.

TO ADMIRAL LORD HOOD.

[Autograph, in the possession of Mrs. Conway.]

Agamemnon, Genoa Mole, September 23rd, 1794.

Mr. Drake is not yet arrived, nor have we any account of his movements since the Letter he wrote the Consul, saying he expected to be here on the 20th. On Sunday evening I waited on the Doge, and, as Mr. Drake was not arrived, I found it absolutely necessary to say something civil, which I did in the following words: ' That I was come to pay my respects to his Serenity, and to assure him, that both by duty and inclination I should pay the strictest attention to the neutrality of Genoa; and should be happy in doing everything in my power to cement the harmony which subsisted between the two Nations.' The Doge was much pleased, and very civil; saying, ' That he thanked me for my expressions of friendship, and begged to assure me, that it should be reciprocal on his part; and that from so pleasing a beginning of our renewal of friendship, he had no doubt of its being lasting; that he was always happy to see English Men-of-War in Genoa; and whatever I found a difficulty in getting, by making it known to him, he would be happy in removing it; and that the gates were always at my disposal.

I was received in some State, the Doge advancing to the middle of the room to receive me, and I had the honors of a Senato. On my departure from the Palace, the orders of the Doge had preceded me to the gates, where the Captain of the Guard told me he had the decree for the gates at whatever time I pleased. I hope your Lordship will think I did right in expressing myself in the manner I did. I can tell your Lordship for your private ear, that never man was so unpopular as Mr. Drake in Genoa—the Nobles, Middle class, and Lowest, equally hate him. Even the boat people speak of him as being so unlike any other Englishman. Yesterday evening I had an application from the Master of an English brig, taken by the French privateers under the guns of a Genoese fort, in March last, and kept with his people in one of the Lazzarettos, till the Genoese Courts determine whether she was taken within the limits of their Coasts. The Master and crew wish my application for them to be liberated in the first instance, and secondly, that an immediate examination of the case may take place, as they are sure, they say, of proving that the Vessel was taken under the guns of the Genoese fort. I told the Merchants that this was more a business for Mr. Drake than myself, but that if Mr. Drake did not soon arrive, I would apply for the Master and crew to be liberated. The Consul, from late circumstances, has no weight. I shall acquaint Mr. D. of the circumstance so soon as he arrives.

TO MRS. NELSON.

[From Clarke and M'Arthur, vol. i. p. 191.]

Genoa, September 27th, 1794.

We are just going to sea with Lord Hood and Admiral Hotham, who came in here four days ago. We are to proceed off Gourjean to look at the French Ships, and thence to Toulon, where the Enemy have six Sail ready for sea, and most probably will soon make an effort to join their other Ships. The French have taken possession of Vado Bay in the Genoese territory, and of course will prevent our Ships

from anchoring; and I have but little doubt, if the Enemy
turn their thoughts to the invasion of Italy, that next Spring
they will accomplish it. The Allied Powers seem jealous of
each other, and none but England is hearty in the cause.
Lord Hood goes from the Fleet to Corsica, whence he sails for
England.

Yours, &c.

HORATIO NELSON.

TO ADMIRAL LORD HOOD.

[From a Copy, in the Nelson Papers.]

Agamemnon, at Sea, October 2nd, 1794.

My Lord,

Not any notice having been taken in the Public List of
Wounded at the Siege of Calvi, of my eye being damaged, I
feel it but justice to myself to transmit to your Lordship two
Certificates, one from the Surgeon General of his Majesty's
Forces, the other, from the Physician of the Fleet, and the
Surgeon landed for the care of the Seamen; and I have to
request that your Lordship will take such measures as you
may judge proper that my Sovereign may be informed of my
loss of an eye in His Service: nor do I think that his Majesty
will consider that I suffered the less pain from my determination to do my duty in twenty-four hours after the accident,
that those laborious duties intrusted by your Lordship to my
direction might not slacken.

I submit my Case entirely to your Lordship,[5] resting assured you will mention me in this matter as I deserve, and
will do ample justice to the gallant Officers and Seamen employed under me.

I am, with great respect,
Your Lordship's most obedient Servant,

HORATIO NELSON.

---

[5] Lord Hood did not fail to recommend his case in the strongest manner to the
first Lord of the Admiralty. Vide Lord Hood's Letter to Nelson, of the 1st of
December, 1794, p. 502 post.

CERTIFICATES.

These are to Certify, that Horatio Nelson, Esquire, Commander of his Majesty's Ship Agamemnon, did, on the 10th day of July 1794, while Commanding the Seamen before Calvi, receive a wound of the iris of the right eye, which has occasioned an unnatural dilatation of the pupil, and a material defect of sight.

Given under our hands, on board his Majesty's ship Victory, off Calvi, this 9th day of August 1794.

JOHN HARNESS,
Physician to the Fleet.
MICHAEL JEFFERSON,
Surgeon attending on Shore.

These are to Certify that Captain Horatio Nelson of his Majesty's Ship Agamemnon, now serving on Shore at the Siege of Calvi, was on the 10th day of July last, wounded in the face and right eye, much injured by stones or splinters, struck by shot from the Enemy. There were several small lacerations about the face; and his eye so materially injured, that in my opinion, he will never recover the perfect use of it again.

W. CHAMBERS,
Surgeon to the Forces in
the Mediterranean.

Calvi, August 12th, 1794.

TO MRS. NELSON.

[From Clarke and M'Arthur, vol. i. p. 193.]

Off Gourjean, October 3rd, 1794.

Lord Hood[6] is gone to Leghorn to receive his dispatches by a messenger, who is arrived from England, and most pro-

---

[6] On the 30th of September Lord Hood directed Captain Nelson to proceed off Gourjean, and place himself under the orders of Vice-Admiral Hotham, or if he had not arrived, of Vice-Admiral Goodall. In a Private Letter of that date Lord Hood said:

"My dear Nelson,—My letters by the return of the courier I sent to Leghorn,

bably we shall only see him to take leave. Admiral Hotham
will be Commander-in-Chief; and with new men, new
measures are generally adopted, therefore I can at present
say nothing about myself, except that I am in most perfect
health. We have here eleven Sail of the Line, the Enemy
have fourteen; seven here, and seven at Toulon. They will
probably before the winter is over effect a junction, when our
Fleet will be kept together; but whenever they choose to
give us a meeting, the event I have no doubt will be such as
every Englishman has a right to expect.

October 10th.—Lord Hood is to join us in a few days; I
fear I have no chance whatever of going Home. My Ship's
company are by no means recovered; and we are destined to
keep the sea, until both Ship and Crew are rendered unfit for
service. Pray let me hear often from you: it is my greatest
comfort.

October 12th.—Lord Hood left us yesterday: therefore
our hopes of my going Home at present are at an end; however, we must not repine: at all events I shall cheat the
winter, and, as I understand I am to have a cruise, it may
possibly be advantageous. Lord Hood is very well inclined
towards me; but the service must ever supersede all private
consideration. I hope you will spend the winter cheerfully.
The Wolterton family, I am sure, will be happy to receive
you for as long a time as you please. Do not repine at my
absence; before Spring I hope we shall have Peace, when we
must look out for some little cottage: I assure you I shall
return to the plough with redoubled glee.

October 15th.—Two of my opponents, whom I fell in with
last year about this time, are now in England, or near it,
the St. Fiorenzo, late La Minerve, and La Melpomene, both

make it necessary for me to go to that Port immediately, having reason to believe a
messenger will be there before me with Dispatches of great importance for me to
get as soon as possible. You will therefore herewith receive an order to proceed
off Gourjean and put yourself under the command of Vice-Admiral Hotham,
or Vice-Admiral Goodall, in his absence. So soon as I get my Dispatches you
shall hear from me. I send you two Newspapers, by which you will see that
Cunningham was arrived. You will give them to Admiral Hotham. Ever, my
dear Nelson, most faithfully yours, Hood."—*Original*, in the Nelson Papers.

40 guns, 18-pounders, two as fine Frigates as are in the world.[1] I have been fortunate in being present at the taking and destroying of that whole Squadron; and which, but for our disabling them, intended to have returned to France: they are now better disposed of.

Yours, &c.
HORATIO NELSON.

TO CAPTAIN WILLIAM LOCKER, LIEUTENANT-GOVERNOR, GREENWICH HOSPITAL.

[Autograph, in the Locker Papers.]

Agamemnon, October 10th, 1794. Off Gourjean Bay.

My dear Friend,

I am just favoured with your letter of 3rd September, for which I sincerely thank you. My constitution is not the least impaired by my fag, which I assure you has been very great. I was almost the only person, in Army or Navy at the Siege of Calvi, who was not completely knocked up. Out of 2,000 men we have had died upwards of 300; and the others were so reduced that we had only 400 to take possession. My Ship's company, who were all landed, suffered with the others; nor can I get the better of the fever. Our Sick-list is now seventy-seven, almost all objects for the Hospital. What is to become of us I cannot guess, we are here making a show, but certainly unfit for a long cruise. The French Ships in the Bay are so fortified, that we cannot get at them without a certainty of the destruction of our own Fleet. At Toulon six Sail of the Line are ready for sea in the outer Road, and two nearly so in the Arsenal. When Victory is gone we shall be thirteen Sail of the Line, when the Enemy will keep our new Commanding Officer in hot water, (Hotham,) who missed, unfortunately, the opportunity of fighting them, last June.[2]

The French, if something capital is not done by the Austrians in the Piedmontese Territory, will in the spring over-

---

[1] Captured at the Surrender of Calvi.
[2] Vide p. 476.

run Italy, now they have got and fortified Vado Bay, and every Town belonging to the Genoese, as they advance. We shall lose the benefit of Port Especia if the Austrians do not make haste; and if the French get it, their Fleet may lay there with the greatest safety, and Italy is lost to us. Leghorn will fall in a week. Some of the French are more active [*a word torn*] than ourselves. We offend [*torn*] proceed, and then retreat. This [*torn*] our conduct respecting Genoa, a war against her would have starved the Southern Provinces. Our *Allies* in these Seas are useless to us, as I believe they are in all other parts of the world. My paper is full. Kind remembrances to Miss Eliza, and your Sons. Holloway of the Britannia, and John Sutton of the Egmont, desire to be remembered to you. Believe me your most affectionate Friend,

H. N.

Josiah is very well, and thanks you for your inquiries after him.

TO VICE-ADMIRAL HOTHAM.

[From a Copy, in the Admiralty, transmitted by Vice-Admiral Hotham, on whom the temporary command of the Fleet in the Mediterranean had devolved in consequence of Lord Hood's return to England.]

Agamemnon, at Sea, 17 October, 1794.

Sir,

In obedience to your directions desiring me to inquire of Mr. William Bolton[8] on what grounds he had written a letter to his relations in Suffolk, stating as a fact that Lieutenant Day and the crew of his Majesty's Ship Ardent,[9] were prisoners in France, I have the honour to acquaint you, that I find from Mr. Bolton that he had heard such a report, and had written it to his friends, but that he was satisfied long since there was no truth in it.

I have the honour to be, &c.

HORATIO NELSON.

[8] Then a Midshipman of the Agamemnon; afterwards Captain Sir William Bolton. Vide p. 342, ante.

[9] The fate of the Ardent was never ascertained. It was supposed that she was blown up.

TO MRS. NELSON.

[From Clarke and M'Arthur, vol. i. p. 194.]

Leghorn, October 24th, 1794.

What changes, my dearest Fanny, our life is subject to. The other day, when I wrote, I was going up the Levant : now that is gone by, and I am under different orders. We came in here to get a few refreshments for my people, seventy of whom are still very ill, and I go to sea on the 26th to join the Fleet again. We have but little news here. I wish we could make a Peace on any fair terms, for poor England will be drained of her riches to maintain her Allies, who will not fight for themselves.

[Apparently in continuation.]

Leghorn, October 31st.

It is an ill wind that blows nobody any good : being obliged by a gale to put back last night, I in consequence received your letter of September 30th, which gave me infinite pleasure. Why you should be uneasy about me, so as to make yourself ill, I know not. I feel a confident protection in what-ever service I may be employed upon ; and as to my health, I don't know that I was ever so truly well : I fancy myself grown quite stout. My Ship, and Ship's company, though not in half the strength as when I left Spithead, several of my guns that were landed at Corsica having been destroyed, yet I am sure feel themselves equal to go alongside any 74 out of France. Lord Hood sends me word he shall come out here again ; I own I don't think so, although he retains the Chief Command. It rejoices me to hear Maurice[1] is so well off. Admiral Hotham cannot keep the sea much longer ; the Fleet must return into some Port. We have had three gales of wind in thirteen days, all very strong ; neither sails, ships, nor men can stand it. In the Channel, the Fleet goes instantly into Torbay, here we always keep the Sea.

Yours, &c.,

HORATIO NELSON.

---

[1] His eldest Brother.

TO THE RIGHT HONOURABLE SIR GILBERT ELLIOT,
VICEROY OF CORSICA.

[Autograph, in the Minto Papers.]

Agamemnon, Leghorn, October 24th, 1794.

My dear Sir,

Since your Excellency has taken upon yourself the
Viceroyship of Corsica, I have not had an opportunity of
wishing you a most happy Government; and I sincerely
hope, from your mild Administration, that Corsica, hitherto
torn to pieces by its own intestine divisions, will become an
united and happy Country. Sure I am, without a compliment unmerited, that if they do not, under your Excellency,
unite and be happy, they will not deserve to be so. My stay
here will be very few days more; but should Lady Elliot
and your family arrive here (which I am told is possible)
during my stay, the Agamemnon shall convey her Ladyship
to Corsica, and I am certain that any Captain who may be
here will immediately receive her, and convey her to Bastia,
with the greatest pleasure.

Believe me, dear Sir,
Your most faithful
HORATIO NELSON.

TO THE REVEREND MR. NELSON, HILBOROUGH.

[Autograph, in the Nelson Papers.]

Leghorn, October 26th, 1794.

My dear Brother,

I have not heard from you this age : not more than three
or four letters since I left England. You are become a noto-
rious bad correspondent, and hardly deserve a letter from
me. You may now, perhaps, thank a rainy day, and all
their letters finished. I own I should like to hear from you,
and all your Hilborough and Swaffham news, more interesting to me than all the Public news, probably because more
difficult to be got at. This is not the case with you, who, I
know, wish for Public news, and authentic. Then, I will
send you a list of the French fleet in these Seas.

Sans Culotte 120, Duquesne 74, Généreux 74, Tonnant 80, Commerce de Bordeaux 74, Censeur 74, Heureux 74, four Frigates, one Corvette, in Gourjean Bay; Languedoc 80, Ca Ira 80, Conquerant 74, Guerrier 74, Mercure 74, two Frigates, and Scout brig, in the outer road of Toulon, ready for sea; Barras 74, Souveraine 74, Alcide 74, (Hardi 64, intended for Toulon guard-ship,) the others fitting, and nearly ready; two new Frigates fitting. Thus have the Enemy a Fleet, in point of number superior to ours, we having only fourteen Sail of the Line. The junction of the two Squadrons off Gourjean and Toulon may be made whenever they please, for in the winter we cannot blockade them. What object they may have in view no one can tell, but if it is Italy, no Action will take place here before February, for before their Army can risk being cut off, there must be a Sea Action to force us into Port, when, if we are not completely victorious—I mean, able to remain at Sea whilst the Enemy must retire into Port—if we only make a Lord Howe's victory, take a part, and retire into Port, Italy is lost. Of the event of an Action I have no doubt, and only hope, they will be mad enough to make the trial speedily. It will end our heavy fag: it is the only event we have to wish for. The weather continues so bad and heavy gale of wind that we are riding forecastle in; and a foul wind, therefore cannot get out. I desire I may hear from you very soon. You will not forget to remember me kindly to Mrs. Nelson, my Aunt, and the little ones. Compliments to all our friends at Swaffham, and believe me,

Your most affectionate Brother,

HORATIO NELSON.

TO WILLIAM SUCKLING, ESQ.

[From "the Athenæum."]

Agamemnon, Leghorn, October 31st, 1794.

My dear Sir,

Being driven back to this Port last night by a gale of wind, I got Mrs. Nelson's letter, dated from Kentish Town. Your kindness to her will never be forgotten by me; and to Mrs. Suckling and Miss Suckling I feel infinitely obliged. I shall

only tell you, what may not be believed in England, that the
French have put together a Fleet at Toulon, which could
hardly be credited. Although many of them are old, yet
they have fitted them well enough for an Action, if it should
be necessary. I send you a list of them on the other side.
We don't seem to make much of the war. Our Allies are our
burden. Had we left the Continent to themselves, we should
have done well, and at half the expense. The gale moderates, and I am just going to get under weigh again.

Believe me, with every affectionate wish and regard,

Your obliged

Horatio Nelson.

I beg to be kindly remembered to every part of your
family; compliments to Mr. Mentz.

Sans Culotte 120, Tonnant 80, Duquèsne 74, Commerce
de Bourdeaux 74, Généreux 74, Censeur 74, Heureux 74,
four Frigates, one Corvette, in Gourjean Bay. Languedoc 80,
Ca Ira 80, Conquerant 74, Guerrier 74, Mercure 74, two
Frigates, and Schooners, in the outer road of Toulon, and
ready for sea. Barras 74, Souverain 74, Alcide 74, are ready
for sea in the inner harbour, and two new Frigates; Hardi
64, guard-ship, at Toulon.

TO H. R. H. THE DUKE OF CLARENCE.

[From Clarke and M'Arthur, vol. i. p. 194.]

Agamemnon, at Sea, November 7th, 1794.

Since I had the honour of writing to your Royal Highness,
my time has been fully occupied in endeavouring to reinstate
the health of my Ship's company, which had been miserably
torn to pieces by, without vanity, I hope I may be allowed to
say, as hard service as a Ship's crew ever performed. I have
lost fifty of my best men since I left Calvi; nor can the others
be got round to their proper health, so entirely are their constitutions destroyed. I had been sent into Leghorn for some
stores at the latter end of October, and did not leave Admiral
Hotham off Gourjean Bay until the 3rd of November in the

morning, when I found the Enemy's Fleet had given us the slip[2] and that it was determined to unite our Fleet at St. Fiorenzo; the French having given out, that they would eat their new-year's dinner in Corsica. I was immediately detached to look into Hieres Bay and Toulon, and to examine into the state of their Fleet, and where they were got to. On the 5th of November, not finding them in Hieres Bay, I stood close into Toulon Harbour, where are twenty-two Sail of Ships in the inner Harbour: we could only look over a point of land, therefore cannot say how many were of the Line. I see plainly they will keep us in hot water the whole winter, and I think it probable may detach small Squadrons to get, for a few days at intervals, in the track of our Trade upward-bound. Your Royal Highness has probably read the list handed about of their Fleet, fifteen Sail of the Line, ten Frigates, and Corvettes. Many we know must be in very bad condition; but still they may bear a few hours at Sea, which is sufficient for their purpose. Believe me ever with the highest respect,

Your Royal Highness's most dutiful Servant,

HORATIO NELSON.

TO THE RIGHT HONOURABLE SIR GILBERT ELLIOT,
VICEROY OF CORSICA.

[Autograph, in the Minto Papers.]

Agamemnon, St. Fiorenzo, November 10th, 1794.

My dear Sir,

As I have been sent by the Admiral to examine into the state of the Enemy's Fleet at Toulon, I think it will be acceptable to your Excellency to have a copy of my Report, more especially as it is given out that Corsica is their object of attack, and very many in our service believe it. I own myself of a different opinion. Neither Calvi, St. Fiorenzo, or Bastia can be attacked by them, unless—what I hope no Englishman will credit—that they are able to beat

----

[2] The Fleet which took refuge in Gourjean Bay, "afterwards succeeded, owing in a great degree to the stormy state of the weather, in eluding the blockading force, and reached in safety the road of Toulon."—James' Naval History, vol. i. p. 193.

our Fleet. We know from experience that an Army, thrown ashore without the possibility of being supported by a Fleet to land all the requisites for a Siege, (which are many,) however numerous they may be, cannot subsist long in an Enemy's country. The Corsicans, if we keep them out of fortified places, would harass them to death.

I shall take this opportunity of saying a word of Ajaccio. If the Enemy have an intention of getting a hold in Corsica, that is the place they will attempt; and should they succeed, we shall find it a difficult matter to drive them out again. I never was there; but it strikes me, that by numbers landed, and the appearance of their Fleet for a few hours, they may succeed; for I believe the Corsicans understand nothing of the art of defending fortified Towns.

You will, I am sure, receive what I am going to say as it is meant, *well*, and believe that all my wishes and desires are to see our Country successful, and the schemes of our Enemies frustrated. I am well aware it may be said, and with truth, that we have not Troops in the Island to defend any one place properly. I admit it; but in answer I say— and am satisfied in my mind it will turn out so—if the Enemy make an attempt, that a few Troops and Artillery stationed at Ajaccio, to keep the gates shut for a few days, would render abortive any schemes they may have for establishing themselves there. I think three hundred men, and some Artillery to keep the Guns in order, to which if a Guard-ship was added, the seamen, in time of need, could go on shore to man the works; (for if the Enemy get Ajaccio, they may lay there with their whole Fleet, or leave a single Frigate, neither of which we could attack; for in the Gulph there is no sounding, and a sea setting constantly in, which would make us keep at a distance.) With this defence, I am confident the place, and I believe I may say the Island, would be perfectly safe, till our Fleet could get to the Enemy, when the event, I have no doubt, would be what every Briton might expect; besides, we have the incitement, (if any is wanted,) of our Home Fleet,[2] and we shall not like to be outdone by any one.

---

[2] The Victory of the 1st of June.

I have taken the liberty of mentioning my idea of the importance of Ajaccio, only in the belief which I have, that your Excellency will receive it as a *private* communication, (my situation does not entitle me to give any public opinion on such a point); as such I send it, and shall be happy if it gives rise to a serious consideration of its importance, when, I doubt not, much more proper modes of defence and security will be thought of than I have suggested. But, however that may be, I am bold to say, none can exceed me in the earnest desire of serving well my King and Country; and of convincing your Excellency how much I am, on every occasion, your most sincere, humble Servant,

HORATIO NELSON.

STATE AND SITUATION OF THE FRENCH FLEET IN TOULON, NOVEMBER 5TH, 1794.

1.
2. } In the Arsenal, with their top-gallant-masts struck.
3.

INNER ROAD.

1. Topmasts just pointed through the cap.
2. Top-gallant-mast up.
3. Do.   do.
4. Topgallant-mast struck.
5. Topmasts up—no top-gallant-masts.
6. Topgallant-masts up—Flag at mizen top-mast-head.
7. Topgallant-masts up.
8. Do.   do.   Broad Pendant at maintopgallant-mast head.
9. Topgallant-masts up.
10. Topgallant-masts struck.
11. Do.   do.
N. B. None of these Ships have their sails bent.

OUTER ROAD.

1. Frigate—topgallant-masts down.

2. Frigate—topgallant-masts up.

3.
4.
5. } Of the Line, sails bent, some with topgallant-yards
6.   across.
7.

8. Cannot tell whether of the Line or Frigate.

N. B. No. 5, with a Pendant forward, all the others with Pendants at the maintop-gallant-mast-heads. Seven Sail of our Transports laying in a Tier under Cape Sepet above the Naval Hospital, with their Truce flag hoisted forward, and the English Colours at the mizen-peak. Yards and topmasts struck, topsail-yards down.

HORATIO NELSON.

TO MRS. NELSON.

[From Clarke and M'Arthur, vol. i. p. 196.]

St. Fiorenzo, November 12th, 1794.

I have been sent, since I wrote to you last, to look after the French Fleet, who had again given Admiral Hotham the slip. I found them in Toulon, sixteen Sail of the Line and several Frigates, and came in here two days afterwards. The French say they will have Corsica again. There has been a most diabolical report here, of Agamemnon's being captured and carried into Toulon, owing to my running into the Harbour's mouth. I hope it has not reached England. Never believe anything you may see in the Papers about us, and rest assured, that Agamemnon is not to be taken easily; no two-decked Ship in the world, we flatter ourselves, is able to do it.

November 15th.—Agamemnon begins to look miserably without a mizen-mast, and will soon be without a main-mast. I am in the best possible health, yet I don't like to be any longer kicked about, I am tired. The lying in Port is misery to me. I have just received a letter from the Viceroy of Corsica, in which are the following flattering expressions to me, I am certain they will give you pleasure;—it was on the subject of Corsica being attacked : ' I know that

you, who have had such an honourable share in this acquisition, will not be indifferent at the prosperity of the Country
which you have so much assisted to place under his Majesty's
government.'—Whether these are words of course, and to be
forgotten, I know not; they are pleasant, however, for the
time.

Yours, &c.
HORATIO NELSON.

TO H. R. H. THE DUKE OF CLARENCE.

[From Clarke and M'Arthur, vol. i. p. 196.]

November, 1794.

Sir,

Our Transports, which had been detained at Toulon since
the time they carried over the Garrison of Calvi, arrived on
the 22nd.   No reason was ever given for detaining them;
but their sails were taken from them, and during their stay
not a man was suffered to go on shore. They were, however,
treated tolerably, until the arrival of Jean Bon St. André,
who, to the Officer's modest and proper requests, gave insolent
answers, the true characteristic of little minds; a generous
Enemy would have disdained the withholding medical assistance
from the unfortunate, whom chance had put in their power.
At eight o'clock in the evening of the 20th, their sails were
sent alongside, and a message, that if they were not out of the
harbour by twelve o'clock next day, they would keep them.
The English, poor fellows, wanted no spur to clear them of
such wretches; one Transport, who got aground, they left
behind, and she is not yet arrived.   The Enemy have fifteen
Sail of the Line ready for Sea, with which, they say, they
mean to fight our Fleet; and as Admiral Hotham sailed from
Fiorenzo on the 25th, to go off Toulon with thirteen Sail of
the Line, they will have the opportunity.   As to the event
I have no doubt it will be victory on the side of the English.
My heart, I assure you, is almost broke to find Agamemnon lying here, little better than a wreck: we hope to get
fitted in about three weeks.   I own my sincere wish, that
the Enemy would rest quiet until we are ready for Sea, and
a gleam of hope sometimes crosses me, that they will.   At

Toulon seven Sail of the Line are to be launched by next March; they get well supplied with timber by the Genoese vessels.

I am, &c.

HORATIO NELSON.

TO WILLIAM SUCKLING, ESQ.

[Autograph, in the possession of John Young, Esq. Printed in "the Athenæum."]

Agamemnon, Leghorn, November 28th, 1794.

My dear Sir,

Perhaps you will say, I am but little obliged for this letter, as it encloses one for my dear wife; but I believe you will give me credit for writing as often as my situation will admit. I shall tell you our news, which will soon be interesting. Matters are fast drawing to a crisis in this Country. Our Transports, which have been detained at Toulon, since they carried over the Garrison of Calvi, were liberated on the 20th November; their sails, which had been taken from them, being sent on board, and sixteen hours allowed them to depart. Not a man was allowed to go on shore during their stay, and the answers of Jean Bon St. André were insolent in the highest degree to modest and proper requests. He sent a message to Lord Hood,[3] not

---

[3] Lord Hood arrived in England on the 21st of September, and on the 1st of December wrote to Nelson respecting his Services and Wound.

"(Private.)   Devizes, December 1st, 1794.

"My dear Nelson,—I arrived at Spithead on the 21st and in London on the 23rd, orders having been lodged not to put the Victory under quarantine. On my getting out of my coach Lord Chatham came to me, and I took the earliest opportunity of explaining to his Lordship the very illiberal conduct of General Stuart in not mentioning you in his Public Letter, and put into his hands your Letter to me with the accompanying Certificates, [vide p. 488 ante,] which he will show the King, so that you may be perfectly easy upon that subject.

"Five sail are now under orders for the Mediterranean; three are to come home, the Bedford, your Ship, and another. I am so far in my way to Bath, in order to get myself into health to return to the Mediterranean in the Spring. After I got into my coach I received a note from Lord Grenville, informing me he should dispatch a messenger to Florence to-morrow, and as my engagement to call upon my good friend the Speaker near Reading, and an accident befalling a coach-horse and the postilion, I did not get here for some hours so soon as I

knowing of his departure, that, if he sent any more Flags
to the Port of the Mountain, he would burn the Vessels.
They have fifteen Sail of the Line ready for sea, with which
they say they will fight our Fleet. Now, as Admiral Hotham is gone off Toulon with thirteen Sail of the Line, they
may if they please. I am, as you will believe, uneasy enough,
for fear they will fight, and Agamemnon not present,—it will
almost break my heart; but I hope the best—that they are
only boasting at present, and will be quiet till I am ready.

The Admiral will return here, and I hope to be ready to
accompany him the next time he goes to sea: it is misery for
me to be laid up dismantled. Our friends in Corsica think
the French intend them a visit. I am of a different opinion
from the whole Fleet, Army, and Viceroy. Port Especia is
their object, I am convinced; and, if they get it, they
will plague us more than ever. They have seven Sail of the
Line on the stocks at Toulon, which will all be launched next
March, when they will have twenty-two Sail of the Line for
the whole of next summer. The Genoese supply them with
everything, and England has submitted to be humbled by
such a paltry State. The Danes and Swedes are for
ever entering Toulon with timber. If they are stopped, they
are bound to Genoa and Leghorn, from which place the wood,
&c., is sent with little expense. The rascality of Neutral
Powers we all know; therefore I have only to say, they are
as bad as ever.

I beg you will present my kindest remembrances to Mrs.
Suckling, Miss Suckling, and the rest of the family. Is Captain Suckling[1] still abroad? My remembrance to him when
you write, and don't forget me to Mr. Rumsey, and my
friends at Hampstead, and believe me ever

Your most affectionate

HORATIO NELSON.

expected; consequently lost the mail from Bath, and must send an express, as I
should be sorry the messenger should arrive at Florence without a few lines to
you. Lady Hood is with me, and unites in all good wishes, with, my dear Nelson, yours very faithfully, HOOD." *Original*, in the Nelson Papers.

[1] Afterwards Lieutenant-Colonel, to whom Letters will be found in subsequent volumes: he was a natural son of Mr. Suckling.

TO JOHN M'ARTHUR, ESQ.

[Autograph, in the possession of Mrs. Conway.]

Agamemnon, Leghorn, November 28th, 1794.

My dear Sir,

I dare say you inquired at Gibraltar about the expense of the Corn vessel, and have directed Littledale and Broderip to pay the amount, although the letter is not yet arrived. This letter is on the subject of our Bastia and Calvi Prize-money.

What I have got at present is nothing : what I have lost is, an eye, 300*l.*, and my health, with the satisfaction of my Ship's company being completely ruined : so much for debtor and creditor. It is absolutely necessary you should know how the Prize-money is to be distributed. It may be necessary, and I think must be finally determined by the King in Council. Shall those who were present at the commencement, those who only came time enough to see the Enemy's flags struck, share equal to us who bore the burden of the day? It must be considered as very different to sharing Prize-money at sea. There the object, if resistance was made, could be assisted : with us it was quite different. Far be it from me to be illiberal. Those Ships who rowed guard the whole time, as Victory, Princess Royal, and Fortitude, and Agamemnon, are the only Ships who remained the whole Siege ; Gorgon, great part ; L'Imperieuse, certain ; and Fox Cutter. How the others are to be discriminated, I cannot say.

I think you ought to get the opinion of two good Counsel, and from their opinion you may form some judgment what may be necessary to be done. Colonel Villettes and myself have talked the matter over, and think, as we were joined together in the same service, that we should be considered as different from the others. Then Brereton and the Captains who block-aded the Port, and served on shore—under what head those [Ships] who accidentally assisted for one moment and were gone the next, is not for me to determine. If it is thought right these points ought, and I must desire may be, inquired into. I know no reason why every one that pleases is to share with us. It may be necessary to speak to Lord

Hood on the subject, who, I am sure, will recommend what
is just, and that I would have you pursue.　Believe me,

Your very obedient humble Servant,

HORATIO NELSON.

TO MRS. NELSON.

[From Clarke and M'Arthur, vol. i. p. 197.]

December, 1794.

We have our fears[2] for some Frigates of ours on the coast
of Barbary : one is arrived who escaped from six Frigates,
but we have not heard of the other two.　The French have
sent over, as a present to the Bey of Tunis, a Xebec completely armed : thus by trifling presents they keep up their
influence, whilst England sends nothing; of course, they are
the well-wishers of one, and dislike the other, and give the
Enemy every information respecting our Cruisers, whilst we
are in total ignorance.

December 19th.—Our Fleet is arrived, and I shall be ready
to go to Sea with them again.　We sail to-morrow on a
cruise, therefore I can only scribble a line to say, I never
was better: I have no doubt but good fortune will attend us.
Most probably early in the Spring we shall be in England,
and I really believe Peace is not far distant at this moment.
God bless you, and give us a happy meeting, says your most
affectionate husband,

HORATIO NELSON.

---

[2] These fears proved to be without foundation.

END OF VOL. I.

LONDON :

PRINTED BY G. J PALMER, SAVOY STREET, STRAND.

1741383R0033

Printed in Great Britain
by Amazon.co.uk, Ltd.,
Marston Gate.